Scripture and Theology

Theologische Bibliothek Töpelmann

―

Edited by
Bruce McCormack, Friederike Nüssel
and Judith Wolfe

Band 201

Scripture and Theology

Historical and Systematic Perspectives

Edited by
Tomas Bokedal, Ludger Jansen and Michael Borowski

DE GRUYTER

ISBN 978-3-11-221404-6
e-ISBN (PDF) 978-3-11-076841-1
e-ISBN (EPUB) 978-3-11-076849-7
ISSN 0563-4288

Library of Congress Control Number: 2023939416

Bibliographic information published by the Deutsche Nationalbibliothek
The Deutsche Nationalbibliothek lists this publication in the Deutsche Nationalbibliografie;
detailed bibliographic data are available on the internet at http://dnb.dnb.de.

© 2025 Walter de Gruyter GmbH, Berlin/Boston
This volume is text- and page-identical with the hardback published in 2023.
Printing and binding: CPI books GmbH, Leck
Typesetting: Ludger Jansen

www.degruyter.com

Contents

Foreword —— VII

Tomas Bokedal, Ludger Jansen, Michael Borowski
Scripture and Theology in Context: An Introduction —— 1

Part 1: Scripture and the Web of Meanings

Jeanine Mukaminega
An Anthropological Analysis of Ezekiel 13:17–21 —— 35

Torleif Elgvin
Messiahs and Redeemer Figures in Postexilic Texts —— 57

Luuk van de Weghe
Early Divine Christology: Scripture, Narrativity and Confession in Luke-Acts —— 89

Tomas Bokedal
Why is the New Testament Called "New Testament"? —— 119

Francis Borchardt
Disassembling Provenance: Origin Stories and Why They Matter for Scripture —— 149

Part 2: The Bible at Work: Historical Case Studies

Beatrice Victoria Ang
Power Dynamics in the Preached Word: A Fourth Century Case Study —— 165

Willibald Sandler
Augustine without a Theodicy of a Condemning God —— 195

Ludger Jansen
Philosophy in Aquinas' Exegetical Work and Its Meta-Theological Implications —— 235

Knut Alfsvåg
Hamann between Luther and Hume —— 261

Alison Milbank
Let Everything that Hath Breath Praise the Lord —— 283

Brandon K. Watson
The Divine Forwards: Karl Barth's Early Exegesis of the Pauline Epistles —— 305

Georg Fischer
Karl Rahner's Use of the Bible —— 327

Part 3: Informing Theological Discourse: Systematic Perspectives

Boubakar Sanou and John C. Peckham
Canonical Theology, Social Location and the Search for Global Theological Method —— 345

Hans Burger
Quadriga without Platonism —— 375

Arnold Huijgen
Reinventing the Quadriga —— 397

Mark W. Elliott
The Theological Art of Scriptural Interpretation: Lessons from von Balthasar —— 415

Ida Heikkilä
The Holy Scriptures as a Recognition- and Witnessing-Authority —— 433

Elisabeth Maikranz
The Relationship of Scripture and Tradition in the Light of God's Revelation —— 453

Michael Borowski
Deriving Theology from Scripture —— 473

List of Contributors —— 487

Foreword

> Und jedem Anfang wohnt ein Zauber inne
> Der uns beschützt und der uns hilft zu leben.
>
> In all beginnings dwells a magic force
> For guarding us and helping us to live.
>
> Hermann Hesse

"In all beginnings dwells a magic force." Hermann Hesse was certainly right. Yet, it is never *only* magic in the beginning – often there is also labour, for instance, and sometimes downright confusion. The development of this volume involved some magic, extensive labour, and, if not confusion, the constant push for orientation – for if scholars from different academic, geographic, cultural and denominational backgrounds seek to talk with each other about Scripture and theology, initial orientation is essential.

This present anthology is witness to such a push towards initial orientation. It represents an unusual collection of peer reviewed essays in several respects. It does not only seek to bridge the two key domains in Divinity, biblical studies (or Scripture) and theology; it also includes contributions from senior and junior scholars of various professional and denominational backgrounds. The bulk of the twenty chapters included in the book stems from presentations at the Scripture & Theology workshops held in Bologna in 2019 and digitally in 2020 at the Annual Conferences of the European Academy of Religion (EuARe). The spectrum of theological and methodological style embraced spans a wide range of scholarly approaches. Some of the contributions employ traditional historical and literary methods, others are primarily constructive-theological or critical-emancipatory in their approach, while still other papers reflect a particular church context, or a wider ecumenical horizon, as the platform for theological and historical exploration. Thus, the book as a whole is a polyphonic response to the question how Scripture relates to theology. It collects voices from various disciplines and confessional backgrounds. Each of the authors is responsible for their own contribution.

In the process of completing the volume, we, the editors, made new friends. We are grateful towards the EuARe for their continuing efforts to foster dialogue where there was none. We thank the Scripture & Theology Advisory Board for their willingness to support our annual panels in various ways. We also thank the presenters and authors, as well as our reviewers and proofreaders – especially Dr. Mark Nixon – for their critical, yet constructive feedback on the papers. We further extend our thanks to NLA University College for funding proofreading of the present volume, and to de Gruyter – in particular, Dr. Albrecht Döhnert – for their willingness towards and support for this somewhat unusual volume. Likewise, we are grateful to our authors for following through with the demands and shifts connected with this publication. Finally, we want to thank Prof. Dr. Friederike Nüssel, Prof. Dr. Bruce McCormack and the late Prof. Dr. Christoph Schwöbel for their willingness and support to include the volume in the *Theologische Bibliothek Töpelmann*. In line with this, we also want to acknowledge that one of our presenters – Prof. Dr. Corneliu Constantineanu, Professor of Theology at Arad University, Romania – sadly passed away due to a Covid-19-infection. Corneliu's manuscript "Justice and Reconciliation: The Use of Scripture in Public Theology" could not be recovered. Corneliu himself is sincerely missed.

We see this volume as a first attempt to bring together Scripture and theology within a renewed discussion among a diversity of scholarly voices and interests. Future publications, we hope, will relate to this initial orientation, yet will not be able to reduce the complexity involved in the inherent connection between Scripture and theology. And it is this connection, with its potential for good scriptural, historical and constructive theology, that may also be "guarding us and helping us to live".

Aberdeen/Bergen, Brixen/Rostock, Amsterdam/Bielefeld
May 2023
TB, LJ, MB

Tomas Bokedal, Ludger Jansen, Michael Borowski
Scripture and Theology in Context: An Introduction

Abstract: The chapter sets the stage for the volume by describing the state of the art and the particular contribution of the present book. The opening paragraphs outline the history of the interrelations between Scripture and biblical studies with theology in the pre-modern, modern and late-modern periods. This is followed by a brief introduction to each of the book's chapters.

Keywords: Scripture, Theology, Biblical Studies, Exegesis, Hermeneutics, History of interpretation

1 A Broken Relationship?

Christianity relates to the Bible. Yet here the questions begin: How can theology be derived from Scripture, how can faith be gained from text? These questions can be asked in biblical, historical and systematic perspectives: What is the theological status of the Bible? How have the Scriptures been received theologically through the centuries? And how should they be appropriated today? How can biblical studies, on the one hand, and systematic and constructive theology, on the other, interact in productive ways and be fruitful for the Christian faith in a 21st century context? These are the book's leading questions.

For a long time in the past, biblical studies and systematic, or doctrinal, theology were closely linked to one another. However, in the modern period they became gradually separated which led to increasing subject specialization but also to a lamentable lacuna within the various branches of theology as the lack of dialogue between biblical studies and the various other theological sub-disciplines increased.[1] In the recent past, the British New Testament scholar Fran-

---

[1] Cf. Roy A. Harrisville and Walter Sundberg, *The Bible in Modern Culture: Baruch Spinoza to Brevard Childs* (Grand Rapids: Eerdmans, 2002, 2nd ed); and Jonathan Sheehan, *The Enlightenment Bible: Translation, Scholarship, Culture* (Princeton, NJ: Princeton University Press, 2005).

Tomas Bokedal, NLA University College, Norway; University of Aberdeen, UK; tomas.bokedal@nla.no
Ludger Jansen, University of Rostock, Germany; and PTH Brixen, Italy, ludger.jansen@pthsta.it
Michael Borowski, VU Amsterdam, The Netherlands, michael.borowski@gmx.de

cis Watson and others have expressed concerns about the mutual isolation vis-à-vis one another of the theological sub-disciplines Old Testament, New Testament and systematic theology.[2] Separating the two domains of Scripture and theology is not always indicative of a healthy division of labour. According to Watson, this split between sub-disciplines also deeply affects biblical studies as such, where scholars of the Hebrew Bible, the Old Testament, typically have little, if any, need of the New Testament. On a similar note, traditional New Testament studies only rarely pursue serious engagement with Patristic exegesis, early Christian doctrine or liturgical theology. Systematic theology in the past decades, on its part, has frequently undertaken major advancements quite independent of the biblical material or the longstanding dialogue with biblical scholarship.

However, cross-disciplinary approaches increasingly have found their way into the theological sub-disciplinary curricula, helping to set new agendas for how Scripture and theology may relate to one another. In a variety of contexts, scholars have sought to re-establish the time-honoured bonds between the disciplines. The present volume is part of this intellectual response, with contributions from scholars of various professional and denominational backgrounds. The book's chapters together seek to reinvigorate the crucial interdisciplinary dialogue, involving particularly biblical, historical and systematic-theological perspectives. The anthology offers a cross-disciplinary academic response to various facets of what has often been perceived as a broken relationship between the domains. In this introduction, we will shortly sketch this situation and its historical genesis (sections 2–4) and explain how the chapters in this volume address it (sections 5–8).

Given the long tradition of Christian theology, the aforementioned divide between Scripture and theology is a relatively recent one. How did it come about? Somewhat oversimplifying, in the interest of conciseness and simplicity, we divide the history of biblical interpretation into three phases to situate the chapters of the present volume in a broad historical context: the pre-modern period (pre-Christian period–1500 CE), the modern period (1500–present), and, as its end-phase, the late-modern period (1970–present). For each of these three periods we will briefly characterize the Scripture-and-theology dynamic. In telling this story, we make transparent the framework we operate within, and how the chapters of this volume are connected to this framework.

---

[2] Francis Watson, *Text and Truth: Redefining Biblical Theology* (Edinburgh: T&T Clark, and Grand Rapids: Eerdmans, 1997). See also Stephen E. Fowl, *Engaging Scripture: A Model for Theological Interpretation*, Challenges in Contemporary Theology (Oxford: Blackwell, 1998).

2 The Pre-modern Period

Pre-modern scriptural interpretation, whether through the eyes of an Irenaeus, Origen or an Aquinas, was attentive to the theological world of the Scriptures as received in the Jewish and Christian faith communities. In the case of the former two church teachers, representing pre-Nicene theologizing, we can note a key phenomenon, underlined by the German theologian Wolfhart Pannenberg – namely that the early church *presupposed* the truth of dogmas. This is reflected in the *Epistle to Diognetus* (5.3) and in Origen (*In Matt.* 12.23): As "the Christian faith does not rest on human teaching", it follows that Christian doctrines can be described as divine dogmas (*dogmata theou*), with God as guarantor for their claims to truth.[3] This early revelatory view of theology was further affiliated with a unified view of the Scriptures, as noted by the Patristic scholar Frances Young: "The unity of the scriptures is recognised to have been a 'dogma' among the Fathers."[4] For the Christian faith communities and their leaders, these Scriptures were perceived as canonical[5] and triune[6] in character, associated with the triune Rule of Faith/Truth (*regula fidei/veritatis*). As the Church Father Irenaeus underscores, "Whoever keeps the Rule of Truth, which they received through baptism, unchanged in their heart, will know … [the things taught] from the Scriptures" (*Haer.* III, 4.1). Both Irenaeus (*Haer.* I, 9.4–10.1; III, 1.2) and Tertullian (*Praescr.* 19) are representative voices of this faith, "the faith of those who believe in the Father and Son and Holy Spirit" (Tert. *Prax.* 2), referring to the sum content of apostolic teaching.[7] Similarly, Clement of Alexandria, who also

---

[3] Wolfhart Pannenberg, *Systematic Theology*, vol. 1, trans. Geoffrey W. Bromiley (Edinburgh: T&T Clark 1991), 9–10.

[4] Frances M. Young, *Biblical Exegesis and the Formation of Christian Culture* (Cambridge: Cambridge University Press, 1997), 7.

[5] See, e.g., Bruce M. Metzger, *The Canon of the New Testament: Its Origin, Development, and Significance* (Oxford: Clarendon Press, 1987); and *The Biblical Canon Lists from Early Christianity: Texts and Analysis*, edited by Edmon L. Gallagher and John D. Meade (Oxford: Oxford University Press, 2017).

[6] See, e.g., Tomas Bokedal, *The Formation and Significance of the Christian Biblical Canon: A Study in Text, Ritual and Interpretation* (London: Bloomsbury T&T Clark, 2014).

[7] For a historical treatment, see Tomas Bokedal, "The Rule of Faith: Tracing Its Origins," *Journal of Theological Interpretation* 7.2 (2013): 233–55; and, for systematic-theological reflection, cf. Robert W. Jenson, *Systematic Theology*, vol. 1, *The Triune God* (New York: Oxford University Press, 1997), 46: "the phrase 'Father, Son, and Holy Spirit' is simultaneously a very compressed telling of the total narrative by which Scripture identifies God and a personal name for the God so specified; in it, name and narrative description not only appear together, as at the beginning of the Ten Commandments, but are identical. […] The church is the community

associates the church's Rule, or Ecclesiastical Canon, with the Old and New Testament Scriptures and their interpretation. Clement writes: "The Canon of the Church is the agreement and unity of the Law and the Prophets with the [New] Testament delivered at the coming of the Lord."[8] To Irenaeus, Clement and other early exegetes and theologians, Christological and triune textual highlighting was further visible in the Greek Old and New Testament manuscripts themselves by means of *nomina sacra* ("sacred names") demarcations; i.e., a delimited selection of specially sacred words, such as the Greek terms for "God", "Jesus" and "Spirit".[9] British palaeographer C. H. Roberts nicely characterises these textual markers as "the embryonic creed of the first Church".[10] The early triune Rule-of-Faith structure, perceivable in text, liturgy and theology eventually took on a widely accepted expression in the Apostles' Creed and, even more so, in the ecumenical Nicene Creed (C).[11]

On a more general note, the overall strong Christological focus in the faith communities, indicated through the *regula fidei*, *nomina sacra* demarcations and otherwise, was brought to bear specifically on the church's Scriptures, and their interaction with theology. In Origen's phrasing, "All the Scriptures are one book because all the teaching that has come to us about Christ is recapitulated

---

and a Christian is someone who, when the identity of God is important, names him 'Father, Son, and Holy Spirit'. Those who do not or will not belong to some other community."

[8] Clem. *Strom.* VI, 15.125.3: κανὼν δὲ ἐκκλησιαστικός ἡ συνῳδία καὶ συμφωνία νόμου τε καὶ προφητῶν τῇ κατὰ τὴν τοῦ κυρίου παρουσίαν παραδιδομένῃ διαθήκῃ. See further Bengt Hägglund, "Die Bedeutung der 'regula fidei' als Grundlage theologischer Aussagen," *Studia Theologica* 12 (1958): 1–44.

[9] For *nomina sacra* demarcations (here in SMALL CAPS), such as GOD (θεός, θ̄c̄), LORD (κύριος, κ̄c̄), JESUS (Ἰησοῦς, ῑc̄), CHRIST (χριστός, χ̄c̄), and SPIRIT (πνεῦμα, π̄ν̄ᾱ), their emergence and significance, see Larry W. Hurtado, *The Earliest Christian Artifacts: Manuscripts and Christian Origins* (Grand Rapids and Cambridge: Eerdmans, 2006), 95–154. For a brief overview of their appearance in early Bible manuscripts, see also the presentation in Tomas Bokedal, "What Was the First Bible Like?" *The Conversation*, 30.08.2018, https://theconversation.com/what-was-the-first-bible-like-102005.

[10] C. H. Roberts, *Manuscript, Society and Belief in Early Christian Egypt* (Oxford: Oxford University Press, 1979). In the Codex Sinaiticus, for example, over 95 percent of these *nomina sacra* are written in their contracted forms in the Greek Old and New Testaments. Images of the codex can be found at https://codexsinaiticus.org/en/manuscript.aspx. For the description of the *nomina sacra* as a visible creed, see also R. Kendall Soulen, *The Divine Name(s) and the Holy Trinity*, vol. 1, *Distinguishing the Voices* (Louisville: Westminster John Knox Press, 2011).

[11] For an overview of various creedal texts, see J. N. D. Kelly, *Early Christian Creeds* (New York: Longman Publishing, 1972); and *Faith in Formulae: A Collection of Early Christian Creeds and Creed-related Texts*, edited by Wolfram Kinzig, 4 vols. (Oxford: Oxford University Press, 2017).

in one single whole" (*Ioa. Comm.* V, 6).¹² Similarly, Origen's teacher, Clement, when in his *Stromateis* he connects Christ with Scripture: "For in the Lord we have the first principle of our teaching (ἀρχὴ τῆς διδασκαλίας), both by the prophets, the Gospel, and the blessed apostles." (*Strom.* VII, 16.95)¹³

As for variations of exegetical-theological approaches among early scriptural expositors, we can notice the commitment to Christological fulfilment of prophecy (exemplified by Justin Martyr¹⁴); exegesis in line with the Rule of Faith (exemplified by Irenaeus and Tertullian;¹⁵ differently in Marcion¹⁶ and Gnostic biblical interpreters¹⁷); hermeneutical appeal to the literal, moral and spiritual meanings of Scripture (exemplified by Origen¹⁸); engagement with figurative, literal and Christian meanings of Scripture (exemplified by Augustine¹⁹); and theoretical discussion on the literal sense – and its relation to other senses – of Scripture (exemplified by Thomas Aquinas²⁰). In the fourfold sense of Scripture reading (literal, allegorical, tropological and eschatological) that arose from the time of Augustine onwards, the historian David Steinmetz suggests that the three non-literal senses correlate with the three theological virtues:

---

12 Origène, *Commentaire sur Saint Jean: Livres I–V*, edited by Cécile Blanc, Source chrétiennes 120, 383f. (Paris: Éditions du Cerf, 1966); cited from Enrique Nardoni, "Origen's Concept of Biblical Inspiration," *The Second Century* 4 (1984): 9–23, here 14.
13 *The Ante-Nicene Fathers*, edited by Alexander Roberts and James Donaldson (Peabody: Hendrickson, 1885–1887), vol. 2, 550, modified.
14 See, e.g., Oskar Skarsaune, *The Proof from Prophecy: A Study in Justin Martyr's Proof-Text Tradition. Text-Type, Provenance, Theological Profile* (Leiden: Brill, 1987).
15 See, e.g., Heinz Ohme, *Kanon ekklesiastikos: Die Bedeutung des altkirchlichen Kanonbegriffs*, Arbeiten zur Kirchengeschichte 67 (Berlin: de Gruyter, 1998), 61–121; and Mark Edwards, *Catholicity and Heresy in the Early Church* (Farnham: Ashgate, 2009), 4–5, 43.
16 See, e.g., Metzger, *The Canon of the New Testament*, 91–94.
17 See, e.g., Birger A. Pearson, *Ancient Gnosticism: Traditions and Literature* (Minneapolis: Fortress Press, 2007), 101–33; and Edwards, *Catholicity and Heresy in the Early Church*, 11–33; cf. also Andreas Köstenberger and Michael J. Kruger, *The Heresy of Orthodoxy: How Contemporary Culture's Fascination with Diversity Has Reshaped Our Understanding of Early Christianity* (Wheaton: Crossway, 2010).
18 See, e.g., Joseph W. Trigg, *Origen*, The Early Church Fathers (London: Routledge, 1998), 32–35; William Yarchin, *History of Biblical Interpretation: A Reader* (Peabody: Hendrickson, 2004), 41–50; and Martin Westerholm and Stephen Westerholm, *Reading Sacred Scripture: Voices from the History of Biblical Interpretation* (Grand Rapids: Eerdmans, 2016), 67–100.
19 See, e.g., Yarchin, *History of Biblical Interpretation*, 61–75; and *Augustine: On Christian Doctrine and Selected Introductory Works*, edited by Timothy George, Theological Foundations (Nashville: B&H Academic, 2022), 9–165.
20 Yarchin, *History of Biblical Interpretation*, 93–96; and Westerholm and Westerholm, *Reading Sacred Scripture: Voices from the History of Biblical Interpretation*, 162–97.

The allegorical sense taught about the Church and what it should believe, and so it corresponded to the virtue of faith. The tropological sense taught about individuals and what they should do and so it corresponded to the virtue of love. The anagogical sense pointed to the future and wakened expectation, and so it corresponded to the virtue of hope.[21]

Along these lines – at least in principle – the Scriptures, either together with church tradition and the office of episcopacy (the early church, Orthodox and Catholic churches), or on their own (the early church, and later many Protestant churches), functioned normatively vis-à-vis the Christian movement.[22] A major incentive behind their success as Holy Writ in the church universal, and beyond, was their continuous use for public reading and exposition in corporate worship, from the first century onwards.[23]

3 The Modern Period

In the modern period (1500–present) many of the pre-modern assumptions of biblical interpretation, including the relationship between Scripture and theology outlined above, were, on the one hand, continued and deepened in the Orthodox, Catholic and Protestant church traditions up till the present.[24] On the

---

21 David C. Steinmetz, "The Superiority of Pre-Critical Exegesis," in *The Theological Interpretation of Scripture: Classic and Contemporary Readings*, edited by Stephen E. Fowl (Oxford: Blackwell, 1997), 29; quoted from Treier, *Introducing Theological Interpretation of Scripture*, 51.

22 Cf. *Didascalia Apostolorum*, ch. 4 (Connolly, R. H., *Didascalia Apostolorum, the Syriac Version translated and accompanied by the Verona Latin Fragments* [Oxford: Oxford University Press, 1929], 34), which discusses one of the major episcopal tasks, pertaining to scriptural interpretation, urging the bishop "to compare the Law and the Prophets with the Gospel, so that the sayings of the Law and the Prophets may be in accord with the Gospel"; cf. also the *Gelasian Decree* (nn. 350–4; Denzinger, *Enchiridion symbolorum definitionum et declarationum de rebus fidei et morum* [Freiburg im Breisgau: Herder, 1991], 162–5): "propheticae et evangelicae atque apostolicae scripturae, quibus ecclesia catholica per gratiam Dei fundata est" ([it is] the prophetic, evangelical and apostolic Scriptures, on which the catholic church by God's grace is founded).

23 See Hughes Oliphant Old, *The Reading and Preaching of the Scriptures in the Worship of the Christian Church*, vol. 1, *The Biblical Period* (Grand Rapids: Eerdmans, 1998); for communal reading in the first century, see Brian J. Wright, *Communal Reading in the Time of Jesus: A Window into Early Christian Reading Practices* (Minneapolis: Fortress Press, 2017).

24 Alan J. Hauser and Duane F. Watson (eds), *A History of Biblical Interpretation*, vol. 2, *The Medieval through the Reformation Periods* (Grand Rapids: Eerdmans, 2009); John Breck, *Scripture in Tradition: The Bible and Its Interpretation in the Orthodox Church* (Yonkers, NY: St. Vladimir's Seminary Press, 2001); Edith M. Humphrey, *Scripture and Tradition: What the Bible*

other hand – as a parallel and largely academic development – they were variously and gradually amended, critiqued, deconstructed, and reformulated to fit Renaissance, Reformation, Enlightenment and historicist reasoning.[25] A first thing to note in this connection is that around the turn of the 16th century (1500 CE), printed bibles began to replace handwritten manuscripts, which often resulted in a loss of textual information, such as standard inclusion of the supratextual *nomina sacra* demarcations, which disappeared from printed English Bibles.[26]

During the Reformation, special attention was devoted to historical, literal and Christological exegesis of the biblical texts. As things developed in the Western church, a divide arose between the appropriation of Scripture and that of the tradition(s) of the church. As the Reformers stressed the Scripture principle (*sola scriptura*),[27] the Catholics countered by underlining the hermeneutical

---

Really Says (Grand Rapids: Baker Academic, 2013); Gerald Bray, *Biblical Interpretation: Past and Present* (Downers Grove: InterVarsity Press, 1996); Henri de Lubac, *Scripture in the Tradition*, Milestones in Catholic Theology (Wheaton: Crossway, 2000); Craig A. Carter, *Interpreting Scripture with the Great Tradition: Recovering the Genius of Premodern Exegesis* (Grand Rapids: Baker Academic, 2018); and Scott W. Hahn, *Covenant and Communion: The Biblical Theology of Pope Benedict XVI* (Grand Rapids: Brazos Press, 2009).

25 See the *Dictionary of Biblical Interpretation*, edited by John Hayes (Nashville: Abingdon Press, 1999); Yarchin, *History of Biblical Interpretation*; Robert Morgan with John Barton, *Biblical Interpretation*, The Oxford Bible Series (Oxford: Oxford University Press, 1988); William Baird, *History of New Testament Research*, 3 vols. (Minneapolis: Fortress Press, 1992–2013).

26 E.g., the Tyndale Bible and the King James Bible. This transition, from manuscripts to printed bibles, is noted, with a critical remark, by Dietrich Bonhoeffer, as documented in *Finkenwalde 1935–37*, Dietrich Bonhoeffer Werke 14 (Gütersloh: Gütersloher Verlagshaus, 1996), 510. John Henry Newman, another leading theologian, upheld the *nomina sacra* convention in his own writings. See also Dirk Jongkind, *Scribal Habits of Codex Sinaiticus*, Text and Studies: Contributions to Biblical and Patristic Literature, Third Series 5 (Piscataway, NJ: Gorgias Press, 2007); and D. C. Parker, *An Introduction to the New Testament Manuscripts and Their Texts* (Cambridge: Cambridge University Press, 2008).

27 Cf. the description of Luther's view on how Scripture produces faith in Westerholm and Westerholm, *Reading Sacred Scripture: Voices from the History of Biblical Interpretation*, 209: "Note well: 'the Holy Spirit ... through the Gospel': the (external) Word (= the gospel) and (the inner working of) the Spirit together produce faith"; and ibid., 231: "Read at its literal level, the content of Scripture can be divided into two categories: law and gospel. Keeping the categories distinct is crucial to reading Scripture aright." As for John Calvin commenting on Scripture, we may note the following (ibid., 247): "Those who wish to prove to unbelievers that Scripture is the Word of God are acting foolishly, for only by faith can this be known. (*Inst.* 1.8.13)" See further Keith A. Mathison, *The Shape of Sola Scriptura* (Moscow, ID: Canon Press, 2001); and M. D. Thompson, *A Sure Ground on Which to Stand: The Relation of Authority and Interpretive Method in Luther's Approach to Scripture* (Bletchley: Milton Keynes; Wynesboro: Paternoster, 2004).

importance of both Scripture and tradition.²⁸ Renaissance appeal to the sources (*ad fontes*) led to further and deeper textual study among scholars such as the humanist Erasmus of Rotterdam and within the Protestant camps, through the major Reformers, the Pietist movement, and the Lutheran and Reformed scholastic programmes. Scholarly attention to the original biblical languages was a central factor in the renewed interest in the Scriptures, resulting in translations into the vernacular languages – which, however, were at the same time neglected, in favour of the Latin Vulgate in Western Europe. Martin Luther's full translation, from the Greek and Hebrew/Aramaic, of the New Testament (1522) and the Old Testament with Apocrypha (1534) into German, is here pivotal for the new way of scriptural reading and research, with special attention devoted to the letter. Luther's publication as well of Old and New Testament commentaries were soon continued by John Calvin, who further renewed this exegetical trend by producing some forty-five volumes of biblical commentary, reflecting his classical humanist training, by closely attending to the 'plain sense', with special attention dedicated to "grammatical and rhetorical features of the text in its original languages, and in its historical context."²⁹

When this philologically oriented exegesis and theologizing was integrated into doctrinal works, such as Melanchthon's *Loci Communes* or Calvin's *Institutio Christianae Religionis*, the result was an amalgamation of grammatical biblical exegesis and theology, which could be described as a form of Scripture

---

28 *Council of Trent, Concilium Tridentinum diariorum, actorum, epistularum, tractatuum nova collection*, edited by the Societas Goerriesiana, 13 vols. (Freiburg: Herder, 1901–2001), 5:31. "hanc veritatem partim contineri in libris scriptis, partim sine scripto traditionibus"; for a Lutheran response to the decrees embraced by the Council of Trent, see Martin Chemnitz, *Examination of the Council of Trent*, 4 vols., trans. M. and F. Kramer (St. Louis: Concordia, 1971–1986); cf. also Ronald D. Witherup, *The Word of God at Vatican II: Exploring Dei Verbum* (Liturgical Press, 2014), 9–10; and, for tradition and Scripture in the early period, J. N. D. Kelly, *Early Christian Doctrines* (San Francisco: Harper, 1978), rev. ed., 29–51; for an interesting recent ecumenical engagement between Protestant and Catholic theologians, see Kevin J. Vanhoozer's essay "Expounding the Word of the Lord: Joseph Ratzinger on Revelation, Tradition, and Biblical Interpretation" (as well as other essays), in *The Theology of Benedict XVI: A Protestant Appreciation*, edited by Tim Perry (Bellingham: Lexham Press, 2019), 66–86; ibid., 85: "Ratzinger's most enduring legacy may well be his attempt to make good on Vatican II's claim that, the study of the sacred page should be [...] the very soul of theology." (*Dei Verbum*, §24). As for catholic traditions that prevailed among Protestants, Jaroslav Pelikan (*Credo: Historical and Theological Guide to Creeds and Confessions of Faith in the Christian Tradition* [New Haven and London: Yale University Press, 2003], 473) provides the following quote from Benjamin Breckenridge Warfield, who writes that "the Reformation, inwardly considered, was just the ultimate triumph of Augustine's doctrine of grace over Augustine's doctrine of the church."
29 Yarchin, *History of Biblical Interpretation*, 184.

based theological exegesis, or whole-biblical theology, with an emphasis on key biblical passages and doctrines.[30] A further addition to their academic training, characterizing the works of the early Reformers, was the field of Rabbinic and Hebrew scholarship needed for access to the linguistic world of the Hebrew Bible. Yet another area of expertise notable in Melanchthon and others, bolstering scriptural interpretation, was the embrace of Patristic theology and exegesis.[31] The renewed exegetical focus and learning, which emphasised the literal sense of Scripture, had already caused Luther, when studying the OT – with his dual interest in grammatical scriptural exposition and theology (centring on the Ten Commandments, Christology, soteriology and creedal theology) – to distinguish between two different types of literal scriptural meanings, the historical and the prophetical, *sensus literalis historicus*, on the one hand, and *sensus literalis propheticus*, on the other. Another Lutheran impetus that was later played up by historical-critical scholarship, was the partially open approach to the question of biblical canonicity.[32]

When historical criticism entered the scene with scholars such as Johann Philip Gabler and his inaugural address – "On the Proper Distinction between Biblical and Dogmatic Theology and the Specific Objectives of Each" – at Altdorf in 1787,[33] critical reflection on the separation of biblical and dogmatic the-

---

30 See, e.g., Todd R. Hains, *Martin Luther and the Rule of Faith: Reading God's Word for God's People*, New Explorations in Theology (Downers Grove: IVP Academic, 2022); and Carl R. Trueman, *The Creedal Imperative* (Wheaton: Crossway, 2012); for a different emphasis, cf. Loren T. Stuckenbruck, "Johann Philipp Gabler and the Delineation of Biblical Theology," *Scottish Journal of Theology* 52 (1999): 140 and 140n.3 (139–52): "Martin Luther's principle of *sola scriptura*, which broadly characterised the Reformation's critique of medieval scholasticism, was initially not distinguished from dogmatic theology. And so, the study of the biblical text was essentially considered the virtual equivalent for the articulation of the church's teaching on a given subject. [...] Hence, for example, Philipp Melanchthon could refer to Paul's letter to the Romans as a *compendium doctrinae*."
31 See, e.g., Peter Fraenkel, Ld., *Testimonia Patrum: The Function of the Patristic Argument in the Theology of Philip Melanchthon*, Travaux d'humanisme et renaissance 46 (Genève: Librairie E. Droz, 1961).
32 See Jacob A. O. Preus, "The New Testament Canon in the Lutheran Dogmaticians," *The Springfielder* 25 (1961): 8–33; regarding later discussions on the canon, see the important anthology *Das Neue Testament als Kanon*, edited by Ernst Käsemann (Göttingen: Vandenhoeck & Ruprecht, 1970); and, with an emphasis on canonical diversity, rather than canonical unity, see Ernst Käsemann, "The Canon of the New Testament and the Unity of the Church," in idem, *Essays on New Testament Themes*, Studies in Biblical Theology, First Series 41 (London: SCM Press, 1968): 95–107.
33 Johann Philipp Gabler, *De justo discrimine theologiae biblicae et dogmaticae regundisque racte utriusque finibus*; English translation: "On the proper distinction between biblical and dogmatic

ology, which until then had tended to be conflated,[34] was placed at the forefront of the scholarly discussion. Gabler suggested a three-stage process through which to move from historical biblical studies to biblical theology: i) linguistic and historical analysis of biblical texts, ii) identification of ideas common among the biblical writers, and iii) articulation of the Bible's timeless and universal principles. Based on these principles, being inspired by Enlightenment ideas, "biblical theology" was claimed to have been 'founded' in its own right, offering an objective, constant and enduring message, which then could be used also by dogmaticians. However – contrary to beliefs held in the premodern period – in Gabler's view, as phrased by the biblical scholar Loren Stuckenbruck, dogmatics was "a very human enterprise, subject to changes imposed by the specific contexts within which theologians find themselves".[35] This gap posed between historical biblical and theological doctrinal studies, separating text and reader, resulted in the exemplary interpreter being one not initially led by theological commitments and, in the furtherance of historical methodology – in the biblical scholar Joel Green's phrasing – one not guided "by commitments of any kind, other than the bracketing of questions of 'truth' in order to give priority to the question of 'meaning'".[36]

The academic development of biblical interpretation in the 19th and early 20th century was dramatic with the appearance of mythical approaches to scriptural interpretation (Strauss), rational criticism of the life of Jesus (Reimarus), historical-critical analysis of the Old Testament (Wellhausen), liberal Protestantism (Ritschl, von Harnack), the history of religions approach (Weiss, Bousset, Wrede, Troeltsch), and form criticism (Gunkel, Noth, von Rad, Schmidt, Dibelius, Bultmann).[37]

One of the most important contributions to historical-critical analysis was William Wrede's influential *The Task and Methods of 'New Testament Theology'*

---

theology and the specific objectives of each," in John Sandys Wunsch and Laurence Eldredge, "J. P. Gabler and the Distinction Between Biblical and Dogmatic Theology: Translation, Commentary, and Discussion of His Originality," *Scottish Journal of Theology* 33 (1980): 133–58.

34 David R. Law, *The Historical-Critical Method: A Guide for the Perplexed*, Guides for the Perplexed (London: Bloomsbury, 2012), 52.

35 Stuckenbruck, "Johann Philip Gabler," 144. Cf. ibid., 156: "A number of aspects in Gabler's programme are no longer thought to be tenable by biblical theologians. These would include, among others, Gabler's presumption that one can describe the contents and aims of biblical (or any) texts 'objectively', that historical accidents are devoid of any formative theological claims, and that one can arrive through the analysis of such details at a 'pure' biblical theology."

36 Joel B. Green, *Seized by Truth* (Nashville: Abingdon Press, 2007), 63–4.

37 See further Morgan with Barton, *Biblical Interpretation*.

(originally published in German in 1897).[38] In this programmatic work, Wrede presents some of the basic and lasting principles of historical-critical scholarship. We will here list some of the key points with impact on the Scripture–theology dynamic: i) the old doctrine of inspiration is recognized by academic theology to be untenable (69), ii) with the doctrine of inspiration discarded, it is no longer possible to maintain the dogmatic concept of the canon, because, as Wrede put it, "no New Testament writing was born with the predicate 'canonical' attached" (70),[39] iii) the historian "must be guided by a pure disinterested concern for knowledge" (70), iv) the New Testament can no longer "be temporally located in the apostolic period" (71), v) it is questioned whether the New Testament documents can be said to contain "doctrine" (75, 81),[40] vi) the task of New Testament theology is to "lay out the history of early Christian religion and theology," rather than focusing on the religious and ethical content of the New Testament writings (84), and, vii) "the name New Testament theology is wrong in both its terms" (116).

Four decades later, the British biblical scholar C. H. Dodd could present the New Testament scholarly project as a critical task undertaken in five successive stages, culminating in biblical theology, with each new stage building on the results of the previous stages: 1) textual criticism; 2) introductory questions (*Einleitung*); 3) detailed linguistic exegesis; 4) comparative study of ancient Jewish, Hellenistic, and early Christian religious beliefs; and 5) biblical theology.[41] In terms of methodology and subject matter, modern New Testament scholarship had reached a highpoint in regard to scholarly confidence. In Dodd's words, summarizing the modern state of the art of the New Testament

---

38 William Wrede, "The Task and Methods of 'New Testament Theology'," in *The Nature of New Testament Theology: The Contribution of William Wrede and Adolf Schlatter*, edited by Robert Morgan (Eugene: Wipf & Stock; previously published by SCM Press, 1973). A more recent endorsement of Wrede's programme can be found in Heikki Räisänen, *Beyond New Testament Theology: A Story and a Programme*, 2nd ed. (London: SCM Press, 2000).
39 Cf. Frank Thielman, *Theology of the New Testament: A Canonical and Synthetic Approach* (Grand Rapids: Zondervan, 2005), 28, commenting in this connection: "the canonicity of certain texts has no meaning for the historian of early Christianity until the authoritative status of the canonical texts themselves becomes important for early Christianity."
40 According to Wrede (p. 70), "It is only justifiable to speak of doctrine when thoughts and ideas are developed for the sake of teaching."
41 Charles H. Dodd, *The Present Task in New Testament Studies: An Inaugural Lecture Delivered in the Divinity School on Tuesday, 2 June 1936* (Cambridge: Cambridge University Press, 1936); source: Markus Bockmuehl, *Seeing the Word: Refocussing New Testament Study*, Studies in Theological Interpretation (Grand Rapids: Baker Academic, 2006), 28.

discipline, "The major problems had in a measure been solved."[42] Some five decades later, another confident expert – leading historical-Jesus scholar E. P. Sanders – could provide an eye-catching list of facts "almost beyond dispute" that outlined Jesus' life, including "a short list of equally secure facts" about the aftermath of Jesus' life.[43] Despite variations in epistemological approach, the value (of this kind) of historical research also for theology and Christology is indicated by a number of scholars.[44]

4 The Late-modern Period

The late-modern period in biblical interpretation (1970–present) can be said to have begun effectively from the 1970s on. Perhaps the most important scholar in this connection, who set out to break, in part, with standard historical methodology and the modern approach to the discipline, was the American Old Testament scholar Brevard S. Childs.[45] Childs' *Biblical Theology in Crisis*[46] and his *Introduction to the Old Testament as Scripture*,[47] helped to set new and broader agendas in biblical studies, where historical scholarship could be pursued parallel to other approaches. Most noteworthy among these was Childs' own canonical approach, which is open to reception-, effective- and salvation-history (influenced by von Rad and Gadamer), as well as to dogmatics (influenced by Barth). This had implications also for theologians who worked in dialogue with

---

[42] Dodd, *The Present Task in New Testament Studies*, 10; cited from Bockmuehl, *Seeing the Word: Refocussing New Testament Study*, 30.

[43] E. P. Sanders, *The Historical Figure of Jesus* (London: Penguin Books, 1993), 10–11. For a late-modern response to Sanders and other modern scholars on historical Jesus scholarship, see, e.g., *Jesus, Criteria, and the Demise of Authenticity*, edited by Chris Keith and Anthony Le Donne (London: T&T Clark, 2012).

[44] See, e.g., Watson, *Text and Truth*, 10–11; Peter Stuhlmacher, *Jesus of Nazareth – Christ of Faith* (Peabody: Hendrickson, 1993); and Luke Timothy Johnson, *The Real Jesus: The Misguided Quest for the Historical Jesus and the Truth of the traditional Gospels* (San Francisco: Harper, 1996); cf. also Dale C. Allison Jr., *The Historical Christ and the Theological Jesus* (Grand Rapids: Eerdmans, 2009); and James D. G. Dunn, "Remembering Jesus: How the Quest of the Historical Jesus Lost Its Way," in *The Historical Jesus: Five Views*, edited by James K. Beilby and Paul Rhodes Eddy. (Downers Grove: IVP Academic, 2009), 200: "My first protest is directed in the first place against the assumption that 'the Christ of faith' is a perversion of 'the historical Jesus'; that faith is something which prevents a clear historical view of Jesus."

[45] See Yarchin, *History of Biblical Interpretation*, 305–19.

[46] Brevard S. Childs, *Biblical Theology in Crisis* (Philadelphia: Westminster Press, 1970).

[47] Brevard S. Childs, *Introduction to the Old Testament as Scripture* (London: SCM Press, 1979).

biblical scholarship. As a matter of fact, the initial impetus to much of Childs' biblical, and canonical, theological approach was the methodological breakthrough in theological exegesis undertaken by Karl Barth fifty years earlier, with the publication of *Der Römerbrief* in 1919 (1921, 2nd ed.), where Barth focused on the "'subject matter', or 'content' or 'substance' of the text – and therefore, in this case, the being of the eternal God – as having hermeneutical control."[48] Barth's background in writing this highly influential commentary was his frustration when he, as a pastor in 1915, experienced a "lack of anything to preach from the liberal verities of his theology teachers."[49] In his later theological writings, Barth was to produce classical and creative church dogmatics, in close dialogue with theologians and exegetes of the church's past. Barth and Childs are thus central for the subject of the present volume, which is bringing Scripture and theology into dialogue with one another. Other biblical scholars soon followed the example of Childs, such as James A. Sanders and Walter Brueggemann.[50] From the 1970s to the present, a broad range of methods and approaches have entered the domains of biblical studies.

In a situation when a wide spectrum of methods and approaches are available for both theologians and biblical scholars, theological exegesis is an attractive avenue forward for many. However, methodological pluralism comes with several challenges, not least in the biblical guild, where space is offered to a plethora of scholarly approaches, e.g., traditional historical-criticism, tradition-historical criticism, literary criticism, rhetorical criticism, feminist criticism, postcolonial criticism, canonical criticism – and, in addition, methods focusing on Graeco-Roman literature and culture, social history, cultural anthropology, and modern archaeology. In regard to this methodological pluralism that has come to characterize, in particular, the discipline of New Testament studies, the New Testament scholar Markus Bockmuehl notes the "splendid isolation" with which the different methodological approaches often operate vis-à-vis one another as well as the fragmentation regarding scholarly method: "The extraordi-

---

[48] Treier, *Introducing Theological Interpretation of Scripture*, 16. Cf. also Donald Wood, *Barth's Theology of Interpretation*, Barth Studies (London: Routledge, 2016; first published by Ashgate in 2007), 86: "'modernity' is not a basic category for Barth. On his terms, the church that attends to God's revelation can speak meaningfully of specific historical ages and trends."
[49] Treier, *Introducing Theological Interpretation of Scripture*, 14.
[50] Cf. James A. Sanders, *Canon and Community: A Guide to Canonical Criticism* (Philadelphia: Fortress, 1984); James A. Sanders, *From Sacred Story to Sacred Text: Canon as Paradigm* (Philadelphia: Fortress, 1987); and Walter Brueggemann, *The Creative Word: Canon as Model for Biblical Education*, revised and with a foreword by Amy Erickson (Minneapolis: Fortress, 2015).

nary degree of isolation and fragmentation pertains not merely in matters of method, but in virtually every aspect of the discipline."[51] The systematic theologian Robert W. Jenson responds on the cover of Bockmuehl's *Seeing the Word* in a correspondingly solemn key: "What does one do about an academic discipline, 'New Testament studies,' that has almost done away with its own object of study?"[52]

5 Scripture and Theology in a Late-modern Context

As for the Scripture–theology dynamic in the late-modern situation, briefly outlined above, we noted that cross-disciplinary approaches increasingly have found their way into the theological sub-disciplinary curricula, helping to set new promising agendas for how Scripture and theology may relate to one another. During the last decades, we have seen new scholarly emphasis on the following seven dimensions:

(i) Canonical reading,[53] with a renewed focus on canonical approaches towards biblical interpretation. As in much subsequent canonical interpretation, various direct or indirect responses to the 20th century biblical scholar Brevard Childs have been at the forefront.[54] Within New Testament canon

---

[51] Bockmuehl, *Seeing the Word: Refocussing New Testament Study*, 33.
[52] For a different response to the pluralism that characterise the disciplines of biblical studies, see, e.g., "The Interpretation of the Bible in the Church," presented by the Pontifical Biblical Commission to Pope John Paul II on April 23, 1993 (as published in *Origins*, January 6, 1994). https://catholic-resources.org/ChurchDocs/PBC_Interp-FullText.htm, 24.09.2022; and Markus Bockmuehl, "Bible versus Theology: Is 'Theological Interpretation' the Answer?" *Nova et Vetera* 9 (2011): 27–47.
[53] E.g., Craig Bartholomew et al., *Canon and Biblical Interpretation*, Scripture & Hermeneutics Series 7 (Milton Keynes & Wynesboro: Paternoster; Grand Rapids: Zondervan, 2006; cf. also *Verbindliches Zeugnis*, vol. 1, *Kanon – Schrift – Tradition*, edited by Wolfhart Pannenberg and Theodor Schneider (Freiburg: Herder; Göttingen: Vandenhoeck & Ruprecht, 1992); and *Die Einheit der Schrift und die Vielfalt des Kanons. The Unity of Scripture and the Diversity of the Canon*, edited by John Barton and Michael Wolter, Beihefte zur Zeitschrift für die neutestamentliche Wissenschaft und die Kunde der Älteren Kirche 118 (Berlin: de Gruyter, 2003).
[54] Childs, *Introduction to the Old Testament as Scripture*; Brevard S. Childs, *The New Testament as Canon: An Introduction* (London: SCM Press, 1984); idem, *Biblical Theology of the Old and New Testaments: Theological Reflection on the Christian Bible* (Minneapolis: Fortress Press, 1992).

studies, Bruce Metzger's learned contribution from 1987 is another valuable starting point for historical and theological exploration of the canon.[55]

(ii) The interaction between text, history and theology in biblical studies,[56] often involving a wider array of disciplines as well, in which theological elements become part of a serious critical engagement with the biblical texts in their historical, literary, or broader textual, context. To this effect, Donald A. Hagner writes in the Preface of his *The New Testament: A Historical and Theological Introduction*: "A distinguishing mark of the present book is its understanding of the NT within the framework of the history of salvation."[57] Other *Introductions*, bridging the genre of *New Testament Introduction* (*Einleitung in das Neue Testament*) and aspects of theology have appeared, helping to set a broader sub-disciplinary agenda.[58] Appeal for broader methodological scope, beyond the purely historical, in Old and New Testament studies – including literary, reader-oriented and theological approaches – are addressed also in studies such as John Barton's *Reading the Old Testament: Method in Biblical Study*[59] and the essay collection, *Hearing the New Testament: Strategies for Interpretation*, edited by Joel B. Green.[60]

---

55 Metzger, *The Canon of the New Testament*. See also Bokedal, *The Formation and Significance of the Christian Biblical Canon*; John C. Peckham, *Canonical Theology: The Biblical Canon, Sola Scriptura, and Theological Method* (Grand Rapids: Eerdmans, 2016); and *Canon Formation: Tracing the Role of Sub-Collections in the Biblical Canon*, edited by W. Edward Glenny and Darian R. Lockett (London: T&T Clark, 2023).

56 E.g., Donald A. Hagner, *The New Testament: A Historical and Theological Introduction* (Grand Rapids: Baker Academic, 2012). Cf. Udo Schnelle, *The History and Theology of the New Testament Writings* (London: SCM Press, 1998): "The canonical concept is only a later focusing and concentration of a claim already implicit within the documents themselves. It is therefore possible for one to dispense with the specific concept of the canonicity of the documents being studied without surrendering a concern for the substance of their message or negating the theological dimension of the discipline 'Introduction to the New Testament'."

57 Hagner, *The New Testament: A Historical and Theological Introduction*, xi.

58 E.g., N. T. Wright and Michael Bird, *The New Testament in Its World: An Introduction to the History, Literature, and Theology of the First Christians* (London: SPCK, and Grand Rapids: Zondervan Academic, 2019).

59 John Barton, *Reading the Old Testament: Method in Biblical Study* (Louisville: Westminster John Knox Press, 1984, 1996). See also *The Cambridge Companion to Biblical Interpretation*, edited by John Barton (Cambridge: Cambridge University Press, 1998); for a different, practical-theological methodological emphasis, see further John Eaton, *The Psalms: A Historical and Spiritual Commentary with an Introduction and New Translation* (London: Continuum, 2003).

60 See *Hearing the New Testament: Strategies for Interpretation*, edtied by Joel B. Green (2nd ed., Grand Rapids: Eerdmans, 2010). See also *Searching for Meaning: An Introduction to Interpreting the New Testament*, edited by Paula Gooder (London: SPCK; 2008).

(iii) Reception-historical studies,[61] as the new forceful, historically more broadly informed, avenue for the study of biblical and other religious texts of the past. Several influential studies have recently been published in this area, such as Stephen J. Chester's *Reading Paul with the Reformers: Reconciling Old and New Perspectives*.[62] In the near future we may expect further impact of such studies also on more traditional biblical scholarship.[63] This area of scholarship, in the somewhat narrower sense, is also referred to as the use of the Bible in the church,[64] which draws on past scriptural engagement in order to gain refreshing insights on text, exegesis and interpretation for past and present. Biblical scholars interested in reception-history, church historians as well as systematicians can all benefit from this new wave of publications, attending to scriptural usage through the ages.

(iv) Hermeneutically and theologically reflected biblical interpretation, or biblical theology, which provides a more advanced and holistic view of biblical textuality, not least as applied to OT and NT theology,[65] where at the same

---

61 E.g., Brevard S. Childs, *The Struggle to Understand Isaiah as Christian Scripture* (Grand Rapids: Eerdmans, 2004); John Riches, *Galatians through the Centuries*, Blackwell Bible Commentaries (London: Blackwell Publishing, 2008), as well as other volumes in Blackwell Bible Commentaries series; Timothy George, *Reading Scripture with the Reformers* (Downers Grove: IVP Academic, 2011); *A History of Biblical Interpretation*, vols. 1–2, edited by Alan J. Hauser and Duane F. Watson (Grand Rapids: Eerdmans); and *Handbuch der Bibelhermeneutiken: Von Origenes bis zur Gegenwart*, edited by Oda Wischmeyer (Berlin: de Gruyter, 2016).

62 Stephen J. Chester, *Reading Paul with the Reformers: Reconciling Old and New Perspectives* (Grand Rapids: Eerdmans, 2017).

63 Cf. the inclusion of reception-historical and history-of-interpretation reflections throughout Ulrich Luz's renowned commentary on Matthew, *Matthew 1–7*, *Matthew 8–20* and *Matthew 21–28*, Hermeneia, three vols. (Minneapolis: Fortress Press, 2001–2007). See also Stephen Westerholm, *Romans: Text, Readers, and the History of Interpretation* (Grand Rapids: Eerdmans, 2022).

64 Cf., e.g., the series *Interpretation: Resources for the Use of Scripture in the Church*, edited by Patrick D. Miller (Louisville: Westminster John Knox Press), the *Ancient Christian Commentary on Scripture* series, edited by Thomas C. Oden, and the *Reformation Commentary on Scripture* series (both published by IVP Academic, Downers Grove).

65 E.g., Ronald E. Clements, *Old Testament Theology: A Fresh Approach*, Marshall's Theological Library (Basingstoke: Marshall Morgan & Scott, 1978); Brevard S. Childs, *Old Testament Theology in a Canonical Context* (Minneapolis: Fortress Press, 1985); Walter Brueggemann, *Theology of the Old Testament: Testimony, Advocacy, Dispute* (Minneapolis: Fortress Press, 1997); Erhard S. Gerstenberger, *Theologies in the Old Testament* (London: T&T Clark, 2002); R. W. L. Moberly, *Old Testament Theology: Reading the Hebrew Bible as Christian Scripture* (Grand Rapids: Baker Academic, 2013); Ernest W. Nicholson, *God and His People: Covenant and Theology in the Old Testament* (Oxford: Clarendon Press, 1986); Udo Schnelle, *Theology of the New Testament* (Grand Rapids: Baker Academic, 2009); Frank J. Matera, *New Testament Christology* (Louisville: Westminster John Knox Press, 1999).

time the historical issues at stake are taken into account.⁶⁶ Scholarly focus on the theology of individual biblical books, or groups of biblical writings, is linked to this renewed interest in this approach.⁶⁷
(v) Two-horizons initiatives involving biblical studies and systematic theology,⁶⁸ offering continual interdisciplinary engagement and dialogue, with particular attention given to the exegesis and theology of a particular biblical book, Scripture as a whole, and Christian doctrine. Two-horizons projects, with input from both biblical scholars and systematicians, focusing on a particular biblical book, such as the Gospel of John and the Epistle to the Hebrews, here deserve particular mention.⁶⁹
(vi) Theological interpretation of Scripture⁷⁰ is another promising change in scriptural interpretation and theological work, and the mutual interaction and collaboration of the two theological disciplines.

---

66 Cf. the whole-biblical approach by Peter Stuhlmacher in his *Biblical Theology of the New Testament* (Grand Rapids: Eerdmans, 2018); Reinhard Feldmeier and Hermann Spieckermann, *God of the Living: A Biblical Theology* (Waco: Baylor University Press, 2011). Cf. also *Beyond Biblical Theologies*, edited by Heinrich Assel, Stefan Beyerle and Christfried Böttrich (Tübingen: Mohr Siebeck, 2012); and *The Oxford Encyclopedia of the Bible and Theology*, edited by Samuel E. Balentine, 2 vols. (Oxford: Oxford University Press, 2015). For hermeneutically oriented approaches, see further Ben F. Meyer, *Reality and Illusion in New Testament Scholarship: A Primer in critical Realist Hermeneutics* (Collegeville, MN: The Liturgical Press, 1994); and the broad hermeneutical introduction to biblical interpretation in Anthony C. Thiselton, *New Horizons in Hermeneutics: The Theory and Practice of Transforming Biblical Reading* (Grand Rapids: Zondervan, 1992).
67 See, e.g., John Goldingay, *The Theology of the Book of Isaiah* (Downers Grove: IVP Academic, 2014); the *New Testament Theology* series edited by James D. G. Dunn (Cambridge: Cambridge University Press); James D. G. Dunn, *The Theology of Paul the Apostle* (Grand Rapids: Eerdmans, 1998); Joseph A. Fitzmyer, *Paul and His Theology: A Brief Sketch* (Upper Saddle River: Prentice Hall, 1967, 1989); and Udo Schnelle, *Apostle Paul: His Life and Theology* (Grand Rapids: Baker Academic, 2005). See also the more than 30 volumes of the *Jahrbuch für Biblische Theologie* that have appeared since 1986.
68 E.g., *The Two Horizons Old Testament Commentary* series, edited by J. Gordon Conville and Craig Bartholomew (Grand Rapids: Eerdmans); *The Two Horizons New Testament Commentary* series, edited by Joel B. Green and Max Turner (Grand Rapids: Eerdmans); and *SCM Theological Commentary on the Bible*, edited by R. R. Reno et al. (London: SCM Press).
69 E.g., *The Gospel of John and Christian Theology*, edited by Richard Bauckham and Carl Mosser (Grand Rapids: Eerdmans, 2008); and *The Epistle to the Hebrews and Christian Theology*, edited by Richard Bauckham et al. (Grand Rapids: Eerdmans, 2009).
70 E.g., David H. Kelsey, *Proving Doctrine: The Uses of Scripture in Modern Theology* (Valley Forge: Trinity Press International, 1999); *The Theological Interpretation of Scripture: Classic and Contemporary Readings*, edited by Stephen E. Fowl (Oxford: Blackwell Publishers, 1997); *Theological Exegesis: Essays in Honor of Brevard S. Childs*, edited by Christopher Seitz and Kathryn

(vii) Relating Scripture and theology has also been a concern for scholars who seek to conceptualize theological method by addressing theology's sources and construals.[71] Such attempts have been made in both Protestant and Roman Catholic contexts.[72] Yet, despite these honourable interdisciplinary advancements, several of the scholarly sub-disciplines within Divinity are, unfortunately, still largely isolated in relation to one another.

As pointed out above, the chapters of the present volume respond to various aspects of the broken relationship between the domains Scripture and theology that still mark the late-modern scholarly situation. The authors connect in sev-

---

Greene-McCreight (Grand Rapids: Eerdmans, 1998); *Reading Texts, Seeking Wisdom: Scripture and Theology*, edited by David F. Ford and Graham Stanton (Grand Rapids: Eerdmans, 2003); *Dictionary for Theological Interpretation of the Bible*, edited by Kevin Vanhoozer et al. (London: SPCK and Grand Rapids: Baker Academic, 2005); *Scripture's Doctrine and Theology's Bible: How the New Testament Shapes Christian Dogmatics*, edited by Markus Bockmuehl and Alan J. Torrance (Grand Rapids: Baker Academic, 2008); Daniel J. Treier, *Introducing Theological Interpretation of Scripture: Recovering a Christian Practice* (Nottingham: Apollos, 2008); and Joseph K. Gordon, *Divine Scripture in Human Understanding: A Systematic Theology of the Christian Bible* (Notre Dame, IN: University of Notre Dame Press, 2019). For a more historically oriented contribution to this field, see, e.g., *The Bible and Early Trinitarian Theology*, edited by Christopher A. Beeley and Mark E. Weedman (Washington D.C.: The Catholic University of America Press, 2018). There is also a journal specially devoted to theological interpretation, namely, *the Journal of Theological Interpretation*, with the following online description: "Critical biblical scholarship as developed and defined since the mid-eighteenth century has played a significant and welcome role in pressing us to take biblical texts seriously on their own terms and diverse contexts. With the postmodern turn, additional questions have surfaced—including the theological and ecclesial location of biblical interpretation, the significance of canon and creed for biblical hermeneutics, the historical reception of biblical texts, and other more pointedly theological interests. How might we engage interpretively with the Christian Scriptures so as to hear and attend to God's voice? The *Journal of Theological Interpretation* aims to serve these agendas." (Retrieved from https://www.jstor.org/journal/jtheointe on 24.09.2022.)

71 E.g., *The Routledge Companion to the Practice of Christian Theology*, edited by Mike Higton and Jim Fodor (London: Routledge, 2015).

72 See, for instance, John Webster, *The Domain of the Word: Scripture and Theological Reason* (London: Bloomsbury, 2012); Nicholas Lash, *Newman on Development: The Search for an Explanation in History* (Palm Coast, FL: Patmos Press, 1975); Gerald O'Collins and Daniel Kendall, *The Bible for Theology: Ten Principles for the Theological Use of Scripture* (New York/Mahwah, NJ: Paulist Press, 1997); Donald A.D. Thorsen, *The Wesleyan Quadrilateral: Scripture, Tradition, Reason & Experience as a Model of Evangelical Theology* (Grand Rapids: Zondervan, 1990). The issue is often touched upon in fundamental theology and systematic-theological prolegomena. Maybe the most important contribution in this regard has been David H. Kelsey, *The Uses of Scripture in Recent Theology* (Minneapolis: Fortress Press, 1975).

eral ways to the seven dimensions identified in this section. Canonical reading (i) is addressed by Bokedal as well as by Sanou and Peckham. Mukaminega, Elgvin, and Borchard address the interaction between text, history and theology in biblical studies (ii). Ang, Jansen, and Fischer study the reception of Scripture (iii). Hermeneutically and reflected biblical interpretation (iv) is endorsed by Van de Weghe. Sandler, Watson, and Huijgen address two-horizon initiatives (v), while theological interpretation (vi) is addressed by Alfsvåg, by Sanou and Peckham, by Burger, Huijgen, and Elliott. Finally, the last chapters in this volume, by Heikkilä, Maikranz, and Borowski, discuss theological method and the question how to relate Scripture and theology in general (vii).

Some of the chapters include sub-disciplinary dialogue between the two domains quite explicitly (Alfsvåg, Watson), other contributions do so both directly and indirectly (Mukaminega, Bokedal), while still others demonstrate more of an openness towards such dialogue and interdisciplinarity (Elgvin, Borchardt). Other cross-disciplinary emphases of the volume address the dialogue between history and New Testament theology/Christology (Van de Weghe), historical theology and the present (Ang), Thomistic philosophy and exegesis (Jansen), eco-theology and the Bible (Milbank), the use of the Bible in theology (Sandler, Fischer), canonical reading (Sanou and Peckham), the theological art of scriptural interpretation (Elliott), the connection between exegesis and systematic theology via the traditional idea of the fourfold sense of Scripture (Burger, Huijgen), interaction between Scripture and tradition(s) (Heikkilä, Maikranz), and Scripture in doctrinal development (Borowski). Along the lines listed above, the present anthology is taking some first steps towards constructive scholarly dialogue and mutual engagement. By bringing together contributions from various disciplines, and from various confessional and geographic backgrounds into a single volume, we hope to encourage further dialogue outside of one's sub-discipline. The chapters in this book are organised in three parts, which we will now outline: Part 1, "Scripture and the Web of Meaning" (detailed in section 6), Part 2, "The Bible at Work: Historical Case Studies" (section 7), and Part 3, "Informing Theological Discourse: Systematic Perspectives" (section 8).

6 Part One: Scripture and the Web of Meanings

In the opening chapters, five biblical scholars reflect historically, literarily, hermeneutically, and theologically on a selection of ancient canonical and noncanonical texts. Specific themes in two biblical books – emancipatory anthropology in Ezekiel and creative construal of Christology in Luke – are highlighted, while a broader range of canonical and non-canonical literature is explored in the remaining chapters. These dwell on the emergence of messiahship and redeemer figures in postexilic texts, canon formation across the first Christian centuries, and literary origin stories in Jewish and Christian milieus – with potential for, or a view towards, present significance and application. The movement at the core of these chapters in Part One thus is from text and Scripture to fresh perspectives on anthropology, messiahship, the-κύριος-becoming-the-Christ theology, covenantal theology, patterns of biblical intra-textuality, processes of textual canon formation and scriptural authority.

Jeanine Mukaminega critically explores aspects of the anthropology of Ezekiel 13:17–21. She begins with a brief review of previous studies, focusing particularly on issues of gender, of religion, and ties with Ancient Near East cultures. Airing discomfort with some earlier scholarly reflection, Mukaminega analyses the keywords within Ezekiel 13 and notes the issue of silenced voices, before addressing the broader anthropological background of prophetic writings in the Ancient Near East literature. She concludes that in the era of 21st century biblical criticism, Ezekiel's oracle hermeneutics may foster a healthy and creative theological reading. A critical historical re-evaluation may review the anthropology of the long-standing readings.

Torleif Elgvin presents a historical-literary survey of texts on messiahs and redeemer figures in postexilic times, covering writings that in the course of time were classified as biblical, OT apocrypha, OT pseudepigrapha or belonging to the Dead Sea Scrolls. The chapter contrasts individual and collective messianism, and surveys Davidic, priestly, dual, and heavenly messianism. The study is primarily diachronic, at times overruled by thematic considerations. While pre-exilic texts demonstrate the hope for a son of David perceived in earthly categories, exilic and post-exilic times would see a transformation of the hopes for a divinely commissioned leader. In Second Temple times, eschatological and messianic hopes become pluriform and multifaceted. By demonstrating a pluriformity in eschatological outlook and messianic hope, Elgvin argues that biblical texts are not less pluriform as they, too, may be seen as responses to the historical situation of any given place and time.

Luuk van de Weghe assesses Luke's corpus as presenting a complex portrait of Jesus: In terms of his messianic identity, Luke-Acts crafts Jesus in regal and prophetic categories, while it also presents him as the κύριος through various trajectories within the narrative. Van de Weghe starts out by arguing that Luke's reliance on diverse sources could account for this complexity. He moves on by making the case that Luke appears to develop his κύριος Christology in accordance with this complexity, enhancing Jesus' divine lordship in respect to the perspectives within his narrative. Van de Weghe argues that Luke does not merely present a biographical depiction of Jesus, but uses his variegated portrait to present what it is like for the κύριος to become the Christ.

Reflecting historically, theologically and editorially-canonically, *Tomas Bokedal* asks why the New Testament is called 'the New Testament' to begin with. He submits that there are five partly complementary answers to this question. Building on previous scholarly contributions by Theodor Zahn, W. C van Unnik, Hans von Campenhausen, Wolfram Kinzig and David Trobisch, the chapter suggests the relevance of all five answers for a comprehensive, hermeneutically informed understanding of the title. A particular emphasis of the chapter is the historical and theological continuity across first and second century Christian reflection on the new covenant notion based on Jeremiah 31:31–34.

Francis Borchardt compares the stories of discovery in the translator's prologue to Ben Sira, the prologue of the Sibylline Oracles, and the prologue of the Gospel of Nicodemus to illustrate how these prologues function to create the works to which they are attached as fully realized entities in the world. He concludes that these prefatory passages establish that the texts (or the corpora of knowledge) with which they are affiliated bear strong connections to ancient and somehow privileged knowledge. By linking past, present and future, they may be of perennial interest to audiences in various settings.

7 Part Two: The Bible at Work

Moving through the past two millennia, Part Two of this volume presents seven historical case studies which contribute to an engagement with past attempts of doing theology by applying Scripture. The first three chapters in this section address classic theologians: John Chrysostom, Augustine, and Thomas Aquinas.

Beatrice Ang explores the mechanics behind the proclamation of Scripture by drawing on the thought and practice of John Chrysostom. She aims to provide a Chrysostomian perspective into what it means to "preach with power". She analyses two sermons in the light of modern studies on Chrysostom's Christian appropriation of Hellenistic psychagogy for one, and in the light of the fourth century controversy between pro-Nicenes and Arians regarding the implications of power in the essential relationship between the Father and the Son for another. Ang argues that for Chrysostom, the divine authority and ability of the Son must be affirmed if preaching is to have a positive effect on human well-being, and that Chrysostom's reasons have been shaped by practical and political considerations, as well as by Scripture-based theo-anthropological assumptions.

Willibald Sandler addresses Augustine's interpretation of Scripture. He argues that only due to a fatal misunderstanding of Romans 9, Augustine thought he had to accomplish a "theodicy of a damning God". Sandler argues that in view of these and other biblical-theological flaws in the wake of this central misunderstanding, especially in the area of Augustine's theology of original sin and grace, dogmatic theologians are faced with the question of whether they must radically distance themselves from Augustine and from a dogmatic church doctrine based on him in these areas, or whether a differentiated transformative reception is possible which, as in the case of Augustine himself, is guided by biblical-theological insights.

Ludger Jansen assesses the role of philosophy in Aquinas' exegetical work and its meta-theological implications by studying Aquinas' treatment of John 1:14a. He begins by sketching the standard account of Aquinas' meta-theological view, inspired by the first *quaestio* in the *Summa theologiae*, and then moves on to discuss how Aquinas uses philosophy in his interpretation of the famous passage from the Prologue of the Gospel of John where it is said that the Word became flesh. Jansen concludes that while the official meta-theology from the *Summa* stresses the hierarchical structure of sciences and the foundationalist character of the reference to Scripture, Aquinas' exegetical practise is very much non-foundationalist.

The next two chapters attend to authors from early modern Europe. *Knut Alfsvåg* addresses the preconditions of the background from which our theologies are shaped, asking how we can disentangle the metaphysical commitments of modern science from their obvious achievements. Closing in on the issue of a Christian worldview, Alfsvåg focuses on the development of thought in the German theologian Johann Georg Hamann (1730–1788): contextualizing Hamann in an epoch of increasing biblical criticism in the 18th century, Alfsvåg traces the development in seeing the Bible differently by updating some of Luther's emphases.

Alison Milbank studies the reaction of Christian poets to the Cartesian reduction of animals to mere machines. Milbank seeks to demonstrate that in opposition to this well-known approach, Cartesian dualism was questioned at the same time. She shows how the poetry of Henry Vaughan (1621–1695) and Christopher Smart (1722–1771) exemplifies, as she puts it, "a more respectful and theological understanding of the natural order and a different construal of the human role towards it".

The two concluding chapters examine the use of Scripture in two important theologians of the twentieth century, namely Karl Barth and Karl Rahner. *Brandon K. Watson* focuses on Karl Barth's early exegesis of the Pauline letters, honing in on the root of Barth's dogmatic system and development to uncover early evidence of Barth's Trinitarian and Christological understanding of election from within his biblical exegesis. To do so, Watson engages with Barth's early exegetical lectures during his two professorships in Göttingen and Münster, teasing out theological implications from Barth's exegesis of Paul. Additionally, Watson understands Barth to be a rich resource for biblical studies, showing not only that Barth's biblical insights influenced his dogmatic work, but also how his biblical exegesis remains relevant for reflection on God's self-identification with the human Jesus.

Georg Fischer reports on the research project "Karl Rahner and the Bible" that explores the backgrounds and characteristics of Rahner's approach to Scripture by exposing its roots in the *Spiritual Exercises* and his philosophical formation. Fischer concludes that an ambivalence in Rahner's attitude towards the Bible can be seen: While Rahner would have marked the Bible with high esteem, on the one hand, there would be a clear preference for the tradition of the Church, on the other. This affects also Rahner's stance towards the Old Testament and Judaism.

8 Part Three: Informing Theological Discourse

The process of making theological proposals has always been full of challenges. Part Three reflects on a number of current challenges, aiming to provide resources for doing theology today.

Boubakar Sanou and *John C. Peckham* emphasize the social contexts in which theology is pursued and point to a potential conflict between contexts and universalist approaches. In particular, they emphasize that many issues in contemporary theology might be foreign to the 'Majority World'. Sanou and Peckham argue that the privileging of philosophical or theological frameworks would lead at least to two concerns, namely the potential undermining of the uniquely normative authority of Scripture that the vast majority of Christians across the globe affirm, and the danger of imposing particular philosophical, doctrinal, or other frameworks onto Scripture. Canonical theology, Sanou and Peckham argue, can help to deal with these two concerns.

Hans Burger addresses the fourfold sense of Scripture by referring to Hans Boersma and his new evaluation of the *quadriga*, the traditional idea of the fourfold sense of Scripture. While he remains largely positive about Boersma's conception of sacramental ontology as the presupposition of a fourfold typology, Burger takes some issue with the Platonism Boersma requires. Burger concludes that the practice of spiritual reading in search for Christological meaning does not necessarily imply a Platonist worldview with its inherent problems and can be continued today without such Platonism.

Arnold Huijgen seeks to even 'reinvent' the *quadriga* by connecting biblical exegesis and systematic theology via the anagogical-eschatological sense of Scripture. Huijgen identifies three levels on which Eschatology connects biblical studies and systematic theology: (i) the eschatological coming of God fitting to the Old Testament, (ii) the eschatological expectation of the church according to the New Testament, and (iii) the eschatological character of truth explicated in the Christian creed, i.e., Christ's coming to judge the living and the dead. Huijgen concludes that this strategy of using the *quadriga* does not commit to a Platonic worldview.

Mark Elliott takes into focus Hans Urs von Balthasar's theological art of scriptural interpretation: He contextualizes von Balthasar's work with Rahner and Schlier in order to then look at Balthasar's contribution to the Catholic multi-authored volume *Mysterium Salutis* of 1967, before moving to consider six thematic elements in his *Herrlichkeit* (translated as *Glory of the Lord*). Elliott briefly accounts for Balthasar's 1976 reflections on the relationship between biblical exegesis and dogmatics; he concludes with a consideration of the related questions of 'canon' and 'theological encyclopedia'.

Ida Heikkilä addresses the different understandings of the relationship between Scripture and tradition as one of the central reasons for ecclesial tension and division at the beginning of the third millennium. Focusing on the German Catholic–Lutheran dialogue "Communio Sanctorum", she discusses the question of who has the final say in the church and how the different authorities relate to each other.

Elisabeth Maikranz explores the tension between the normative function of Scripture of Protestant theology and the various traditions that developed from the canon. Maikranz starts out by reflecting on various dimensions of 'tradition', and the more recent historical development of this concept. She then turns to Wolfhart Pannenberg as her central interlocutor for elaborating the complexity of the relationship between Scripture and tradition. In connection to his work, Maikranz concludes that the critical function of Scripture is a dynamic process in which inner-biblical processes of interpretation are translated into the present in order to convey the special significance of the biblical events of revelation. This implies, as Maikranz shows, that theology needs to take into account the complexity of tradition in Scripture in an effort to elucidate transmission processes to understand the formation of significance. It also implies that transmitting the content of the revelation of God is always linked to Scripture and seeks expressions to translate its significance into new contexts, and that expressing the salvific reality of God in reference to Scripture and tradition cannot disclose a definite and final expression of this reality.

Finally, *Michael Borowski* addresses the question, How can theology be derived from Scripture? In search for an answer, he analyses Kevin J. Vanhoozer's work on the development of doctrine in order to submit an exemplary outline for doctrinal development: In tracing this theme through Vanhoozer's project on 'being biblical' in one's theology, Borowski characterizes doctrine and its development as the theologian's primary task. For 'doing' theology, he then submits three elements of developing such doctrine: the turn to Scripture, the formulation of doctrine, and the renewal of doctrine.[73]

References

Allison, Dale C., Jr., *The Historical Christ and the Theological Jesus*, Grand Rapids: Eerdmans, 2009.
Assel, Heinrich, Stefan Beyerle and Christfried Böttrich, eds., *Beyond Biblical Theologies*, Tübingen: Mohr Siebeck, 2012.
Baird, William, *History of New Testament Research*, 3 vols., Minneapolis: Fortress Press, 1992–2013.
Balentine, Samuel E., ed., *The Oxford Encyclopedia of the Bible and Theology*, two volumes, Oxford: Oxford University Press, 2015
Bartholomew, Craig et al., *Canon and Biblical Interpetation*, Scripture & Hermeneutics Series 7, Milton Keynes & Wynesboro: Paternoster; Grand Rapids: Zondervan, 2006.
Barton, John, ed., *The Cambridge Companion to Biblical Interpretation*, Cambridge: Cambridge University Press, 1998.
Barton, John, *Reading the Old Testament: Method in Biblical Study*, Louisville, KY: Westminster John Knox Press, 1984, 1996.
Barton, John and Michael Wolter, eds., *Die Einheit der Schrift und die Vielfalt des Kanons. The Unity of Scripture and the Diversity of the Canon*, Beihefte zur Zeitschrift für die neutestamentliche Wissenschaft und die Kunde der Älteren Kirche 118, Berlin: de Gruyter, 2003.
Bauckham, Richard and Carl Mosser, eds., *The Gospel of John and Christian Theology*, Grand Rapids: Eerdmans, 2008.

---

[73] We are indebted to Don Ross and Donald Wood for constructive comments on earlier versions of this introduction.

Bauckham, Richard et al., eds., *The Epistle to the Hebrews and Christian Theology*, Grand Rapids: Eerdmans, 2009.

Beeley, Christopher A. and Mark E. Weedman, eds., *The Bible and Early Trinitarian Theology*, Washington D.C.: The Catholic University of America Press, 2018.

Bockmuehl, Markus, "Bible versus Theology: Is 'Theological Interpretation' the Answer?" *Nova et Vetera* 9 (2011): 27–47.

Bockmuehl, Markus, *Seeing the Word: Refocussing New Testament Study*, Studies in Theological Interpretation, Grand Rapids: Baker Academic, 2006.

Bockmuehl, Markus and Alan J. Torrance, eds., *Scripture's Doctrine and Theology's Bible: How the New Testament Shapes Christian Dogmatics*, Grand Rapids: Baker Academic, 2008.

Bokedal, Tomas, *The Formation and Significance of the Christian Biblical Canon: A Study in Text, Ritual and Interpretation*, London: Bloomsbury T&T Clark, 2014.

Bokedal, Tomas, "The Rule of Faith: Tracing Its Origins." *Journal of Theological Interpretation* 7.2 (2013): 233–55.

Bokedal, Tomas, "What Was the First Bible Like?" *The Conversation*, 30 Aug. 2018, https://theconversation.com/what-was-the-first-bible-like-102005; accessed on 10.10.2022.

Bonhoeffer, Dietrich, *Finkenwalde 1935–37,* Dietrich Bonhoeffer Werke 14, Gütersloh: Gütersloher Verlagshaus, 1996.

Bray, Gerald, *Biblical Interpretation: Past and Present*, Downers Grove, IL: InterVarsity Press, 1996.

Breck, John, *Scripture in Tradition: The Bible and Its Interpretation in the Orthodox Church*, Yonkers, NY: St. Vladimir's Seminary Press, 2001.

Brueggemann, Walter, *Theology of the Old Testament: Testimony, Advocacy, Dispute*, Minneapolis: Fortress Press, 1997.

Brueggemann, Walter. *The Creative Word: Canon as Model for Biblical Education*, revised and with a foreword by Amy Erickson. Minneapolis: Fortress, 2015.

Carter, Craig A., *Interpreting Scripture with the Great Tradition: Recovering the Genius of Premodern Exegesis*, Grand Rapids: Baker Academic, 2018.

Chemnitz, Martin, *Examination of the Council of Trent*, 4 vols., translated by M. and F. Kramer, St. Louis, MO: Concordia Publishing House, 1971–1986.

Chester, Stephen J., *Reading Paul with the Reformers: Reconciling Old and New Perspectives*, Grand Rapids: Eerdmans, 2017.

Childs, Brevard S., *Biblical Theology in Crisis*, Philadelphia: Westminster Press, 1970.

Childs, Brevard S., *Biblical Theology of the Old and New Testaments: Theological Reflection on the Christian Bible*, Minneapolis: Fortress Press, 1992.

Childs, Brevard S., *Introduction to the Old Testament as Scripture*, London: SCM Press, 1979.

Childs, Brevard S., *The New Testament as Canon: An Introduction*, London: SCM Press, 1984.

Childs, Brevard S., *Old Testament Theology in a Canonical Context*, Minneapolis: Fortress Press, 1985.

Childs, Brevard, S., *The Struggle to Understand Isaiah as Christian Scripture*, Grand Rapids: Eerdmans, 2004.

Clements, Ronald E., *Old Testament Theology: A Fresh Approach*, Marshalls Theological Library, Basingstoke: Marshall Morgan & Scott, 1978.

Council of Trent, *Concilium Tridentinum diariorum, actorum, epistularum, tractatuum nova collection*, edited by the Societas Goerriesiana, 13 vols., Freiburg: Herder, 1901–2001.

Denzinger, Hermann, and Peter Hünermann, eds., *Enchiridion symbolorum definitionum et declarationum de rebus fidei et morum*, Freiburg: Herder, 1991.

Didascalia Apostolorum, the Syriac Version translated and accompanied by the Verona Latin Fragments, edited by R. H. Connolly, Oxford: Oxford University Press, 1929.

Dodd, Charles H., *The Present Task in New Testament Studies: An Inaugural Lecture Delivered in the Divinity School on Tuesday, 2 June 1936*, Cambridge: Cambridge University Press, 1936.

Dunn, James D. G., "Remembering Jesus: How the Quest of the Historical Jesus Lost Its Way." In James K. Beilby and Paul Rhodes Eddy, eds., *The Historical Jesus: Five Views*, Downers Grove, IL: IVP Academic, 2009, 199–225.

Dunn, James D. G., *The Theology of Paul the Apostle*, Grand Rapids: Eerdmans, 1998.

Eaton, John, *The Psalms: A Historical and Spiritual Commentary with an Introduction and New Translation*, London: Continuum, 2003.

Edwards, Mark, *Catholicity and Heresy in the Early Church*, Farnham: Ashgate, 2009.

Feldmeier, Reinhard and Hermann Spieckermann, *God of the Living: A Biblical Theology*, Waco, TX: Baylor University Press, 2011.

Fitzmyer, Joseph A., *Paul and His Theology: A Brief Sketch*, Upper Saddle River, NJ: Prentice Hall, 1967, 1989.

Ford, David F. and Graham Stanton, eds., *Reading Texts, Seeking Wisdom: Scripture and Theology*, Grand Rapids: Eerdmans, 2003.

Fowl, Stephen E., *Engaging Scripture: A Model for Theological Interpretation*, Challenges in Contemporary Theology, Oxford: Blackwell Publishing, 1998.

Fowl, Stephen E., ed., *The Theological Interpretation of Scripture: Classic and Contemporary Readings*, Oxford: Blackwell Publishers, 1997.

Fraenkel, Peter, *Testimonia Patrum: The Function of the Patristic Argument in the Theology of Philip Melanchthon*, Travaux d'humanisme et renaissance 46, Genève: Librairie E. Droz, 1961.

Gabler, Johann Philipp, *De justo discrimine theologiae biblicae et dogmaticae regundisque racte utriusque finibus*. English translation: "On the proper distinction between biblical and dogmatic theology and the specific objectives of each." In John Sandys Wunsch and Laurence Eldredge, "J. P. Gabler and the Distinction Between Biblical and Dogmatic Theology: Translation, Commentary, and Discussion of His Originality." *Scottish Journal of Theology* 33 (1980): 133–58.

Gallagher, Edmon L. Gallagher and John D. Meade, eds., *The Biblical Canon Lists from Early Christianity: Texts and Analysis*, Oxford: Oxford University Press, 2017.

George, Timothy, ed., *Augustine: On Christian Doctrine and and Selected Introductory Works*, Theological Foundations, Nashville, TN: B&H Academic, 2022.

George, Timothy, *Reading Scripture with the Reformers*, Downers Grove, IL: IVP Academic, 2011.

Gerstenberger, Erhard S., *Theologies in the Old Testament*, London: T&T Clark, 2002.

Glenny, W. Edward and Darian R. Lockett, eds., *Canon Formation: Tracing the Role of Sub-Collections in the Biblical Canon*, London: T&T Clark, 2023.

Goldingay, John, *The Theology of the Book of Isaiah*, Downers Grove, IL: IVP Academic, 2014.

Gooder, Paula, ed., *Searching for Meaning: An Introduction to Interpreting the New Testament*, London: SPCK and Louisville, KY: Westminster John Knox Press, 2008, 2009.

Gordon, Joseph K., *Divine Scripture in Human Understanding: A Systematic Theology of the Christian Bible*, Notre Dame, IN: University of Notre Dame Press, 2019.

Green, Joel B., ed., *Hearing the New Testament: Strategies for Interpretation*, Grand Rapids: Eerdmans, 2010, 2nd ed.

Green, Joel B., *Seized by Truth*, Nashville, TN: Abingdon Press, 2007.
Hägglund, Bengt, "Die Bedeutung der 'regula fidei' als Grundlage theologischer Aussagen." *Studia Theologica* 12 (1958): 1–44.
Hagner, Donald A., *The New Testament: A Historical and Theological Introduction*, Grand Rapids: Baker Academic, 2012.
Hahn, Scott W., *Covenant and Communion: The Biblical Theology of Pope Benedict XVI*, Grand Rapids: Brazos Press, 2009.
Hains, Todd R., *Martin Luther and the Rule of Faith: Reading God's Word for God's People*, New Explorations in Theology, Downers Grove, IL: IVP Academic, 2022.
Harrisville, Roy A. and Walter Sundberg, *The Bible in Modern Culture: Baruch Spinoza to Brevard Childs*, Grand Rapids: Eerdmans, 2002, 2nd ed.
Hauser, Alan J. and Duane F. Watson, eds., *A History of Biblical Interpretation*, vols. 1–2, Grand Rapids: Eerdmans, 2009.
Hayes, John, ed., *Dictionary of Biblical Interpretation*, Nashville, TN: Abingdon Press, 1999.
Higton, Mike and Jim Fodor, eds. *The Routledge Companion to the Practice of Christian Theology*, London: Routledge, 2015.
Humphrey, Edith M., *Scripture and Tradition: What the Bible Really Says*, Grand Rapids: Baker Academic, 2013.
Hurtado, Larry W., *The Earliest Christian Artifacts: Manuscripts and Christian Origins*, Grand Rapids and Cambridge: Eerdmans, 2006.
Jenson, Robert W., *Systematic Theology*. Vol. 1: *The Triune God*, New York: Oxford University Press, 1997.
Johnson, Luke Timothy, *The Real Jesus: The Misguided Quest for the Historical Jesus and the Truth of the traditional Gospels*, San Francisco: Harper, 1996.
Jongkind, Dirk, *Scribal Habits of Codex Sinaiticus*, Text and Studies: Contributions to Biblical and Patristic Literature, Third Series 5, Piscataway, NJ: Gorgias Press, 2007.
Käsemann, Ernst, ed., *Das Neue Testament als Kanon*, Göttingen: Vandenhoeck & Ruprecht, 1970.
Käsemann, Ernst, "The Canon of the New Testament and the Unity of the Church." In: idem, *Essays on New Testament Themes*, Studies in Biblical Theology, First Series 41, London: SCM Press, 1968, 95–107.
Keith, Chris and Anthony Le Donne, eds., *Jesus, Criteria, and the Demise of Authenticity*, London: T&T Clark, 2012.
Kelly, J. N. D., *Early Christian Creeds*, New York: Longman Publishing, 1972.
Kelly, J. N. D., *Early Christian Doctrines*, San Francisco: Harper, 1978.
Kelsey, David H., *Proving Doctrine: The Uses of Scripture in Modern Theology*, Valley Forge, PA: Trinity Press International, 1999.
Kelsey, David H., *The Uses of Scripture in Recent Theology*, Minneapolis: Fortress Press, 1975.
Kinzig, Wolfram, ed., *Faith in Formulae: A Collection of Early Christian Creeds and Creed-related Texts*, 4 vols., Oxford: Oxford University Press, 2017.
Köstenberger, Andreas and Michael J. Kruger, *The Heresy of Orthodoxy: How Contemporary Culture's Fascination with Diversity Has Reshaped Our Understanding of Early Christianity*, Wheaton, IL: Crossway, 2010.
Lash, Nicholas, *Newman on Development: The Search for an Explanation in History*, Palm Coast, FL: Patmos Press, 1975.
Law, David R., *The Historical-Critical Method: A Guide for the Perplexed*, Guides for the Perplexed, London: Bloomsbury, 52 (Kindle edition).

Lubac, Henri de, *Scripture in the Tradition*, Milestones in Catholic Theology, Wheaton, IL: Crossway, 2000.
Luz, Ulrich, *Matthew 1–7*, *Matthew 8–20* and *Matthew 21–28*, Hermeneia – A Critical and Historical Commentary on the Bible, 3 vols., Minneapolis: Fortress Press, 2001–2007.
Matera, Frank J., *New Testament Christology*, Louisville, KY: Westminster John Knox Press, 1999.
Mathison, Keith A., *The Shape of Sola Scriptura*, Moscow, ID: Canon Press, 2001.
Metzger, Bruce M., *The Canon of the New Testament: Its Origin, Development, and Significance*, Oxford: Clarendon Press, 1987.
Meyer, Ben F., *Reality and Illusion in New Testament Scholarship: A Primer in critical Realist Hermeneutics*, Collegeville, MN: The Liturgical Press, 1994.
Moberly, R. W. L., *Old Testament Theology: Reading the Hebrew Bible as Christian Scripture*, Grand Rapids: Baker Academic, 2013.
Morgan, Robert, with John Barton, *Biblical Interpretation*, The Oxford Bible Series, Oxford: Oxford University Press, 1988.
Nardoni, Enrique, "Origen's Concept of Biblical Inspiration." *The Second Century* 4 (1984): 9–23.
Nicholson, Ernest W., *God and His People: Covenant and Theology in the Old Testament*, Oxford: Clarendon Press, 1986.
O'Collins, Gerald and Daniel Kendall, *The Bible for Theology: Ten Principles for the Theological Use of Scripture*, New York/Mahwah, NJ: Paulist Press, 1997.
Ohme, Heinz, *Kanon ekklesiastikos: Die Bedeutung des altkirchlichen Kanonbegriffs*, Arbeiten zur Kirchengeschichte, Band 67, Berlin: de Gruyter, 1998.
Old, Hughes Oliphant, *The Reading and Preaching of the Scriptures in the Worship of the Christian Church*. Vol. 1: *The Biblical Period*, Grand Rapids: Eerdmans, 1998.
Origen. *Commentaire sur Saint Jean: Livres I–V*, edited by Cécile Blanc, Source chrétiennes 120, Paris: Éditions du Cerf, 1966.
Pannenberg, Wolfhart, *Systematic Theology*, vol. 1, translated by Geoffrey W. Bromiley, Edinburgh: T&T Clark 1991.
Pannenberg, Wolfhart and Theodor Schneider, eds., *Verbindliches Zeugnis 1: Kanon – Schrift – Tradition*, Freiburg: Herder and Göttingen: Vandenhoeck & Ruprecht, 1992.
Parker, D. C., *An Introduction to the New Testament Manuscripts and Their Texts*, Cambridge: Cambridge University Press, 2008.
Pearson, Birger A., *Ancient Gnosticism: Traditions and Literature*, Minneapolis: Fortress Press, 2007.
Peckham, John C., *Canonical Theology: The Biblical Canon, Sola Scriptura, and Theological Method*, Grand Rapids: Eerdmans, 2016.
Pelikan, Jaroslav, *Credo: Historical and Theological Guide to Creeds and Confessions of Faith in the Christian Tradition*, New Haven and London: Yale University Press, 2003.
Pontifical Biblical Commission, "The Interpretation of the Bible in the Church." Presented by the Pontifical Biblical Commission to Pope John Paul II on April 23, 1993 (as published in *Origins*, January 6, 1994). https://catholic-resources.org/ChurchDocs/PBC_Interp-FullText.htm (accessed on 24.09.2022).
Preus, Jacob A. O., "The New Testament Canon in the Lutheran Dogmaticians." *The Springfielder*, 25 (1961): 8–33.
Räisänen, Heikki, *Beyond New Testament Theology: A Story and a Programme*, London: SCM Press, 2000, 2nd ed.
Reno, R. R. et al., eds., *SCM Theological Commentary on the Bible*, London: SCM Press.

Riches, John, *Galatians through the Centuries*, Blackwell Bible Commentaries series, London: Blackwell Publishing, 2008.
Roberts, Alexander, and James Donaldson, eds. *The Ante-Nicene Fathers: Translations of the Writings of the Fathers Down to A.D. 325*. Edited by Alexander Roberts and James Donaldson. 10 vols. Peabody, MA: Hendrickson, 1885–1887.
Roberts, C. H., *Manuscript, Society and Belief in Early Christian Egypt*, Oxford: Oxford University Press, 1979.
Sanders, E. P., *The Historical Figure of Jesus*, London: Penguin Books, 1993.
Sanders, James A. *Canon and Community: A Guide to Canonical Criticism*. Philadelphia: Fortress, 1984.
Sanders, James A. *From Sacred Story to Sacred Text: Canon as Paradigm*. Philadelphia: Fortress, 1987.
Schnelle, Udo, *Apostle Paul: His Life and Theology*, Grand Rapids: Baker Academic, 2005.
Schnelle, Udo, *The History and Theology of the New Testament Writings*, London: SCM Press, 1998.
Schnelle, Udo, *Theology of the New Testament*, Grand Rapids: Baker Academic, 2009.
Seitz, Christopher and Kathryn Greene-McCreight, eds., *Theological Exegesis: Essays in Honor of Brevard S. Childs*, Grand Rapids: Eerdmans, 1998.
Sheehan, Jonathan, *The Enlightenment Bible: Translation, Scholarship, Culture*, Princeton, NJ: Princeton University Press, 2005.
Skarsaune, Oskar, *The Proof from Prophecy: A Study in Justin Martyr's Proof-Text Tradition. Text-Type, Provenance, Theological Profile*, Leiden: Brill, 1987.
Soulen, R. Kendall, *The Divine Name(s) and the Holy Trinity*. Vol. 1: *Distinguishing the Voices*, Louisville, KY: Westminster John Knox Press, 2011.
Steinmetz, David C., "The Superiority of Pre-Critical Exegesis." In: Stephen E. Fowl, ed., *The Theological Interpretation of Scripture: Classic and Contemporary Readings*, Oxford: Blackwell, 1997.
Stuckenbruck, Loren T., "Johann Philipp Gabler and the Delineation of Biblical Theology." *Scottish Journal of Theology* 52 (1999): 139–52.
Stuhlmacher, Peter, *Biblical Theology of the New Testament*, Grand Rapids: Eerdmans, 2018.
Stuhlmacher, Peter, *Jesus of Nazareth – Christ of Faith*, Peabody, MA: Hendrickson Publishers, 1993.
Thielman, Frank, *Theology of the New Testament: A Canonical and Synthetic Approach*, Grand Rapids: Zondervan, 2005.
Thiselton, Anthony C., *New Horizons in Hermeneutics: The Theory and Practice of Transforming Biblical Reading*, Grand Rapids: Zondervan, 1992.
Thompson, M. D., *A Sure Ground on Which to Stand: The Relation of Authority and Interpretive Method in Luther's Approach to Scripture*, Bletchley: Milton Keynes; Wynesboro: Paternoster, 2004.
Thorsen, Donald A.D., *The Wesleyan Quadrilateral: Scripture, Tradition, Reason & Experience as a Model of Evangelical Theology*, Grand Rapids: Zondervan, 1990.
Treier, Daniel J., *Introducing Theological Interpetation of Scripture: Recovering a Christian Practice*, Nottingham: Apollos, 2008.
Trigg, Joseph W., *Origen, The Early Church Fathers*, London: Routledge, 1998.
Trueman, Carl R., *The Creedal Imperative*, Wheaton, IL: Crossway, 2012.

Vanhoozer, Kevin J., "Expounding the Word of the Lord: Joseph Ratzinger on Revelation, Tradition, and Biblical Interpretation." In: in Tim Perry, ed., *The Theology of Benedict XVI: A Protestant Appreciation*, Bellingham, WA: Lexham Press, 2019, 66–86.

Vanhoozer, Kevin J. et al., eds., *Dictionary for Theological Interpretation of the Bible*, London: SPCK and Grand Rapids: Baker Academic, 2005.

Watson, Francis, *Text and Truth: Redefining Biblical Theology*, Edinburgh: T&T Clark and Grand Rapids: Eerdmans, 1997.

Webster, John, *The Domain of the Word: Scripture and Theological Reason*, London: Bloomsbury, 2012.

Westerholm, Martin and Stephen Westerholm, *Reading Sacred Scripture: Voices from the History of Biblical Interpretation*, Grand Rapids: Eerdmans, 2016.

Westerholm, Stephen, *Romans: Text, Readers, and the History of Interpretation*, Grand Rapids: Eerdmans, 2022.

Wischmeyer, Oda, ed., *Handbuch der Bibelhermeneutiken: Von Origenes bis zur Gegenwart*, Berlin: de Gruyter, 2016.

Witherup, Ronald D., *The Word of God at Vatican II: Exploring Dei Verbum*, Liturgical Press, 2014.

Wood, Donald, *Barth's Theology of Interpretation*, Barth Studies, London: Routledge, 2016; first published by Ashgate in 2007.

Wrede, William, "The Task and Methods of 'New Testament Theology'." In *The Nature of New Testament Theology: The Contribution of William Wrede and Adolf Schlatter*, edited by Robert Morgan, Eugene, OR: Wipf & Stock, 2009, previously published by SCM Press, 1973.

Wright, Brian J., *Communal Reading in the Time of Jesus: A Window into Early Christian Reading Practices*, Minneapolis: Fortress Press, 2017.

Wright, N. T. and Michael Bird, *The New Testament in Its World: An Introduction to the History, Literature, and Theology of the First Christians*, London: SPCK and Grand Rapids: Zondervan Academic, 2019.

Yarchin, William, *History of Biblical Interpretation: A Reader*, Peabody, MA: Hendrickson Publishers, 2004.

Young, Frances M., *Biblical Exegesis and the Formation of Christian Culture*, Cambridge: Cambridge University Press, 1997.

Part 1: **Scripture and the Web of Meanings**

Jeanine Mukaminega
An Anthropological Analysis of Ezekiel 13:17–21

Abstract: Ezekiel 13:17–21 is an oracle against "those who prophesy of their own will, *hamitnab'wot*." The oracle is one of the several biblical negative voices towards women. This chapter examines the anthropological portrait of the oracle's characters by scrutiny of its semantics. It aims for a theological renewal of biblical reading for the 21st century, with its multicultural communities and its intersectional individual identities. After an overview of the questions and results of previous studies relating to gender, phenomenology, and links with Ancient Near East documents, the chapter analyses three aspects of the passage that have been little or not at all addressed: the hypothesis of the influence of ancient Egyptian prophetic texts, the anthropology conveyed by the oracle's semantics, and the blindness of traditional hermeneutics to prophetic oracles' negative anthropological view. Instead of a hermeneutic that aligns itself with the worldview of the Bible's scribe and that agrees with the semantic tools discrediting its opponents, the chapter argues for a new awareness of the voices silenced in Ezekiel, and for a reading that recognizes the cultural, anthropological, and theological diversity of the Bible.

Keywords: Ezekiel, Gender, Prophecy, Divination, Ancient Near East culture, Ritual, Renewing theology, Prophetesses, Hermeneutic filters, Anthropological semantics

1 Introduction

Ezekiel 13 seems to mainly focus on two prophecies that are contradictory in their meaning and in the way God is consulted. This work is an attempt to analyse its content and to question the relevance of its theology and anthropology in today's world. In fact, a set of keywords with various declensions would seem to be significant to us on the anthropological level.

Jeanine Mukaminega, Faculté Universitaire de Théologie Protestante de Bruxelles (FUTP), jeanine.mukaminega@protestafac.ac.be

The Old Testament has indeed been subjected to various studies in history since the 18th century but the interest in identifying those addressed by the prophecies of Ezekiel 13:17–21 is recent despite the curiosity their name awakens. In fact, in v. 17, Ezekiel was urged to turn his gaze to the בְּנוֹת עַמְּךָ הַמִּתְנַבְּאוֹת which means *daughters of your people, the prophesiers, or daughters of your people, those who prophesy.* Over the last 20 years, the passage has caught the attention of Bible scholars,[1] yet none has dealt with the literary elements of entrapment and liberation of souls as subjects in theology and anthropology. The issues of gender[2] and religious comparison were given more attention. Yet the question of the relevance of such a theology in the multicultural societies of the 21st century calls for a re-evaluation.

We can better understand the theology and anthropology conveyed by focusing on what is perceived as the crux of the conflict between Ezekiel and those to whom he prophesied. Do Ezekiel and "the daughters of his people" deal with the same issue? Do they address the same people? What type of humanity is referred to in Ezekiel's accusations? To answer these questions, I proceed in four steps: First, a short review of the *status quaestionis* of the research on Ezekiel 13:17–21 shows the results on the main questions raised by the text (four aspects). Second, in view of new perspectives, the content, backed by the key words in the literary context of the book of Ezekiel is revisited. The content and its meanings are extended to the wider context of prophesy and divination as documented in the literature of the Ancient Near East (ANE). Third, I compare the theology and anthropology in Ezekiel 13 with the wider cultural context in ANE. Fourth, I conclude with some suggestions for theological renewal today that derive from the discussion in this chapter.

---

1 See Jonathan Stökl, "The מִתְנַבְּאוֹת in Ezekiel 13," *Journal of Biblical Literature* 132 (2013): 61–76, and its rich bibliography. For classical critical studies cf. George Albert Cooke, *The Book of Ezekiel* (Edinburgh: T&T Clark, 1951), 137–50; Moshe Greenberg, *Ezekiel, 1–20. A New Translation with Introduction and Commentary* (New York: Doubleday, 1986), 232–48; Henry McKeating, *Ezekiel* (Sheffield: Sheffield Academic Press, 1993).
2 Some emblematic facts in the Christian tradition: Jesus and his twelve apostles were all men; the refusal of female priesthood by the Catholic Church.

2 Pre-existing Studies

2.1 Scope and Delimitation

The passage is widely regarded as composite and uncertain because of the differences between various manuscripts, grammatical inconsistencies,[3] heavy style (vv. 18 & 20) and a remarkable use of *hapax legomena* which makes all translations and meanings uncertain. Each study uses a translation based on several arbitrary choices. As for the delimitations of the text, Ezekiel 13:17–21 is part of a larger literary group, Ezekiel 12:21–14:11, which deals more with true and false prophecies.[4] This work deals with a more restricted passage about the "prophesying women" regarded as dishonest and dangerous. The beginning of the chapter (vv. 1–16) deals with supposed false prophets. The two parts have the same language and themes[5]. The passage is followed by Ezekiel 14 where the elders are castigated for idolatry (14:1–3).

According to Herman Gunkel's theory, an autonomous tradition (legend) is characterised by identifiable boundaries (a beginning and an end) and a discernible "literary genre" with independent content. Such an entity still remains coherent even when removed from its current literary body.[6] Ezekiel 13:17–21 perfectly meets these criteria.[7] In fact, in verse 17, we move from prophets to 'prophetesses', in the verses that follow, new groups of people are being denounced in detail. The literary genre is appropriate to the *opposing oracles*. Verses 20–21 present a clear ending and a divine sentence.

---

[3] Jonathan Stökl, "The מִתְנַבְּאוֹת", 63; John Wevers, *The New Century Bible Commentary: Ezekiel* (London: Marshall, Margon & Scott, 1971), 88; Walter Zimmerli, *Ezekiel* (Philadelphia: Fortress Press, 1986), 288–9.

[4] John Wevers, *The New Century*; Moshe Greenberg, *Ezekiel, 1–20*, 232–246; Walter Zimmerli, *Ezekiel*, 285–99; John F. Evans, "Death-Dealing Witchcraft in the Bible? Notes on the Condemnation of the 'Daughters' in Ezekiel 13: 17-23," *Tyndale Bulletin* 65.1 (2014): 57–84.

[5] John F. Evans, "Death-Dealing Witchcraft", 59–60. For Walter Zimmerli, p. 291–2, the structure of the chapter is original.

[6] Cf. Pierre Gibert, *Une théorie de la légende. Hermann Gunkel et les légendes de la Bible*. Paris: Flammarion, 1979.

[7] The classification of traditions as elaborated by Gunkel for the book of Genesis has evolved. It was extended to the Psalms and Prophets by later studies where the use of the concept of legend became more conservative cf. Edgar W. Conrad, *Reading the Latter Prophets: Towards a New Canonical Criticism* (London, New York: T&T Clark International, 2003), 10.

Some authors extend the text unit to verses 22–23.[8] However, literary clues reveal that verses 22–23 are addition to the original text. In verse 22, a transitional term, "because" (*yan*, יַעַן), acts as a later clarification, in line with Fishbane's theory: the "mantological exegesis of oracles".[9] Written by a later hand, in a homiletical style, the content of this verse has an exegetical dimension. Verse 23 is almost a repetition of verse 21, especially of the final formula *and you will know that I am the Lord*. These clues indicate an exegetic activity that aims to elucidate the indeterminate side of the oracle: the profession of "*hamitnab'wot*" and the identity of their victims and recipients.

2.2 Date and Author

The book of Ezekiel has a coherent literary framework with three parts: chapters 1–24 prophesies against Judea and Jerusalem; chapters 25–32 prophesies against the nations and chapters 33–48 are a message of salvation and hope.[10] Looking at the chronological outline, the book is divided into thirteen literary units.[11] The prophecies of chapters 1–24 are believed to come from Ezekiel with some additional editorial rearrangements and additions.[12] He is believed to have spoken them during his early years of exile between 592–587 BC. Several expressions are supposedly unique to Ezekiel. For McKeating, there is a noticeable new language[13] in Ezekiel 8:5: *and you, son of man, lift your eyes to the north, they will know that I am the Lord.*

Yet, scholars have pointed out several literary issues. They have examined the passage's complex writing, transmission, and editing processes, covering several epochs. For example, there are notable differences between the Masoretic tradition and the Septuagint version.[14] Equally, Gunkel has cautioned that prophetic words are supposedly pronounced before being written and rewritten. Although there is a core of Ezekiel's oracles, the author Ezekiel and the date of

---

8 Nancy Bowen, "The Daughters of your People: Female Prophets in Ezekiel 13:17–23," *Journal of Biblical Literature* 118 (1999): 417–33; John F. Evans, "Death-dealing Witchcraft," 67.
9 Michael Fishbane, *Biblical Interpretation in Ancient Israel* (Oxford: Clarendon, 1989), 458–524.
10 Henry McKeating, *Ezekiel*, 15–16.
11 Lena-Sofia Tiemeyer, "The Book of Ezekiel," in *Dictionary of Old Testament Prophets*, edited by Mark Boda and Gordon MacConville (Downers Grove: InterVarsity Press, 2012): 214–29.
12 Lena-Sofia Tiemeyer, "The Book of Ezekiel," 219; Henry McKeating, *Ezekiel*, 53–4.
13 Henry McKeating, *Ezekiel*, 17–18; John F. Evans, "Death-Dealing Witchcraft," 59–60.
14 Christophe Nihan, "Ezéchiel," in *Introduction à l'Ancien Testament*, edited by Thomas Römer et al. (Genève: Labor et Fides, 2009), 439–63.

the book that bears his name are relative. Recent studies have extended research to new issues: gender negativity, religious practices, phenomenology, and links with ancient Near Eastern cultures.

2.3 Studies about Gender

The emergence of critical studies and feminist movements has revealed the extent to which patriarchal culture[15] is entrenched in the Scriptures and in societies. The issue of gender in Ezekiel 13:17–21 was therefore raised, triggered mainly by three literary alerts:
1. the unusual use of *hamitnab'wot* "women who prophesy" instead of prophetesses, which is rare but proven in other parts of the Bible in its singular form (הַנְּבִיאָה *hanebi'ah*);[16]
2. the "*hoy*, woe" formula in a statement involving a soft threat at the end (the threat is soft as the envisioned divine intervention focuses on the liberation of victims rather than on the punishment of the women);
3. the language of diviners and the elements of divination in derogatory wording.

The clear literary indication of contrast is that "daughters of your people" are not mixed with false male prophets of verses 1–16. The gender-based negativity received in the course of the centuries that still strongly inhabits Bible reading communities could be due to this gender contrast and the ignorance of the functions of divination rituals. Without questioning biblical language and traditional hermeneutics, classical commentators, even critical ones,[17] have perpetuated a negative image of the "women who prophesy". Things evolve and the opinion that 'female prophets' are witches is taking a positive turn.[18] The process of

---

15 The Bible attests to rare prophetesses, a judge, but no priestesses, no Elderly women, and no reigning queens, which illustrates its patriarchal nature.
16 Different words refer to a prophet in the Bible: prophet, soothsayer, seer, man of God, sons of prophets. The term "prophetess" is used six times in the Bible with both positive and negative connotations: Ex 15:20 (Miriam); Jdg 4:4 (Deborah); 2Ki 22:14 & 2Ch 34:22 (Huldah); Isa 8:3 (anonymous); Ne 6:14 (Noadiah). Just like in Ezekiel 13, prophetess and prophets were accused of false prophecies in Ne 6:14. *Hamitnab'wot* has the same root as prophet (*nabi'*). Different modes of operation are attested too, including dreams and divination.
17 Walter Zimmerli, *Ezekiel*, 296.
18 See Jonathan Stökl, "The מִתְנַבְּאוֹת," 62, notes 1 and 2 on the question of gender.

deconstruction happens with the help of research on the complex phenomenon called prophesy and divination which has been contextualised.[19]

2.4 Religious Disputes

Finally, we understood that in order to grasp the issue in Ezekiel 13:17–21, it is important to clarify the religious dispute associated with all the rituals practices mentioned here. In some Christian traditions, "prophesying women" or *hamitnab'wot* were considered as "magicians", "diviners", "necromancers", "witches", "fortune-tellers", "demonesses", etc.[20] Such interpretation was influenced by the negativity conveyed by the terms in the passage that are associated to "magic".[21] As ethnological studies develop, the dignity of these cultures is being restored. The progress of studies in the fields of religion and culture of the Near East is beneficial to the "prophesying women" in Ezekiel 13.

According to Jean Marie Durand, who analysed the documents found in Mari (19th to 13th century BC) from the point of view of content, time, places and phenomena, there is no specific word for "prophecy". Similar phenomena existed but doubled as the divination ritual.[22] By deconstructing the paradigm that "magic" and "divination' are bad as opposed to "religion" and "prophecy", Jonathan Stökl delimits the term. He clarifies both terms after emphasising that the boundaries between prophecy and divination are porous and blurred. He considers "divination" as the main two-sided generic term: "technical" divination (dream interpretation, augury) and "intuitive" divination (dream, prophecy).[23] In his article "Female Prophets in the Ancient Near East",[24] the author calls

---

[19] Jonathan Stökl, ibid; John F. Evans, "Death-Dealing Witchcraft;" Nancy Bowen, "The Daughters of Your People," 417–33; Johanna Stiebert, *Fathers and Daughters in the Hebrew Bible* (Oxford: Oxford University Press, 2013); Marjo C. Korpel, "Avian Spirits in Ugarit and in Ezekiel 13," in *Ugarit, Religion and Culture,* edited by Nick Wyatt et al. (Münster, Ugarit Verlag, 1996).

[20] Nancy Bowen, "The Daughters of Your People," 419 and note 9.

[21] Daniel Schwemer, "The Ancient Near East," in *Magic and Witchcraft in the West. From the Antiquity to the Present,* edited by David J. Collins (Cambridge: Cambridge University Press, 2015): 17–51. The term "magic" is associated to the Greek word *mageía* and to the old Persian *maguš*.

[22] Jean-Marie Durand, *Cours et travaux du Collège de France.* Annuaire 111e année (Paris: Collège de France, avril 2012), 379–98.

[23] Jonathan Stökl, "The מִתְנַבְּאוֹת," 67; See Esther J. Hamori, "The Prophet and the Necromancer: Women's Divination for the Kings," *Journal of Biblical Literature* 132 (2013), 827–43; *Prophéties et oracles 1: dans le Proche-Orient ancien,* edited by Jésus Asurmendi et al. (Supplément au Cahiers Evangile 88, Paris: Cerf, 1994): 6. Micha Titiev distinguishes between religious rites (communal and calendar) and magical rites (individual in case of emergency crisis),

a "prophet" one who conveys the message of a deity without the request of the receiver or someone who is identified as a prophet in literature. Then he examines the attested religious social sphere to which the activities of the "prophesying women" of Ezekiel can be associated.

2.5 Rapport with the Cultures of the Ancient Near East

About 140 individual texts have been identified[25] through several corpora such as the Mari corpus of the 18th century BC, the Neo-Assyrian state archives of Nineveh of the 17th century BC, Aramaic inscriptions and controversial texts of prophecy (Ebla, Emar, Ugarit, Hittite and Egypt).[26] The vocabulary and phenomenon vary with the corpus. The comparisons cover various aspects: form-structure, style-language, thematic and literary composition. In this recapitulation of existing studies, we do not intend to recall all the work in these corpora. We will refer mainly to a few researchers whose interest relates to the purpose of this article.

Stökl studies documents where female prophets are referred to as *āpiltu* in ancient Babylonian Akkadian and as *raggintu* in Neo-Assyrian texts.[27] He also explores Emar's documents and concludes that "prophesying women" are the same as *munabbiatu* in the texts of Emar. As for Bowen,[28] she strives to identify the social class of "daughters of your people" and establishes a parallelism of structure and function with the *Maqlû* incantations ritual model as established by Tzvi Abusch.[29] According to her, Ezekiel takes the supposed harmful power of the "prophesying women" away from the community. As for Ezekiel, he is considered as an "exorcist" while the others are witches. Stökl regrets that Bowen maintains the negative view of what, in phenomenological terms, is involved

---

cf. Tzvi Abusch, "The Demonic Image of the Witch in Standard Babylonian Literature: The Reworking of Popular Conceptions by Learned Exorcists," in *Religion, Science and Magic in Concert and in Conflicts*, edited by Jacob Neusner et al. (New York: Oxford University Press,1989): 27–58.
24 Jonathan Stökl, "Female Prophets in the Ancient Near East," in *Prophecy and Prophets in Ancient Israel*, edited by John Day (London, New York: T&T Clark International, 2010).
25 Martti Nissinen et al., *Prophets and Prophecy in the Ancient Near East* (Atlanta: Society of Biblical Literature, 2003).
26 Jonathan Stökl, "Ancient Near Eastern Prophecy," in *Dictionary of Old Testament Prophets*, edited by Mark Boda and J. Gordon MacConville (Downers Grove: InterVarsity Press, 2012), 16–24.
27 Jonathan Stökl, "Female Prophets in the Ancient Near East," 47.
28 Nancy Bowen, "The Daughters for Your People," 421
29 Tzvi Abush, "The Demonic Image of the Witch."

in magic and divination as opposed to prophecy. Considering Bowen's presentation as a whole, the "prophesying women" are witches when considering the classical hermeneutics of the oracle, whereas they can be seen as "medicine women" with regard to similar semantics in other sources. The similarity of language leads Bowen to propose medical rituals associated with pregnancy and childbirth.[30]

For Evans the "prophesying women" practise a certainly "binding" but defensive and therapeutic magic like the Babylonian *āšipu* 'exorcists' and not the magic of the *kaššāptu*, "witches" where people are bound. The author addresses the issue from a pastoral point of view with a concern for efficiency in the Church. He reminds us of Daniel Bodi's study which makes a comparison with Akkadian incantations, *maqlû* and Sumariens'.[31] The author highlights how both *kaššāptu* and *āšipu* make use of binding magic. Secondly, these binding magic rituals can be harmful or curative depending on the person who uses them. For Evans, the Judean elite brought to Babylonia may have had access to cuneiform material concerning binding magic. He does not exclude the possibility of this knowledge being transmitted into Aramean before the exile.[32]

For Korpel and Stökl, "the women who prophesy" are equated with the *munabbīatu* of Emar's texts; they are therefore necromancers. For Durand, the *munabbīatu* refer to mourners during burials. However, for traditional theology, necromancers are negative as in the Bible, for example, in 1Sa 28:3, 9; Isa 8:19 & 1Ch 10:13. Things evolved as Stökl strongly disagrees with the voice of the Bible and proposes to see them as highly respected professionals in their lifetime.[33] For both the author and Evans, they were opponents of Ezekiel who were denigrated through the reception of the text. Despite these views, we still do not know their precise occupations. Were they respected necromancers, valuable female doctors, holy prophetesses or evil witches?

These studies reveal a two-fold subsidiary problem concerning the relationship with the ANE. Firstly, the Middle East is so large with many diverse cultures and changing connections. We cannot determine the exact meaning of Ezekiel's text and the type of work it refers to based on his vocabulary alone. Secondly, the prophetic phenomenon in both the biblical corpus and the ANE texts is complex and involves various terms with specific nuances. ANE literature employs *āpilum*, (which responds) and the ecstatic, *muḫḫūtum* in Old Baby-

---

[30] Nancy Bowen, "The Daughters of Your People," 424
[31] Daniel Schwemer, "The Ancient Near East," 20–21.
[32] John F. Evans, "Death-Dealing Witchcraft," 79.
[33] Jonathan Stökl, "The מִתְנַבְּאוֹת."

lonian and *maḫḫutum* in Neo-Assyrian. The *muḫḫutum/maḫḫutum* (mad ones) are not professional prophets but have various professions attached to a temple including occasional prophecy (lay prophets)[34]. The Bible refers to these people as *roheh* (he that sees), *hozeh* (seer), *nabi'* (prophet) and *qosem* (diviner) (Isa 3:2; Jer 29:8; Mic 3:7). The main term, "prophet" *nabi'* can refer to both intuitive and ecstatic prophets.

Except for short outlines, (2Ki 3:15; 1Sa 10:5) in biblical literature there are no details of prophecy and divination rituals,[35] whereas in the ANE texts there are often manuals describing the rituals, the names of the recipients, the circumstances and the problems dealt with.[36] In both literatures, technical details on the modalities are rarely given. Yet, these details are necessary for the epistemology of scientists who function by dissection and compartmentalisation of the "Reality". The biblical cases are more problematic as the voice of the prophet is removed from its historical contexts. Although there is also the phenomenon of modification,[37] the Near Eastern material is often contemporary with events. For the Bible, one is obliged to consider the editorial reinterpretation of traditions in Judea/Yehud, including strategies to eliminate divergent views.

3 Content and New Perspectives

As noted above, the issues raised in the introduction have been addressed by significant studies.[38] These studies focus on the ritual and semantic aspects of divination/magic.[39] They examine the formal similarities with various Mesopo-

---

[34] For Jean-Marie Durand, *Cours et travaux du Collège de France*, 391, "there are two kinds of prophecy: that which doubles as divination, and which is the work of *âpilum* 'that which speaks afterwards', and that which is spontaneous: it is the *egirrû*, which is the work of a population from the depths of the temple or of simple individuals who claim to have divine instruction". Jonathan Stökl, relates the case of a prophetess of Mari, *Aḫḫatum*, who was delivering divine message in a delusional state, see "Female Prophets," 50–1.

[35] However, many texts mention the existence of these practices and even specify some materials, and the reasons for using them (Deut 18:10–11; 1Sam 28,6–8).

[36] Jean-Marie Durand, "Les 'déclarations prophétiques'," 25–7.

[37] Béatrice André-Salvani, *Babylone* (Paris: Presse Universitaire de France, 2009).

[38] Nancy Bowen, "The Daughters of Your People"; John F. Evans, "Death-Dealing Witchcraft"; Jonathan Stökl, "The מִתְנַבְּאוֹת"; William H. Brownlee, "Exorcising the Souls from Ezekiel 13, 17–23," *Journal of Biblical Literature* 69 (1950): 367–73.

[39] For Nancy Bowen, "The Daughters of Your People," 420, separation is predominately a sociological concern.

tamian rituals, such as the language (ligature, ties, bonds …) and the structure of anti-sorcery incantations. However, these studies contain a threefold gap.

3.1 A Foolproof Prophetic Positivism?

The first issue concerns the supposed absolute positivism of "prophecy", as if nothing could be questioned in the phenomenon as though it was transmitted to us through hermeneutic filters. Therefore it is mandatory for these studies to discuss the boundaries between "prophecy" and "divination" – the former in positive terms and then the latter negatively. The fact is that some anthropological uses and views of the phenomenon of biblical prophecy are questionable. Stökl's distinction[40] may be an improvement, but it is still part of the epistemology of recent Western scholars. His analyses do not capture the anthropological depth that underlies prophecy/divination. The phenomenon belongs to all cultures from the beginning of civilisations to the present day. It refers to something durable in human experience and expressed in a mythological universe not yet truly deciphered. Of course, there are variations across civilisations, places and times: divination by the stars, oracles, animal entrails (chicken, lamb), spontaneous visions, dream interpretation, interpretations of natural phenomena, etc. The variations treat concrete cultural aspects rather than the deeper reality addressed by these practices. The words "religion", "prophecy", "magic" and "divination" must themselves be circumscribed in time, space and domains of knowledge and validation.

All known civilisations have been concerned with communicating with a world beyond our material world while developing logical deductions (concepts and practical wisdom) inspired by empirical experiences or astrological observations.[41] Today's hyper-technological civilisation also bears witness to several groups that claim to connect to cosmic energy (cognitive sciences, e.g., the Noēsis project). In ancient societies, intuitive communication went hand in hand with ritual, and boundaries were elusive. The oracular phenomenon that is associated with "prophecy" has had technical or ritual operating modes like magic. This issue of questioning what is beyond everyday human perception and fate depict an intrinsic anthropological depth and a more inalienable otherness to that which exegetes are dealing with. The scope of the vocabulary on

---

40 Jonathan Stökl, "The מִתְנַבְּאוֹת".
41 Jean Bottéro, *Babylone: À l'aube de notre culture* (Paris: Gallimard, 1994), 100–1; Béatrice André Salvani, *Babylone*, 10.

professions, functions, places, social issues and technical manuals is too wide to recall its implications in a comprehensive way.[42] The second gap concerns the probable reminiscences of Egyptian funerary rituals and predictive texts that are less studied in the consulted studies. That similarity exists between Egyptian "predictive texts" and biblical narrative prophecies is probably mere assumption.[43] The third gap is the question of theology, which is subsidiary and meagre, whereas the oracles of the Bible are supposed to set out theological and ethical ideologies.[44]

The new light we are putting forward aims to examine some facets of the threefold gap. It examines the content of Ezekiel 13:17–21 while accepting the results of existing studies. The ideology of biblical writing and the wider context of the ANE cultures including Egypt and Canaan are briefly revisited. The emphasis is on what is being questioned in the activities of the "prophesying women". Is it their lack of efficiency (their lies)? We are not sure. What can we learn from the structure, the attributes of the characters and the semantics? The next sections are based on two major presuppositions: the first is Gunkel's general advice to scholars that in the literature of the later prophets, the right context for reading 'is to be found outside the book itself'. Ezekiel 13:17–21 is then a small system functioning within other macro-systems on which it depends like a Russian doll. Second, leaving aside the explanation of verses 22–23, which we take to be an addition, the semantics of the passage is definitely ambiguous, textual variations and inconsistencies make the message of the oracle unfixed.

3.2 Structure and Key Words

In terms of structure, considering the utterances of God, the oracle takes the form of a pyramid in three parts:
- Introduction of the messenger, "you, son of man" and the addressees of the oracle: "daughters of your people, those who prophesy (*hamitnab'wot*) on their own initiative" (v. 17).
- The content of the oracle (1): Threat (הוי, woe) and rebuking (vv. 18–19) about their activities: sewing magic wrist bands, making head veils;

---

[42] Jean-Marie Durand, *Cours et travaux du Collège de France*.
[43] Jonathan Stökl, "*Prophecy in the Ancient Near East: A Philological and Sociological Comparison* (Leyde: Brill, 2012); "Ancient Near Eastern Prophecy," 21.
[44] Nancy Bowen, "The Daughters of Your People," 423, assumes that the prophetesses of Ezekiel 13 are condemned because they are "the other" and their practices serve contrary social goals and concerns.

hunting and trapping souls to earn a little barley and bread; causing the wrong souls to die while letting souls who should die live.
- The content of the oracle (2): Announcement of the divine intervention to rescue the souls of God's people (vv. 20–21): God destroys the magic wrist bands and head veils to liberate the ensnared souls therein.

Rolf Rendtorff notes that for Ezekiel, the final formula of the message, parallel to the style of the king in the Near Eastern text, became a formula of recognition: "וִידַעְתֶּן כִּי-אֲנִי יְהוָה *and you will know that I am the Lord*". Similar to a king or judge, the prophet pronounces accusations 'הִנְנִי, *behold*' and passes sentences according to the civil practice of the region.[45]

These statements bear literary elements: "daughters of your people", "entrapping souls", "freeing souls", "on their own initiatives" and "killing", that are indications of a theology and anthropology to be re-evaluated.

These clues, complemented by a close examination of the characters' attributes, reveal that the language of the oracle portrays an overall negative human being (heartless, naive and manipulable). The semantic lead to several directions:
- In the literary proximity of the false prophets (vv. 1–16), the plural designation of the "women who prophesy" – given the legal or popular recognition of various brotherhoods – echoes the expression, "sons of the prophets" (2Ki 2:3, 5, 7, 15; 4:1, 38; 5:22; 9:1) which suggests a professional status in the king's entourage. Could the "prophesying women" be prophetesses who practise similar professions as the sons of prophets?
- To recall Johanna Stiebert's study on the term "daughter", the expression "daughters of your people", v. 17 may make sense if associated with passages with idiomatic constructions using the word "daughter" (Jer 9:19–20, Mic 4:14, Ecc 12:4).[46] The female professions that seem to inspire these texts (singers, mourners, seamstresses) are attested in Near Eastern documentation (doc 1166–1171)[47] in the priestly context. It is clear that the details of these public female professions have disappeared in the biblical canon.
- "וּבְנוֹת גּוֹיִם, *and daughters of the nations*" in Ezekiel 32:18 may echo בְּנוֹת עַמֶּךָ, *daughters of your people*. When the expression "daughters of ..." refers to a

---

45 Rolf Rendtorff, *Introduction à l'Ancien Testament* (Paris: Cerf, 1989), 199–204.
46 Johanna Stiebert, *Fathers and Daughters*, 28.
47 *Documents épistolaires du palais de Mari*, vol. 3, edited by Jean-Marie Durand (Paris: Cerf, 2000), 348–56. Jonathan Stökl, "Female Prophets," 51, note 20.

group (nation, city, tribe), it expresses the social aspect of that group in four categories:
1. the dominant culture such as lust, pride (Isa 3:16–17; Cant 3:5) considered as excessive or even perverse, so as to denounce them as a potential social danger;
2. weeping when bereaved, woe and suffering (Jdg 11:37–40; Eze 32:16; Pss 48:12; 97:8; La 3:51);
3. Heroism: fighting heroes who are celebrated or mourned (2Sa 1:20, 24; Isa 16:2; Eze 16:27, 57);
4. Otherness perceived as negative and a source of idolatry (Ge 27:46; 28:8; Nu 25:1–3).

– "Entrapping, chasing out, releasing souls" can be ideologically linked to the Egyptian language of wrapping in funeral rituals based on the notion of *ba*, heart, *jb* inner or *heart-jb*.[48]
– "Putting souls to death" refers to the cult of the dead attested in the Bible (Jer 16:5–7; 2Ki 23:24) while the veils can be linked to the iconographic cults (statues of gods) attested in Judah with a few allusions in the Bible (Isa 6:1). Moreover, dressing the statues of the gods is a well-known tradition of the Babylonian priesthood (*Baruch* 6, 10–11) and Canaan (2Ki 23:7).
– Declaring doom *hoy* is common in the context of the fall of the king's power (e.g. the inscription on the prism of Sennacherib).
– "Prophesying women, מִתְנַבְּאוֹת" – the masculine form is attested as referring to ecstatic prophets (Nu 11:27; 1Sa 10:5; Jer 14:14; 1Ki 22:10 and 2Ch 18:9), but the feminine participle form *hitpael* is a hapax. 1Sa 10:5 clearly refers to them as cultic prophets because they are linked to a sanctuary as in the ANE documents. In Nu 11:27 and 1Sa 10:5, they are not seen as false prophets.

These parallels suggest that the oracle is a typical story recognised in the regional culture with a specific function: to distort the meaning of traditions. Those who wrote the book of Ezekiel transmitted it scathingly. This Ezekiel's oracle assigns a negative identity to women by invoking and depreciating all the attributes that usually valorised them.

---

[48] The practice of wrapping conjures up death as a catastrophe. cf. Youri Volokhine, "Tristesse rituelle et lamentations funéraires en Egypte ancienne," *Revue de l'histoire des religions* 2 (2008): 179–82. The cultural influence of Egypt in Judah is well proven. For example the Egyptian *ankh* on the seal of Hezekiah (716–687 BC), king of Judah (Michaël Langlois, "Le sceau d'un roi de la Bible découvert à Jérusalem," 04.10.2015, https://michaellanglois.fr/fr/missions/#mission1).

3.3 Places

The oracle asks whether *the women who prophesy*, also called *the daughters of your people*, are part of the exiled community or whether they are in the land of Judah. In Eze 3:11; 33:2, 12, 17, 30 we see five times *towards the son of your people*, אֶל־בְּנֵי עַמֶּךָ referring to the exiled community while once, in Eze 37:18 it refers to Judah and Israel. Hence, the location is again unclear.

Biblical texts where women are engaged in prophecy/divination activities (Ex 15:20–21; 1Sa 28:5–6; 2Ki 22:14; Pr 6:26; Isa 57:3–5; Na 3:4; Jdg 4:4) often tell the places and circumstances: the king's palace, shrines, battlefields in crisis, and festival celebrations. Were the "prophesying women" "prophetesses" of the cult or of the king in late Judah as in the Neo-Assyrian documents?[49] In Judah, some women were called prophetesses before the exile of 597. We can cite an anonymous prophetess in Is 8:3 and Huldah at the same time as Jeremiah; both women were advisors to the king. But also, groups of elite women were brought to Babylonia with elite men like Ezekiel himself. Thus, from the reign of Saul and David (the woman of En-Dor in 1Sa 28:5–15, Nathan, Gad) through the reign of Josiah (Huldah, Jeremiah) to the Persian era (Noadiah), the Bible testifies that kings consulted female diviners, prophetesses and prophets.

If divination and Canaanite rituals are the real background of Ezekiel 13, the oracle condemns the culture of Canaan, particularly related to the ancient sanctuaries considered as obstacles to centralisation. There are significant indications that Canaanite culture has been systematically erased by the writer's editing. Researchers observe that religious centres such as Shiloh and Mitspah with a strong priesthood throughout history and linked to great figures have no aetiology![50] Divinatory texts have been found in Judea near Jerusalem.[51] Many other passages can be recalled, e.g. Jeremiah 23:13–16 and Ezekiel 16:1–8 where verses 2–3 remind us that – before entering the covenant (vv. 6–8) – Jerusalem was formerly Canaan, a potential seat of idolatry.

If the "prophesying women" are exiled elite women, they may be associated with those false prophets denounced by Jeremiah 29 with reference made about induced dreams (incubation). The term הַמִּסְפָּחוֹת *veils* (v. 18) can refer even to historical figures. It makes one think of Qammatum, a priestess of the god Da-

---

[49] John W.Hilber, *Cultic Prophecy in the Psalm* (Berlin: de Gruyter, 2005).
[50] Lukasz Niesiolowski-Spanò, *The Origin Myths and Holy Places in the Old Testament* (London: Routledge, 2014).
[51] Michaël Langlois, "La Bible parle-t-elle encore aujourd'hui?" *Radio Télévision Belge Francophone Présence Protestante*, 11.10.2020, https://www.youtube.com/watch?v=AQa5_zNm4v4.

gan of Terqa, characterised by her headdress.⁵² Her message was about tying the net against the enemies during the crisis with Eshnunna.⁵³ The socio-political context of Qammatum seems similar to that of our 13th chapter of Ezekiel. If we translate הַמִּסְפָּחוֹת as headwrap or headband, this may refer to an object attested to the musical high priestess Enheduanna in the sanctuary of Ninna during the reign of Sargon (18ᵗʰ BC).⁵⁴ Although we lack enough evidence, the term could refer to an object that was used by the priesthood in Canaan or Babylonia. In Tzvi Abusch's description of the functions of the *āšipu*,⁵⁵ it was about tying knots to free patients, applying amulets as protective devices, which may be related to the material and activities of "the women who prophesy". The author notes that in the popular social world, witches are not always negative or guilty; it depends on which side you are on.⁵⁶

4 Theology and Anthropology in ANE and in Ezekiel 13:17-21

4.1 The World Vision of the Ancient Near East.

Biblical and ANE anthropology have the same vision of the human being: since the very beginning of the earth, man is made of dust (clay) and God's matter (spirit in the Bible and flesh and blood in the poem *Atrahasis*). This duality is the basis of the magical and theological worlds of both literary works. The oracles of Ezekiel share this mythological Worldview which is deeply rooted in the cultures of the region. There, human life and history are linked to the cosmic heartbeat.⁵⁷ There is an interconnection between the constituents of the universe. When individuals, families or communities go through crisis, it is a part of their connection with the world of the gods. For Glassner, professionals con-

---

52 Jean-Marie Durand, "Les 'déclarations prophétiques'," 24; Jonathan Stökl, "Female Prophets in the Ancient Near East," 50.
53 Jean-Marie Durand, "Les 'déclarations prophétiques'," 24, 33, 58–9.
54 Nele Ziegler, "Femmes inspiratrices en Mésopotamie: les musiciennes de cour," *Journal Asiatique* 303 (2015), p. 198.
55 Tzvi Abusch, "The Demonic Image of the Witch."
56 Tzvi Abusch, "The Demonic Image of the witch," 32.
57 Jean-Jacques Glassner, "Les temps de l'histoire en Mésopotamie," in *Israël construit son histoire. L'historiographie deutéronomiste à la lumière des recherches récentes*, ed. Albert de Pury et al. (Genève: Labor et Fides, 1996): 167–89.

nect the past, present and future through three main activities: writing down significant events of the past (history reports through divination), performing rituals punctuated by festivals, and questioning the gods (divination-prophecy) about what is to come when change is suspected. According to Glassner, we can say that Ezekiel and the "prophesying women" are competing to stop, change or redirect the fate of their people.[58] Both points of view are rooted in the same transcendent Worldview but diverge in views specific to their respective social backgrounds.

In terms of skills for deciphering cosmic signs, rituals operate in different modes. In the analyses of many divination model livers found in Mari, divination is intended to be a descriptive and rational science.[59] Glassner notes that the interpretation is not literal but rather a judicious reuse of ancient observation where history seems self-referential. Therefore, the ancient Near East was a world where subjectivity was strongly recognised. Researchers cannot access the subjectivity of these ancient diviners, despite their legacy attested by numerous tablets. This same Worldview is emphasised in Ezekiel 13, depicting a rivalry between specialists to decipher the causes of the present event, the fall of Jerusalem and its consequences. The question is: what cosmic law is violated in their society?

Dt 28:68 and 2Ki 25:26, for example, describe the crisis in Judah during Ezekiel's lifetime as the shame of returning to Egypt. It conveys an ideology with Egypt as a symbol of slavery and domination. If we go by Glassner's theory,[60] time is a circle of sequential segments with overlapping flows. A crisis, a destruction of a city, a war, an illness, an exile ... are a jump to the next segment, a kind of transfer. Similarly, Jacques Chopineau observes biblical time as a sinusoidal repetition/continuity of life processes.[61] Rituals are natural modalities for transfers to happen. This is why the ANE's prophecies were brought to the attention of the king for wise decisions. The oracles of Ezekiel are an invitation to this kind of transfer in a time of dominating empires, unfortunately in a monolithic way.

Mesopotamian diviners omit specific names (person or space), change grammar (past becomes present or future, plural becomes singular and vice versa) to give a different time, character and place.[62] This changes the whole

---

58 Ibidem, 168.
59 Jean-Jacques Glassner, "Les temps de l'histoire en Mésopotamie", 183.
60 Jean-Jacques Glassner, "Les temps de l'histoire en Mésopotamie", 172–5.
61 Jacques Chopineau, *Quand le texte devient parole*, Analecta Bruxellensia 6 (2001): 32–3.
62 Bernard Levinson, *L'Herméneutique de l'innovation* (Bruxelles: Lessius, 2006), 24–30.

context and meaning⁶³. Abusch's study attests to the revision of incantations by scribes who specialised in writing, *āšipu*.⁶⁴ Given the grammatical inconsistency, could this also apply to Ezekiel 13? Especially since we know that biblical prophets appeal to past traditions; transform and use them (Jer 31). Here Ezekiel refers to a popular Canaanite tradition of divination held by women to disparage it in the name of Yahweh. Protective tools are made to become destructive. This process of polarisation is also attested to in the *maqlû* incantations.⁶⁵

4.2 A Specific Biblical Worldview?

Like in Mesopotamia, in the biblical world, human beings, nature, demons, angels and deities live together, with the possibility of conflict, offence and mutual damage. Both the diviner and the prophet have some knowledge of giving meaning to the variety of events in human history. Let us recall three aspects of Deuteronomistic ideology that are at work in the prophetic traditions: (i) the exile is the consequence of the breaking of the covenant, (ii) the leaders and the people bear the responsibility, (iii) Yahweh offers a new covenant. In such a view of reality, the Deuteronomic renewal⁶⁶ cannot be analysed as a rationally planned future as in the manner of our culture. Ezekiel 13 remains in an established subjective environment where individuation as self-maturation is suspected or seen as the intrusion of the god.

Unlike the Mesopotamian diviners, in our passage the writers of the Bible erase all traces leading to the contemporary event. For Bowen, Ezekiel 13 testifies to a theology of discontinuity where diversity is no longer allowed. The comprehensive purge leads to a new identity, the end of the old relationship between social groups and a new tendency to think of the future in a monolithic direction. The new system must adapt to the current expansion of emerging empires, tribal diversity that is no longer effective, where each has its own sanctuary and practices.

In this World Vision, divination, prophecy, priesthood and kingship are a powerful sphere, an arena for choosing kings, religious figures and traditions that can be passed on in times of crisis. Documentation from Mari provides us

---

63 Jean-Jacques Glassner, "Les temps de l'histoire en Mésopotamie",182–5.
64 Tzvi Abusch, "The Demonic Image of the Witch."
65 Ibidem, 35.
66 Gods abandoning their cities and being able to return without granting reconstruction are known from the mythological story of Era (Jean-Jacques Glassner, "Les temps de l'histoire en Mésopotamie," 187).

with cases where the diviners even tried to have international authority (see also the case of Balaam in the book of Numbers). The dispute between Ezekiel and 'the prophesying women' dominates this choice arena.[67] The theological ideology through the theme of "liberation of souls" without a concrete context is curious. The link to the experiential situation has been broken. The text presents Ezekiel's view as a supposed security. And for what anthropological situation? According to this theological view, the past must be revisited by interpreting the Law of Moses. So, what Law of Moses *did the daughters of your people transgress*? The text may repeat the other two occurrences of אֶל־בְּנוֹת, *towards the daughters of* (Ge 6:4; Nu 25:1), which lead to the theme of lewd behavior. Profaning God is an allusion to Canaanite religious practices.

5 Conclusion: Renewing 21st Century Theology

The oracle of Ezekiel 13:17–21 features three social categories wherein only Ezekiel, with God's word, may speak. The biblical scribe grants neither "prophesiers" nor the people the right to express themselves. The reader can thus only guess at what these silent characters had to say. Researchers must make do with the vague allusions made in the text and in outside sources. This explains the slow reorientation of biblical theology over the past four centuries, in the era of biblical criticism. It has become either more rational – joining with sociology and psychology – or metaphoric and symbolic. It has also supported theologies linked to mythological and mystical concerns.

To be effective, the hermeneutics of Ezekiel´s oracle must offer meaning to historical communities. Traditional interpretations have upheld a biased judgment, aligning themselves with Ezekiel's voice. Such interpretations have proved enormously destructive to the image of women over the centuries and remain even today solidly ingrained in a number of communities.[68] Theology itself would benefit by adopting the invaluable practice of relativizing atavistic interpretations. It must ask itself how these kinds of oracles can inspire questions about the phenomenon of multiple, minority, and intersectional identities, specific to our civilization.

---

67 Alan Linzi and Jonathan Stökl, *Divination, Politics and Ancient Near East Empires.* (Atlanta: Society of Biblical Literature Press, 2014): 54.
68 John F. Evans, "Death-Dealing Witchcraft."

The concept of "saving" souls has been passed down as a binary one, wherein the People must be saved from the clutches of "those who prophesy, *hamitinab'wot*", designating these professionals as an Evil. Such an interpretation relies heavily on a dangerous assumption. In Ezekiel 13:17–21 everything takes place as if in a moment of crisis – there is a good side and an evil side – even as reality reveals its greater complexity. Trigano here offers two models that may explain the birth of ideas and systems: a chronological process and a process based on an order of realities, which is to say a shared fundamental and foundational experience of humanity, freed from the passage of time.[69] The biblical oracles are meant to take place in the latter and should be understood within a specific framework of social organization. The social "truth" linked to this ancient structure and its foundational experiences as recorded in the Bible, has become skewed but has not disappeared entirely. Theological theses must remain attentive to this new understanding.

The oracular phenomenon and its functional arrangements (a special space in sanctuaries or during festivals, incantations, repetitions, chants ...) may be the distant ancestor of certain contemporary phenomena. Might there be an underlying pattern shared by the ancient soothsayers and contemporary interpreters of dreams, astrological theories, and synchronicity? In any event, it can only be worthwhile to relativize traditional interpretations, while at the same time recognizing the anthropological foundations of the ancient methods of consulting the gods. Theology can follow a middle way, such as by researching spiritual aspirations that may span cultures and time periods, by resuscitating voices that have been reduced to silence, by highlighting diversity, and by questioning the scribe's linguistic tools, thereby opening space to theological creativity.

References

Abusch, Tzvi. "The Demonic Image of the Witch in Standard Babylonian Literature: The Reworking of Popular Conceptions by Learned Exorcists." In *Religion, Science and Magic in Concert and in Conflicts*, edited by Jacob Neusner et al., New York: Oxford University Press: 1989, 27–58.
Abusch, Tzvi. *The Witchcraft Series Maqlû*. Atlanta: Society of Biblical Literature Press, 2015.
André-Salvani, Béatrice. *Babylone*. Paris: Presse Universitaire de France, 2009.
Asurmendi. Jesus, et al., eds. *Prophéties et oracles 1: dans le Proche-Orient ancient*. Supplément au Cahiers Evangile, vol. 88. Paris: Cerf, 1994.

---

[69] Cf. *Controverse sur la Bible*, edited by Shmuel Trigano (Paris: In Press, 2012): 63–70.

Boda, Mark and Gordon MacConville, eds. *Dictionary of Old Testament Prophets*. Downers Grove, IL: InterVarsity Press, 2012.

Bottéro, Jean. *Babylone. À l'aube de notre culture*. Paris: Gallimard, 1994.

Bowen, Nancy. "The Daughters of Your People: Female Prophets in Ezekiel 13:17–23." *Journal of Biblical Literature* 118 (1999): 417–33.

Brownlee, William H. "Exorcising the Souls from Ezekiel 13, 17–23." *Journal of Biblical Literature* 69 (1950): 367–73.

Chopineau, Jacques. *Quand le texte devient parole*, Analecta Bruxellensia 6 (2001).

Conrad, Edgar W. *Reading the Latter Prophets: Towards a New Canonical Criticism*. London, New York: T&T Clark International, 2003.

Cooke, George Albert. *The Book of Ezekiel*. Edinburgh: T&T Clark, 1951.

Durand, Jean-Marie. "Les 'déclarations prophétiques' dans les lettres de Mari". In *Prophéties et oracles 1: dans le Proche-Orient ancient*, edited by Asurmendi. Jesus, et al. Supplément au Cahiers Evangile, vol. 88. Paris: Cerf, 1994, 8–74.

Durand, Jean-Marie, ed. *Documents épistolaires du palais de Mari*. Vol. 3. Paris: Cerf, 2000.

Durand, Jean-Marie. *Cours et travaux du Collège de France. Annuaire 111e année*. Paris: Collège de France, avril 2012, 379–98.

Evans, John F. "Death-Dealing Witchcraft in the Bible? Notes on the Condemnation of the 'Daughters' in Ezekiel 13: 17-23." *Tyndale Bulletin* 65.1 (2014): 57–84.

Fishbane, Michael. *Biblical Interpretation in Ancient Israel*. Oxford: Clarendon, 1989.

Gibert, Pierre. *Une théorie de la légende. Hermann Gunkel et les légendes de la Bible*. Paris: Flammarion, 1979.

Glassner, Jean-Jacques. "Les temps de l'histoire en Mésopotamie." In *Israël construit son histoire. L'historiographie deutéronomiste à la lumière des recherches récentes*, edited by Albert de Pury et al., Genève: Labor et Fides, 1996, 167–89.

Greenberg, Moshe. *Ezekiel, 1–20. A New Translation with Introduction and Commentary*. New York: Doubleday & Co, 1986.

Hamori, Esther J. "The Prophet and the Necromancer: Women's Divination for the Kings." *Journal of Biblical Literature* 132 (2013), 827–43.

Hilber, John W. *Cultic Prophecy in the Psalm*. Berlin: de Gruyter, 2005.

Korpel, Marjo C. "Avian Spirits in Ugarit and in Ezekiel 13." In *Ugarit, Religion and Culture: Proceedings of the International Colloquium on Ugarit Religion and Culture, Edinburgh, July 1994*, edited by Nick Wyatt et al. Münster: Ugarit Verlag, 1996.

Langlois, Michaël. "Le sceau d'un roi de la Bible découvert à Jérusalem", https://michaellanglois.fr/fr/missions/#mission1. 04.10.2015.

Langlois, Michaël. "La Bible parle-t-elle encore aujourd'hui ?" RTBF Présence Protestante, 11.10.2020, https://www.youtube.com/watch?v=AQa5_zNm4v4.

Levinson, Bernard. *L'Herméneutique de l'innovation*. Bruxelles: Lessius, 2006.

Linzi, Alan and Jonathan Stökl. *Divination, Politics and Ancient Near East Empires*. Atlanta: Society of Biblical Literature Press, 2014.

McKeating, Henry. *Ezekiel*. Sheffield: Sheffield Academic Press, 1993.

Niesiolowski-Spanò Lukasz. *The Origin Myths and Holy Places in the Old Testament*. London: Routledge, 2014.

Nihan, Christophe. "Ezéchiel." In *Introduction à l'Ancien Testament*, edited by Thomas Römer et al., Genève: Labor et Fides, 2009, 430–63.

Nissinen, Martti et al. *Prophets and Prophecy in the Ancient Near East*. Atlanta: Society of Biblical Literature, 2003.

Ramsey, Georges. "Speech-Forms in Hebrew Law and Prophetic Oracles." *Journal of Biblical Literature* 96/1 (1977): 45–58.
Rendtorff, Rolf. *Introduction à l'Ancien Testament*. Paris: Cerf, 1989.
Schwemer, Daniel. "The Ancient Near East." In *Magic and Witchcraft in the West. From the Antiquity to the Present*, edited by David J. Collins. Cambridge: Cambridge University Press, 2015.
Stiebert, Johanna. *Fathers and Daughters in the Hebrew Bible*. Oxford: Oxford University Press, 2013.
Stökl, Jonathan. *Prophecy in the Ancient Near East: A Philological and Sociological Comparison*. Leiden: Brill, 2012.
Stökl, Jonathan. "Female Prophets in the Ancient Near East", in *Prophecy and Prophets in Ancient Israel*, edited by John Day. London, New York: T&T Clark International, 2010.
Jonathan Stökl, "Ancient Near Eastern Prophecy." In *Dictionary of Old Testament Prophets*, edited by Mark Boda and J. Gordon MacConville, Downers Grove, IL: InterVarsity Press, 2012, 16–24.
Stökl, Jonathan and Corrine Carvalho. *Prophets Male and Female: Gender and Prophecy in the Hebrew Bible, the Eastern Mediterranean and Ancient Near East*. Atlanta: Society of Biblical Literature Press, 2013.
Stökl, Jonathan. "The מִתְנַבְּאוֹת in Ezekiel 13." *Journal of Biblical Literature* 132 (2013): 61–76.
Tiemeyer, Lena Sofia. "The Book of Ezekiel." In *Dictionary of Old Testament Prophets*, edited by Mark Boda and Gordon MacConville, Downers Grove, IL: InterVarsity Press, 2012.
Trigano, Shmuel, ed. *Controverse sur la Bible*. Paris: Éditions In Press, 2012.
Volokhine, Youri. "Tristesse rituelle et lamentations funéraires en Égypte ancienne." *Revue de l'histoire des religions* 2 (2008): 163–97.
Wevers, John W. *The New Century Bible Commentary: Ezekiel*. London: Marshall, Margon & Scott, 1971.
Ziegler, Nele. "Femmes inspiratrices en Mésopotamie: les musiciennes de cour." *Journal Asiatique* 303 (2015): 197–204.
Zimmerli, Walter. *Ezekiel*. Philadelphia: Fortress Press, 1986.

Torleif Elgvin
Messiahs and Redeemer Figures in Postexilic Texts

Abstract: The chapter presents a historical-literary survey of texts on messiahs and redeemer figures in postexilic times. The coverage is primarily diachronic, at times overruled by thematic considerations. The first part discusses texts that became biblical, followed by texts from the Old Testament Apocrypha and the Dead Sea Scrolls. While preexilic texts demonstrate the hope for a son of David perceived in earthly categories, exilic and postexilic times would see a transformation of the hopes for a divinely commissioned leader. In Second Temple times, eschatological and messianic hopes become pluriform and multifaceted. The chapter contrasts individual and collective messianism, and surveys Davidic, priestly, dual, and heavenly messianism. It discusses texts that became biblical in dialogue with other texts from the second and first centuries BCE, a hermeneutical dimension often overlooked in scholarship. It includes a discussion of the temple-centered eschatology related to the Heliopolis temple built by Judean exiles in the 160s and suggests a second-century editorial layer in Zech 12–14.

Keywords: Messianism, Prophetic literature, Septuagint, Greek Isaiah, Davidic Psalter, Balaam oracle, Son of Man, Enochic Parables, Sirach, Tobit, Antiochus Epiphanes, Qumran messianism, Hasmonean history, Heliopolis temple

1 Introduction

There are preexilic precursors for postexilic messianism.[1] Judahite texts from the ninth to the seventh century expect a righteous son of David as a God-sent future

---

[1] The chapter surveys a selection of relevant postexilic texts. For a more comprehensive discussion with ample references to secondary literature, see Torleif Elgvin, *Warrior, King, Servant, Savior. Messianism in the Hebrew Bible and Early Jewish Texts* (Grand Rapids: Eerdmans, 2022). Biblical texts are quoted or adapted from NRSV or JPS; LXX from NETS, at times I provide my own translation. For Qumran texts I give my own translation. I try to break new scholarly ground in the discussion of texts such as Num 24; Jer 30; Ps 110:3; 1QS 9; and 4Q246, and on issues such as presentic and futuric eschatology around the high priest Onias and the Heliopolis temple, Hasmonean and anti-Hasmonean messianism, and Hasmonean-time updating of the Scriptures to conform them with reality on the ground.

Torleif Elgvin, NLA University College, Oslo, Norway, torleif.elgvin@nla.no

https://doi.org/10.1515/9783110768411-003

ruler. In first temple times, the son of David is perceived in earthly categories.[2] However, exilic and postexilic times will see a transformation of the hopes for a future God-sent leader. An ideal Judean king dominating the neighbouring nations can now – in some texts – be perceived as a world emperor with global rule. At the same time, hopes about future redeemer figures become more pluriform.

A radical change of course is evident with Deutero-Isaiah: The anointed ruler and temple builder is Cyrus, no son of David is mentioned, and the nation is heir to the Davidic promises (55:1–5). I see Cyrus as the anointed servant of 42:1–9 and 49:1–9*.[3] With the growth of Second Isaiah, two songs envisage a suffering servant who will bring hope through his propitiatory suffering—either Israel suffering for the nations, or an individual bringing redemption to the nation. In the following I will present a survey of the pluriform hopes of redeemer figures in postexilic times.

2 Development of Prophetic Books

2.1 Haggai, Zechariah, Jeremiah 30: A Davidide and a Priest

Haggai and Zechariah reflect Judean restoration and hopes under the leadership of Zerubbabel—grandson of king Jehoiachin and Persian governor in the province of Yehud, responsible for rebuilding the temple together with the high priest Joshua during the years 520–515.

Haggai ends with a kind of messianic declaration to Zerubbabel: "On that day, says Yhwh of hosts, I will take you, Zerubbabel my servant, son of Shealtiel, and make you like a signet ring, for I have chosen you, says Yhwh of hosts." Terms such as "my (Davidic) servant," "I will take you," "I have chosen

---

[2] A typical example is GJer 23:5–6, which should be dated around the time of Zedekiah (596–587): "Behold, days are coming, says the Lord, when I will raise up for David a righteous dawn. This king shall reign, he will have insight and execute justice and righteousness in the land. In his days Judah will be saved and Israel encamp in confidence. And this is the name by which he will be called, 'the Lord Yhwh is righteousness'."

[3] For Cyrus as the servant of Isa 42:1–9, see Reinhard Kratz, *Kyros im Deuterojesaja-Buch: Redaktionsgeschichtliche Untersuchungen zu Entstehung und Theologie von Jes 40–55*, FAT 1 (Tübingen: Mohr Siebeck, 1991); Kim Lan Nguyen, "Cyrus. A Righteousness," in *The History of Isaiah. The Formation of the Book and its Presentation of the Past*, edited by Jacob Stromberg and J. Todd Hibbard, FAT 150 (Tübingen: Mohr Siebeck, 2021), 475–92; Pieter van der Lugt, *The Rhetorical Design of Isaiah 40–48/55. Zion's Incomparable Savior and His Servants*, OS 82 (Leiden: Brill, 2022), 195–201.

you," and "signet ring" reveal a belief that the Davidic dynastic line would be renewed in Jerusalem.

For Zechariah, Zerubbabel is the promised Davidide, the elect Shoot (3:8; 6:12). In Zech 4, the prophet is given a vision of two olive trees flanking the menorah. The seven-branched oil lamp symbolizes the presence of Yhwh, while the two olive trees are "the two sons of oil who stand by the Lord of the whole earth" (4:14). The "two sons of oil" refer to Zerubbabel and Joshua, the Davidide and the priest, with essential roles in establishing the temple and the temple service.

Zech 6:10–14 describes a ceremony where crowns are given to the high priest. 6:11 and 6:14 refer to crowns in the plural, 6:12–13 talks about the Shoot who shall build the temple and rule from his throne alongside the priest on his throne, while 6:11 reports the crowns (plural) being set only on the head of Joshua the priest. An earlier version of the text clearly had crowns being set on both leaders (cf. the hypothethic addition in italics below).

> ¹¹Take the silver and gold and make crowns, which you shall set on the heads of [*Zerubbabel son of Shealtiel and*] the high priest Joshua son of Jehozadak, ¹²and say to him: Thus says Yhwh of hosts: Here is a man whose name is Shoot: below him it shall shoot forth, he shall build the temple of Yhwh. ¹³He is the one that shall build the temple of Yhwh, he shall bear royal honor and sit and rule on his throne. There shall be a priest by his throne, with peaceful understanding between the two of them. ¹⁴And the crowns shall be in the custody of Heldai, Tobiah, Jedaiah, and Josiah, son of Zephaniah, as a memorial in the temple of Yhwh.

This text suggests that Zerubbabel indeed was regarded as the promised Davidide and that he, later on, was removed from the governor's seat. Subsequently, an editor of Zechariah had to take this into account and project the expected Shoot far into the future. Zerubbabel faded out of history; there are no further records about his fate.

Zech 4 and 6 became formative for dual or priestly messianism in later texts. Some scribes would stress the expectation of the anointed ruler, others that of the anointed priest. The hope for seeing a Davidic ruler on the throne in the present or close future had been crushed with the disappearance of Zerubbabel, and a Davidic hope would have to be postponed to a utopic future. With the high priest as political leader of the province in Hellenistic times, we might expect that hopes centred around the temple or a priestly messiah would more easily come to the surface than Davidic expectations.

The composite chapters Jer 30 and 33 thematize the future time of salvation. The earlier G version of 30:20–22 foresaw a future ruler dedicated to the Lord (lit., "he has set his heart to return to me"): "'I will gather them, and they shall

return to me, for who is this one, who dedicates his heart to me?' says the Lord."
In M, the text is recast:

> ²¹Its chieftain shall be one of its own,
> its ruler shall come from its midst,
> I will bring him near, he shall come near to me,
> for who is this one, who stakes his life coming near to me, says Yhwh.
> ²²And then you shall be my people, and I will be your God.

The words "I will bring him near" (√*qārab* in *hiphil*) bring us into the priestly, sacrificial realm. Coming into Yhwh's presence, the leader will pledge his life. Compared with G, M adds a new verse containing the covenant formula "and then you shall be my people, and I will be your God." The ruler's daring act in God's presence is done for the sake of the people and will lead to a renewed covenantal relation. The leader comes out of the people: he is "its chieftain" and "ruler" (*môšēl*). Perhaps for the first time in Scripture, *môšēl* is used for the priest—probably a reflection of present political reality in the province of Yehud in Hellenistic times.

The extended Masoretic version of Jeremiah betrays knowledge of political development in Egypt around 300 BCE.[4] I suggest that MJer 30:20–24 uses the present priestly leader in Jerusalem as type for a future priestly figure who in the end times (cf. 30:24) would risk his life in a sacrificial act before God. Whether he will die in Yhwh's presence is left open, but Isa 53:10–11 may play in the background.

This text goes alongside other passages in the proto-Masoretic recension of Jeremiah that foresee a future son of David. But it is the noble priestly ruler who will be the tool for the renewal of the covenant people, when God by his wrath fulfills his will toward the nations.

Zechariah's "two sons of oil" would find an echo in MJer 33:17–22, absent in the earlier Greek recension. This text affirms Yhwh's covenant both with David and the ministering Levites: "There shall not be an end to men of David's line who sit upon the throne of the House of Israel. Nor shall there be an end to the line of the levitical priests before me, of those who present burnt offerings and

---

[4] Pierre-Maurice Bogaert, "La datation par souscription dans les rédactions courte (LXX) et longue du livre de Jérémie," in *L'apport de la Septante aux études sur l'Antiquité: Actes du colloque de Strasbourg, 8–9 novembre 2002*, edited by Jan Joosten and Philippe Le Moigne, LD 203 (Paris: Cerf, 2005), 137–59; Armin Lange, "The Textual Plurality of Jewish Scriptures in the Second Temple Period in Light of the Dead Sea Scrolls," in *Qumran and the Bible: Studying the Jewish and Christian Scriptures in Light of the Dead Sea Scrolls*, edited by Nora Dávid and Armin Lange, CBET 57 (Leuven: Peeters, 2010), 43–96 at 77–82.

turn the meal offering to smoke and perform sacrifices" (vv 17–18, JPS adapted). The Davidide is possibly set into the future—his tasks are not explicated—while the anointed priestly line is represented by the ongoing priestly ministry in the temple.

A similar vague description of the role of the future son of David appears in the combination of oracles in Jer 30. Jer 30:5–7 and 30:16–17 preserve an authentic oracle from the prophet: through war and distress Jacob will ultimately see salvation, God will heal their wounds and crush those who plundered them. Here, Yhwh is the only redemptive actor. Subsequently, 30:12–14 would explicate the trials God allowed when he struck the nation through enemy armies. Finally, vv. 8–9 were added, introduced by the formula "on that day." Here, the nation "will serve Yhwh their God and David their king"—but any job description for the Davidic king is not provided.

Only the early oracle 23:5–6 keeps a job description for the coming Davidide: he will reign as king and execute justice and righteousness in the land. Inspired by other prophetic books, the reworked M recension would introduce a new messianic term into the book of Jeremiah. The earlier "I will raise up for David a righteous dawn" (G) now appears as "I will raise up for David a righteous *Shoot*"—a term echoing Zech 3:8 and 6:12 and likely alluding to Isa 11:1. In a close to identical form, this oracle was subsequently pasted into MJer 33:14–16 (not in G), introducing 33:19–22 on the ongoing temple ministry and a future Davidide.

A different perspective surfaces in Zech 9:9–10, a text from the early Hellenistic period:

> ⁹Rejoice greatly, O daughter Zion!
> Shout aloud, O daughter Jerusalem!
> Lo, your king comes to you,
> triumphant and victorious is he,
> humble and riding on a donkey,
> on a colt, the foal of a donkey.
> ¹⁰I will cut off the war chariot from Ephraim
> and the war horse from Jerusalem,
> and the battle bow shall be cut off.
> He shall command peace to the nations,
> his dominion shall be from sea to sea,
> from the Great River to the ends of the earth.

Zech 9:9–10 expects a future king radically different from the David of DtrH and the king of the royal psalms. In the process of restoration, God will demolish the nation's military in a way reminiscent of the end-time vision of Isa 2:1–5. He will enable the humble king to rule an empire in peace, an empire reaching "to the ends of the earth." This description of a nonmilitary king appears as a contrast to most Hellenistic rulers and transcends the nature of earthly kings.

2.2 Serving David their King and Yhwh their God

Ezek 34:23–24; 37:24–25; Jer 30:8–9; and Hos 3:5—all mention "David their king/prince" and "Yhwh their God," These oracles show a Davidic hope in late Persian Yehud. In contrast to Isa 11:1–5 and Mic 5:1–5[2–6], their job description for the Davidic ruler is remarkably vague.

Ezekiel did not include David in his visions for God's restoration. With the term *nāśî'*, his blueprint for a new temple referred to a leader with a sacrificial office. It may be a priestly editor who inserted passages on a Davidic shepherd and viceroy alongside Yhwh in the salvation oracles of Ezek 34 and 37, to conform these chapters with other scriptures. The earlier Greek text refrains from using the term "prince" (David is only their "ruler"), so this scribe acknowledges that the prophet used *nāśî'* for a priestly office (45:7–8; 46:1–18). In contrast, M's "prince" reflects a later redaction. For the first scribe, the viceroy is ruler only, while his successor shared an expressed royal Davidic hope, using the terms "prince" and "king" in MEzek 34:24; 37:24.

Another postexilic scribe specified his royal hope with inserts in the books of Jeremiah and Hosea. Instead of using the terms "ruler" or "prince," two texts declare that the nation shall seek or serve "Yhwh their God and David their king" (GJer 37:8–9 // MJer 30:8–9; Hos 3:5).

3 David and the End-time in the Psalms

3.1 Royal Psalms

The royal psalms 2, 21, 72, and 110 have their roots in preexilic times. During the time of the Judean kingdom they presented an ideal of the Davidic king, ruling in the land and dominating the neighboring countries. This ideal would be in marked contrast to political reality in the early Levant, where Judah remained a tiny kingdom in the shadow of the empires.

When these psalms were reread and edited during the Second Temple period, they presented a utopic ideal. In the shadow of the Persian and Hellenistic empires, any vision of the son of David's rule would have to be postponed to an indefinite future.

Psalm 72 would easily be read on a messiah transcending the nature of an earthly king. With Zenger, I separate 72:8–11, 15, 17b as postexilic additions with new perspectives (below rendered in italic font):[5]

> *⁸Let him rule from sea to sea,*
> *from the Great River to the ends of the earth.*
> *⁹Let desert dwellers kneel before him,*
> *and his enemies lick the dust.*
> *¹⁰Let kings of Tarshish and the islands pay tribute,*
> *kings of Sheba and Seba offer gifts.*
> *¹¹Let all kings fall down before him,*
> *and all nations serve him.*
> *¹⁵So let him live, and receive gold of Sheba,*
> *let prayers for him be said always,*
> *blessings on him invoked at all times.*
> ¹⁷ªMay his name endure forever
> and get offspring as long as the sun lasts.
> *¹⁷ᵇLet men invoke his blessedness upon themselves,*
> *let all nations pronounce him blessed.*

In the earlier core of Ps 72, the king is the mediator of blessings, the movement is outward—from the king, while in the postexilic verses there is a movement inward—from the nations toward the king. While Pss 2, 110 and prophetic oracles such as Mic 5:4–8[5–9] describe the king as a conquering warlord, the reign of this king is peaceful and characterized by abundance in the fields and happiness among men. The preexilic core was a prayer for the king ruling the land on God's behalf. Here, the messiah has worldwide dominion and is honored as an ancient Near Eastern emperor by his subordinate vassal kings. The earthly Judean king has been transformed into a messianic king with worldwide dominion, a source of blessing for the nations.

With its description of a luxurious royal wedding (of Solomon?), Ps 45 stands out among the royal psalms. I regard 45:11–16[10–15] as a postexilic addition to an earlier royal hymn. The earlier poem addresses the king in the second person, a court poet praises the king's divinely given office, with the relation between God and the king in focus. From postexilic times onwards, the full psalm would be read on the messianic king, in consort with Pss 2, 21, 72, and 110, and metaphorically on the wedding between God or a heavenly messiah and Zion/the elect community.

---

5 Frank-Lothar Hossfeld and Erich Zenger, *Psalms 2: A Commentary on Psalms 51-100* (Minneapolis: Fortress, 2005), 207–8.

Ps 132 is prominent among postexilic Zion and David psalms. Here the election of David and the election of Zion go together, and the David theology is subordinate to the cultic theology of the temple. Similar to Chronicles, David primarily appears as originator of the temple cult. In contrast to 2 Sam 7, the election of David is intimately connected with David's transfer of the ark to Zion.

David's oath to Yhwh to provide him with a dwelling place (vv 2–5) corresponds to Yhwh's oath to provide a dynasty for David and protect it against enemies (vv 11–12). Yhwh vows to dwell in the temple of Zion, walk with its priests, and feed the people. The psalm is celebrated in the temple, with priests ministering and faithful ones around—they are actors in the present, while the Davidic promise is set in the future.

Ps 132:12 reflects on the behavior of preexilic kings and the experience of the exile: "If your sons keep my covenant and my decrees that I teach them, then their sons also shall sit forever on your throne." In contrast to 2 Sam 7, the divine pledge to David on a lasting dynasty is conditional. While recognizing that the failure of Davidic kings led to the exile and end of the kingdom, the psalm upholds the promise of a future for the house of David: "I will make a horn sprout for David and set up a lamp for my anointed" (Ps 132:17). The horn is a symbol of power and specifically of royal power. Thus, the future Davidide is not the peaceful ruler of Zech 9:9–10 and the postexilic stratum in Ps 72:8–11, 15, 17b, but a monarch with political and military might. In the present, the nation continues to celebrate its liturgies in the temple—which again point to a successor to David, the temple's founding father, far into the future.

3.2 Davidic-Messianic Editing of 2 Samuel and 11QPs[a]

2 Sam 20:23–24:25 contains eight appendices to the Deuteronomistic History, all connected to David, the last seven arranged in a chiastic pattern.[6] A material reconstruction of the last columns of the early-Herodian scroll 1QSamuel (1Q7) suggests that it contained only three of these eight appendices: the record of the Philistine wars and their heroes (2 Sam 21:15–22), David's last words (23:1–7), and one of the lists of David's warriors (23:8–23).[7] Compared with the canonical recension, we lack the list of David's officials (20:23–26), the two stories on

---
[6] (A) offense of Saul and expiation, (B) list of heroes, (C) David's hymn of praise, (C′) David's last words, (B′) two lists of heroes, (A′) offense of David and expiation.
[7] Torleif Elgvin, "1QSamuel—A Pre-canonical Shorter Recension of 2Samuel," *ZAW* 132 (2020): 281–300; idem, "More on 1QSamuel and the Theory of Literary Growth. Response to Benjamin Ziemer," *ZAW* 133 (2021): 1–8.

royal guilt and expiation (21:1–14; 24:1–25), Ps 18 (= 2 Sam 22), and the second list of David's warriors (23:24–39).

A comparison with M demonstrates that Davidic appendices were added to 2 Samuel in stages. Post-Deuteronomistic scribes wanted to bring to the forefront the figure and image of David—a reflection of a vivid Davidic hope in Hellenistic times. "David's last words" (23:1–7), one of the earlier of these additions, is particularly instructive:

> ¹The oracle of David, son of Jesse,
> the oracle of the man whom God exalted,
> the anointed of the God of Jacob,
> the pleasant one among the singers of Israel:
> ²The spirit of Yhwh speaks through me,
> his word is upon my tongue.
> ³... The Rock of Israel has said to me:
> One who rules over people justly,
> ruling in the fear of God,
> ⁴is ... like the sun rising on a cloudless morning ...
> ⁵ᵃIs not my house like this with God?
> For he has made with me an everlasting covenant,
> ordered in all things and secure.

"David's last words" underlines central features of an ideal image of David: he is Yhwh's elect and anointed, rules justly in the fear of God, and is the founder of the "house of David." Different from earlier Davidic oracles or royal psalms, he is "the pleasant one among the singers of Israel"—a reference to Davidic psalms and psalm scrolls circulating at this time. He is also a *prophet*: Yhwh speaks through him, and the poem is stylized as a prophetic oracle.

A comparison with the end of 11QPsᵃ is illustrative. "David's last words" are here followed by "David's compositions" (XXVII 2–11) and Ps 140, and the scroll originally concluded with 134:1–3 and the biographical David-psalms 151A (XXVIII 3–12) and 151B (opening in XXVIII 13–14).[8] Similar to "David's last words," the Hebrew text of Ps 151A/B presents David as a singer, anointed as prince and connected to God's covenant:

---

8 Pss 151A/B were likely included in some scrolls of the Psalter during the second century, before the early-first-century translation into Greek. In 11QPsᵃ, 151A is preserved in full, but less than two lines of 151B is extant. The Septuagint conflated the first psalm and the beginning of the second into one composition, placed at the end of the Psalter. Some Syriac Bibles include Ps 151 as well as four other nonbiblical psalms from 11QPsᵃ.

> ³Hallelujah! Of David, son of Jesse.
> I was smaller than my brothers, youngest of my father's sons.
> He made me ⁴shepherd of his sheep and ruler over his goats.
> My hands fashioned a pipe, my fingers a lyre, and I glorified Yhwh.
> ... He sent his prophet to anoint me, Samuel, ⁹to magnify me.
> ... He took me ¹¹who followed the flock and anointed me with holy oil.
> He set me as prince of his people and ruler over the children of ¹²his covenant.

This liturgical scroll, copied by a sectarian scribe, was carefully formatted with a Davidic-messianic ending. The placement of "David's last words" together with Ps 151A/B may be more original than its late canonical setting with the appendices to DtrH in 2 Sam 21–24. I tentatively date the 1Q7 recension of 2 Samuel to the late third or early second century (post-Chronicles) and the further growth in the M recension to the second century. With "David's last words," there is a messianic edge already in the 1Q7 recension.

The evidence of 1QSam and 11QPs^a shows that editors of the Samuel scrolls around 200 found it pertinent to close 1–2 Samuel with three Davidic appendices, and their successors brought in four more. 2 Sam 24 (pasted from 1 Chr 21 and an earlier source) would underline David as founder of the temple cult; the others would point to David as type for the coming messiah.

3.3 Editing and Growing Together of Psalm Scrolls

The book of Psalms reflects a process of editing and growing together of smaller psalm scrolls during the postexilic period. A "Davidization" with a messianic edge is transparent throughout the process. The translation of 151 psalms into Greek in Egypt in the early first century demonstrates that the collection had reached its full size at this time.[9] The book would be divided into two major scrolls (1–72, 73–150) since one scroll would be too large to handle easily. The double "Amen" that closes 72:19 and the colophon of 72:20 marks the conclusion of the first scroll, which programmatically ended with the royal/messianic Ps 72, with words of the everlasting fame of the messiah and a messianic age where God's glory will fill the whole world.

As part of the initial growth of the Psalter, the early scroll of Pss 3–41 was combined with Pss 42–50 and Pss 51–72 into a collection opening and closing with two Davidic/messianic psalms, Ps 2 and Ps 72. Around 200, other editors

---

[9] The reference to Moab and Idumea in GPs 59:9–10 [M60:9–10[7–8]] and 107:9–10 [M108:9–10[8–9]] suggests a time after the Hasmonean conquest of Idumea in 107.

would extend the frame with the wisdom psalms 1 and 119, presenting the Psalter as a book to be read and meditated upon in dialogue with the Mosaic Torah (cf. Ps 1:2), not only being a collection of psalms to be sung in the temple. As part of the programmatic beginning of the Psalter, Ps 2 would remain a lasting testimony to singers and readers about the Davidic hope of the people of Judah.

In Ps 18, the editors framed an existing psalm with a biographical David-intro and a messianic closure (18:51 [18:50]). The added "postlude" changes a royal hymn to a messianic psalm. It proclaims a future hope for the Davidic line: "Great triumphs he gives to his king, and shows steadfast love to *his anointed*, to David and his *descendants* forever." It is in this later form it was appended into 2 Sam 22.

The superscriptions of Davidic psalms display David in a role different from king, ruler, and prototype for a future king. Here David appears as instigator of the temple cult and ideological type for Levite temple singers and praying Judeans. Thus, with the disappearance of Davidic rulers, the figure of David remained important for the temple community as cultic fellowship. But the two images of David existed side by side in third- and second-century Jerusalem, while some circles would stress one more than the other.

4 Second-century Texts

4.1 A Restored Zion without a Son of David

In their scenarios for the future, some early-second-century texts envisage a glorious temple in a restored Jerusalem without paying attention to the future son of David. This holds true for the Zion hymns in Sir 36:13–19[13–22], Tob 13:9–17, and 11QPs^aZion. In Ben Sira's time, the high priest was the religious and civil leader of the Judeans. The panegyric praise of the high priest Simon in Sir 50 hardly allows for a Davidic ruler at the side of the priest in the close future. However, the section on David and Solomon in Ben Sira's praise of the fathers could suggest a possible fulfilment of Davidic promises far into the future.[10]

---

[10] "The Lord ... exalted his [i.e., David's] horn forever, he gave him a royal covenant and a glorious throne in Israel. ... But the Lord would not go back on his mercy, or undo any of his words. He would not obliterate the issue of his elect, nor destroy the stock of the man who loved him; and he granted a remnant to Jacob, and to David a root springing from him" (47:11, 22). However, Sir 45:24–26 makes the covenant with Aaron greater than that with David. The Hebrew version of 45:25 limits the Davidic promise to Solomon, while the covenant with Aaron

11QPs^aZion does not mention the temple; the focus is the glorious restoration of Zion. None of these psalms speak about the anointed end-time high priest, so, in contrast to many Qumran texts, there is no expressed priestly messianism here. These texts can be compared to the collective messianism in 4Q246 and some Yahad texts (see below).

4.2 Yhwh in Egypt: Onias, Greek Isaiah, Joseph and Aseneth, Zech 12–14

In the 160s, a group of Judean exiles built a temple for Yhwh in Heliopolis, a temple functioning until Vespasian in 74 gave orders to close it down. Josephus gives two contrasting versions of the fate of the high priest Onias III, ousted from his office by the Hellenizing Jason in 175. According to *War* (1.31–33; 7.421–36), Onias III, well and alive, led a group of Judeans to Egypt and became the temple builder in Heliopolis. In *Antiquities*, however, Onias III was killed in Antioch around 171, and it is his son, Onias IV, who leads his group into the Egyptian exile (*Ant.* 12.237–38, 387; 20.235–36). The latter version concurs with 2 Macc 4:32–35.

According to Josephus, the exiles saw themselves as fulfilling an Isaianic prophecy of Isa 19:18–22 about a Yhwh presence in Egypt: According to the Greek, "the Lord will send them a *man* who will save them" (v. 20)—this man must be Onias (M "He will send them a redeemer who will fight and save them").

Seeligmann argues that Heliopolis traditions were included in the Greek translation of Isaiah, made in Alexandria in the 140s.[11] In addition to GIsa 19:18–22, Seeligmann finds a reference to the flight of Onias IV to Egypt in GIsa 8:8 and 10:24. Isaiah's repeated references to "the king of Assyria" are either read directly as prophecies of the ungodly king ruling from Damascus or consciously given a secondary meaning in a new historical context (Isa 7:17, 20; 8:4, 7; 10:12; 20:4, 6).[12] In 8:8 and 10:24, the M hypotext is transformed into a prophecy of

---

is lasting: "And there is also a covenant with David, son of Isai, from the tribe of Judah; while the inheritance of a man [i.e., David] is to his son alone, the inheritance of Aaron is also to his seed" (Genizah ms B).

11 Isac Leo Seeligmann, with Robert Hanhart and Hermann Spieckermann, *The Septuagint Version of Isaiah and Cognate Studies*, FAT 40 (Tübingen: Mohr Siebeck, 2004), 50, 233–51.

12 Qumran pesharim interpret Isaiah in the same way (4QpIsa^a [4Q161] frgs 2–4, 6–10; 4QpIsa^c [4Q163] frgs 2–3; frgs 4–7 II 2–6, 21 [interpretation of Isa 8:7; 10:12–13, 24–27]).

Antiochus beating Jerusalem and causing the righteous and legitimate high priest into an Egyptian exile.

Bohak convincingly argues that the fascinating novel Joseph and Aseneth has its origin in the priestly milieu of Heliopolis.[13] Chs 16–17 are an allegory on priests leaving their dwelling and source of life to find refuge with Aseneth, the future wife of the patriarch Joseph (Gen 41:50). The Jerusalem temple of Jason and Menelaus is spiritually corrupt and destined for destruction, while the true priests will settle with Aseneth, who will be a City of Refuge, pointing to a future city of God in Egypt. With its temple, Aseneth's City of Refuge will be the only true Zion in the coming eschaton, "the City of Righteousness" about which the prophets had spoken.

In the moderate messianism of Joseph and Aseneth, the anointed high priest will, with his colleagues, establish a city that will be the end-time Jerusalem. Its temple will be the dwelling of God and a source of life and immortality, for Judeans and Egyptian converts. The true sons of the Living God will be "called from darkness to light ... from death to life ... be renewed by God's spirit ... and the chosen ones will live in God's eternal life forever and ever" (8:10–11). This temple-centered eschatology may be compared with Sir 36, Tob 13, and 11QPs^{a}Zion.

Daniel 7–12 is commonly dated to the 170s and 160s, reflecting the third-century wars of the Diadochi, the campaigns of Antiochus IV, and the Maccabean uprising. These upheavals should also be considered as background for the completion of the book of Zechariah. I here suggest that Zech 13:7–9 in a symbolic way retells the story of the killing of Onias III in Antioch in 171 (2 Macc 4:34–36; *Ant.* 12.237–38; 20.235–36) and the subsequent trials under Antiochus IV:

> [7]Sword, awake against my close friend,[14]
> the man who is my associate, says Yhwh of hosts.
> Smite the shepherd, so that the flock will be scattered
> when I turn my hand against the small ones.
> [8]In the whole land, says Yhwh,
> two-thirds shall be cut off and perish,
> one-third shall be left alive.
> [9]I will put this third into the fire,
> refine them as one refines silver,
> and test them as one tests gold.
> He will call on my name,

---

13 Gideon Bohak, Joseph and Aseneth and the Jewish Temple in Heliopolis (Atlanta: Scholars Press, 1996).
14 Reading *rēʿî* ("my close friend") for the Masoretic pointing *rōʿî* ("my shepherd").

> and I will answer him.
> I will say, "He is my people,"
> And he will say, "Yhwh is my God."

Scholars struggle to interpret this enigmatic passage and suggest a fitting historical setting in the fourth or third century. However, if prophetic books could be updated during the second century, an Oniad-Epiphanes dating of this passage could solve the crux. *Rēʿî* ("my close friend") would be a fitting designation for the high priest, who could be considered in line with the heavenly temple in his sacrificial service (cf. 1QSb III 25–26; IV 22–26). Since the high priest in the Hellenistic period functioned as civil leader of the Judeans, the term "shepherd" (for his flock) in the third member of v. 7 would also be fitting.

According to the text, a catastrophic fallout for the nation would follow the death of the shepherd, and only a third of the people will survive. Such a decimation of the people is not recorded between the destruction of the First Temple and the campaigns of Antiochus IV, and even the persecutions of the latter did not lead to such a gruesome slaughter. The concluding stichs envisage that, through trials and refinement, the nation will be led to a renewed covenant relation with God, perhaps with both Jerusalem and Heliopolis in view.

The text closely parallels Daniel passages that symbolically recast the history of the 160s: thousands shall be slayed during times of trials (7:21, 23; 11:41; 12:1), an anointed one is being cut off (commonly identified with Onias III; 9:26), and the trials will ultimately lead to a renewed relation of the nation with God (7:18, 27).

My interpretation of Zech 13:7–9 suggests that scribes in Judea or Heliopolis saw the need to update and actualize Zech 12–14 in light of the murder of Onias III and the upheavals of the 160s. In their eyes, the hypotext was unfinished and in need of a continuation. The subsequent 14:2–5 may have been polished in the same editorial stage and refer to Antiochus's twofold sacking of Jerusalem in 169–168 and the flight of the Onias group to Egypt.[15] A comparison of Zech 13–14 with Dan 7, 9, 11, 12 suggests that all these chapters in different ways contain symbolic reflections of the bloody history of Judah and Jerusalem in the decade following the murder of Onias III.[16]

---

[15] Zech 14:2–5 can be compared with Dan 7:9–10, 12:1. The oracle concludes, "Then Yhwh my God will come, and all the *holy ones* with him"—the only occurrence in Zechariah of the term *qədōšîm*—a term well known from Dan 7, cf. 1 En 1:9, "the Great Holy One will appear with his heavenly armies, he comes with myriads of *holy ones*."

[16] For a discussion of the enigmatic pierced figure of Zech 12:10–12, see Elgvin, *Warrior, King*, 97, 130, 191, 303–6, 311, 314.

4.3 A Mighty Messiah with Heavenly Powers

The throne vision in Dan 7:9–10, 13–14 would have a great impact on subsequent tradition. In this judgment scene, heavenly thrones are set for the Ancient of Days and the Son of Man—after the latter has arrived with the clouds of heaven. Then, the Ancient of Days gives the Son of Man ultimate power over all the earth:

> ¹⁴Dominion, glory, and kingship were given to him,
> all peoples and nations of every language must serve him.
> His dominion is an everlasting dominion that shall not pass away,
> and his kingdom shall not be destroyed.

A postexilic reading of two early royal psalms may provide some background for the Son of Man in Dan 7. In Ps 110, the earthly Davidic king is enthroned alongside God's heavenly throne. In the likely postexilic addition of 110:4, he is bestowed with a priestly office and ministry. Psalm 2 describes a close union between "Yhwh and his anointed" (v. 2). The divine proclamation to the king, "You are my son; today I have begotten you" (v. 7), would have potential to inspire reflections on a heavenly status of the messiah.

I tend to see the Son of Man as an exalted messianic figure.[17] The authority he is given over peoples and nations is easiest read in light of biblical texts on the future or universal rule of the Davidic king. We should note the royal terminology of 7:14: "kingship" (*malkû*) is given to the Son of Man, his "kingdom" (*malkût*) shall not be destroyed.

Further, biblical texts before Dan 7 do not afford angelic figures with universal rule or a large empire. And we should keep in mind that the earliest interpretative traditions—4Q521 (second half of second century) and the Enochic Similitudes (around the turn of the era)—read the Son of Man as a messiah. A much-discussed Qumran text casts light on early understanding of the Danielic vision:

> ¹[For hea]ven and earth will obey his anointed one,
> ²[and nothing th]at is in them will turn away from the commandments of the holy ones.
> ³Be strong, you who seek the Lord, when you serve him!
> ⁴Indeed, in this you will find the Lord, all you who hope in your hearts

---

17 John J. Collins lists three main lines of interpretation for the Son of Man: (a) an exalted human being; (b) a collective symbol (cf. 7:15–27, where the reign is given to the people of God); (c) a heavenly being (Collins' preferred option) (*Daniel. A Commentary on the Book of Daniel* [Philadelphia: Fortress, 1993], 304–10).

> ⁵that the Lord will attend to the pious and call the righteous by name.
> ⁶Over the poor his spirit will hover, with his strength he will restore the faithful,
> ⁷on the throne of the eternal kingdom, he will honor the pious,
> ⁸he who sets prisoners free, opens the eyes of the blind, and raises up those who are bo[wed down.
> ⁹[ ] .. I shall hold fast [to the Lord
> ¹⁰[ ] .. and by his loving kindness .. [ ]
> ¹¹the fru[it of good dee]ds(?) to a neighbor shall not tarry.
> ¹²The Lord shall do glorious things that have never been done, just as he said.
> ¹³For he shall heal the badly wounded, revive the dead, and proclaim good news to the afflicted.
> ¹⁴He shall satis[fy the poo]r, guide the uprooted, and enrich the hungry. (4Q521 2 II + 4 1–14)

4Q521 (4QMessianic Apocalypse) was copied around 100 and likely authored sometime during the second half of the second century. The text does not bear features characteristic of the Yahad and should be read as a midrash on Dan 7, Ps 146, and 1 Sam 2. The text appears as a sequel to Dan 7:13–14, as it attributes universal lordship to "his anointed one" (*məšîḥô*), that is, *the* messiah. Whatever the original meaning of "son of humankind," Dan 7:13–14 is here read as a heavenly inauguration of Israel's Davidic messiah.

While the messiah is the central figure in lines 1–3, God himself is the acting subject in lines 4–14, which closely follow Ps 146:7–10 as hypotext. However, the mighty deeds that God will do belong to the messianic age.

In Dan 7:9–14, the focus is the reign given to the Son of Man, while in 7:15–27, it is the restoration of the people of God and the reign given to it by divine intervention. This twofold structure recurs in 4Q521, where lines 1–3 have the messiah in focus, while lines 4–14 describe how God will restore and redeem the elect community. In 4Q521, the enthronement of a messiah in heaven will lead to a renewal of God's people on earth.[18]

4.4 An Interlude: The Enochic Son of Man

The full text of 1 Enoch is only known from Ethiopian manuscripts from the fifteenth century onward, and the book would necessarily undergo textual and literary changes during its odyssey from Aramaic (partly preserved in eleven

---

18 As many interpreters note, this text (or the tradition it represents) receives sequels in the Gospels, Matt 11:2–6 // Luke 7:18–23 and 4:18–19. However, this writer may be the first to note that the closest textual echo of "[for hea]ven and earth will obey his anointed ... when you serve him" is the last words of Jesus in Matt 28:18: "All authority in heaven and on earth has been given to me," preceded by "they worshiped him" (28:17).

fragmentary Qumran manuscripts that cover less than 1/5 of the text) through Greek to Ethiopic, and the Ethiopic textual tradition is also dynamic.[19] Apart from the fragmentary Aramaic evidence, this ancient Jewish textual collection has survived through Christian transmission.

While there is no messiah in the Book of Watchers (from the third and early second century), this will change in the last section of 1 Enoch, the Book of Parables, 1 En 37–71. In 1 En 45–69, Enoch sees a heavenly viceroy, a "Son of Man" walking alongside God ("the Lord of Spirits," "the Head of Days") and being set by God on the heavenly throne.

The Parables are absent from the Aramaic and Greek manuscripts and are not quoted in patristic literature.[20] A *caveat* is needed: while the core of Parables may be dated around the turn of the era or in the late first century CE, details in the text known to us could be colored by Christian scribes in the Greek and Ethiopic traditions.

Different biblical images converge in the Parables' image of the Son of Man. The title and heavenly character echo Dan 7:13–14. The heavenly enthronement represents a development of the Danielic text as well as Ps 110. "My chosen one" and "light for the nations" (1 En 45:3–4; 48:6; 49:2; 51:3; 61:5, 8) point to the servant of Yhwh (Isa 42:1, 6). Righteousness dwells with the Son of Man, similar to the messianic shoot and suffering servant in Isaiah (1 En 46:3; 49:2; Isa 11:1–5; 53:11). He is "the anointed one" like the royal messiah (1 En 48:10; Ps 2:2).

In 1 En 45, 61, 62, and 69, the Son of Man is set on the throne of glory, receives praise and laudation, and presides at the end-time judgment—it is the Son of Man who sits on the throne, not the Head of Days. Sinners and iniquity will be destroyed, while the righteous will be resurrected to a blessed life on a renewed earth.

---

[19] Loren Stuckenbruck, Ted M. Erho, "The Significance of the Ethiopic Witnesses for the Text Tradition of 1 Enoch: Problems and Prospects," in *Congress Volume Aberdeen 2019*, edited by Grant Macaskill, Christl M. Maier and Joachim Schaper, SupVT 192 (Leiden: Brill, 2022), 416–34.
[20] Many would date the Parables between 40 and 1 BCE, while a minority suggests a date between 1 CE and 70 CE. See the contributions of Suter, Eshel, Hannah, and Arcari in *Enoch and the Messiah Son of Man. Revisiting the Book of Parables*, edited by Gabriele Boccacini (Grand Rapids: Eerdmans, 2007); George W.E Nickelsburg and James C. VanderKam, *1 Enoch 2. A Commentary on the Book of 1 Enoch, Chapters 37–82* (Minneapolis: Fortress, 2012), 58–63. Enoch and Jubilees were translated from Greek to Geez around the sixth century as part of the larger project of translating the Bible into this Ethiopian language. Richard Bauckham now dates the Parables to the late first century CE; cf. his *Son of Man*, vol. 1, *Early Jewish Literature*, Grand Rapids: Eerdmans, forthcoming.

Toward the end of the literary growth of the Parables, an appendix (1 En 70–71) was added. Here, Enoch receives the surprising message that the enthroned Son of Man is no other than himself.

> [14]You are the Son of Man who was born for righteousness,
> and righteousness dwells on you ...
> [16]And all will walk on your path ...
> with you will be their dwellings and with you, their lot,
> and from you they will not be separated forever and ever.
> [17]And thus, there will be length of days with that Son of Man,
> and there will be peace for the righteous ...
> in the name of the Lord of Spirits forever and ever. (1 En 71:14, 16–17)

The Parables understand Dan 7:9–14 as an unfinished hypotext in need of a continuation. According to 7:14, "all shall serve him"—recurring in the worship of the Son of Man (1 En 48:5; 62:6–9). In 1 En 45–71, the Son of Man is portrayed as mediator between God and humankind, a heavenly source of redemption and righteousness. While subordinate to the Lord of Spirits, he has godlike or divine features. He is preexistent and hidden in God's abode (48:3–6; 62:7); his glory will last forever (48:2); all who dwell on the earth will fall down and worship before him (48:5; 61:11–12; 62:6–9). These features of the Ethiopic text do not necessarily go back to the Jewish *Vorlage*, they may represent Christian polishing of the text in patristic and medieval times.

However, the identification of the Son of Man with Enoch himself in ch. 71 remains a strange element in a text transmitted through centuries by Christian scribes. Is it a leftover from the Aramaic-Jewish tradition or could it represent a late stage in the editorial growth of the Ethiopian recension?

4.5 The People of God as the End-Time Messianic Community

The texts of Sir 36, Tob 13, and 11QPs[a]Zion envision a glorious future for Jerusalem without any mention of the son of David. Then there are texts that continue biblical traditions of Yhwh as the sole actor in the end-time drama (e.g., 1 En 1–11). In some texts, the people of God appear as the eschatological messianic community (cf. Isa 55:1–5, where the Davidic promises are bequeathed to the nation in its return to Zion). In Dan 7:15–27, the sequence of the vision of the Son of Man, the end-time actor is the people of the holy ones (those allied with the angels) who is refined through trials and given eternal reign.

In a collective messianism, redemption occurs through the action of the people of God. Here, later texts draw on biblical passages on the last days/the time to come without mention of a redeemer figure. A Daniel-related text from the second century is a prime example of this line of interpretation. Of the scroll 4Q246 (4QapocrDaniel ar) a column and a half is extant. The text, with my suggested reconstructions, runs as follows:

```
I.1[                    fear] came [u]pon him. He fell before the throne of
 2[the king       and said, "Live,] O king, forever! Wrath comes, and your years
 3[are counted      revealed in] your vision, everything that shall come forever.
 4[                     be b]attles, and oppression will come over the earth.
 5[                carnage in the land], and great slaughter in the provinces,
 6[                    brought about by] the king of Assyria, [and E]gypt²¹
 7[will be hit hard                    this king] will be great on the earth,
 8[                              him all will] worship and all will serve,
 9[    son of the g]reat [God] he shall call himself, by his name he shall designate himself.
II.1He shall call himself son of God, and they shall call him son of the Most High.
Like the meteors ²that you saw, so shall their rule be changi[ng]:
they shall rule over ³the earth and trample everything down:
people shall trample upon people, province trample upon [pro]vince—
 4   until the people of God will rise and make everything rest from the sword.
⁵Its/his kingdom shall be an everlasting kingdom and all its/his paths in righteousness.
It/he shall jud[ge] ⁶the land in truth and make everything whole.
The sword shall cease from the earth, ⁷and all the provinces shall pay it/him homage.
The great God is its/his strength, ⁸he himself shall wage war for it/him.
He shall give peoples in its/his hand and ⁹cast them all down before it/him.
Its/his dominion shall be an everlasting dominion, and all the deeps of [
```

This text is a sequel to Dan 7:7–9, 11–12, 15–27, possibly authored soon after 164. In the text, a prophetlike person is called to the court to interpret the king's vision, similar to Joseph before pharaoh. The imaginary king could be the Ptolemaic ruler.

The parallels with Dan 7 indicate that the main figure in I 4–II 1 is neither a messiah nor a heavenly being, but rather an ungodly king. The boasting king and adversary of God's people is modelled on Antiochus Epiphanes. In the second century, the Isaianic term "king of Assyria" is reinterpreted as the contemporary king in Damascus and concretely as Antiochus Epiphanes.

The parallels with Luke 1:32–35 do not make the ruler of 4Q246 I 4–II 1 a messiah. They rather demonstrate the closeness between Luke's messianic terminology and royal ideology in the ancient Near East. The Gospels were written

---

21 Most scholars read "the king of Assyria and Egypt" or "the kings of Assyria and Egypt." My interpretation of lines 6–7 would fit the intrusions by Antiochus, "the king of Assyria," into Egypt in 170–169 and 168.

at a time when the imperial cult was intensified, not least in the eastern parts of the Roman Empire (cf., e.g., Josephus, *War* 4.168). The words of the annunciation certainly relate to Davidic texts in the Bible. But this Lukan text also vibrates with tension vis-à-vis Roman imperial ideology.[22] As an expression of oriental royal ideology, 4Q246 remains important for the interpretation of Luke 1:32–35 and New Testament proclamation of Jesus as messiah.

4Q246 II 4–9 presents a crux. The earthly actor who has God as his strength is consistently referred to with a singular suffix—its/his, which can be read either as a divinely blessed king or the end-time people of God. I prefer the latter option. Line 4 opens with a paragraph marker (a *vacat*), which indicates the new era, the restoration of the people of God. The text of col. II is complete, no king or messiah is introduced before lines 5–9 which elaborate on the end-time kingdom given to God's people. As in Dan 7:15–27, the people of God, who have been through turmoil and suffering, emerge as the victor of the end time. In this text, the restored people of the end time is portrayed as God's messianic community.

4.6 The Hasmonean Kingdom and Messianic Expectations

The Maccabean project started as a guerrilla revolt for Torah, temple, and Israelite purity. It developed into a state-building project with an organized army, territorial ambitions, and a military expansionist policy vis-à-vis the surrounding nations. With the military conquests of Hyrcanus, Aristobulus, and Jannaeus, an Israelite state was established that matched the biblical accounts of the United Kingdom. Such remarkable achievements after more than four hundred years of subjugation under world empires would lead to messianic fervor in some circles and to critical reflection in others.

With its first recension from the 120s, 1 Maccabees is a consistent apology for the Hasmoneans as elect deliverers of the Judean nation. They are the "men to whom was given salvation to Israel by their hand," as David was in his time (1 Macc 5:62, echoing 2 Sam 2:17). 1 Macc 13:41 ("the yoke of the gentiles was lifted from Israel") sees the liberation from the Seleucid Empire—the latter-day Assyria—by the hand of Simon, as fulfilment of Isa 10:27 and 14:25.

---

22 Cf. Morten Hørning Jensen, "The Gospel of Reconciliation in the Gospel of Mark," in *Reconciliation: Christian Perspectives—Interdisciplinary Approaches*, edited by Tobias Faix, Johannes Reimer, and Cobus J. van Wyngaard (Wien/Zürich: LIT, 2020), 23–44 at 26–32, 38.

The Hasmoneans saw themselves as an integral part of biblical history, walking in the footsteps of David and Solomon. This is evidenced in two poetic eulogies honoring Judah the Maccabee and Simon after their deaths (1 Macc 3:3–9; 14:4–15), which contain echoes and allusions to biblical texts on the son of David and the future Davidic kingdom. These anointed priestly rulers were hailed as small messiahs, bringing to some kind of fulfilment Davidic oracles as well as general prophecies on God turning the fate of his people.[23]

By their deeds, the Hasmoneans established themselves not only as rulers, but also as legitimate high priests. 1 Macc 2:24–28 sets Phinehas's zeal for the purity of Israel as a paradigmatic ideal. By repeating the deeds of "Phinehas our father," Mattathias and his sons earn God's favor: "And he became zealous in the law as Phinehas had done" (2:26, 54). The covenant of Phinehas, which gave legitimacy to the high priesthood of the house of Zadok, was superseded by the new covenant with the house of the Hasmoneans.

From 152, the Hasmonean rulers occupied the double office of high priest and civil leader. During the Ptolemaic and Seleucid periods, the high priest had been both civil and religious leader of the Judean province. Ruling priests who downplayed the hope of a Davidic messiah were, therefore, no *novum* with the Hasmoneans. In 142, the Judean assembly gave full powers to Simon:

> The Judeans and the priests were pleased that Simon would be their *leader* and high *priest* forever, until a trustworthy *prophet* would arise, and that he would be commander over them . . . And Simon accepted and was pleased to be high priest and commander and ethnarch of the Judeans and priests and to protect them all. (1 Macc 14:41, 47)

The words "leader and high priest forever" consciously echo the royal/messianic Ps 110:4: "You are a priest forever according to the order of Melchizedek." Psalm 110 is here used as legitimization for the Hasmonean rulers and priests.[24]

Simon's edict acknowledges the three offices of ruler, priest, and prophet: two of them already in function, while the office of prophet was postponed to the future. Two Josephus texts suggest that Hyrcanus countered opposition by claiming also the third office, that of the prophet. Josephus and his pro-Hasmonean source saw Hyrcanus "accounted by God worthy of three of the

---

23 See Elgvin, *Warrior, King*, 215–18.
24 Ps 110:3 evinces scribal censoring of an earlier mythological text describing the king's divinely given "birth" (cf. G, Syr) to the knotty text of M that hails a powerful young king with his people mustering for battle. This scribal change is commonly dated to the third century. A dating in the time of the warring Hasmonean rulers Simon (142–135) and John Hyrcanus (135–105) makes more sense.

greatest privileges: the rule of the nation, the office of high priest, and the gift of prophecy" (*Ant.* 13.299–300). Elsewhere Josephus reports a prophetic revelation given to Hyrcanus in the temple during his priestly service (*Ant.* 3.282–83), a tradition positively affirmed in the Tosefta (t. *Sotah* 13.5).

A composite Balaam oracle in Num 24 reflects textual polishing in Hasmonean times. The final wording seems to reflect Hasmonean triumph, subjugation of Idumea, and the demise of the Seleucid empire:

> [17]What I see is not yet,
> what I behold is not near:
> A star shall come out of Jacob,
> a scepter shall rise out of Israel,
> he shall crush the borderlands of Moab,
> and the territory of all the Shethites.
> [18]Edom will become a possession,
> Seir a possession of his enemies,
> while Israel does valiantly.
> [19]One out of Jacob shall rule,
> and destroy the survivors of the city.
>
> [23]Again he uttered his oracle, saying:
> Alas, who shall live when God does this?
> [24]Ships shall come from Kittim
> and afflict Asshur and Eber,
> also he shall perish forever.

These verses fit Israelite dominion over their neighbours only with the ninth-century Omri dynasty's expansion into Edom or in Hasmonean times. Balaam indeed sees far into the future when a princely ruled Israel shall subdue the neighboring nations to the east. The Nabateans ("his enemies") had pushed the Edomites westward from the fourth/third century, and Israel indeed "did valiantly" when Hyrcanus conquered the northern part of Perea after 129 and subjugated Idumea in 107. Further, the War Scroll likely preserves an earlier and shorter version of Num 24:18–19 without mention of Edom or Seir (1QM XI 6–7).[25]

---

[25] Helen S. Jacobus, "Strangers to the 'Biblical Scrolls': Balaam's Fourth Oracle (Num 24:15–19) and its Links to Other Unique Excerpted Texts," in: *Is there a Text in this Cave? Studies in the Textuality of the Dead Sea Scrolls in Honour of George J. Brooke*, edited by Ariel Feldman, Maria Cioată, and Charlotte Hempel, STDJ 119 (Leiden: Brill, 2017), 226–257 at 244–49. The 1QM text runs: "He shall descend from Jacob and destroy the survivors of the city. The enemy will become a possession, while Israel does valiantly."

The last oracle of Balaam (Num 24:23–24) foresees that "ships from Kittim" will afflict Asshur. In Qumran scrolls, the Kittim are identified with the Romans and their armies. The "ships of Kittim" appear in a Danielic oracle of salvation (11:25–35 at 11:30). This force is commonly identified with the Roman fleet that caused Antiochus Epiphanes to retreat from Cyprus and Egypt during his second Egyptian campaign in 168. Thus, the term "ships of Kittim" has second-century flavor.

Second-century texts such as Greek Isaiah can use "Asshur" for Seleucid Syria—with Antiochus IV taking the role of the violent king of Asshur. And Seleucid Syria remained the main military enemy of the Hasmoneans throughout the second century. Vv. 23–24 hardly fit preexilic times, the oracle expects ships from the west (= the Romans) to confront Asshur (= Seleucid Syria), which will suffer and thereafter come to an end as a kingdom. These verses were likely added to the Balaam cycle when the empire gradually fell apart after the death of Antiochus VII in 129 (in 63 it finally fell to Pompey).

Within the Balaam cycle, the king of Israel appears in the oracles of ch. 24 (24:3–9, 15–19, 20, 21, 23–24). Vv. 18 and 24 (possibly also v. 19) show a messianic rereading and extension of the oracles with the Hasmonean conquest of Idumea in 107 and the falling apart of the hostile Seleucid empire. The Hasmonean princely rulers represent a fulfilment of Balaam's prophecy.

5 Messianism in Yahad Texts

5.1 A Prophet and Two Anointed Ones

We now turn to messianism in relevant texts authored within the Yahad. The vision in Zech 4 of two sons of oil was foundational for the dual messianism we encounter in three important texts of the Yahad: the final version of the Community Rule, the Rule of the Congregation, and 4QTestimonia.

The thematic collection of scriptures in 4QTestimonia (4Q175) outlines the offices of prophet like Moses (lines 5–8: Deut 18:18–19), Davidic ruler (lines 9–13: Num 24:15–17), and priest (lines 14–20: Deut 33:8–11). 4QTestimonia may be construed as a critical response to the twofold office of Hasmonean rulers, reflected in Simon's edict from 142 that proclaimed Simon and his descendants as high priests and rulers of the Judeans, "until a trustworthy prophet would arise" (1 Macc 14:41), and, as noted above, Hyrcanus may have claimed all three offices. The collection of scriptures in 4Q175 represents a silent protest: the officially anointed leadership is illegitimate; the Yahad still waits for the right prophet together with the anointed ones of Aaron and Israel. The same threefold hope is expressed in the Community Rule, as it appears in its final recension from Cave 1.

> At that time, the men ⁶of the Yahad shall set apart a holy house for Aaron, to form a most holy community and a house of communion for Israel [...] the men of holiness [...] shall depart from none of the teachings of the law [...] but shall be ruled by the original precepts by which the men of the Yahad were first instructed, ¹¹until there shall come the prophet and the anointed ones of Aaron and Israel. (1QS IX 5–6, 8–11)

The clause "until there shall come the prophet and the anointed ones of Aaron and Israel" appears as a later attachment to a long section of regulations (cf. the shorter and earlier recension in 4QS^d (4Q258) 2 II 6–9). The scribe who prepared the master copy of 1QS saw the need to qualify these statutes with a proclamation of the end-time hope of the Yahad. At an earlier stage this eschatological clause was not part of the Serekh tradition.

The first appendix to 1QS, 1QSa (1Q28a) opens with a blueprint for the military organization in the end-time war. The last section describes the sacred meal when the royal messiah appears, a meal presided by the anointed high priest. Thus, the text introduces two anointed ones in the end time:

> ¹¹This is the order of the [ass]embly of the men of renown, [summoned] for the gathering, for the council of the community: when [God] fathers ¹²the messiah among them: [the Priest,] head of the entire congregation of Israel, shall enter first, trailed by all ¹³[his] brot[hers, the sons of] Aaron [...]. They are to sit ¹⁴be[fore him] by rank. Then the [mess]iah of Israel may en[ter,] and the heads ¹⁵of [their] th[ousands] are to sit before him by rank, according to [their] st[anding] in their camps and their marches [...].
> W[hen] they gathe[r at the tabl]e of the community [...] nobody [should stretch out] his hand to the first portion ¹⁹of the bread or [the new wine] before the Priest. For [he] shall [bl]ess the first portion of the bread ²⁰and the new win[e and stretch out] his hand for the bread first. And afterw[ard,] the messiah of Israel [shall st]retch out his hands ²¹to the bread. [Finally,] the entire congregation of the community [shall bl]ess, each o[ne] according to his rank. This regulation shall govern ²²every me[al,] provided at least ten men are ga[t]hered together. (1QSA II 11–22, excerpted)

In the table liturgy, the high priest of the end times is ranked above the messiah of Israel. The breaking-in of the last days is the time "when [God] fathers the messiah among them." As co-presider at the eschatological banquet the messiah appears in a peaceful role, but a military role for the messiah would be presupposed (cf. 1QSa I).

Since 1QSa had a literary prehistory (cf. the shorter recension of 4Q249a), I suggest that it was the joining of this appendix to the Community Rule that caused the scribe to add "until there come the prophet and the anointed ones of Aaron and Israel" to the prescriptions in 1QS IX. Thus, 1QSa II is no sequel to

1QS IX 11 as hypotext; rather, it was 1QSa that caused the introduction of "the anointed ones of Aaron and Israel" into 1QS.

During this literary process, the terms "the Priest" and "messiah of Israel" (1QSa) were rephrased into "the anointed ones of Aaron and Israel" (1QS). Further, the tradition we encountered in 4QTestimonia and 1 Macc 14:41—three end-time figures—was known to the scribe of 1QS and caused him to include the eschatological prophet in the short clause of the last days. The Community Rule was penned as a master scroll on costly parchment around 100, close in time to the reign of Hyrcanus, a ruler claiming that God had blessed him with the offices of ruler, priest, and prophet. The theological confrontation with the Hasmoneans caused Yahad circles to supplement the collective messianism of the Serekh texts with the expectation of three end-time agents still to come and deliberately attach the Messianic Rule (1QSa) as an appendix to this scroll.

This literary development suggests that, during the first two generations of the Yahad, some texts advocated a collective messianism with the community as the central end-time actor (see below on 1QS), while other texts (such as 1QSa) reflect a dual messianism, foreseeing two individual figures of redemption. The focus on the Shoot of David as the main eschatological agent, exhibited in exegetical texts of the first century BCE, may be a later development.

5.2 The Shoot of David

Some sectarian texts foresee a royal messiah, a Davidide, without mentioning (at least in the preserved parts) any priestly messiah. This goes for 4QCommentary on Genesis A (4Q252):

> ¹*The scepter [shall not] depart from the tribe of Judah* [Gen 49:10]. Whenever Israel rules, ²*there shall [not] fail to be a descendant of David upon the throne* [Jer 33:17], for *the staff* is the covenant of kingship, ³... until the messiah of *righteousness comes, the Shoot of David* [Jer 23:5]. ⁴For to him and his seed is granted the covenant of kingship over his people for everlasting generations, since ⁵he observed the [... statutes and precepts of] the law with the men of the Yahad. For ⁶[... *the obedience of the people]s* is the assembly of the men of ⁷[the Yahad who submit to him(?)]. (4Q252 V 1–7)

The Davidic messianism is underlined by bringing in Jer 33:17 and 23:5 as supporting references to Gen 49:8–12—a hypotext on the lion of Judah that suggests a messiah at war. Toward the end of the preserved passage, we learn that the dynastic promise to David was given because of his Torah observance: "Since he observed the [... statutes and precepts of] the law with the men of the Yahad"—which means that David and the community shared the same interpretation of the law.

Sectarian pesharim, commonly dated to the first half of the first century BCE, exhibit a similar messianism. For 4Q161 (4QpIsa[a]), Isa 10:22–34 refers to the end-time war of the gentiles (the Kittim = the Romans) against Jerusalem. During the war, the Prince of the Congregation (*neśî' hā'ēdâ*) will return to Zion from the wilderness of the nations (II 14–15). Then follows the commentary on Isa 11:1–5:

> [17][this is the Shoot of] David who shall arise at the end o[f days, . . . [18]. . .] his enemies; and God will support him with [a spirit of] strength [. . . [19]. . . and will give him] a throne of glory, a crown [of holiness,] and elegant garments. [20][. . . He will put a scepte]r in his hand, and he shall rule over all the n[atio]ns, even Magog [21][. . .] his sword shall judge [all] the nations. The words *he will not* [22]*[judge by what his eyes see] or pass sentence by what his ears hear* mean that [23][he will be advised by the Zadokite priests,] and as they instruct him, so will he judge, and as they order, [24][so will he pass sentence.] One of the priests of renown shall go out with him. (4Q161 III 17–24, excerpted)

The hypotext Isa 11:1–5 portrays a peaceful messiah, ruling and judging his people in the land in righteousness.[26] However, the sectarian scribes read 11:1–5 together with the preceding verses (that refer to war) as a joint prophecy on the last days, which would necessarily imply a military role for the messiah, who will judge and rule the nations with his sword. "He will not judge by what his eyes see or pass sentence by what his ears hear" (11:3) means that the king should relate to what *others* would see and hear, i.e., the messianic king would need to listen to and submit to the advice of a group of priests, and "priests of renown" would likely come out of the Yahad.

The thematic pesher 4Q174 (4QFlorilegium) includes commentary on Davidic passages from Scripture:

> [I,10]*The Lord decl[ares] to you that he will build you a house* [2 Sam 7:11c]; *and I will raise up your offspring after you* [2 Sam 7:12b]; *and I will establish the throne of his kingdom* [11]*[fore]ver. I will be a father to him, and he will be my son* [2 Sam 7:13b–14a]—this is the Shoot of David, who shall arise with [12]the Interpreter of the Torah, who will [arise] in Zi[on in the la]st days, as it is written, *And I shall raise up the booth of David that is fallen* [Am 9:11]—this is the fallen booth of [13]David that will arise to deliver Israel. . . .
> [18][Why] *do the nations [con]spire, and the peoples plo[t] in vain? The kings of the earth s]et themselves, [and the ru]lers take counsel together against Yhwh and his* [19]*[anointed one* (Ps 2:1–2). Its in]terpretation: [that the na]tions [shall set themselves] and con[spire vainly

---

[26] A fitting sequel to Isa 11:1–5 is the Davidic hymn in Ps. Sol. 17:21–46, a text from the mid-first century BCE.

against] the chosen ones of Israel in the last days—^{II.1}this is the time of trials that is to co[me upon the house of J]udah. (4Q144 I 10–II 1)

In this text, the Davidide is accompanied by the "Interpreter of the Torah"— likely the high priest. Neither of these two figures are called "anointed," and the "anointed one" of Ps 2:2 is identified with the elect nation threatened by the attack of the nations. The terminology is clearly different from "the anointed ones of Aaron and Israel" in 1QS IX 11. Thus, the text advocates both collective and individual messianism—the latter with two end-time figures.

The same terminology appears in the Damascus Document, but here with another hypotext, the Balaam oracle, Num 24:17 (as in 4QTestimonia): "The *star* is the Interpreter of the Torah, who shall come to Damascus as it is written, *A star shall come out of Jacob, a scepter shall rise out of Israel*. The *scepter* is the Prince of all the Congregation. When he comes, he shall *crush all the Shethites*" (CD-A VII 18–21). The word pair "scepter" and "star" of Num 24:17 is used as argument for a dual messianism. For the pesher, the *star* refers to the end-time Interpreter of the Torah who will stand alongside the Prince of the Congregation, the scepter in the Balaam prophecy.

A royal messiah appears in 4Q285 (4QSefer ha-Milhamah):

²[... Prin]ce of the Congregation and all Isr[ael ... ³... just as it wa]s written [in the book of Ezekiel the prophet, *And I will strike your bow from your left hand]* ⁴*[and bring down your arrows from your right. You shall fall] upon the mountains of I[srael, you and all your troops and the peoples that are with you* [Ezek 39:3–4] ... ⁵... the king of the] Kittim and [... ⁶... the Pr]ince of the Congregation [shall pursue them] all the way to the [Great] Sea [... ⁷...] And they [shall flee] from Israel at that time [... ⁸... And] he shall stand against them and they shall be stirred against them [... ⁹...] and they shall return to the dry land at th[at] time [... ¹⁰...] then they shall bring him before the Prince of [the Congregation ...] (4Q285 4 2–10)

In this text we encounter a messiah at war, similar to Ps 2 and Ps 110. As in 4Q161, he is "Prince of the Congregation" (*neśî' hā'ēdâ*), but he also musters the forces of "all Israel." The royal messiah, coming out of the Yahad and leading all Israel, will muster his armed forces against the Kittim (= the Romans) in battle. The fragment ends with the leader of the enemy forces being brought before the messiah to receive his judgment.

5.3 A Sacrificing and Suffering Priest

The motif of a sacrificing and suffering priest appears in a pre-sectarian Aramaic text, 4Q541 (4QapocrLevi^b?):

> ¹[all] the children of his generation [... ²...] his [w]isdom. He shall make atonement for all the children of his generation, and he shall be sent to all the children of ³his peo[ple]. His words are like the words of heaven, and his teaching like the will of God. His everlasting sun will shine, ⁴its fire will give warmth unto the ends of the earth. It will shine on darkness, darkness will vanish ⁵from the earth and mist [fr]om the dry land.
> They will speak against him many words and many ⁶[lie]s, invent fables about him, and speak all kinds of shameful things about him. His generation will be evil and perverted ⁷[so that] it will be [rejected.] Lies and violence will be his office, in his days the people will go astray and be confounded. (4Q541 9 I 1–7)

The second paragraph must here refer to a period before the breakthrough of universal renewal. There is internal strife in the people, the priest is controversial and a victim of slandering and perhaps persecution. Isaiah 53 plays in the background. This Levitical priest shall make atonement for all of "his generation"—perhaps a reference to the eschatological day of atonement. The priest's teaching and sacrificing ministry will lead to a cosmic renewal.

A sequel to the image of the eschatological priest in 4Q541 appears in the sectarian Self-Glorification Hymn. This Hebrew text is preserved in two recensions and four manuscripts: two copies of the Thanksgiving Hymns and two texts from the Milhamah (War Scroll) tradition (1QHª XXV–XXVI; 4QHª [4Q427] 7 I; 4Q491 11; 4Q471b):

> ¹ Praise him in]wondrous awe[...
> ⁴ as inheritance he gave me, in the midst of] those who walk in ⁵perfection,
> a mighty throne in the angelic council [for]ever,
> where the kings of the east never shall sit, and their nobles not have a dwelling.
> [Their] glory cannot ⁶ be compared to mine,
> none has been exalted save myself, no one can reach up to me.
> From among the poor I was delivered up to the heavens.
> There is none ⁷[like me among]the nobles.
> I am reckoned with the angels, my dwelling is in the holy council.
> [My] fo[rm] is not like flesh, all glory is mine,
> my communion is with the mighty ⁸[angels in] the holy [dwel]ling.
> [W]ho has been reckoned as despised like me,
> yet who is like me in my glory?
> ... ⁹... Who has born[e a]fflictions and seen evil like me,
> None has bor[ne suf]fering like me.
> Yet no teaching compares ¹⁰[to mine,]
> [Who can] op[en their mouth and admonish] or correct me?
> Who can match what drips from my mouth,
> who can, [with his tongue], summon me or equal my judgments?
> ¹¹[... Fo]r I am seated with the angels,

my glory is with the sons of the king.
My fo]undation is] neither of gol]d nor refined gold [(4Q491 frg 11 i 1, 4–11 with frgs 12, 23)²⁷

Most recent scholars see the imagined singer of this hymn as the high priest of the last days. In contrast, Qimron suggests to read the song as a hymn of praise by the *maskil*, the priestly leader of the community. These two interpretations are not mutually exclusive. The singer's unique teaching suggests a priestly figure, as teaching was part of the job description of the priests. As in 4Q541, this teacher experiences trials and suffering, there are clear allusions to Isaiah 53.

The exalted teacher of the hymn may be identified with the one who would "teach righteousness at the end of days" (CD-A VI 11) (as the Teacher of Righteousness had done in his days) and the end-time "Interpreter of the Law" of 4QFlorilegium. The singer's elevation to the heavens does not eliminate his humanity. In his officiating ministry he performs before the heavenly king and is enthroned on high, but his teaching ministry is still vis-à-vis other humans.

A textual variant in 1QIsaᵃ casts light on the elevation of the singer. The scribe who penned the second half of the large Isaiah scroll may have deliberately added a *yod* to the text of his *Vorlage* in Isa 52:14, to make it clear that the suffering servant is anointed, like Cyrus (45:1) and the prophet proclaiming his own vocation in 61:1: "So I anointed [*māšaḥtî*] his appearance above any man, and his form above any sons of man" (1QIsaᵃ 52:14). With such a reading, the anointed servant of the Isaiah text would prefigure the priestly Teacher of Righteousness and the end-time high priest, both anointed servants of God.

5.4 The Messianic Community of the Last Days

The War Scroll (1QM) is a detailed description of the coming end-time war where the sons of light confront the sons of darkness, the army of Belial. At a certain stage of the war, the Balaam oracle on the star of Jacob is brought as proof text (XI 6–7). The interpretation of the oracle does not focus on a royal messiah but reads the oracle as a prophecy of the end-time war with the destruction of Moab, the sons of Seth, and other enemies. David appears earlier in this column, but only as an example and ideal of warriors who trust in God's intervention. The high priest is given a liturgical role in columns XII–XVIII, appearing as leader of the corps of army chaplains following the battle. The War Scroll thus advocates a collective messianism. The restored nation—identified with the sons of light—appears as the

---

27 Readings and reconstruction mainly with Elisha Qimron: "Thanksgiving of a leader (4Q491)," *Meghillot. Studies in the Dead Sea Scrolls* 14 (2018–19): 13–24 [in Hebrew].

messianic actor. Redemption will be brought forth through the action of the people of God, assisted by the angels with whom they are in communion.[28]

In the Serekh scrolls the collective messianism is more reflected and pronounced. The Community Rule sees the Yahad as a spiritual temple and God's agent in the eschatological history. They are "the everlasting plantation, the house of holiness for Israel and assembly of supreme holiness for Aaron," "the precious cornerstone" of Isa 28:16, "the house of perfection and truth in Israel," who shall be "a sacrifice and atone for the land" (1QS VIII 5–10, par. 4Q258, 4Q259).

6 Concluding Reflections

Throughout the present survey, we have seen that Yahad texts demonstrate a remarkable pluriformity when it comes to eschatological outlook and messianic hope. Some texts interact critically with pro-Hasmonean theology that saw the Hasmonean state as fulfilment of biblical promises.

Biblical texts are not less pluriform. From a theological perspective one could say that Yhwh "kept the cards close to his chest." As history would be rolling its way, he would face different choices and only in time put the cards on the table and show the trump. In a biblical perspective, God's way is not predetermined but is crystallized during his co-wandering with his people through history. One could compare this with a later rabbinic dictum appearing in the midst of a messianic "smorgasbord" in b. Sanhedrin 97–99:

> Rabbi Joshua ben Levi opposed two verses, as it is written, *See, one like a Son of Man came with the clouds of heaven* (Dan 7:13), while elsewhere it is written, *See, your king comes to you, humble and riding upon an ass* (Zech 9:7). This means, if they are meritorious, he will come with the clouds of heaven; if not, humble and riding on an ass. (b. Sanh. 98a)

In the interpretative exegesis of the New Testament writings, a wide range of messianic passages and Old Testament themes are connected with the Jesus event and the early Jesus movement. In a transtextual analysis, passages in the New Testament writings can be characterized as *continuations* of an unfinished

---

[28] A particular "heavenly eschatology" is advocated by three priestly texts, the Aramaic 4QVisions of Amram (4Q543–549), the Songs of the Sabbath Sacrifice, and 11QMelchizedek: the priestly angel Melchizedek is the leader of God's heavenly armies and fighting the sons of darkness and their angelic prince. The elect community on earth appears as a more passive recipient of salvation (Elgvin, *Warrior, King*, 252–55).

hypotext, *sequels* that offer new episodes following a complete hypotext, or *transformations*, where plot, characters, and motifs in a narrative are transferred to a new textual context.[29] Also extra-biblical traditions and texts, such as those surveyed above, belong to the Judean heritage of the NT writers.

References

Bauckham, Richard. *Son of Man*, vol. 1: *Early Jewish Literature*. Grand Rapids: Eerdmans, forthcoming.

Boccacini, Gabriele, ed. *Enoch and the Messiah Son of Man. Revisiting the Book of Parables*. Grand Rapids: Eerdmans, 2007.

Bogaert, Pierre-Maurice. "La datation par souscription dans les rédactions courte (LXX) et longue du livre de Jérémie." In *L'apport de la Septante aux études sur l'Antiquité: Actes du colloque de Strasbourg, 8–9 novembre 2002*. Edited by Jan Joosten and Philippe Le Moigne. LD 203, 137–59 Paris: Cerf, 2005.

Bohak, Gideon. *Joseph and Aseneth and the Jewish Temple in Heliopolis*. Atlanta: Scholars Press, 1996.

Collins, John J. *Daniel. A Commentary on the Book of Daniel*. Philadelphia: Fortress, 1993.

Elgvin, Torleif. "1QSamuel—A Pre-canonical Shorter Recension of 2Samuel." *Zeitschrift für Alttestamentliche Wissenschaft* 132 (2020): 281–300.

Elgvin, Torleif. "More on 1QSamuel and the Theory of Literary Growth. Response to Benjamin Ziemer." *Zeitschrift für Alttestamentliche Wissenschaft* 133 (2021): 1–8.

Elgvin, Torleif. *Warrior, King, Servant, Savior. Messianism in the Hebrew Bible and Early Jewish Texts*. Grand Rapids: Eerdmans, 2022.

Genette, Gérard. *Palimpsests: Literature in the Second Degree*. Translated by Channa Newman and Claude Doubinsky. Lincoln: University of Nebraska Press, 1997.

Hossfeld, Frank-Lothar, and Erich Zenger. *Psalms 2: A Commentary on Psalms 51–100*. Minneapolis: Fortress, 2005.

Jacobus, Helen S. "Strangers to the 'Biblical Scrolls': Balaam's Fourth Oracle (Num 24:15–19) and its Links to Other Unique Excerpted Texts." In *Is there a Text in this Cave? Studies in the Textuality of the Dead Sea Scrolls in Honour of George J. Brooke*. Edited by Ariel Feldman, Maria Cioată, and Charlotte Hempel. STDJ 119, 226–57. Leiden: Brill, 2017.

Kratz, Reinhard. *Kyros im Deuterojesaja-Buch: Redaktionsgeschichtliche Untersuchungen zu Entstehung und Theologie von Jes 40–55*. FAT 1. Tübingen: Mohr Siebeck, 1991.

Lange, Armin. "The Textual Plurality of Jewish Scriptures in the Second Temple Period in Light of the Dead Sea Scrolls." in *Qumran and the Bible: Studying the Jewish and Christian Scriptures in Light of the Dead Sea Scrolls*. Edited by Nora Dávid and Armin Lange. CBET 57, 43–96 Leuven: Peeters, 2010.

---

29 Gérard Genette, *Palimpsests: Literature in the Second Degree*. Translated by Channa Newman and Claude Doubinsky (Lincoln: University of Nebraska Press, 1997), 1–10.

Nickelsburg, George W.E., and James C. VanderKam. *1 Enoch 2. A Commentary on the Book of 1 Enoch, Chapters 37–82*. Minneapolis: Fortress, 2012.

Nguyen, Kim Lan. "Cyrus. A Righteousness." In *The History of Isaiah. The Formation of the Book and its Presentation of the Past*. Edited by Jacob Stromberg and J. Todd Hibbard. FAT 150, 475–92 Tübingen: Mohr Siebeck, 2021.

Qimron, Elisha. "Thanksgiving of a leader (4Q491)." *Meghillot. Studies in the Dead Sea Scrolls* 14:13–24 [in Hebrew], 2018–19.

Seeligmann, Isac Leo, with Robert Hanhart and Hermann Spieckermann. *The Septuagint Version of Isaiah and Cognate Studies*. FAT 40. Tübingen: Mohr Siebeck, 2004.

Stuckenbruck, Loren, and Ted M. Erho. "The Significance of the Ethiopic Witnesses for the Text Tradition of 1 Enoch: Problems and Prospects." in *Congress Volume Aberdeen 2019*. SupVT 192. Edited by Grant Macaskill, Christl M. Maier, and Joachim Schaper, 416–34. Leiden: Brill, 2022.

Van der Lugt, Pieter. *The Rhetorical Design of Isaiah 40–48/55. Zion's Incomparable Savior and His Servants*. OS 82. Leiden: Brill, 2022.

Luuk van de Weghe
Early Divine Christology: Scripture, Narrativity and Confession in Luke-Acts

Abstract: Luke's corpus presents a complex portrait of Jesus. In terms of his messianic identity, Luke-Acts crafts Jesus in regal and prophetic categories, while it also presents him as the κύριος (Lord) through various trajectories within the narrative. First, it is argued that Luke's reliance on diverse written and oral sources could account for this complexity. Second, it is argued that Luke appears to develop his κύριος Christology in accordance with this complexity, enhancing Jesus' divine lordship in respect to the perspectives within his narrative. Overall, Luke presents not merely a biographical depiction of Jesus, but through his variegated portrait he presents what it looks like for the κύριος to become the Christ.

Keywords: Eyewitness testimony, Christology, Biography, Luke-Acts, Peter, Mary, Beloved Disciple

1 Introduction

This chapter springs from my interest in Luke's use of eyewitness testimony, which has led to several publications on the topic.[1] One such publication is an onomastic study demonstrating that the accuracy and sophistication of the personal naming patterns in Luke-Acts is reflected in the biographical compositions of Josephus, Plutarch, and Suetonius, i.e., in the Graeco-Roman biographies that mark the apex of that genre.[2] Within this apex, the sophisticated naming patterns reflect the historical concern and the reliance on source-material that set these works apart.

---

[1] Some are forthcoming. Luuk van de Weghe, *The Historical Tell: Eyewitness Testimony in the Gospel of Luke and Acts* (Chillicothe, Ohio: DeWard, 2022); idem, "The Beloved Eyewitness," *New Testament Studies* 66.3 (2022): 351–7; idem, "Name Recall in the Synoptic Gospels," *New Testament Studies* (2023). I use "Luke" and the names of the other Evangelists as a mere shorthand for the Gospel authors without necessarily implying traditional attributions.
[2] Van de Weghe, *The Historical Tell*, Ch. 2; idem, "Name Recall."

Luuk van de Weghe, University of Aberdeen, Scotland, Luukvandeweghe@gmail.com

https://doi.org/10.1515/9783110768411-004

Likewise, Luke's prologue (Luke 1:1–4), when situated amongst the Graeco-Roman historical writings, would communicate to Theophilus (1:3) not merely a reliance on written sources but also a reliance on oral informants, among whom were likely understood to be the key eyewitnesses within Luke's narrative.³ Within Luke's βίος, we see a concentration of vividness, minor variations from Luke's Markan template, and Semitisms within pericopae that centre around key individuals. I argue elsewhere that this convergence is best explained by Luke's reliance on oral informants – not exclusive to his reliance on broader written/oral traditions.⁴

The likelihood of Luke's reliance on oral sources will rest on arguments and publications beyond this chapter, and therefore, although we often suggest possible eyewitness influences in Luke's Gospel, the centrality of our argument here will not rest on their particular identities. Rather, the argument will rest on the manner in which Luke appears to adapt divergent portraits of Jesus into a consistent lordship Christology. In terms of structure and method, we will survey the Christologies of three major sections of Luke's Gospel and, moving through these sections sequentially, we will observe that they capture distinct perspectives of Jesus. Surveying these Christological portraits, we can appreciate that the movement of Luke's Gospel, which captures Jesus' lordship even with the Infancy Narrative (e.g., Luke 1:43, 2:11), moves the reader to understanding this identity in terms of Jesus' messianic roles and characteristics, culminating in Jesus' servanthood and death. Luke's Gospel provides a new hermeneutic for understanding divine lordship in terms of Jesus' messianic ministry, clarifying our understanding, I will argue, of Acts 2:36 (κύριον αὐτὸν καὶ χριστὸν ἐποίησεν ὁ θεὸς τοῦτον τὸν Ἰησοῦν ὃν ὑμεῖς ἐσταυρώσατε, "God made this Jesus, whom you crucified, both Lord and Messiah").⁵

Due to space constraints, in what follows I will be forced at times to oversimplify my case. Clearly, Luke's Christology is variegated, possibly balancing Synoptic and Johannine perspectives, incorporating written and oral traditions, capturing various movements of Christological understandings, and attempting to synthesize these. This is what one would expect if Luke conserved various interpretations of Jesus' ministry. In this chapter, I want to ask how such an

---

3 See Van de Weghe, *The Historical Tell*, Ch. 1; John Peters, *Luke Among the Ancient Historians* (Eugene: Pickwick, 2022); idem, "Luke's Source Claims in the Context of Ancient Historiography," *Journal for the Study of the Historical Jesus* 18.1 (2020): 35–60.
4 Van de Weghe, *The Historical Tell*, Ch. 8.
5 Unless otherwise noted, biblical translations in this chapter are from the New International Version (NIV) and Greek texts are from the Tyndale House Greek New Testament (THGNT).

understanding of Luke's text might bear on Christological questions. Can we speak of a consistent Lukan Christology? And if so, is such a Christology in conformity with the earliest traditions of Jesus?

2 The Ambiguous Image

Our aim here is to demonstrate how a sensitivity to Luke's possible use of eyewitness materials could enrich our understanding of what we might call his "theography" of Jesus – this is, of a biography that presents a new, creative portrait of Yahweh as much as it does a historical, conservative portrait of Jesus. We will explain Luke's diverse Christological perspectives considering possible familial, Petrine, and Johannine influences. Luke's Gospel not only organizes itself organically around such perspectives, as we will attempt to show, but Luke cumulatively develops his Christology through them, showing both historically and theologically that the answer to the question, "What is Yahweh like?", is answered by the ministry and vindication of Jesus the Messiah-κύριος.

Luke's approach here can be likened to an experiment by Peter Brugger, a psychiatrist from the department of neurology in the University Hospital in Zürich, who has published several studies on Jastrow's famous ambiguous image, the duck-rabbit illustration (see Fig. 1).[6]

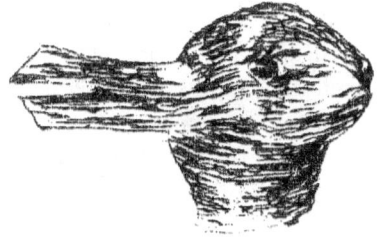

Fig. 1: The Duck-rabbit

---

[6] The experiment was conducted and published with the help of Peter's wife, Suzanne (Peter Brugger, Suzanne Brugger, "The Easter Bunny in October: Is it Disguised as a Duck?" *Perceptual and Motor Skills* 76.2 (1993): 577–8. His other article on Jastrow's duck-rabbit is Peter Brugger, "One Hundred Years of an Ambiguous Figure: Happy Birthday, Duck/Rabbit!" *Perceptual and Motor Skills*. 89.4 (1999): 973–7. Joseph Jastrow's image in Figure 1 was published in the article, "The Mind's Eye," *Popular Science Monthly* 54 (1899): 299–312, although previously published in *Fliegende Blätter* (a popular satiric publication).

Most interpretations of the image and its later variants are duck dominant.[7] Peter and his wife, Suzanne, however, conducted an experiment to see if certain background considerations might impact the interpretation of the image. In 1993, they asked individuals entering the Zürich Zoo to identify the image. One group, consisting of two subgroups (based on age), was asked to make the identification in October; the other group was asked to make the identification at Easter. In October, both children under age ten and older individuals identified the variant of Jastrow's image as a bird, with identifications ranging from a duck to a stork, a flamingo, and other unspecified/specified birds. At Easter, however, the overwhelming interpretation of the image was that of a rabbit.

This is an excellent illustration of what Luke accomplishes in his narrative. Various perspectives identify Jesus as Messiah, prophet, or Isaianic servant, but the narrative background leads the reader to see each of these portraits, especially in light of the Hebrew scriptures, as a description of the κύριος/LORD. The dominant realization of Jesus-as-LORD is new, of course, in the same sense that the rabbit identification of Easter might be novel, but the identification is consistent with, even resultant from, the same features of the image that led to the previous identifications. These other identities – king, prophet, etc. – are not the ultimate identification Luke wants us to associate with Jesus, but they form part of the ultimate picture of how Luke wants us to see, define, and understand the Easter κύριος through the prior categories of Jesus' messiahship.

Even if one is reluctant to attach the label of Graeco-Roman biography to Luke's Gospel, Luke's incidental comment in Acts 1:1 that his prior work concerned all that "*Jesus* began to do and teach" leads us, nevertheless, to the inevitable concession that a focus on Jesus lies at the heart of Luke's project. In this regard we should assume that Luke would have fashioned his composition to illuminate – both overtly and through subtle artistry – the character of his subject, as aptly and famously described by Plutarch when referring to the aim of his biography of Alexander:

> For it is not Histories that I am writing, but Lives; and in the most illustrious deeds there is not always a manifestation of virtue or vice, nay, a slight thing like a phrase or a jest often makes a greater revelation of character than battles where thousands fall, or the greatest armaments, or sieges of cities. Accordingly, just as painters get the likenesses in their portraits from the face and the expression of the eyes, wherein the character shows itself, but make very little account of the other parts of the body, so I must be permitted to devote

---

7 Brugger, "One Hundred Years of an Ambiguous Figure," 976.

myself rather to the signs of the soul in men, and by means of these to portray the life of each, leaving to others the description of their great contests (*Alex.* 1:2–3).[8]

The lack of significant parallels notwithstanding,[9] there is every reason to believe that Luke was no less adept than Plutarch in overlaying, so to speak, his well-ordered historical portrait of Jesus with subtleties to accentuate the "true" nature of Jesus' identity. It is in this very endeavour, however, that many scholars have found Luke wanting. Delbert Burkett, for example, concedes that "not all of what Luke says about Jesus is completely consistent," while Geoffrey Lampe sees Luke's portrait as "somewhat untidy and ill-defined."[10] Even a brief glance at monographs on the topic confirms a disparate perspective: *The Davidic Messiah in Luke-Acts: The Promise and its Fulfilment in Lukan Christology* (Strauss), *Der Sühnetod Des Gottesknechts - Jesaja 53 im Lukasevangelium* (Mittmann-Richert), *Luke's Christology of Divine Identity* (Henrichs-Tarasenkova).[11] This latter title invites us into yet another layer of discussion around Luke's picture of Jesus. Not only is Jesus' relationship to his designation as χριστός (Messiah) under dispute, but Jesus' relationship to his identity as κύριος (Lord) also remains a point of contention. Notable contributors of the twentieth century, e.g., Hans Conzelmann and Jacob Jervell, opted for a "low Christology" in Luke-Acts, well summarized by Jervell: "Jesus is not divine, not

---

8 Plutarch, *Lives: Demosthenes and Cicero. Alexander and Caesar*, translated by Bernadotte Perrin, Loeb Classical Library 99, vol. 7 (Cambridge, MA: Harvard University Press, 1919).
9 One obvious discrepancy is found between the time of composition and the lifetime of the subject; where Luke arguably wrote within living memory of Jesus, Plutarch was centuries removed from the life of Alexander the Great.
10 Delbert Burkett, "Jesus in Luke-Acts," in *The Blackwell Companion to Jesus*, edited by Delbert Burkett (London: Wiley-Blackwell, 2011), 47; Geoffrey Lampe, "The Lucan Portrait of Christ," *New Testament Studies* 2.3 (1956): 160–75, esp. 160; Lampe notes that there is no "real inconsistency" between Luke's Christology and Peter's apparently adoptionist speech on the day of Pentecost, noting similarity to the Phil. 2:6–11 passage regardless of the potential for many of the earlier Christological designations from the Infancy Narrative onwards to be proleptic (Lampe, "The Lucan Portrait of Christ," 170–71).
11 Mark Strauss, *The Davidic Messiah in Luke-Acts: The Promise and its Fulfilment in Lukan Christology* (Sheffield: Sheffield Academic Press, 1995); Ulrike Mittmann-Richert, *Der Sühnetod des Gottesknechts: Jesaja 53 im Lukasevangelium*, Wissenschaftliche Untersuchungen zum Neuen Testament 220 (Tübingen: Mohr Siebeck, 2008); Nina Henrichs-Tarasenkova, *Luke's Christology of Divine Identity*, Library of New Testament Studies 542 (London: Bloomsbury T&T Clark, 2016).

pre-existent, not incarnated, not the creator or tool of creation, not the universal reconciler, not the *imago dei* etc."[12]

A significant contribution to cast doubt on Luke's low Christology is C. Kavin Rowe's *Early Narrative Christology: The Lord in the Gospel of Luke*, based on his doctoral dissertation from Duke University under the supervision of Richard Hays.[13] This work is later supplemented by his *New Testament Studies* article, "Acts 2.36 and the Continuity of Lukan Christology," which applies his dissertation's narrative approach to Peter's comment in Acts 2:36 that "God made this Jesus, whom you crucified, both Lord and Messiah," emphasizing, naturally, the awkward import of "made" (ἐποίησεν) here in the context of a speech regarding Jesus' resurrection.[14] Rowe's analysis merits enough significance to function as a springboard for our discussion, yet it suffers from several weaknesses.

Rowe's first deficiency is of a general nature. As noted by Darrell Bock, Rowe sometimes underappreciates the diversity of Luke's portrait of Jesus by under-emphasizing the character-level perspective of Jesus as Messiah.[15] The central thesis of Rowe's approach is that Luke has molded his narrative to develop his portrait of Jesus as the κύριος, that this title is somehow controlling, and that it also relates – in an undefined manner – to the divine κύριος of the Hebrew Bible. Often throughout the narrative, the characters in Luke's Gospel address Jesus in the vocative, κύριε, and even in such cases, argues Rowe, they may be saying more than they know, for Luke is using their stories to craft his own larger picture of what it means for Jesus to be κύριος through the narrative's progression.[16]

Rowe claims that his narrative approach should be brought to bear on a crucial text such as Acts 2:36, where Peter is claiming that God has "made" Jesus "both Lord and Messiah." After discussing both patristic and modern

---

12 Hans Conzelmann, *Die Mitte der Zeit: Studien zur Theologie des Lukas*, Beiträge zur historischen Theologie 17 (Tübingen: Mohr Siebeck, 1954), esp. 172.; Jacob Jervell, *The Theology of the Acts of the Apostles* (Cambridge: Cambridge University Press, 1996), 30. For a brief overview of Conzelmann's contribution to Lukan Christology, see Henrichs-Tarasenkova, *Luke's Christology of Divine Identity*, 6–11.
13 C. Kavin Rowe, *Early Narrative Christology: The Lord in the Gospel of Luke*, Beihefte zur Zeitschrift für die Neutestamentliche Wissenschaft 139 (Berlin and New York: de Gruyter, 2006).
14 C. Kavin Rowe, "Acts 2.36 and the Continuity of Lukan Christology," *New Testament Studies* 53.1 (2007): 37–56.
15 Darrell Bock, *A Theology of Luke and Acts: God's Promised Program, Realized for All Nations*, Biblical Theology of the New Testament Series (Grand Rapids: Zondervan, 2012), 153–4, n. 16.
16 See Rowe, *Early Narrative Christology*, 88, 100; Cf. Bock, *A Theology of Luke and Acts*, 154, n. 17.

approaches to this text, Rowe keenly observes that the core of ancient as well as modern discussions revolve around the word ἐποίησεν.[17] While many exegetes showcase this text as a prime example of either 1) Luke's use of a traditional text that is at odds with his own Christology or 2) Luke's placement of these words onto the lips of Peter, in light of historiographical parallels, so as to allow Peter to "say what he would have said" (although Luke disagrees with Peter's alleged position), Rowe argues that either option would cut against Luke's broader narrative project, which paints Jesus as κύριος from his birth (e.g., Luke 1:43) and even designates him as the χριστὸς κύριος ("The Messiah, the Lord," Luke 2:11) in the Infancy Narrative.[18] Rowe naturally focuses his argument on how Luke develops the idea of κύριος throughout his Gospel while neglecting Luke's development of χριστός, which seems just as relevant to the discussion. He opts, ultimately, for an interpretation of Acts 2:36 which reads ἐποίησεν, anticlimactically, as "manifested," although this is a position he initially mentions without giving it much credence.[19] In my mind, Rowe does not do justice here to the thrust of Peter's use of ἐποίησεν, especially since Luke could easily have placed a cognate form of ἀποδείκνυμι on Peter's lips – as he does in Acts 2:22 – to communicate "manifested" or "set forth."

3 Χριστός and Κύριος

Below, I present a different interpretation through a demonstration of how incorporating Luke's creative engagement with traditional material can shed more satisfying light on this interpretive puzzle – that is, on the question of what Peter means when he says, in Acts 2:36, that God has made Jesus "both Lord and Messiah" at his resurrection. The word "creative" may not be the best word to use for Luke's κύριος Christology, since according to Luke the concept of Jesus' lordship, even as it might relate to his divine identity on some level, does not remain on the upper levels of Luke's narrative, so to speak. This is to say, it is not merely that Luke identifies Jesus as Lord through his narrative voice only (although he frequently does this) and that Luke, through allusions from the characters in his narrative, equates this concept of κύριος with the deeds/actions/claims of Yahweh (cf. 1:78; 3:1–6; 8:39, 9:43; 13:34; 17:11–19;

---

[17] Rowe, "The Continuity of Lukan Christology," 42.
[18] Rowe, "The Continuity of Lukan Christology," 51.
[19] Rowe, "The Continuity of Lukan Christology," 55; Rowe passes over this reading swiftly without further comment in a brief paragraph on p. 41.

etc.), but that these allusions and experiences, according to Luke's own assertions (Luke 1:1–4) must have had some meaning already to the eyewitnesses in his Gospel.[20] The concept of Jesus' Lordship-Christology is hardly a linear progression within Luke's narrative. It appears to vary within specific sections of his text. To illustrate the point, we can take the pericope in which Peter is introduced to Jesus (5:1–11).[21] Here, Luke highlights Peter's vocative address to Jesus as "Lord" (significantly, ἐπιστάτα before the miracle (5:4) but κύριε (5:8) after the miracle). Yet the actions performed by Peter in this very pericope, some of which find a close parallel in Isaiah's response to Yahweh in Isaiah 6 – his declaration (cf. Isa 6:5, Luke 5:8), his prostration (cf. Isa 6:1, Luke 5:8) – communicate that the idea of Jesus' potential identification alongside Yahweh not merely haunts the upper levels of Luke's narrative but often descends into the lower levels of the claimed experiences of Luke's eyewitnesses.[22] The meaning and significance of this will only become clearer as we demonstrate how this expresses itself in Luke's Gospel, and its impact on Luke's Christology and the interpretation of Acts 2:36 should become apparent along the way.

Luke's Christology does have a lower level, of course, and this is determined by the prior categories that would have been held by Luke's sources. This level relates to various interpretations of Jesus as χριστός, which, as we will show, has regal, prophetic, and priestly implications based on the traditions that Luke is engaged with. As these categorize Jesus along various messianic lines, each individual category is nuanced in some capacity by an emerging idea that is without prior categories – that the κύριος himself is taking on these messianic roles. This is the general movement – with different, various trajectories within each perspective – so that Peter's comment that at the resurrection Jesus became κύριον καὶ χριστόν is not an adoptionist expression that communicates a new understanding of Jesus as much as it is a theological expression that communicates something new about God; while on the lower level Luke's biography is the story of how Jesus was exalted to the right of hand of God, with the implication that this tells us something about Jesus, on the upper level Luke's biography is the story of the LORD expressing himself savingly in

---

20 For a brief overview of salient occasions, see Richard B. Hays, *Reading Backwards* (Waco: Baylor University Press, 2014), 55–74, as well as our further discussion below.
21 Simon is incidentally mentioned already in Luke 4:38, but Luke 5:1–11 marks his focused introduction to the reader, providing more detailed insight into Simon's background, partnerships, occupation, and, most importantly, his developing relationship with Jesus.
22 Rowe notes something else of interest – that this passage is paired with Isa 6:1–8 in the Revised Common Lectionary. He comments: "both Peter and Isaiah experience their own sinfulness in the presence of the κύριος" (*Early Narrative Christology*, 99).

the life/death/resurrection of Jesus, with the implication that this tells us something new about God. But we will develop this in much more detail. Figure 2 shows a simplified summary of our reading.

We will survey Luke's developing Christology now as we move through his Gospel, interacting with the "lower level" messianic perspectives of Luke's eyewitnesses on the one hand while also discussing how these lower levels become increasingly consonant with the upper level of a κύριος Christology in particular, unique ways.

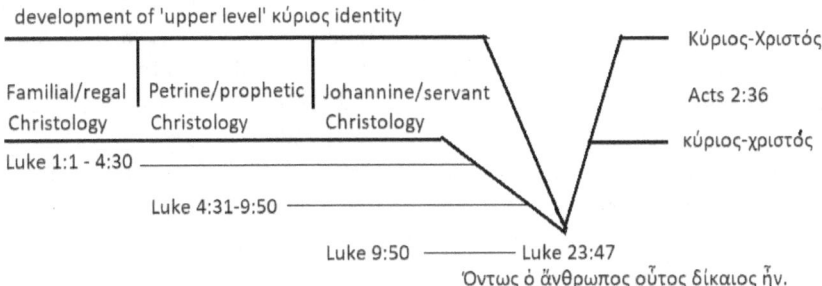

Fig. 2: Development of Lukan Christology

4 Familial/Regal Christology

The general perspective of Luke 1:1–4:30 (i.e., from Jesus' birth through his Nazareth sermon) shows several signs of a familial origin. Strong reasons exist – although none are conclusive – for seeing at least portions of Luke's Infancy Narrative as derived from written source material, whether of Hebrew or Greek origin.[23] Stephen Farris' analysis concluded that this portion of Luke's text is more Septuagintal than the Septuagint itself.[24] What relationship does this have to the comments of Luke 2:19 and 2:51 (that Mary "treasured all these things in her heart")? Ben Meyer, while not denying that the comments could have a historiographical import, dismisses the suggestion out of hand because Meyer

---

[23] See Chang-Wook Jung, *The Original Language of the Lukan Infancy Narrative*, Journal for the Study of the New Testament: Supplement Series 267 (London: T&T Clark International, 2004); Stephen Farris, *The Hymns of Luke's Infancy Narratives: Their Origin, Meaning and Significance* (London: Bloomsbury Academic, 1985).
[24] Farris, *The Hymns*, 57.

believes Luke likely received these comments in the form of written traditions (esp. 2:19, upon which he believed 2:51 to be dependent): "If the notice in 2:19 had derived from the evangelist's redaction, we might have more reason to attach a special historiographical significance to it. However, as it is more likely to have originated in a pre-Lucan source, we conclude that the notice has no more historiographical significance than its parallel in 1:65; that is, it has no historiographical significance."[25]

Of course, many believe that Luke 1–2 could have been the literary creation of Luke in its entirety or at least that it has been so refined by him that any source would be beyond recognition. An onomastic observation made by Richard Fellows, however, bears repeating, although no commentator to date has interacted with it. Significantly, it is able to stand regardless of the exact nature of Luke's general source material for Luke 1–2.[26] Fellows observes that Μαριάμ, the Semitic (indeclinable) variant of Mary's name, likely occurs in all Lukan and Matthean texts based upon the available data across the spectrum of manuscript traditions (considering that a declinable form in the first declension genitive also acts as a suppletive for this Semitic form[27]). Two exceptions, however, are particularly noteworthy. The first is in Acts 1:14, where Luke used the Greek variant of Mary's name, Μαρία. Fellows conjectures reasonably that Luke here is using the form of Mary's name that he would have been accustomed to using and that his audience, likewise, might be familiar with. The other occurrence, quite relevant to our discussion, is Luke 2:19 (ἡ δὲ Μαρία πάντα συνετήρει τὰ ῥήματα ταῦτα συνβάλλουσα ἐν τῇ καρδίᾳ αὐτῆς, "But Mary treasured up all these things and pondered them in her heart."), the only occurrence of Mary's name within the comments bearing on Mary's personal reflections. This indeed, as Fellows suggests, lends credence to the idea that these are not part of the written tradition Luke may have received – if, indeed, he received any written traditions – but are instead Luke's own editorial comments and, if editorial comments, reveal a unique personal insight into Mary's state of mind.

Bauckham is not persuaded that Mary herself could be the source of Luke's Infancy Narrative, but he does note that the genealogy of Luke 3 shows signs of

---

[25] Ben F. Meyer, "'But Mary Kept All These Things...' (Lk 2:19, 51)," *Catholic Biblical Quarterly* 26.1 (1964): 31–49, esp. 49.
[26] This brief discussion is based on Richard Fellows, "Mariam became Maria and, with that name, was Luke's source for the infancy narrative," Paul and Co-workers (Blog), 5.01.2021, http://paulandco-workers.blogspot.com/2021/01/mariam-became-maria-and-with-that-name.html.
[27] See Peter Williams, "Christmas Variants (3)," Evangelical Textual Criticism (Blog), 12.12.2005, http://evangelicaltextualcriticism.blogspot.com/2005/12/christmas-variants-3.html.

primitivity and, when aligned with comments from Africanus and the Book of Jude, develops a larger case that it goes back to the family of Jesus in some capacity (he believes, likely through James the brother of Jesus).[28]

Regardless, the early portions of Luke's text reflect a cohesive regal Christology, which is otherwise in line with the comments from Africanus (quoted by Eusebius, *Hist. Eccl.* 1.7.14) that Jesus' family members were intent on preserving Jesus' genealogy, likely to prove Jesus to be the Messianic Son of David.[29] As Bock has remarked, the titles of Jesus in this section (esp. 1:32, "Son of the Most High"; 1:35, "Holy One," and "Son of God") while bearing an apparent flavour of the divine, can and should likely be read in strictly messianic terms.[30] Indeed, these "lower-level" messianic expectations allow for the most consistent interpretation of the pericope found in Luke 4:14–30, in which Jesus reads from Isaiah 61:1–2 the passage which introduces his activity throughout the Galilean ministry (4:31–9:50):

> πνεῦμα κυρίου ἐπ' ἐμέ, οὗ εἵνεκεν ἔχρισέν με εὐαγγελίσασθαι πτωχοῖς, ἀπέσταλκέν με κηρύξαι αἰχμαλώτοις ἄφεσιν καὶ τυφλοῖς ἀνάβλεψιν, ἀποστεῖλαι τεθραυσμένους ἐν ἀφέσει, κηρύξαι ἐνιαυτὸν κυρίου δεκτόν.
> The Spirit of the Lord is on me, because he has anointed me to preach good news to the poor, to preach release to the captives, to give eyesight to the blind, to send the oppressed away in freedom, and to preach the Lord's acceptable year. (Luke 4:18–19, my translation)

---

28 See Richard Bauckham's discussion in "Luke's Infancy Narrative as Oral History in Scriptural Form," in *The Gospels: History and Christology: The Search of Joseph Ratzinger-Benedict XVI*, edited by Bernardo Estrada, Ermenegildo Manicardi and Armand Puig i Tàrrech, vol. 1 (Vatican City: Libreria Editrice Vaticana, 2013), 399–417; see, also, Richard Bauckham, *Jude and the Relatives of Jesus in the Early Church* (Edinburgh: T&T Clark, 1990), Ch. 7.
29 For another brief discussion on this by Richard Bauckham, see "The Relatives of Jesus," *Themelios* 21.2 (1996): 18–21.
30 Bock notes, "In a difference of nuance, it is C. Kavin Rowe's failure in his *Early Narrative Christology* to mention how the key announcement of Luke 1:31–35 sets up Luke's portrait of Jesus that causes him to highlight 'Lord' at the expense of Messiah. He is correct to criticize me for underemphasizing the role of Lord early on in Luke in my *Proclamation from Prophecy and Pattern: Lucan Old Testament Christology* (JSNTSup; Sheffield: Sheffield Academic Press, 1987), but he missed my narrative point in his critique on p. 8. It was that 'Lord' is introduced without as much development in the infancy material as the image of 'Messiah' receives; Luke's initial emphasis is on Jesus' role as the promised Davidite [sic]. Rowe's treatment of 1:43 argues that Jesus is shown to be Lord as a result of a special birth, defining that role. I argued that the role of Jesus there was ambiguous. Narratively, Rowe is correct here, but the movement of the story in the understanding of the characters reflects the ambiguity I argued for. Mary, Zechariah, and Simeon praise Jesus for his role as messianic deliverer, not something more" (Bock, *A Theology of Luke and Acts*, 176, n. 16).

In this passage, Jesus' messianic identity is fused with the prophetic in a way that only heightens the expectation of grace which is about the be bestowed on this tiny hamlet in the Galilean countryside. The residents' proclamation, "isn't this Joseph's son?" (4:22), is then by no means a rejection to Jesus' covert claims of divinity (cf. Mark 6:2, Matt. 13:54) but is instead a reflection of this community's desire to seize Jesus' messianic *euangelion* for their own advantage. Jesus' response in Luke 4:23, "Surely you will quote this proverb to me: 'Physician, heal yourself!' And you will tell me, 'Do here in your hometown what we have heard that you did in Capernaum,'" makes sense within this setting. Jesus' comment in Luke 4:24, "no prophet is acceptable in his hometown," which differs from Mark (6:4) and Matthew (13:57) by replacing the οὐκ...ἄτιμος (not...without honor) with δεκτός (acceptable), likewise is not in reference to Jesus' rejection at Nazareth. Jesus is clearly not rejected in Luke 4:22, and neither were Elijah or Elisha rejected by the Israelites when God sent them to Sidon and Syria, respectively, as Jesus goes on to highlight (Luke 4:26, 27). Jesus' use of δεκτός here in Luke 4:24 ties back to the final word in Jesus' Nazareth sermon, which reads, ... κηρύξαι ἐνιαυτὸν κυρίου <u>δεκτόν</u> (lit., "to preach [the] year of [the] Lord [which is] <u>acceptable</u>"). Jesus is likely not saying then, according to Luke, that no prophet is acceptable to his *own people* in his hometown, but rather that no prophet is acceptable *to God* in his hometown. In other words, the nature of a God-pleasing prophetic ministry like that of Elijah and Elisha is outward-focused, because a prophet of God is not bound by the borders of his hometown, just as the grace of God's message (cf. Luke 4:22, τοῖς λόγοις τῆς <u>χάριτος</u>, lit., "...words of grace") is free to extend to the unexpected recipient. Jesus is not Nazareth's prophet, but God's![31]

This brief exegesis merely serves to highlight how a coherent lower-level reading can be achieved by a strict focus on a messianic identity yet unclouded by later Christological importation. Nevertheless, this is not all that can be said, nor is it all that Luke wants to say about Jesus at this early stage. And what is more important, the additional things Luke wants to say are not and cannot be stated apart from the regal/prophetic identity that Luke has painted of Jesus thus far.

---

31 My observations here are indebted to many helpful studies: see, for example: Caleb C. Afulike "Luke's Portrayal of the Social Dimension in the Ministry of Jesus and the Apostles (Luke-Acts) According to Isaiah's Message of Social Justice in Chapters 61:1–2 and 58:6," *Journal of Religious & Theological Information* 17:2 (2018): 41–54; Paul Hertig, "The Jubilee Mission of Jesus in the Gospel of Luke: Reversals of Fortunes," *Missiology* 26.2 (1998): 167–79; David Hill, "The Rejection of Jesus at Nazareth (Luke IV 16-30)," *Novum Testamentum* 13.3 (1971): 161–80; James A. Sanders, "Isaiah in Luke," *Interpretation* 36.2 (1982): 144–55.

Tab. 1: Jesus–Augustus Parallels[32]

Topic	Traditions about Jesus in Luke	Augustus Parallels
Prophecy/portents prefigure birth	1:26–38	Suetonius, Aug. 94
Miraculous conception	1:34–35	Cassius Dio 45.1.2
Cultic context	1:8–11	Suetonius, Aug. 94
Declared ruler/king at birth	1:32–33; 2:10–11	Suetonius, Aug. 94
Shepherds herald birth	2:8–20	Virgil, Ecl. 1:6–8
Birth is good news	2:10	Priene Inscription
Proclaimed saviour	2:11	Ibid.
Called Lord	2:11	Ibid., Acts 25:26
Bringer of age of peace	2:14	Ovid, Fast. 2. 127-44
Son of God	1:35	Tacitus, Ann. 1.11–13
Qualities at age twelve	2:41-52	Suetonius, Aug. 8

Several recent studies argue that Luke appears to have composed his Infancy Narrative as a counter-alternative to the birth accounts of Caesar Augustus.[33] Table 1 highlights the most relevant points.

These connections further highlight the significance of certain points of Luke's narrative. Unlike the despots of the Roman empire, Jesus is born to a young virgin named Mary. While Zechariah (1:5–9), Elizabeth (1:5–7), even Joseph (1:27), are imbued with pedigrees and descriptors of honor and cultural esteem within the narrative – e.g., their old age, their cultic associations, their links to the priesthood, their lineages to Aaron and to David – Luke's main character, Mary, brings nothing to convey an esteemed status to Luke's audience.[34] Nevertheless, she is fronted in conversation (2:34), given words of prophecy (2:35), and granted narrative insight (2:19, 51), and we are led to be-

---

[32] Based on Table 1 in Billings, "At the Age of 12," 85–86.
[33] Christian Blumenthal, "Augustus' Erlass und Gottes Macht: Überlegungen zur Charakterisierung der Augustusfigur und ihrer erzählstrategischen Funktion in der lukanischen Erzählung," *New Testament Studies* 57.1 (2011): 1–30; Michael Kochenash, "'Adam, Son of God' (Luke 3.38): Another Jesus–Augustus Parallel in Luke's Gospel," *New Testament Studies* 64.3 (2018): 307–25; Bradly S. Billings, "'At the Age of 12': The Boy Jesus in the Temple (Luke 2:41–52), the Emperor Augustus, and the Social Setting of the Third Gospel," *Journal of Theological Studies* 60.1 (2009): 70–89.
[34] For further discussion, see: Joel Green, "The Social Status of Mary in Luke 1,5-2,52: A Plea for Methodological Integration," *Biblica* 73.4 (1992): 457–72.

lieve that God's blessing upon her is a reflection of a systematic divine reversal of sorts (1:46–55). Likewise, the Roman roads which bore the propaganda of the Roman empire are now being subjugated by the herald of the coming of the Lord (3:4–6), and even the historically problematic census of Caesar Augustus which went out across the world really serves only to bring God's true king to the town of God's promise (cf. 2:1).[35] Luke's use here of "Augustus" in its transliterated form of the Latin, as noted by Morris, is telling.[36] Luke knows that the meaning of this title (which Luke treats as a meaningless name here in 2:1) is σεβαστός, commonly translated as the "majestic one" or "worshipful." Commentators have neglected to ask why Luke used the transliterated form here, especially since he otherwise translates it (cf. Acts 25:21, 25). Further, Luke generally removes Latinisms,[37] and no other Greek writers for a period of several hundred years use Luke's transliterated form, Αὐγοῦστος.[38] The likely explanation, however, is that Luke is trying to emphasize the worshipfulness and majesty of someone in this text – but it is not Augustus. It is, rather, a baby born in a manger (Luke 2:7). This baby is referred to by Simeon as the ἀνατολὴ ἐξ ὕψους ("the rising [sun] from on high," Luke 1:78), which, as Simon Gathercole has observed, is a veiled reference to pre-existence.[39] Jesus' sonship, likewise, goes beyond the regal and appears to have familial implications for his relationship to God (e.g., Luke 2:49).[40] Again, the Baptist prepares the way for Jesus in the fulfilment of Isaiah 40:3–5 (cf. Luke 3:4–6) which speaks of a forerunner prepar-

---

35 Edward Meadors, "'Isaiah 40.3 and the Synoptic Gospels' Parody of the Roman Road System," *New Testament Studies* 66.1 (2020): 106–24.

36 Royce Morris, "Why ΑΥΓΟΥΣΤΟΣ? A Note to Luke 2.1," *New Testament Studies* 38.1 (1992): 142–44.

37 See Friedrich Blass and Albert Debrunner, *A Greek Grammar of the New Testament and Other Early Christian Literature*, trans. R. W. Funk (Chicago: University of Chicago Press, 1964), 4; cited by Morris, "A Note to Luke 2:1," 143.

38 The transliteration does not occur in Greek writings prior to Luke and nowhere in the papyri prior to 223 CE; indeed, Morris notes: "that it later became a proper name is not in dispute; but it is clearly apparent that it became a proper name because of Luke's use of the word in the Gospel, and it also seems obvious that it became a proper name because it was unintelligible otherwise to his Greek audience" ("A Note to Luke 2:1," 143).

39 Simon Gathercole, "The Heavenly ἀνατολή (Luke 1:78–9)," *Journal of Theological Studies* 65.2 (2005), 471–88.

40 For further discussion on this, see: Brendan Byrne, "Jesus as Messiah in the Gospel of Luke: Discerning a Pattern of Correction," *Catholic Biblical Quarterly* 65.1 (2003): 80–95, esp. 84–86. This study demonstrates how Luke shows Jesus to be a transcendent Messiah by subtle redactions/features which correct possible perceptions that Jesus' charges – that he was a messianic pretender – might have been justified.

ing the way for Yahweh.⁴¹ Out of the twenty-five usages of κύριος in the Infancy Narrative, twenty-three relate clearly to God but two relate clearly to Jesus (Luke 1:38, 43), creating ambiguity.⁴² Not merely is the "lower level" of the text supplemented, then, with a separate "higher level" Christology, but the κύριος Christology descends upon the lower level and affects it, in fact accentuating the literary contrast that Luke is making about Jesus: while Augustus Caesar was adopted to become the Son of God (i.e. the son of the dead, deified Julius) through oppression and exploitation, Jesus became a son of man through his implicit adoption by Joseph (Luke 3:23) as an act of humility. Jesus in Luke 4:14–30 is a lover of the outsider and the marginalized, not as a concession but as an outworking of a messianism that is – at this point, however subtly – God's messianism.

5 Petrine/Prophetic Christology

The variegation of Luke's lower level becomes more acute as his Gospel progresses. This is indicated acutely in Luke's Petrine perspective of Jesus' Galilean ministry. This section (4:31–9:50) neatly fulfills the parameters of ministry laid out by Jesus in his Nazareth sermon (i.e., Luke 4:18/Isaiah 61:1–2: to proclaim good news to the poor, free the oppressed, recovery of sight for the blind, etc.). The messianic nature of these activities and their accomplishment by Jesus are echoed again in Luke 7:22, in which Jesus responds to a question from John the Baptist about whether he is the Messiah. Jesus says, "Go back and report to John what you have seen and heard: The blind receive sight, the lame walk, those

---

41 Richard Hays comments, "Luke's extended citation of Isaiah 40:3–5 functions as a programmatic introduction to the narrative of Jesus' ministry (Luke 3:4–6); it frames his activity in terms of Isaiah's visionary prophecy of the end of Israel's exile and thereby serves as a 'hermeneutical key for the Lukan program.' Particularly significant is the fact that Luke concludes his citation of Isaiah 40 with the climactic declaration that 'all flesh will see the salvation of God.' ... Luke has taken the keynote passage from Isaiah 40 that declares the salvific coming of Israel's God and worked it narratively into an announcement of the imminent coming of Jesus as the one who would bring 'the salvation of God' (3:6, citing Isa 40:5 LXX). Luke's citation of the extended block of material from Isaiah 40: 3–5 strongly suggests that he is aware of the full context of Isaiah 40. If so, this identification of Jesus as the one in whom 'all flesh will see the salvation of God' is hermeneutically momentous, for it is precisely in Isaiah 40 that we find one of the most radical declarations in all of Scripture of the incomparability of God..." (*Reading Backwards*, 63–4).
42 For further discussion, see Rowe's discussion in *Early Narrative Christology*, 42–43.

who have leprosy are cleansed, the deaf hear, the dead are raised, and the good news is proclaimed to the poor."

This section is bracketed by pericopae revolving around Peter: his initial call (Luke 5:1–11) and then his experience of the transfiguration (9:28–50), sections which both – as I have discussed elsewhere – contain probable features of eyewitness testimony.[43] Two things are important to observe. First, Jesus takes on the prerogatives of Yahweh the κύριος through almost every feature by which he defined his messianic prerogative as outlined by Luke 4:18/7:22, whether through word or through deed. Jesus commissions Peter, as discussed, in the same manner that the κύριος commissioned Isaiah (cf. Is 6:1–8); he forgives sins as the Lord forgives sins (Luke 5:17–26, 7:44–50); he has authority over Sabbath regulations as established by Yahweh (Luke 6:1–11); and in a staccato-like fashion, he demonstrates his authority over death, disease, nature, and evil within a span of four short pericopae (8:22–56). As Rowe highlights, in several cases Luke sharpens the Markan context to emphasize the divine identity of Jesus.

In Luke 5:21, wherein the Pharisees and Scribes attribute blasphemy to him, they ask τίς δύναται ἁμαρτίας ἀφεῖναι εἰ μὴ μόνος ὁ θεός ("Who is able to forgive sins if not God alone?"); In this case, Luke has slightly modified Mark's εἷς ὁ θεός, replacing it with the weightier form, μόνος ὁ θεός (cf. 4 Kgdms 19:15, Is 37:16, 2 Macc 7:37, etc.). Luke uses this form, Rowe argues, to emphasize the key issue involved in Jesus' alleged blasphemy. It was not merely that Jesus forgave sins – an issue which is God's prerogative – but that in doing so he placed himself in the eyes of the Pharisees as a rival to God's uniqueness.[44]

Luke's trend is yet more clearly seen in Luke 6:5: καὶ ἔλεγεν αὐτοῖς· κύριός ἐστιν τοῦ σαββάτου ὁ υἱὸς τοῦ ἀνθρώπου, "Then he [Jesus] said to them, "The Son of Man is Lord of the Sabbath." Here Luke has removed the following sections (in bold) from Mark 2:27–28: "Then he said to them, 'ced**The Sabbath was made for man, not man for the Sabbath. So** the Son of Man is Lord **even** of the Sabbath.'" This redaction by Luke de-emphasizes the general applicability of Jesus' teaching (i.e., the Sabbath was made for humanity, not vice versa) and instead places the justification of the action of Jesus' disciples – specifically, the plucking grain on the Sabbath – squarely upon the identity of him as the κύριος. By deleting both the connective ὥστε ("so") and the καί (in this context,

---

[43] Van de Weghe, *The Historical Tell*, Ch. 8; see also, Colin Hemer, *The Book of Acts in the Setting of Hellenistic History*, Wissenschaftliche Untersuchungen zum Neuen Testament 49 (Tübingen: Mohr Siebeck, 1989), 356–57.
[44] Rowe, *Early Narrative Christology*, 113.

"even"), which formed part of Jesus' argument in Mark, Luke restructures the phrase to emphasize the identity of Jesus as κύριος. Rowe remarks:

> In Mark the principle that negotiates the relation between human beings and the Sabbath allows him to emphasize that the Son of Man is Lord even (καί) of the Sabbath. By contrast, Luke emphasizes that the Lord of the Sabbath is the Son of Man. That is to say, the alterations and movement of the Lukan text itself press for a way of reading the sentence which recognizes and emphasizes the authority of the Son of Man over the Sabbath precisely in his identity as κύριος.
> The best English translation, therefore, of the Lukan version, κύριός ἐστιν τοῦ σαββάτου ὁ υἱός τοῦ ἀνθρώπου, is not the common "the Son of Man is lord of the Sabbath," but rather "the Lord of the Sabbath is the Son of Man." This latter translation captures better the particularities of the Lukan text and thereby allows the potential theological resonance to be heard.[45]

This sudden, sharp emphasis on Jesus' divine identity is only our first observation. The more exceptional feature is the general thrust of Luke's Petrine perspective. Luke's Petrine perspective does not move the reader from seeing Jesus as a prophet to seeing Jesus on par with Yahweh the κύριος. The audience is confronted with Jesus' divine association *at the time when* Peter is commissioned by his Lord (Luke 5:1–11). The experiences within the narrative build toward a climax in the revelation of Jesus' identity, which is seen in the transfiguration (9:28–36).[46] This pericope is of supreme importance to Luke. Not only does he add significant details to Mark's account, but it marks the main transitionary event into Luke's Travel Narrative (9:51–19:44). What I am emphasizing here is that it is significant, however, not so much in what it tells us about Jesus' divine identity, but rather what it reveals to us – in embryonic form – of how that divine identify manifests itself in Jesus' messiahship.

Jesus' climactic question to his disciples, "who do you say I am?" (Luke 9:20), which results in Peter's declaration, "you are God's messiah" (9:20), sets the stage for the meaningful definition not of what that prophetic messiahship means for Jesus' divine identity but for what that prophetic messiahship means for the concept of divine lordship, which in the Travel Narrative is expressed in Jesus' grace toward outsiders, leading to his rejection and death.

---

45 Rowe, *Early Narrative Christology*, 112.
46 The event was significant to the Early Church and appears to have played a legitimizing role for the Sons of Zebedee and Simon Peter; see David Wenham and A. D. A. Moses. "'There Are Some Standing Here...': Did They Become the 'Reputed Pillars' of the Jerusalem Church? Some Reflections on Mark 9:1, Galatians 2:9 and the Transfiguration," *Novum Testamentum* 36.2 (1994): 146–63.

As others have noted, Luke removes any doubt that the transfiguration should be equated with a theophany of greater significance than Moses' experience at the top of Mt. Sinai.[47] Luke adds these key components into his recollection: the sense of "glory" (9:31–33, esp. Jesus' glory: "when they became fully awake, they saw his glory," 9:32), the focus on Jesus' ascent (9:28), the descent of the cloud (9:34), the fear of the disciples (9:34), the shining face of Jesus (9:29).[48] Luke also reverses Mark's ἀκούετε αὐτοῦ (Mark 9:7) into αὐτοῦ ἀκούετε (Luke 9:35) in the command from the Father concerning Jesus: "This is my beloved son, *listen to him*," to echo Deut. 18:15 more closely (c.f. Acts 3:22), highlighting Jesus' identity as a prophet greater than Moses.[49]

All of this is, surprisingly, only the window dressing. Embedded within the Father's command to his disciples is a subtle change of only a single word from Mark's text: my *beloved* son (ἀγαπητός, Mark 9:7) to my *chosen* son (ἐκλελεγμένος, Luke 9:35). This change is as artful as it is revealing, for it designates Jesus' messianic identity explicitly in terms of the Isaianic servant of Isaiah 42:1 (LXX, ὁ ἐκλεκτός μου).[50] To this alteration is added Luke's comment that the topic of discussion was Jesus' upcoming suffering and death, his exodus (ἔξοδος, 9:31), so that what is both echoed and anticipated by the command "listen to him!" is Jesus' increased identification of himself with a certain type of messianic identity: the suffering servant of Isaiah. What is important in all of this is, again, the movement of the text. It moves from divine identity to servant

---

47 Heinz Schürmann, *Das Lukasevangelium: Kommentar zu Kap. 1,1–9,50*, Herders theologischer Kommentar zum Neuen Testament 3/1 (Freiburg: Herder, 1990), 556–557; John P. Heil, *The Transfiguration of Jesus Narrative Meaning and Function of Mark 9:2–8, Matt 17:1–8 and Luke 9:28–36*, AnBib 144, (Rome Pontificio Istituto Biblico, 2000), 272; David M. Miller, "Seeing the Glory, Hearing the Son: The Function of the Wilderness Theophany Narratives in Luke 9:28–36," *Catholic Biblical Quarterly* 72.3 (2010): 498–517; Gregory R. Lanier, "Luke's Distinctive Use of the Temple: Portraying the Divine Visitation," *Journal of Theological Studies* 65.2 (2014): 433–62.
48 Miller, "Hearing the Son," 503, Lanier, "Portraying the Divine Visitation," 451–2.
49 Miller, "Hearing the Son," 502. For the identification of the Isaianic Servant with the Prophet-like-Moses from Deut. 18:14, see Gordon P. Hugenberger, "The Servant of the Lord in the 'Servants Songs' of Isaiah: a Second Moses Figure," in *The Lord's Anointed. Interpretation of Old Testament Messianic Texts*, edited by P.E. Satterthwaite, R.S. Hess, G.J. Wenham (Carlisle: Paternoster; Grand Rapids: Baker, 1995), 105–40.
50 C. François Bovon, *L'Évangile selon Saint Luc 1-9* (Genève: Labor et Fides, 1991), 488–89; Robert F. O'Toole states that this is a reference to the Hebrew text of Is 42:1 ("How Does Luke Portray Jesus as Servant of Yhwh?," *Biblica* 81.3 (2000): 328–46; That Luke quotes texts aligned more closely with the Proto-MT has recently been suggested by Kai Akagi, "Luke 1:49 and the Form of Isaiah in Luke: An Overlooked Allusion and the Problem of an Assumed LXX Text," *Journal of Biblical Literature* 138.1 (2019): 183–201, see esp. 192–3.

identity. The new, surprising twist in the story is not Jesus' divine connection. The twist is rather another glimmer of the same trajectory displayed through the familial Christology of the Infancy Narrative: divine lordship is not a development out from messianism; messianism is a development, whether regal or prophetic, out from divine lordship.

6 Johannine/Servant Christology

I have elsewhere discussed the historical connections between the Third and Fourth Gospels, especially within their Passion accounts, indicating the likelihood that Luke may have used the Beloved Disciple as a source for some of his material.[51] Allusions to the Isaianic servant become increasingly stronger throughout Jesus' Passion in Luke's Gospel, occurring upon the lips of Jesus (22:37), through details shared with the other evangelists (Mark 10:42–45; cf. Luke 22:24–27), and through Luke's own literary allusions (Luke 22:24–27; 23:35; 23:47).[52] These allusions continue into the speeches of Acts (3:13, 26; 4:27, 30; 8:32–33; cf. Is 53:7–8 LXX), demonstrating Luke's further interest in the motif. Although direct citations in the Passion narrative are scarce, this is likely due to Luke's historical interest; here Luke chose to depend, as David Seccombe argues, "on the 'witness' of those present to establish his case"; nevertheless, as Vincent Taylor has noted and many have affirmed, Luke's Passion narrative "depicts Jesus as the Servant of the Lord without using the name."[53] In this narrative, Luke intentionally refuses to designate Jesus as κύριος although he

---

[51] Van de Weghe, *The Historical Tell*, Ch. 9; idem, "The Beloved Eyewitness."
[52] For the significance of the Servant of the Lord in Luke's depiction of Jesus' death, see: Joel B. Green, "The death of Jesus, God's servant," in *Reimaging the Death of the Lukan Jesus*, edited by Dennis D. Sylva, Bonner Biblische Beiträge 73 (Frankfurt: Hain, 1990), 1–28; Mittmann-Richert, *Jesaja 53 Im Lukasevangelium*, which not only argues that Is 53 is the controlling linchpin in Lukan theology but also redeems a perspective of Luke's theology much more in line with Paul's: "Das Lukasevangelium ist im Vier-Evangelien-Kanon das paulinische Evangelium," 313; John Kimbell, *The Atonement in Lukan Theology* (Cambridge: Cambridge Scholars Publishing, 2014); Christopher Hutson, "Enough for What?: Playacting Isaiah 53 in Luke 22:35-38," *Restoration Quarterly* 55 (2013): 35–51; T. S. Ferda, "Reason to Weep: Isaiah 52 and the Subtext of Luke's Triumphal Entry," *Journal of Theological Studies* 66.1 (2015): 28–60.
[53] David Seccombe, "Luke and Isaiah," *New Testament Studies* 27.2 (1981): 252–59, esp. 258; Vincent Taylor, *The Passion Narrative of St. Luke*, edited by O. E. Evans, Society of New Testament Studies Monograph Series 19, (Cambridge: Cambridge University Press, 1972), 13.

makes every opportunity to highlight this throughout the rest of his Gospel.⁵⁴ It is the sacred moment when Luke's Gospel crashes into the historical reality of Jesus' humiliation.

This "sacred silence" in the passion of Jesus, with the narrative left comment-free, is likewise mirrored in the Gospel of John, as I have discussed elsewhere.⁵⁵ Although generally less recognized, there are three ways that the Travel Narrative of Luke's Gospel, along with Luke's Passion Narrative, are influenced by a κύριος Christology, and each has a parallel in the Johannine emphasis.

The first springs from Kenneth Bailey's study of the parables of Luke 15, each of which relates to the other and is designed to highlight the prodigal nature of God, who loves ἀσώτως ("prodigally," i.e., with self-abandon, recklessly); Bailey highlights this emphasis in opposition to the traditional focus on the prodigal nature of the son (cf. the traditional readings of Luke 15:11–31, based on ζῶν ἀσώτως in 15:13). Indeed, each parable has its focus, whether on the shepherd (15:3–7), the woman (15:8–10), or the father (15:11–31), on the one who receives the glory and the benefit of retrieving their lost items. Bailey argues that the issue of atonement is woven throughout these parables, esp. Luke 15:11–31.⁵⁶ Given the context of the honour-shame culture of Jesus' environment, each act that the father does in approaching his lost son, for example – of running for him, which would involve hiking up his garment, 15:20 (a humiliating act); granting him his signet ring, 15:22; giving him the best robe (his own robe), 15:22; and giving up the best sacrifice, 15:23 – is merely another sacrifice of degradation and personal abandonment while, as Bailey shows, these acts occur apart from his son's repentance and are, therefore, unconditionally given over.⁵⁷ Bailey makes similar observations about sacrifice within the other parables. The older son in the final parable (15:11–31), Bailey argues, typifies the persons to whom the parables are directed. These parables, according to Bailey, are in themselves Jesus' invitation to his interlocuters to receive the grace of God.⁵⁸ In the setting of Luke's Gospel, however, it is not God's actions that are being questioned, but rather Jesus' actions of eating and dining with sinners and tax

---

54 Rowe, *Early Narrative Christology*, 194–6.
55 Luuk van de Weghe and John Battle, "Truth and Semantic Change in the Gospel of John," *Bulletin for Biblical Research* 31.2 (2021): 211–27.
56 Kenneth Bailey, *The Cross and the Prodigal: The 15th Chapter of Luke, Seen through the Eyes of Middle Eastern Peasants* (St. Louis: Concordia, 1973; 2ⁿᵈ edition, Downers Grove: InterVarsity Press, 2005).
57 Kenneth Bailey, *Finding the Lost Cultural Keys to Luke 15* (St. Louis: Concordia, 2005), 132–50.
58 Ibid., 189. See also my forthcoming publication, *For People Like Us: God's Search for the Lost of Luke 15* (Eugene: Wipf & Stock, 2023).

collectors (15:1–2). Jesus, nevertheless, answers an accusation against himself with a three-fold set of parables about what God is like. The thrust of the message is undoubtedly echoed in much Johannine literature, as Bailey explicitly notes:

> Some of the same theological meaning here created by parable [of Luke 15:11–31] is affirmed in other NT writings using other language. In the parable the father as head of the house and the father at the edge of the village are one person. In John's gospel Jesus says, "The Father and I are one" (10:30). Also in the parable the father becomes a suffering servant in order to reconcile his son to himself. St. Paul writes, "God was in Christ reconciling the world unto himself" (2 Cor. 5:19 KJV). What is said conceptually in John and in 2 Corinthians appears metaphorically in Luke 15.[59]

The second relevant text is one found at the end of Luke's Travel Narrative, while Jesus was walking "along the border between Samaria and Galilee" (Luke 17:11–19).[60] Here, Jesus meets ten lepers, nine of which are Israelites while one is a Samaritan. Like John's account of Jesus with the woman at the well in John 4:1–26, the Gerizim temple and the proper place of worship lingers within the context.[61] In Luke's account, Jesus heals the ten lepers and tells them to go and "show yourselves to the priests" (17:14). Only one leper, the Samaritan, returns, and when he does so he worships at Jesus' feet (17:15–16). Jesus then makes a stunning, albeit cryptic, remark. He says what appears to be an ill-mannered statement: "Has no one returned to give praise to God except this foreigner (ἀλλογενής)?" (17:18). ἀλλογενής is a *hapax* in the New Testament and is a term exclusive to Jewish literature; it has its occurrence prominently in one place within Jewish antiquity: upon the signs that separated the Court of the Gentiles

---

59 Ibid., 151.
60 For another argument favouring yet another connection to the Elisha narrative (2 Kgs 5:8–19) with this pericope, see: Wilhelm Bruners, *Die Reinigung der zehn Aussätzigen und die Heilung des Samariters, Lk 17,11-19: Ein Beitrag zur lukanischen Interpretation der Reinigung von Aussätzigen*, Forschung zur Bibel 23 (Stuttgart: Katholisches Bibelwerk, 1977). Our brief discussion leans on Dennis Hamm's terrific article, "What the Samaritan Leper Sees: The Narrative Christology of Luke 17:11–19," *Catholic Biblical Quarterly* 56.2 (1994): 273–87.
61 After surveying the relevant literature on the Samaritans, Hamm comments: "Quite strikingly, what one learns from a reading of our information about Samaritans amounts to the very same three themes evoked in John 4: (1) Samaritans and Jews share a common tradition (the Torah and a claim to descend from Abraham); (2) they have a history of enmity; and (3) they are divided mainly by the concern for the right place to worship Yahweh: Jerusalem or Gerizim. This preoccupation with the right place to worship the Hebrew God may be the main thing we need to know to understand Luke's special interest in the ethnicity of the grateful leper" ("What the Samaritan Leper Sees," 282).

in the Jerusalem temple from the sacred space reserved only for Jews – the inscriptions that forbade any foreigner from entering upon the pain of death.[62] Jesus then, in Johannine fashion, appears to consider this leper's encounter with *him* as a substitute for the temple, whether in Jerusalem or on Mt. Gerizim, but Jesus here, unlike the Jerusalem temple, receives the Samaritan's worship at his feet as an expression of the leper's healing/salvation (17:19). The entire account becomes reminiscent of Jesus' discussion in John 4:21–26. Dennis Hamm concedes: "Luke's Christology could be said to be on a 'trajectory' towards that of the Fourth Gospel."[63]

Third, Gregory Lanier has demonstrated how Luke portrays Jesus' journey to the temple in Jerusalem as the divine visitation of Yahweh.[64] He notes – and this is uncontroversial – Luke's focus on the temple despite its potential irrelevance for his post-70 CE audience.[65] Further, Lanier shows the manner that Luke emphasizes the temple throughout his narrative, specifically redacting Markan/Q material to reveal how Jesus embodied the presence of Yahweh and his subsequent return to his temple as reminiscent of prophetic visions from Ezek 8–11. Below are his most telling points:

---

62 Ibid., 284.
63 Ibid., 287.
64 Lanier, "Portraying the Divine Visitation."
65 This focus in Luke's Gospel has been studied by many who come to conclusions similar to Lanier's: Cornelius van der Waal, "The Temple in the Gospel according to Luke," *Neotestamentica* 7.1 (1973): 49–59; Michael Bachmann, *Jerusalem und der Tempel: Die geographisch-theologischen Elemente in der lukanischen Sicht des jüdischen Kultzentrums*, Beiträge zur Wissenschaft vom Alten und Neuen Testament 6 (Stuttgart: Kohlhammer, 1980); Dennis D. Sylva, "The Temple Curtain and Jesus' Death in the Gospel of Luke," *Journal of Biblical Literature* 105.2 (1986): 239–50; Klaus Baltzer, "The Meaning of the Temple in the Lukan Writings," *Harvard Theological Review* 58.3 (1965): 263–77; J. Bradley Chance, *Jerusalem, the Temple, and the New Age in Luke–Acts* (Macon, GA: Mercer University Press, 1988); Joel B. Green, "The Demise of the Temple as 'Cultural Center' in Luke-Acts: An Exploration of the Rending of the Temple Veil (Luke 23.44–49)," *Revue Biblique* (1994): 495–515; John H. Elliott, "Temple versus household in Luke-Acts: A contrast in social institutions," *Hervormde Teologiese Studies* 47.1 (1991): 88–120. Nicholas H. Taylor comments: "With the coming of John the Baptist the temple ceases to function as the locus of divine presence on earth. Jesus becomes the primary manifestation of divine presence during his ministry, but the status of the temple as divine residence is not refuted until the moment of Jesus' death. However, it is noteworthy that, whereas Matthew and Mark record the rending of the veil immediately after the death of Jesus (Mt 27:50-51; Mk 15:37-38), in Luke it precedes Jesus' death. For Luke the status of the temple as divine residence has already ended with the commencement of the Gospel, and is not brought about by the death of Jesus" ("The Jerusalem Temple in Luke-Acts," *Hervormde Teologiese Studies* 60.1/2 (2004): 459–85, esp. 481).

- The themes of visitation and glory are prominent in the Infancy Narrative – themes which carry strong associations throughout the LXX of the presence of Yahweh.[66]
- These themes are reemphasized in Luke's baptism and transfiguration accounts; while strengthening the connections between God's presence and the person of Jesus, Luke shuffles Jesus' temptations so that the final action before his ministry is the departure from the temple (Luke 4:10), allowing a recapitulation of Ezekiel's vision of Yahweh departing from his temple (Ezek 8–11) within Luke's narrative.[67]
- At the midpoint of Jesus' departure/return to the Jerusalem temple, in Luke 13:35a, Jesus utters the statement, "Look, your house is left to you desolate," amid several judgments similar to Ezek 8:5–11.[68]
- Luke uniquely has Jesus arrive *directly* at the temple (19:45a) rather than in Jerusalem more generally (cf. Matt 21; Mark 11), coming down specifically from the Mt. of Olives (ἤδη πρὸς τῇ καταβάσει τοῦ ὄρους τῶν ἐλαιῶν, 19:37); this is in fulfilment of the expectations of Yahweh reversing his temple departure up the Mt. of Olives in Ezek 11:23 (καὶ ἀνέβη ἡ δόξα κυρίου ἐκ μέσης τῆς πόλεως καὶ ἔστη ἐπὶ τοῦ ὄρους, LXX; cf. Ezek 43:2–4); this explains why Jesus laments over the city with the comment, "for you did not know the time of your visitation" (19:44), aligning his own rejection by the Jerusalemites with the destruction of their city and their rejection of God himself.[69]

These "upper-level" connections to Johannine Christology, like in the previous regal and prophetic portions of Luke's narrative, occur prior to the narrative focus on Jesus' messiahship and set the context for its deeper understanding. In Luke, this is well-demonstrated in the centurion's comment at Jesus' death.[70]

---

66 Lanier, "Portraying the Divine Visitation," 447–51.
67 Ibid., 453.
68 Ibid., 453, 456.
69 Ibid., 456–9.
70 This comes at the end of a masterful literary parallel drawn between Barabbas and the crowd to emphasis Jesus' substitutionary death (see the excellent article by Monique Cuany, "Jesus, Barabbas and the People: The Climax of Luke's Trial Narrative and Lukan Christology (Luke 23:13–25)," *Journal for the Study of the New Testament* 39.4 (2017): 441–58. Given that Luke uses narrative technique here to highlight Jesus' substitutionary atonement, as well as allusions to Isa 53 and other Isaianic servant passages, it is all the more puzzling why Luke would neglect to include Mark 10:45 if he wished to emphasize this theme. For a reasonable solution, see: David Moffitt, "Atonement at the Right Hand: The Sacrificial Significance of Jesus' Exaltation in Acts," *New Testament Studies* 62.4 (2016): 549–68.

The centurion states: "Surely this man was righteous/innocent (δίκαιος)," an implicit reference to Is. 53:11 (τῇ συνέσει δικαιῶσαι δίκαιον εὖ δουλεύοντα πολλοῖς, LXX; cf. Luke 23:47b, Acts 3:14, 26). Both Mark 15:37 and Matthew 27:54 record the centurion's comments as, "Surely this man was the Son of God!" The question we must ask is, "What did Jesus' death demonstrate?" Was it that he was the Son of God (Mark 15:37, Matt. 27:54)? Or was it that he was the righteous/just servant (Luke 23:47b)? All that we've discussed leads us to Luke's likely answer, which would have been, "Yes," to both questions.

7 Χριστός and Κύριος in Acts 2:36

We are now prepared to consider again Peter's claim in Acts 2:36 that in the resurrection God made Jesus both χριστός and κύριος. First, there is a "lower-level" reading that could make sense of this claim. The resurrection of Jesus was God's divine reversal of the human "no" to Jesus. The Jewish people killed their Messiah (Acts 2:23), but God granted him power and dominion in accordance with the Psalms: a status of a Davidic type but then accentuated further and higher (Acts 2:25–32). Under this reading, it is best to remove any high Christological claims from Peter's sermon. Jesus was exalted simply because the Jewish people were wrong to kill him, presumably because Jesus' teachings and actions were reflective of what was acceptable to God (Luke 4:24; Acts 2:22). Jesus' resurrection was a result of God's vindication of Jesus and no more.

To this "lower-level" reading we could add some deeper nuance that may not have theoretically been captured by Peter's audience. In related speeches Peter goes out of his way to confirm that Jesus was not merely declared righteous/innocent at his trial and death (23:4, 14, 22, 47), but that his righteousness appears to have been part of his identity as the messianic, Isaianic servant (Acts 3:14, 26). His exaltation (Acts 2:33; cf. Isa 52:13) would then be part of this motif as echoed by Acts 8:32–33 as one of the scriptural paradigms that made sense of not only Jesus' resurrection (Acts 2:32) but also his ascension to God's throne at his right hand (Acts 3:33), which as David Moffitt has shown, could have both regal and priestly connotations.[71]

Indeed, in Peter's speeches the resurrection/ascension of Jesus are a basis upon which people can repent and be saved (Acts 2:36–38), and Peter links this fact with prophecies from the book of Joel, which read:

---

[71] Moffitt, "Atonement at the Right Hand."

> In the last days, God says, I will pour out my Spirit on all people. Your sons and daughters will prophesy, your young men will see visions, your old men will dream dreams [...]. And everyone who calls on the name of the Lord will be saved. (Acts 2:17, 21; cf. Joel 2:28, 32)

At this point we are confronted yet again with a κύριος Christology, for as people call upon the name of Jesus they fulfill a prophecy related to a people who will call upon the name of Yahweh, and this is only accentuated as one moves further throughout Acts, wherein a total of thirty-three out of a hundred usages of κύριος are ambiguous in regards to their referent as being either Jesus or Yahweh.[72] Throughout Acts, the anarthrous form of κύριος (as in the LXX, where it translates יהוה) typically refers to God, but Acts 2:36 and 10:36 are clear exceptions;[73] the latter usage (10:36) designates Jesus as "Lord over all" (πάντων κύριος), while the former usage (2:36) is our text in question.

What are we to make, then, of Peter's claim that God made Jesus both κύριος and χριστός (Acts 2:36)? It has been my burden to stress that we ought to take Luke's use of eyewitness traditions seriously in our understanding of this text. If so, we see a consistent movement through a diversity of perspectives. Yet through each messianic perspective, whether regal or prophetic or Isaianic, it is not the Messiah who is made more lordly but it is the Lord who is made to take on new messianic functions. God (ὁ θεός – read, "father") made Jesus both Lord and Christ, then, in the sense that he confirmed ultimately Jesus' interpretation of his own divinity in terms of suffering and servanthood.

References

Afulike, Caleb C. "Luke's Portrayal of the Social Dimension in the Ministry of Jesus and the Apostles (Luke-Acts) According to Isaiah's Message of Social Justice in Chapters 61:1–2 and 58:6." *Journal of Religious & Theological Information* 17:2 (2018): 41–54.
Akagi, Kai. "Luke 1:49 and the Form of Isaiah in Luke: An Overlooked Allusion and the Problem of an Assumed LXX Text." *Journal of Biblical Literature* 138.1 (2019): 183–201.
Bachmann, Michael. Jerusalem und der Tempel: Die geographisch-theologischen Elemente in der lukanischen Sicht des jüdischen Kultzentrums. Beitrage zur Wissenschaft vom Alten und Neuen Testament 6. Stuttgart: Kohlhammer, 1980.

---

[72] James D. G. Dunn, "ΚΥΡΙΟΣ in Acts," in *Jesus Christus als die Mitte der Schrift*, edited by. C. Landmesser et al. (Berlin: de Gruyter, 1997), 363–78, esp. 369–72.
[73] Larry Hurtado, "God or Jesus? Textual Ambiguity and Textual Variants in Acts of the Apostles," in *Texts and Traditions: Essays in Honour of J. Keith Elliott*, edited by Peter Doble and Jeffrey Kloha (Leiden/Boston: Brill, 2014), 239–54, esp. 242.

Bailey, Kenneth. *The Cross and the Prodigal: The 15th Chapter of Luke, Seen through the Eyes of Middle Eastern Peasants*. St. Louis: Concordia, 1973. Second Edition, Downers Grove: InterVarsity Press, 2005.

Bailey, Kenneth. *Finding the Lost Cultural Keys to Luke 15*. St. Louis: Concordia, 2005.

Baltzer, Klaus. "The Meaning of the Temple in the Lukan Writings." *Harvard Theological Review* 58.3 (1965): 263–77.

Bauckham, Richard. *Jude and the Relatives of Jesus in the Early Church*. Edinburgh: T&T Clark, 1990.

Bauckham, Richard. "The Relatives of Jesus." *Themelios* 21.2 (January 1996): 18–21.

Bauckham, Richard. "Luke's Infancy Narrative as Oral History in Scriptural Form." In *The Gospels: History and Christology: The Search of Joseph Ratzinger-Benedict XVI*, edited by Bernardo Estrada, Ermenegildo Manicardi and Armand Puig i Tàrrech. Vatican City: Libreria Editrice Vaticana, 2013, vol. 1, 399–417.

Billings, Bradly S. "'At the Age of 12': The Boy Jesus in the Temple (Luke 2:41–52), the Emperor Augustus, and the Social Setting of the Third Gospel." *Journal of Theological Studies* 60.1 (2009): 70–89.

Blass, Friedrich and Albert Debrunner. *A Greek Grammar of the New Testament and Other Early Christian Literature*, trans. Robert W. Funk. Chicago: University of Chicago Press, 1964.

Blumenthal, Christian. "Augustus' Erlass und Gottes Macht: Überlegungen zur Charakterisierung der Augustusfigur und ihrer erzählstrategischen Funktion in der lukanischen Erzählung." *New Testament Studies* 57.1 (2011): 1–30.

Bock, Darrell. *A Theology of Luke and Acts: God's Promised Program, Realized for All Nations*. New Studies in Biblical Theology. Grand Rapids: Zondervan, 2012.

Bock, Darrell. Proclamation from Prophecy and Pattern: Lucan Old Testament Christology. Journal For the Study of the New Testament Supplement 12. Sheffield: Sheffield Academic Press, 1987.

Bovon, C. François. *L'Évangile selon Saint Luc 1-9*. Genève: Labor et Fides, 1991.

Brugger, Peter. "One Hundred Years of an Ambiguous Figure: Happy Birthday, Duck/Rabbit!" *Perceptual and Motor Skills*. 89.4 (1999): 973–77.

Brugger, Peter, and Suzanne Brugger. "The Easter Bunny in October: Is it Disguised as Duck?" *Perceptual and Motor Skills* 76.2 (1993): 577–78.

Burkett, Delbert. "Jesus in Luke-Acts." In *The Blackwell Companion to Jesus*, edited by Delbert Burkett. London: Wiley-Blackwell, 2011, 47–63.

Byrne, Brendan. "Jesus as Messiah in the Gospel of Luke: Discerning a Pattern of Correction." *Catholic Biblical Quarterly* 65.1 (2003): 80–95.

Chance, J. Bradley. *Jerusalem, the Temple, and the New Age in Luke–Acts*. Macon, GA: Mercer University Press, 1988.

Conzelmann, Hans. *Die Mitte der Zeit: Studien zur Theologie des Lukas*. Beiträge zur historischen Theologie 17. Tübingen: Mohr Siebeck, 1954.

Cuany, Monique. "Jesus, Barabbas and the People: The Climax of Luke's Trial Narrative and Lukan Christology (Luke 23:13–25)." *Journal for the Study of the New Testament* 39.4 (2017): 441–58.

Dunn, James D. G. "ΚΥΡΙΟΣ in Acts." In *Jesus Christus als die Mitte der Schrift*, edited by Christof Landmesser et al. Berlin: de Gruyter, 1997, 363–78.

Elliott, John H. "Temple versus household in Luke-Acts: A contrast in social institutions," *Hervormde Teologiese Studies* 47.1 (1991): 88–120.

Farris, Stephen. *The Hymns of Luke's Infancy Narratives: Their Origin, Meaning and Significance*. London: Bloomsbury Academic, 1985.

Fellows, Richard. "Mariam became Maria and, with that name, was Luke's source for the infancy narrative," Paul and Co-workers (Blog), 5.01.2021, http://paulandco-workers.blogspot.com/ 2021/01/mariam-became-maria-and-with-that-name.html.

Ferda, Tucker S. "Reason to Weep: Isaiah 52 and the Subtext of Luke's Triumphal Entry." *Journal of Theological Studies* 66.1 (2015): 28–60.

Gathercole, Simon. "The Heavenly ἀνατολή (Luke 1:78–9)." *Journal of Theological Studies* 65.2 (2005), 471–88.

Green, Joel B. "The Death of Jesus, God's Servant." In *Reimaging the Death of the Lukan Jesus*, edited by Dennis D. Sylva. Frankfurt: Hain, 1990, 1–28.

Green, Joel B. "The Social Status of Mary in Luke 1,5-2,52: A Plea for Methodological Integration." *Biblica* 73.4 (1992): 457–72.

Green, Joel B. "The Demise of the Temple as 'Cultural Center' in Luke-Acts: An Exploration of the Rending of the Temple Veil (Luke 23.44–49)," *Revue Biblique* (1994): 495–15.

Hamm, M. Dennis. "What the Samaritan Leper Sees: The Narrative Christology of Luke 17:11–19." *Catholic Biblical Quarterly* 56.2 (1994): 273–87.

Hays, Richard B. *Reading Backwards: Figural Christology and the Fourfold Gospel Witness*. Waco, TX: Baylor University Press, 2014.

Heil, John P. *The Transfiguration of Jesus Narrative Meaning and Function of Mark 9:2–8, Matt 17:1–8 and Luke 9:28–36*. Analecta Biblica 144. Rome: Pontificio Istituto Biblico, 2000.

Hemer, Colin. *The Book of Acts in the Setting of Hellenistic History*. Wissenschaftliche Untersuchungen zum Neuen Testament 49. Tübingen: Mohr Siebeck, 1989.

Henrichs-Tarasenkova, Nina. *Luke's Christology of Divine Identity*. Library of New Testament Studies 542. London: Bloomsbury T&T Clark, 2016.

Hertig, Paul. "The Jubilee Mission of Jesus in the Gospel of Luke: Reversals of Fortunes." *Missiology* 26.2 (1998), 167–79.

Hill, David. "The Rejection of Jesus at Nazareth (Luke IV 16-30)." *Novum Testamentum* 13.3 (1971): 161–80.

Hugenberger, Gordon P. "The Servant of the Lord in the 'Servants Songs' of Isaiah: a Second Moses Figure." In *The Lord's Anointed. Interpretation of Old Testament Messianic Texts*. Carlisle: Paternoster; Grand Rapids: Baker, 1995, 105–40.

Hurtado, Larry. "God or Jesus? Textual Ambiguity and Textual Variants in Acts of the Apostles." In *Texts and Traditions: Essays in Honour of J. Keith Elliott*, edited by Peter Doble and Jeffrey Kloha. Leiden/Boston: Brill, 2014, 239–54.

Hutson, Christopher. "Enough for What? Playacting Isaiah 53 in Luke 22: 35–38." *Restoration Quarterly* 55 (2013): 35–51.

Jastrow, Joseph. "The Mind's Eye." *Popular Science Monthly* 54 (1899): 299–312.

Jervell, Jacob. *The Theology of the Acts of the Apostles*. Cambridge: Cambridge University Press, 1996.

Jung, Chang-Wook. *The Original Language of the Lukan Infancy Narrative*. Journal for the Study of the New Testament Supplement 267. London: T&T Clark International, 2004.

Kimbell, John. *The Atonement in Lukan Theology*. Cambridge: Cambridge Scholars Publishing, 2014.

Kochenash, Michael. "'Adam, Son of God' (Luke 3.38): Another Jesus–Augustus Parallel in Luke's Gospel." *New Testament Studies* 64.3 (2018): 307–325.

Lampe, Geoffrey H. "The Lucan Portrait of Christ," *New Testament Studies* 2.3 (1956): 160–75.

Lanier, Gregory. "Luke's Distinctive Use of the Temple: Portraying the Divine Visitation," *Journal of Theological Studies* 65.2 (2014): 433–62.
Meadors, Edward. "'Isaiah 40.3 and the Synoptic Gospels' Parody of the Roman Road System." *New Testament Studies* 66.1 (2020): 106–24.
Meyer, Ben F. "'But Mary Kept All These Things...' (Lk 2:19, 51)." *Catholic Biblical Quarterly* 26.1 (1964): 31–49.
Miller, David M. "Seeing the Glory, Hearing the Son: The Function of the Wilderness Theophany Narratives in Luke 9:28–36." *Catholic Biblical Quarterly* 72.3 (2010): 498–517.
Mittmann-Richert, Ulrike. *Der Sühnetod des Gottesknechts: Jesaja 53 im Lukasevangelium*. Wissenschaftliche Untersuchungen zum Neuen Testament 220. Tübingen: Mohr Siebeck, 2008.
Moffitt, David. "Atonement at the Right Hand: The Sacrificial Significance of Jesus' Exaltation in Acts." *New Testament Studies* 62.4 (2016): 549–68.
Morris, Royce. "Why ΑΥΓΟΥΣΤΟΣ? A Note to Luke 2.1." *New Testament Studies* 38.1 (1992): 142–44.
O'Toole, Robert F. "How Does Luke Portray Jesus as Servant of Yhwh?" *Biblica* 81.3 (2000): 328–46.
Peters, John. "Luke's Source Claims in the Context of Ancient Historiography." *Journal for the Study of the Historical Jesus* 18.1 (2020): 35–60.
Peters, John. *Luke Among the Ancient Historians*. Eugene, OR: Pickwick, 2022.
Plutarch. *Lives: Demosthenes and Cicero. Alexander and Caesar*, trans. Bernadotte Perrin. Loeb Classical Library 99, vol. 7. Cambridge, MA: Harvard University Press, 1919.
Rowe, C. Kavin. *Early Narrative Christology: The Lord in the Gospel of Luke*. Beihefte zur Zeitschrift für die neutestamentliche Wissenschaft 139. Berlin and New York: de Gruyter, 2006.
Rowe, C. Kavin. "Acts 2.36 and the Continuity of Lukan Christology." *New Testament Studies* 53.1 (2007): 37–56.
Sanders, James A. "Isaiah in Luke." *Interpretation* 36.2 (1982): 144–55.
Schürmann, Heinz. *Das Lukasevangelium: Kommentar zu Kap. 1,1–9,50*. Herders Theologischer Kommentar zum Neuen Testament 3/1. Freiburg: Herder, 1990.
Seccombe, David. "Luke and Isaiah." *New Testament Studies* 27.2 (1981): 252–59.
Strauss, Mark L. The Davidic Messiah in Luke-Acts: The Promise and its Fulfilment in Lukan Christology. Sheffield, England: Sheffield Academic Press, 1995.
Sylva, Dennis. "The Temple Curtain and Jesus' Death in the Gospel of Luke." *Journal of Biblical Literature* 105.2 (1986): 239–50.
Taylor, Nicholas H. "The Jerusalem Temple in Luke-Acts." *Hervormde Teologiese Studies* 60.1 (2004): 459–85.
Taylor, Vincent. *The Passion Narrative of St. Luke*, edited by O. E. Evans. Supplement for the Study of the New Testament 19. Cambridge: Cambridge University Press, 1972.
Van de Weghe, Luuk, and John Battle. "Truth and Semantic Change in the Gospel of John," *Bulletin for Biblical Research* 31.2 (2021): 211–27.
Van de Weghe, Luuk. "The Beloved Eyewitness." *New Testament Studies* 66.3 (2022): 351–57.
Van de Weghe, Luuk. The Historical Tell: Eyewitness Testimony in the Gospel of Luke and Acts. Chillicothe: DeWard, 2022.
Van de Weghe, Luuk. "Name Recall in the Synoptic Gospels." *New Testament Studies* (2023).
Van de Weghe, Luuk. *Holy and Tender: God's Search for the Lost of Luke 15*. Eugene, OR: Wipf & Stock, 2023.
Van der Waal, Cornelius. "The Temple in the Gospel according to Luke," *Neotestamentica* 7.1 (1973): 49–59.

Wenham, David and A. D. A. Moses. "'There Are Some Standing Here...': Did They Become the 'Reputed Pillars' of the Jerusalem Church? Some Reflections on Mark 9:1, Galatians 2:9 and the Transfiguration," *Novum Testamentum* 36.2 (1994): 146–63.

Williams, Peter. "Christmas Variants (3)," Evangelical Textual Criticism (Blog), 12.12.2005, http://evangelicaltextualcriticism.blogspot.com/2005/12/christmas-variants-3.html.

Tomas Bokedal
Why is the New Testament Called "New Testament"?

Historical, Editorial and Theological Dimensions

Abstract: This chapter offers an account as to why the New Testament book collection is labelled "New Testament." It argues that the original Greek title ἡ καινὴ διαθήκη (Latin *novum testamentum*) is deeply historically, theologically and editorially rooted, and that it therefore continues to play a key role as the latter half of the dual title "Old" and "New Testament." The following explanations for the collective title are explored: (I) it is a neutral label without any particular meaning – the New Testament just happens to be called "the New Testament"; (II) it is the traditional and, reception-historically, most popular designation; (III) it reflects the two-covenant theology prevalent at the time of its adoption; (IV) as an intrascriptural link to "new covenant" language, influential Christian editors introduced the title into the biblical manuscript tradition to provide an overall designation for the specifically Christian portion of the Scriptures; and (V) as part of the canon formation, it helped presenting the Christian Bible as a book in two parts, with each part relating to the Christ event in its own unique way. Building on and critiquing previous scholarly contributions, the chapter elaborates on these explanations, suggesting the relevance of all five explanations (but especially II–V) for a comprehensive understanding of the title.

Keywords: καινὴ διαθήκη, *Novum testamentum*, Two-covenant theology, Jer 31:31–34, Book title, Second century, Scripture, Canon, Biblical theology

1 Introduction

Why is the New Testament called "the New Testament"? In the present chapter, five different, yet partly complementary answers – or features of the New Testament title – are presented. I. The New Testament just happens to be called "New Testament" – that is, it is a neutral label which is used without any par-

---

Tomas Bokedal, NLA University College, Norway; University of Aberdeen, UK;
tomas.bokedal@nla.no

ticular meaning (neutral label); II. the title is employed because it happens to be the traditional title, namely the title which was the most popular and commonly used overall designation for the main collections of "apostolic" writings in the early church (traditional label); III. a third reason for the use of this peculiar, and perhaps even unexpected, title for the specifically Christian Scriptures is theologically grounded and relates to the understanding of the notions of covenant and two-covenant theology in the first- to early-third-century faith communities, when the labels καινὴ διαθήκη and *novum testamentum* for the new Scriptures were coined (theological label); IV. a fourth rationale for the increasingly popular designation was its likely introduction as overall title into the New Testament text collection by influential second-century Christian editors – functioning as an intra-scriptural link to "new covenant" language (editorial label); and V. a further potentially significant reason for the enduring preference for the title was its particular function in the canon formation process, facilitating a form of balance between the two main Christian text corpora regarding their respective relation to the Christ event (canonical label). The title appears to have been introduced into, and/or associated with, the manuscript tradition by editors of the collection of New Testament writings, and by others, from the late second century on. The scholarly contribution of the chapter lies in the critical evaluation of previous scholarship and in the comprehensive approach to the topic, elaborating on the five listed features (I–V). I shall elaborate on these in the following: Features I–II in sections 3 and 4; and Features III–V in sections 2, 4 and 5. First, however, a review of previous research on the preferred designation καινὴ διαθήκη introduces the discussion on the reasons behind the title (section 2). Some concluding remarks round off the chapter (section 6).

2 A Brief History of Research

Approaching the question as to why the New Testament writings received the collective Greek and Latin title καινὴ διαθήκη/*novum testamentum* from the late second or early third century onwards, I shall first review some previous scholarly suggestions. As Kinzig points out in his important 1994 article on the topic, most scholars on the canon spend very little time on the issue and notice more or less only the obvious, namely that a transition in meaning seems to have taken place as διαθήκη/*testamentum* was ascribed as book title to the scriptural corpus. However, these scholars do not "attempt an explanation of how exactly this came about."¹ Only a handful of attempts have been achieved to that effect. First that of Theodor Zahn more than a century ago, second that of W. C. van Unnik in 1961, and third that of Hans von Campenhausen in 1968. A fourth major attempt to explain the title was undertaken by Wolfram Kinzig in 1994. Before exploring καινὴ διαθήκη further in dialogue with a wider range of scholarship (2.5 and 5 below), we shall first briefly review these four scholars' respective suggestions (2.1–4).²

2.1 Zahn: A Popular Misunderstanding of the Theological Term διαθήκη

In 1888, when Theodor Zahn published the first volume of his monumental history of the New Testament canon,³ he included a section on the various designations of the Christian Scriptures used by the early church, such as "the Prophets and Apostles," and "the Law, the Prophets, the Gospels and the Apostles." As Kinzig points out, as Zahn analysed these labels he also noticed that the two titles "Old" and "New Testament" had prevailed. In Zahn's view, however, these titles did not correspond to the original meaning of these scriptural terms. For

> in the Bible διαθήκη meant the covenant established by God, the order of the relationship between God and the community given by Him, and καινὴ διαθήκη a re-organization of this relationship by Christ which was reserved for the end of times, hence not the *document* of the revelation, but *revelation* itself.⁴

---

1 Wolfram Kinzig, "καινὴ διαθήκη: The Title of the New Testament in the Second and Third Centuries," *JTS* 45.2 (1994), 519. Similarly, W. C. van Unnik, "Ἡ καινὴ διαθήκη – a Problem in the early History of the Canon," in *Sparsa Collecta: The Collected Essays of W. C. van Unnik*, vol. 2 (Leiden: Brill, 1980): 159: "Little attention [...] is given to [...] [the] question, why these books were assembled under the title of a διαθήκη."
2 Other, monograph-length, studies that discuss the notion of διαθήκη include Ernst Kutsch, *Neues Testament – Neuer Bund? Eine Fehlübersetzung wird korrigiert* (Neukirchen-Vluyn: Neukirchener Verlag, 1978); and Petrus J. Gräbe, *New Covenant, New Community: Significance of Biblical and Patristic Covenant Theology for Contemporary Understanding* (Bletchley, Milton Keynes, UK: Paternoster, 2006).
3 Theodor Zahn, *Geschichte des Neutestamentlichen Kanons*, vol. 1 (Erlangen: Verlag von Andreas Deichert, 1888).
4 Zahn, *Geschichte des neutestamentlichen Kanons*, 103 (trans. Kinzig, "καινὴ διαθήκη," 520): "Bezeichnete doch διαθήκη in der Bibel den von Gott gestifteten Bund, die von Gott der Gemeinde gegebene Ordnung ihres Verhältnisses zu ihm, und καινὴ διαθήκη eine der Endzeit

Thus, for Zahn the titles "Old" and "New Testament" as labels for the bipartite Christian Bible "are ultimately a popular misunderstanding of the theological term, a misunderstanding which 'sensitive' theologians such as Origen and Augustine still objected to."[5]

To some degree Zahn may be right in his estimation, but on two key points in his analysis he needs amendment. First, concerning his estimation of a misunderstanding of the titular use of the term διαθήκη, such misinterpreting may arguably not have taken place, if "sensible" editors of the Christian Scriptures were *de facto* responsible for the inauguration of the new term as book title. Secondly, with regard to Zahn's conclusion that διαθήκη could not denote a written document, this seems to be a misjudgement. Paul, for example, uses διαθήκη to designate a "last will and testament" (cf. Gal 3:15, 17;[6] Heb 9:16f.) and this meaning of the term was used as a standard meaning of the word both before and after Paul, including as well in Philo and several early church writers.[7] More generally, it can be noted that already in the Old Testament, διαθήκη is used in the LXX rendering of 2 Chronicles 25:4 for, or in close association with, the Hebrew word בָּתוּב, *katuv*, "what is written" (κατὰ τὴν διαθήκην τοῦ νόμου κυρίου, καθὼς γέγραπται, 2 Chron 25:4 LXX).[8] And in 2 Cor 3:14 Paul appears to refer to the Torah by the label "Old Testament" as something written, when he discusses the veil covering the face of his fellow Jews "at the reading of the Old Covenant/Testament" (ἐπὶ τῇ ἀναγνώσει τῆς παλαιᾶς διαθήκης; 2 Cor 3:14).[9] Quoting H. Windisch, Hans von Campenhausen stresses that in 2 Cor 2:14 παλαιὰ διαθήκη is "undoubtedly thought of as a written document."[10]

---

vorbehaltene, durch Christus gestiftete Neuordnung dieses Verhältnisses, also nicht Offenbarungsurkunde, sondern Offenbarung."

5 Kinzig, "καινὴ διαθήκη," 521.

6 See Richard B. Hays, "The Letter to the Galatians: Introduction, Commentary, and Reflections," in *The New Interpreter's Bible Commentary*, vol. IX (Nashville: Abingdon Press, 2002, 2015), 1092–93; and Kinzig, "καινὴ διαθήκη," 521.

7 See further Levi S. Baker, *New Covenant Documents for a New Covenant Community: Covenant as an Impetus for New Scripture in the First Century* (PhD diss., Southeastern Baptist Theological Seminary, Wake Forest, NC, 2021), 154, 155n.156, 265n.19, and 287n.66.

8 TDNT, vol. 2, 106. The Greek words γράφω and διαθήκη occur in the LXX Rahlfs in the same verse on twelve occasions, namely in Exod 34:27, 28; Deut 4:13; 29:19, 20; 31:9; 2 Kings 23:3, 21; 2 Chron 25:4; 34:31; Jer 38:33, and Dan 9:13 (in these twelve verses διαθήκη appears fifteen times and γράφω 12 times, with the sum of the occurrences of the two words being 27 [3 x 3 x 3], a potential 'alphabetical fullness' numeral). For similar arithmetical observations, see footnotes 35, 49, 55 and 65 below.

9 Zahn (*Geschichte des Neutestamentlichen Kanons*, 103), too, appears to note this in Paul: "Allerdings hatte schon Paulus den Namen auf die geschriebene Urkunde übertragen, wenn er

In addition to these examples, the label διαθήκη could also be used for a range of Jewish-Christian writings, such as the *Testaments of the Twelve Patriarchs* (which may even make up a specific genre) as well as for pagan writings bearing the title "Last Will and Testament."[11]

Again, and on a related note, to the extent that the Christian adoption of the title καινὴ διαθήκη can be ascribed to the Christian scribal culture, perhaps the inauguration of the designation is less a popular misunderstanding, as Zahn claimed, but instead communicates an editorial/scribal aspect of the scriptural canon formation process, inspired not least by Paul's application of the titles in 2 Cor 3:4–18 and the appropriation of the new covenant notion in Hebrews (see further 5.2 and 5.5 below).

2.2 Van Unnik: Conveying a Second-Century Theology of the Covenants

In 1961, the New Testament scholar Wilhelm C. van Unnik offered an alternative explanation to that of Zahn, accounting for the new title.[12] In his view "the title under discussion prevailed because it was a consequence of the theology of the covenants as developed towards the end of the second century."[13] In his article, van Unnik helpfully points, first of all, to the significance of the notion of διαθήκη Χριστοῦ, "the covenant of Christ," around 175 CE, when asking for "the

---

von einem Lesen des alten Bundes sprach. Aber er verstand darunter doch nur die Thora, nicht das AT"; cf. Baker, *New Covenant Documents for a New Covenant Community*, 228: "In 2 Cor 3:14, 15 Paul reveals that he, like other 2T Jews, receives the Torah as a covenant document, because 'reading the old covenant' is equivalent to 'reading Moses.'" In connection with 2 Cor 3:14, Baker here critiques Harry Y. Gamble's (*The New Testament Canon: Its Making and Meaning* (Philadelphia: Fortress, 1985), 19–20) and James Barr's (*Holy Scripture: Canon, Authority, Criticism* (Philadelphia: Westminster Press, 1983), 12) interpretations of the Spirit/letter dichotomy in 2 Cor 3:6–8.

10 Hans von Campenhausen, *The Formation of the Christian Bible* (Philadelphia: Fortress Press, 1972), 264n.283; German original: *Die Entstehung der christlichen Bibel* (Tübingen: Mohr Siebeck, 1968, 2003).

11 Kinzig, "καινὴ διαθήκη," 523–24.

12 Van Unnik, "Ἡ καινὴ διαθήκη."

13 Kinzig, "καινὴ διαθήκη," 521. A similar treatment of the notion καινὴ διαθήκη as that of van Unnik, focussing on the second- and early-third-century church setting is found in Everett Ferguson, "The Covenant Idea in the Second Century," in idem, *The Early Church at Work and Worship*, vol. 1: *Ministry, Ordination, Covenant, and Canon* (Cambridge: James Clarke & Co, 2013), 173–200.

meaning of καινὴ διαθήκη in its application to that collection of early Christian books which we usually call 'the New Testament' and which under that name influenced the church and the world in an absolutely unique manner" (see further 5.4 below).[14] He then critiques Adolf von Harnack's view of the new title when understood apart from the Old Testament and to whom the "relation with the O.T. was just an afterthought."[15] Instead, van Unnik stresses that "the idea of a 'new covenant' cannot be separated from the O.T., because it originated there and is completely unintelligible without the O.T."[16] Significantly, he then poses an interesting question that already von Harnack had raised: "Was it true that this idea of a *BUND* [Covenant] itself suggested a document?"[17]

2.3 Von Campenhausen: A Theologically Significant Dual Concept

Towards the end of the decade, in 1968, the German church historian Hans von Campenhausen again treated the question of the New Testament book title afresh in his renowned monograph *The Formation of the Christian Bible* (German original: *Die Entstehung der christlichen Bibel*). He argued that the labels "Old" and "New Testament" "prevailed over all others because of the very nature of the Bible as a book in two parts: 'They denoted a comprehensive and theologically very significant dual concept, in which nevertheless each group of Scriptures had its clearly defined place.'"[18] In addition to this account for the emergence of the designations, he also adopted van Unnik's previous conclusion that the book title "New Testament" was a result of the covenantal theology

---

14 Van Unnik, "Ἡ καινὴ διαθήκη," 158.
15 Van Unnik, "Ἡ καινὴ διαθήκη," 161.
16 Van Unnik, "Ἡ καινὴ διαθήκη," 161.
17 Cf. Adolf von Harnack, *The Origin of the New Testament and the Most Important Consequences of the New Creation*, trans. J. R. Wilkinson (London: Williams & Norgate, 1925), 33–34: "It is [...] certain that a compilation of writings is always in danger of disintegration if it is not in some way limited, in *idea* at least. A hundred years ago Novalis advanced the very reasonable question: 'Who declared the Bible (the Canon of the New Testament) to be closed?' Our answer to the question is: The idea, firmly held, that the new books were fundamental documents *of the Second Covenant* which God had established through Jesus Christ, was the intellectual originator of the 'closed' *instrumentum novum*."
18 Cited from Kinzig, "καινὴ διαθήκη," 521; von Campenhausen, *The Formation of the Christian Bible*, 263.

developing around this time.[19] For Campenhausen, the precise name for the collection was "the last feature still wanting for the accomplishment of the bipartite Christian Bible."[20] For von Campenhausen, too, it seems, the question of supplying a title to the new collection of Christian Scripture was associated with some kind of anticipation, if not inevitability.[21]

2.4 Kinzig: The Church's Adoption of a Marcionite Title

Wolfram Kinzig, whose presentation of previous scholarship has been a guide for the aforementioned history of research, offered his own particular interpretation in 1994, in an article entitled "καινὴ διαθήκη: The Title of the New Testament in the Second and Third Centuries." In line with some previous influential German scholarship, such as von Harnack's and von Harnack's student Hans von Campenhausen's, Kinzig takes the view that Marcion has been a major source of influence for the formation of the Christian New Testament.[22] The question he rises with renewed emphasis in his 1994 article is whether Marcion may have labelled his collection of writings "New Testament," that is a Marcionite "New Testament" consisting of a modified Gospel of Luke and ten Pauline letters. Most scholars in the past, such as von Harnack, von Campenhausen and Bruce Metzger, were sceptical as to this possibility.[23] Kinzig, however, argues that Marcion's emphasis on "newness" in various respects prepared the way also for the new title for his scriptures.[24] Quoting von Harnack, Kinzig writes

---

19 Cf. von Campenhausen, *The Formation of the Christian Bible*, 268; Kinzig, "καινὴ διαθήκη," 521.
20 Von Campenhausen, *The Formation of the Christian Bible*, 262.
21 On this theme, see further Baker, *New Covenant Documents for a New Covenant Coummunity*.
22 Kinzig, "καινὴ διαθήκη," 535.
23 See Kinzig, "καινὴ διαθήκη," 536, for additional scholars who adhere to this traditional view, with which Kinzig disagrees.
24 On the theme of newness in Marcion, Kinzig comments ("καινὴ διαθήκη," 537): "According to Marcion, the unknown God is a God of mercy who is diametrically opposed to the God of justice of the Old Testament. In Marcion's view this can especially be seen from the 'new doctrines of the new kind of mercy of the new Christ, in which Christ himself distinguished that which is 'new' from that which is 'old'. [...] Christ proclaimed a 'new kingdom' (cf. Luke 10:9). His proclamation itself was 'a new manner of speaking', since it consisted in parables and answering of questions. This proclamation, however, was also materially new, because it announced the forgiveness of sins and the love of one's enemy, which were both, in Marcion's view, unknown to the Old Testament."

that in the *Antitheses* composed by Marcion "no catchword appears to have occurred more frequently than 'new.'"[25] In Kinzig's opinion

> [t]he Greater Church did not take over Marcion's canon. It did, however, adopt its name Καινὴ διαθήκη. Owing to Marcion's influence, the term had probably become popular in the Church at large, before the 'orthodox' canon took its final shape. The *Église savante* initially tried to fend off this new designation. This explains why it is found neither in Justin nor in Irenaeus. At a later stage it was adopted by theologians such as Tertullian, Origen and Augustine only with considerable reluctance – precisely because they were unaware of its origin. The theology behind this designation, however, was taken over already by Justin, because it suited him well in his own controversy with Judaism.[26]

Though Kinzig is here making some good points, backing up his argument in his more detailed analysis of especially Tertullian's response to Marcion, I still find his position unconvincing, and I agree with previous scholarship that chose not to go down this route, noting the significance of the (two-)covenant notion already in Paul, Hebrews and *Barnabas* (see 5 below). However, for the sake of the argument of the present chapter, it may not matter much who actually introduced the label as book title. Moreover, I do not agree with Kinzig's hypothesis that Marcion further "downgraded" the Jewish Bible by calling it the "Old Testament."[27] What matters more is the way the church went about in employing a dual title for its Scriptures, "Old" and "New Testament" – and Marcion was most likely not the originator of both these titles anyway (contra Kinzig); and in terms of their mutual relation as labels indicating both discontinuity and continuity, other theologians than Marcion, such as Paul (2 Cor 3:6, 14), the author of Hebrews (Heb 8:7, 13; 10:9), anonymous Christian Scripture

---

25 Adolf von Harnack, *Marcion: das Evangelium vom fremden Gott; eine Monographie zur Geschichte der Grundlegung der katholischen Kirche*. Neue Studien zu Marcion (Darmstadt: Wissenschaftliche Buchgesellschaft, 2nd ed, 1924), 87; Kinzig, *Novitas Christiana: Die Idee des Fortschritts in der Alten Kirche bis Eusebius* (Göttingen: Vandenhoeck & Ruprecht, 1994), 126.
26 Kinzig, "καινὴ διαθήκη," 543; idem, *Novitas Christiana*, 128: "Justin ist der erste nachneutestamentliche Autor, der in seinem 'Dialog mit Tryphon' (geschrieben 155–160) eine Zwei-Testamente-Theologie entwickelt." Cf. Hermann von Lips, *Der neutestamentliche Kanon: Seine Geschichte und Bedeutung* (Zürich: Theologischer Verlag Zürich, 2004), 186.
27 Kinzig, "καινὴ διαθήκη," 544. What is old was often considered more valuable, or authoritative, than that which is new in the ancient world; cf. in this regard, e.g., Josephus, *Antiquitates iudaica*. See also Tomas Bokedal, *The Formation and Significance of the Christian Biblical Canon: A Study in Text, Ritual and Interpretation* (London: Bloomsbury T&T Clark, 2014), 175–92.

editors, Justin, Irenaeus and Clement, appear to be among the main players, with the new covenant promise in Jer 31:31–34 at the core of the discussion.[28]

2.5 Previous Scholarship and a Way Forward

From this critical overview of previous scholarship on the new title, the following points are worth underscoring as I continue the discussion:

(1) Zahn was on a good track when contextualising παλαιὰ/καινὴ διαθήκη as book titles, used in parallel with other comparable labels, such as "the Law, the Prophets, the Gospels and the Apostles." Within this textual setting the notions of "Law," "Gospel" and "Covenant" all seem to have an oral as well as a written component associated with the respective concepts. For the purposes of this chapter, I notice in particular that "Law," "Gospel," and "New Covenant/Testament" were all used as scriptural book titles around 200 CE. On a critical note, I pointed out above that Zahn wrongly presumed that a διαθήκη could not refer to a document and that his estimation that the new book title represented a misunderstanding of the concept was questionable. Rather, the second-century collective title καινὴ διαθήκη may very well have been introduced into the manuscript tradition by theologically well-informed editors responsible for the production of Christian Scripture (cf. Feature IV above: the title as editorial label).

(2) The covenantal theology, and in particular the two-covenant theology, that became popular in the second century is most certainly related to the appropriation of the new major book titles, as pointed out by van Unnik, von Campenhausen and Kinzig. I shall argue below that a two-testament theology can be linked to the New Testament writings themselves, and, as van Unnik stressed, that the expression καινὴ διαθήκη should be closely interconnected to Jer 31:31–34 (cf. Feature III above: the title as theological label).

(3) An additional point, emphasized in particular by von Campenhausen, is also most certainly in agreement with the historical development, namely that the titles "Old Testament" and "New Testament" prevailed over all others because of the very nature of the Bible as a book in two parts: "They de-

---

[28] The "Old Testament" is strongly focused in the polemics of Justin, Irenaeus and Tertullian against Marcion and his negative treatment of everything Jewish, including the Scriptures. In John Barton's phrasing (*The Spirit and the Letter* (London, SPCK, 1997), 58): "Marcion emphatically did not cause the Church to have a New Testament; he did cause it to have an 'Old Testament,' that is, to correlate the old Scriptures with its (already more or less formed) collection of Christian books."

noted a comprehensive and theologically very significant dual concept, in which nevertheless each group of Scriptures had its clearly defined place"[29] (cf. Feature V above: the title as canonical label).

To anticipate what will be discussed in section 5 below, we can here note as well an early pre-critical Christian voice that appears to implicitly incorporate all three of the above remarks (1–3), namely Clement of Alexandria's (ca. 150–215 CE) phrasing in *Stromateis*, pertaining to the Ecclesiastical Canon, or Rule of Faith.[30] Clement famously writes: "The Canon of the Church is the agreement and unity of the Law and the Prophets with the [New] Testament delivered at the coming of the Lord."[31] "The [New] Testament (διαθήκη) delivered at the coming of the Lord" may be regarded as both oral and written, but since it is here placed in close relationship with the Law and the Prophets – which are written documents – the written character of the Testament seems to be underscored. Thus, Clement's phrasing arguably relates primarily 1) to written documents, 2) to a two-covenant theology, with implicit reference to Jer 31:31–34 (cf. *Strom*. VI, 5.41.5–6), and 3) to the emergent textuality of the Christian Bible as a book in two parts (Law and Prophets, on the one hand, and the [New] Testament delivered at the coming of the Lord, on the other), which should be inner-biblically

---

[29] Von Campenhausen, *The Formation of the Christian Bible*, 521.

[30] As for the notions Ecclesiastical Canon and Rule of Faith in Clement of Alexandria, see Tomas Bokedal, "The Rule of Faith: Tracing Its Origins," *Journal of Theological Interpretation* 7.1 (2013): 233–55.

[31] Clem. *Strom*. VI, 15.125.3: κανὼν δὲ ἐκκλησιαστικός ἡ συνῳδία καὶ συμφωνία νόμου τε καὶ προφητῶν τῇ κατὰ τὴν τοῦ κυρίου παρουσίαν παραδιδομένῃ διαθήκῃ. Heinz Ohme, *Kanon Ekklesiastikos: Die Bedeutung des altkirchlichen Kanonbegriffs* (Berlin: de Gruyter, 1998): 143, comments on this passage in Clement: "Die 'Richtschnur der Wahrheit' wird nun auch explizit angesprochen als das entscheidende *Auslegungsprinzip* und der *hermeneutische Schlüssel* zur Erkenntnis der einen Wahrheit in den Schriften des Alten und Neuen Testamentes. Diese Regel der Schriftauslegung stamme von Christus selbst, werde in der Kirche bewahrt und ist deshalb auch 'kirchlicher Kanon': 'Die kirchliche Richtschnur besteht aber im Zusammenklang und in der Übereinstimmung des Gesetzes und der Propheten mit dem bei der Anwesenheit des Herrn geschlossenen Neuen Bund' (VI 15.125.3)". Cf. also ibid., 131. Von Campenhausen, *The Formation of the Christian Bible*, 266, further remarks: "Clement who has read Irenaeus, speaks very frequently of the two covenants, the old and the new, and of the higher unity which they constitute together. This is still along conventional lines. In addition, however, there are passages in which it would be arbitrary not to refer this same word *diatheke* directly to the old and new Scriptures. Thus, on one occasion he says that we have to believe in the Son of God even 'without probable and compelling proofs', since this is 'proclaimed and described by the old and by the new *diatheke*.'"

balanced with one another in agreement with the scripturally aligned Ecclesiastical Canon, or Rule of Faith.³²

With the above research overview on the New Testament title as my point of departure, I shall now discuss the five features of the title mentioned in the Introduction (I. neutral, II. traditional, III. theological, IV. editorial, and V. canonical label) in an attempt to answer the question, Why is the New Testament called "New Testament"?

3 A Title without Significant Meaning (in the Latin West)?

The English title "New Testament" is a translation of the Latin *novum testamentum* in the Latin Vulgate,³³ which in its turn is a translation of the Greek ἡ καινὴ διαθήκη. On the title page of the Elzevir Greek New Testament of 1624 we thus find both the Greek and the Latin titles: ἡ καινὴ διαθήκη and *novum testamentum*. Other previous, and later, editions of the New Testament similarly contain what from early on became the standard title for the "apostolic" collection of Scriptures, that is ἡ καινὴ διαθήκη, *novum testamentum*, or the more recent, English, rendering, "the New Testament." As far as I am aware, the first time we find the Greek title visibly recorded in an extant manuscript, heading the list of New Testament books, is in the Table of Contents of the fifth- or sixth-century Codex Alexandrinus.³⁴ Recent eclectic editions of the Greek New Testament, like NA28 (German Bible Society, 2012) and the Tyndale House Greek New Testament (Crossway and Cambridge University Press, 2017; henceforth THGNT), however, choose to omit the Greek title.³⁵

---

32 Ohme (*Kanon Ekklesiastikos*, 144) quotes Bengt Hägglund in this connection (Hägglund, "Die Bedeutung der 'regula fidei' als Grundlage theologischer Aussagen," *Studia Theologica* 12 (1958) 1–44: 34), who describes the *regula fidei* as follows: "'ein Masstab der Auslegung', der 'den Hauptinhalt der Schrift, von welchem her alles andere beurteilt und gedeutet werden muss', bezeichnet." See also Bokedal, "The Rule of Faith."
33 Prior to Jerome, who was responsible for the Latin Vulgate, Tertullian and others had made use of the Latin rendering *novum testamentum* of the Greek title ἡ καινὴ διαθήκη for the new collection of Christian Scriptures.
34 See the reproduction at http://www.csntm.org/manuscript/View/GA_02, image GA_02_1881_ VOL1_EXTRA_0007a.jpg (accessed on 01.06.2020).
35 NA28 and THGNT have retained other book titles associated with the 27 books of the New Testament, introduced at various points in the canonical process. As a result of the omission of

As we face the problem of translation, the first suggestion made above – about the title's lack of real significance (cf. Feature I above: the title as neutral label) – appears to be hidden between the lines, namely in the process of translating the title from the Greek to the Latin. Van Unnik helpfully comments in this regard:

> It cannot be denied that the terms "Old" and "New" Testament respectively or the pre-Christian and Christian part of the Bible have become neutralized. The word "testament" in this connection has become a hollow shell to most Christians which is used without any meaning. This happened for western christendom, when *testamentum* was adopted as a translation for διαθήκη.[36]

---

the book title ἡ καινὴ διαθήκη for the full corpus of NT writings, i) the expression καινὴ διαθήκη (with that Greek word order; see further 5.5 below) appears on three occasions in the NT (Luke 22:20; 1 Cor 11:15 and 2 Cor 3:6), rather than on four occasions (which potentially may signify universality; cf. Irenaeus' emphasis on the numeral four in relation to the fourfold Gospel; Iren. *Haer.* III, 11.8); ii) the word διαθήκη occurs only 33 times in the NT, instead of 34 times [2 x 17] (cf. the potential significance of 17 as associated with an archaic form of the divine Name – the numerical value of AHWH being 17 – and as a triangular base (17) in the triangular numeral 153 (where 153 is the sum of the first 17 natural numbers); see Richard Bauckham, "The 153 Fish and the Unity of the Fourth Gospel," *Neotestamentica* 36 (2002): 82. In this connection we may also note that διαθήκη appears 17 times in Hebrews. Regarding the two titular terms in καινὴ διαθήκη, we may further notice the following figures in the full NT text of Textus Receptus and the family 35 textform (Majority Text): In the seven NT verses in which the two words occur together (Matt 26:28; Mark 14:24; Luke 22:20; 1 Cor 11:25; 2 Cor 3:6; Heb 8:8; and Heb 9:15) the total occurrences of the two terms (καινός and διαθήκη) amount to 15. If to these seven passages an eighth instance is added (potentially indicating new creation; cf. 1 Pet 3:20), namely the collective title καινὴ διαθήκη for the NT Scriptures as a whole, the total number of occurrences of the two terms amounts to 17 (which may have been invested with numerical significance by the Byzantine editors of the New Testament (the Majority Text/Textfamily 35/Textus Receptus)). For similar arithmetical observations, see further footnotes 8, 49, 55 and 65.

36 Van Unnik, "Ἡ καινὴ διαθήκη," 158. With reference to the monographs of Johannes Behm, *Der Begriff Διαθήκη im Neuen Testament* (Leipzig, 1912) and Ernst Lohmeyer, *Diatheke. Ein Beitrag zur Erklärung des neutestamentlichen Begriffs* (Leipzig, 1913), van Unnik further comments on the title's neutralized function (continuing the quote in the main text): "This happened for western christendom, when *Testamentum* was adopted as a translation for διαθήκη. In itself this was quite correct from the point of view of ordinary Greek usage, but it missed the particular connotations of biblical Greek." Hans von Campenhausen here follows van Unnik; see von Campenhausen, *The Formation of the Christian Bible*, 267: "the transition into Latin made it virtually impossible to prevent what was now a technical term from becoming rigid and lifeless. The normal rendering for the *diatheke* of the Greek bible was *testamentum*, a term which with its hard, juristic overtones could really comprehend only the idea of a 'testamentary' deposition or instrument, but not the whole breadth and elasticity of the Greek concept."

As a consequence, the rich biblical and theological meaning of the Greek notion of διαθήκη, "covenant,"[37] including its use as book title, was largely lost – despite the fact that its NT (but not its OT) usage normally translated into Latin as *testamentum*.[38] Instead of "the New Covenant," as the English rendering of the Greek expression, the novel label for the Christian part of the Bible, which was dependent on the Latin phrasing, thus became "the New Testament."

4 A Traditional Title Handed Down in the Church

We encounter the expression ἡ καινὴ διαθήκη, "the New Testament"/"the New Covenant," as a Greek book title for the first time around the year 200 CE. The earliest explicit connection between ἡ καινὴ διαθήκη and Christian literature is testified by an anonymous writer refuting Montanism in 192–193 CE (Eusebius *Hist. Eccl.* V, 16.3).[39] As a title for the collection of the new apostolic writings, the Greek ἡ καινὴ διαθήκη is then used a handful of times by Clement of Alexandria (ca. 150–215 CE) in Egypt (*Strom.* I, 5.28.2), and the Latin rendering *novum testamentum* by Tertullian of Carthage (ca. 160–220 CE) in North Africa (*Marc.* IV, 1).

Tertullian uses the Latin terms *testamentum* and *instrumentum* to denote the main sections of the bipartite Christian Bible in his book *Against Marcion* between 207 and 210/11 CE. As a designation for the new specifically Christian writings, being placed on a par with the Jewish Scriptures, the title may have been used prior to Clement and Tertullian by Melito of Sardis (d. ca. 180 CE) as early as 170 CE, and — as suggested by J. N. D. Kelly and others — also by Irenaeus of Lyons (ca. 125–202 CE; *Haer.* IV, 9.1). However, whether Irenaeus and Melito used the term "New Testament"/"New Covenant" as book title in the last two or three decades of the second century is regarded as uncertain by most scholars (see further 5.5 below).[40]

We are on more firm ground when trying to understand Melito's use of the expression παλαιὰ διαθήκη, "Old Testament" or "Covenant." According to Eusebius (*Hist. Eccl.* IV, 26; V, 16.3), Melito may be employing the designation ἡ παλαιὰ διαθήκη, "the Old Testament" or "the Old Covenant," as a title for the

---

37 Basic lexical meaning of διαθήκη: covenant; last will and testament; contract.
38 Cf. Gräbe, *New Covenant, New Community*, 13.
39 Cf. von Campenhausen, *The Formation of the Christian Bible*, 265 and 265n.290; 230–31.
40 See J. N. D. Kelly, *Early Christian Doctrines* (Harper Collins, 1978, rev. ed.), 56, who refers to Iren. *Haer.* IV, 9.1; and David Trobisch, *The First Edition of the New Testament* (Oxford: Oxford University Press, 2000), 44, 131n.168.

collection of the Jewish Scriptures, i.e., the Christian "Old Testament." However, in the case of Melito, this is less certain since his use of the Greek phrasing τὰ τῆς παλαιᾶς διαθήκης βιβλία is somewhat ambivalent and can be translated both as "the books of the Old Testament/Covenant," that is the books with that common title, or as "the books of the old covenant," referring to the theological concept "old covenant," that is the books that *contain* the old covenant.[41] In my view, however, the first rendering is more likely, due to the literary context in the *Extracts* of Melito, as they discuss the listing of books to be included in the Jewish canon. Furthermore, since the same use of the genitive τῆς παλαιᾶς διαθήκης is found also in Origen, and *there* clearly functions as a title for the first part of the bipartite scriptural corpus (*Hom. Ier.* 1.7, *bis*; 4.6, τὰ βιβλία τῆς διαθήκης), this gives some further support to the traditional understanding of Melito's employment of τῆς παλαιᾶς διαθήκης, as referring to the book title "the Old Testament" (or "the Old Covenant"). In this connection, we may notice, as well, a comment made by J. Ligon Duncan III:

> The question is not whether Melito intends τῆς παλαιᾶς διαθήκης to indicate 'a collection of OT books' in the sense in which we use the term OT. [Wolfram] Kinzig makes much of the fact that Melito uses the genitive and that therefore the meaning of the phrase is clouded [...]. But this misses the point. Whether Melito means τῆς παλαιᾶς διαθήκης itself to refer to a list of books, or as a theological concept (the time or administration in which the said books were written), it is beyond question that he is employing it here as at least part of a designation of a list of books! [Theodor] Zahn, [Adolf von] Harnack and even Kinzig seem to miss this obvious point in their detailed musings on διαθήκη as a title for the Scriptures.[42]

Duncan is right here in his critique of previous scholarship by making this more nuanced point, which also takes the textual context into proper account. Duncan's remark is moreover helpful for the broader argument of the present chapter as it seeks to bridge – historically and theologically – previous first- and second-century associations with the notion of διαθήκη with the term διαθήκη once it began to be employed more generally as the major title for the collection of "apostolic" Scriptures before or around the turn of the century (200 CE; cf. Features II–V above: the title as traditional, theological, editorial and canonical label).

However, even if some minor uncertainties still surround the earliest appearance of the titles "Old" and "New Testament/Covenant" as dual title for the scriptural canon in the final decades of the second century, there is little reason

---

41 Cf. Kinzig, "καινὴ διαθήκη," 528.
42 J. Ligon Duncan III, "The Covenant Idea in Melito of Sardis: An Introduction and Survey," *Presbyterion* 28.1 (2002): 32–33.

for doubt as to their popularity and success from the early third century onwards as the more common and increasingly prevalent titles for the Christian Bible. Early-third-century theologians and exegetes, such as Origen, repeatedly make use of the designation (ἡ καινὴ) διαθήκη as title for the New Testament. In Origen's *Commentaries on John* and *on Matthew*, as well as in his *Homilies on Jeremiah*, διαθήκη is definitely used as book title some 17 times, and possibly on as many as 44 occurrences.[43] Nevertheless, for some reason Origen still expresses some hesitation with regard to this novel usage of the term διαθήκη. Accordingly, in a few cases he talks of "the so-called 'Old Testament'" and "the so-called 'New Testament' (τὴν λεγομένην παλαιὰν/καινὴν διαθήκην)."[44] In the works of some other church teachers, the new book designations do not occur at all, as is the case in the *Testimonies* by Cyprian of Carthage (200–258 CE), Origen's contemporary in the West.[45]

Nonetheless, the designations become increasingly popular, to which also Origen testifies. His mention of "the so-called Old and New Testament/Covenant" demonstrates that they are *so* called by many others, presumably including key editors of the Christian Scriptures. On a reception-historical note, already Tertullian around 210 CE tells us that the new titles are the most commonly used labels for the two-part Christian Bible. To this effect, Augustine, too, a little later, thus can say in his *Revisions* that "[i]n calling (these books) 'Old Testament' I have followed the usage with which the Church speaks. The Apostle, however, seems to call 'Old Testament' only what was given on Mount Sinai" (*Retr.* 2,4,3).[46] By observing the narrower use of "old covenant/testament" in Paul's Galatian and Corinthian correspondence (Gal 4:24, "these women are two covenants"; 2 Cor 3:14, "Indeed, to this day, when they hear the reading of the old covenant (ἐπὶ τῇ ἀναγνώσει τῆς παλαιᾶς διαθήκης), that same veil is still there"), Augustine, too – due to prior Pauline usage (not Marcionite usage; cf above) – appears to express some potential reservation with regard to the popular and common usage of the new Christian titles, thus repeating what Origen had already written before him. Likewise, Tertullian, prior to Origen and

---

43 Kinzig, "καινὴ διαθήκη," 531.
44 *Joa. Com.* V, 4; *De Orat.* 22; referred to by Zahn, *Geschichte des Neutestamentlichen Kanons*, 103; Kinzig, "καινὴ διαθήκη," 532.
45 Kinzig, "καινὴ διαθήκη," 533.
46 Kinzig, "καινὴ διαθήκη," 533–34, comments: "Augustine here appears to allude either to 2 Cor. 3: 14 or to Gal. 4: 24, where Hagar is identified with the covenant 'from Mount Sinai', or to a combination of both passages. We may conclude from his remark that, at the time of Augustine, Vetus Testamentum as a title for the books of the first part of the Christian Bible was common in the Church at large."

Augustine, refers to the label *novum testamentum* as the more common and popular title, whereas he himself apparently favoured also other designations such as *novum instrumentum* for the apostolic writings. However, in his case, the situation is somewhat different, of course, as compared to Origen, since in Tertullian we are also dealing with a translation of the term into Latin.[47]

The use of the dual title as the standard label for the Christian (Old and New Testament) Scriptures soon can be seen more frequently in the Christian literature. The third- and fourth-century writer Lactantius (240–325 CE), who was an advisor to Constantine I, provides a fine editorial-canonical summary when he says that "all Scripture is divided into two Testaments [...]. That which preceded the advent and passion of Christ – that is the law and the prophets – is called the Old; but those things which were written after His resurrection are named New Testament." (*Inst.* IV, 20.4; cf. Features III–V above: the title as theological, editorial and canonical label).[48] Pertaining to the attributes "old" and "new," this, of course, gives a particular Christological textual twist to our inquiry into the approved designation for the NT and OT collections.

Again, despite Tertullian's, Origen's and Augustine's possible reservation towards the titles (see further 5 and 6 below), they nevertheless make a concession to an increasingly established church, and emergent Christian scriptoria, tradition, which endorses the new titles. In the end, these writers, too, make frequent use of the novel labels "Old" and "New Testament/Covenant." As Augustine underlines: "In calling (these books) 'Old Testament' I have followed the usage with which the Church speaks" (*Retr.* II, 4.3).

This, again, gives voice to the second proposed feature above (Feature II: the title as traditional label) accounting for the query posed in the chapter heading, namely: Popular usage of the label is due to the fact that it already happens to be the increasingly established title handed down in the church, presumably endorsed also by the Christian scribal/scriptoria culture – i.e., the title had already become the most popular, commonly used and accepted designation for the collection of "apostolic" writings.

Having discussed the New Testament title as a neutral and a traditional label (Features I and II), in the next section, I shall elaborate on the three additional facets of the title mentioned in the Introduction: theological (III), editorial (IV), and canonical features (V). To better understand the potential significance of the New Testament title, I shall approach these three facets (Features III–V) by briefly exploring the Hebrew and Greek terms בְּרִית, *berith*, and διαθήκη (5.1),

---

47 Cf. Kutsch, *Neues Testament – Neuer Bund?*, 165.
48 ANCL; quoted from Kinzig, "καινὴ διαθήκη," 533.

the Pauline concept of covenant/testament (5.2), the New Testament notion of newness based on Jer 31:31–34 (5.3), second-century theologies of the covenant (5.4) and the title's editorial and canonical intra-scriptural links (5.5).

5 The Biblical Context of καινὴ διαθήκη and Early Christian Covenantal Theology

5.1 The Term διαθήκη

Before proceeding with the wider biblical and early Christian use of the notion of καινὴ διαθήκη, I shall dwell first on the basic meaning of the key term διαθήκη. What, more precisely, is meant by this word. Just as with the Latin *testamentum*, in Hellenistic Greek, διαθήκη signifies "testament" or "last will." This connotation of the word is seen twice already in the New Testament, in Gal 3:15 and Heb 9:16–17. When we turn to the Septuagint, διαθήκη is used as a translation of the Hebrew *berith*, בְּרִית,[49] which sometimes signifies a "treaty" or

---

[49] בְּרִית, "covenant," appears 22 times in Joshua, possibly indicating alphabetical fullness or completeness (for similar numerological figures, see Tomas Bokedal, "The Bible Canon and Its Significance: Textual Comprehensiveness, Function, Design and Delimitation," in *Canon Formation: Tracing the Role of Sub-Collections in the Biblical Canon*, edited by W. Edward Glenny and Darian R. Lockett (London: Bloomsbury T&T Clark, 2023): 7–32, where alphabetical multiples (22/27 and 24) and divine-Name related multiples (26, 17 and 15) are especially noted. Cf. the 22 consonants in the Hebrew alphabet (representing fullness)), 66 times [3 x 22] in the Former Prophets, 14 times in 1–2Sam (a potential numerological reference to the Davidic number 14; cf. note 65 below), 14 times in 1 Kings and 26 times in 1–2 Kings (a potential reference to the numerical value of the Tetragrammaton, which is 26), and 286 times [13 x 22 = 11 x 26] in the full Masoretic Text (a potential reference to alphabetical completeness and the divine Name). In LXX Göttingen διαθήκη occurs 85 times [5 x 17] in the Pentateuch, 26 times in Gen, 28 times [2 x 14] in Deut, and 15 times in the Twelve Prophets. In LXX Rahlfs διαθήκη occurs 26 times in Gen, 17 times in Exod, 28 times [2 x 14] in Deut, 17 times in 1–2 Sam, 24 times in 1–2 Kings, 15 times in 1 Chron, 48 times [2 x 24] in the Poetical Books (excluding Odes and Psalms of Solomon), 15 times in the Twelve Prophets, and 340 times [20 x 17] (excluding Odes and Psalms of Solomon)/345 times [23 x 15] (including Odes and Psalms of Solomon) in the full text of LXX Rahlfs. Διαθήκη <AND> κύριος (search in Accordance 13 on this form; textual scope: verse) demonstrates the following results (LXX Göttingen): Deut 52 times [2 x 26] and Pentateuch 88 times [4 x 22]. Corresponding results for LXX Rahlfs are: the full text of LXX Rahlfs 352 times [4 x 4 x 22], Deut 52 times [2 x 26], the Pentateuch 88 times [4 x 22], 1 Sam 14 times, 1–2 Sam 22 times, 1–2 Kings 45 times [3 x 15], 1 Chron 30 times [2 x 15], the Prophets 66 times [3 x 22]. For similar arithmetical observations, see footnotes 8, 35, 55 and 65.

"covenant," "a two-sided contract or agreement between partners of equal standing." Yet, as Reidar Hvalvik points out, the normal Greek word for such a treaty would, however, be συνθήκη rather than διαθήκη.[50] When the LXX translators selected διαθήκη, this was probably due to the fact that this word was also used in the general sense "regulation" or "decree." And this Greek LXX rendering comes close to the meaning of the Hebrew in most cases in the Old Testament.[51] As for the Hebrew term, in Kinzig's summary account, "בְּרִית does not originally signify a covenant of two equal contracting partners, but, rather, means a unilateral 'ordinance,' 'obligation' – as an obligation imposed by oneself or by somebody else."[52] As בְּרִית, "covenant; ordinance," denotes a one-sided obligation, it can also, for example, signify a promise. It is thus not surprising that διαθήκη can occur more or less as a synonym for "promise" and "oath," as exemplified in Luke 1:69–73, especially vv. 72–73: "He has raised up a mighty savior for us in the house of his servant David [...]. Thus he has shown the mercy promised to our ancestors, and has remembered his holy covenant promise (μνησθῆναι διαθήκης ἁγίας αὐτοῦ), the oath that he swore to our ances-

---

50 Reidar Hvalvik, *The Struggle for Scripture and Covenant: The Purpose of the Epistle of Barnabas and Jewish-Christian Competition in the Second Century*, WUNT 2/82 (Tübingen: Mohr Siebeck, 1996), 149.
51 So Kutsch, *Neues Testament – Neuer Bund?*, 58: "Wie wir gesehen haben, wird das hebräische Wort *bᵉrît* von der Septuaginta – bei nur zwei Ausnahmen (Gen 14,13; 1Kön 11,11) – mit διαθήκη wiedergegeben. Für die griechischen Übersetzer hat also ganz offensichtlich dieses Wort wie kein anderes seiner hebräischen Vorlage *bᵉrît* entsprochen. Dies erscheint überraschend angesichts des Sachverhaltes, daß in der Umwelt der Übersetzer διαθήκη im Sinn von 'letztwilliger Verfügung (die mit dem Tod des Testators in Kraft tritt)', 'Testament' verwendet wurde. Diesen Sinn hat das hebr. *bᵉrît* nie und nirgends gehabt, weder im Alten Testament noch in irgendeinem anderen hebräischen Text. Wie konnte da διαθήκη als Äquivalent für *bᵉrît* verwendet werden? Die Erklärung für diesen Vorgang ergibt sich aus der Beobachtung, daß in dem Begriff 'Testament', διαθήκη, zwei Momente vereinigt sind, nämlich das Moment der einseitigen Setzung, Verfügung: der Testator bestimmt allein, was in einer gewissen Angelegenheit geschehen soll, und das Moment des Letztwilligen: der Testator trifft die Bestimmung für den Fall seines Todes, also mit der Intention, daß diese Bestimmung in der betreffenden Angelegenheit als seine letzte Entscheidung gilt. Von diesen beiden Momenten entspricht das erste der Bedeutung von *bᵉrît*; und indem die Septuaginta διαθήκη für *bᵉrît* gesetzt hat, hat sie in διαθήκη ebendieses Moment der einseitigen Setzung, Bestimmung, Verfügung aufgenommen. Das zweite Moment, das Moment des Letztwilligen, trat dabei zurück, ja wurde ganz ausgeschaltet. Diese 'Einschränkung' war um so eher möglich, als das Wort διαθήκη selbst ja keinerlei Bezug auf das Moment des Letztwilligen enthält. Mit anderen Worten: διαθήκη wurde von den Übersetzern der Septuaginta in dem ursprünglichen Sinn des Wortes gebraucht."
52 Kinzig, "καινὴ διαθήκη," 520.

tor Abraham" (Luke 1:69, 72–3; NRSV, modified). H. Hegermann further comments on the Greek OT and NT rendering of the Hebrew:

> In the theological *berith* sayings of the OT a bilateral commitment is established along with the one-sided obligatory actions, as in the pattern of relationship to a sovereign. Thus the translation 'covenant' should be maintained, but also made more precise with phrases that allow differentiation, such as "covenant promise" and "covenant of obligation."
>
> In all instances the emphasis lies on irrevocable commitment. This is indeed the case for διαθήκη in the sense of *last will and testament*: what is of significance is that what is irrevocable is valid (Gal 3:15), coming to be "in force" after death (Heb 9:17). God has firmly obligated himself to his people in his holy *covenant promise* to Abraham (Luke 1:72f.).

5.2 Covenant/Testament in the Corpus Paulinum

In Paul, two of the meanings of διαθήκη listed in the third edition of BDAG are utilised:[53] (i) "last will and testament", and (ii) "covenant," corresponding to the Hebrew term בְּרִית. Dispite the scarcity of this crucial word in the Pauline Corpus,[54] the 26 occurrences of the term in the full 14-letter corpus (including Hebrews) and the 17 occurrences in Hebrews may perhaps connect arithmetically to the two numerical values commonly associated with the divine Name (YHWH/AHWH), 26 and 17 – thus underscoring the divine aspect and initiative of διαθήκη.[55] Be that as it may, the few occurrences of the word in Paul are none-

---

53 W. Bauer, *A Greek-English Lexicon of the New Testament and Other Early Christian Literature*, revised by F. W. Danker (Chicago: University of Chicago Press, 3rd ed, 2000); referred to as BDAG.
54 As for the term's central place in Paul, see, e.g., N. T. Wright, *The Climax of the Covenant: Christ and the Law in Pauline Theology* (Minneapolis: Fortress Press, 1991).
55 For similar argumentation applied to a broader range of New Testament terms, especially the *nomina sacra* word-group, see Bokedal, "The Bible Canon and Its Significance." YHWH, *yod* (= 10) + *he* (= 5) + *waw* (= 6) + *he* (= 5) = 26; AHWH, *aleph* (= 1) + *he* (= 5) + *waw* (= 6) + *he* (= 5) = 17. Cf. Casper J. Labuschagne's phrasing ("General Introduction to Logotechnical Analysis (Rev.)," University of Groningen, 2016, 4; 28.07.2022, https://core.ac.uk/download/pdf/148314126.pdf): "The divine name number **17** can of course be explained as the sum of the *digits* of the numbers 10, 5, 6 and 5 (1 + 0 + 5 + 6 + 5 = **17**), but it is also possible that **17** is the numerical value of a conjectured *'ahweh*, אהוה, which is *to 'ehyeh* אהיה, "I am" (Ex. 3:14), as *yahweh*, יהוה, is to *yihyeh*, יהיה, "he is": **17** = ' h w h, יהוה = 1 + 5 + 6 + 5." For comparison and for interesting corresponding NT word-frequencies for the Greek term λόγος, "word; message; speech," the following figures may also be noted – all of which are multiples of either 26 or 17 – present in various canonical sub-units (THGNT, NA28): λόγος (all forms of the word): 1 Cor 17 occurrences, 1–2 Cor 26 occurrences; λόγος (forms of the word in nominative singular): John 17 occurrences, Gospels+Acts 34 occurrences [2 x 17], the full NT 68 occurrences [4 x 17]; λόγος

theless central for the present chapter, as they lay the ground for the two key connotations of the term, and for the emerging two-testament theology (cf. Feature III above: the title as theological label). In Gal 3:15–17, the basic meanings "last will and testament" and "covenant" both appear to be incorporated into the text (as reflected in NRSV);[56] 2 Cor 3:6 speaks explicitly of a "new covenant," 2 Cor 3:14 refers to a written "Old Covenant," and Gal 4:24 outlines two covenants (two covenants are presumed also in 2 Cor 3:4–18).[57] The notion of an "old" and a "new covenant" is here clearly presumed within the Pauline circle, but also by other early Christian authors addressing the subject.[58] Paul's introduction to the (new) covenant concept, including references to the old and the new covenants, is further elaborated by the author of Hebrews, in whom the more neutral labels πρῶτος, "first, former," and δεύτερος, "second, latter," pertaining to covenant surface (Heb 8:7; 10:9), together with less neutral terminology (8:13). Pertaining to the Corpus Paulinum, the reader thus encounters two of the five features mentioned in the Introduction that arguably were em-

---

(forms of the word in the nominative): John 17 occurrences, the full NT 78 occurrences [3 x 26]; ὁ λόγος (arthrous forms of the word in the nominative): John 17 occurrences, the full NT 68 occurrences [4 x 17]; λόγος (forms of the word in the singular): the full NT 85 occurrences [5 x 17]; ὁ λόγος (arthrous forms of the word in the singular): Praxapostolos (Acts+Catholic Epistles) 51 occurrences [3 x 17]; λόγος (forms of the word in the genitive): the full NT 17 occurrences; λόγος (forms of the word in the dative): Luke-Acts 17 occurrences; Gospels+Acts 26 occurrences; λόγος (forms of the word in the accusative): the full NT 153 occurrences [9 x 17]; λόγον (accusative singular): the full NT 130 occurrences [5 x 26]; and λόγοις (dative plural): the full NT 17 occurrences. See also footnotes 8, 35, 49 and 65. See further Tomas Bokedal, *Christ the Center: How the Rule of Faith, the Nomina Sacra, and Numerical Patterns Shape the Canon* (Bellingham, WA: Lexham Academic, forthcoming 2023).

56 See Stanley E. Porter, "The Concept of Covenant in Paul," in *The Concept of the Covenant in the Second Temple Period*, edited by Stanley E. Porter and Jacqueline C. R. de Roo, Supplements to the Journal for the Study of Judaism 71 (Atlanta: Society of Biblical Literature & Leiden: Brill, 2003), 277: Referring to the lexical definition in BDAG, Porter comments that the meaning 'last will and testament' (the Hellenistic meaning of διαθήκη) applies to Heb 9:16–17, and to Gal 3:15 – "rendered 'a will that has been ratified' – and 17. It [BDAG] also acknowledges that in v. 17 the meaning 'shades into mng. 2', which is the translation of διαθήκη for ברית in the Hebrew Bible."

57 Porter, "The Concept of Covenant in Paul," 269. In terms of the status of the old covenant title, it may be considered secondary also in the sense that, based on Jer 31:31–34, it is derived from the designation "new covenant." If there is or will be a "new covenant" there may also be, by implication, implicitly or indirectly, the existence of an "old covenant." In Paul's reflections in 2 Cor 3:6 and 3:14 this internal logic seems to play out.

58 So Hvalvik, *The Struggle for Scripture and Covenant*, 92. Hvalvik provides the following references: 2 Cor 3:6, 14; Heb 8:6–10; Justin, *Dial.* 24.1; 34.1; Irenaeus, *Haer.* IV, 9.1; IV, 33.14; IV, 34.4; and also adds the comment (ibid. 92n.43): "Despite a varied terminology, nobody expressed the traditional two-covenant theology in terms of one-covenant thinking!"

braced by the inauguration of the New Testament book title: Feature III: the title as theological label, and Feature IV: the title as editorial label, intra-textually connecting the title to the letter corpus.

5.3 Newness in the New Testament and the New Covenant in Jeremiah 31:31–34

When we approach the broader theme of newness in the New Testament,[59] the new covenant concept based on Jer 31:31–34 (LXX 38:31–34) is at the heart of the discussion. Key to the scholarly exploration of the themes "old" and "new" is here the question of continuity and discontinuity relating to formative Judaism and early Christianity. One of the main issues, according to Donald Hagner, seen from an early Christian perspective, relates to the temporary role that the law had to play in pursuit of righteousness, and that "that role has come to an end with the coming of Christ. As in so much of what the NT has to say, a key turning point has now been reached in the history of salvation."[60] Similarly Roy Harisville: The "new" that Jesus embodies in Matt 13:52 and elsewhere "is not merely the chronologically new, but above all, the *eschatologically new*. The element of continuity between new and old is indeed present, but it is a continuity which must not be allowed to deprive the new of its uniqueness (its contrast with the old), its finality, and its dynamic, i.e., its eschatological character."[61]

Underlying its various claims to newness, the Christian church, from the earliest years onwards, "claimed the promise of Jer. 31:31–34 and understood itself to be the people of the new covenant."[62] In this connection, in his treatment of the

---

[59] See Donald A. Hagner, *How New is the New Testament? First-Century Judaism and the Emergence of Christianity* (Grand Rapids: Baker Academic, 2018); and Roy A. Harrisville, *The Concept of Newness in the New Testament* (Augsburg Publishing House, 1960); cf. also ibid. 47: "it is the conviction of the New Testament authors that the new covenant inaugurated by Jesus is qualitatively different from the way in which God ordered His relation to men in the past, a supreme and final arrangement between God and His community, never to be supplanted or surpassed."
[60] Hagner, *How New is the New Testament?*, 4. For a discussion of the so-called New Perspective on Paul and Judaism in this connection, see ibid., 1–21.
[61] Harisville, *The Concept of Newness*, 28. Quoted from Hagner, *How New is the New Testament?*, 19–20. Cf. also Roy Harisville, "The Concept of Newness in the New Testament," *Journal of Biblical Literature* 74 (1955): 79: "Four distinctive features are found to be inherent in the concept of newness: the elements of contrast, continuity, dynamic, and finality." Cited from Trobisch, *The First Edition of the New Testament*, 137n.49.
[62] Jack R. Lundbom, *Jeremiah 21–36*, The Anchor Yale Bible (New Haven & London: Yale University Press, 2004), 474.

new covenant notion in Jer 31:31–34, Georg Fischer argues for the interpretation of a truly new conception, which I will keep to in the following.[63] God's people have broken the covenant (31:32), it is only God who can take the initiative for newness and restoration in this situation. Relating to the Jeremianic presentation of the new covenant in 31:31–34, the following theological themes become crucial for the subsequent Christian appropriation of the concept: the theme of inclusion (cf. Rom 11:26), the theme of internalisation of the law (cf. 1 Thess 4:9; 1 John 2:27), the theme of forgiveness (cf. Matt 26:28), and, indirectly, also the theme of blessing (cf. Gal 3:10–14).[64] These theological emphases served the early church (and arguably the New Testament editors) as potential intra-textual thematic links relating to the new book title ἡ καινὴ διαθήκη (cf. Features III and IV above: the title as theological and editorial label).

5.4 Second-Century Theologies of the Covenant

In the *Epistle of Barnabas*, written sometime between 70 and 135 CE, the centrality of the biblical concept διαθήκη is discussed.[65] In 13.1 the author writes: "Now let us see whether this people [that is the Christians] are the heirs, *or* the former people [the Jews], and whether the covenant relates to us [Christians] *or* to

---

[63] The question of continuity and discontinuity vis-à-vis the new covenant notion in Jeremiah is treated differently by scholars. See, e.g., Georg Fischer, *Jeremia 26–52*. Herders Theologischer Kommentar zum Alten Testament (Freiburg: Herder, 2005), 175. David G. Peterson (*Transformed by God: New Covenant Life and Ministry* (Nottingham: IVP, 2018), 29–30), similarly to Fischer, comments: "The formal structure of the oracle in [Jer] 31:31–34 also stresses discontinuity: 'not like the covenant' (v. 32) is followed by 'but this is the covenant' (v. 33), and 'no longer' is opposed by 'for they shall all know me' (v. 34). This suggests that the word 'new' in the expression 'new covenant' indicates 'radical discontinuity.'" Cf. ibid., 29: "In Jer 31:23–26, 35–38 there is stress on continuity with the past, whereas in Jer 31:27–30, 31–34 and 38–40, the stress is on discontinuity." On Paul's approach to the law/covenant, cf. also A. Andrew Das, *Paul, the Law and the Covenant* (Peabody, MA: Hendrickson Publishers, 2001), 94: "Paul refuses to admit any life-giving or salvific capacity in the Mosaic covenant and its law. [...] Paul's own thinking has moved decidedly beyond covenantal nomism: no longer does the old covenant serve as a gracious, salvific framework for the law."
[64] Cf. Lundbom, *Jeremiah 21–36*, 474–79; and Fischer, *Jeremia 26–52*, 175–80; and Just. *Dial.* 11.2–4, quoted below.
[65] The noun διαθήκη appears 14 times in *Barn.*, which may be a numerical reference to the Davidic number 14 (The sum of the three radicals in the Hebrew name דוד, *Dawid*, is 14: *dalet* (= 4) + *waw* (= 6) + *dalet* (= 4) = 14; cf. Matt 1:17 and the 14th position of David's name in Matthew's genealogy). See also footnotes 8, 35, 49 and 55 above.

them."⁶⁶ When discussing Jewish-Christian relations and issues along these lines, the theological concept of covenant receives prime of place in the *Epistle of Barnabas*. A little later, in Justin, the reader encounters some more advanced thoughts pertaining to διαθήκη, in the form of a two-covenant theology that before long came to further influence the Christian conception of a two-covenant/two-testament Bible (cf. Features III and V above: the title as theological and canonical label).⁶⁷ Staged in the mid-130s, Justin says in his (fictive) dialogue with the Jew Trypho that

> he has read that there should be a definitive law and a covenant more binding than all others [...]. The law promulgated at Horeb is already obsolete, and was intended for you Jews only, whereas the law of which I speak is simply for all human beings [...]. An everlasting and final law, Christ himself, and a trustworthy covenant has been given to us, after which there shall be no law, or commandment, or precept. [...] [Christ] is indeed the New Law, the new covenant [ἡ καινὴ διαθήκη], and the expectation of those who, from every nation, have awaited the blessings of God. (*Dial.* 11.2–4)⁶⁸

We can here detect an interesting first- and second-century Christian development of the covenant notion, which is found already in the *Epistle of Barnabas*, where Christ is more than the giver of the covenant; he himself is the covenant. "I have made you a covenant with the people" (*Barn.* 14.7; Isa. 42 applied to Christ). The notion of Christ himself as the new covenant is found several times also in Justin (*Dial.* 11.2–4; 51.3; 122.5) and elsewhere. This idea of Christ as the Covenant/New Covenant is the highpoint of first- and second-century covenantal theology as found in *Barnabas*, Justin and elsewhere. It is within this covenantal theological milieu that second-century editors of the Christian Scriptures introduce the new label ἡ καινὴ διαθήκη. I shall now briefly discuss the editorial inauguration of the title and its potential intra-textual and canonical ramifications (cf. Features III and IV above: the title as theological and editorial label).

5.5 The NT Title's Editorial and Canonical Intra-Scriptural Links

The New Testament scholar David Trobisch suggests the existence of a second-century archetype collection of the New Testament that set the agenda for the

---

66 Cited from Hvalvik, *The Struggle for Scripture and Covenant*, 92.
67 Cf. Kinzig, *Novitas Christiana*, 128.
68 St. Justin Martyr, *Dialogue with Trypho*, trans. Thomas B. Falls; revised and with a new introduction by Thomas P. Halton, edited by Michael Slusser (Washington DC: Catholic University of America Press, 2003), 20–21 (modified).

major subsequent Greek New Testament manuscript tradition. "The archetype of the collection," he writes, "most probably was entitled ἡ καινὴ διαθήκη, 'The New Testament.' [...]. The uniform evidence of the extant [manuscript] tradition [...] strongly suggests that this was the title of the archetype."[69] Whether we should here speak of an "archetype," following Trobisch, or rather of an early consistent and wide-reaching editorial practice, either way, a good case can be made for a close connection between the editorial choice of title in early manuscripts and the reference to the title in church teachers like Clement, Tertullian and Origen. It is here worth noticing that titular stability, or standardisation – with only minor editorial variations – can be observed for the early superscriptions for the Gospels and the Pauline and Catholic Epistles.[70] From this manuscript data, we have reasons to expect further editorial stability also with respect to the two overall book titles – "The Old" and "The New Testaments" – ascribed to the bipartite Christian Scriptures. To the above list of teachers (Clement, Tertullian and Origen), interestingly, Trobisch further adds Melito of Sardis, who writes that he "learnt accurately the books of the Old Testament," especially "how many they are in number, and what is their order." In Trobisch's view: Even if the term "New Testament" is not explicitly used here by Melito, "it is implied by the designation *Old Testament*, which is introduced without explanation."[71] Trobisch further places the alleged early editorial inauguration of the New Testament title in broader editorial context, includ-

---

69 Cited from Trobisch, *The First Edition of the New Testament*, 43–44.

70 See Trobisch, *The First Edition of the New Testament*, 38–43; Benjamin P. Laird, *The Pauline Corpus in Early Christianity: Its Formation, Publication, and Circulation* (Peabody, MA: Hendrickson Academic, 2022); Martin Hengel, *The Four Gospels and the One Gospel of Jesus Christ: An Investigation of the Collection and Origin of the Canonical Gospels* (London: SCM Press, 2000), 48–56; and ibid., 170: "all New Testament book titles and not just those of the Gospels display a considerably 'conservative' capacity for persistence. Here the earliest textual tradition knows virtually no basic variants. Although this tradition was still relatively variable in the first half of the second century, by comparison with later 'apocryphal' texts the protection of liturgical usage nevertheless kept it relatively constant, more constant than the text of the essentially older Septuagint, which had run wild as a result of numerous Jewish and Christian recensions. This constancy is true not only of the text and especially of the titles but also of the new external form of the codex (as opposed to the scroll), and is connected with the persistence of the early Christian writers or scriptoria. Only in the very much later manuscripts, like the minuscules, did the titles have to be expanded by decorative elaborations and learned additions."

71 Trobisch, *The First Edition of the New Testament*, 44. To Trobisch's observation, I would like to add the following: To the extent that the notion of old covenant is dependent on Jer 31:31–34 (LXX 38:31–34), the notion of *new covenant* is not only presupposed, but appears to be the primary and explicitly mentioned concept of the two—*new* and *old*.

ing/addressing the use and standardisation of *nomina sacra*, the codex form used for the Christian Scriptures, the formulation of book titles for the individual books of the New Testament and "the evidence indicating that the collection was called 'New Testament' from the very beginning." Trobisch concludes: "All of these elements [...] are evidence of a careful final redaction. These editorial features did not originate with the authors of the individual writings. They serve to combine disparate material into a collection and to create the impression of a cohesive literary unit for readers of the work."[72]

Now, as I here presume a close link between the title ἡ καινὴ διαθήκη in the manuscript tradition, on the one hand, and professional and popular use of the title reflected in second- and third-century theologians, on the other, some further textual observations may be made. First, the concrete manuscript employment of the collective Old and New Testament titles intra-textually connects with seven Greek biblical passages, one of which contains the expression παλαιὰ διαθήκη (2 Cor 3:14), three of which contain the phrasing διαθήκη καινή (Jer 38:31 LXX, Heb 8:8 and 9:15) and three further verses that contain the expression καινὴ διαθήκη (Luke 22:20, 1 Cor 11:25 and 2 Cor 3:6). Only one of these passages contains the exact phrase ἡ παλαιὰ διαθήκη (τῆς παλαιᾶς διαθήκης, in the genitive, in 2 Cor 3:14),[73] while two of the seven passages (in the nominative) contain the exact phrase ἡ καινὴ διαθήκη – the wording soon to be employed also as collective book title – namely the words of institution presented in Luke 22:20 and 1 Cor 11:25. Of these two, it is only Luke 22:20 which conveys the expression as expressed directly by Jesus himself – and in that connection, the phrase refers to the last supper.[74] In terms of the original Hebrew phrasing בְּרִית חֲדָשָׁה, "new covenant," this expression features only in Jer 31:31 – a passage which seems to be inner-biblically involved in the other seven biblical references already mentioned. With the editorial choice of the dual book heading ἡ παλαιὰ καὶ ἡ καινὴ διαθήκη, as readers, we are here arguably intra-textually directed to these altogether seven or eight passages, with Jer 31:31–34 at the hermeneutical centre of this miniature intra-textual network (Jer 31:31/LXX 38:31; Luke 22:20; 1 Cor 11:25; 2 Cor 3:6, 14; Heb 8:8 and 9:15) – with implications

---

[72] Trobisch, *The First Edition of the New Testament*, 44.
[73] Cf. Trobisch, *The First Edition of the New Testament*, 138n.60: "That the editors wanted to refer to 2 Corinthians 3 by choosing the title *Old Testament* is supported by the observation that 2 Corinthians 3 is the only passage in the Christian Bible where the expression παλαιὰ διαθήκη is used."
[74] For textcritical considerations pertaining to Luke 22:20, see, e.g., I. Howard Marshall, "The Last Supper," in *Key Events in the Life of the Historical Jesus: A Collaborative Exploration of Context and Coherence*, edited by Darrell L. Bock and Robert L. Webb (Grand Rapids: Eerdmans, 2009): 529–41.

for ongoing reflection upon the title's potential significance (Feature IV: the title as editorial label). Finally, we may note as well the very special, or textually privileged, status in the New Testament of Jer 31 (LXX 38):31–34 in terms of textual space, as these Jeremianic verses (in the Greek) make up the longest Old Testament quotation within the New Testament text corpus (Heb 8:8–12 cites the text in full; and 10:16–17 in abridged form).

6 Concluding Remarks

Wilhelm van Unnik, one of the scholars dialogued with in this chapter, describes the impact of the new book title by pointing to the significance of the notion of διαθήκη Χριστοῦ, "the covenant of Christ," around 175 CE, when asking for "the meaning of καινὴ διαθήκη in its application to that collection of early Christian books which we usually call 'the New Testament' and which under that name influenced the church and the world in an absolutely unique manner."[75] Associated with the Christ-event, the title, no doubt, became the standard designation for the new Scriptures. Surprising perhaps to some, however, the Greek book title did not – as of yet – find its way into recent critical editions of the New Testament, such as NA28 and THGNT. In my view, this (i.e., inclusion of *some* first- and second-century book labels pertaining to the New Testament, exclusion of *others*) deserves further scholarly discussion.

Why is the New Testament called "the New Testament"? As I explored this question from a historical, editorial and theological perspective, five partly complementary features were proposed for a fresh comprehensive answer (Features I–V above). Even if there is truth to the claim that the expression "New Testament" (in the Latin West) has become a largely neutral label, without any specific meaning (I), when used as collective title for the "apostolic" portion of the Christian Scriptures, I argued throughout the chapter primarily in favour of the four alternative options (II–V). By implication, although the designation *prima facie* may appear insignificant (I), scholarly immersed analysis of the topic (II–V), serves as encouragement for ongoing engagement with the designation and its (potential) significance as book title.

In my discussion, it became clear that the two-covenant theology of the first and second century, with particular focus on Jer 31:31–34 (with its stress on forgiveness and an internalised law) was crucial for the adoption of the title

---

[75] Van Unnik, "Ἡ καινὴ διαθήκη," 158.

(Feature III: the title as theological label), and that, reception-historically, the designation καινὴ διαθήκη/*novum testamentum* had become the most popular designation for the second main part of the Christian Scriptures around 210 CE (Feature II: the title as traditional label), with possible knowledge of the dual title "Old" and "New Covenant/Testament" implied already in Melito of Sardis around 170 CE, or shortly thereafter. The prompt and universal appropriation of the dual book title, from the late second century on, is arguably reflected in the explicit awareness shown by Origen and Augustine of the different indicated meanings of the concept's biblical usage in Paul and elsewhere, on the one hand, and in the titular employment of διαθήκη/*testamentum*, on the other. The proposal of the present chapter regarding these church teachers' depiction of "the so-called *New Testament/Covenant*" goes in another direction than some earlier scholarly suggestions. Rather than viewing the new designation as a misunderstanding of the biblical concept, there is reason to view the new textual label in terms of the scriptural status attained, or claimed, for the incorporated writings, alongside that of "the Law" and "the Gospel." In all three cases ("Law," "Gospel," "Covenant"), these labels were used to designate both an oral and a written/textual aspect pertaining to revelation. As for the textual aspect of διαθήκη/*testamentum* when used as book title, three components were arguably in play, in addition to features discussed in relation to Feature I (the alleged insignificance of the title in the Latin West) and Feature II (the title as traditional label): a second-century two-testament theology (Feature III); editorial introduction of the title, intra-scripturally involving a selection of highlighted scriptural passages and themes (Feature IV); and an editorial/canonical element (Feature V). The latter point on the canon, von Campenhausen helpfully described as follows: The labels "Old" and "New Testament" prevailed over all others because of the very nature of the Bible as a book in two parts: "They denoted a comprehensive and theologically very significant dual concept, in which nevertheless each group of Scriptures had its clearly defined place." In the early church, a similar thought was expressed by Lactantius: "all Scripture is divided into two Testaments/Covenants [...]. That which preceded the advent and passion of Christ – that is the law and the prophets – is called the Old; but those things which were written after His resurrection are named New Testament/Covenant" (*Inst.* IV, 20.4). A major objective of the present chapter has been to demonstrate the likelihood that this articulated comprehension of the new title(s) was theologically and editorially/canonically grounded in the first- and second-century Christian textual culture, including in the Old and New Testament writings themselves.

Around 200 CE, Clement of Alexandria seems to give implicit and explicit expression to key aspects of what has been argued in this chapter, by attending in concise form to Features III–V on theological (III), editorial (IV) and canonical (V) facets of our query: "The Canon of the Church is the agreement and unity of the Law and the Prophets with the [New] Testament/Covenant delivered at the coming of the Lord." (*Strom.* VI, 15.125.3). Thus, Clement's phrasing arguably relates primarily to written documents, to a two-covenant theology with implicit reference to Jer 31:31–34 (Feature III), and to the emergent textuality of the Christian Bible as a book in two main parts (Features IV and V) – which Clement claims should be inner-biblically balanced with one another in line with the scripturally aligned Ecclesiastical Canon, or Rule of Faith (Features III and IV).[76]

References

Baker, Levi S. *New Covenant Documents for a New Covenant Community: Covenant as an Impetus for New Scripture in the First Century*. PhD diss. Wake Forest, NC. Southeastern Baptist Theological Seminary, 2021.
Barr, James. *Holy Scripture: Canon, Authority, Criticism*. Philadelphia: Westminster Press, 1983.
Barton, John. *The Spirit and the Letter* (London, SPCK, 1997).
Bauckham, Richard. "The 153 Fish and the Unity of the Fourth Gospel." *Neotestamentica* 36 (2002): 77–88.
Bauer, Walter. *A Greek-English Lexicon of the New Testament and Other Early Christian Literature*. Rev. and ed. F. W. Danker. Chicago: University of Chicago Press, 3rd ed, 2000.
Behm, Johannes. *Der Begriff Διαθήκη im Neuen Testament*. Leipzig, 1912.
Bokedal, Tomas. "The Bible Canon and Its Significance: Textual Comprehensiveness, Function, Design and Delimitation." In *Canon Formation: Tracing the Role of Sub-Collections in the Biblical Canon*, edited by W. Edward Glenny and Darian R. Lockett, 7–32. London: Bloomsbury T&T Clark, 2023.
Bokedal, Tomas. *Christ the Center: How the Rule of Faith, the* Nomina Sacra, *and Numerical Patterns Shape the Canon*. Bellingham, WA: Lexham Academic, forthcoming 2023.
Bokedal, Tomas. *The Formation and Significance of the Christian Biblical Canon: A Study in Text, Ritual and Interpretation*. London: Bloomsbury T&T Clark, 2014.
Bokedal, Tomas. "The Rule of Faith: Tracing Its Origins." *Journal of Theological Interpretation* 7.1 (2013): 233–55.
Campenhausen, Hans von. *The Formation of the Christian Bible*. Philadelphia: Fortress Press, 1972 (German original: *Die Entstehung der christlichen Bibel*. Tübingen: Mohr Siebeck, 1968, 2003).
Das, A. Andrew. *Paul, the Law and the Covenant*. Peabody, MA: Hendrickson Publishers, 2001.

---

[76] I would like to thank Ludger Jansen and an anonymous reviewer for valuable comments on an earlier draft of the present chapter.

Duncan, J. Ligon. "The Covenant Idea in Melito of Sardis: An Introduction and Survey." *Presbyterion* 28.1 (2002): 12–33.

Ferguson, Everett. "The Covenant Idea in the Second Century," in idem, *The Early Church at Work and Worship*, vol. 1: *Ministry, Ordination, Covenant, and Canon*. Cambridge: James Clarke & Co, 2013, 173–200.

Fischer, Georg. *Jeremia 26–52*. Herders Theologischer Kommentar zum Alten Testament. Freiburg: Herder, 2005.

Gamble, Harry Y. *The New Testament Canon: Its Making and Meaning*. Philadelphia: Fortress, 1985, 19–20).

Gräbe, Petrus J. *New Covenant, New Community: Significance of Biblical and Patristic Covenant Theology for Contemporary Understanding*. Bletchley, Milton Keynes, UK: Paternoster, 2006.

Hägglund, Bengt. "Die Bedeutung der 'regula fidei' als Grundlage theologischer Aussagen." *Studia Theologica* 12 (1958): 1–44.

Hagner, Donald A. *How New is the New Testament? First-Century Judaism and the Emergence of Christianity*. Grand Rapids: Baker Academic, 2018.

Harrisville, Roy A. *The Concept of Newness in the New Testament*. Augsburg Publishing House, 1960.

Harrisville, Roy A. "The Concept of Newness in the New Testament." *Journal of Biblical Literature*, 74 (1955): 69–79.

Harnack, Adolf von. *Marcion: Das Evangelium vom fremden Gott; eine Monographie zur Geschichte der Grundlegung der katholischen Kirche*. Neue Studien zu Marcion. Darmstadt: Wissenschaftliche Buchgesellschaft, 2nd ed., 1924.

Harnack, Adolf von. *The Origin of the New Testament and the Most Important Consequences of the New Creation*, trans. J. R. Wilkinson. London: Williams & Norgate, 1925.

Hays, Richard B. "The Letter to the Galatians: Introduction, Commentary, and Reflections." In *The New Interpreter's Bible Commentary*, vol. IX. Nashville: Abingdon Press, 2002, 2015.

Hengel, Martin. *The Four Gospels and the One Gospel of Jesus Christ: An Investigation of the Collection and Origin of the Canonical Gospels*. London: SCM Press, 2000.

Hvalvik, Reidar. *The Struggle for Scripture and Covenant: The Purpose of the Epistle of Barnabas and Jewish-Christian Competition in the Second Century*. WUNT 2/82. Tübingen: Mohr Siebeck, 1996.

Justin Martyr. St., *Dialogue with Trypho*, trans. Thomas B. Falls. Revised and with a new introduction by Thomas P. Halton, edited by Michael Slusser. Washington DC: Catholic University of America Press, 2003.

Kelly, J. N. D. *Early Christian Doctrines*. Harper Collins, rev. ed., 1978.

Kinzig, Wolfram. "καινὴ διαθήκη: The Title of the New Testament in the Second and Third Centuries." *JTS* 45.2 (1994).

Kinzig, Wolfram. *Novitas Christiana: Die Idee des Fortschritts in der Alten Kirche bis Eusebius*. Göttingen: Vandenhoeck & Ruprecht, 1994.

Kutsch, Ernst. *Neues Testament – Neuer Bund? Eine Fehlübersetzung wird korrigiert*. Neukirchen-Vluyn: Neukirchener Verlag, 1978.

Labuschagne, Casper J. "General Introduction to Logotechnical Analysis (Rev.)." University of Groningen, 2016, https://core.ac.uk/download/pdf/148314126.pdf.

Laird, Benjamin P. *The Pauline Corpus in Early Christianity: Its Formation, Publication, and Circulation*. Peabody, MA: Hendrickson Academic, 2022.

Lips, Hermann von. *Der neutestamentliche Kanon: Seine Geschichte und Bedeutung*. Zürich: Theologischer Verlag Zürich, 2004.

Lohmeyer, Ernst. *Diatheke. Ein Beitrag zur Erklärung des neutestamentlichen Begriffs*. Leipzig, 1913.

Lundbom, Jack R. *Jeremiah 21–36*. The Anchor Yale Bible. New Haven & London: Yale University Press, 2004.

Marshall, I. Howard. "The Last Supper." In *Key Events in the Life of the Historical Jesus: A Collaborative Exploration of Context and Coherence*, edited by Darrell L. Bock and Robert L. Webb, 481–588. Grand Rapids: Eerdmans, 2009.

Ohme, Heinz. *Kanon ekklesiastikos: Die Bedeutung des altkirchlichen Kanonbegriffs*. Berlin: de Gruyter, 1998.

Peterson, David G. Transformed by God: New Covenant Life and Ministry. Nottingham: IVP, 2018.

Porter, Stanley E. "The Concept of Covenant in Paul." In *The Concept of the Covenant in the Second Temple Period*, edited by Stanley E. Porter and Jacqueline C. R. de Roo. Supplements to the Journal for the Study of Judaism 71, 269–85. Atlanta: Society of Biblical Literature & Leiden: Brill, 2003.

Trobisch, David. *The First Edition of the New Testament*. Oxford: Oxford University Press, 2000.

Van Unnik, W. C. "Ἡ καινὴ διαθήκη – a Problem in the Early History of the Canon," in *Sparsa Collecta: The Collected Essays of W. C. van Unnik*, vol. 2, 157–71. Leiden: Brill, 1980.

Wright, N. T. *The Climax of the Covenant: Christ and the Law in Pauline Theology*. Minneapolis: Fortress Press, 1991.

Zahn, Theodor. *Geschichte des neutestamentlichen Kanons*, vol. 1. Erlangen: Verlag von Andreas Deichert, 1888.

Francis Borchardt
Disassembling Provenance: Origin Stories and Why They Matter for Scripture

Abstract: In the context of early Jewish and Christian prologues, stories of discovery are ubiquitous. Sometimes these stories of discovery claim a special access and agency for the translator, allowing them to take credit for the work, and by extension earn favor with potential readers and with God. Yet these tales are present even when the one who claims to translate or otherwise adapt the text is anonymous, and desirous of neither prayer nor any other reward for their efforts. This evidence suggests that such fictions may serve a different rhetorical function. This chapter argues that these fictions of provenance serve to realize the texts to which they are attached. The stories of provenance conjure the idea that the texts they introduce have existed long before, continue to exist now, and will continue to exist in the future. They do so by telling tales of unique access to writings, a special skill or opportunity that allows for the necessary transformation of the text, and a manufactured legacy that ties the writing back to a hoary past. In telling these stories they reveal a set of ancient Jewish and Christian values around scriptural writings. This chapter compares the stories of discovery in the translator's prologue to Ben Sira, the prologue of the Sibylline Oracles, and the prologue of the Gospel of Nicodemus to illustrate how these prologues work to create the works to which they are attached as fully realized entities in the world.

Keywords: Gospel of Nicodemus, Acts of Pilate, Prologues, Provenance

1 Introduction

In her recent work on the poetics of textual discovery, Eva Mroczek makes a convincing plea to turn our scholarly attention toward myths of manuscript finds.[1] She masterfully highlights the ways in which such stories participate in

---

[1] Eva Mroczek, "True Stories and the Poetics of Textual Discovery," *Bulletin for the Study of Religion* 45 (2016): 21–31; eadem, "Batshit Stories: New Tales of Discovering Ancient Texts," *Marginalia: Los Angeles Review of Books*, 22 June, 2018, https://marginalia.lareviewofbooks.

Francis Borchardt, NLA University College; francis.borchardt@nla.no

tropes that reveal the values and expectations surrounding revelatory and scriptural literature.[2] Significantly, Mroczek points out how these values can be concerned with the place of the scholar within the chain of transmission of the text (as with the Nag Hammadi, Dead Sea Scrolls, and Cairo Geniza find stories) and with the fragmentary nature of knowledge from and about the past (as with the 9th century letter of Timothy I, 2 Enoch 47, and 2 Macc 2:1–8).[3] From Mroczek's perspective these myths express ideas not just about one's relationship to a given text, but to textuality writ large. They display concern not just about the role of the figure who discovers a manuscript, but about the role of scholars as subjects who are able and responsible for the preservation and curation of texts as objects. Although she acknowledges that many such stories can function as paratexts, authorizing some text or corpus, Mroczek's program is explicitly concerned with treating these stories as objects of analysis in themselves, rather than simply as authorizing fables or historical data about how a given text or corpus becomes available.[4] In this sense she shifts from treating these discovery accounts as paratexts to treating them as texts.[5] In doing so, Mroczek assembles a grand theory of how these myths work from antiquity to the contemporary world of scholarship on ancient Jewish and Christian writings.

My aim is less ambitious, but it takes Mroczek's goal of focusing on the poetics of discovery as a point of departure. For this essay, I aim to investigate a particular type of provenance narrative that makes claims to having changed older texts in the ancient world. This type of discovery myth is found in prefatory writings connected with ostensibly adapted texts.[6] It tends to weave together an intricate matrix of motifs that form a trope wherein texts are unearthed from

---

org/batshit-stories-new-tales-of-discovering-ancient-texts; eadem, "Truth and Doubt in Manuscript Discovery Narratives," in *Rethinking 'Authority' in Late Antiquity: Authorship, Law, and Transmission in Jewish and Christian Tradition*, ed. A.J. Berkovitz and Mark Letteney (London: Routledge, 2018), 139–60.

2 Mroczek, "Truth," 153; eadem, "True," 29–30.
3 Mroczek, "True," 24; eadem, "Truth," 152.
4 Mroczek, "Truth," 153; eadem, "True," 21–2. For this use of paratext see Gérard Genette, *Paratexts: Thresholds of Interpretation*, trans. Jane Lewin (Cambridge: Cambridge University Press, 1997).
5 Adrian Wilson, "What is a Text?" *Studies in the History and Philosophy of Science* 43 (2012): 341–58, esp. 346–7, convincingly argues that the status of "text" has become a way of conceiving a writing, picture, object, or experience so that meaning is found therein. It follows in his definition that status as text is conferred by a given reader.
6 On the terminology of prefatory writings as opposed to prologues, see Genette, *Paratexts*, 161, who suggests that any introductory text, regardless of position, reflecting on the text that follows or precedes it should be included under the category of prefatory writings.

a distant past, are revealed to be imperfect or at risk of loss, but are finally adapted so that they will not only be read, but survive into the future. Along with Mroczek, I am interested in what these discovery stories have to say about the values associated with literary works and the figures who work on them. In particular, I am attempting to argue that these narratives create a sense of eternal presence around texts so that they have an apparent existence beyond any particular historical setting. In making this claim, I examine specifically how these stories use the notions of adaptation and change, compositional agency, and presence/absence of the past to create the idea of a text that travels beyond the limits of the book itself.

In the Hellenistic, Graeco-Roman, and Byzantine literary worlds, prologues containing such find narratives are relatively commonplace. For this essay I shall primarily focus on the stories of discovery within the prologues introducing the Greek translation to Ben Sira, the ostensible Greek translation to the Gospel of Nicodemus, and one of the anthologies of the Sibylline Oracles. I shall assert that these writings betray a common set of literary and scholarly values about the relationship between scripture and eternal presence. I shall further show how these tales of discovery enlist the finding figures in an intricate biographical fiction. The stories craft finding figures that take responsibility for the survival of the text, both through their discovery of a preexistent writing, and through their exertions to adapt that writing so that it promises to survive into the future. In these cases, the scholarly finding figure is thus positioned as a savior, not of souls, but of texts.[7] As such, the very specific interaction between these figures and the writings on which they work creates or deepens the biography of a given text, realizing it as continually present, and therefore perennially valuable.

2 The Greek Prologue to Ben Sira

The Greek prologue to Ben Sira is the earliest prefatory writing we are examining.[8] It contains a rather mundane story of discovery as far as these myths go. The

---

[7] Or put another way, they are "mythic heroes", as Mroczek, "True," 24, aptly names her scholars.
[8] On the Greek prologue and its presence in manuscripts, see Joseph Ziegler, *Septuaginta: Vetus Testamentum Graecum 12/2: Sapientia Iesu Filii Sirach* (Göttingen: Vandenhoeck & Ruprecht, 1980), 123–6. The Greek prologue is found in all but seven Greek manuscripts of Ben Sira, and all but one Latin manuscript (S 339). It is absent in the GKII tradition, and in one

prologist, who famously claims that Jesus Ben Sira is his ancestor (SirPr, 7), holds back from overloading his account with the type of exoticizing or miraculous elements that Mroczek has noted are typical of such stories.[9] There is nothing of following animals into caves, rescuing scroll sheets from an ignorant or destructive bearer, or even revealing a once hidden text from a secret location. Instead the prologist writes simply that he found a decent quality manuscript while he was sojourning in Egypt in the 38th year of Ptolemy Euergetes (SirPr, 27–29). Nothing more specific is said of where he might have found the manuscript, or under what conditions. From what we know about ancient circulation of manuscripts it could be a bookseller, but it would be much more likely to be in a private or public library.[10] The prologist's story is just unremarkable enough to be some version of what actually happened. Despite the mundane appearance of this discovery story, however, there remain in this narrative, and in the broader matrix of the prologue, elements familiar from more fantastical accounts.

One such element is that the work the prologist claims to have found in Egypt has a palpable connection to the distant past. This assertion may seem odd, especially if one understands the prologist to speak of Ben Sira as his grandfather, rather than a more distant male ancestor. But, my argument does not rely on a reading that widens the gap between the prologist cum translator and Ben Sira. Instead, I am suggesting that the way in which the prologue frames Ben Sira's work assures the reader that it is an epitome of Israel's ancient education and wisdom. The work, as the prologist presents it, is not new or innovative. It reaches back into the past, even beyond Ben Sira's grandfather, and into Israel's ancestral history.[11] This can be deduced from the series of statements made in the prologue. First, the prologist notes that Israel is to be

---

notable manuscript of that tradition (ms. 248) it is replaced by a different prologue. It is also absent in the Ethiopic and Armenian versions.

9 Note that most commentators translate the term πάππος, which is used by the prologist to refer to Ben Sira, as grandfather. However, according to "πάππος," *LSJ*, 1302, the term can refer generally to any male ancestor. Because the prologue never provides any more detail about the relationship, and based on the content of the translation on the one hand (50:1–21) and the prologue on the other (Pr. 27–30), the number of generations between the two figures is unclear, I prefer to use the more general sense of the term.

10 See Bernard van Groningen, "ΕΚΔΟΣΙΣ," *Mnemosyne* 16 (1963): 1–17; Raymond Starr, "The Circulation of Literary Texts in the Roman World," *Classical Quarterly* 37 (1987): 213–23; idem, "The Used-Book Trade in the Roman World," *Phoenix* 44 (1990): 148–57, most broadly on this topic.

11 Elias Bickerman, *The Jews in the Greek Age* (Cambridge: Harvard University Press, 1988), 204, notes that Ben Sira himself channels the voice of tradition when he presents his teachings in the book.

praised for its education and wisdom as they are found through the law, the prophets, and the others that follow them (SirPr, 1–3). Second, Ben Sira is said to devote himself to reading the law and the prophets and the other ancestral books, thereby acquiring great skill in them (SirPr, 7–11). Third, the prologist asserts that, because of his proficiency, Ben Sira was led to write something himself about education and wisdom in order to lead people in a more lawful life (SirPr, 12–14). Taken together, these assertions aver that Ben Sira's writing is not simply the work of a wise sage, or the product of individual genius. It is, in fact, the culmination of a life spent immersing himself in ancient teachings of Israel's ancestors.[12] So, even though Ben Sira's work might have been composed only two generations prior to his ostensible grandson finding a copy of it in Egypt, the work is itself presented as a compendium of what is best of the ancestral tradition. It bears the very same wisdom and education as the texts that he studies and re-presents.

This, of course, could be understood as an authorizing statement. Ben Sira's work is valuable because it distills the knowledge, and possesses the same qualities found in earlier works that are already highly valued. That much is obvious. But, limiting our enquiry to this type of analysis ignores *why* such a statement works. The answer appears to be that the knowledge of the ancestors, particularly the sort of knowledge that has reached the contemporary audience, is perennially important. It does not rely on being bound to one place, time, or situation. The prologue claims that Israel's wisdom and education has continually been proven valuable from antiquity into the reader's contemporary era. The value comes both from the prospect of its continued curation through time, and possibly also its perceived rarity in the contemporary world.[13] It has been transmitted through the ancestral lineage of Israel culminating with Ben Sira.

---

[12] This is specifically the reading endorsed by Armin Lange, "'The Law, the Prophets, and the Other Books of the Fathers' (Sir. Prologue) Canonical Lists in Ben Sira and Elsewhere?" in *Studies in the Book of Ben Sira: Papers of the Third International Conference on Deuterocanonical Books, Shime'on Centre, Pápa, Hungary, 18–20 May, 2006*, ed. Géza Xeravits and József Zsengeller (Leiden: Brill, 2008), 55–80.

[13] On the importance of reliable transmission and implied obedience for the value of knowledge see Carol Newsom, "Woman and the Discourse of Patriarchal Wisdom: A Study in Proverbs 1–9," in *Gender and Difference in Ancient Israel*, ed. Peggy Day (Minneapolis: Fortress, 1989), 142–60; Benjamin Wright, "From Generation to Generation: The Sage as Father in Early Jewish Literature," in *Biblical Traditions in Transmission: Essays in Honor of Michael Knibb*, ed. Charlotte Hempel and Judith Lieu (Leiden: Brill, 2006), 309–32; Jacqueline Vayntrub, "The Book of Proverbs and the Idea of Ancient Israelite Education," *ZAW* 128 (2016): 96–114. On the ways in which inaccessibility of knowledge and text bears within it the potential for knowledge of the highest value, see Mroczek, "Truth," 152.

And now, Ben Sira has become the figure through whom the knowledge might be accessed. It is he, after all, who gains mastery over Israel's past and produced a text transmitting all he has learned.

But, the chain of transmission does not end there. As knowledgeable as Ben Sira might be, and as useful as his work is, when the prologist encounters his manuscript in Egypt, it is apparently languishing, unread and perhaps unknown by the Greek-speaking Jews who live abroad (SirPr, 30–36). In this find story, the work *might as well* have been sitting in a cave. The knowledge from the distant past is being ignored, and at risk of being lost. Yet, as luck would have it, the figure most suited to the task "discovers" the manuscript and rectifies the situation. The prologist, as Ben Sira's descendant, is presumably heir to his teachings, and bears the implicit responsibility to internalize his ancestor's knowledge.[14] Moreover, he demonstrates his knowledge and skill in the task of translation, when he discusses how the Greek translations of other Hebrew texts like the law and prophecies and the rest of the works differ in rhetorical quality from their original language.[15] So, by his own account, the prologist sets to work exploiting his unique access to the text, his special connection to Ben Sira, and his skill in Greek and Hebrew. The result is that he produces a Greek translation of his ancestor's work that makes Israel's ancestral knowledge available to the wider world. He transforms the languishing wisdom and education of Israel's ancient ancestors from an entity at risk into one that can once again be enjoyed by an even larger audience. In this rather mundane prologue, we nevertheless have the finding figure emerge as a savior of the text. He has saved it from its precarious place in a little-read language and exerted his control over the text thereby establishing it as an object that will continue to reach an even wider public. In so doing, he has also placed himself as the authority over Israel's past through whom all Greek readers, at least, must access the treasures of Jewish antiquity. The prologist's very contribution, like that of his grandfather, and presumably those who preceded even Ben Sira, demonstrates that the wisdom and education of Israel remains relevant for all, regardless of time and place. The entire story of discovery and prologue within which it is found transform this newly produced translation of a little-read work into a text with a long history that precedes its current appearance. It demands that its value be acknowledged because it presents itself as a transformation and continuation of Israel's ancestral knowledge.

---

14 Wright, "From Generation," 328–30.
15 Benjamin Wright, *Praise Israel for Wisdom and Instruction: Essays on Ben Sira and Wisdom, the Letter of Aristeas and the Septuagint* (Leiden: Brill, 2008), 262–4.

3 The Prologue to the Gospel of Nicodemus

A similar story can be told when we turn to the prologue of the Gospel of Nicodemus.[16] This preface, spoken in the voice of a Pro-Praetor's bodyguard, Ananias (NicPr, 2), once more reveals a fascination with an antique body of knowledge that is ostensibly both obscure and inaccessible for an implied target audience. Like the prologue to Ben Sira, it tells this story without resorting to the more fantastical and esoteric imagery familiar from the find stories Mroczek has examined. Yet, it too does the same work as those stories in much the same way as does the prologue of Ben Sira. In the case of this discovery account, which dates itself to the late fourth century, in the reigns of Theodosius I and Valentinian II, the special knowledge comes in a work over three centuries old.[17] The manuscript that Ananias alleges to have discovered is Nicodemus' eyewitness account of Jesus' passion and resurrection, which was then given to the Jewish authorities at that time (NicPr, 5). The ostensible antiquity of the text here is thus not only manufacturing temporal distance between Ananias and the text's origins, but also importantly placing the composition of that text within a crucial historical setting. The prologue's claim essentially establishes the text as the oldest account of the trial and passion of Jesus. This fictional setting, though, maintains the persistent value associated with prolonging and expanding a text's biography as part of a discourse that extends the reader's ability to capture knowledge of the fragmentary past.

Just as with the discovery narrative in the Greek prologue of Ben Sira, however, the access to the past through the manuscript is hindered. Twice the prologue emphasizes that the gospel that has been discovered is written in Hebrew

---

16 Bart Ehrman, Zlatko Plese, *The Apocryphal Gospels: Texts and Translations* (2011), 419–20, discusses the identification of this work alternatively as the Acts of Pilate and the Gospel of Nicodemus. According to Ehrman and Plese, the work circulated under both names, depending on manuscript. The identification of the work with Nicodemus appears to come from the prologue under examination here.

17 On the date of the text, see Michael Zellman-Rohrer, "A New Coptic Witness to the *Acts of Pilate (Gospel of Nicodemus)*: P. Newark Museum Acc. 75.98" *JTS* 69 (2018): 611–27, esp. 613–4, especially in the context of the Coptic manuscript that he first publishes in the article. He notes that the gospel likely comes from the fourth century CE, and that his earliest Coptic manuscript dates from no later than the sixth century CE. This counters the claims of G.C. O'Ceallaigh, "Dating the Commentaries of Nicodemus" *HTR* 56 (1963): 21–58, esp. 58, who asserts that the text comes from no earlier than the mid-sixth century CE, and that no manuscripts come from earlier than the eighth century. O'Ceallaigh, however, does note that the prologue dates the work to 440 CE.

letters (NicPr, 1, 5). This means that it is essentially inaccessible for the Greek speaking implied audience established by the find narrative itself. For this audience, a manuscript find that is written in Hebrew is no find at all. The text remains just as inaccessible as it had been before Ananias encountered it in the official records. It is a relic of the past, but it is not complete. What this means is that a crucial part of the discovery narrative in this case is also the transformation that Ananias brings to the text. In this formulation of find stories, the discovery takes place in two phases, both of them necessary. The first is the actual physical encounter with an ancient text. The second is the transformation of that text so that it is revealed to the Greek-speaking world. In both the prefaces of the Gospel of Nicodemus and the Greek translation of Ben Sira, it is important that the translation is from what is perceived of as a particular language to what is perceived of as a universal language.[18] It is, in itself, an activity that removes the text from hiding. It also places the scholar, as mediator, in a primary position to reveal that text to the world. This is as much the case with Ben Sira's descendant as it is with Ananias in the Gospel of Nicodemus.

The writing, ostensibly lost for over three centuries could only be found and then disseminated because of the peculiar biography with which Ananias is endowed. Presumably, he would not have access to this ancient official text were he not in the service of the Pro-Praetor. Although the prologue is not explicit on this point, it seems rather likely that it is supposed to be the Pro-Praetor of Syria–Palestina, as is made clear in the text itself.[19] This places Ananias in a setting within which he might have access to official archives related to judicial trials.[20] His name, being a Hellenized from of Hananiah, also implies his Judean heritage and by extension, his mastery over the Hebrew language (NicPr, 1, 5).[21] Moreover, his prolonged statement regarding his knowledge of

---

18 Philip Fackler, "Adversus Adversus Iudaeos? Countering Christian Anti-Jewish Polemics in the Gospel of Nicodemus" *JECS* 23 (2015): 413–44, esp. 425–6, notes how Ananias' role brings the text out of the supposed obscurity of the Hebrew language into the wider world of the Greek language.

19 Zbigniew Izydorczyk, "Introduction," in *The Medieval Gospel of Nicodemus: Texts, Intertexts, and Contexts in Western Europe*, ed. Zbigniew Izydorczyk (Tempe, AZ: Arizona State University, 1997), 1–20, esp. 4–6 shows the extent to which Pilate is involved in various versions of the text.

20 Fackler, "Adversus," 426.

21 On the presence of this name as evidence of Jewish presence in a population, see e.g. Willy Clarisse, "The Jewish Presence in Graeco-Roman Egypt: The Evidence of the Papyri since the Corpus Papyrorum Judaicarum," in *Israel in Egypt: The Land of Egypt as a Concept and Reality for Jews in Antiquity and the Early Medieval Period*, ed. Alison Salvesen, Sarah Pearce, Miriam Frenkel (Leiden: Brill, 2020), 305–25, esp. 309–10.

Jesus Christ through scripture and baptism establishes him as a reliable tradent for the story of Jesus' passion and resurrection for an implied audience that is both Greek-speaking and Christian.[22] Even Ananias' request to readers for prayer on his behalf (NicPr, 2–3) places him in the role of a loyal and dependable servant of Jesus. The peculiar mix of access to the text through his office, knowledge of language through his upbringing, and devotion to attaining the truth of Jesus' trial through his commitments makes it so that a figure like Ananias emerges as the necessary mediator of this text. Without him, the writing would remain lost, unreadable for Greek speakers, and would therefore never have its value realized. As in the case of the Ben Sira find story, then, the writing only actually has value for the implied audience specifically because of the scholar figure responsible for its transformation. Ananias, like Ben Sira's descendant becomes the savior of essential knowledge. Through the find story connected to Ananias, the newly-produced writing gains a biography of its own. It attains an origin in the past, a location where it was stored/hidden, and a means by which it was made available for the present and the future. The discovery narrative transforms the text once more into a writing that is continually appropriate in all times and places.

4 The Prologue to the Sibylline Oracles

A slightly different type of transformation comes in the early sixth century prologue to a collection of Sibylline oracles.[23] Here, we find the same tropes we

---

22 Fackler, "Adversus," 426, makes this point specifically. He notes that the preface alone removes the fiction of Jewish participation in the dissemination and circulation of the text.
23 Johannes Geffcken, *Die Oracula Sibyllina* (Leipzig: J. C. Hinrichs'sche Buchhandlung, 1902), XXI–XXIII, whose edition of the Sibylline Oracles is considered the standard, identifies manuscripts A, S, P, and B as part of the same φ family. He does not know of manuscript D. Aloisius Rzach, "Sibyllinische Orakel," *PW*, 2.2:2103–83, esp. 2121–2, notes the existence of D, but does not sufficiently describe it so as to determine whether it contains all of the prologue, as in A and S, part of the prologue, as in P, or no prologue, as in B. Rieuwerd Buitenwerf, *Book III of the Sibylline Oracles and its Social Setting: With an Introduction, Translation, and Commentary* (Leiden: Brill, 2003), 66, n.3, reasons that because Rzach does not mention anything concerning the contents, that it must have contained the prologue. This conclusion seems less than certain. On the sixth century date see John Collins, "Sibylline Oracles: A New Translation and Introduction," in *Old Testament Pseudepigrapha, Volume I: Apocalyptic Literature and Testaments*, ed. James Charlesworth (Garden City, NY: Doubleday, 1983), 317–472, esp. 322; Rzach, "Sibyllinische," 2119–20, Buitenwerf, *Book III*, 86.

have already noticed, even as the way the text is changed differs. As the prologue introduces the φ manuscripts of the oracles as an anthology, it is again concerned with establishing the perennial value of Sibylline books 1–8 and with the role of the collector in that process. The antiquity of these writings is established in two central sections of the prologue wherein both a setting for oral performance and literary production are introduced, and wherein the precarious situation of these texts is highlighted.

The first of these sections (SibPr, 29–50) introduces a list of ten Sibyls that plays with a literary canonization of known sibyls known first from Varro, but then in various versions from Lactantius and the *Tübingen Theosophy*.[24] In this list, the sibyls are presented sequentially beginning with the Chaldean sibyl, who is said to be from the family of Noah, and by the eighth sibyl reaches the time of Cyrus and Solon.[25] The final two sibyls are not placed in a historical context, but the antiquity of these prophetesses is nonetheless established. The impression is that each of them have arisen in succession and spoken prophecy about any number of subjects, whether the Trojan wars, Alexander the Great, or indeed, as stated elsewhere in the prologue, Jesus' death and resurrection.[26] In the case of

---

[24] H.W. Parke, *Sibyls and Sibylline Prophecy in Classical Antiquity*, ed. B.C. McGing (London: Routledge, 1988), 29–35, notes both that the traditional selection of ten sibyls goes as far back as Marcus Terentius Varro's *Antiquitatem humanarum et divinarum* (with considerable variations). A similar list of sibyls, with some variations can be found in Lactantius, *Divine Institutes*, I.6.7–12 and later in the so-called *Tübingen Theosophy*, which is an apologetic treatise in four books that employs oracles and knowledge from the Graeco-Roman world in order to demonstrate the truth of its monophysite Christian positions. The third book of the *Theosophy* is dedicated to reproducing oracles of the sibyls that contribute to this larger project. A portion of book three of the *Theosophy* (III.7–59, 69–80, 82, 85–91) is believed to have been copied in full into the sibylline prologue. There are two critical editions of the *Theosophy*. The most current edition of the *Theosophy* is to be found in Pier Franco Beatrice, *Anonymi Monophysitae Theosophia: An Attempt at Reconstruction* (Leiden: Brill, 2001). An earlier edition is to be found in Hartmut Erbse, *Theosophorum Graecorum Fragmenta*, (Stuttgart: Teubner, 1995).

[25] Parke, *Sibyls*, 30.

[26] On the positive use of sibylline divination by apologists and church fathers see Bard Thompson, 'Patristic Use of the Sibylline Oracles', *Review of Religion* 6 (1952): 115–36; Parke, *Sibyls*, 152–73; and John Bartlett, *Jews in the Hellenistic World: Josephus, Aristeas, the Sibylline Oracles, Eupolemus* (Cambridge: Cambridge University Press, 1985), 36; On Lactantius' use of non-Christian oracles in his apologetic writing see Stefan Freund, "Christian Use and Valuation of Theological Oracles: The Case of Lactantius' *Divine Institutes*," *Vigiliae Christianae* 60 (2006): 269–84, esp. 281–2. But see also the caution to place the use of the sibyl in a broader context by Mischa Hooker, 'The Use of Sibyls and Sibylline Oracles in Early Christian Writers', (PhD diss. University of Cincinnati, 2007), 60–1. Ashley Bacchi, *Uncovering Jewish Creativity in Book III of the Sibylline Oracles: Gender, Intertextuality, and Politics* (Leiden: Brill, 2020), 68,

this story of discovery, the antiquity of the oracles seems to be important because they are constructed as an external confirmation of what is found in Christian scriptures. As such they need to be realized as old enough to be free from any influence of Christian writings. In addition, the list establishes a canon of sibyls whose writings are not only antique, but known to various figures through history. Their ideas are returned to by such illustrious figures as Euripides, Vergil, and Plato, and thereby have a patina of continual trustworthiness.

A second passage establishing the antiquity of the sibyls comes in SibPr, 51–74. Here, the Cumaean sibyl is the focus. In this part of the prologue a story familiar from Dionysius of Halicarnassus and a number of other sources relates how the Cumaen Sibyl approached the Roman King Tarquinius (either Superbus or Priscus, depending on the version) with her nine books of oracles.[27] She is denied access to the king twice before he finally assents to read them. This results in the destruction of six of the nine books. The king then realizes the great value of the remaining three books and has them stored away and collects as many other oracles from around the world as possible. This setting within the reign of the sixth century BCE Roman monarchy both establishes antiquity and through it also furthers the theme of trust already seen. But, more importantly, this also establishes how these important oracles become "lost". This is, after all, yet another narrative of discovery. Obviously, the six books that were burned are not recoverable, but those that are stored away by the king instantly become inaccessible. Moreover, there is an impression that similar texts to these, coming from other sibyls, are scattered throughout the world, and can be found. So, although these are ancient writings that are clearly valuable, they are also established as in a precarious position vis-à-vis their continuous survival without the work of curators working to collect them.

This all fills out the background for the efforts of the anonymous voice of the collector in the prologue. Unlike the Gospel of Nicodemus or Ben Sira, the prologist's voice here makes no claims whatsoever about their identity. Nevertheless, their efforts are established as necessary in order to access these oracles. Without

---

discusses how this is present and part of the cultural hybridity of Ptolemaic Egypt in the early Jewish milieu of book 3 of the Sibylline Oracles.

27 On top of the sibylline prologue, the story is found in the *Theosophy* 3.29–39; Lactantius, *Divine Institutes* I.6.10–11; Aulus Gellius, *Attic Nights* 2.19, Pliny, *Natural History* 13.88; and Dionysius of Halicarnassus, *Roman History* 4.62.2–4. Olivia Stewart Lester, *Prophetic Rivalry, Gender, and Economics: A Study in Revelation and Sibylline Oracles 4–5* (Tubingen: Mohr Siebeck, 2018), 162, 203–7, points out the way in which these passages establish a sibylline discourse as political discourse that is critical of Rome, and the ways the story demonstrates value by using economic language and an economic transaction to describe the oracles.

their work toward collection and anthologization, the oracles are likely to remain scattered, or even worse, destroyed. The impression in the prologue is that the oracles are at constant risk of being lost. Therefore, when the voice of the anthologizer claims to have set down the oracles so that they are easily read, the prologist becomes yet again a salvific figure. They ensure that the timeless oracles reach the audience in a state wherein they can be accessed and engaged together. In addition, their actions bring the knowledge of the distant past into the present, and promise that it will continue to be read in the future.

5 Conclusion

By way of conclusion, I would only like to highlight what the poetics of discovery have shown in these three prologues. The prefatory passages establish that the text and/or corpus of knowledge with which they work bears strong connections to ancient, and somehow privileged knowledge. This is true whether it is the sum of knowledge of Israel's ancestors, the eyewitness testimony of a follower of Jesus, or the utterances of a number of prophetic speakers throughout Mediterranean history. This aspect of discovery stories, in part, lends value to the text being transmitted. Yet, these stories of discovery also highlight the fragility of this ancient knowledge that arises specifically because of its antiquity and foreignness. In so doing, such stories erect a long prehistory for their newly-produced texts. That prehistory establishes these texts as real entities that have a biography outside of the prologue or manuscript itself. The grandson's translation captures Israel's ancestral wisdom and education, including the knowledge and effort of his grandfather, Ben Sira. The Gospel of Nicodemus takes the knowledge gathered from a specific moment in time and places it in an official archive, underlining the fact that it has been secured and vetted in some way before it comes into the possession of Ananias. The Sibylline anthologist gathers together oracles from ancient prophetesses that have been scattered across the known world. These stories all show that the texts they introduce pre-existed their own efforts, but must be adapted so that they might be saved. The finding figure then arises as the hero, as the compositional agent of consequence, precisely because the figure has enacted change. He links past, present, and future. Taken together, these stories reveal that a desirable literary value surrounding such texts is that they are perennially of interest to audiences in various settings.

References

Bacchi, Ashley. *Uncovering Jewish Creativity in Book III of the Sibylline Oracles: Gender, Intertextuality, and Politics.* Leiden: Brill, 2020.
Bartlett, John. *Jews in the Hellenistic World: Josephus, Aristeas, the Sibylline Oracles, Eupolemus.* Cambridge: Cambridge University Press, 1985.
Beatrice, Franco. *Anonymi Monophysitae Theosophia: An Attempt at Reconstruction.* Leiden: Brill, 2001.
Bickerman, Elias. *The Jews in the Greek Age.* Cambridge: Harvard University Press, 1988.
Buitenwerf, Rieuwerd. *Book III of the Sibylline Oracles and its Social Setting: With an Introduction, Translation, and Commentary.* Leiden: Brill, 2003.
Collins, John. "Sibylline Oracles: A New Translation and Introduction." In *Old Testament Pseudepigrapha, Volume I: Apocalyptic Literature and Testaments*, edited by James Charlesworth. Garden City, NY: Doubleday, 1983, 317–472.
Ehrman, Bart; Plese, Zlatko. *The Apocryphal Gospels: Texts and Translations* Oxford: Oxford University, 2011.
Erbse, Hartmut. *Theosophorum Graecorum Fragmenta*, Stuttgart: Teubner, 1995.
Freund, Stefan. "Christian Use and Valuation of Theological Oracles: The Case of Lactantius' *Divine Institutes*." *Vigiliae Christianae* 60 (2006): 269–84.
Geffcken, Johannes. *Die Oracula Sibyllina.* Leipzig: J. C. Hinrichs'sche Buchhandlung, 1902.
Genette, Gérard. *Paratexts: Thresholds of Interpretation.* Translated by Jane Lewin. Cambridge: Cambridge University Press, 1997.
Hooker, Mischa. *The Use of Sibyls and Sibylline Oracles in Early Christian Writers.* PhD dissertation, University of Cincinnati, 2007.
Lange, Armin. "'The Law, the Prophets, and the Other Books of the Fathers' (Sir. Prologue) Canonical Lists in Ben Sira and Elsewhere?" In *Studies in the Book of Ben Sira: Papers of the Third International Conference on Deuterocanonical Books, Shime'on Centre, Pápa, Hungary, 18–20 May, 2006*, edited by Géza Xeravits and József Zsengeller. Leiden: Brill, 2008, 55–80.
Lester, Olivia Stewart. *Prophetic Rivalry, Gender, and Economics: A Study in Revelation and Sibylline Oracles 4–5.* Tubingen: Mohr Siebeck, 2018.
Mroczek, Eva. "True Stories and the Poetics of Textual Discovery." *Bulletin for the Study of Religion* 45 (2016): 21–31.
Mroczek, Eva. "Batshit Stories: New Tales of Discovering Ancient Texts," *Marginalia: Los Angeles Review of Books*, 22 June, 2018, https://marginalia.lareviewofbooks.org/batshit-stories-new-tales-of-discovering-ancient-texts.
Mroczek, Eva. "Truth and Doubt in Manuscript Discovery Narratives." In *Rethinking 'Authority' in Late Antiquity: Authorship, Law, and Transmission in Jewish and Christian Tradition*, edited by A.J. Berkovitz and Mark Letteney. London: Routledge, 2018. 139–60
Newsom, Carol. "Woman and the Discourse of Patriarchal Wisdom: A Study in Proverbs 1–9." In *Gender and Difference in Ancient Israel*, edited by Peggy Day. Minneapolis: Fortress, 1989, 142–60.
Parke, H.W. *Sibyls and Sibylline Prophecy in Classical Antiquity*, edited by B.C. McGing. London: Routledge, 1988.
Rzach, Aloisius. "Sibyllinische Orakel," *Pauly-Wissowa Realencyclopädie der classischen Altertumswissenschaft*, 2.2:2103–83.

Starr, Raymond. "The Circulation of Literary Texts in the Roman World." *Classical Quarterly* 37 (1987): 213–23.
Starr, Raymond. "The Used-Book Trade in the Roman World." *Phoenix* 44 (1990): 148–57.
Thompson, Bard. "Patristic Use of the Sibylline Oracles." *Review of Religion* 6 (1952): 115–36.
Van Groningen, Bernard. "ΕΚΔΟΣΙΣ." *Mnemosyne* 16 (1963): 1–17.
Vayntrub, Jacqueline. "The Book of Proverbs and the Idea of Ancient Israelite Education." *Zeitschrift für die Alttestamentliche Wissenschaft* 128 (2016): 96–114.
Wilson, Adrian. "What is a Text?" *Studies in the History and Philosophy of Science* 43 (2012): 341–58.
Wright, Benjamin. *Praise Israel for Wisdom and Instruction: Essays on Ben Sira and Wisdom, the Letter of Aristeas and the Septuagint.* Leiden: Brill, 2008.
Wright, Benjamin. "From Generation to Generation: The Sage as Father in Early Jewish Literature." In *Biblical Traditions in Transmission: Essays in Honor of Michael Knibb*, edited by Charlotte Hempel and Judith Lieu. Leiden: Brill, 2006, 309–32.
Ziegler, Joseph. *Septuaginta: Vetus Testamentum Graecum 12/2: Sapientia Iesu Filii Sirach.* Göttingen: Vandenhoeck & Ruprecht, 1980.

Part 2: **The Bible at Work:
Historical Case Studies**

Beatrice Victoria Ang
Power Dynamics in the Preached Word: A Fourth Century Case Study

Abstract: Preaching is an important Christian practice where we see the Bible being used. This chapter explores the mechanics behind the proclamation of scripture by drawing on the thought and practice of the celebrated preacher and Church Father, John Chrysostom (ca. AD 349–406). The aim is to provide a Chrysostomian perspective into what it means to "preach with power." Because preaching is always situational, a theological-historical methodology is employed. For this purpose, two sermons that Chrysostom delivered as bishop of Constantinople are analysed in the light of (1) insights from modern studies on his Christian appropriation of Hellenistic psychagogy; and (2) the controversy between pro-Nicenes and Arians regarding the implications of power in the essential relationship between the Father and the Son. The analysis shows that Chrysostom's multifaceted discourse on power is situated in his social, political, and religious context. For Chrysostom, the divine authority and ability of the Son must be affirmed if preaching is to have a positive effect on human well-being. His reasons have been shaped by practical and political considerations, as well as scripture-based theo-anthropological assumptions.

Keywords: John Chrysostom, Preaching, Scripture, Divine authority, Divine ability

1 Introduction

John Chrysostom, whose moniker means golden-mouth, is widely recognised as one of early Christianity's most prolific and gifted preachers.[1] He was born in

---

[1] Chrysostom's surviving sermons of varying genres (e.g., exegetical, polemical, and panegyrical), delivered in both Antioch and Constantinople, total over 800 and are distributed among 2,000 manuscripts. Majority of his sermons, based on Bernard Montfaucon's 18th century edition, can be found in volumes 47–64 of Jacques Paul Migne's *Patrologia Graeca*. Only 48 of his sermons have so far had modern critical editions, and these can be found in 11 volumes of *Sources Chrétiennes*. See James Daniel Cook, *Preaching and Popular Christianity: Reading the Sermons of John Chrysostom* [Oxford: Oxford University Press, 2019], 5, 23–4.

Beatrice Victoria Ang, Biblical Seminary of the Philippines, beatrice.ang@bsop.edu.ph

https://doi.org/10.1515/9783110768411-007

Antioch ca. AD 345–49 and later served as a presbyter there for about 11 years.[2] His skill in preaching, together with his virtuous character, was reportedly the reason for his election to the episcopal seat of Constantinople in either late AD 397 or early 398.[3] The sermons that are the subject of this chapter were the second and third sermons that Chrysostom preached after his episcopal ordination.[4] *Contra anomoeos homilia* 11 and *De Christi divinitate* were delivered only days apart,[5] and, as we shall see, share the same themes and aim. In them, Chrysostom touches on three facets of the power of Christ, upon which the power of preaching rests: power as authority (ἐξουσία); power as ability (δύναμις);

---

[2] See John Norman Davidson Kelly, *Golden Mouth: The Story of John Chrysostom—Ascetic, Preacher, Bishop* (Ithaca, NY: Cornell University Press, 1995), 296–8. Chrysostom became a presbyter in AD 386 but was a deacon for six years prior (ibid., 38).

[3] Sozomen, *Hist. eccl.* 8.2 (edited by Joseph Bidez et al., SC 516, 238); Socrates, *Hist. eccl.* 6.2 (edited by Günther C. Hansen, SC 505, 260–4).

[4] His first sermon, unfortunately, has not been preserved. See Paul Harkins, introduction to *St. John Chrysostom. On the Incomprehensible Nature of God* (Washington, D.C.: Catholic University of America Press, 1984), 33–5, 270n2. The likely existence of a first sermon is due to Chrysostom's opening remark in *Anom.* 11: "Μίαν ὑμῖν διελέχθην ἡμέραν, καὶ ἀπὸ τῆς ἡμέρας ἐκείνης οὕτως ὑμᾶς ἐφίλησα ὡς ἐξ ἀρχῆς καὶ ἐκ πρώτης ὑμῖν συντραφείς [...]" (edited by Anne Marie Malingrey, SC 396, 286).

[5] *Christ div.* is also known as *Anom.* 12. Despite the title, *Anom.* 11 and 12 were unlikely to have been aimed only against *anomoeans*. Malingrey, who prepared the critical edition for *Sources Chrétiennes*, informs us that it was Montfaucon who put all 12 sermons together and designated them *Contra Anomoeos*. Early manuscripts only put *Anom.* 1–5, 1–6, or 1–8 together. The problem with Montfaucon's decision, as Malingrey rightly points out, is that while *Anom.* 1–6 are evidently against *anomoeans*, i.e., naming them specifically in certain places and dealing with the incomprehensibility of God (which was the main point of controversy), the same cannot be said for *Anom.* 7–12. In the latter, the references are to "heretics" in general. I add that Chrysostom does name certain "heresies" but only as minor adversaries (e.g., Marcionites, Manichaeans). There is a main adversary mentioned and likened to Goliath, but this group is not named (*Anom.* 11.61–91 [SC 396, 292–4]). Moreover, *Anom.* 7–12 focus on defending the equality of the Father and the Son (I add, the divinity of the Son), which other groups besides the *anomoeans* denied (introduction to SC 396, 21–9). For sure, there are thematic links between *Anom.* 7–12 and 1–6, as Malingrey points out. Examples of this are Chrysostom's reference to "the glory of the only Begotten" and his use of συγκατάβασις and ταπεινοφροσύνη (ibid., 27–8). I think it cannot therefore be ruled out that Chrysostom saw the homilies as thematically related, even if he did not deliver all of them as a polemic strictly against the *anomoeans*. Indeed, there would have been a gap of 11 years between *Anom.* 1 and *Anom.* 11–12 since he delivered the latter when already bishop of Constantinople. The passing of time, as well as differences in setting and audience, would account for some of the changes in Chrysostom's expression and thought. However, some consistency would have also remained if his theological approach and the main threat as he saw it (i.e., the denial of Christ's divinity) remained the same. I discuss his adversaries further in relation to the Arian presence in Constantinople in section 2 below.

and power at work, or in operation, affecting something (ἐνέργεια). In the context of this paper, therefore, power dynamics refer to Chrysostom's demonstration of the connection between Christ's divine *authority* and the concrete expression of his divine *ability* through preaching, which *effects* spiritual healing. To an equally crucial but smaller extent, the roles of the preacher and of laypeople on the whole operation of preaching is also discussed.

2 The Historical Context of *Anom.* 11 and *Christ div.*

Chrysostom's aims in *Anom.* 11 and *Christ div.* are explicit. First, he wants to instruct his congregation on the equality of the Father and the Son. Proving this from scripture, as we shall see later, takes up the lion's share of his discourse. Second, he wants to persuade his listeners to come to church consistently. This is an exhortation Chrysostom constantly repeats. For example, in a revealing passage towards the end of *Anom.* 11, Chrysostom urgently exhorts his congregation to "cover over" the "poverty" of the Church of Constantinople not only "by coming [to Church] constantly" but by bringing their whole families, particularly their children, as new converts.[6] Chrysostom also appears to be very concerned about numbers. At the beginning of *Anom.* 11, he extols the fervent faith of the Constantinopolitan congregation but by comparing them to the "larger" congregation of Antioch.[7] Later, he reminds his congregation of the beginnings of the church in the book of Acts, saying it started with eleven members (minus Judas), then one hundred and twenty, then three thousand, then five thousand, then "they filled the whole world with the knowledge of God."[8] And then, in *Christ div.*, he ecstatically praises the increase in church attendance since his last sermon.[9]

The two points—instruction in Nicene orthodoxy and concern for church attendance—are very much related, for Chrysostom was shepherding the pro-Nicene church of Constantinople. Chrysostom has two reasons for insisting on

---

6 John Chrysostom, *Anom.* 11.39–41 (Harkins, trans., *Incomprehensible*, 284–5).
7 Ibid. 11.1–2 (270–1). Antioch's congregation is larger, but Constantinople's "patience and endurance" are greater. As we shall see, Chrysostom understood the difficulties that the church of Constantinople faced. He praises them for their fortitude but does not hide his desire to see them grow in numbers.
8 Ibid. 11.37 (283).
9 John Chrysostom, *Christ div.* 1 (Harkins, *Incomprehensible*, 286).

Nicene orthodoxy and church attendance—one is political, and the other is pastoral. Since the pastoral reason is explicitly what the two sermons are about, I will discuss it in greater depth later. The political reason, however, is more implicit, and so I will give a background here as to its importance.

The problem was that although the pro-Nicene church had been the imperially sanctioned church in Constantinople for at least 17 years prior to Chrysostom's arrival,[10] there were immense challenges to its growth and stability. As Justin Pigott has persuasively pointed out, the church of Constantinople was far from a well-established institution in the 390s. Constantinople was previously an insignificant city and only rose to prominence because of Constantine's imperial decree. The pro-Nicene church was new and lacked an institutional lineage and theological tradition that would have given it some stability in the face of competing faiths and frequent political shifts. Indeed, after Constantine, the pro-Nicene church underwent periods of intense prohibition and persecution under Arian-leaning emperors (e.g., Constantius and Valens), causing their numbers to dwindle down. In addition, because of the huge influx of people from across the empire (incentivised by the Constantinian and Theodosian dynasties), Constantinople was home to diverse ethnicities and religious faiths—pagans, *homoians*, Apollinarians, Novatians, Eunomians, etc. Even after Theodosius I became emperor and groups that did not affirm Nicene orthodoxy were technically "outlawed", there were still influential pagans and non-Nicenes working in his court. The same was likely true during the reign of his son, Arcadius, who was the emperor during Chrysostom's tenure.[11] Despite what the law said, therefore, the influence and status of the pro-Nicene church were not necessarily secure.

---

10 I.e., since AD 380, when Theodosius I's edict, *Cunctos Populos*, made Nicene Christianity the official faith of the empire (*Cod. Theod.* 16.1.2 [Clyde Pharr, trans., *The Theodosian Code and Novels and the Sirmondian Constitutions*, edited by Clyde Pharr et al. (Princeton, NJ: Princeton University Press, 152), 440]).

11 See Justin Pigott, "Capital Crimes: Deconstructing John's 'Unnecessary Severity' in Managing the Clergy of Constantinople," in *Revisioning John Chrysostom: New Approaches, New Perspectives*, edited by Chris L. De Wet and Wendy Mayer (Leiden: Brill, 2019), 743–6, 753–6. In the case of Theodosius I, Pigott points out that secret Eunomians (followers of the teachings of the *anomoean*, Eunomius) were discovered in his court and dealt with quite leniently. As for Arcadius, his general and later enemy, Gainas, was an Arian Goth (ibid. 750–2). And Arcadius's powerful prefect, Eutropius, although probably a pro-Nicene (we have no evidence to indicate otherwise), sometimes worked in favour of the pro-Nicene church and sometimes opposed it (John Chrysostom, *Eutrop.* 3 [PG 52.393–4]).

Of the non-Nicenes, Chrysostom's fiercest competitors were the Arians. Two groups of Arians are relevant to our study of *Anom.* 11 and *Christ div.*, namely the *homoians* and the *anomoeans*. The *homoians* held that the Son is "like" the Father but not in essence. From AD 360, the bishop of Constantinople was a *homoian*, Eudoxius. He ruled for 19 years and was succeeded by Demophilus, who was bishop during AD 381, the same year when Theodosius I banned heretics from holding assemblies inside the city.[12] In Chrysostom's time, there were still a good number of these *homoians* in Constantinople, as I will detail in due course.

The second group of Arians were the *anomoeans* or Eunomians, who held that the Son could not be "like" the Father in essence. The founders of this group were Aetius and Eunomius, who had previously been friends with Eudoxius but had to part ways with him because many of the *homoian* party did not accept the teachings of Eunomius.[13] Eunomius's teachings were apparently erudite and influential enough—not only in Constantinople but in surrounding regions—that they prompted responses from pro-Nicenes like Basil of Caesarea and Gregory of Nyssa.[14] We can therefore understand his appeal to the educated elite of Constantinople and, indeed, he was said to have taught in private houses there before he was finally banished by Theodosius I.[15] While we do not have evidence of a strong cohort of Eunomians still around during Chrysostom's tenure in Arcadius's reign (as we do have of the *homoians*), it is not unreasonable to assume that there were Christians, even from among Chrysostom's own congregation, who were familiar with Eunomius's teachings, especially since, in the process of arguing against him, Basil and Gregory preserved some of his doctrinal points in their polemic.

Chrysostom's aim to grow the pro-Nicene church would not, therefore, be easily achieved. Rival groups were in operation that kept potential believers away and even tempted some of his flock astray. If Chrysostom could sustain imperial backing for the pro-Nicene church, then more Constantinopolitans might join his church and support its ministries. But one way to sustain imperial favour was to show strong and consistent numbers. These considerations are

---

12 Socrates, *Hist. eccl.* 4.1, 14, 35; 5.3, 7, 12 (SC 505, 22–140, 154–86); cf. Sozomen, *Hist. eccl.* 7.2, 5, 14, 17 (SC 516, 74–158); *Nullus haereticus* (*Cod. Theod.* 16.5.6 [*Theodosian Code*, 451]).
13 Socrates, *Hist. eccl.* 4.13 (SC 505, 62).
14 For the critical edition of Eunomius's works of which only fragments have been preserved, see *Eunomius. The Extant Works*, edited and translated by Richard Paul Vaggione (Oxford: Clarendon Press, 1987). Basil of Caesarea's *Contra Eunomium* is available in SC, vols. 299 and 305, as is Gregory of Nyssa's *Contra Eunomium* (SC 521, 551).
15 Sozomen, *Hist. eccl.* 7.17 (SC 516, 150–8); Socrates, *Hist. eccl.* 5.20 (SC 505, 208–10).

evident in an important encounter between Chrysostom's pro-Nicene church and the *homoians* reported by the fifth-century historians, Socrates and Sozomen. Despite the aforementioned ban Theodosius I had instituted against heretics assembling in the city, the *homoians* found a way to make their presence and influence felt. At nighttime during solemn festivals, on Saturdays, and on Sundays, they would meet at public porticoes and hold processions from the city to their churches outside. As they did so, they would sing about their dogma antiphonally and also chant against the pro-Nicenes, "Where are those who say that the Three Persons constitute one Power?" Apparently "fearful lest any of his own church people should be led astray by witnessing these exhibitions," Chrysostom fought back by establishing his own processions with the funding of the empress and the administrative support of her eunuch, Briso. This back and forth between the two processions ultimately ended in violence, so that the emperor put a stop to the Arian processions.[16]

This story suggests that while imperial law favoured the pro-Nicenes, concessions were shown to other religious groups in practice. As scholars like Jonathan Stanfill and Nathanael Andrade have shown, processions in the ancient world were incredibly significant—a way for individuals and groups to make public statements about themselves and to recreate the meaning of the civic spaces around them.[17] What would the flourishing of *homoian* processions, with their intentionally provocative message, have communicated to their participants and to observers if not the threat that, in the ever-shifting religio-political landscape of late antiquity, a reversal of fortune is always imminent? And what does it say that, at least up until the eruption of violence, such processions were permitted? It is possible that the concession afforded to the *homoians* was simply an expression of imperial benevolence but it could also have been a diplomatic concession to a group that was influential because it still had a solid number of devoted adherents. Because of imperial support, Chrysostom was able to win the procession wars. His processions were much grander and were ultimately allowed to continue whereas the *homoian* processions were suppressed. How-

---

[16] Sozomen, *Hist. eccl.* 8.8 (SC 516, 270–2; Chester D. Hartranft, trans., NPNF 2/2:404); cf. Socrates, *Hist. eccl.* 6.8 (SC 505, 294–8). The Arians referred to here are *homoians* and not Eunomians, because the historians refer to Eunomians as a separate group elsewhere. See, for example, Sozomen, *Hist. eccl.* 7.12 (SC 516, 118)—Demophilus is called the president of the Arians and Eunomius the representative of the Eunomians.

[17] See, for example, Jonathan Stanfill, "The Body of Christ's Barbarian Limb: John Chrysostom's Processions and the Embodied Performance of Nicene Christianity," in De Wet and Mayer, *Revisioning Chrysostom*, 674–6; Nathanael Andrade, "The Processions of John Chrysostom and the Contested Spaces of Constantinople," *JECS* 18, no. 2 (2010): 161–89.

ever, if Chrysostom were to totally eclipse his rivals, he also needed strong public support. Preaching was a means for him to persuade people to join his cause.

And so, in *Anom.* 11 and *Christ div.*, Chrysostom makes full use of his persuasive powers to defend Nicene orthodoxy and to demonstrate its impact on the lives of his listeners. But before doing that, he gives the upstart church of Constantinople a sense of continuity with the apostolic church that hinges on their embrace of the Nicene faith. Because they embrace the true faith, they are members of the true church. They are not, after all, totally lacking in theological tradition. Their church may neither be as large nor as ancient as Antioch's (it was common knowledge that Antioch had apostolic ties), but their faith is more fervent.[18] In what sense? Their faith is like the faith demonstrated by God's followers in scripture. Like God's followers in scripture, they, too, face many adversaries and are sustained by grace. Thus, Chrysostom describes the church of Constantinople as 1) a flock of sheep surrounded by wolves on every side; 2) a ship encircled by storms and waves; 3) an olive tree standing in the midst of a furnace, threatened by the fires of heresy on every side. Yet the flock is not destroyed; the ship is still afloat; and the trees, enjoying the blessing of a heavenly dew, bloom and bear fruit.[19] He furthermore likens their church to David, who, fortified only by his faith, stood against the armed and armoured Goliath and "shone forth from within with the grace of the Spirit."[20] Chrysostom's words here are meaningful in light of the religio-political context in Constantinople that we had just discussed. He reinforces the divide between the pro-Nicene church and other faiths, and, in view of his repeated exhortations to church attendance, his sermons feel like a metaphorical "call to arms". The pro-Nicene church must grow, and, by its growth, demonstrate the superiority of the Nicene faith.

Having said all this, we must not neglect that Chrysostom also had pastoral reasons for defending the Nicene faith and encouraging people to regularly come to church. We must not dismiss that he had very real beliefs about the nature of human beings and their relationship with their creator rooted in his Christian worldview. That is, for Chrysostom, Christian teachings were not merely rhetorical constructs to aid him in his religio-political goals. He saw himself, as scholars like David Rylaarsdam and Wendy Mayer have extensively demonstrated, as a Christian philosopher.[21] That is, Chrysostom, in the tradition

---

18 John Chrysostom, *Anom.* 11.1–2 (Harkins, *Incomprehensible*, 270–1).
19 Ibid. 11.3 (271–2).
20 Ibid. 11.4–5 (272).
21 David Rylaarsdam, *John Chrysostom on Divine Pedagogy: The Coherence of His Theology and Preaching* (Oxford: Oxford University Press, 2014); Wendy Mayer, "Shaping the Sick Soul: Reshap-

of classical philosophers (like Socrates and Plato), practiced psychagogy, a means of using rhetoric to lead souls (or people) to truth with the goal of making them into good and virtuous citizens. In Chrysostom's psychagogy, however, Christianity is the true philosophy, Christian scripture is the formative literature, and virtue is defined as living a "heavenly way of life."[22] *Anom.* 11 and *Christ div.* confirm these findings. In the two sermons, Chrysostom defends the divinity of Christ using scripture and demonstrates how acknowledging this truth has a tangible impact on human well-being and the pursuit of virtue. It is to this discussion that we shall now turn.

3 Scripture and the ἐξουσία of Christ

As we noted in the previous section, Chrysostom opens *Anom.* 11 by comparing the church of Constantinople to David, who faced Goliath "fortified only by his faith." Chrysostom will take David's "faith" and apply it to his congregation not in the general sense of belief or trust in God but specifically to the role of scripture and Nicene orthodoxy in human well-being.

Chrysostom begins by directing his congregation's attention to the "stone" that David used to defeat Goliath. He interprets it allegorically, calling it the "cornerstone" and the "spiritual rock," which, in various places in the New Testa-

---

ing the Identity of John Chrysostom," in *Christians Shaping Identity from the Roman Empire to Byzantium: Studies Inspired by Pauline Allen*, edited by Geoffrey Dunn and Wendy Mayer (Leiden: Brill, 2015), 140–64. A growing number of Chrysostom scholars, confirming and supporting this view of Chrysostom as a Christian philosopher who practiced psychagogy, are changing the way Chrysostom is read. For example, Courtney Wilson VanVeller, *Paul's Therapy of the Soul: A New Approach to John Chrysostom and Anti-Judaism* (PhD diss., Boston University, 2015); Junghun Bae, *John Chrysostom on Almsgiving and the Therapy of the Soul* (Leiden: Brill Schöningh, 2021). These studies are built on the seminal work of Margaret Mitchell, who extensively demonstrated the influence of Greek *paideia* in Chrysostom's various interpretation and usage of the person and work of the Apostle Paul. Cf. Margaret Mitchell, *The Heavenly Trumpet: John Chrysostom and the Art of Pauline Interpretation* (Louisville: Westminster John Knox, 2002).

[22] See Rylaarsdam, *Pedagogy*, 13–48. The "heavenly way of life" for Chrysostom connotes many things which are beyond the scope of this paper. It is worth noting, however, that he connects it with the life of monks and of virgins, people who strive to live like angels on earth and who should be emulated, in a manner where moderate living and having control over the passions is key. See, for example, Pak-Wah Lai, "The Monk as Christian Saint and Exemplar in St. John Chrysostom's Writings," in *Saints and Sanctity*, edited by Peter Clarke and Tony Claydon (Suffolk: Boydell & Brewer, 2011), 21–7. Section 5 below touches a little bit on practical expressions of virtue.

ment, have been used to refer to Christ. In 1 Cor 10:4, for example, the apostle Paul gives a spiritual interpretation of the Old Testament story of Moses miraculously bringing forth water from a rock (Exod 17; Num 20). Paul teaches that the rock from which the wandering Israelites drank was a "spiritual rock," and that this rock was Christ. Because of the interpretive precedent set by Paul, Chrysostom argues that he, too, is justified in thinking of David's stone not just as an ordinary stone. Just as, in the case of Moses's rock, it was not the "nature of the visible stone" but the "power of the spiritual stone" that sent forth water, so David defeated Goliath not by "the visible stone" but by "the spiritual stone."[23]

Chrysostom's spiritualised interpretation of David's stone would ultimately also point to Christ. But he does not say that the stone itself is Christ—rather, the stone is scripture.[24] Picking up on the dichotomy between the visible and the spiritual, he quotes Paul again, this time from 2 Cor 10:4–5: "Our weapons are not merely carnal but spiritual, demolishing sophistries and reasoning and every proud height that raises itself against the knowledge of God." Claiming to follow the directive of this verse, Chrysostom promises that his discourse will not be "based on reasoned arguments (ἀπὸ λογισμῶν)" but "arguments from the Scriptures" (ἀπὸ τῶν Γραφῶν).[25] He carefully qualifies that he does *not* mean that it is impossible to arrive at truth through λογισμῶν. However, even if it were possible, "the reasonings of mortals are timid" (Wis 9:14). That is to say, even if something is proved true by reasoned arguments, such arguments could not "provide an assurance that is full enough" (πληροφορίαν) nor "faith which is sufficient" (πίστιν ἱκανήν) for the soul.[26] It is not, therefore, that Chrysostom is against λογισμῶν. He simply sees a lack or deficiency in human reasoning that only scripture can fill.

To fully grasp Chrysostom's comments here, we must mention that he does not think of assurance and faith for the soul as pertaining only to the acceptance of right doctrine. To be sure, believing in sound doctrine is part of what gives the soul πληροφορίαν and πίστιν ἱκανήν. But the gist of Chrysostom's argument in *Anom.* 11 and *Christ div.* is that while scripture testifies to

---

23 John Chrysostom, *Anom.* 11.6 (Harkins, *Incomprehensible*, 272).
24 In fact, although Chrysostom calls David's stone the "spiritual rock" and the "cornerstone," he intentionally leaves out that, in the NT, these terms are explicitly made in reference to *Christ* (and not scripture *per se*). Either Chrysostom forgot—or, more likely, he felt that it would detract from the connection he wanted to make between David's stone and scripture being a Christian's greatest "weapon" against heresy.
25 John Chrysostom, *Anom.* 11.48–49, 59–60 (SC 396, 290–2); *Anom.* 11.6–7 (Harkins, *Incomprehensible*, 273).
26 Ibid. 11.56–58 (SC 396, 292); *Anom.* 11.7 (Harkins, *Incomprehensible*, 273).

Nicene orthodoxy (this being correct knowledge), Nicene orthodoxy validates the power of scripture to positively affect human souls, leading Christians to "join the rightness of [their] way of life and the deeds [they] do to the correctness of the teaching [they] embrace so that what pertains to [their] salvation may not be divided in two."[27] That is, for Chrysostom, right knowledge is incomplete if not joined to right way of living. By λογισμῶν, one can arrive at some truths, but it will not lead to that perfect marriage between right knowledge and virtuous living that are the characteristics of a healthy soul. Scripture is needed for that.

But why? What is it about scripture that gives it such power over the soul? For Chrysostom, the source of scripture's power is the divine authority of Jesus Christ. He particularly defends the Old Testament because its connection to Christ has been doubted by several heretical groups,[28] as well as by Jewish communities. On the contrary, Chrysostom argues, "the glory of the only begotten shines forth with a great abundance of light not only in the words of the evangelists and apostles but also in what the prophets said and in the entire Old Testament."[29] In fact, Christ himself said: "If you believed Moses, you would believe me for he wrote about me."[30] For Chrysostom, Christ more than approves the OT. In other works, he goes so far as to refer to the whole of scripture as "the word of Christ" (ὁ λόγος τοῦ Χριστοῦ). For example, in his homily on Colossians 3, where Paul exhorts his readers, "Let the word of Christ dwell in you richly," Chrysostom stresses, "Hearken ye [...] how to you too [Paul] commits especially the reading of the Scriptures; and that not to be done lightly [...] but with much earnestness." And, later, he exhorts his audience: "[G]et you at least the New Testament, the Apostolic Epistles, the Acts, the Gospels for your constant teachers. [...] This is the cause of all evils, the not knowing the Scriptures."[31]

The advantage of Chrysostom's Christ-centred view of scripture is that it allows him to see scripture as a whole and therefore to harmonise his interpretation of various biblical passages. In *Anom.* 11 and *Christ div.*, this helps him build a strong case for Christ's divinity, which will be very important to his later argument that the human soul needs scripture.

---

27 Ibid. 11.28 (Harkins, *Incomprehensible*, 280).
28 He mentions the "heretics," Marcion, Manichaeus, and Valentinus, and also mentions "the Manichaeans" as a group.
29 Ibid. 11.8 (273).
30 Ibid. 11.11 (274).
31 John Chrysostom, *Hom. Col.* 9.1 (PG 62.361–2; John Broadus, trans., NPNF 1/13:300–1).

How, then, does Chrysostom defend Christ's divinity? It must be noted that, despite being a *homoousion*, Chrysostom consistently avoided drawing inferences from scripture about divine essence.³² He affirmed the *homoousion* formula: God is one θεότητα in three ὑποστάσεις, wherein the difference in ὑποστάσεις is a difference in προσώποις and not in οὐσίας.³³ However, as is the case here in *Anom.* 11 and *Christ div.*, he focused on proving the equal power of the Father and the Son. Arguably, Chrysostom's objection to *homoianism* and *anomoeanism* is that their denial of the divine persons' equality of essence compromises their equality of power. As Michel Barnes has pointed out, there were complex debates among Nicenes and Arians on what is meant by scripture when it refers to Christ as the "power of God" (1 Cor 1:24). For example, Athanasius believed that the Son is by nature the power of God (this being the proof of his divinity), and that the Son alone is the power of God. However, others, like Eusebius of Nicomedia and Asterius the Cappadocian, argued that Christ is just one of God's many powers referenced in scripture. Asterius is an example of one who saw God as having two kinds of powers—that which was his own and that in reference to his ministers. Christ is the most important of God's powers, but he is still a minister.³⁴ Eunomius, meanwhile, believed that God's essence is simple and ingenerate. Therefore, any product of his must also be simple and ingenerate. Non-essential creation is impossible for him. Eunomius thus ascribed creative authority to the Father but creative activity only to the Son. Since the Son is both ingenerate and can create, he cannot be God.³⁵ As we shall see, Chrysostom would not have accepted views similar to Asterius's or Eunomius's. For him, the Son must have both divine ability and divine authority. It is on these that scripture's impact on human well-being rests. If Christ is not God, then his words neither have power over the human soul nor need to be obeyed. The meaning of this will get clearer as we move along. First, let us see how Chrysostom defends the divine authority of Christ and how it relates to scripture.

---

32 For example, John Chrysostom, *Anom.* 2.32 (Harkins, *Incomprehensible*, 83–4): "He gave freedom to you so that you might give glory to him. But whenever a man is meddlesome and inquisitive about God's essence, he insults God."
33 John Chrysostom, *Sac.* 4.4.78–80 (SC 272, 260).
34 There are, of course, differences in its implication and usage among different Nicenes and Arians. See full discussion in Michel Rene Barnes, *The Power of God: Δύναμις in Gregory of Nyssa's Trinitarian Theology* (Washington, D.C.: Catholic University of America Press, 2001), 125–72.
35 I am simplifying Eunomius's argument here to focus on what Chrysostom found objectionable. Barnes, again, gives a fuller discussion of the intricacies of Eunomius's argument about divine power. See *Power*, 177–219.

Chrysostom begins his defence by pointing to the divine work of the creation of human beings. In performing this divine act, God said: "Let us make man in our image and likeness." Chrysostom argues that God must have been saying these words to someone who shared an "equality of honour" with him, for he did not use the simple command "Make!" (ποίησον) as he would have done if speaking to a servant, but "Let us make" (ποιήσωμεν) as though engaging in consultation (τῆς συμβουλῆς).[36] The strength of Chrysostom's interpretation, as we said, depends on harmonisation. He makes the following arguments:

1. Scripture sometimes says that "God has no counsellor [σύμβουλον]" (cf. Isa 40:13; Rom 11:33–34; Wis 9:13). So how can the Son be his counsellor? Chrysostom argues that scripture says the former whenever it wishes to convey that God needs no one. On the other hand, here in Genesis, scripture refers to the Son as God's counsellor because it wishes to convey their equal honour (cf. Isa 9:5).[37]
2. To show that there is a difference between how one speaks to a servant and to an equal, Chrysostom brings up the NT story of the centurion who asked Jesus to heal his servant (Matt 8:5–13). Though Jesus offered to come to the centurion's house to perform the healing, the centurion, believing himself unworthy to have Christ come under his roof, refused. He reasoned that Jesus only had to say the word and his servant would be healed, for the centurion, too, had subordinates and servants under him who were quick to obey his word. Chrysostom takes this as a demonstration of the man's faith, particularly that he recognised the superiority of Jesus as master [τοῦ Δεσπότου]).[38] And Jesus affirmed the centurion's insight by not correcting him. Jesus did not say, "The opinion you have of me is greater than what belongs to me. [...] You think that I give orders because I have authority (αὐθεντίας), but I have no authority."[39] Instead, Jesus said, "Amen, I say to you, I have not found such great faith in Israel."[40] Chrysostom argues,

---

36 John Chrysostom, *Anom.* 11.115–18 (SC 396, 296); *Anom.* 11.12–13 (Harkins, *Incomprehensible*, 274–5).
37 Ibid. 11.118–24 (SC 396, 296–8); *Anom.* 11.13–17 (Harkins, *Incomprehensible*, 275–6).
38 Ibid. 11.156–57 (SC 396, 300); *Anom.* 11.18–20 (Harkins, *Incomprehensible*, 276–7).
39 Ibid. 11.171–74 (SC 396, 302); *Anom.* 11.21 (Harkins, *Incomprehensible*, 277–8). Chrysostom uses αὐθεντία and ἐξουσία interchangeably in this text (see point 3). Both words connote legitimate authority. Chrysostom uses ἐξουσία, however, to express the identical nature of the Father's and the Son's authority or power. He switches to αὐθεντία for illustrative purposes, since αὐθεντία is a word for authority that stylistically corresponds to the identification of Jesus as a δεσπότης.
40 Ibid. 11.22 (Harkins, *Incomprehensible*, 278).

"Therefore the master's praise ratified what the centurion had said. No longer are they words spoken by the centurion; they now express a declaration from the master."[41]

3. Returning to Genesis, Chrysostom notes that Christ did not just make man with the Father but that man was made in their single image (μίαν εἰκόνα), since the Father said, "According to *our* image and likeness [ital. mine]."[42] It is tempting to think of "image" here as referring to "essence." However, in Chrysostom's *Homilies on Genesis*, he explicitly interprets the *imago Dei* as authority or dominion over creation which human beings received from God.[43] He makes the same emphasis on authority here. As proof that Christ shares a single image with the Father, he points out that Christ is described multiple times in scripture as sitting at the Father's right hand. Why? To show that "they are the same in honour [τὸ ὁμότιμον] and exactly alike in power [τῆς ἐξουσίας τὸ ἀπαράλλακτον]. For a subordinate does not sit with his superior but stands alongside him."[44] While angels are always standing alongside or around God, attending to Him (Dan 7:9–10; Isa 6:1–2; 1 Kgs 22:19), the Son is seated at the Father's right hand. So, Chrysostom insists of Christ, "You must realize that his dignity is that of a master possessing authority [αὐθεντίαν]."[45] Quoting Heb 1:7 which says, "Of the angels he says, 'He makes his angels spirits, and his ministers flaming fire; but of the Son, 'Your throne, O God, is forever and ever'," Chrysostom says of Paul (to whom he attributes the epistle to the Hebrews): "By means of the throne he is showing us the Son's kingly power."[46]

With such proofs, then, Chrysostom defends Christ's divine authority. Immediately afterwards, he gives this exhortation:

> Therefore, since our discourse has proved by all these texts that the Son is not valued as one who ministers but has the dignity of a master, let us worship him as our master because he is equal in honour to the Father. He himself commanded us to do this when he said: "So that all men may honour the Son just as they honour the Father." Let us join the

---

41 Ibid.
42 Ibid. 11.192 (SC 396, 304); *Anom.* 11.23–24 (Harkins, *Incomprehensible*, 278).
43 John Chrysostom, *Hom. Gen.* 8.3–4 (PG 53.72–3); 16.4 (PG 53.130).
44 John Chrysostom, *Anom.* 11.195–96 (SC 396, 304); *Anom.* 11.24 (Harkins, *Incomprehensible*, 278–9).
45 Ibid. 11.25–26 (Harkins, *Incomprehensible*, 279).
46 Ibid. 11.27 (Harkins, *Incomprehensible*, 279–80); διὰ τοῦ θρόνου τὴν βασιλικὴν ἡμῖν ἐξουσίαν δηλῶν (*Anom.* 11.219–20 [SC 396, 306]).

rightness of our way of life and the deeds we do to the correctness of the teaching we embrace so that what pertains to our salvation may not be divided in two.[47]

In this brief statement, Chrysostom thus gives the reason why Christ's divine authority (to which "the correctness of the teaching we embrace" pertains) is important to recognise. Recognition of it necessitates worship and worshipful action on the part of believers. But what sort of action does Chrysostom expect from them? In *Anom.* 11, at least, it is that they constantly come to church. But church attendance is not the goal in itself. Chrysostom highlights attending church specifically to hear the preaching of the Word. He asserts, for instance, "But nothing can set your lives straight and make them exactly right so much as can your constant attendance at the church and your eager attention in listening to what is said here."[48] And, "we reap benefit because we refresh our souls with the word of God."[49] And also, "What food is to the body, the teaching of God's word is to the soul" (cf. Matt 4:4).[50] Chrysostom turns his congregations' attention, therefore, from obligation (i.e., come to church to worship) to advantage (i.e., come to church to refresh your souls). Now this advantage also rests on the theological premise that presupposes the divinity of Christ. Chrysostom discusses it in more detail in the next sermon, *Christ div.*, where he continues his discourse on Christ's divine power. However, in *Christ div.*, he shifts his focus from power as divine authority to power as divine ability.

4 The δύναμις of Christ and the Healing of the Soul

At the opening of *Christ div.*, Chrysostom delightedly observes the increase in church attendance since his last sermon a few days ago. Using an agricultural metaphor, he attributes this increase to God's grace, saying that grace enables spiritual sowing to produce crops very quickly. But while grace tends and cultivates, the speed of harvest also depends on whether the souls being cultivated are "rich and fertile".[51] Joyful at receiving rich returns from his congregation after only a little labour on his part, he thus promises to resume his task of "cul-

---

47 Ibid. 11.28 (Harkins, *Incomprehensible*, 280).
48 Ibid. 11.29 (280).
49 Ibid. 11.33 (281–2).
50 Ibid. 11.29 (280).
51 John Chrysostom, *Christ div.* 3 (Harkins, *Incomprehensible*, 287).

tivation" with full attention.⁵² Thus we have Chrysostom identifying three key "players" in the operation of preaching: 1) the preacher who cultivates faith by his preaching; 2) the listener who hears and responds through action; and, 3) God, who enables growth. Of these three, it is the role of God that is quite abstract and mysterious. What is it that God does that causes people to be responsive? What is this grace that he gives? Chrysostom successfully concretises God's work by showing its ties to scripture and its power to heal.

Before going into his exegetical discourse, Chrysostom first reminds his congregation of the harmony between the OT and the NT. This will be important later. Quoting John 5:46 (Christ: "If you believed Moses, you would believe me") and Deut 18:15 (Moses: "The Lord your God shall raise up for you a prophet from among your brethren as he raised up me; to him shall you listen"), Chrysostom asserts, "Christ sent the Jews back to Moses so that, through Moses, he might draw them to himself. [...] let us believe in whatever Christ does or says, both in all other things and also in that miracle which you heard in today's reading."⁵³

The miracle in question was the healing of the paralytic at the pool of Bethesda. The story, recorded in John 5, begins as follows: During one of the Jewish feasts, Jesus went up to Jerusalem to the pool called Bethesda. At certain times, an angel would go down into the pool and stir the waters. The first person to jump into the pool after the surging of the water was cured, no matter what sickness he had. So, in those five porticoes by the pool, a multitude of sick, blind, and lame people lay in wait for the water to be stirred up.⁵⁴

What was Christ's purpose for coming to Jewish feasts? Chrysostom immediately seizes on this detail, asserting that Christ intentionally went to where he knew people would gather as he was eager to heal the sick. In the Greek, Chrysostom says of Christ, Ὅτε τοίνυν πλήρης ὁ σύλλογος αὐτῶν ἦν καὶ ἀπηρτισμένον τὸ θέατρον, τότε εἰς μέσον ἐρχόμενος τὰ πρὸς τὴν σωτηρίαν τῆς ἐκείνων ψυχῆς ἐπεδείκνυτο. Paul Harkins translates this as Chrysostom saying that Christ "used to come into [the people's] midst and show them the truths that bring salvation to their souls."⁵⁵ However, the Greek does not have "truths" as the object of the verb "show" (ἐπεδείκνυτο). Since ἐπεδείκνυτο is in the middle voice, it is better to think of it as Christ giving an exhibition of himself, i.e., through his healing power. The emphasis here is not on Christ imparting "truths" or "teaching" *per se* but performing wonders. This is supported by

---

52 Ibid. 4 (287).
53 Ibid. 5–6 (287).
54 Ibid. 6 (287–8).
55 Ibid. 60–62 (SC 396, 324); *Christ div.* 7 (Harkins, *Incomprehensible*, 288).

Chrysostom emphasising that Christ was there to *cure* and also the fact that Chrysostom metaphorically refers to the gathering of sick people as a θέατρον. In this imagery, Christ takes on—in a striking reversal of the usually negative sense that the theatre connotes in Chrysostom—the role of a performer.[56]

For Chrysostom, the divine δύναμις of Christ manifests itself in his ability to heal. Christ's healing, and therefore his power, is unique and superior to that of a mere angel or minister. Chrysostom compares the healing granted through the pool of Bethesda to the healing of Christ in "the pool of the waters of baptism."[57] The healing administered through a servant (i.e., an angel) could heal only one person,[58] while the master's (i.e., Christ's) healing in baptism can cure as many people as necessary. The servant's healing only "healed imperfections and mutilations of the body, [but] the master cures the wickedness of the soul."[59] The servant had to come down and stir the waters of Bethesda, but it is enough, in the baptismal waters, to evoke the master's name "so to bestow on them the entire cause of their power to cure."[60] Chrysostom's stress on Christ as master again points to his divinity. Chrysostom is adamant that Christ is not just one of God's many powers. He is not one of the angels sometimes described in scripture as "principalities and powers" (Eph 6:12). For Chrysostom, there is no in-between. Either Christ's power is God's, which makes him God—or it is not, which makes him a minister.

In the course of the sermon, Chrysostom therefore shows further proof of Christ exhibiting authority and power that only God can. Chrysostom gives an extensive discussion of the manner by which Christ healed the paralytic. Why, Chrysostom asks, did Christ heal the paralytic by commanding him to "take up his mattress and walk" when he knew it was the Sabbath and the Jewish religious leaders would complain?[61] Chrysostom gives two interrelated answers. First, intending to free the Jews from observing the Law of Moses, Christ was, little by little, bringing the observation of the Sabbath to an end.[62] Second, because some were slandering his miracles, Christ wanted to show that the mira-

---

56 As Blake Leyerle, *Theatrical Shows and Ascetic Lives: John Chrysostom's Attack on Spiritual Marriage* (Berkeley, CA: University of California Press, 2001) has demonstrated, Chrysostom used theatrical commonplaces to ridicule monks and virgins who lived together in a so-called "spiritual marriage" (211).
57 Ibid. 8 (Harkins, *Incomprehensible*, 289).
58 Ibid.
59 Ibid. 10 (288–9).
60 Ibid. 10 (289).
61 John Chrysostom, *Christ div.* 24 (Harkins, *Incomprehensible*, 294).
62 Ibid. 24 (295).

cle was not done by human skill but by divine power (θεία δύναμις). That is, onlookers would have realised that the paralytic's healing was not fake, for "[u]nless his limbs had been made solid and his joints held fast, he would not have been able to support the weight on his shoulders."[63] Moreover, while an ordinary human physician could not possibly perform an instantaneous healing of such a grave disability, in the case of Christ, "[a]s soon as the sacred word was uttered by his holy tongue, the sickness fled, the word became deed, and the whole illness was completely cured."[64] The connection between the "sacred word" and the paralytic's healing is crucial. Chrysostom contends: "[T]he word of Christ accomplished all this. Yet the words were not mere words but the words of God. [...] For if God's words made man when man did not exist, much more will they make him whole again and restore him to health even though he has grown feeble and weak with disease."[65]

We thus arrive at the crux of Chrysostom's argument. In *Anom.* 11, he had argued that the Father and the Son created the first man together. Since Christ possesses the same creative power as the Father, it is a simple thing for him to restore that which he, in the first place, created. Unlike Eunomius, however, who contended that the Son created only by the authority of the Father, Chrysostom insists that Christ possesses both the creative power and the authority. Hence, he points out that Christ both *healed* and *commanded*, as the healed paralytic himself later testified to the Jews: "He who made me well said to me, 'take up your mattress and walk.'" This is a confession by the healed man, Chrysostom claims, that Christ was both his physician (τὸν ἰατρὸν) and the lawgiver (τὸν νομοθέτην) who was worthy of his trust (ἀξιόπιστόν).[66] Chrysostom's designation of Christ as physician and lawgiver, then, is highlighting two sides of Christ's power. Christ's role as physician highlights his divine *ability*, whereas his position as a lawgiver signifies his divine *authority*. Indeed, with the designation of Christ as lawgiver, we realise why Chrysostom earlier mentioned that one of Christ's aims was the eventual abrogation of the Sabbath. This, too, is a statement of Christ's divinity and his authority. Seeing that God gave the Law of Moses to the Jews, only God can set them free from it as well.

The connection between Christ's divine authority and divine ability is that the latter is an expression and proof of the former. Chrysostom demonstrates this in his discussion of Jesus's answer to the Jews who confronted him for

---

[63] Ibid. 221–23 (SC 396, 336); *Christ div.* 25–26 (Harkins, *Incomprehensible*, 295–6).
[64] Ibid. 27–28 (Harkins, *Incomprehensible*, 296–7).
[65] Ibid. 29 (297).
[66] Ibid. 269–71 (SC 396, 338); *Christ div.* 31–32 (298).

breaking the Sabbath. Jesus declares, "My Father works even until now, and I work."[67] Such a claim, Chrysostom argues, would not have helped Christ's case if he had been inferior in authority to the Father. An ordinary person would not escape punishment, for example, if he dared to put on a purple robe or crown befitting only a king. And only an emperor can pardon criminals who have committed heinous crimes—a judge will be punished if he dared do this without the emperor's approval.[68] Chrysostom thus concludes that only one who is "himself an emperor or one who has the same dignity [...] will feel quite confident in saying that he is only doing what the emperor does. Just as their pre-eminence is one and the same [ἡ τῆς ἀρχῆς μία ὑπεροχή], so, too, their power [ἡ ἐξουσία] would naturally be one and the same."[69]

The claim of divine authority is then backed up by the work to which Christ refers – a work only God, who created human being, is capable of doing. Through a command, Jesus instantaneously restored a human being to a state of wholeness and health. This act of restoration or healing is part of what Chrysostom perceives as God's providential work. For, Genesis says, God rested after six days of creation. The ongoing divine work to which Christ must therefore be referring is "God's daily providence [τὴν καθημερινὴν πρόνοιαν]."[70] That is, Chrysostom explains, God is holding together what he produced. All creatures (angels or powers, visible or invisible) enjoy the benefit of His providence. Deprived of God's providential action, creatures "waste away, they perish, they are

---

[67] This verse was an important verse in the pro-Nicene debates against the Eunomians. Basil of Caesarea used it to defend the Son's equality with the Father by saying their equality is an "identity of power." That is, "all the Father's power is contained in [the Son];" hence, "whatsoever He should see the Father doing, these same the Son does likewise" (*Cont. Eunom.* 1.23 [Mark Delcogliano and Andrew Radde-Gallwitz, trans., *St. Basil of Caesarea. Against Eunomius* (Washington D.C.: Catholic University of America Press, 2011), 124–5]). See also Pak Wah Lai, who argues and demonstrates that Chrysostom may have learned the "principle of equivalence" from Basil, i.e., proving Christ is divine because he shares the same knowledge, authority, and power as the Father ("John Chrysostom's Reception of Basil of Caesarea's Trinitarian Theology," *Scrinium* 15, no. 1 [July 2019]: 74–7).
[68] John Chrysostom, *Christ div.* 44–45 (Harkins, *Incomprehensible*, 302–3).
[69] Ibid. 392–93 (SC 396, 348); *Christ div.* 46–50 (Harkins, *Incomprehensible*, 303–5).
[70] Ibid. 424 (SC 396, 350). Chrysostom's position here is slightly similar to Gregory Nazianzen. Nazianzen also thinks that the work to which Christ is referring is creation and "the government and preservation of the things which He has made." The difference between them is that Nazianzen does not see a "likeness of things done" between Christ's miracles and the Father's creative work. They are alike only "in respect of the Authority" (*Or.* 30.11 [Charles Gordon Browne, trans., NPNF 2/7:313]). Chrysostom, however, as we have seen, sees a parallel between speaking human beings into creation and speaking to restore them to health.

gone." Christ is distinguishing between those who exercise providence and care (in the context, the Father and the Son) and those who are sustained by it (i.e., all creation). Christ is claiming to be of the former and not of the latter. Hence, he is equal to the Father.[71] Implicit also in Chrysostom's argument is that the seventh day is a Sabbath for human beings but not for God, who "rested" from creation but in fact goes on working. The act of healing that Christ did is simply part of that providential work, in that part of keeping his creation together is mending the broken parts.

Chrysostom's insistence on Christ's divine authority in addition to his ability is crucial to his pastoral aims. Christ's words heal, but they are like medicine that must be received by the patient if they are to positively impact the human soul. If Chrysostom were to emphasise Christ's ability only, this would minimise human responsibility to heed and obey Christ's words. If he were to emphasise authority only, then it would be like asking human beings to heal themselves without the aid of grace. But, in fact, the word of Christ works its power on fertile souls, and fertility is evinced not just in cognitive assent but purposeful action. Why is this the case and how does the preached Word affect human souls? This will be the subject of our last section.

5 The ἐνέργεια of the Preached Word

Our focus in the previous sections was on Chrysostom's arguments in *Anom.* 11 and *Christ div.* about the divine authority and ability of Christ. We also noted that Chrysostom tied that authority and ability to Christ's words. Chrysostom was especially keen to associate Christ's words with scripture in the ministry of the church. We had already discussed two reasons. First, in order to sustain imperial favour and increase public regard for the pro-Nicene church, he desired to see more consistent attendance in church. Second, theologically, Nicene orthodoxy protected the efficacy of scripture for spiritual healing by anchoring its power in the divine authority and ability of Christ.

In discussing the ἐνέργεια of the preached Word in the human person, we must stress the significance of human action and response in Chrysostom. As we had noted earlier, Chrysostom saw himself as a philosopher in the tradition of classical philosophers. As such, he also saw himself as a doctor of the soul. This self-perception, as Mayer has most cogently argued, is important to our

---

71 John Chrysostom, *Christ div.* 51–52 (Harkins, *Incomprehensible*, 305).

understanding of why and how Chrysostom preached. In Chrysostom's anthropology, the boundaries between body and soul, and so also of their state of sickness and health, are blurred. Things that affect the soul affect the body and vice versa.[72] Chrysostom's preaching was a form of therapy for the soul wherein he used speech to help the soul resist the passions. Thus, in his preaching, Chrysostom does not just correct his audience's rational belief—he includes exhortations to physical discipline (e.g., fasting) and the overcoming of physical vices. Put another way, he preached from scripture with the goal of effecting transformation in the *whole* of the listener's person—this approach being possible because human beings are *embodied* souls. When transformed holistically in this way, listeners become what Mayer calls "living embodied hermeneutic exemplars," because they imitate and live out what was preached to them.[73]

Chrysostom's exhortations in *Anom.* 11 and *Christ div.* reflect and confirm Mayer's findings. Chrysostom (as the preacher) makes an effort not just to give his congregation doctrinal information but invites them to see the whole of their life, including their simple presence in church, as part of the operation of preaching. The theological premise for lay participation in preaching is set forth in Chrysostom's interpretation of the actions of the paralytic of Bethesda. The paralytic's patient endurance of suffering, his response to Christ's question ("Do you want to be healed?"), how he was healed, and his response to the Jewish leaders' criticism after, all demonstrate how Chrysostom viewed the ἐνέργεια of Christ's words on an individual and the community around him. Indeed, Chrysostom makes the paralytic into something of an exemplar for his congregation to contemplate and emulate:

> Let all men listen carefully, all who live with the weakness of their infirmity, all who endure the crises of worldly affairs, all who have lived with the surging storms of unexpected troubles. This paralytic lies before us a haven open to all, as a safe port from human disasters.[74]

Chrysostom's argument here is intentionally provocative in that he uses language that is not normally used to describe sick people in abject poverty. It is usually those who have wealth that are described as "safe ports" and it is the

---

[72] Mayer, "Shaping," 146–7.
[73] Wendy Mayer, "The Homiletic Audience as Embodied Hermeneutic: Scripture and Its Interpretation in the Exegetical Preaching of John Chrysostom," in *Hymns, Homilies and Hermeneutics in Byzantium*, edited by Sarah Gador-Whyte and Andrew Mellas (Leiden: Brill, 2021), 11–29.
[74] John Chrysostom, *Christ div.* 12–13 (Harkins, *Incomprehensible*, 290–1).

poor and the sick that depend on their alms and mercy to survive.[75] Yet, here, Chrysostom is reversing the situation. The hapless paralytic is described as a safe haven for the congregation of Constantinople, which, given that the city was the emperor's base, must have counted rich and powerful people among its members.[76] Yet Chrysostom could justify such a reversal to his audience because he presents the paralytic as a kind of holy man or ascetic. It was common for holy men and monks to serve as spiritual patrons or teachers to the wealthy, who in turn sustained them or their ministry with material provisions. But these spiritual teachers normally *chose* poverty.[77] The paralytic did not, yet Chrysostom still paints him as a person of virtue who had strength of soul (τὸν τόνον τῆς ψυχῆς).[78] Though the paralytic did not choose to be sick and poor, Chrysostom commends him for bearing his situation well. Chrysostom thus transforms the despised paralytic into someone from whom his congregation may learn. Indeed, he asserts that Christ saw the paralytic's virtue and asked him if he wanted to get well not because Christ did not know the answer but to give the man an opportunity to speak about his tragic life, so that he may become a teacher of patience (γενέσθαι διδάσκαλον ὑπομονῆς) to others.[79] Chrysostom praises the man's endurance of soul (τῆς ψυχῆς τὴν καρτερίαν).[80] For, though sick people are normally sullen and surly, the paralytic was not angered by Christ's question. Rather, "with great reasonableness" (μετὰ πολλῆς τῆς ἐπιεικείας),[81] due to the "virtue and discipline of his whole way of life" (τὴν φιλοσοφίαν καὶ τὴν ὑπομονὴν ἅπασαν),[82] the paralytic simply replied, "Yes, Lord, but I have no one to put me into the pool when the water is stirred."[83] And despite the fact that the paralytic would each year be disappointed in his hopes (because someone else gets into the water before him), for thirty-eight years, he never gave up coming.[84] As a result of his virtue and discipline, the paralytic

---

75 For example, John Chrysostom, *Laz.* 2.5 (PG 48.989–90).
76 For examples of Chrysostom's partnership with the wealthy, see Wendy Mayer, "Constantinopolitan Women in Chrysostom's Circle," *VC* 53, no. 3 (1999): 265–88.
77 See Wendy Mayer, "Poverty and Generosity Toward the Poor in the Time of John Chrysostom," in *Wealth and Poverty in Early Church and Society*, edited by Susan R. Holman (Grand Rapids, MI: Baker Academic, 2008), 140–58.
78 John Chrysostom, *Christ div.* 118 (SC 396, 328).
79 Ibid. 136–39 (330).
80 Ibid. 141 (330).
81 Ibid. 157 (330).
82 Ibid. 121–23 (328); literally: "his philosophy and total endurance".
83 Ibid. 14–19 (Harkins, *Incomprehensible*, 291–3).
84 Ibid. 20–22 (293–4). Most people, Chrysostom points out, quickly give up when their prayers go unanswered.

"received his cure with greater glory," in that it was not just an angel that cured him but Christ, the master of the angels.[85]

As Chrysostom moves from a description of the paralytic's suffering to his healing, we see the latter's exemplar portrait also undergo a shift. If, in the beginning, the paralytic was only an exemplar of patient endurance, he afterwards becomes a monument (τρόπαιον) of Christ's power. But he is not passive even in the moment of being healed. Chrysostom makes much of the fact that Christ told the man to carry his own bed. Not only would the paralytic's identity be confirmed by him carrying his bed,[86] if the paralytic could lift his bed, he would be "exhibiting a monument to the defeat of his disease and an indisputable proof of his return to health."[87] When the man is later confronted by the Jews for carrying his mat on the Sabbath, he responds by affirming the healing done to him. As we noted previously, Chrysostom interprets his words ("The man who healed me said to me, 'Take up your mattress and walk'") as a confession that Christ had both authority and ability to heal him and that Christ is, therefore, God. So, then, by his testimony, Chrysostom proclaims,

> The paralytic becomes an *evangelist*, a teacher of those unbelievers, a *physician* and a herald to put them to shame and condemn them. He was a physician not by his words alone but by his actions. He did not heal by what he said but by what he did. What did he do? He carried about with him a clear and indisputable proof; by his cured body he established the truth of the testimony he gave.[88]

Besides the fact that Chrysostom also describes priests as physicians and evangelists, particularly as they exercise the ministry of preaching,[89] Chrysostom's emphasis on the paralytic healing not "by what he said but by what he did" hearkens back to an exhortation he makes in *Anom*. 11. In there, Chrysostom, after noting how preaching refreshes the soul, asks his congregation to contemplate how much their presence in church similarly refreshes the souls of their fellow believers. "Do you say that you cannot preach a long discourse, that you have no instruction to give? Merely be present here in the church, and you have

---

85 Ibid. 22 (294).
86 Ibid. 25 (295–6).
87 Ibid. 214 (SC 396, 334); *Christ div.* 25 (Harkins, *Incomprehensible*, 295).
88 Ibid. 37–38 (Harkins, *Incomprehensible*, 300–1).
89 For example, John Chrysostom, *Sac.* 4.2.96–4.3.47 (SC 272, 246–52). To be precise, regarding the term "evangelists", assuming that we are not talking of the Gospel writers, Chrysostom sees them as similar to pastors-teachers except that they only preach the Gospel, which by no means makes them inferior. His example of evangelists are Priscilla and Aquila (*Hom. Eph.* 11.2 [PG 62.83]; cf. Acts 18).

done everything you have to do."⁹⁰ While preaching is normally apprehended through hearing, Chrysostom puts emphasis on the act of seeing also, so that Christ's words penetrate the soul through the sense of sight as well as that of hearing. This is the reason why church attendance is very important. Christians attending Chrysostom's pro-Nicene church, by their attendance, are already professing what they believe. Participants therefore preach Christ's divinity to one another. Similarly, their absence can negatively affect their fellow believers. A person, Chrysostom argues, might come to church ready and willing, but if he "sees" (ἴδῃ) only a few people, what he sees will quench his desire. He will grow numb, feel more hesitant, and then go away. In this way, little by little, the whole congregation will grow weaker and more indifferent. On the other hand, if he "sees" (ἴδῃ) people running together with earnestness and zeal, streaming in from every side, the readiness of these others will make him eager and willing, even if his heart has grown sluggish and slack.⁹¹ Thus, Chrysostom describes the participation of believers in *Anom.* 11 in much the same way as he does the paralytic in *Christ div.*, who could be considered an evangelist for simply testifying to Christ's power through the picking up of his mat.

However, while Chrysostom values attendance, much more important to him is the transformation of life that comes through preaching. He points out that the healing of the paralytic did not end in bodily healing. Jesus later found him again to say to him: "See, you are cured. Sin no more, so that nothing worse may happen to you." Chrysostom interprets this as Jesus giving "timely exhortation and advice." Christ did not remind the man of his sins while he was sick and his soul was distressed, as such reminders would not have helped him. But after Christ had "proved by his deed his power and his concern for him, he gave him timely exhortation and advice." Why? Because Christ had already shown by the very things he did that he now deserved to be believed."⁹² Put another way, Christ held off on correcting the man's life until he had shown the man by his power that he is indeed God, and his words are worth listening to.

We already noted how strongly Chrysostom emphasised in *Anom.* 11 that preaching refreshes the soul. But in what sense does it refresh the soul? Although much of *Anom.* 11's exhortation is on coming to church, near the end, Chrysostom tells his congregation,

---

90 John Chrysostom, *Anom.* 11.34 (Harkins, *Incomprehensible*, 282).
91 Ibid. 11.273–80 (SC 396, 310); *Anom.* 11.35 (Harkins, *Incomprehensible*, 282).
92 John Chrysostom, *Christ div.* 39–40 (Harkins, *Incomprehensible*, 301).

> Let us run here to be present at each assembly. If lustful desire burns in your heart, the mere sight of this house of prayer will easily enable you to quench the flames. If you are in a fit of rage, you will have no trouble in laying that wild beast to rest. If some other passion besets you, you will be able to quell the storm and bring much calm and peace to your soul.[93]

The theme of overcoming the passions and pursuing virtue is emphasised much more in *Christ div.* There, Chrysostom repeats his argument, "Nothing contributes to a virtuous and moral way of life as does the time you spend here in church."[94] He then expands on this argument by returning to his opening metaphor in the sermon, likening the congregation's souls to land that needs to be cultivated by the farmer to produce crops in abundance. While, in the opening metaphor, he only mentioned the grace of God as having a role in the production of crops, here he concretises God's work by stressing the role of scripture. That is, Chrysostom identifies the water that produces the fruit of the Holy Spirit (cf. Gal 5:22–23) in Christians as "the words of God." Without the watering of scripture, the soul will become dry and grow thistles and thorns, which have the natural characteristics of sin, for, "where there are thorns, there you will find snakes, serpents, scorpions, and every power of the devil."[95] Chrysostom does not go on to give examples of sinful behaviour but he does give detail of the opposite, which is to describe what virtue looks like outside the church and in the context of the household.[96] Chrysostom imagines that spouses who come home from church perceive each other as more worthy and desirable. For, what is taught in church is virtue of soul, i.e., chastity, sobriety, goodness and virtue, and the firm fear of God.[97] These characteristics echo the reasonableness, moderation, and discipline that Chrysostom saw in the paralytic.[98]

---

[93] John Chrysostom, *Anom.* 11.42 (Harkins, *Incomprehensible*, 285).
[94] John Chrysostom, *Christ div.* 53 (Harkins, *Incomprehensible*, 305).
[95] Ibid. 56 (306).
[96] As we have repeatedly noted, Chrysostom saw Christian philosophy as affecting the whole of life.
[97] Ibid. 56 (306).
[98] Of course, it may be argued that Chrysostom's view of virtue is too ascetically inclined. This is likely at least partly because of the Christian ascetic influences in his own life. For example, as a young man, he was a student at the *asketerion* of Diodore of Tarsus, who was an ascetic. See Andrea Sterk, *Renouncing the World Yet Leading the Church: The Monk-Bishop in Late Antiquity* (Cambridge, MA: Harvard University Press, 2004),143–4. Nonetheless, it is true that ascetic themes (e.g., chastity, sobriety, moderation) are present in scripture—e.g., 1 Cor 9:27; Matt 19:11–12; Eph 5:18—even if they do not necessarily represent the whole of scripture's teachings on virtue.

But it is, of course, in first listening to preaching in church that the lives of his congregation will be transformed. Indeed, if Chrysostom could get his congregation to come to church regularly, he could ensure that his members had constant interaction with scripture, especially in those days when whole bibles were more expensive to keep. And even those that kept some texts of scripture may not always have had time or motivation to regularly peruse them at home. Chrysostom was all too aware of the distractions that living in the city furnished Christians, be these in relation to work or entertainment.[99] But "Here [in church]," Chrysostom argues, "the apostles and prophets wipe clean and beautify the face, they strip away the marks of senility left by sin, they apply the bloom of youth, they get rid of every wrinkle, stain, and blemish from our souls."[100] Such beauty of soul is unlike physical beauty in that it "cannot be marred by time, disease, old age, death, or any other such thing. It stays constantly in bloom. [...] it draws God himself to love it.[101] We must note, though, that developing virtue from scripture is not merely an intellectual exercise for Chrysostom. It requires action on the part of the hearer to obey. Hence, Chrysostom's exhortations are in the form of commands, such as when he says of Christ's equality with the Father: "Keep this in your mind and guard it will all possible care. Make your way of life a robe which is woven together from good moral conduct and correct doctrine."[102] His last words in *Christ div.*, similarly, are not just exhortations to listen to preaching. He joins together receiving the Word and acting on it, repeating that the way to "wipe away every stain" in one's soul is "by reading the Scriptures, by prayer and almsgiving, by peace and concord with one another."[103]

Therefore, to speak of the ἐνέργεια of the preached word in Chrysostom's theology is not to talk of an operation shrouded in mystery. Chrysostom conceives of it in very practical, concrete terms. At the crux of it is the recognition of the divine identity of Christ and of scripture as his words. The divine authority and ability belong to Christ and not to scripture *per se*, but Christ's power operates through his words. Because Christ's words are the words of the God who made and sustains human beings, scripture (or discourse from scripture) is able

---

99 See Dayna S. Kalleres, *City of Demons: Violence, Ritual, and Christian Power in Late Antiquity* (Oakland, CA: University of California Press, 2015), 57–65.
100 John Chrysostom, *Christ div.* 57 (Harkins, *Incomprehensible*, 306–7).
101 Ibid. 58 (307).
102 Ibid. 53 (305); ταῦτα δὲ μέμνησθε καὶ φυλάττετε μετὰ ἀκριβείας ἁπάσης καὶ τὴν ἀπὸ τῆς πολιτείας φιλοσοφίαν τῇ τῶν δογμάτων ὀρθότητι συνυφαίνετε (*Christ div.* 12.434–36 [SC 396, 352]).
103 Ibid. 59 (Harkins, *Incomprehensible*, 307).

to comfort the soul; inform the soul of what is true and moral; and nurture and deepen the mutual love between God and the soul. For Chrysostom, all these are best fostered in the church, particularly the pro-Nicene church to which he belonged. There, Christ is worshipped as God and one member preaches scripture to another not only in the actual exchange of words but in the profession of orthodox faith through faithful and attentive attendance and virtuous living.

6 Conclusion

The two sermons discussed in this chapter show how Chrysostom viewed "preaching with power." From a Chrysostomian perspective, power in preaching refers to the recognition of Christ's divine authority and ability, upon which the authority, cohesion, and effectivity of scripture rests. Because scripture is Christ's words, it operates for the divine creator as a means to restore or maintain the health of human souls. Such health, for Chrysostom, is seen through belief in right doctrine and virtuous living. Members of the church participate in the ἐνέργεια of the preached Word in concrete ways. Chrysostom does not discuss the role of the priest much but, by his example, we see how the preacher discourses with and from scripture, heightening the experiential aspects of the congregation's encounter with God's words. The priest cultivates the fertile souls of his congregants through his exegetical and homiletical efforts. He exhorts, warns, and instructs both to protect his flock from heresies and to prod them to apply the medicine of scripture to their souls. The members participate in preaching, too—if not in words, then through their presence in church (a confession of right doctrine) and through living out the teachings of scripture in their day-to-day lives. By rooting his approach in the theology of creation and providence, Chrysostom makes scripture indispensable not only to faith but to the whole of human life.

It is worth repeating that Chrysostom's historical context influenced his view and practice of preaching. In the case of *Anom.* 11 and *Christ div.*, it was his goal to grow the pro-Nicene Church which struggled despite its status as the official church of Constantinople. Preaching was Chrysostom's means to kindle faith and enthusiasm and amass public support for the pro-Nicene church. Not only was preaching his personal strength but his view and practice of it were rooted in solid anthropological assumptions about rationality and will, the link between body and soul, and the power of God over his creation. Chrysostom's rhetoric, therefore, has theological depth and was not employed only for style or enjoyment. As such, *Anom.* 11 and *Christ div.* are excellent examples of Chrysostom using his persuasive powers to their full extent.

Recognising these two points, namely, (1) that the notion of preaching with power is mysterious but not inexplicable, and (2) that powerful preaching rests on both practical considerations and theo-anthropological foundations, has several benefits for churches in the present day. While learning from Chrysostom does not entail doing things precisely as he did them, we can allow the principles behind his practice to challenge us as we reflect on preaching in our times.

First, the Chrysostomian perspective both reinforces the indispensable place of preaching in the Christian life and challenges us to expand our definition of it. Preaching is indispensable in that it encourages discourse on Christ's words. For while Christ's words permeate the liturgy (e.g., in hymns, scripture reading, the consecratory words of the sacrament), it is in preaching that the congregation is most explicitly called to participate in the interpretation, appreciation, and application of divine truth. In preaching, preachers explore scripture, clarify doctrine, and discuss scripture's relevance to their congregation's lives, hoping that the congregation will then take this exhortation, mull it over, discuss it with others, and live out its implications in their day-to-day. It is this psychosomatic engagement with scripture as the word of God, cultivated by the preacher, that makes preaching a potent medicine for the soul. If this is how preaching is defined, however, we must consider that preaching goes beyond the confines of delivering sermons. Bible study meetings, for example, can be classified as preaching, and might, in some contexts, not just supplement pulpit preaching but replace it. Bible study meetings may be more effective in contexts where conversation and dialogue are more valued; where there is indifference toward or suspicion of organised religions; where, for economic or political reasons, Sunday worship may be impossible; or, where there is a greater need to cultivate friendships. In such a setting, preachers engage the congregation with their preaching not only by teaching but by creating space for church members to preach to one another. Bible study meetings can be conducted less formally and may be a better avenue for encouraging members to publicly share how their knowledge of doctrine and scripture impacts their lives.

Second, for those that are insecure about their ability to preach (formally or informally, in a big group or even in friendly conversations), the Chrysostomian perspective can give both comfort and challenge. Some preachers are considered "gifted" because they have a natural or instinctual affinity for preaching well. Without having to work out the theological logic behind preaching as we have done here, they practice it well. For those that struggle to communicate, however, knowing the theo-anthropological reasons behind preaching is useful, as it suggests that powerful preaching can be learned. To be sure, it is not an easy skill to learn. There needs to be a conscious effort to continually reflect on divine commands in relation to the human condition, both in the general sense and specifically to one's times, experience, and culture. Communicating these reflections to different kinds of people in a manner that invites action and response is an additional challenge. As such, the Chrysostomian perspective on preaching can be demanding, but it also promises that a person who actively studies, practices, and communicates the word of God can be an effective preacher. Indeed, while still developing one's skills in areas like scriptural interpretation and verbal communication, one can rest assured that there are other ways of preaching with which one can easily engage. For instance, one can honestly live out what it means to be a Christian, not just by being a shining example of virtue but by acknowledging one's weaknesses and need of God's grace, of which being present and involved in the life of the church through fellowship with believers is a wonderful demonstration.

References

Andrade, Nathanael. "The Processions of John Chrysostom and the Contested Spaces of Constantinople," *JECS* 18, no. 2 (2010): 161–89.

Bae, Junghun. *John Chrysostom on Almsgiving and the Therapy of the Soul*. Leiden: Brill-Schöningh, 2021.

Barnes, Michel Rene. *The Power of God: Δύναμις in Gregory of Nyssa's Trinitarian Theology*. Washington, D.C.: Catholic University of America Press, 2001.

Basil of Caesarea. *Contra Eunomium*. Bernard Sesboüé, Georges-Matthieu de Durand, and Louis Doutreleau, eds. *Contre Eunome*. SC 299, 305. Paris: Éditions du CERF, 1982–83. English translation by Mark Delcogliano and Andrew Radde-Gallwitz, *St. Basil of Caesarea. Against Eunomius*. Washington D.C.: Catholic University of America Press, 2011.

Cook, James Daniel. *Preaching and Popular Christianity: Reading the Sermons of John Chrysostom*. Oxford: Oxford University Press, 2019.

Gregory of Nazianzus. *Oratio* 30. Paul Gallay and Maurice Jourjon, eds. *Grégoire de Nazianze. Discours 27–30*. SC 250. Paris: Éditions du CERF, 1978. English translation by Charles Gordon Browne, NPNF 2/7:309–318.

Gregory of Nyssa. *Contra Eunomium*. Jaeger, Wernerus, ed. *Gregorii Nysseni Opera. Vol. I et II: Contra Eunomium Libri*. Leiden: Brill, 1960.

Harkins, Paul, trans. *St. John Chrysostom. On the Incomprehensible Nature of God*. Washington, D.C.: Catholic University of America Press, 1984.

John Chrysostom. *Contra Anomoeos homilia* 11. In *Jean Chrysostome. Sur l'égalité du Père et du Fils. Contre les anoméens Homélies VII–XII*, edited by Anne-Marie Malingrey, SC 396, 286–314. Paris: Éditions du CERF, 1994. English translation by Harkins, *Incomprehensible*, 270–85.

John Chrysostom. *De Christi divinitate = Contra Anomoeos homilia* 12. Malingrey, *Sur l'égalité*, 318–356. Eng. trans. by Harkins, *Incomprehensible*, 286–307.

John Chrysostom. *De Lazaro conciones* 1–7. PG 48.963–1054.

John Chrysostom. *De sacerdotio*. In *Jean Chrysostome. Sur le sacerdoce [Dialogue et Homélie]*, edited by Anne-Marie Malingrey. SC 272, 60–363. Paris: Éditions du CERF, 1980.

John Chrysostom. *Homiliae in Genesim*. PG 53.21–54.580.

John Chrysostom. *In epistulam ad Colossenses homilia* 9. PG 62.299–392. English translation by John Broadus, NPNF 1/13:257–321.

John Chrysostom. *In epistulam ad Ephesios homilae* 1–24. PG 62.9–177.

John Chrysostom. *In Eutropium*. PG 52.391–96.

Kalleres, Dayna S. *City of Demons: Violence, Ritual, and Christian Power in Late Antiquity*. Oakland, CA: University of California Press, 2015.

Kelly, John Norman Davidson. *Golden Mouth: The Story of John Chrysostom—Ascetic, Preacher, Bishop*. Ithaca, NY: Cornell University Press, 1995.

Lai, Pak-Wah. "John Chrysostom's Reception of Basil of Caesarea's Trinitarian Theology." *Scrinium* 15, no. 1 (July 2019): 62–78.

Lai, Pak-Wah. "The Monk as Christian Saint and Exemplar in St. John Chrysostom's Writings." In *Saints and Sanctity*, edited by Peter Clarke and Tony Claydon, 19–28. Suffolk: Boydell & Brewer, 2011.

Leyerle, Blake. *Theatrical Shows and Ascetic Lives: John Chrysostom's Attack on Spiritual Marriage*. Berkeley, CA: University of California Press, 2001.

Mayer, Wendy. "Constantinopolitan Women in Chrysostom's Circle." *VC* 53, no. 3 (1999): 265–88.

Mayer, Wendy. "Poverty and Generosity Toward the Poor in the Time of John Chrysostom." In *Wealth and Poverty in Early Church and Society*, edited by Susan R. Holman, 140–58. Grand Rapids, MI: Baker Academic, 2008.

Mayer, Wendy. "Shaping the Sick Soul: Reshaping the Identity of John Chrysostom." In *Christians Shaping Identity from the Roman Empire to Byzantium: Studies Inspired by Pauline Allen*, edited by Geoffrey Dunn and Wendy Mayer, 140–64. Leiden: Brill, 2015.

Mayer, Wendy. "The Homiletic Audience as Embodied Hermeneutic: Scripture and Its Interpretation in the Exegetical Preaching of John Chrysostom." In *Hymns, Homilies and Hermeneutics in Byzantium*, edited by Sarah Gador-Whyte and Andrew Mellas, 11–29. Leiden: Brill, 2021.

Mitchell, Margaret. *The Heavenly Trumpet: John Chrysostom and the Art of Pauline Interpretation*. Louisville, KY: Westminster John Knox, 2002.

Pigott, Justin. "Capital Crimes: Deconstructing John's 'Unnecessary Severity' in Managing the Clergy of Constantinople," in *Revisioning John Chrysostom: New Approaches, New Perspectives*, edited by Chris L. De Wet and Wendy Mayer, 733–78. Leiden: Brill, 2019.

Rylaarsdam, David. *John Chrysostom on Divine Pedagogy: The Coherence of His Theology and Preaching*. Oxford: Oxford University Press, 2014.

Socrates. *Historia ecclesiastica*. Hansen, Günther C., ed., Pierre Périchon and Pierre Maraval, trans. *Socrate de Constantinople. Histoire ecclésiastique*. SC 477, 493, 505, 506. Paris: Éditions du CERF, 2003–2007.

Sozomen. *Historia ecclesiastica*. Bidez, Joseph, Bernard Grillet, Guy Sabbah, and André-Jean Festugière, eds., and trans. *Sozomène. Histoire ecclésiastique*. SC 306, 418, 495, 516. Paris: Éditions du CERF, 1983–2008.

Stanfill, Jonathan. "The Body of Christ's Barbarian Limb: John Chrysostom's Processions and the Embodied Performance of Nicene Christianity." In *Revisioning John Chrysostom: New*

Approaches, New Perspectives, edited by Chris L. De Wet and Wendy Mayer, 670–97. Leiden: Brill, 2019.

Sterk, Andrea. *Renouncing the World Yet Leading the Church: The Monk-Bishop in Late Antiquity*. Cambridge, MA: Harvard University Press, 2004.

The Theodosian Code, trans. Clyde Pharr. In *The Theodosian Code and Novels and the Sirmondian Constitutions*, edited by Clyde Pharr, Theresa Sherrer Davidson, and Mary Brown Pharr, 11–476. Princeton, NJ: Princeton University Press, 1952.

Vaggione, Richard Paul, ed., and trans. *Eunomius. The Extant Works*. Oxford: Clarendon Press, 1987.

Wilson VanVeller, Courtney. *Paul's Therapy of the Soul: A New Approach to John Chrysostom and Anti-Judaism*. PhD dissertation. Boston University, 2015.

Willibald Sandler
Augustine without a Theodicy of a Condemning God

His Misunderstanding of Romans and Resulting Transformations of Predestination, Original Sin, Freedom and Grace

Abstract: Augustine's reading of Romans 9 radically transformed his theology. In *Ad Simplicianum* (397) he developed a new understanding of grace and freedom together with original sin and predestination, laying the foundations for his later anti-Pelagian theology. This theological transformation, however, is marred by a fatal misunderstanding of Rom 9. A misguided "theodicy of a condemning God" threw Augustine's theology into an imbalance that led contemporary liberal theologians to reject his theological system and the Church's teaching on it as a whole. This thesis is supported by an examination of recent exegesis on Romans 9–11, as well as a theological analysis of *Simplician* and Augustine's earlier *Propositions from the Epistle to the Romans*. The liberal criticism of Kurt Flasch and Thomas Pröpper is thus partially confirmed. However, the polarising dilemma posed by Flasch between an irresponsible eclectic reception and a complete rejection of Augustine's theology based on the *Simplician* by contemporary dogmatics is rejected. Instead, a third way of a transformative reception is methodically developed. Finally, a possible path for such a transformative reception of Augustine, based on a proper understanding of Romans 9, is outlined.

Keywords: Augustine, Ad Simplicianum, Grace and freedom, Original sin, Predestination, Theodicy, Method of dogmatic theology, Rom 9–11, Rom 5:12

1 Introduction

Augustine is considered to be the most important Church teacher of grace. But his theology of grace is inextricably linked with a highly problematic doctrine of predestination. Correspondingly, God is so free and powerful in his choice of grace that he leads some of humanity safely to eternal salvation—through unde-

Willibald Sandler, Theological Faculty, University of Innsbruck, willibald.sandler@uibk.ac.at

served election even in the womb—while he withholds this grace from others without reason, so that they inevitably go to eternal damnation. The harshest statements of Augustine's doctrine of predestination are to be found in his latest works – especially in *Rebuke and Grace* (c. 427) and *On the Predestination of the Saints* (429) – but the beginnings go back much further. In 397, fourteen years before his controversies with Pelagius began, Augustine completed a book in response to questions from his former mentor and friend, Bishop Simplician. The questions referred to difficult biblical passages, particularly from Romans, which threatened to obscure God's goodness and justice. Augustine, who by this time had already written much on Romans – notably his *Propositions from the Epistle to the Romans* (394) – initially reacted helplessly. He then came to the conclusion that he had to revise his earlier interpretations of Romans 9 and, as a consequence, important parts of his previous theology. In his book *Ad Simplicianum*, he not only reinterpreted the passages in question, but also outlined a new system of freedom and grace, predestination and original sin, which contained some extreme conclusions.

The systematic response that Augustine developed in this work, and sharpened in his later Pelagian controversies, is viewed very critically in parts of contemporary Catholic dogmatics, especially in the German-speaking world. A major influence was the philosopher Kurt Flasch, who in 1990 published the first German-language edition of the most problematic parts of Augustine's *Simplician*, together with a scathing commentary.[1] Flasch accused Augustine of designing with the *Simplician* a *logic of terror*, as he titled his book, which would determine not only his later theology but also the church doctrine and even Christianity to this day. His accusation could be summed up as follows: Augustine's *Simplician* is a "logic of *terror*" because Augustine legitimises a terrible image of God and man in an almost cynical way; and it is a "*logic* of terror" because here Augustine links grace and predestination in an almost compelling way with a doctrine of original sin that – on the basis of a prenatal complicity with the fallen Adam – categorically denies human beings a free will to do good by nature; and because Augustine presents a God as just and merciful who consigns a majority of people to hell.

Flasch's criticism of Augustine has been confirmed as accurate and irrefutable in parts of German-speaking systematic theology. Especially Thomas Pröpper in his highly regarded *Theological Anthropology*[2] – although much more differentiated than Flasch's deliberate polemic (cf. ibid., 242) – relies primarily on

---

1 Kurt Flasch, *Logik des Schreckens. Augustinus*, edited by Kurt Flasch (Mainz: Dieterich, 1995).
2 Cf. Thomas Pröpper, *Theologische Anthropologie*, 2 vols. (Freiburg: Herder, 2016).

Flasch's razor-sharp analyses to critically reconstruct Augustine's doctrine of original sin. From this, Pröpper draws consequences for the Church's doctrine of original sin, which is strongly influenced by Augustine. He concludes that "the theory of original sin, at least in the form developed by Augustine, [...] is indeed *unacceptable* – unacceptable on both *moral* and *theological* grounds. For guilt [...] can only ever be one's *own* fault."[3]

In this chapter I elaborate on the legitimate concerns of this critique of Augustine's theological turn in *Simplician* and trace it back to a fatal misunderstanding in his interpretation of Romans 9: Augustine now understood the statement "I have loved Jacob, but I have hated Esau" (Rom 9:13)[4], which Paul attributes to God in the prophet Malachi (Mal 1:2f), as a divine election of Jacob to eternal salvation and a divine rejection of Esau amounting to eternal damnation. My thesis is, first, that Augustine in the *Simplician* and also earlier (in his *Propositions form the Epistle to the Romans* of 395) engaged in a "theodicy of a condemning God", i.e. that he tried to justify the justice and goodness of an eternally electing or also rejecting God. Second, I argue that significant distortions of Augustine's theology of grace, freedom and original sin emerged in *Simplician* and even earlier, in the context of and because of this attempted theodicy.

To this end, in the second section of this chapter I will show, taking into account recent exegesis, how the texts of a predestining rejection of persons by God in Rom 9 stand in the broader context of Rom 9–11, where Paul, especially in Rom 11:25f, proceeds to reveal a "mystery" according to which "all Israel will be saved" in the end. This, as will be shown, is to be interpreted in such a way that the rejection of Esau and many others can no longer be understood as a definitive rejection for eternity. Thus, in the second section, I want to show that Augustine's unquestioning assumption of the eternal rejection of Esau and the greater part of Jesus-rejecting Israel is in fact wrong, and that it is rather a question of a salvation-historical role to which God freely elects or rejects people and nations, without this necessarily leading to eternal salvation or damnation. Thus, Augustine's theodicy of a condemning God proves unnecessary and misleading.

This objection not only against Augustine's exegesis of the Letter to the Romans, but also against a central motive of his theological turn, will allow me in the third and fourth sections to critically examine those texts before and in the *Simplician* where, in connection with an attempted theodicy of a condemning God, he arrives at problematic conclusions and a correspondingly distorted theological system-building with regard to grace and freedom as well as original sin.

---

[3] Ibid., vol. 2, 1024; my translation.
[4] Unless otherwise stated, biblical quotations are from the New Revised Standard Version (1989).

On the basis of this analysis, in the fifth chapter I partly agree with Flasch's and also Pröpper's sharp criticism of Augustine's "theological system", but I reject the dilemma posed by Flasch, either as a systematic theologian to faithfully and theologically inconsistently accept Augustine's *Simplician*, or to consistently and openly break with Augustine and the church dogmas based on him, especially on original sin. Beyond this false dilemma, I argue for the middle way of a "transformative reception of Augustine", which I justify methodologically in the fifth section. In the sixth section, I offer an outlook on how such a transformative reception of Augustine might be developed in the context of a biblically grounded "dramatic-kairological" theology of grace and original sin.

2 Double Predestination or Universal Hope for Salvation? The Challenge of Rom 9–11

2.1 The Salvation-Optimistic Framing of Rom 9 by Rom 9–11. New Perspectives in Recent Exegesis

Until the 20th century, in the wake of Augustine and under the influence of the Reformers, Rom 9 was repeatedly isolated from the context of Rom 9–11 and interpreted in the way of double predestination.[5] This was especially the case with Rom 9:21–23. Thereby, the salvation-optimistic outlook in Rom 11 often remained unconsidered. The "mystery" that "all Israel will be saved" (11:25–26) and that "God has imprisoned all in disobedience so that he may be merciful to all" (11:32) was related to the Church as "spiritual Israel" with Rom 9:6 ("not all who are of Israel"). This is a spiritualising view which we already find in Augustine.[6]

In the 20th century the interpretation of Rom 9–11 changed. Not least under the shocking impression of the Shoah, a differentiated theology of Israel and a Jewish-Christian dialogue emerged, which also influenced the exegesis of Rom 9–11.[7] Rom 9–11 was increasingly read in terms of ethnic Israel. This contrasted

---

5 Cf. Klaus Haacker, "Das Thema von Römer als Problem der Auslegungsgeschichte," in *Between Gospel and Election. Explorations in the Interpretation of Romans 9–11*, ed. Florian Wilk and J. Ross Wagner, 55–72 (Tübingen: Mohr Siebeck, 2010), 58.
6 Cf. civ. 21,24; Otto Kuss, *Der Römerbrief. 3. Lieferung: Röm 8,19–11,36* (Regensburg: Pustet, 1978), 828–934, with a long excursus on predestination in the history of interpretation of Rom 9–11, beginning with the Church Fathers.
7 Cf. Eduard Lohse, "Gottes Gnadenwahl und das Geschick Israels", in *Rechenschaft vom Evangelium. Exegetische Studien zum Römerbrief* (Berlin: de Gruyter, 2007), 29–42.

sharply with Paul's assessment of the salvific destiny of that larger part of Israel who had not embraced Christ. Paul referred to this in Rom 9:6–11:10 and especially harshly in Rom 9:22 where he applied the phrase "vessels of wrath prepared for destruction" to this larger part of Israel.[8] Did Paul intend this to be an irreversible divine rejection that would inevitably lead to eternal damnation? And if this were the case: Did Paul *claim* such damnation, or did he only consider it in order to finally reject it when he spoke of "all Israel" being saved (Rom 11:26) or in order to integrate it into a more comprehensive salvation-optimistic framework? Both alternatives to Paul's claim of Israel's damnation are supported by the fact that the "vessels of wrath prepared for destruction" (Rom 9:22) are placed in an incomplete if-clause. In contrast, Paul speaks in Rom 11:25 of a temporary hardening, "until the full number of the Gentiles has come in". But in this way "all Israel will be saved" (11:26). In contrast to a replacement theological application of "all Israel" to the church, most commentators today assume that "all Israel" refers to ethnic Israel and includes, at least to a large extent, those Israelites who were or are "hardened" against Christ. In this context, "all Israel" is usually not understood numerically in the sense of "all Jews without exception", but in the sense of a qualified majority representing Israel.[9]

Such considerations presuppose a salvation-historical and eschatological interpretation of Rom 11:25f: "A hardening has come upon part of Israel, *until* the full number of the Gentiles has come in. And *so* all Israel will be saved", whereby "until" and "so" can refer to the entire world time until the expected parousia. According to Michael Wolter, Paul expects an end-time work by God to end the hardening of the non-Christian majority of Israel, though without any hint or idea of how this might happen.[10]

However, such a salvation-historical and eschatological interpretation is not shared by all exegetes. For example, Zoccali in his overview of various interpretations of "all Israel" (Rom 11:26) rejects the eschatological interpretation

---

8 Quoted according to the New American Standard Bible (1977).
9 With reference to a similarly oriented text from the Mishna. Cf. Douglas J. Moo, *The Epistle to the Romans* (Grand Rapids: Eerdmans, 2009), 722–3; Eduard Lohse, *Der Brief an die Römer* (Göttingen: Vandenhoeck & Ruprecht 2003), 320. Moreover, it is discussed whether "all Israel" diachronically refers to the Israel of different times or synchronically only to the Israel of the last generation before the parousia. Cf. Moo, *The Epistle to the Romans*, 723.
10 According to Wolter, this is precisely the mystery of which Paul speaks in Rom 11:25. Cf. Michael Wolter, "Ein exegetischer und theologischer Blick auf Röm 11,25–32," *New Testament Studies* 64 (2018): 123–42, and Michael Wolter, *Der Brief an die Römer. Teilband 2: Röm 9–16* (Ostfildern: Patmos, 2019), 199–215.

in favour of a "total national elect interpretation"[11], according to which "all Israel" does not refer numerically to all the members of historical Israel, but only to those who are elected by God and thus belong to the true Israel in the sense of Rom 9:6, where it says that "not all who are descended from Israel are Israel" (NIV).[12] This hypothesis has the undeniable advantage of eliminating the seeming contradiction between the salvation-pessimistic statements about Israel in Rom 9:6–11:10 and the salvation-optimistic "mystery", which Paul reveals in Rom 11:25–32. In doing so, however, this hypothesis levels the dramatic tension in the biblical text between a rejection of Christ's offer of salvation, a resulting hardening, and a dramatic overcoming of this tension with the help of the conversion of the Gentiles, which leads at least many of the hardened Jews to salvation through a salutary "jealousy". The "total national elect interpretation" obscures this drama of salvation history with a harmonising, logically flawless, but banal and basically tautological thesis.[13] Such a discovery would certainly not have required Paul to reveal a "mystery" (Rom 11:25).[14] Thus, moreover, Paul's dramatic struggle in Rom 9–11, with its outcome of a drama of salvation that sustains both the hope of salvation and the severity of hardening, would be dissolved into a rather shallow doctrine of predestination.

Recent exegesis largely rejects harmonising interpretations of Rom 9–11 and emphasises Paul's struggle with different solutions, which he considers and sometimes rejects, modifies or integrates into a broader perspective that he reveals as a mystery (Rom 11:25).[15] In any case, however, the tense overall text of

---

[11] The term was coined by Christopher Zoccali, "'And so all Israel will be saved': Competing Interpretations of Romans 11:26 in Pauline Scholarship," *Journal for the Study of the New Testament* 30 (2008): 303–18.

[12] Cf. Zoccali, "And so all Israel will be saved," and John K. Goodrich, "Until the Fullness of the Gentiles Comes In: A Critical Review of Recent Scholarship on the Salvation of 'All Israel' (Romans 11:26)," *Journal for the Study of Paul and His Letters* 6 (1996): 5–32.

[13] The first objection to the *total national elect hypothesis* favoured by Zoccali, with which he has to deal, is that it is undramatic or, as he puts it, "anti-climactic". Cf. Zoccali, "And so all Israel will be saved," 310. The tautology in this thesis is this: For all who are ultimately saved, it is true that they belong to the true Israel in the face of God, which in turn will ultimately be recognisable by the fact that they are saved. Cf. Moo, *The Epistle to the Romans*, 722: "Some have dismissed this interpretation because it would turn Paul's prediction into a purposeless truism: after all, by definition those who are elect will be saved." However, Moo does not consider this objection decisive.

[14] Cf. Leon Morris, *The Epistle to the Romans* (Grand Rapids: Eerdmans, 1994), 421.

[15] Cf. Haacker, "Das Thema von Römer als Problem der Auslegungsgeschichte," 82–5; Charles H. Cosgrove, "Rhetorical Suspense in Romans 9–11: A Study in Polyvalence and Hermeneutical Election," *Journal of Biblical Literature* 115 (1996): 271–87.

Rom 9–11 forbids to speak of a God-caused "hardening" (Rom 9:18) or of a "determination to destruction" in the way of a double predestination towards eternal damnation.[16] Such an interpretation is championed only by a few Calvinist commentaries today[17] and is also deeply questioned by at least one author from the Calvinist tradition.[18]

However, it must be taken into account that the predestinarian interpretations of Romans e.g. by Moo and Schreiner do not simply adopt positions from their dogmatics, but are presented with exegetical arguments that are to be taken seriously. A dogmatic-theological reception would therefore do well not to push these positions aside simply because of differently oriented confessional and dogmatic positions but to integrate their justified concerns as best as possible. For this, a more differentiated concept of predestination could be helpful, which could account for legitimate concerns of double predestination by considering that God predestines people rather for limited periods of their lives. The hopeful mystery that Paul presented to the Corinthians indeed consists in a temporal limitation of predestination: "I want you to understand this mystery: a

---

16 The idea that Paul advocated a double predestination in Rom 9–11 is either rejected by the majority of today's exegetes on Rom 9–11 or is no longer considered at all. An interpretation of Rom 9–16 in terms of double predestination is rejected in principle by: James D. Dunn, *Romans 9–16* (Grand Rapids: Zondervan, 1988), 567; Lohse, *Der Brief an die Römer*, 281; Robert J. Jewett, *Romans: A Commentary* (Minneapolis, Minn.: Fortress Press 2006), 598; Ulrich Wilckens, *Der Brief an die Römer, 2. Teilband: Röm 6–11* (Neukirchen-Vluyn: Neukirchener Verlag), 1980, 181–95 (with a restriction of "double predestination" to an inner-historically limited "salvation-historical" perspective); Peter Stuhlmacher, *Der Brief an die Römer* (Göttingen: Vandenhoeck & Ruprecht, 1989), 131; Norbert Baumert, *Christus – Hochform von "Gesetz": Übersetzung und Auslegung des Römerbriefes* (Würzburg: Echter, 2012), 172, 186, 244; Haacker, "Das Thema von Römer als Problem der Auslegungsgeschichte," 58, 64, 72; Mark Reasoner, "Romans Moves from Margin to Center, from Rejection to Salvation: Four Grids for Recent English-Language Exegesis," in *Between Gospel and Election. Explorations in the Interpretation of Romans 9–11*, ed. Florian Wilk, and J. Ross Wagner, 73–87 (Tübingen: Mohr Siebeck, 2010), 79, 83; Wolter, *Der Brief an die Römer. Teilband 2*, 73, 77, 83.
17 Cf. especially Moo, *The Epistle to the Romans*, 608, on Rom 9,22f: "Paul is clear here, as he is elsewhere: some people receive God's mercy and are saved, while others do not receive that mercy and so are *eternally condemned*" (emphasis mine). Similarly Thomas R. Schreiner, *Romans* (Grand Rapids: Baker, 1998), 510: "One cannot elude the conclusion that Paul teaches double predestination here". Schreiner is strongly influenced here by John Stephen Piper, *The Justification of God: An Exegetical and Theological Study of Romans 9:1–23* (Grand Rapids: Baker, 2nd edition 1993); with the 'classic' problem, already present in Augustine, of treating this text without connection to Rom 11.
18 Cf. Cosgrove, Rhetorical Suspense in Romans 9–11.

hardening has come upon part of Israel, *until* the full number of the Gentiles has come in" (Rom 11:25).

Thus, Rom 9:13 ("Jacob I loved, but Esau I hated") or 9:22 ("the vessels prepared for destruction") could be understood as a double predestination limited within history, which will be embraced and surpassed by the "mystery" (Rom 11:25) of an ultimate salvation, so that the final and actual predestination is no longer double. This is the direction taken by Ulrich Wilckens, who states in relation to Esau and Jacob (Rom 9:13):

> Paul is thus heading towards a double predestination, not in a cosmological but in a salvation-historical sense, namely to emphasise the complete, absolute freedom in which God constitutes and advances the history of his chosen people within the history of the world.[19]

This results in a temporally limited "double predestination" (Rom 9:13.22) for Rom 9–11, with a view to an eternal predestination that is no more "double", but is all about salvation (Rom 11:26). Nevertheless, this outlook does not necessarily amount to an apocatastasis (not even limited to Israel), but to an election of "all Israel", in the sense of a qualified majority. No 'automatic' salvation can be derived from this. Dogmatic theology can be inspired by this Pauline "mystery" to an ultimate hope of salvation not only for Israel but for all humanity, so that eternal salvation and damnation are not equally probable alternatives, but there is a decisive hope of salvation.

Not only the majority of contemporary exegetes but also some theologians of the "Innsbruck Dramatic Theology", to which I count myself, reject an interpretation of Rom 9–11 as double predestination. On Rom 9:12 ("Jacob I loved, but Esau I hated"), Raymund Schwager stated in 1986 in an essay on the soteriology of Augustine:

> These statements, however, do not refer to the question of the eternal salvation or damnation of the two brothers. Rather, they justify why Jacob and not Esau (despite his birthright) became the progenitor of Israel and thus a bearer of the divine promise. According to Paul, there is no reason for this election in any human merit. It arises from the pure counsel of God. However, since nothing is said about the eternal salvation or damnation of Esau and Jacob, this Pauline text offers no biblical proof of a final restrictive election of God's grace.[20]

The concept of salvation-historical roles in dramatic theology leads from a perspective of individualistic salvation, which often afflicted earlier dogmatics in

---

[19] Wilckens, *Der Brief an die Römer*, 195f (my translation).
[20] Cf. Raymund Schwager, *Der wunderbare Tausch. Zur Geschichte und Deutung der Erlösungslehre*, Gesammelte Schriften 2 (Freiburg: Herder, 2015), 226, my translation.

their interpretation of Rom 9, back to the biblically central question of Israel's calling and the different roles that various persons (Jacob, Esau, Pharaoh) have in this context. Salvation-historical roles are sovereignly determined by God, and God gives people freedom to fulfil or not fulfil their roles in different ways. The fact that these latitudes are not arbitrarily available but sovereignly given by God is a legitimate concern of various theologies of predestination: if a person fails to fulfil a calling, God won't be surprised by this. Rather, we must assume that every free human rejection of God, as well as the diversions that result from this, are encompassed in advance by a more comprehensive plan of God. We can and must therefore assume a divine 'master plan' which is fundamentally invisible to us, but of which God may reveal to us more or less limited partial perspectives as "his plan". From this point of view it can be stated without contradiction

(1) that people – like Esau, Pharaoh or the Jews who rejected Jesus although they recognised him – made wrong decisions on their own responsibility;
(2) that Paul, in his despair over the fate of his beloved native people, received a deeper insight from God, according to which these wrong decisions of his fellow brothers and sisters did not thwart his plan, but rather that God himself determined some people from the beginning – before they had been born (Rom 9:11) – in such a way that it was easy for them to accept his offer of salvation, while God did not show this grace to others, so that in this sense he "hardened" them (Rom 9:18), or – figuratively speaking – made them vessels "for ordinary use" (Rom 9:21) and "prepared them for destruction" (Rom 9:22);
(3) that Paul was later allowed by God to catch an even deeper glimpse of his divine plan and was thus able to share with his brothers a "mystery" (Rom 11:25) according to which God uses the hardening of the Jews for a more comprehensive plan of salvation according to which "all Israel will be saved" (Rom 11:26),
(4) whereby even this is only a limited glimpse of God's overarching plan, so that Paul can hope for his people without relieving them of their responsibility. God's 'master plan' thus remains a "mystery" (Rom 11:25), even though Paul shares a deep glimpse of it with the readers of his letter.

2.2 Without a "Theodicy of a Condemning God": Augustine's Theology Needs a Further Transformation

A key thesis of this chapter is that Augustine in *Simplician*, due to a misunderstood Pauline doctrine of predestination in Rom 9, mistakenly thought he had to provide a theodicy for a God who predestines people to eternal damnation. To do justice to Augustine, the assertion of such a "theodicy of a condemning God" requires some clarifications that I would like to make in advance:

(1) Augustine rarely says explicitly that God condemned Esau and others to hell by his predestination.[21] But throughout he takes for granted that Paul is dealing with a predestination to eternal salvation – as with Jacob – or to eternal damnation in the case of Esau, Pharaoh and the hardened majority of Israel (exemplary for a larger part of humanity).[22]

(2) In *Simplician*, Augustine tries to mitigate the harshness of such seemingly groundless divine condemnation by distinguishing that God never actively plunges humans into ruin. God only does not give the grace necessary for them to escape hell (cf. Simpl. 1,2,16). But because man cannot escape hell without God's electing grace, his non-electing amounts in fact to damnation. Therefore, it seems to me justified to speak of Augustine's theodicy of a condemning God which is fundamentally unnecessary.

(3) Augustine does not explicitly state in the *Simplician* that predestination to eternal damnation affects the majority of people. However, he concludes this from the biblical statement that is important for him: "Many are called, but few are chosen" (Mt 22:14; cf. Simpl. 1,2,13). In his later work, Augustine will emphasize more strongly a particularism of salvation with a smaller number of the saved.[23]

In what follows, I will argue that in order to bring about this theodicy of a condemning God, Augustine had to sharpen his theology of original sin from a theology of *hereditary misery* – with the assumption that all human beings, as a result of Adam's sin, are limited in their freedom to do good and are subject to the power of death – into a definitive theology of *hereditary guilt* which is theologically unacceptable. This has the fatal consequence that even unborn children are guilty before God in such a way that they justly deserve hell. And I will show that Augustine distorted the relationship between divine grace and human free will when he pursued a theodicy of a condemning God which – with a correct understanding of Rom 9–11 – would not be necessary at all.

---

[21] Augustine is most explicit in Simpl. 1,2,18, where in connection with Esau he speaks of the fact that "God hates sinfulness. Therefore he punishes it in some by condemnation (*per damnationem*), in others he removes it by justification" (my translation).
[22] It should be noted that Augustine never assumes a direct condemnation by God, but rather an election by God which, according to his plan, is not an "adequate calling" (*vocatio congrua*), so that it is not sufficient to be accepted by faith. This inadequate vocation therefore amounts to eternal condemnation. Cf. section 3.3.
[23] Cf. civ. 21,21; corrept. et gr. 10,28.

3 Theological Distortions Due to a Theodicy of a Condemning God (1): Grace and Freedom

3.1 A New Understanding of Grace in Augustine's *Simplician*

It was not only in *Simplician* that Augustine found himself compelled to a theodicy of a condemning God. Three years earlier, in his *Propositions from the Epistle to the Romans* (exp. prop. Rm., 394)[24] he had blamed Esau's unbelief for his eternal damnation by means of a problematic auxiliary theological consideration: Although God does not choose or reject people depending on their works, he does so depending on their belief or unbelief. Accordingly, God rightly condemned Esau already in the womb because God had *foreseen* his later unbelief (cf. exp. prop. Rm. 52[60]). This way out was blocked for Augustine since his writing of *Simplician* due to his deeper reading of the Pauline letters: "What do you have that you did not receive? And if you received it, why do you boast as if it were not a gift?" (1 Cor 4:7; cf. Simpl. 1,2,9)

Augustine realised that his earlier interpretation of the letter to the Romans, which saw faith as a purely human achievement, was incompatible with this biblical text. For then Jacob would have been able to boast of his faith, since he had not received it from God, but had performed it entirely by his own strength; and this was in clear contradiction to 1 Corinthians 4:7.

So, in *Simplician*, Augustine corrected his previous theology of grace: not only good works, but also faith, are wrought by God. According to this, there is no act relevant to salvation – not asking for God's help through grace, not accepting the offer of grace in faith, and not persevering in the good – that man can do of his own accord without at the same time being supported by God's grace.

3.2 Grace and Freedom: Overcoming or Intensifying Competition?

This grace-theological turn, which Augustine had made in *Simplician* almost a decade before his controversies with Pelagius, was to shape the Church's theology of grace with its rejection of Pelagianism and Semipelagianism. In doing so,

---

24 Cf. Augustine, "Expositio quarundam propositionum ex epistula apostoli ad Romanos," in *Augustine on Romans*, Text and Translation by Paula Fredriksen Landes, 2–49 (Chico, Cal.: Scholars Press, 1982).

Augustine escaped a competing determination of the relationship between grace and human freedom, which was symptomatic of Pelagian and semi-Pelagian approaches when they believed that human freedom was to be ensured by acts that were autonomous in the sense that they were *not* at the same time borne by God's grace.

And yet, in the context of Augustine's late work *Predestination of the Saints* (429), there is a notorious statement that seems to prove a competitive relationship between God's grace and human freedom. Referring to his struggle with Rom 9 in *Simplician*, Augustine retrospectively stated:

> In resolving this question I worked hard in defense of the free choice of the human will, but the grace of God conquered.[25]

With the *Simplician*, in which Augustine pushed through to overcoming a competitive relationship between grace and freedom, he became involved in an intensified competitive thinking between divine and human activity in another respect. This is also reflected in the reception of Augustine, with conflicting assessments of whether Augustine's theology of grace since the *Simplician* overcame or intensified a competing determination of grace and freedom. Thomas Pröpper, for example, agrees with Gisbert Greshake that "Augustine was ultimately only able to conceive of the relationship between divine and human freedom in terms of competing causes"[26] and thus disagrees with Otto Hermann Pesch, who understands Augustine to mean that human freedom "cannot compete with God" because it is supported and released by God's grace – at least as freedom for the good.[27]

In what follows I will show that Augustine does in fact think repeatedly in the direction of such a mediation of grace and freedom in a process of divine-human encounter, but that he inevitably misses it whenever he strives for a theodicy of a condemning God. But if his mediation of grace and freedom failed, as Augustine freely admitted in retrospect in his later work, then Pröpper is right that Augustine remained trapped in a competitive thinking between divine grace and human freedom. Indeed, he even intensified this competitive think-

---

[25] Praed. sanct. 8; translation: Augustine, *Answer to the Pelagians, vol. 4*, edited by Roland J. Teske and John E. Rotelle (Hyde Park: New City Press, 1999). 155. Augustine here reproduces his statement from retr. 2,1,1. In the following section 3.3.2, I will develop the meaning of this sentence in a more differentiated way.

[26] Thomas Pröpper, *Theologische Anthropologie*, vol. 2, 1014, my translation.

[27] Otto Hermann Pesch and Albert Peters, *Einführung in die Lehre von Gnade und Rechtfertigung* (Darmstadt: Wissenschaftliche Buchgesellschaft, 1981) 23f, my translation.

ing in comparison with a Pelagian or semi-Pelagian division between the divine and human spheres of action, as he himself did in his early interpretation of Romans. For, since the *Simplician*, he has tended to replace the human choice between faith and unbelief with a divine choice that predestines human beings, by choosing between a vocation that is strong enough to irresistibly obtain the believing consent of humans and a vocation that is insufficient for this. This will be clarified in the following two sections.

3.3 Distortions in Augustine's *Propositions from the Epistle to the Romans* (394)

With both approaches – his earlier *Propositions from the Epistle to the Romans* (394) and the *Simplician* (397) that corrected it – Augustine missed the golden mean which understands the relation between God's grace and human freedom as *a process of encounter* where God's gracious calling resonates in the souls of the hearers, making possible its acceptance as well as its rejection. Yet Augustine in his early expositions on Romans was in principle open to such a balanced mediation of grace and freedom:

> For neither can we will unless we are called, nor after our calling, once we have willed, is our will and our running sufficient unless God both gives strength to our running and leads where he calls (exp. prop. Rm. 54[62],3).

According to Thomas Ring, Augustine determines here "the decision to believe as an independent act of the human will, but not an absolute one, but a conditionally independent one, which has the preceding calling of God as an indispensable condition"[28]. The crucial question here is how strong or weak one should imagine this divine conditionality of the independent human act of will. Here is the minimum that has to be said: If one understands faith, as Augustine did in his early interpretation of Romans, as a positive response to God's call, and unbelief as a refusal to respond to this call, then it follows logically that neither faith nor unbelief is possible if there has been no divine call. But does God's call also move people to respond by faith?

Everything we know from the Bible about God's calling encounter with people speaks to this. This is especially evident in the mediation of God's call

---

28 Thomas Gerhard Ring, "Erläuterungen," in Augustinus, *An Simplicianus zwei Bücher über verschiedene Fragen.* Sankt Augustinus – Der Lehrer der Gnade. Prolegomena, vol. 3, ed. Thomas Gerhard Ring (Würzburg: Augustinus Verlag, 1991), 284f; my translation.

through Jesus' proclamation of the kingdom of God in the Gospels. People are thus partially torn out of their habitual ways of perceiving, thinking, judging and acting, and placed into the dynamic of a dawning Kingdom. In this situation they are challenged by Jesus to accept the revealing God through faith and repentance.[29] Thus the decision of faith with which people accept God's call proves to be based on God's grace.

One might think that Augustine shares this view in his earlier treatise on Romans, when he states that for our will to respond to the divine call, "our will and our running [are not sufficient] unless God also gives the running powers and leads where he calls them" (exp. prop. Rm. 54[62],3, see above). But in the preceding chapter 53(61), Augustine has already committed himself to a Pauline interpretation according to which, in the sequence of divine calling (1), faith decision to accept the calling (2) and good works (3), calling and good works are indeed given by God's grace, but the faith decision for or against the divine calling is the exclusive responsibility of humans: "Belief is our work, but good deeds are his who gives the Holy Spirit to believers" (exp. prop. Rm. 52[60],12). That "God both gives strength to our running and leads where he calls", the early Augustine (before *Simplician*) thus refers only to good works, not to the decision to believe.

In this way, Augustine fell behind a balanced mediation of grace and freedom as a process of encounter between God and man, as already laid out in his text. Instead, he resorted to a division between divine and human spheres of activity, which, however, effectively determines the relationship between the two in the manner of division and competition: "It is we who believe and will, but he who gives to those believing and willing the ability to do good works through the Holy Spirit" (exp. prop. Rm. 53[61],7). This relapse was due to a theodicy of a condemning God, which Augustine developed in exp. prop. Rm 52f(60f), in order to reject Manichean objections based on Rom 9:11–13:

> Here Paul shows that there is no iniquity with God, as certain people can say when they hear "Before they were born, Jacob I loved, but Esau I hated." (exp. prop. Rm. 53[61],1)

---

[29] This is precisely how the anticipatory summary of Jesus' kingdom message in the Gospel of Mark is to be understood: "The time is fulfilled, and the kingdom of God has come near; repent, and *believe* in the good news" (Mk 1:15). Cf. Willibald Sandler, "Divine Action and Dramatic Christology: A Rereading of Raymund Schwager's Jesus in the Drama of Salvation," *Religions* 14/3 (2023): 15f.

Through his two theses of Esau's exclusive responsibility for his unbelief and of divine foreknowledge of this unbelief, Augustine was able to make God's "hatred of Esau" appear as a just punishment for his unbelief.

3.4 Distortions in the *Simplician* (397)

Both theses had to be abandoned by Augustine in the *Simplician*, and this caused his theodicy of a condemning God to collapse. In order to carry it out successfully after all, he could only fall back on an event of human guilt, which again preceded the divine predestination in the womb (according to Rom 9:11). Such an event is found by Augustine in the *Simplician* with a new theological trick, as ingenious as it is devastating, which puts his doctrine of original sin on a new footing: Even before a person– be it Jacob or Esau, an Israelite from the elect of Israel or from the hardened rest (Rom 11:7)–was chosen or rejected by God before her birth, she had already sinned in Adam and thus lost her original goodness she had received through creation (cf. section 4.1).

Thus, in the *Simplician*, Augustine lost the balance between God's work of grace and the free human decision of faith in the opposite direction compared to his earlier interpretation of Romans: away from the free human decision of faith and towards an all-dominant, predetermining work of God. Although Augustine first corrected the imbalance of his earlier interpretation of Romans by attributing the decision to believe – in a balanced way by distinguishing between different levels of activity – to both God and man: "For he has willed that our willing be both his and ours – his by calling and ours by following."[30]

However, Augustine could not develop this balanced mediation of grace and freedom any further, because in *Simplician* he had to restore in a new way his theodicy of a condemning God, which had failed in its earlier form. His doctrine of original sin, which was sharpened for this purpose, had the anthropological consequence that every human being had fallen in Adam and was therefore no longer *per se* capable of any good deed relevant to salvation. Thus, according to Augustine since his *Simplician*, after Adam's fall human beings are entirely dependent on divine election with regard to their capacity for good. So the difference between some people accepting God's call with faith and others rejecting it – unbelieving and hardening themselves – can only be attributed to

---

[30] Simpl. 1,2,10; translation: Aurelius Augustine, *Responses to Miscellaneous Questions*, trans. Boniface Ramsey, vol. I/12, The Works of Saint Augustine: A Translation for the 21st Century (Hyde Park: New City Press, 2008), 193.

God. Hence, for Augustine, the difference between acceptance and rejection, faith and unbelief is no longer based on a free and ultimately responsible human choice, but – because "God has mercy on no one in vain" (Simpl. 1,2,13) – on God's predetermining choice whether to call humans in an insufficient or in a sufficient way ("congruenter").[31] An adequate vocation ("vocatio congrua"), according to Augustine, means that God creates in a person such a strong desire for her that rejection is no longer within the horizon of her freedom.

Later systematisation tended to term the salvific freedom that opens man to a life fulfilled in God "libertas" and to distinguish it from freedom of choice as "liberum arbitrium" – as is often, but not always, the case with Augustine.[32] Using this terminology in a more systematic way, we can say that Augustine in *Simplician* conceived of a *libertas* without *liberum arbitrium* (i.e. without free choice between alternatives). It is in this sense that Augustine's late admission is to be understood according to which in *Simplician* grace triumphed over his effort for the freedom of the human will (see above, section 2.2): "In resolving this question [regarding Rom. 9, W.S.] I worked hard in defense of the free choice [liberum arbitrium!] of the human will, but the grace of God conquered."[33]

This concession by Augustine that his efforts to safeguard human freedom in the *Simplician* had failed must be understood in a qualified way: It does not refer to the redeemed freedom ("libertas") which sets human beings free towards God and the good but to a *freedom of choice* ("liberum arbitrium") in the sense of an ability to decide between the alternatives of accepting and rejecting God's calling. But can there be a *libertas* without *liberum arbitrium*?[34] Certainly it

---

[31] With Rom 8:28 (Vulgate), Augustine speaks in Simpl. 1,2,4 of a vocation "secundum propositum". In Simpl. 1,2,13 he speaks of persons who are called in an appropriate way (*congruenter vocati*). For a distinction between the two terms, see Ring, "Erläuterungen," 300–4.

[32] "Augustine does not draw a clear and consistent distinction between liberum arbitrium, and libertas [...]; 'libertas' often denotes the qualified freedom established by grace, which consists in consenting to the will of God [...], while 'liberum arbitrium' means the decision-making authority even in fallen man [...]." Volker Henning Drecoll, "Gratia," in *Augustinus Lexikon*, vol. 3, 182–242 (Basel: Schwabe, 2010) 209, n. 205; my translation. A more systematic application of the two terms *libertas* and *liberum arbitrium* in Augustine is given by Karl-Heinz Menke, *Das Kriterium des Christseins: Grundriss der Gnadenlehre* (Regensburg: Pustet, 2003), 38–9.

[33] Praed. sanct. 8; translation: Augustine, *Answer to the Pelagians*, IV 4, 155. Cf. section 3.2.

[34] This question is discussed with regard to Augustine in the form of whether he has a libertarian or a compatibilist conception of freedom. Johannes Brachtendorf summarises: "On the whole it must be said that the early Augustine, especially in *De libero arbitrio*, begins with a rather libertarian conception of freedom, but then tends towards compatibilism to the extent that he takes into account the determining power of grace and tries to make it compatible with

exists in the sense of a "consolidated freedom", preceded by a free choice between possible alternatives,[35] but not without it.

3.5 A More Balanced Relationship between Grace and Freedom in Other Works of Augustine

Where Augustine did not feel compelled to carry out a theodicy of a condemning God, he approached a more balanced understanding of vocation as an event of grace that does not replace but enables human freedom to accept or reject God's offer of grace; this is the case in texts before and after the *Simplician*. Thus, shortly before the *Simplician*, Augustine, in his *Eighty-Three Varied Questions* (div. qu., completed in 396), emphasised the necessity of a divine drive and calling for the human will for the good as well as a human freedom of choice to accept or reject one's vocation:

> [...] since a person cannot will unless he has been alerted and called, either interiorly where no one sees or exteriorly by audible words or some visible signs, it happens *that God works in us even this very willing*. For not all of those who were called willed to come to that supper which the Lord says in the gospel had been prepared [See Lk 14:16–24], and those who did come would have been unable to come unless they had been called. And so those who came must not attribute it to themselves that, having been called, they came; *and those who chose not to come must attribute it to no one but themselves*, since they had been called to come in free will.[36]

This text gives us a glimpse of a transitional phase in which Augustine seems to have left behind his concept of faith as an exclusively human act from his *Proposition from the Epistle to the Romans* two years earlier, but without linking it again to a theodicy of a condemning God, as was the case a year later in *Simplician*.

Fifteen years later, in his new approach to a theology of grace, *The Spirit and the Letter* (spir. et litt., 412), Augustine again asked whether Paul's rejection of all boasting made a free choice of human will in response to God's offer of grace

---

human freedom" Johannes Brachtendorf, "Einleitung," in Augustinus, *De Libero Arbitrio – Der Freie Wille*, edited by Johannes Brachtendorf, Paderborn 2006, 7–69 (Paderborn: Schöningh, 2006), 65, my translation.

35 In this sense, Augustine stated in corrept. et gr. 11,32: "But what will be more free (*liberius*) than free choice (*libero arbitrio*) when it will no longer be able to be a slave to sin? For this freedom would also have been for Adam the reward of his merit, as it has become that of the holy angels." English Translation by Han-Luen Kantzer Komline, *Augustine on the Will: A Theological Account* (New York: Oxford University Press, 2020). 396.

36 Div. quaest. 68.5; transl.: Augustine, *Responses to Miscellaneous Questions*, 120; my emphasis.

impossible; and he came to a very conclusion from the *Simplician*. Now Augustine, following closely the passage just quoted from Diversis quaestionibus, emphasises both to the utmost: on the one hand, God's call of grace as a necessary condition for its faithful acceptance, and on the other hand, man's free and responsible decision for or against God's call. Again, he begins with the first:

> Let that person pay attention and see that this will is to be attributed to God's gift, not only because it arises from the free choice which is created in us as part of our nature, but also because God brings it about by the enticements of our perceptions that we will and that we believe. He does this either externally through the exhortations of the gospel [...]. Or he does this internally where none have control over what comes into their minds, though to assent or dissent is in the power of their will. God, then, works in these ways with the rational soul so that it believes him. For it cannot so much as believe anything by free choice, if there is no enticement or invitation which it can believe. *God, then, certainly produces in human beings the will to believe, and his mercy anticipates us in every respect.* [cf. Ps 59:11].[37]

This human will (which is wholly wrought by God) to accept God's calling with faith, is now understood by Augustine in the manner of a free will, not only (as in *Simplician)* as a freedom ("libertas") open towards God and the true good, but also as a genuine freedom of choice ("liberum arbitrium") between the alternatives of acceptance and rejection:

> *But to assent to God's invitation or to dissent from it is, as I said, in the power of one's will.* This fact not only does not weaken the words, "What do you have that you have not received?" (1 Cor 4:7), but rather confirms them. The soul can, of course, receive and have the gifts about which it hears this only by assenting. Accordingly, what it has and what it receives come from God, but the receiving and the having certainly come from the one who receives and has them.[38]

Here, Augustine not only asserts a maximum divine power of grace and human freedom at the same time, but also moves from a concurrence between grace and freedom (as still in *Simplician*, where grace predominated over freedom) to a *direct proportionality* of both, since it is God's power of grace that releases human freedom of choice, which has been weakened by sin. "Free choice is not done away with by grace, but strengthened, because grace heals the will by which we freely love righteousness".[39]

---

37 Spir. et litt. 60; translation: Augustine, *Answer to the Pelagians*, vol. 1, 192; emphasis mine.
38 Ibid., continuation of the previous quote; emphasis mine.
39 Spir. et litt. 52; translation: Augustine, *Answer to the Pelagians*, vol. 1, 185. Is this release of freedom of choice not only in terms of content (in that it gains God and true good as its object),

It is a pity that Augustine subsequently lost this balanced approach again, due to the worsening anti-Pelagian controversy and the resulting polarizations. He rejected the *external grace (gratia externa)* favoured by Pelagius, to which the human being is much more likely to take a position in freely decided acceptance or rejection[40] and favoured the *internal grace (gratia interna)*,[41] which reaches the human will in a depth area where this will is constituted, so that a free choice regarding this inner call to grace can hardly be imagined. Augustine increasingly emphasized the irresistibility of divine grace, but then also had to give more space to external grace – for example, through exhortations – in order to counteract exaggerations of his radical theology of grace.[42]

It follows that the imbalance of Augustine's later theology of grace was not caused by his controversy with Pelagius, but arose more than fourteen years earlier in the *Simplician*, due to Augustine's predestinationist misunderstanding of Romans 9, combined with a deeper understanding of Pauline texts (esp. 1 Cor 4:7; cf section 3.1). But the polarization of the Pelagian controversy hindered Augustine from consolidating and deepening a balanced solution of the grace-freedom relationship that he had already achieved in *Spirit and the Letter*.[43] Rather, he quietly distanced himself from it.

---

but also formally given as a real possibility of choice? This is suggested by Augustine in these most open passages, but not further explained by him. This is where a contemporary theology of grace inspired by Augustine would have to continue. In a planned follow-up to this chapter, I intend to make a proposal in this regard. See the outlook in section 6.3.

40 This is contrary to the previously quoted texts from div. qu. and spir. et litt. where Augustine explicitly addressed both an inner and an exterior grace and also in contrast to his autobiographical testimonies in the *Confessiones*: the encounter with courageous converts spurred him on to his conversion. Here, inner grace does not work without external grace, mediated by the world and other persons.

41 The schematised terminology of a *gratia externa* and a *gratia interna* is alien to Augustine, to Pelagius and their contemporaries, but not the matter expressed with it (on Augustine, see the previous note). Later systematising reflection in the history of theology characterises above all Pelagius' understanding of grace as that of a mere *gratia externa*, mediated by external models and by laws, whereby the example of Christ plays an outstanding role. This also corresponds to Augustine's critique (without the corresponding terminology) when he accuses Pelagius of a merely external work of grace in view of Jesus' teachings and a corresponding learning from the Gospel and when he insists on an inwardly transforming work of God's grace connected with it. On Augustine about human learning in sharp correction of Pelagius, cf. De natura et gratia 40,47, and on Jesus' teaching, cf. De gratia Christi et de peccato originali 1,13,14.

42 So overall in corrept. et gr.

43 Drecoll, on the other hand, interprets spir. et litt. 60 in line with *Simplician*: "The subsequent statement consentire vel dissentire propriae voluntatis est (agreeing or disagreeing is a matter of one's own will) cannot, because of this context, be understood as if Augustine were suddenly

4 Theological Distortions Due to a Theodicy of a Condemning God (2): Original Sin

4.1 "A Single Mass of Sin in Adam": Augustine's New Construct of Original Sin

In *Simplician*, Augustine fatally connected this theological imbalance of grace with his predestination-theological misunderstanding of Rom 9: If God had not only predestined Esau's bad works but also his unbelief by non-election, then apparently God alone was responsible for Esau's damnation. Accordingly, Augustine thought he had to defend God against the suspicion of an arbitrary damnation of a majority of people into eternal damnation. In order to free God from this suspicion, Augustine had to find a comprehensible[44] reason for God condemning people – if not because of a later unbelief foreseen by God, then because of a shortcoming that preceded their birth.

For here the Manichaean solution offered itself dangerously, according to which there was an evil human nature that could be traced back to an evil divine power. Augustine has fought against such a dualistic and fatalistic consequence since his conversion. Akin to this is the idea of double predestination, according to which God would be free to create bad vessels whose destruction is up to him. Had not Paul also spoken of this in Rom 9:21–22? But this basically Manichaean variant was unacceptable to Augustine due to his theology of creation. Against this he argued in *Simplician* with a strong text from the Book of Wisdom:

---

making a turnaround here by advocating an independent contribution of the human will; rather, he interprets agreeing and disagreeing as movements of the will that are directly influenced by God." Volker Henning Drecoll, "De spiritu et littera," in *Augustin Handbuch,* ed. Volker Henning Drecoll (Tübingen: Mohr Siebeck, 2014), 332; my translation. However, this is a harmonizing interpretation which is not compelling and unlikely due to Augustine's strong echoes of div. quaest. 84. Another argument against this is that Augustine here emphasizes the tension between grace and freedom, which would simply be dissolved in the sense of *Simplician* as explained by Drecoll. This tension is evident in the whole layout of spir. et litt. 60, as well as in the key statement: "*sed* consentire vel dissentire propriae voluntatis est" (emphasis mine). In his explanation, Drecoll omitted the "sed" and lost the tension in Augustine's statement.

44 In *Simplician* and in his later work, Augustine assumes that God has a reason for electing some and condemning others, but that this reason is entirely incomprehensible to us. Nevertheless, according to Augustine, we need comprehensible reasons for God's justice and mercy in order to trust him. Cf. Simpl. 1,2,16.

> For you love all things that exist, and detest none of the things that you have made, for you would not have made anything if you had hated it (Wis 11:24, cf. Simpl. 1,2,8).

How could Augustine combine this confession of an infinitely loving Creator God with a justification for the same God "not loving but hating" a larger part of humanity like Esau, which, according to Augustine's misunderstanding of Romans 9, must mean that he condemns them to hell? And Augustine thought he had to justify that God had damned these people even before they were born, without any bad decisions or actions foreseen by God being the decisive factor. Nevertheless, Augustine wanted to maintain that these same damned people were good and loved by God from creation.

In the *Simplician*, Augustine attempted to square this circle with a sharpened version of his theology of original sin, which he was already developing at the time. His basic idea: *Before* their birth (and therefore before and independently of any self-responsible sinning of their own free will as born, individual human beings) and yet *after* their creation as good beings loved by God, all human beings had fallen into a guilt that would earn them eternal damnation. They would have incurred this guilt through and in Adam by participating in his Fall:

> Therefore, all human beings – since, as the Apostle says, all die in Adam (1 Cor 15:22), from whom the origin of the offense against God spread throughout the whole human race – are a kind of single mass of sin ["una quaedam massa peccati"] owing a debt of punishment to the divine and loftiest justice, and whether [the punishment that is owed] be exacted or forgiven, there is no injustice.[45]

As a result of Adam's Fall, every human being would only face eternal hell. In view of this universal misery, it would be a gesture of Gods's extraordinary generosity not to allow all human beings to perish, but to select a remnant for salvation – without any merit whatsoever and on the basis of a divine plan whose reasons remain obscure to us. This is why the part of Augustine's letter to Simplician devoted to Rom 9 ends in an exuberant praise of God:

> If you do not repay what is owed, you have reason to be grateful; if you do repay it, you have no reason to complain. [...] Let us say "Alleluia" and join in the canticle [...][46]

This conclusion of the *Simplician* was the central impetus for Kurt Flasch's condemnation of this work as a "logic of horror" (cf. section 1).

---

45 Simpl. 1,2,16; translation: Augustine, *Answer to the Pelagians*, vol. 1, 198.
46 Simpl. 1,2,22; translation: Augustine, *Answer to the Pelagians*, vol. 1, 207.

4.2 A Serious Deficit: Augustine's Theology of Original Sin Isolates Adam from All Other Human Beings

Augustine's unnecessary and unworkable theodicy of a damning God, which he undertook in the *Simplician*, forced him to drive a wedge between Adam and all other human beings. For if he reduced Adam's sin – like the sin of all other human beings – ultimately to God's predestination, Augustine could no longer hold to the original goodness of creation, which he passionately defended against Manichaeism. Consequently, he had to assume that Adam, before his Fall, had a freedom of choice regarding God's offer of salvation, which he, in opposition to Pelagius, denied to all other human beings. In *Rebuke and Grace* (426), Augustine wrote about the divine help of grace that Adam had before the Fall:

> This help was, of course, such that he could abandon it if he willed to and could remain in it if he willed to, not such that it would make him to will this. This is the first grace which was given to the first Adam [...].[47]

In *Simplician*, Augustine thought he had to exclude precisely this freedom for all other human beings, since for him it was incomprehensible "that God is merciful to no avail unless we will. For if God is merciful, we also will."[48]

But why should this have been different for Adam (and Eve) before the Fall? If Augustine had consistently applied the same to Adam as to all other human beings, then ultimately God would have been the reason for Adam's Fall and Augustine's theodicy of a damning God would collapse. Augustine would have ended up in double predestination and thus would no longer have been able to defend the belief in a good creation and thus in a good, just and merciful Creator. Thus Augustine was forced to assert a fundamental opposition between the free will of Adam and that of all other human beings.

This grace-theological contradiction between Adam and all other human beings was later exacerbated by the polarisation of the Pelagian controversy.

---

[47] Corrept. et gr. 11,31; translation: Augustine, *Answer to the Pelagians*, vol. 4, 139.
[48] Simpl. 1,2,12; translation: Augustine, *Responses to Miscellaneous Questions*, 194. Behind this assumption lies Augustine's theological turn towards grace: There must be nothing that man can accomplish exclusively of himself (not even the faith with which he accepts his calling) because, according to 1 Cor 4:7, there is nothing of which man can boast: not the faithful acceptance of God's call and, correspondingly, not its rejection. In section 2.2, I showed that Augustine's efforts at a theodicy of a condemning God prevented him from a balanced determination of the relationship between grace and freedom.

For now Adam stood for the human being sovereignly capable of good and evil – a concept of humanity to which Pelagius referred in his moral sermons and which, according to Augustine, does not correspond at all to the human being under original sin (cf. above, section 2.2).

A particular problem of Augustine's theology of grace – starting with the *Simplician* and intensified in the Pelagian controversy – thus lies in the fact that he, too, cannot do without a human freedom of choice with regard to God's offer of salvation, but reserves this exclusively for Adam (and Eve) before the Fall. In this way, Adam, the exemplary human being as the Bible understands him, becomes a counterexample to all other human beings – at least with regard to how he carries out his freedom under God's grace and in relation to it.

Accordingly, for Augustine's doctrine of original sin, the contrast between Adam's *peccatum originale originans* (through a freely induced fall into sin, which would not be possible in this way for all other human beings) and our *peccatum originale originatum*[49] – a state of, as it were, inherited guilt, which makes us appear as victims rather than perpetrators of Adam's sin – solidified after the *Simplician*.

With this, however, Augustine, in the wake of his *Simplician*, gets into another contradiction with the Bible after his misunderstanding of Romans 9. The Bible sees Adam (and Eve) as exemplary for human beings. The story of the Fall shows how people fall away from God again and again – without any lack and without any reason recognisable to us – such as David with Bathsheba, Solomon with his pagan wives or even the people of Israel in the desert, after a lot of trusting experiences of being provided for by God.[50] The Bible knows not just one, but a lot of "Falls of Man",[51] and the Fall of Adam and Eve at the beginning

---

49 This schematising terminology was not yet used by Augustine, but it excellently shows the fracture in his theology of original sin, which he laboriously tried to patch up through different approaches to the transmission of original sin from Adam to other human beings which were incoherent among themselves. Cf. Urs Baumann, *Erbsünde? Ihr traditionelles Verständnis in der Krise heutiger Theologie* (Freiburg: Herder, 1970), 28–36.

50 Cf. Willibald Sandler, *Der verbotene Baum im Paradies: Was es mit dem Sündenfall auf sich hat* (Kevelaer: Topos, 2009), 26–34.

51 Accordingly, Norbert Lohfink speaks of a plurality of original sins. Cf. Norbert Lohfink, "Die Ursünden in der priesterlichen Geschichtserzählung," in *Die Zeit Jesu. FS für Heinrich Schlier*, ed. Günther Bornkamm, and Karl Rahner (Freiburg: Herder 1970): 38–57. An inclusive-exemplary understanding of Adam is, as far as I can see, taken for granted rather than reflected in contemporary Old Testament exegesis. Georg Fischer, in his new commentary on Gen 1–11, succinctly states, "Exemplarily and for the first time, Gen 3 shows, on the one hand, how human beings fail [...]": Georg Fischer, *Genesis 1–11*. Herders theologischer Kommentar zum Alten Testament (Freiburg: Herder 2018), 272; my translation. In the 1960s, on the other hand, there

of humanity is a *story of meaning*, a wisely composed teaching narrative that is supposed to explain, in the manner of a radical *origin story*, how humans again and again squander a good relationship with God and his creation for apparently no reason.[52]

This problem, too, arose only from the shifts in Augustine's theology from the Simplician onwards. A few years earlier, in his dispute with Fortunatus (392), Augustine had still explicitly considered the role of Adam as an exemplary human being: We all sin again and again like Adam (cf. section 6.1.1).

4.3 Conclusion: Augustine's Doctrine of Hereditary Guilt in the *Simplician* is Theologically Untenable

With regard to Augustine's theology of original sin and subsequently to the Church's doctrine of original sin, Thomas Pröpper concluded that "the theory of original sin, at least in the form developed by Augustine, [...] is indeed *unacceptable* – unacceptable on both *moral* and *theological* grounds. For guilt [...] can only ever be one's *own* fault."[53]

Basically, I agree with Pröpper's judgement, which is momentous for a ecclesiastical theology of original sin. I share his criticism that with his *Simplician*, Augustine crossed the line into a definitive theology of hereditary guilt – with the fatal consequence that children who are still unborn must be considered to be so unrighteous that a God who condemns them to eternal damnation can still be understood as a just and merciful God. Augustine attempted such a proof in *Simplician*, and what came out of it, in my opinion, really amounts to a "logic of terror". This also applies to Augustine's argument that the condemned can still fulfil a salvation-historical benefit for the elect in the way of a deterrent (cf. Simpl. 1,2,18). With his doctrine of hereditary guilt as developed in his *Simplician*, Augustine crossed a boundary beyond which one can no longer responsibly follow him as a systematic theologian. Indeed, many theologians today share the criticism of Augustine's doctrine of original sin outlined here. However, one must then take into account the danger that, in view of Augustine's strong logical interlocking of various teachings on freedom, grace, original sin and predestination, a merely selective reception of Augustine becomes logically inconsistent.

---

was still a discussion (still alive in recent dogmatics) about Adam as a corporate personality or progenitor, which seems outdated in today's Old Testament exegesis.
52 Cf. Sandler, *Der verbotene Baum im Paradies*, 26–30.
53 Pröpper, *Theologische Anthropologie*, vol. 2, 1024; my translation. Cf. section 1.

4.4 "Love it or Leave it": The Problem of a Polarising Critique of Augustine and of Church Dogma Based on Him

On the other hand, Flasch – and with him Pröpper – exaggerated the logical coherence of an Augustinian system or even Augustinianism[54] which would have prevailed with Augustine since his *Simplician*. Not only theologians who are faithful to the Church doctrine of original sin, but also Flasch and Pröpper are guilty of a selective reception of Augustine, albeit with reversed signs, in that they nail Augustine down to particularly problematic statements, especially from the *Simplician* and from his late work.[55] More balanced approaches by Augustine to the relationship between grace and human freedom *after* the *Simplician* (cf. section 2.4) are not considered by neither Flasch or Pröpper. Pröpper attests that Augustine, until just before the *Simplician*, still has a convincing concept today, "because it takes the sinner's responsibility seriously, does not underestimate the dialectic of the weakened will and at the same time still counts on God as the advocate of human freedom"[56]. But for Augustine from the *Simplician* onwards, Pröpper, in accord with Flasch, sticks to undifferentiated negative sweeping judgements: "Freedom, since 397, is no longer something that belongs to the essence of the human spirit [...]; it becomes a secondary aspect of grace."[57]

Flasch confronts today's theologians with the false dilemma of "love it or leave it": for him, to "love" Augustine's theology necessarily means accepting a radically pre-modern attitude, including religious fanaticism up to and including the Inquisition,[58] while to "leave it", must consequently amount to a rejection of the Church's doctrine of grace and original sin based on Augustine.

---

54 "It [the *Simplician*] is nothing less than the founding document of Augustinianism." Flasch, *Logik des Schreckens*, 51; my translation.
55 Cf. Drecoll's criticism of Flasch, with further references in Drecoll, "Gratia," 187.
56 Pröpper, *Theologische Anthropologie*, vol. 2, 1009, my translation.
57 Ibid. 1013, with a quotation from Flasch, *Logik des Schreckens*, 123; my translation.
58 Cf. Flasch, *Logik des Schreckens*, 15, 137.

5 Methodological Reflection: A Transformative Reception of Augustine's Theology

5.1 Not Rupture, but Transformation by a "Conversion of Thought"

Flasch and Pröpper claimed that the *Simplician* signified a rupture in Augustine's theology. In contrast to this, I prefer to speak of transformations. A transformation does not exclude a rupture, but with Augustine it is a theologically processed rupture. One could call this *a theological conversion of thought*.[59] An extreme biblical example of this is Paul's conversion, which also shattered his previous theology, but then led to a reformulation of his theology around the centre of a previously passionately rejected faith in Christ as the Risen One.[60] A new insight or revelation[61] is adopted even though it seems incompatible with central assumptions within the framework of previous thinking and therefore breaks the previous system of thinking. In the aftermath of such a "thought quake" ("Denkbeben"[62]), the elements that have been scattered far and wide are gradually rearranged and brought into a new system in such a way that the new insight or revelation occupies a central place in it.

Such a "conversion of thought" is the catastrophic form of a transformation. Usually, transformations proceed more quietly. A living system of thought that is open for learning also grows by ongoing minor transformations, by discarding what has been disproved, absorbing new knowledge and rearranging parts of a system of thought to integrate change.

5.2 Transformations *in* Augustine's Theology

Such transformational processes play an important role in Augustine's distinctly systematic, argumentative and coherent thinking. Even before the *Simplician*,

---

[59] On the theological method of a "conversion of thought", see Sandler, "Divine Action and Dramatic Christology," 6–10.
[60] Cf. Willibald Sandler, *Charismatisch, evangelikal und katholisch. Eine theologische Unterscheidung der Geister* (Freiburg: Herder, 2021), 286f.
[61] Augustine explicitly described his key insight for the *Simplician* with 1 Cor 4 as a "revelation of God." Cf. praed. sanct. 8.
[62] Cf. Flasch, *Logik des Schreckens*, 17. I am adopting Flasch's accurate term here, who however uses it exclusively polemically.

Augustine continually modified and developed his ideas of free will and its limitations. In his early writings on free will[63] he argued philosophically and made little use of biblical texts. His main concern was to refute Manichaeism by grounding evil in human free choice, without tracing their sinful volitional decisions – and thus evil itself – back to a Creator God, which would obscure his justice, goodness and omnipotence.[64] Augustine's primary interest in a theodicy resulted from this anti-Manichaean concern.

Subsequently, Augustine took increasing account of biblical texts that seemed to question a person's autonomous free will, and with which the Manichaeans confronted him. These include, above all, the despair of the law-bound human being in Romans 7, who recognises and desires the good without being able to achieve it.[65]

From such contexts, Augustine's early conception of free will can be understood as a philosophically argued basic insight that he gradually modified theologically, as Han-Luen Kantzer Komline has convincingly argued in a comprehensive monograph on free will in Augustine.[66]

5.3 Interim Summary: A Transformative Reception of Augustine is Necessary and Possible

Just as Augustine transformed his previous theology in the *Simplician* on the basis of a transformed understanding of Paul's letters, so today's systematic theologians should be able to take up this theological system in a transformative way, by breaking it down and reassembling it in such a way that the resulting theology corresponds to a transformed understanding of Rom 9–11 (cf. sections 2 and 3). What must be rejected in Augustine's interpretation of Paul is his unquestioned assumption that the Pauline texts in Rom 9 about a divinely caused hardening and rejection of Esau, Pharaoh and above all of a larger part of the Jewish people – exemplary for most humans in general – amount to their eternal damnation: if

---

[63] This is especially the case in the first book of *De libero arbitrio*, or also in the anti-Manichaean *De duabus animarum*. Cf. Kantzer Komline, *Augustine on the Will*, 15–77.
[64] Cf. especially Augustine's *Contra Fortunatum*. On this cf. Kantzer Komline, *Augustine on the Will*, 77–87.
[65] Augustine was challenged on this by the Manichaean Fortunatus, who introduced Rom 7 as an argument for his dualistic view. Cf. Kantzer Komline, *Augustine on the Will*, 82, with reference to c. Fort. 19.
[66] Cf. Kantzer Komline, *Augustine on the Will*.

not through a direct predestination to hell, then through an "insufficient calling" (cf. section 3.3), so to speak through a denial of assistance.

In sections 3 and 4 I have shown that highly problematic exacerbations of Augustine's theology of grace and original sin in *Simplician* are due to a theodicy with which he attempted to justify the justice and goodness of such a condemning God in order to be able to reject fatalistic and dualistic interpretations of Scripture by the Manichaeans. In section 5 I argued that justified concerns about exaggerated Augustinian criticism in the work of the philosopher Kurt Flasch and, exemplarily, in the work of the systematic theologian Thomas Pröpper, who is highly influential in German-speaking theology, are based on this unnecessary and also unworkable theodicy of a condemning God. If this cornerstone is removed from Augustine's *Simplician* theology – which in turn constitutes his later theology of grace and freedom, predestination and original sin – then a large part of Augustine's theological system is bound to collapse. And this in turn shakes traditional church teaching where it is based on Augustine, which also applies to central Catholic dogmas of grace and especially of original sin.

This raises a dilemma for a dogmatic theology that understands itself as ecclesial. In my critique of Kurt Flasch's anti-Augustinian polemic, I argued that Flasch drives his readers into the fallacy of a false dilemma regarding Augustine and Augustinian Church doctrine: "love it or leave it" (cf. section 4.4). This critique can only be confirmed by systematic theology if it shows a viable third way between adhering to Augustine's theological transformations with their far-reaching consequences since the *Simplician* and rejecting them altogether up to Catholic dogma. That such transformations are possible was impressively demonstrated to us by Augustine with his own radical reconstruction of his theology in the *Simplician*. Here we find the high ethos of a theology that is ready to be broken by a deeper understanding of God's biblically mediated revelation, without irrationalistically abandoning itself, and thus to reassemble the fragmented parts in a deepened effort of a *fides quaerens intellectum*.[67]

To carry out such a transformation is beyond the scope of this chapter. Nevertheless, the proposal made here would remain in limbo if I did not at least indicate how I think such a transformative reinterpretation is possible. I begin

---

[67] Whether and to what extent Augustine also reflected this understanding of a theology in listening to biblical revelation would have to be examined separately. Anselm of Canterbury did an excellent methodological work in this regard, following Augustine in many respects. Cf. Michel Corbin's interpretation of Anselms method, and on this: Sandler, "Divine Action and Dramatic Christology," 6–8.

with Augustine's theology of original sin, which is particularly challenging and controversial for a reception in contemporary dogmatics.

6 Towards a Transformed Reception of Augustine on Original Sin, Grace and Freedom

6.1 Starting Point: Augustine's Understanding of Original Sin Shortly before the *Simplician*

As shown in section 4.1, in the *Simplician* Augustine has sharpened his earlier doctrine of Adam's Fall into a definitive doctrine of hereditary *guilt*, thereby legitimising as just and merciful God's seemingly unwarranted condemnation of human beings along the lines of Esau, Pharaoh and the majority of Israel in Rom 9–11. My discussion of these Pauline texts and their recent exegesis (cf. section 2.1) has led to the conclusion that they do not deal with the eternal salvation or damnation of human beings, but with a limited role in the history of salvation, which is surpassed by a broader perspective of predestination, especially in Rom 11:25–26 for Israel. But this all-embracing predestination, which transcends any predestination of a salvation historical role, is no longer a double predestination; it refers entirely to election but not to damnation. For this reason, Augustine's attempted theodicy of a damning God proves unnecessary. Equally unnecessary, therefore, is the tightening of the doctrine of original sin that Augustine undertook for this purpose in the *Simplician*. This finding necessitates a transformation of Augustine's concept of original sin, the first step of which is a return to its status immediately before the *Simplician*.

Until then, Augustine had developed his "doctrine of original sin" (in the broad sense of a doctrine on the effects of Adam's original sin on all other human beings) in a sequence of two "theological differentiations"[68] or "complexifications"[69] of his decided doctrine of free will.

---

[68] Kantzer Komline, *Augustine on the Will*, 77, speaks here explicitly of theological differentiations.
[69] "*Contra Fortunatum* reveals new layers of complexity to Augustine's conception of will" (Ibid. 82).

6.2 Falling into the Compulsions of Bad Habit: Analogy between Adam's Sin and our Sinning (c. Fort. 392)

In his public debate with the Manichaean Fortunatus (in the year 392), Augustine first repeated his doctrine of free will: "I say that it is not sin if we do not sin with our own will."[70] He defended this position against Fortunatus, who countered him with Pauline statements about the broken will in Rom 7. Augustine interpreted these passages in such a way that the original free will is compelled by bad habits caused by one's own sins. To make this clear, Augustine referred to Adam's Fall:

> He was of such a nature that nothing at all [*nihil omnino*] could oppose his will if he wanted to keep the commandments of God. But after he himself sinned of his own free will, we who are descended from his lineage have been plunged into necessity.[71]

That it is so, according to Augustine, is comprehensible to all of us from our own experience, when in any matter we forfeit an initial freedom to do good by yielding to temptations.[72]

With a few strokes, Augustine sketches out a "doctrine of original sin" that still leaves the connection between Adam's sin and a will bound by compulsion rather vague. An effect of Adam's Fall on us is suggested but only a temporal sequence is stated. We fall into a similar unfree situation of compulsion like Adam, after we ourselves have sinned like him. This is not causality, but only a weak analogy of proportionality: by sinning *like Adam*, we damage our freedom of will to do good and, *like Adam*, deliver ourselves to the power of sin and death. However, Augustine keeps open the possibility that this repetition of sin is suggested by a resonance of Adam's sin in all human beings.[73]

---

[70] C. Fort. 21, my translation.

[71] C. Fort. 22; my translation.

[72] "But each of us, with moderate reflection, can see that what I am saying is true. For today we have the free choice to do or not to do something before we get entangled in any practice of our action. But when we have done something with this freedom and the corrupting sweetness and lust of the act has held the soul, it is so entangled in its own habit that it cannot later defeat what it has manufactured by its sinning" (c. Fort. 21; my translation).

[73] Yet Augustine does not say that the effect of Adam's sin is that we sin in the same way as he did. He only says that we sin in a similar way and can therefore understand the constraint ("the necessity") that was imposed over Adam's original free human will. Cf. c. Fort. 22. The effects of the Fall on others, to which I refer here with the metaphor „resonance", are unfolded in: Sandler, *Der verbotene Baum im Paradies*, 117–64.

6.3 Defusing the Mistranslation of Rom 5:12

This open-ended determination of the relationship between Adam's fall into sin and our tendency, like Adam, to bind our freedom by the compulsion of the sinful habit, as Augustine outlines against Fortunatus, could be formulated in such a way *that we sin like Adam in the wake (or under the influence) of Adam*. If we understand "Adam" in a broader sense, so that we include in this term a sphere of influence resonating from his Fall,[74] then the notorious mistranslation of Rom 5:12 as "Adam [...] *in whom (in quo)* all have sinned", can make passable sense.[75] "In Adam", would then mean (not according to Augustine's later, but according to his early doctrine of original sin from 392 against Fortunatus): In the sphere of the resonating consequences of Adam's Fall, all other people sin *like* him. Such a limbo between Adam's influence and individual guilt corresponds well to the biblical meaning of Rom 5:12 when the verse is read in the context of Rom 5:12–21.[76] For an effect from Adam on all humans is mentioned several times in Rom 5:16–19. In Rom 5:12, however, the Greek expression "eph' hō" (with the Latin mistranslation "in quo [omnes peccaverunt]") is usually translated *causally* today: "Therefore, just as sin came into the world through one man, and death came through sin, and so death spread to all *because* all have sinned [...]." (Rom 5:12 NRS)

Thus, the reason for all people being subject to a death power of sin is not stated to be the sin of Adam, but the sin of every individual. This is certainly the best translation according to philological standards.[77] However, to conclude from this that this is not about original sin would mean isolating the verse from its context. Therefore, a *consecutive* translation ("*so that* all sinned"), as favoured by

---

[74] In the third book of *De libero arbitrio*, Augustine explains what I call here "resonate", analogous to an inner-personal evil habituation, which now radiates to other people. Cf. section 6.3.

[75] Augustine applied this mistranslation since his first anti-Pelagian writing (pecc. mer. 9–20) from the years 411–412 in the sense of a definite doctrine of original sin, which I reject here. It was adopted in the Church's dogma of original sin (Can. 2 of the Synod of Carthage: DH 223; Can. 2 of the Synod of Orange: DH 372) and also retained in the Council of Trent (DH 1512 and 1514) despite and against the philological refutation by Erasmus. For Thomas Pröpper, this represents the remarkable singular case of an obviously wrong Bible translation in the – according to Catholic understanding, infallible – dogma. Cf. Pröpper, *Theologische Anthropologie*, vol. 2, 965.

[76] Cf. Wolter, *Der Brief und die Römer. Teilband 1: Röm 1–8*, Evangelisch-Katholischer Kommentar zum Neuen Testament (Ostfildern: Patmos, 2014), 340–361.

[77] Wolter convincingly justifies this with the chiastic structure of Rom 5:12a–d. Cf. ibid., 344.

Joseph A. Fitzmyer,[78] captures the context of the Rom 5:12 and Paul's intention well. It may be a bad translation,[79] but it is certainly a good paraphrase.

In precisely this sense, the mistranslation "in quo omnes peccaverunt" can now also be tolerated with regard to the intention of the *in quo omnes*–formula in the Dogma, but also of *eph' hō* within the setting of Rom 5:12–19, if we understand "in Adam" as "under the resonating consequences of his Fall" – quite in the sense of Augustine's early version of his doctrine of original sin in *Contra Fortunatum*. This still does not correspond to the isolated statement of Rom 5:12, but it paraphrases well the context in which it stands. If we take the formulation as a shorthand for Rom 5:12–19, then the sense of this statement fits again, but this is only so if we understand it not in the sense as Augustine did according to his sharpened doctrine of original sin since *De Peccatorum Meritis* (412; cf. pecc. mer. 1.9.10), but as suggested here in line with its early version from *Contra Fortunatum*. Such a return to Augustine's earlier doctrine of original sin (as a first step of a transformative reception, in the sense of an "unbuilding") is necessary for the biblical-theological reasons developed above (cf. the beginning of section 6.1).

6.4 "Analogous Sin" (*De Libero Arbitrio* III; 394–395)

In section 6.1.1 I noted that Augustine, in *Contra Fortunatum*, five years before his *Simplician*, made only an unclear connection between Adam's sin and an impairment of our freedom to do good. He suggested the possibility that we sin *like Adam* under the influence of Adam's sin. However, Augustine did not unfold here how this influence could work.

Augustine goes a step further in the third book of his important work *On Free Will* (lib. arb., 395). Here he assumes a "carnal habituation" that affects people even before any single act of free will, as if they themselves had sinned: they no longer clearly recognise the true good, and when or insofar as they recognise it, they no longer have the capacity to put it into practice (cf. lib. arb. 3,19,54.). However, Augustine did not yet assume here that this impairment would be a personal guilt that makes one reprehensible and punishable before God. He did not take this fateful step until the *Simplician*.

---

[78] Cf. Joseph Fitzmyer, "The Consecutive Meaning of ΕΦ' Ω in Romans 5.12," *New Testament Studies* 39 (1993): 321–33.
[79] At least if one follows Michael Wolter's argumentation in *Der Brief an die Römer. Teilband 1*, 344.

Nevertheless, even in *De libero arbitrio* III Augustine wants to speak of a sin (peccatum) that is in us from Adam's sin. But he understands this "hereditary sin" explicitly in an analogous sense:

> Wrong actions done by anyone from ignorance and the inability to perform good acts that he wants to, are called sins for the very reason that they have their origin in the first sin [i.e. of Adam and Eve; W. S.], which was voluntary, and it is this previous sin which has merited these consequences.[80]

This corresponds to an understanding of original sin as *sin in an analogous sense*[81] as we find it, for example, explicitly in Karl Rahner.[82] Thomas Pröpper dismisses Rahner's approaches to a modern understanding of original sin as "fraudulent labelling"[83] because they pretend to interpret the dogmatised Church doctrine of original sin, whereas this Church doctrine – with recourse to Augustine – would hold a decided concept of hereditary *sin and guilt* in a univocal sense. With regard to this verdict of Pröpper, it can be stated from what I have said so far:[84] At least Augustine's third volume of *De libero arbitrio* (about two years before the *Simplician*) corresponds excellently to Rahner's approach. Whether a transformative reception of Augustine, as is outlined here, is also suitable for a reception of the Church's doctrine of original sin, would have to be examined separately.[85]

---

[80] Lib. arb. 3,19,54; translation: Augustine, *The Teacher; the Free Choice of the Will; Grace and Free Will*, trans. Robert P. Russell (Washington: Catholic University of America Press, 1968), 213–4.

[81] Unlike c. Fort. where Augustine assumed a weak *analogia proportionalitatis* between Adam's sin and ours, in lib. arb. III he explicitly advocates an analogy of attribution *(analogia attributionis)*. On these different forms of analogy cf. Joachim Track, "Analogie," in *Theologische Realenzyklopädie*, vol. 2 (Berlin: de Gruyter, 1978): 625–50, in particular 628f.

[82] According to Karl Rahner, "we must speak of original sin in a sense that is, however, merely *analogous*, although it is a moment in the situation of freedom and not in the freedom of an individual as such." Karl Rahner, *Grundkurs des Glaubens*. Sämtliche Werke 26 (Freiburg: Herder, 1999), 113, emphasis and translation mine.

[83] For Pröpper, *Theologische Anthropologie*, vol. 2, 1090, most recent developments of the church's doctrine of original sin are "sailing under a false flag". Georg Essen explicitly confirms this in his guest contribution to the book with reference to Karl Rahner and Piet Schoonenberg (ibid. 1147).

[84] Despite all the differences, this line of argument is quite compatible with Pröpper because it takes his criticism (as well as that of Flasch) seriously and also corresponds to Pröpper's positive assessment of the pre-Simplician Augustine. Cf. Pröpper, *Theologische Anthropologie*, vol. 2, 1009.

[85] In section 6.1.2 I made such a suggestion in view of Augustine's mistranslation of Rom 5:12.

6.5 Outlook: "Dramatic-Kairological" Transformations of Augustine's Theology of Grace, Freedom and Original Sin

What might a transformative reception of Augustine's *Simplician* theology of grace and freedom look like? In particular, what about the *irresistible grace* – in line with his conviction that "God has mercy in no one in vain" [86] – that Augustine has assumed since the *Simplician*? And what about the seemingly irreconcilable counterposition of human free will to reject God's offer of salvation, which Augustine had to accept for Adam if his theodicy of a condemning God was not to fail? Is it simply a matter of rejecting the former and accepting the latter? Or is a transformative reception of Augustine possible, which combines the legitimate concerns of both sides and could thus contribute to a depolarisation of the still smouldering conflict between Augustinianism and Pelagianism?

This should be possible if we take into account how God acts through Jesus Christ according to the testimony of the Gospels (cf. section 3.3.1). According to a dramatic Christology, as outlined by Raymund Schwager in *Jesus in the Drama of Salvation* and taken up and developed in the *Innsbruck Dramatic Theology*,[87] this divine salvific action through and in Jesus Christ can only be grasped in a complex dramatic process that unfolds in several acts, the transitions of which are essentially shaped by the decisions of the persons involved. Of the five acts of the drama of salvation, I will only briefly mention the first and second in order to give an idea of how the seemingly insoluble tension between Augustine's irresistible grace and the human possibility of free choice in relation to God can be developed without contradiction.

Accordingly, at the beginning (in the "first act") there is a new salvific action of God, mediated by Jesus' powerful proclamation of the divine kingdom, which brings people, unasked and in spite of an opposing history of guilt, into salvific situations – in biblical language: *kairoi* – where they are so seized by God's glory that they initially cannot help but consent.[88] In certain salvific events brought about by Jesus, the kingdom of God is not only close enough to be chosen or even rejected by people, but it has already arrived (cf. Lk 11:20). From this first aspect of a kairological salvific action of God, we can reconstruct

---

[86] Cf. Simpl. 1.2.12f, and above, section 3.1.3.2.
[87] Raymund Schwager, *Jesus in the Drama of Salvation: Toward a Biblical Doctrine of Redemption* (New York: Crossroad Publishing Company, [1989] 1999); Sandler, "Divine Action and Dramatic Theology," subtitled: "A Rereading of Raymund Schwager's *Jesus in the Drama of Salvation*".
[88] Cf. Lk 4:22a: "All spoke well of him", and my analysis of this in Sandler, "Kairos und Parusie," 13–5.

Augustine's justified concern for an *irresistible grace* and a *libertas without liberum arbitrium* released towards God (cf. section 3.3.2). But the Gospels also testify to how such a kairos of grace brings people into a decision situation in which it is also possible to reject the offer of salvation, indeed with dramatic consequences. For, metaphorically speaking, the person touched by God does not simply stand before the door of the kingdom of God to decide freely whether to enter or not; rather, she stands in the doorway and, under the impression of God's flashing presence, must decide whether to go on or to go back, rejecting what she had experienced as thoroughly good.[89] In Schwager's five-act reconstruction of the salvation drama of Jesus, the latter corresponds to the second act as a situation of judgement, which is to be understood in the sense of a self-judgment.[90] Such connections between Augustine's theology of grace and a dramatic interpretation of the Gospels, which I have only briefly touched on here, will be developed in a later essay. The compatibility between an initially undeniable experience of grace in the first act and a situation of decision leading to a self-judgment in the second act would have to be developed not only in dramatic theology, but also in a phenomenology of a momentary event of grace and a temporally extended kairos that develops from it.[91]

From there, a dramatic-kairological transformation of Augustine's theology of original sin is also possible. A transformative reception of Augustine's theology of original sin should, in my view, begin with its stage of development just before *Simplician* (cf. sections 6.1.1 and 6.1.3), but should also take up elements of his later doctrine of original sin, albeit in such a way that they correspond to biblical presuppositions that fall short in Augustine. In addition to a correct translation of Romans 5:12 (cf. section 6.1.2), this includes above all the exemplary, inclusive understanding of Adam in the Bible (cf. section 4.2). It corresponds to this if we assume, according to dramatic kairology, that people are placed in a situation of a new beginning through an event of grace, in which they are to some extent freed from old fetters and can act in a salutary way that is otherwise closed to them. In such situations of a graciously opened new beginning, we are to some extent like Adam, which also means that we can *fall like*

---

[89] Accordingly, Jesus tells the listeners of the Sermon on the Mount that they are the light of the world (cf. Mt 5:14). But this does not mean that they have already achieved their goal. For now everything depends on their putting this light not under a bushel but on a lampstand (cf. Mt 5:1): in a new way of life which corresponds to a practical conversion (cf. Mk 1:15), so that this may challenge them to the utmost. This can then lead to the rejection of this effective offer of grace, even though it is recognised as thoroughly good. Cf. Sandler, *Bergpredigt und Gnadenerfahrung*.
[90] Cf. Schwager, *Jesus in the Drama of Salvation*, 53–81.
[91] Cf. Sandler, "Divine Action and Dramatic Christology," 15–9.

Adam, rejecting the Kingdom of God that has been rudimentarily opened to us. It follows that everyone is like Adam – not always, but time and again:[92] called to let the salvation of a new beginning received in a kairos spread to others (Mt 5:15) and warned against a sin that is of a different quality from everyday sinning. It is a freely answered sin of rejecting and betraying the salvation received, so that from there the gracefully experienced new beginning dramatically perverts into a *peccatum originale originans* that affects many in the way of a *peccatum originale originatum.*

References

Augustinus, Aurelius. "Acta contra Fortunatum Manichaeum," edited by Joseph Zycha, in *CSEL* 25/1, 81–112. Wien: Verlag der Österreichischen Akademie der Wissenschaften, 1891. = c. Fort.

Augustine, Aurelius. *Answer to the Pelagians,* edited by Roland J. Teske and John E. Rotelle. The Works of Saint Augustine: A Translation for the 21st Century Vol. I/24–I/27, Hyde Park: New City Press, 1990–1999.

Augustinus, Aurelius. *De civitate Dei. The City of God against the pagans. In seven volumes.* Loeb Classical Library. London: Heinemann, 1957–1972.

Augustinus, Aurelius. "De correptione et gratia," edited by Sebastian Kopp. In: *Schriften gegen die Semipelagianer,* vol. 7, 160–238. Würzburg: Augustinus Verlag, 1955. = corrept. et gr.

Augustinus, Aurelius. *De diversis quaestionibus octoginta tribus,* translated by Carl Johann Perl. Paderborn: Schöningh, 1972. = div. qu.

Augustinus, Aurelius. "De duabus animabus." In *Aurelius Augustinus, Nutzen des Glaubens. De utilitate credendi. Die zwei Seelen. De duabus animabus,* translated by Carl Johann Perl, 109–66. Paderborn: Schöningh, 1966. = duab. an.

Augustinus, Aurelius. *De libero arbitrio,* edited by Johannes Brachtendorf. Augustinus Opera 9. Paderborn: Schöningh, 2006. = lib. arb.

Augustinus, Aurelius. "De peccatorum meritis et remissione et de baptismo parvulorum. Strafe und Nachlassung der Sünden," translated by Rochus Habitzky. In *Schriften gegen die Pelagianer,* vol. 1, 55–301, Würzburg: Augustinus Verlag, 1971. = pecc. mer.

Augustinus, Aurelius. "De praedestinatione sanctorum. Die Vorherbestimmung der Heiligen," edited by Adolar Zumkeller. In *Schriften gegen die Semipelagianer,* vol. 7, 240–327. Würzburg: Augustinus Verlag, 1955. = praed. sanct.

Augustinus, Aurelius. *Die Retractationen in zwei Büchern. Retractionum libri duo,* edited by Carl Johann Perl. Paderborn: Schöningh 1976. = retr.

Augustinus, Aurelius. *Ad Simplicianum. An Simplicianus zwei Bücher über verschiedene Fragen,* edited by Thomas Gerhard Ring. Würzburg: Augustinus Verlag, 1991. = Simpl.

---

92 This corresponds to Augustine's understanding of original sin in *Contra Fortunatum.* Cf. above, sections 6.1.1 and 6.1.2.

Augustinus, Aurelius. "De spiritu et littera," edited by Sebastian Kopp. In: *Schriften gegen die Pelagianer,* vol. 1, 303–436. Würzburg: Augustinus-Verlag, 1971. = spir. et litt.

Augustinus, Aurelius. "Expositio quarundam propositionum ex epistula apostoli ad Romanos. Die Auslegung einiger Fragen aus dem Brief an die Römer. " In *Augustine on Romans. Propositions from the Epistle to the Romans; unfinished commentary on the Epistle to the Romans,* Text and Translation by Paula Fredriksen Landes, 2–49. Chico: Scholars Press 1982. = exp. prop. Rm.

Augustine, Aurelius. *Responses to Miscellaneous Questions,* translated by Boniface Ramsey. The Works of Saint Augustine: A Translation for the 21st Century, vol. I/12. Hyde Park: New City Press, 2008.

Augustine, Aurelius. *The Teacher; the Free Choice of the Will; Grace and Free Will,* translated by Robert P. Russell. The Fathers of the Church: A new translation, vol. 59. Washington: Catholic University of America Press, 1968.

Baumann, Urs. *Erbsünde? Ihr traditionelles Verständnis in der Krise heutiger Theologie.* Freiburg: Herder, 1970.

Baumert, Norbert. *Christus – Hochform von "Gesetz": Übersetzung und Auslegung des Römerbriefes.* Würzburg: Echter, 2012.

Brachtendorf, Johannes. "Einleitung," in Augustinus, *De Libero Arbitrio. Der Freie Wille,* edited by Johannes Brachtendorf, 7–69. Paderborn: Schöningh, 2006.

Cosgrove, Charles H. "Rhetorical Suspense in Romans 9–11: A Study in Polyvalence and Hermeneutical Election." *Journal of Biblical Literature* 115 (1996): 271–87.

Denzinger, Heinrich, and Hünermann, Peter, and Hoping, Helmut, Eds. *Kompendium der Glaubensbekenntnisse und kirchlichen Lehrentscheidungen.* Freiburg: Herder, 2017 (45th edition) = DH.

Drecoll, Volker Henning, ed. *Augustin Handbuch,* Tübingen: Mohr Siebeck, 2014.

Drecoll, Volker Henning. "De spiritu et littera." In *Augustin Handbuch,* edited by Volker Henning Drecoll, 328–34. Tübingen: Mohr Siebeck, 2014.

Drecoll, Volker Henning. "Gratia." In *Augustinus Lexikon,* vol. 3, 182–242. Basel: Schwabe, 2010.

Dunn, James D. G. *Romans 9–16.* Word Biblical Commentary. Grand Rapids: Zondervan, 1988.

Fischer, Georg. *Genesis 1–11.* Herders theologischer Kommentar zum Alten Testament. Freiburg: Herder 2018.

Fitzmyer, Joseph. "The Consecutive Meaning of ΕΦ' Ω in Romans 5.12." *New Testament Studies* 39 (1993): 321–39.

Flasch, Kurt, ed. *Logik des Schreckens. Augustinus von Hippo: De diversis quaestionibus ad Simplicianum I 2.* Translated by Walter Schäfer. Commentary by Kurt Flasch. Mainz: Dieterich. 2nd edition, 1995.

Goodrich, John K. "Until the Fullness of the Gentiles Comes In: A Critical Review of Recent Scholarship on the Salvation of 'All Israel' (Romans 11:26)." *Journal for the Study of Paul and His Letters* (2016): 5–32.

Haacker, Klaus. "Das Thema von Römer als Problem der Auslegungsgeschichte." In *Between Gospel and Election. Explorations in the Interpretation of Romans 9–11,* edited by Florian Wilk and J. Ross Wagner, 55–72. Tübingen: Mohr Siebeck, 2010.

Jewett, Robert J. *Romans: A Commentary.* Hermeneia – A Critical and Historical Commentary on the Bible. Minneapolis, Minn.: Fortress Press 2006.

Kantzer Komline, Han-Luen. *Augustine on the Will: A Theological Account.* Oxford: Oxford University Press, 2020.

Kuss, Otto. *Der Römerbrief.* 3. Lieferung: Röm 8,19–11,36. Regensburg: Pustet, 1978.

Lohfink, Norbert. "Die Ursünden in der priesterlichen Geschichtserzählung." In *Die Zeit Jesu. Festschrift für Heinrich Schlier*, edited by Günther Bornkamm and Karl Rahner, 38–57. Freiburg: Herder, 1970.
Lohse, Eduard. *Der Brief an die Römer*. Kritisch-exegetischer Kommentar über das Neue Testament. Göttingen: Vandenhoeck & Ruprecht, 2003.
Lohse, Eduard. "Gottes Gnadenwahl und das Geschick Israels." In: Eduard Lohse, *Rechenschaft vom Evangelium. Exegetische Studien zum Römerbrief*, 29–42. Berlin: de Gruyter, 2007.
Menke, Karl-Heinz. *Das Kriterium des Christseins. Grundriss der Gnadenlehre*. Regensburg: Pustet, 2003.
Moo, Douglas J. *The Epistle to the Romans*. The new international commentary on the New Testament. Grand Rapids: Eerdmans, 2009.
Morris, Leon. *The Epistle to the Romans*. A Pillar Commentary. Grand Rapids: Eerdmans, 1994.
Pesch, Otto Hermann and Peters, Albert. *Einführung in die Lehre von Gnade und Rechtfertigung*. Darmstadt: Wissenschaftliche Buchgesellschaft, 1981.
Piper, John Stephen. *The Justification of God: An Exegetical and Theological Study of Romans 9:1–23*. Grand Rapids: Baker, 2nd edition, 1993.
Pröpper, Thomas. *Theologische Anthropologie*. 2 vols. Freiburg im Breisgau: Herder, 2016.
Rahner, Karl. *Grundkurs des Glaubens*. In *Sämtliche Werke* 26. Freiburg: Herder, 1999.
Reasoner, Mark. "Romans Moves from Margin to Center, from Rejection to Salvation: Four Grids for Recent English-Language Exegesis." In *Between Gospel and Election. Explorations in the Interpretation of Romans 9–11*, edited by Florian Wilk and J. Ross Wagner, 73–87. Tübingen: Mohr Siebeck 2010.
Ring, Thomas Gerhard. "Erläuterungen." In: Augustinus, *An Simplicianus zwei Bücher über verschiedene Fragen*. Sankt Augustinus – Der Lehrer der Gnade. Vol. 3, Gesamtausgabe seiner antipelagianischen Schriften: Prolegomena, edited by Thomas Gerhard Ring, 177–376. Würzburg: Augustinus Verlag, 1991.
Sandler, Willibald. "Augustinus – Lehrer der Gnade und Logiker des Schreckens? Ein nötiger Schnitt in der Rezeption von 'An Simplician' aus der Perspektive der dramatischen Theologie." In: Willibald Sandler, *Skizzen zur dramatischen Theologie. Erkundungen und Bewährungsproben*, 335–77. Freiburg: Herder, 2012, http://theol.uibk.ac.at/itl/852.html.
Sandler, Willibald. "Bergpredigt und Gnadenerfahrung als Fundamente für eine christliche Spiritualität des gewaltlosen Widerstandes." In *Politik des Evangeliums. Politics of the Gospel*, forthcoming.
Sandler, Willibald. *Charismatisch, evangelikal und katholisch. Eine theologische Unterscheidung der Geister*. Freiburg: Herder, 2021.
Sandler, Willibald. "Divine Action and Dramatic Christology: A Rereading of Raymund Schwager's Jesus in the Drama of Salvation." *Religions* 14/3 (2023): 1–25.
Sandler, Willibald. "Kairos und Parusie. Kairos als Ereignis des in Christus angekommenen und angenommenen Gottes." *Zeitschrift für Katholische Theologie* 136 (2014): 10–31.
Sandler, Willibald. *Der verbotene Baum im Paradies. Was es mit dem Sündenfall auf sich hat*. Kevelaer: Topos, 2009, http://theol.uibk.ac.at/itl/800.html.
Schreiner, Thomas R. *Romans*. Baker Exegetical Commentary on the New Testament. Grand Rapids: Baker, 1998.
Schwager, Raymund. *Jesus in the Drama of Salvation: Toward a Biblical Doctrine of Redemption*. New York: Crossroad, 1999.
Schwager, Raymund. *Der wunderbare Tausch. Zur Geschichte und Deutung der Erlösungslehre*. Gesammelte Schriften 2, Freiburg: Herder, 2015.

Stuhlmacher, Peter. *Der Brief an die Römer*. Das Neue Testament deutsch. Göttingen: Vandenhoeck & Ruprecht, 1989.
Track, Joachim. "Analogie." In *Theologische Realenzyklopädie*, vol. 2, 625–50. Berlin: de Gruyter, 1978.
Wilckens, Ulrich. *Der Brief an die Römer, Teilband 2: Röm 6–11*. Evangelisch-Katholischer Kommentar zum Neuen Testament. Neukirchen-Vluyn: Neukirchener Verlag, 1980.
Wolter, Michael. *Der Brief an die Römer. Teilband 1: Röm 1–8*. Evangelisch-Katholischer Kommentar zum Neuen Testament. Ostfildern: Patmos, 2014.
Wolter, Michael. *Der Brief an die Römer. Teilband 2: Röm 9–16*. Evangelisch-Katholischer Kommentar zum Neuen Testament. Ostfildern: Patmos, 2019.
Wolter, Michael. "Ein exegetischer und theologischer Blick auf Röm 11.25–32." *New Testament Studies* 64, no. 2 (2018): 123–42.
Zoccali, Christopher. "'And so all Israel will be saved': Competing Interpretations of Romans 11:26 in Pauline Scholarship." *Journal for the Study of the New Testament* 30 (2008): 289–318.

Ludger Jansen
Philosophy in Aquinas' Exegetical Work and Its Meta-Theological Implications

A Case Study on Aquinas' Commentary on John 1:14a

Abstract: It is well known that Aquinas is heavily influenced by Aristotle, and it has recently been noted that also his biblical interpretation is influenced by Aristotelian philosophy. In this chapter, I argue that use of philosophy in exegesis has important meta-theological implications. To show this, I analyse Aquinas' interpretation of John 1:14a, and demonstrate the heavy use Aquinas makes of philosophical teachings in the interpretation of this verse. Though only implicitly and tacitly, Aquinas uses Aristotelian philosophy of language, metaphysics, and, most prominently, psychology, in order to understand the incarnation statement. I discuss the presuppositions of Aquinas approach to biblical interpretation and argue that Aquinas' exegetical practice indicates a meta-theological shift from foundationalism to coherentism.

Keywords: Aquinas, Biblical Interpretation, Meta-Theology, Coherentism, John 1:14

1 Introduction

The last decades have seen a rise in research on medieval exegesis in general, and in the exegetical works of Aquinas in particular. As Aquinas is renowned as both a theologian and a philosopher, and as the great synthesizer of Aristotelianism and Catholic Theology, it is not without interest what role, if any, philosophy plays in Aquinas' exegetical works. The Aristotelian influence on Aquinas' exegesis is widely acknowledged, but there is no consensus on its magnitude and relevance. Henning Graf Reventlow, in his monumental *Epochen der Bibelauslegung*, showcases the influence upfront, when he calls his chapter on Aquinas "The Bible and Aristotle". He sketches the general influence of Aristotle on Aquinas, but also the use of Aristotle in his exegesis, where Aquinas does not only employ Aristotelian terms (like cause or form), but also approvingly cites

---

Ludger Jansen, PTH Brixen, Italy; and University of Rostock, Germany; ludger.jansen@pthsta.it

https://doi.org/10.1515/9783110768411-009

ethical or anthropological teachings from Aristotle – but only, Graf Reventlow says, in contexts where these citations are not essential for the understanding of the biblical content.[1] In contrast, I argued in an earlier paper that Aquinas coherently integrates teachings of Aristotle into his exegetical practice, to the consequence that revelation turns into a source of knowledge deeply dependent on philosophy.[2] With respect to the quantitative dimension, Thomas Prügl has argued that Aquinas uses Aristotle "quite sparingly",[3] while Jörgen Vijgen was able to collect no less than 164 explicit references to Aristotle, also known as "the philosopher", from Aquinas' exegetical work. Vijgen describes how Aquinas cites Aristotle to define concepts, to exclude certain readings, to overcome seeming contradictions, to corroborate what is said in Scripture, but also to point to the differences between Aristotle's teachings and the Christian faith.[4] As Vijgen concludes, "Aristotle is Aquinas's primordial intellectual collocutor whenever he, as a theologian, is seeking an understanding of the difficulties of the biblical text", and that Aquinas combines with ease "the natural level of Aristotle's philosophical insights with revealed Scripture".[5]

In this chapter, I go beyond Vijgen's findings in two respects. First, I add to Vijgen's source material by looking at a passage in which Aristotle is used but not mentioned. Second, I think that Aquinas' use of philosophy in his exegetical practice is an important source for his meta-theological views that hitherto has been unduly neglected.

The passage on which I will focus here is Aquinas' interpretation of John 1:14a. I first discuss the position Aquinas ascribes to verse 14a in the context of the gospel (section 2), before going into the details of Aquinas' interpretation (section 3). After this close reading of Aquinas' interpretation, I discuss the

---

[1] Henning Graf Reventlow, *Epochen der Bibelauslegung*, vol. 2, *Von der Spätantike bis zum ausgehenden Mittelalter* (München: Beck 1994): 195–212 ("Bibel und Aristoteles: Thomas von Aquin"). See his page 204 (general influence) and page 210 (use in exegesis): "Die Philosophie des Aristoteles wird von Thomas wie selbstverständlich verwendet, ohne daß sie jedoch auf das inhaltliche Verständnis einen entscheidenden Einfluss gewinnt."

[2] Ludger Jansen, "Was hat der inkarnierte Logos mit Aristoteles zu tun? Thomas von Aquins Gebrauch der Philosophie in der Auslegung des Johannesprologs und eine 'holistische' Interpretation seiner Schrifthermeneutik," *Theologie und Philosophie* 80 (2000): 89–99.

[3] Thomas Prügl, "Thomas Aquinas as Interpreter of Scripture," in *The Theology of Thomas Aquinas*, edited by Rik van Nieuwenhove and Joseph Wawrykow (Notre Dame: Notre Dame University Press 2005): 386–415, esp. 399.

[4] Cf. Jörgen Vijgen, "Aristotle in Aquinas' Biblical Commentaries," in *Reading Sacred Scripture with Thomas Aquinas. Hermeneutical Tools, Theological Questions and New Perspectives*, edited by Piotr Roszak and Jörgen Vijgen (Turnhout: Brepols 2015): 287–346, 337.

[5] Vijgen, "Aristotle in Aquinas' Biblical Commentaries" (see note 4), 338.

hermeneutic presuppositions of Aquinas' approach (section 4). In conclusion, I compare Aquinas' approach to his 'official' meta-theology from the *Summa theologiae* and argue that there is a tension between Aquinas' theory of theological knowledge and his exegetical practice (section 5). Somewhat anachronistically, I will borrow from philosophical epistemology the contrast between foundationalism and coherentism, with an interesting result: With certain provisos, Aquinas might be a card-carrying foundationalist with respect to religious knowledge in the *Summa*, but he turns out to being a practising coherentist in his exegetical works.

Before embarking on the analysis of Aquinas' commentary of John 1:14a, I should say that Aristotle was certainly not the only source of philosophical doctrine that influenced Aquinas. He has as well been influenced by neo-Platonist approaches, mediated to him through the Church Fathers and Arab authors. There are also traces of this influence in the commentary on John.[6] Due to the neo-Platonic commentaries on Aristotle, Aquinas also read Aristotle from a neo-Platonic perspective. These are historically important provisos, yet they are not central for the following argument: Even a neo-Platonist, or a neo-Platonically read Aristotle, is still a heathen philosopher entering theological discourse from the outside. The detailed analysis of these sources is thus outside of the scope of the present paper.

2 The Division of the Text: John 1:14a in Context

Et Verbum caro factum est – the Word has become flesh. These words from John 1:14a are considered a "classic testimony of New Testament understanding of the incarnation".[7] For Bultmann, it prototypically represents the "annoyance" ("Ärgernis") of biblical revelation.[8] Aquinas gives it due consideration, and it is the interpretation of this half verse, to which I will now turn as a case study for Aquinas' use of philosophy in his exegetical work.

Typical elements of Aquinas' exegesis are the focus on the meaning intended by the author or speaker at stake, and a filigree structuring of the text (the

---

[6] Cf., e.g., *Super Io.*, Prol. n.5: "isti fuerunt Platonici".
[7] Ulrich B. Müller, *Die Menschwerdung des Gottessohnes. Frühchristliche Inkarnationsvorstellungen und die Anfänge des Doketismus* (Stuttgart: Katholisches Bibelwerk 1990), 7: "klassisches Zeugnis neutestamentlichen Inkarnationsverständnisses".
[8] Rudolf Bultmann, *Das Evangelium des Johannes. Kritisch-exegetischer Kommentar über das Neue Testament*, 16th edition (Göttingen: Vandenhoeck & Ruprecht 1959), 30.

divisio textus) that reflects its author's intention. The specific concern of the fourth Evangelist is, in Aquinas' eyes, to portray the divinity of Christ.[9] Accordingly, Aquinas structures the fourth gospel in two parts: Similar to a treatise, the first part (consisting in the first chapter) *claims* Christ's divinity, while the longer second part (Jn 2–21) *proves* this claim – both through what Christ did, and said, during His life (Jn 2–11), and through His suffering and resurrection (Jn 12–21). Despite the change in literary form, the first part comprises both the Prologue and the remainder of the first chapter. According to Aquinas' *divisio*, Jn 1 is broken up into three parts: first, it states the divinity of the Word (1:1–5), then its incarnation (1:6–14b), and finally the way how we came to know of the Word (1:14c–51), namely by seeing (1:14c–e) and hearing (1:15), especially by the apostles (1:16–18) and the baptist (1:19–51). Our verse 14a thus belongs to the second part of the Prologue that states the incarnation of the Word of God. Verses 6–8 deal with the witness or forerunner of the Word, namely John the Baptist, while verses 9–14b deal with the incarnated Word itself, or with the coming of the Word (*adventus verbi*) into the world. In this passage, the cause of the coming of the Word is revealed to the reader: The coming of the Word was necessary, but this necessity does not stem from a deficiency of God or a weakness of the Word. Rather, the cause lies in the world, more precisely in the fact that people do not sufficiently recognize God: *mundus eum non cognovit* (1:10b).[10]

Once it is clear that the Word had to come into the world because human beings lack insight into the nature of God, the benefit of the coming of the Word for humans is presented in 1:11–13 (*nobis utilitatem ex adventu Verbi*). According to Aquinas' analysis, these verses deal with the advent of the light (*lucis adventum*) in 1:11a, the reaction of humans (*hominum occursum*) in 1:11b–12a, and the "fruit", or outcome, of the coming for humans (*fructum ex adventu lucis allatum*) in 1:12b–13. The advent of the light is identical with the coming of the Word, since, as Aquinas pointed out in the interpretation of 1:4b–5, being light is the specific effect of the Word for human beings (*virtus specialiter quantum ad homines*).

People react in two ways: although the Word experiences rejection by those who are his (1:11b), there are also people who receive the Word (1:12a). To these people, who believe in his name (1:12c), he gives the wonderful fruit of sonship

---

9 Cf. *Super Io.*, Proemium.
10 For Aquinas' discussion of the *Cur Deus homo* question cf. Walter Mostert, *Menschwerdung. Eine historische und dogmatische Untersuchung über das Motiv der Inkarnation des Gottessohnes bei Thomas von Aquin* (Tübingen: Mohr 1978).

to God (1:12b). The new children of God are not born physically, but spiritually (1:13).[11]

The first part of the Prologue about the incarnation ends with the first half of verse 14. As the concluding verse of this part, it also plays an important role in Aquinas' structure, even if Aquinas does not emphasize this verse as much as modern exegetes do. According to Aquinas' division, verse 14a states the way in which the Word comes into the world (*veniendum modum*), namely both the way of coming into the world itself (1:14a) and the way of life of the incarnated Word in the world (*conversatio Verbi incarnati*; 1:14b). That is, Aquinas wants to interpret verse 14a, *Verbum caro factum est*, as providing information about the manner of the Word's coming: the Word comes by becoming flesh, i.e., the coming of the Word is an incarnational event.

Aquinas notes that he diverges from both Chrysostom and Augustine in his interpretation.[12] According to Aquinas, Chrysostom understands verse 14a as a continuation of Jn 1:12b; he reads verse 14a as an answer to the question: how could Christ make it possible for humans to become children of God? The answer then is: Christ gave humans the possibility to become children of God through the incarnation. In contrast, Aquinas says, Augustine understands verse 14a as a continuation of Jn 1:13: *sed ex Deo nati sunt*. In his eyes, the message of verse 14a is to say, do not be surprised that human beings are born of God, because the Word became flesh, i.e., God became a human being Himself. For Augustine, then, one paradox of faith is surpassed here by another: Not only does John dare to claim that human beings can be born of God, he even claims that God and the divine Word became human.

According to Aquinas' own interpretation, however, verse 14a is a continuation (*continuatur*) and explanation of Jn 1:11a. It is said that the Word of God comes unto his own (*in propria venit*). But in what way does it get there? Verse 14a gives the answer: The Word does not come unto his own by a change of place (*locum mutando*), that is, not by first being in another place and then coming "unto his own". Rather, the Word comes unto his own *per incarnationem* by becoming flesh.

---

11 *Super Io.* I 6, n.160–161: "Non carnaliter, sed spititualiter filii Dei fiunt. [...] Sic ergo generatio filiorum Dei non est carnalis, sed est spiritualis."
12 Cf. Augustine, *Trin.* II 5,8 und II 4,28 bzw. Chrysostomos, *In Io. hom.* 11,1 (= PL 59, 78–79).

3 Aristotelian Psychology and the Incarnation

After this brief overview, I will now consider Aquinas' interpretation of Jn 1:14a in detail. I will pay special attention to how Aquinas unfolds his line of reasoning, and which resource he adduces for this purpose.

Verbum caro factum est. The Word became flesh, God became a human being. Aquinas does not see his task fulfilled in merely highlighting the theological importance of this statement. Rather, he wants to make this statement more precise through the dogmatic confrontation with earlier heresies. For the Christological disputes in the early Church show that the incarnation of God can be thought of in quite different ways. On this historical background, it is not surprising that Aquinas notes that 14a has not been well understood by some interpreters, giving rise to many errors.[13] As Aquinas discusses four of these heretical readings, his interpretation of the verse is almost like a dogma-historical outline on the doctrine of the two natures of Christ. Aquinas discusses the four heresies in the order of their strength. He begins with the strongest position, i.e., the one that deviates most from Catholic dogma, and then proceeds step by step through the other heresies until, finally, he concludes by interpreting the verse in light of the Christological confessions of the early Church. As if in a funnel tapering downward, he thus arrives at his own interpretation, which is aimed at being in full agreement with Catholic dogma.

3.1 Refutation of Monophysitism

The first misinterpretation of John 1:14a Aquinas deals with is Monophysitism. For this position Aquinas refers to Eutyches (b. 378, d. after 451):[14] The latter understood the incarnation in such a way, Aquinas says, that the Word itself or a part of the Word was transformed into flesh, just as flour is transformed into bread or air into fire.[15] This opinion, or so Aquinas continues, is clearly false (*huius opinionis falsitas manifeste apparet*). For it is said in Jn 1:1 that the Word is God, and hence this interpretation is in contradiction to divine immutability

---

[13] Cf. *Super Io.* I 7, n.166: "Notandum quod hoc quod dicitur Verbum caro factum est, quidam male intelligentes, sumpserunt occasionem erroris."
[14] Cf. *Super Io.* I 7, n.166: "Et hic fuit Eutiches, qui posuit commixtionem naturarum in Christo, dicens in eo eamdem fuisse Dei et hominis naturam."
[15] Cf. *Super Io.* I 7, 166: "Quidam namque posuerunt Verbum ita carnem factum esse ac si ipsum vel aliquid eius sit in carnem conversum, sicut cum farina fit panis, et aer ignis."

(*immutabilitas*), which is revealed elsewhere in Scripture, where it says: *Ego Deus, et non mutor* (Mal 3:6). This verse is one of the 'classical' references for God's immutability.[16] (If we look at the context of Mal 3:6, this verse merely demands God's faithfulness to the contract with his people, and not his absolute immutability. For the understanding of Aquinas' argument, however, this does not pose any difficulty.)

If God does not change at all, He does also not change his nature. So it is not possible that the Word has become flesh in a substantial change, Aquinas says, like the flour becomes bread or the air becomes fire. For if the flour becomes bread, it is just bread and no longer flour (in this case, not even potentially). Analogously, according to the traditional doctrine of the four elements, air that turns into fire is no longer air.[17] But since God cannot change, it is especially impossible that He (or a part of Him) loses His divinity. This, however, would be necessary, if the incarnation were modelled after the paradigm of the baked bread, i.e., if the Word and the flesh relate to each other like flour and bread, or air and fire. It must be noted that Aquinas alludes to the theory of the four elements without further ado; he seems to presuppose that his hearers in Paris are acquainted with it (and they probably were).

Aquinas counters the false reading with a formula of his own coinage. He suggests understanding verse 14a as saying: The Word has taken on the flesh (*assumpsit*), without the Word itself having been transformed into flesh.[18] Doing so, he can highlight the Aristotelian insight that there are different varieties of beings,[19] and hence different varieties of changes.[20] Not all changes are substantial changes. Aquinas considers qualitative change a better fitting analogy: it would be very unnatural to explain the sentence "That man has become white" in such a way that the man we knew before is now that white colour (*albedo*) which we now see – and no longer a man. Rather, we would say that that the man is now still a man, but his hair has now taken on white colour.

It seems, though, that Aquinas' new paradigm is itself in conflict with the immutability of God. To this, however, Aquinas could reply that becoming white

---

16 It is cited by Augustine, *Conf.* I 6, by Aquinas, *STh* I q.9 a.1 s.c., as well as by Eleonore Stump, Norman Kretzmann, "Eternity," *Journal of Philosophy* 78 (1981): 429–458, 429 n.1.
17 Cf., e.g., *Metaphysics* I 8, 989a2–18; for a more detailed discussion of the elements cf. *De generatione et corruptione* II 1–5 und *Meteorologica* I 2 and IV.
18 Cf. *Super Io.* I 7, n.166: "Est ergo dicendum contra Eutichem Verbum caro factum est: Verbum carnem assumpsit, non quod ipsum Verbum sit ipsa caro; sicut si dicamus: "Homo factus est albus", non quod ipse sit ipsa albedo, sed quod albedinem assumpsit."
19 Cf., notably, *Metaphysics* V 7 and VII 1.
20 Cf. Aristotle, *Physics* V 2 and VII 2.

is not a change in the essence of human beings, but in one of their accidents – not, that is, in human qua human, but rather in human qua having a hair colour. Likewise, then, the incarnation is not a change in God himself: not Christ qua God changes, but only Christ qua human.[21] Aquinas actually touches on this problem at the end of his discussion of verse 14a:

> But that it is said that the Word was made flesh, does not mean any change in the Word, but only that the nature was assumed anew into the unity with the divine person. And the Word was made flesh – through a union with the flesh. But union is a relation. The relations of God with respect to creatures do not imply a change on the part of God, but on the part of the creature that is in a new way related to God.[22]

Incarnation, therefore, does not require a change in the Word. The incarnation of the Word is rather to be thought of as a union (*unio*). In this case, the union is a dyadic relation between the human nature and the divine nature. Incarnation is therefore a relational change, and the change of a relation results, according to Aristotle, from the change of at least one of the things related.[23] According to Aquinas, the unification of the natures is not due to a change of God; the divine nature remains unchanged. The relational change is rather to be attributed to a change of the human nature newly incorporated into the *unitas personae divinae*. Thus, the incarnation occurs as human nature relates to divine nature in a new, previously unprecedented way (*novo modo*). As human nature is a contingent created nature, Aquinas tells us, such a change is absolutely possible.

3.2 Refutation of Arianism

So far, Aquinas suggested the formulation *Verbum carnem assumpsit* as a paraphrase of verse 14a. However, this paraphrase is not as clear as one may wish: Several heretics would still be happy with this wording. Therefore, Aquinas takes the next step, and discusses the heresies which concord with this formulation. Again, Aquinas starts with the strongest assertion, which is that of Arius (c. 260–336). Aquinas motivates it as follows: Since John wrote *caro factum* and

---

21 This point is also defended by Stump and Kretzmann, "Eternity" (see note 16).
22 *Super Io.* I 7, n.172: "Hoc autem quod dicitur Verbum caro factum est, non aliquam mutationem in Verbo, sed solum in natura assumpta de novo in unitatem personae divinae dicit. Et Verbum caro factum est, per unionem ad carnem. Unio autem relatio quaedam est. Relationes autem de novo dictae de Deo in respectu ad creaturas, non important mutationem ex parte Dei, sed ex parte creaturae novo modo se habentis ad Deum."
23 Aristotle, *Physics.* V 2, 225b 11–13; cf. also *Metaphysics* XIV 1, 1088a 29–35.

not *caro cum anima factum*, Arius had assumed that the Word had taken on inanimate flesh. According to Arian, the place and the task of the human soul had been taken over by the Word of God. Then, of course, God would not really have become human, but would only have had a human shell.[24] Aquinas refutes this position with three arguments:

(1) First of all, Aquinas says, this position is in contradiction to Scripture, which reports certain passions of Christ's soul (*quaedam passiones animae*). For example, the Scripture says that Christ was sad (*contristari et maestus*; Mt 26:37) – and sadness is a state of the soul. Moreover, Christ's soul is even explicitly mentioned in Scripture: *Tristis est anima mea usque ad mortem* (Mt 26:38).

(2) Second, neither God nor the angels can be the form of a body at all, as this is the soul, which is united with the body as its form. For God and angels are by their nature incorporeal beings. Therefore, the Word of God (which is God according to Jn 1:1) cannot be the form of a body.[25] Here, if not before, it becomes clear how much Aquinas does not only phrase the various heresies by means of Aristotelian terminology, but also argues against them on the ground of Aristotelian psychology. For Aristotle, the soul relates to the body as a seal impression relates to the wax into which it is impressed. Like body and soul, seal and wax form a unity. In this analogy, the seal impression corresponds to the form and the wax to the matter.[26] The whole argument is, thus, formulated on the background of Aristotle's hylomorphic theory of living beings as constituted by matter (*hylê*) and form (*morphê*), or body and soul.[27] This implies that the soul does not only determine as an individuation principle what kind of living being the organism belongs to, it is also the principle of the activities and changes of the living being.[28] No soul 'fits' to every type of body, however, because every form presupposes matter of a certain kind. Aquinas now applies this principle to God and the angels: The

---

24 Cf. *Super Io.* I 7, n.167: "Fuerunt etiam alii qui, licet crederent Verbum non in carnem mutatum sed quod eam assumpsit, tamen dixerunt ipsum assumpsisse carnem sine anima; nam si carnem animatam assumpsisset, dixisset Evangelista: Verbum caro cum anima factum est. Et sic fuit error Arii, qui dixit quod in Christo non erat anima, sed Verbum Dei erat ibi loco animae."
25 Cf. *Super Io.* I 7, n.167: "[...] Deus non potest esse forma alicuius corporis; nec etiam angelus corpori uniri potest per modum formae, cum secundum naturam a corpore sit separatus; anima autem unitur corpori sicut forma."
26 Aristotle, *De anima* II 1, 412b6–8.
27 Cf., notably, Aristotle, *De anima* II 1–2.
28 Aristotle, *De anima* II 1, 412b4–6.

form of God and the forms of the angels are essentially incorporeal, so they do not 'fit' to any body at all.[29]

(3) Third, there is no flesh without a soul. A living being cannot exist without a soul, because the soul is its life principle. Flesh without soul is not flesh in the real sense, because flesh is essentially part of a living being. Without soul, however, there is no living being, consequently also no flesh as part of a living being. Flesh without a soul is, thus, not in the same sense flesh as ensouled flesh; it is only equivocally (*aequivoce*) called flesh – only "in the butcher's sense, not the physiologist's", as Peter Simons nicely puts it.[30] But the flesh that the Word took on was part of a living being, namely the human being Jesus of Nazareth. Hence, the Word must also have taken on animate flesh.

Throughout, these arguments use Aristotelian ideas and Aristotelian terminology. First, Aquinas makes use of the idea that emotions are affections of the soul. This is a very generic position that might have been suggested by many authors, and maybe even by common sense. In any case, it is very much in tune with, and probably inspired by what Aristotle says about emotions in his *Ethics*.[31] Second, Aquinas makes use of Aristotle's idea that the soul is the form of the body, and that there must be a certain fit between body and soul.[32] Finally, Aquinas makes use of the equivocity of terms, famously defined by Aristotle at the beginning of his *Categories*, and of Aristotle's mantra that body parts detached from the body keep their name only equivocally.[33] All this Aquinas presupposes tacitly, without mentioning Aristotle's name. We can assume that his hearers in Paris were well acquainted with the theories alluded to, and that they were able to supplement the references by themselves.[34] Because Aquinas can assume a certain acquaintance of his hearers with Aristotle's philosophy, Henning Graf Reventlow has suggested mainly didactic reasons for Aquinas' refer-

---

[29] Cf. *STh* I q.3 a.1 (God) and *STh* I q.50 a.1 (angels).
[30] Peter Simons, *Parts. A Study in Metaphysics* (Oxford: Oxford University Press 1987), 334.
[31] Cf. Aristotle, *Nicomachean Ethics* I 12 and II 4.
[32] Cf. Aristotle, *De anima* I 3, 407b20–26 and II 1–2.
[33] Cf. Aristotle, *Categories* 1 with *De anima* II 1, 412b19–21 (eye) and *Metaphysics* VII 10, 1035b24–25 (finger).
[34] Cf. Joseph P. Wawrykow, "Theologian," *The Westminster Handbook to Thomas Aquinas* (Louisville: Westminster John Knox Press 2005): 149–154, 150: "Students of theology did not study Aristotle as part of their theological training; they had already done so, and so were able to bring to bear that knowledge in their preparation for, and eventual doing, of theological work [...]."

ences to Aristotle.³⁵ Aquinas' discussion here, however, shows that the Aristotelian premises on which his arguments are built are not only didactic devices to convey a message that could also be phrased without them. They are, rather, integral parts of the whole dialectic setup presented here.

During Aquinas' time, Aristotle's teaching of the soul was the gold standard in philosophical psychology. In spite of this (or, maybe, because of this), Aristotle's psychology was hotly debated. In particular, during Aquinas' second teaching period, Aquinas was deeply involved in polemical discussions about the human soul with the Averroistically minded philosophers at the arts faculty in Paris, as witnessed prominently by Aquinas' short treatise on the unity of the intellect.³⁶ The Parisian Averroists argued that all humans share numerically one intellect. This debate is chronologically close to the passage analysed here, as there is considerable consensus that Aquinas gave his lectures on the Gospel of John also during this period.³⁷ The particular Aristotelian teachings cited here, however, do not touch on the subtleties of the intellect in Aristotle. They are so basic that they were probably common ground between the Averroists and the non-Averroists.

3.3 Refutation of Apollinaris

So far, Aquinas has argued that the Word must have taken on animate flesh. Aquinas tell us, that such arguments moved Apollinaris of Laodiceia (d. 382) to weaken the position of Arius: Apollinaris assumes that the Word has taken on animate flesh. However, or so Aquinas tells us, Apollinaris assumes that this flesh was animated with an *anima sensitiva* only, not with an *anima intellectiva*.³⁸ Again, the false doctrine is tacitly represented in terms of Aristotelian psychology: The soul is the form of an animated body, i.e., a plant, an animal or a human being. But while a plant is only able to take in food and to grow, animals have a sensitive soul, carrying with it the capacities for perception and locomo-

---

35 Cf. Graf Reventlow, *Epochen der Bibelauslegung*, vol. 2 (see note 1), 211: "vor allem pädagogische Gründe".
36 For a survey, cf. Jean-Pierre Torrell, *Saint Thomas Aquinas*, vol. 1, *The Person and His Work* (Washington: Catholic University of America Press 1996): 179–96.
37 Cf. Torrell, *Saint Thomas Aquinas*, vol. 1 (see note 36), 199.
38 *Super Io.* I 7, n.168: "Fuerunt autem alii, qui, ex hoc moti, dixerunt Verbum carnem quidem animatam assumpsisse, sed anima[m] sensitiva[m] tantum, non intellectiva[m], loco cuius in corpore Christi dixerunt Verbum esse." (The Marietti edition reads three times "-am", while Busa reads "-a" here.)

tion.³⁹ Finally, human beings participate in the divine *nous* and are capable of thinking because of their intellectual soul.⁴⁰ According to Aquinas' account, Apollinaris now lets the divine Word take the place of the intellectual soul, so that the flesh assumed by the Word is animated with the 'animal' sensitive soul only. Aquinas states three reasons why this interpretation of 1:14a cannot be the correct one:

(1) First, the Apollinarian position, too, contradicts certain statements in the Bible. For in the Gospel of Matthew it is reported that Jesus was astonished: *Audiens autem Iesus miratus est* (Mt 8:10). But astonishment is an activity of the intellectual soul. It presupposes that the person astonished is able to reason, because astonishment is the desire to recognize the hidden cause of a visible effect.⁴¹ Causal explanations are structured logically, according to Aristotle's *Posterior Analytics*, so they presuppose the rational faculty of the human soul.⁴² Just as sadness forced the reader of the gospel to assume a sensitive soul in Christ, thus contradicting Arius, so astonishment forces the reader to assume an intellectual soul in Christ, contrary to Apollinaris' assertion.⁴³

(2) Second, Aquinas says, the untenability of the Apollinarian position can be seen *per rationem*, i.e., without appeal to other scriptural passages. For just as no flesh exists without a soul, as Aquinas explained against Arius, so no human flesh can exist without a human soul, i.e., without an *anima intellectiva*. If the flesh had only a sensitive soul, then God would not have become human at all.⁴⁴

(3) Third, had the flesh only a sensitive soul, God would have become therefore not a human, but a brute animal. But the Word wanted to take on human nature, because this was the best way to restore human nature. Thus, the Word renewed that which it assumed. Had it not taken on human flesh, it would not have restored humanity and thus would not have brought forth

---

39 Cf. *De anima* II 2, 413a22–b4.
40 Cf. *De anima* III 4–5 in combination with *Metaphysics* XII 7, 1072b26–30.
41 Cf. Aristotle's remark in *Metaphysics* I 2, 983a11–20, that philosophy begins with wonder and astonishment (as has also been said in Plato, *Theaetetus* 155d), but then proceeds to cognize the causes of the things perceived.
42 Cf. Aristotle, *Analytica posteriora* I 4.
43 Cf. *Super Io.* I 7, n.168: "admiratio autem est passio animae rationalis et intellectivae, cum sit desiderium cognoscendi causam occultam effectus visi. Sic igitur, sicut tristitia cogit in Christo ponere partem animae sensitivam, contra Arium; ita admiratio cogit ponere in ipso partem animae intellectivam, contra Apollinarem."
44 Cf. *Super Io.* I 7, n.168: "Si ergo Verbum assumpsit carnem animatam anima sensitiva tantum, et non rationali, non assumpsit carnem humanam: et ita non poterit dici: Deus factus est homo."

fruit for human beings.⁴⁵ This, however, contradicts Jn 1:12, which, after all, says that due to the coming of the Word it is possible that humans become the children of God.

In the discussion with Apollinaris, the meaning of the incarnation statement has thus been further clarified: *Verbum caro factum est* means that the Word has taken on flesh animated with a rational soul. Again, the argument refers to the intellect as a faculty of the *anima intellectiva*. Nevertheless, it is independent from any particular account of it and would be acceptable to Averroist hearers in his Paris audience, too.

3.4 Why Is John Silent about the Soul?

Having clarified the meaning of verse 14a so far, Aquinas anticipates two objections against his interpretation, which he answers in the form of small *quaestiones*. First, he asks why John does not mention the soul when he meant ensouled flesh. Aquinas gives four reasons that might have led John to his formulation:

(1) First, John might have opposed the false doctrines of the Manichaeans, who taught that the Word had only apparently taken on flesh. For the Manichaeans believed that the real flesh was a creation of the devil and therefore it would not be fitting for the Word of the good God to take on such flesh. Therefore, the Word did not take on real flesh, but only imaginary flesh (*phantasticam tantum*).⁴⁶ In order to exclude this false doctrine, according to Aquinas, John could have particularly emphasized the flesh,⁴⁷ as Jesus also did to his disciples in the Gospel of Luke: *spiritus carnem et ossa non habet, sicut me videtis habere* (Lk 24:39). Since it can easily be argued that the flesh needs to have a soul (as Aquinas has just argued against Arian and Apollinaris), John did not explicitly need to mention the soul. It might be for this reason that he mentions the flesh only in order to emphasize that the Word has actually, and not only apparently, taken on flesh.

---

45 Cf. *Super Io.* I 7, n.168: "Praeterea ad hoc Verbum humanam naturam assumpsit, ut eam repararet. Ergo id reparavit quod assumpsit. Si ergo non assumpsit animam rationalem, non reparasset eam: et sic nullus fructus proveniret nobis ex Verbi incarnatione, quod falsum est."
46 Cf. *Super Io.* I 7, n.169: "Primo ad ostendendum veritatem incarnationis contra Manichaeos, qui dicebant Verbum non assumpsisse veram carnem, sed phantasticam tantum, cum non esset conveniens ut boni Dei Verbum assumeret carnem, quam ipsi dicebant diaboli creaturam."
47 Cf. *Super Io.* I 7, n.169: "fecit de carne specialiter mentionem".

(2) Second, John might have wanted to point out the greatness of the divine goodness by mentioning the flesh. For the rational soul is very similar to God (*magis conformis*), while the flesh is completely foreign to Him. Therefore, God's condescension to human flesh is especially great and a very special sign of God's love.[48] It is *multo amplioris, immo inaestimabilis pietatis indicium*.[49]

(3) Third, John might also have wanted to express the uniqueness of Christ. For a spiritual union with God is also found in the prophets and the pious.[50] The union in Christ is unique, because in Christ the body is also united with God – a uniqueness that, according to Aquinas, is also described in Ps 140:10 and Job 28:17. Therefore, John may have emphasized the flesh.

(4) Fourth, John may have intended to point out the appropriateness of the coming of the Word to restore human nature, which has been weakened by the flesh (cf. Rom 8:3).[51]

In this step of the discussion, there is no obvious use of Aristotelian teachings involved. It is, however, exciting to see how radical Aquinas is in his rational reconstruction of John's intention as an author.

3.5 Why Is John Silent about Taking on the Flesh?

The second objection that Aquinas deals with is the question why John did not write *Verbum carnem assumpsit* – if this is what he meant according to Aquinas' interpretation.[52] Aquinas gives us two possible reasons for this.

(1) First and foremost, Aquinas sees John here taking a stand against the heretic doctrine of Nestorius (381–451) who taught the separateness of the two natures in Christ. Nestorius' heresy would be compatible with the *assumpsit* formulation. If Nestorius were correct, however, the person of the Word would be distinct from the person of the human being. On the other hand, the *factum* formulation holds: What becomes something is this afterwards.

---

48 In *Super Io.* I 7, n.169, Aquinas refers to 1 Tm 3:16: "Et manifeste magnum est pietatis sacramentum quod manifestatum est in carne".
49 *Super Io.* I 7, n.169.
50 Cf. Wisd 7:27: "Per nationes in animas sanctas se transfert, amicos Dei et prophetas constituens."
51 Cf. *Super Io.* I 7, n.169: "adventum Verbi congruum esse nostrae reparationi". Of course, the soul is implicitly included here, too; cf. argument (3) in section 3.2.
52 Cf. *Super Io.* I 7, n.170.

By contraposition, what never is cannot have been the object of a becoming. Thus, if God had not been a human, one could not say that he became one. Aquinas implicitly bases this on the following principle: If there was a change from *A* to *B*, then there must have been a time at which *B* prevailed. If *B* never prevailed, it follows by *modus tollens* that there never was a change from *A* to *B*. Now, this principle can also be applied to a change from not being human to being a human. Thus, the phrase *Verbum caro factum est* implies that God has indeed been a human being, which excludes the Nestorian heresy.

(2) Second, John may want to be clear about the difference between the incarnation and the temporary function-related *assumptio* of a prophet.[53] For the election of the prophets (*assumptio Prophetarum*) does not lead to a substantial unity (*unitas suppositi*) but only to the prophetic act. Therefore, a stronger phrase is acceptable to describe the *assumptio* of the Word. It might have been for this reason that John chose the formulation: *caro factum est*. This would certainly not be said of a prophet.

Again, Aquinas pictures John as deeply reflective about the precise wording of the Gospel. Aquinas tentatively reconstructs the arguments John might have contemplated, and this time Aquinas even ascribes some principles of Aristotle's analysis of change to the Evangelist.

3.6 Refutation of the Two-Persons Theory

Finally, Aquinas deals with another heresy, which he does not assign to any particular heretic, but which has great similarities with Nestorius's doctrine of the separateness of two natures in Christ that Aquinas has mentioned a few sentences earlier (and that was discussed in the last subsection). As his source, Aquinas explicitly refers to the *Sentences* of Peter Lombard. There, the position is described thus:

---

[53] Cf. *Super Io.* I 7, n.170: "unio Verbi ad carnem non est talis qualis est assumptio Prophetarum, qui non assumebantur in unitatem suppositi, sed ad actum propheticum: sed est talis quod Deum vere faceret hominem, et hominem Deum, idest quod Deus esset homo."

> While they say that a human being subsists of a rational soul and human flesh, they do not admit that he is composed of two natures, namely, the divine and the human; nor are the parts of it two natures, but only the soul and the flesh.[54]

Aquinas does not use a literal quotation for reporting this heresy. Rather, Aquinas formulates the heresy in his own terms:

> There were also others who, not understanding the mode of the incarnation, asserted that the aforesaid assumption was terminated in the truth of the person, confessing in God one person of God and of human; but yet they say that in him there were two hypostases, or two *supposita*, one created by the human nature and the temporal, the other by the uncreated and eternal divine.[55]

This position continues the 'funnel' of heresies. The followers of this heresy admit everything Aquinas has deduced up to here: The Word took on flesh without changing itself, and the flesh was animated with a rational soul. However, according to the present heretical interpretation, the divine and human nature in Christ were separated from each other, so that in Christ there were not only two natures, but also two persons or hypostases.

To refute this position, Aquinas makes tacit use again of Aristotelian ideas. This starts with talk about the *suppositum* – a Latin equivalent of the Greek term *hypostasis*. While the term is derived from the Greek Church Fathers, Aquinas' use of it is informed by Aristotle. For a *suppositum* is a subject to which properties are ascribed, but which cannot itself be ascribed as a property to others.[56] Then one could not say that God is human, because this would attribute the *suppositum* of "God" as a property to another *suppositum*, namely that of "human". But this is not possible. For Aquinas, in touch with tradition, the sentence "*Deus factus est homo*" is true, while the second sentence, "*Homo factus est Deus*", is false.[57] According to the heretical position in question, the first statement, "*Deus factus est homo*", would be false, too. This is because this

---

54 Cf. Peter Lombard, *Sententiae* III d.6 c.2 (= PL 192, 768): "Cumque dicant illum hominem ex anima rationali et humana carne subsistere, non tamen fatentur ex duabus naturis esse compositum, divina, scillicet, et humana; nec illius partes esse duas naturas, sed animam tantum et carnem."
55 *Super Io.* I 7, n.171: "Fuerunt et alii, qui non intelligentes modum incarnationis, posuerunt quidem assumptionem praedictam esse terminatam ad veritatem personae, confitentes in Deo unam personam Dei et hominis; sed tamen dicunt in ipso fuisse duas hypostases, sive duo supposita, unum naturae humanae creatum, et temporale, aliud divinae increatum, et aeternum."
56 Cf. Aristotle, *Categories* 2 and 5. Cf. *In De Un.* a.2, s.c.2: "eorum quae differunt suppositio, unum de altero non praedicatur."
57 Cf. *STh* III 17,6 (on "Deus factus est homo") and *STh* III 17,7 (on "Homo factus est Deus").

position claims that "*Deus est homo*" is false at all times, and then "*Deus factus est homo*" must also be false. Thus, if Deity and humanity merely coexist in Christ, it would not be adequate to say that God became a human being. Again, one would come into conflict with Jn 1:12. As an additional authority, Aquinas cites the Fifth Ecumenical Council, the Second Council of Constantinople in 553, which rejected this position.[58]

3.7 The Positive Answer

After all these arguments, going through the whole 'funnel' of heresies, Aquinas ends up with his own interpretation of verse 14a: The Word has neither partially nor completely transformed itself into the flesh, but has taken on flesh. The Word did not take on inanimate flesh, but animate flesh. This flesh was ensouled with a full human soul, including the rational faculty. And finally, the divine nature in Christ is not separate from the human nature instantiated in flesh and soul, but the divine nature and the human nature come to be one and the same *suppositum* in Christ (i.e., the same *hypostasis* or person). The Word, Aquinas can now say, is therefore human in the same way as any other human being, namely, by having a human nature (*habens humanam naturam*).[59] However, while in Jesus Christ God and human form one person, the two natures are not numerically identical. One cannot say that the Word "is" the human nature. Rather, the incarnation consists in the union of the divine with human nature.

As I already said, there is no explicit reference to Aristotle or his works in the whole passage on Jn 1:14a. Nevertheless, as I have shown, both Aquinas' paraphrase of the different interpretative options, and his complex arguments against the opposing views, are clothed in Aristotelian terms, and the arguments heavily draw on Aristotelian doctrines.

---

[58] Cf. Denzinger-Hünermann 426 with *Super Io.* I 7, n.171: "Si quis in Domino Iesu Christo unam personam, et duas hypostases dixerit, anathema sit." It is sometimes assumed that Aquinas had access to the documents of the Catholic councils in Montecassino or Orvieto; cf. David Berger, *Thomas von Aquin begegnen* (Augsburg: St. Ulrich 2002), 51.

[59] Cf. *Super Io.* I 7, n.172: "Si vero quaeris quomodo Verbum est homo, dicendum quod eo modo est homo quo quicumque alius est homo, scilicet habens humanam naturam. Non quod Verbum sit ipsa humana natura, sed est divinum suppositum unitum humanae naturae."

4 Presuppositions of Aquinas' Argument

In the interpretation of Jn 1:14a examined in this case study, Aquinas follows a peculiarly polemic method. He develops his interpretation by confronting Christological heresies and refuting them one after the other. As I have analysed in detail in the preceding section, Aquinas arranges the heresies in a funnel-like fashion, so to speak: He begins with the position that deviates most from dogma and then works his way closer and closer to the dogma. In doing so, he treats the heresies as if they were both genetically and logically successive positions. Aquinas assumes that Nestorius himself was moved to his position by arguments against Arian similarly to those brought forward by Aquinas.[60]

One can think of this structure as a fictitious dialogue between Aquinas and the heretics, whereby in the case of refutation of one of these theories, the heretics retreat to the next weaker claim to challenge the orthodox interpretation. This, then, is the next one for Aquinas to refute, until finally in all points the fictitious disputation partner must agree with the dogma: The Word did not become flesh; it took on flesh. Mustering heretic interpretations, Aquinas reaches his own interpretation step by step: The Word did not take on inanimate flesh, but animate flesh. This flesh was ensouled with a human soul. The divine nature was not separated from the human nature.

Aquinas pictures John as avoiding or combatting these heresies. Now it would be obscure to assume that the historical author of the gospel reacted to heretics that appeared only after him in history. We should not ascribe such a view to Aquinas. More probably, Aquinas held the view that John foresaw all the possible misunderstandings that later manifested themselves in the history of Christological dogmas, and that he has cautiously chosen his words to, if not avoid these misunderstandings, then at least to give the reader some clues that these are not intended.

Doing so, we must abstract from the fact that John did not write his gospel in Latin. Aquinas is aware that he interprets a translation, and occasionally he uses his knowledge of the original Greek terminology, often acquired from the Church Fathers, to explain biblical names and terms.[61] Most times, however, he

---

60 Cf. *Super Io.* I 7, n.168: "Et hic fuit error Apollinaris, qui quandoque Arium secutus est, tandem propter auctoritates praedictas coactus fuit ponere aliquam animam in Christo [...]."
61 For example, when commenting on John, he explains the equivalence of *Messiah–Christus–unctus* (*Super Io.* I 15, n.301; IV 2, n.617; VI 8, n.1004; XI 4, n.1520), that *metros* means *mensura* (*Super Io.* II 1, n.356), and that *probaton* means *ovis*, matching to *Bethsaida*, which means literally "House of the birds" (*Super Io.* V 1, n.702). Aquinas also tells his readers that *caenos*

acts on the assumption that the Latin confers enough of the refinements of the original text in order to base such sophisticated interpretations on it. Aquinas is also well aware that there are competing versions of the Latin Bible, and at times he discusses the different readings of various Latin translations.[62]

Aquinas' approach to the interpretation of Jn 1:14a is made possible by the fact that, for the medieval interpreter of the Bible, questions of fact are always also questions of interpretation. Because of the inerrancy of the Bible assumed by Aquinas, everything that Scripture says has to be true.[63] For this reason, truth is closely connected with the question of what John intends to say. Therefore, Aquinas can proceed by refuting the heretical interpretation of the verse by refuting the heresy. He does this both by pointing to contradictions with other passages of Scripture and by systematic reasoning. By thus proving the heretical teachings to be false and untenable, Aquinas shows at the same time that John could not have meant them.

The factual issue that is at stake in the interpretation of Jn 1:14a is a decidedly theological problem, since it concerns the mystery of Incarnation. Aquinas throughout refers to Aristotelian philosophy, and in particular to the doctrine of the parts of the soul and their functions according to Aristotle's psychology. This is possible because the theological problem also touches on questions of the nature of the human soul in general. For this, again, the corresponding profane science is to be consulted, and thus its main authority, newly emerging in the thirteenth century: Aristotle.

Even if Aristotle is not mentioned explicitly in the passage discussed, it is evident that Aquinas' whole argument is informed by Aristotelian philosophy, in particular by his psychology. It should also be clear that in this passage, the reference to philosophy is crucial. It is not mere decoration, but drives the argument. The aim of the argument is not to show that the literal reading is false

---

means *novum* and *encaenia* as much as *innovation* to explain the name of the Feast of Dedication of the temple (*Super Io.* X 5, n.1433), that *angelus* means *nuntius* (*Super Io.* XX 2, n.2499), and that *Dydimus* means *geminus* (*Super Io.* XX 5, n.2546). In many of these cases, Church Fathers are explicitly mentioned as sources, and most of this information is also reported in Aquinas' *Catena aurea*, a compilation from the texts of the Church Fathers.

62 A phrase search in the *Corpus Thomisticum* (corpusthomisticum.org) returns 88 finds for "secundum aliam litteram". Cf., e.g., *Super Io.* I 4, n.120 on the different version of Is. 7:9 derived from the Hebrew and Septuagint version („si non credideritis, non permanebitis" vs. „nisi credideritis, non intelligetis"), and *Super Io.* I 8, n.184 on the different translations of Ex 34:29 („splendida" vs. „cornuta").

63 Cf. *Quodl.* XII q.17: "quidquid in sacra Scriptura continetur, verum est; alias qui contra hoc sentiret, esset haereticus."

and must be replaced by a non-literal reading. The aim is rather to decide which of several possible literal readings of Jn 1:14a is the correct one. All but one are rejected by Aquinas, because there are important arguments against them – in particular, they are in contradiction with Aristotelian psychology. Thus, the argument is heavily invested in Aristotelian philosophy. This comes, of course, with a number of presuppositions that should be noted.

First, it is no surprise that the various interpretations are discussed on the background of Aristotle's teaching about the soul, given that the interpretations themselves make use of the language of this theory: A reader not acquainted with Aristotelian psychology, and with the Christological discussions clothed in its language, would not easily reach these possible interpretations. The question itself, as well as Aquinas' phrasing of the various readings of the text already presuppose philosophical terminology and background theories. It is not so much important whether this use of Aristotelian philosophy reflects the historical Aristotle, or the neo-Platonic Aristotle of the commentators. Most of the material borrowed from Aristotle will be common ground for all of these versions of Aristotle anyway. Aquinas, at least, famously notes that his primary interest is in factual questions, and not in historic trivia about the worldviews of ancient philosophers.[64]

Second, Aquinas presupposes that an interpretation of the Bible can be dismissed if it is in contradiction with, say, Aristotelian psychology. For sure, this presupposition cannot be generalised. This is clear, for example, from the fact that Aquinas does not dismiss a literal understanding of creation which is in conflict with Aristotle's doctrine of the eternity of the world. One does not have to look far for a passage critical of heathen philosophy. Only some pages earlier Aquinas says that Jn 1:1 is in fact instrumental in refuting "all of the errors of heretics and philosophers", including Aristotle's claim about the eternity of the world.[65]

This idea is, third, based on the presupposition that something cannot be at the same time false and the intended message of the Bible. In the background, there is of course the assumption that God is the principal author of the Bible

---

[64] Cf. *In De caelo* I 22, n. 288: "studium philosophiae non est ad hoc quod sicatur quid homines senserint sed qualiter se habeat veritas rerum."
[65] Cf. *Super Io.* I 1, n.64: "Si quis ergo recte consideret has quatuor propositiones, inveniet evidenter per eas destrui omnes haereticorum et philosophorum errores. [...] Aristoteles vero posuit in Deo rationes omnium rerum, et quod idem est in Deo intellectus et intelligens et intellectum; tamen posuit mundum coaeternum sibi fuisse. Et contra hoc est quod Evangelista dicit *hoc*, scilicet *verbum* solum, *erat in principio apud Deum*; ita quod ly hoc non excludit aliam personam, sed aliam naturam coaeternam."

(*auctor sacrae Scripturae est Deus*).⁶⁶ God is at the same time omniscient and benign, i.e., both able and willing to confer true revelations to the readers of the Bible. This requires a very strict application of hermeneutical charity: The reader may not assume that any falsehood is contained in the biblical messages.⁶⁷ Aquinas is quite explicit about this when he says that if something has been found to be false by means of sound argument, this can no longer be said to be an interpretation of Scripture.⁶⁸

As is clear from my exposition of Aquinas' arguments in section 3, the evidence for selecting the true interpretation does not come from Aristotle alone: As I have shown, Aquinas also collects from the Gospels information about the mental life of Jesus. Hence, Aquinas uses general psychological teachings plus information about Jesus Christ, in order to infer what to believe about the kind of soul that informed the flesh into which the Logos was incarnated. While philosophical theories are the fruits of human reasoning, the information about Christ comes from revelation – more precisely, from the Jesus event as reported in the Bible. Reason and revelation thus work together here to understand correctly what to believe. Revelation is not, then, something that is separate from reason and an addition to it that leaves reason unchanged. To the contrary, reason has to get involved with revelation in order to understand what is being revealed.

5 A Coherentist Outlook?

This result is in contrast to the 'official' meta-theological picture in the *Summa theologiae*, as exposed in its first *quaestio*. The picture there invites us to see revelation as a given foundation on which we can built theological theories by means of reason and argument. This very much resembles what in epistemology is called foundationalism, i.e., the idea that there is an infallible level of self-justifying beliefs from which all other beliefs must be inferred in order to be justified. In philosophical epistemology this role is usually played by reports

---

66 *STh* I q.1 a.10. Cf. *Super Gal.* VII 7, n.254: "Cum enim eius [= sacrae Scripturae] auctor sit Deus [...]."
67 Cf. *STh* I q.68 a.1: "Primo quidem, ut veritas Scripturae inconcusse teneatur."
68 Cf. *STh* I q.68 a.3: "Sed quia ista positio per veras rationes falsa deprehenditur, non est dicendum hunc esse intellectum Scripturae."

about one's own sense perceptions, whereas it is taken over by revealed scripture in the axiomatic-deductive picture to be found in the *Summa*.[69]

Foundationalism can be motivated as a solution to the so-called trilemma of Agrippa. The trilemma is inspired by the ancient sceptic Agrippa, who is credited for having canonised the five sceptical tropes of Pyrrhonism.[70] The trilemma runs as follows: In order to know some proposition p, we seem to need a justification for p. When asked to give such a justification, we can (1) remain silent and say nothing, or (2) say something new, or (3) say something we previously claimed to know and are now obligated to justify, e.g., p. All three options seem to be unattractive. If we remain silent (option 1), we go dogmatist. If we say something new (option 2), this will itself be in need for justification, and thus we enter an infinite regress. For, of course, in order to justify that we know some proposition p to be true, we should proceed from premises that we also know to be true. Finally, if we say something which we currently try to justify (option 3), we enter a vicious circle in our justification. In any case, no justification seems to be possible, and thus there is no knowledge at all.

Foundationalism tries to solve this trilemma by embracing a certain variant of its first horn. For, or so the foundationalist claims, there are some propositions which we can know without further justification, e.g., basic logical laws or propositions about our sensory experience. From this foundation, all other knowledge needs to be derived inferentially.

Modern epistemology is primarily interested in the justification of empirical knowledge, like my belief that I have two hands. Religious belief is clearly different. Nevertheless, the analogy to foundationalism has some appeal: In both cases, there seems to be a set of foundational propositions that is not itself in need for justification. In the one case, these propositions derive from revelation, in the other case they derive from logical intuition or sensory input. Second, by means of logic, other propositions are derived from this foundation. The metatheological theory sketched in the *Summa theologiae* thus seems to be foundationalist in essence. From this perspective, it is no wonder that some interpreters have considered Aquinas a foundationalist.[71] Others have criticised this

---

[69] It should be noted that even in the *Summa* the axiomatic-deductive picture is supplemented by a dialectic embedding of theological argumentation. I discuss these two aspects along with Aquinas' exegetical practise in a forthcoming paper on "Science, Scripture, and Theology: Three Meta-Theological Perspectives from Aquinas".

[70] Cf. Diogenes Laertius, *Vitae* IX 88, and Sextus Empiricus, *Pyrrh. hyp.* I 15.

[71] Cf. notably Alvin Plantinga, "Reason and Belief in God," in *Rationality, Religious Belief and Moral Commitment: New Essays in the Philosophy of Religion*, edited by Robert Audi and William J. Wainwright (Ithaca: Cornell University Press 1986): 16–93; Nicolas Wolterstorff, *Reason*

classification, though. For one, Anna Williams has pointed to the role Aquinas ascribes to figurative language in Scripture, be it metaphors or the spiritual senses,[72] and concludes that this imports an element of fragility as well as a provisional element into the theological epistemology of Aquinas.[73]

There is more to this. For it is not only the delicateness of metaphorical language as such that makes interpretation difficult. The reader also has to decide whether a passage in question is to be taken literally or not. The Arianist readers refuted by Aquinas (see section 2.2) could as well be unmoved by Aquinas reference to Christ's soul being mentioned in Mt 26:38. They could simply declare that this has to be understood metaphorically. This move is not possible, however, when facing a philosophical argument against their interpretations. Philosophy, thus, becomes an essential part of biblical interpretation.

Given the possibility of such a rejoinder, it is maybe not surprising that the meta-theological picture that transpires from the present case study of Aquinas' exegetical practice seems to lack the foundationalist outlook of the *Summa*. Aquinas' exegetical practice rather reminds one of epistemological position of coherentism. Coherentism embraces the third horn of Agrippa's trilemma and opts for a variant of the circularity option (3) in order to solve it. The fundamental motivation for coherentism is the observation that you cannot justify any single proposition in isolation, but only together with several other propositions. Instead, the coherentist says, it is always our entire 'web of belief' that is at stake,[74] and we are called to keep it in good order with respect to consistency and coherence.

To assign Aquinas a place in the foundationalist–coherentist dichotomy is not trivial. There are always pitfalls lurking when anachronistically applying contemporary concepts to an earlier author. First, as I already said, philosophical epistemology is mainly concerned with our empirical beliefs about the material world, while what is at stake here is Aquinas' meta-theological point of view. Second, both positions may come with a cognitive overload for real per-

---

within the Bounds of Religion, second edition (Grand Rapids: Eerdmans 1999); Scott MacDonald, "Theory of Knowledge," in *The Cambridge Companion to Aquinas*, edited by Norman Kretzmann and Eleonore Stump (Cambridge: Cambridge University Press 1993): 160–95.

72 Cf. *STh* I 1,9 for metaphors and *STh* I 1,10 for the spiritual senses.

73 Cf. Anna N. Williams, "Is Aquinas a Foundationalist?" *New Blackfriars* 91 (2009): 20–45. Also arguing against Aquinas being a foundationalist is Eleonore Stump, "Aquinas and the Foundations of Knowledge," *Canadian Journal of Philosophy*, supplementary volume 17 (1991): 125–58.

74 For this metaphor, cf. Willard Van Orman Quine and Joseph Ullian, *The Web of Belief* (New York: Mcgraw-Hill 1978).

sons. The foundationalist has the problem that translating our (fallible) talk about material things into talk about (infallible) sense data is at least very complex, if not impossible. In contrast, the coherentist has the problem that it is very difficult for us to judge our entire set of beliefs at once, being unable to take a stance outside of this set of beliefs.

Most crucially, there seems to be a tension between the meta-theological theory as described in the *Summa theologiae*, and Aquinas' practice in the biblical commentaries. The meta-theological picture in the *Summa* has a foundationalist appearance: Scripture provides a set of revealed truths as the foundation, upon which theological propositions are built. In contrast, the case study on John 1:14a shows that Scripture can be misread, and hence it does not always speak clearly on its own. It needs the help of argument, and of non-scriptural premises. In the case of John 1:14a, Aquinas derives these premises from Aristotle's philosophy, in particular from Aristotle's teachings on language, metaphysics, and psychology – that is, from philosophical theories that have been developed historically by heathen thinkers. This means that Scripture, in isolation, cannot serve as a foundation for religious beliefs. Aquinas' exegetical practice, thus, is very much non-foundationalist, and thus coherentist.

A fortiori, it is absurd to claim that the Bible is the *sole* source of knowledge, as is surprisingly claimed by Henning Graf Reventlow.[75] One would expect a typographical slip here (a missing negation, maybe, or a missing restriction to some truths relevant for salvation), but the claim is repeated on the next page.[76] Among other things, this is at odds with Aquinas' use of Aristotle described by Graf Reventlow himself (as reported in section 1 above). While for Aquinas all truths derive from God,[77] this does not hinder that some truths have been (and can be) conceived without the help of the Bible, e.g., that I am sitting now, that the sum of the internal angles of a triangle are two rights or that God exists.[78]

Note that I do not say anything about Aquinas' actual argumentative practise in the *Summa* or about his overall goal in that work. There might be a general description that covers both his endeavour there and in the commentary passage under scrutiny here, e.g., "to explain and defend the articles of faith with the help of philosophy".[79] Moreover, just like the Johannine Prologue

---

[75] Cf. Graf Reventlow, *Epochen der Bibelauslegung*, vol. 2 (see note 1), 201.
[76] Cf. Graf Reventlow, *Epochen der Bibelauslegung*, vol. 2 (see note 1), 202: "Daß die Schrift für ihn [*sc.* Aquinas] *ausschließliche* Quelle der Wahrheit ist" (italics in the original).
[77] Cf. *De ver.* 1,8.
[78] For the latter, cf. *STh* I 2,2.
[79] I borrow these words from an anonymous referee to whom I am indebted for this point.

stands out from the remainder of the four Gospels in literary form and theological density, Aquinas' commentary on the Prologue stands out in his use of philosophy. The commentary on verses 1 and 14 are particularly dense in this respect, and the commentary on Jn 1:14a stands out in its dense polemic structure. This means that the present study does not show that use of philosophy is obligatory or always needed for Aquinas when interpreting a biblical text. But it does show what is possible in Aquinas' eyes, and how far the use of philosophy in biblical exegesis can go. It also shows that one misses the full picture of the use of philosophy in Aquinas' biblical commentaries, if one looks at the explicit references only.

Using Aristotelian sources in biblical interpretation, Aquinas shows a truly interdisciplinary outlook on exegesis. However, referring to a theory from another discipline comes with an epistemic risk: The theory might be false. Or it might be debated. Or it may go out of fashion. The latter is indeed the fate of, e.g., Aristotelian psychology. Psychologists today no longer study Aristotle's writings. This does not mean that Aristotle has nothing to say to contemporary philosophy, or contemporary theology. To the contrary, Aristotle can still teach us a lot. But there is a decisive change in the dialectical setting: Aristotle is no longer the decisive authority in psychology. In Aquinas' days, its basic concepts were acceptable for virtually all parties involved in a debate. Today, this is no longer the case. The theory might not even been heard of, let alone provide a shared ground for debate. From the information that Jesus was at some time sad and at another time able to marvel, neuroscientists of the 21st century would, maybe, simplistically infer that he had a complex brain. This is, of course, not within the horizon of Aquinas. Nevertheless, I assume that he would not have hesitated to use this as an argument, had he known a heretic who doubted that Christ lacked this part of the human body.[80]

References

Berger, David. *Thomas von Aquin begegnen*. Augsburg: St. Ulrich, 2002.
Bultmann, Rudolf. *Das Evangelium des Johannes. Kritisch-exegetischer Kommentar über das Neue Testament*, 16th edition. Göttingen: Vandenhoeck & Ruprecht, 1959.

---

[80] Many thanks to audiences in Bressanone, Italy, and at the virtual conference of the European Academy of Religion for inspiring questions, and to Radim Beranek, Burkhard Reis and anonymous reviewers for helpful comments on earlier versions of the paper.

Denzinger, Heinrich, and Peter Hünermann, eds. *Enchiridion symbolorum definitionum et declarationum de rebus fidei et morum*, 40th edition, Freiburg: Herder, 2009.

Graf Reventlow, Henning. *Epochen der Bibelauslegung*. Vol. 2, *Von der Spätantike bis zum ausgehenden Mittelalter*. München: Beck, 1994.

Jansen, Ludger. "Was hat der inkarnierte Logos mit Aristoteles zu tun? Thomas von Aquins Gebrauch der Philosophie in der Auslegung des Johannesprologs und eine 'holistische' Interpretation seiner Schrifthermeneutik." *Theologie und Philosophie* 80 (2000): 89–99.

Jansen, Ludger. "Science, Scripture, and Theology: Three Meta-Theological Perspectives from Aquinas." Presented at the conference of the European Academy of Religion in Münster, September 2022, forthcoming.

MacDonald, Scott. "Theory of Knowledge." In *The Cambridge Companion to Aquinas*, edited by Norman Kretzmann and Eleonore Stump. Cambridge: Cambridge University Press 1993, 160–95.

Mostert, Walter. *Menschwerdung. Eine historische und dogmatische Untersuchung über das Motiv der Inkarnation des Gottessohnes bei Thomas von Aquin*. Tübingen: Mohr, 1978.

Müller, Ulrich B. *Die Menschwerdung des Gottessohnes. Frühchristliche Inkarnationsvorstellungen und die Anfänge des Doketismus*. Stuttgart: Katholisches Bibelwerk, 1990.

Plantinga, Alvin. "Reason and Belief in God." In *Rationality, Religious Belief and Moral Commitment: New Essays in the Philosophy of Religion*, edited by Robert Audi and William J. Wainwright. Ithaca: Cornell University Press, 1986, 16–93.

Prügl, Thomas. "Thomas Aquinas as Interpreter of Scripture." In *The Theology of Thomas Aquinas*, edited by Rik van Nieuwenhove and Joseph Wawrykow. Notre Dame: Notre Dame University Press, 2005, 386–415.

Quine, Willard Van Orman, and Joseph Ullian. 1978. *The Web of Belief*. New York: Mcgraw-Hill, 1978.

Simons, Peter. *Parts. A Study in Metaphysics*, Oxford: Oxford University Press, 1987.

Stump, Eleonore. "Aquinas and the Foundations of Knowledge." *Canadian Journal of Philosophy*, supplementary volume 17 (1991): 125–58 (= *Aristotle and His Medieval Interpretors*, edited by Richard Bosley and Martin Tweedale).

Stump, Eleonore, and Norman Kretzmann. "Eternity." *Journal of Philosophy* 78 (1981): 429–458.

Torrell, Jean-Pierre. *Saint Thomas Aquinas*. Vol. 1, *The Person and His Work*. Washington: Catholic University of America Press, 1996.

Vijgen, Jörgen. "Aristotle in Aquinas's Biblical Commentaries." In *Reading Sacred Scripture with Thomas Aquinas. Hermeneutical Tools, Theological Questions and New Perspectives*, edited by Piotr Roszak and Jörgen Vijgen. Turnhout: Brepols, 2015, 287–346.

Wawrykow, Joseph P. "Theologian." In *The Westminster Handbook to Thomas Aquinas*. Louisville: Westminster John Knox Press, 2005, 149–54.

Williams, Anna N. "Is Aquinas a Foundationalist?" *New Blackfriars* 91 (2009): 20–45.

Wolterstorff, Nicolas. *Reason within the Bounds of Religion*, second edition. Grand Rapids: Eerdmans, 1999.

Knut Alfsvåg
Hamann between Luther and Hume

On the Relation between Biblical Exegesis and Theology in the Thought of Johann Georg Hamann

Abstract: Premodern biblical interpretation presupposes a strong theology of creation. According to this world view, God is active in the world, and events therefore have theological significance. As a result of what has been called the nominalist revolution, events in the world lost their significance as instruments for the mediation of divine presence, though the philosophers of the Enlightenment still felt entitled to establish a reason-based world view. This construction was challenged by David Hume, who maintained that an observer, from experience-based inductions, will never attain universal, necessarily true conclusions. Making use of Hume's critique of Enlightenment rationality, Johann Georg Hamann argues that it should be replaced by a world view founded on the divine light of creation. The world is divine communication and should be interpreted accordingly. History, primarily but not exclusively as recorded in the Bible, thus becomes transparent for transcendence. This is a view of the Bible Hamann had learned from Luther and other premodern Bible interpreters, and he is critical towards the approach of the Enlightenment Bible scholars, the predecessors of modern Bible scholarship, as they made themselves dependent on the secular world view of the Enlightenment.

Keywords: Johann Georg Hamann, Martin Luther, David Hume, Nominalism, Rationalism, Biblical exegesis

1 From Luther to Hamann

Martin Luther is undoubtedly among the most influential figures in the history of biblical interpretation. His emphasis on the clarity of the Scripture as the power that renews the person and allows the recreated human being to participate in divine predicates like justice, power, wisdom, and honour transformed

---

Knut Alfsvåg, VID Specialized University, Stavanger, Norway. knut.alfsvag@vid.no

https://doi.org/10.1515/9783110768411-010

the area of biblical interpretation.[1] However, during the 17th and 18th centuries, Protestant exegesis moved in directions at variance with what had been suggested by the Reformer, and neither Lutheran nor Reformed Orthodoxy, intent as they were at maintaining and refining the emphases of their 16th century heroes, were equal to the task of stemming the tide. Johann Georg Hamann, an 18th century Lutheran who was educated more as a philologist than a theologian, was arguably better informed concerning the presuppositions and implications of Enlightenment exegesis. He was not able to permanently alter the course of the development any more than the Orthodox theologians, but he presented an informed critique that in retrospect has been found highly relevant.[2] The biblical scholars Hamann dialogued with and criticized were the predecessors of 19th century historical biblical criticism. Even from a contemporary perspective, then, the arguments of their 18th century critic deserve a closer inspection.

What I propose to do in this article is, firstly, to briefly sketch the development of biblical criticism during the time between Luther and Hamann. I will then present how Hamann came to see the Bible differently and how he developed his dissenting perspective by updating some of Luther's emphases through the discussion with his own contemporaries. In closing, I will reflect on the significance of Hamann's approach from a current perspective.

2 Nominalism and the Secularization of Biblical Interpretation

A presupposition for pre-modern biblical interpretation including the one given by Luther and the Reformers is a strong theology of creation. This does not necessarily entail a detailed exposition of divine predicates from the principles of natural theology – indeed pre-modern biblical interpretation is generally quite restrained as far as rational predicates of God are concerned. But it entails a worldview according to which events in the world have ultimate significance, particularly, but not exclusively, as far as the events recorded in the biblical

---

[1] Knut Alfsvåg, "'These Things Took Place as Examples for Us': On the Theological and Ecumenical Significance of the Lutheran Sola Scriptura," *Dialog* 55 (2016): 202–9, https://doi.org/10.1111/dial.12256.
[2] John R. Betz, *After Enlightenment: The Post-secular Vision of J. G. Hamann* (Malden, MA; Oxford; Chichester: Wiley-Blackwell, 2009); Oswald Bayer, *A Contemporary in Dissent: Johann Georg Hamann as Radical Enlightener*, trans. Roy A. Harrisville and Mark C. Mattes (Grand Rapids: Eerdmans, 2012).

narrative are concerned. They are the work of the Creator. The implication of this worldview is that God and the world do not exist in the same way as God is the precondition for the existence and intelligibility of all there is.³

This presupposition came under attack for the first time in the history of Christian thought during the 14th century with the demand for univocity and unambiguity concerning the concept of being applied even across the difference between God and the world. William Ockham, the most important proponent of this view, did not doubt that God and humans differed, but in his view an appreciation of this difference depended on its being investigated within a common frame of reference.⁴ The doctrine of creation thus changed its status from being the precondition for the adequate exploration of the world to one of its possible outcomes⁵ and salvation was no longer seen on Augustinian terms as a divine work in the human but as the result of a negotiated deal between two equal partners.⁶

Luther reacted strongly against both implications,⁷ but the movement he initiated could in the long run not withstand the power of what has been called the nominalist revolution. The implication of this revolution is that the significance of facts and events can no longer be explored with reference to the divine as the condition for their reality and intelligibility. They are rather seen as brute facts whose significance is explored by means of concepts established through abstractions from their perceptions in the human mind and related to each other through mathematical equations interpreted as descriptions of the world as a compilation of mechanical contrivances. Facts and events have, therefore, no inherent value; they are only significant as experienced and manipulated for the sake of human well-being. Knowledge is no longer seen as the appreciation

---

3 For an investigation of the understanding of divine difference from its origin in the Bible and Plato through European intellectual history, see Knut Alfsvåg, *What no Mind has Conceived: On the Significance of Christological Apophaticism*, Studies in philosophical theology 45, (Leuven, Paris, Walpole: Peeters, 2010).
4 Alfsvåg, *What no Mind has Conceived*, 109–15; Paul Tyson, *Returning to Reality: Christian Platonism for Our Times* (Eugene, Oregon: Cascade Books, 2014), 64–75.
5 Theo Kobusch, "Nominalismus," in *Theologische Realenzyklopädie*, ed. Gerhard Müller (Berlin, New York: de Gruyter, 1994), 589–604, 592.
6 Bengt Hägglund, *History of Theology*, trans. Gene J. Lund (St. Louis, Mo.: Concordia Publishing House, 2007), 200.
7 Knut Alfsvåg, "Contra Philosophos. The Lutheran Reformation as Critique of the Rationality of Modernity," in *Justification in a Post-Christian Society*, ed. Göran Gunner and Carl-Henrik Grenholm (Eugene: Pickwick Publications, 2014), 192–206.

of divine presence but as the power to manipulate the external world for the benefit of the human.[8]

The outcome of this development was that it was no longer possible to see the events narrated in the Bible as instruments for the mediation of divine presence.[9] They were (more or less reliable) records of historical events; nothing more, nothing less.[10] The understanding of God, the world and the human could thus no longer be established through the investigation of the biblical narrative as the manifestation of the divine origin of the world. Metaphysics (the meaning of everything) could then only be established in the same way as one established the meaning of singular facts, i.e., through the rational exploration of human perception.[11] According to the influential 18th century German philosopher Christian Wolff, this leads to an appreciation of the following facts: The world exists and must, like all existing beings, have a cause; in the case of the world, this cause is called God. Both God and humans are supposed to strive for perfection; hence the value of goodness as a moral norm and the idea of God rewarding the good ones and punishing the evil ones.[12] The biblical narrative is to be commended as far as it corresponds to this worldview. The elements in it that to us seem contrary to reason are seen as appropriate accommodation on the part of Jesus and the apostles (who supposedly were as rational as the Enlightenment philosophers themselves) to what their audience was able to grasp.[13]

---

8 Amos Funkenstein, *Theology and the Scientific Imagination from the Middle Ages to the Seventeenth Century* (Princeton, N.J.: Princeton University Press, 1986, 1986), 27 uses the expression "the nominalist revolution"; Brad S. Gregory, "No Room for God? History, Science, Metaphysics and the Study of Religion," *History and Theory* 47 (2008): 495–519.
9 The details of this development are recorded in Scott W. Hahn and Benjamin Wiker, *Politicizing the Bible: The Roots of Historical Criticism and the Secularization of Scripture 1300–1700* (New York: Crossroad, 2013).
10 Hence Lessing's famous insistence on the great ditch between contingent, historical truths and necessary, reason-based truths (Christoph Bultmann, "Early Rationalism and Biblical Criticism on the Continent," in *Hebrew Bible / Old Testament: The History of Its Interpretation II: From the Renaissance to the Enlightenment*, ed. Magne Sæbø (Göttingen: Vandenhoeck & Ruprecht, 2008), 875–901, 897).
11 Robert Alan Sparling, *Johann Georg Hamann and the Enlightenment Project* (Toronto: University of Toronto Press, 2011), 5, gives the following summary: "The Enlightenment entails a unitary view of truth and nature as fundamentally knowable and controllable." For this reason, "it demands that all authority be subject to reason's rule" (p. 12).
12 See Anthony Kenny, *A New History of Western Philosophy* (Oxford: Oxford University Press, 2010), 573–4.
13 John H. Hayes, "Historical Criticism of the Old Testament Canon," in *Hebrew Bible/Old Testament: The History of Its Interpretation II: From the Renaissance to the Enlightenment*, ed.

A part of the appeal of the new experience and reason-based religion was the apparent collapse of the traditional one. The disintegration of post-Reformation Europe in Catholic, Lutheran, Reformed, Anglican, Puritan and Anabaptist factions all claiming to represent the authority of the Bible and more or less traditional church doctrine let several thinkers appeal to human reason as the only possible foundation of a new unity.[14] One thus tried to build a system of universal truths on abstractions from human experience. However, the perceptions are dependent on context and perspective, and the inductive abstractions drawn from them are never necessarily true. A reason-based system based on human rationality alone will therefore always be inherently unstable. This was well understood by the ancient Greeks, but this lesson was lost on the Enlightenment thinkers.[15]

The Enlightenment philosopher who restored the wisdom of the ancients in this respect was the Scottish 18th century thinker David Hume.[16] Radicalizing the nominalist assumption of humans' impressions and ideas built exclusively on their perceptions, he maintained that on this assumption any notion of the participation of human thought in external reality had to be abandoned. The notion of causality, which is essential for humans making sense of how events in the world are connected, is thus nothing but an impression in the human mind established by custom. It has no relationship to the real relation of things.[17] Experience and rational necessity are incompatible entities; there is thus no such thing as a reason-based metaphysics with content. The attempt to solve the problem by appeal to religion – for Hume this means miracle-based, supernatural revelation – he considers futile.[18] Our sense of the world within which we find ourselves is, therefore, for Hume based on what he calls belief,[19] which

---

Magne Sæbø (Göttingen: Vandenhoeck & Ruprecht, 2008), 985–1005, 1002 (on Johann Salomo Selmer).
14 This was, for example, a very important aspect of the work of Gottfried Wilhelm Leibniz; see Kenny, *History of Philosophy*, 554–6.
15 The first to argue this point in the context of European intellectual history, was Plato; see Lloyd P. Gerson, *Ancient Epistemology* (Cambridge: Cambridge University Press, 2009), 23; Kenny, *History of Philosophy*, 123–9.
16 Kenny, *History of Philosophy*, 562–6.
17 Kenny, *History of Philosophy*, 653–5.
18 Thomas Brose, *Johann Georg Hamann und David Hume: Metaphysikkritik und Glaube im Spannungsfeld der Aufklärung*, vol. I (Frankfurt a M; Berlin; Bern; Bruxelles; New York; Oxford; Wien: Lang, 2006), 223–330; Kenny, *History of Philosophy*, 738–40.
19 David Hume, *An Enquiry Concerning Human Understanding*, ed. Peter Millican, Oxford World's Classics, (Oxford: Oxford University Press, 2007), 34–7. In what follows, I refer to this work with an "E" and section and paragraph number. This reference here is to E 5,10–15.

is established in ways we cannot hope to control rationally though he seems after all to have some tolerance for the attempt to prove God's existence through the argument from design.[20]

This is the thought world within which Hamann was educated. What did he make of it?

3 Hamann's London Experience

Educated at the University of Königsberg in Eastern Prussia, Johann Georg Hamann (1730–1788) was already in his youth sceptical towards one-sided Enlightenment rationality.[21] Wolff's rational metaphysics he found to be narrow-minded and sectarian.[22]

As one of the few Germans who spoke English well, Hamann was in 1757 sent to London on a trade mission which eventually failed miserably. Alone and destitute in his lodgings, he started to read the Bible and in doing so he had, in March 1758, an experience that changed his life forever. In reading the Bible, he writes,[23] he had "recognized his own crimes in the history of the Jewish people", the implication of which was that even God's patience with this people also applied to him. While pondering the commandment "you shall not kill!" in Deut 5, he came to think of Cain and felt that he, through his resistance to the divine calling, had murdered the Son of God thus carrying the same guilt as Cain. Despite the resistance he in this way had shown against the Spirit of God, the same Spirit now proceeded to reveal more and more of "the secret of the divine love and the blessing of the faith in our gracious and unique Saviour".

---

20 Kenny, *History of Philosophy*, 741–2.
21 For an overview of Hamann's work, see Knut Alfsvåg, *Christology as Critique: On the Relation between Christ, Creation and Epistemology* (Eugene: Wipf and Stock, 2018), 53–107. For a thorough investigation of his intellectual thinking before the London experience, see Brose, *Hamann und Hume*, I, 47–103.
22 Brose, *Hamann und Hume*, I, 87–8.
23 See "Gedanken über meinen Lebenslauf", published after Hamann's death and now accessible in Johann Georg Hamann, *Sämtliche Werke*, ed. Josef Nadler, 6 vols. (Wien: Verlag Herder, 1949–1957) (hereafter quoted as N and volume number), vol. 1, 9–54; the central experience is retold pp. 40–1. The writings from London have been republished in Johann Georg Hamann, *Londoner Schriften*, ed. Oswald Bayer and Bernd Weissenborn (München: C. H. Beck, 1993) (quoted as BW); the actual passage is here found on pp. 343–4. Parts of "Gedanken" are translated in Ronald Gregor Smith, *J. G. Hamann: A Study in Christian Existence* (London: Collins, 1960), 139–57. The actual passage is also quoted in Bayer, *Contemporary in Dissent*, 50.

Hamann thus discovered the blessing of finding his misery uncovered in the biblical story in a way that restructured his life around the hope this story manifests. He had experienced the despair of a life overwhelmed by guilt and was still carried by the infinite depth of divine love embodied in the story of Christ and brought to him by the work of the Spirit. The implication of Hamann's discovery was thus not the truism that the Bible contained divine revelation. The important thing was that it exposed the essence of his own existence and that this essence consisted in the realities of his own sinfulness and of divine, infinite love. It is thus not difficult to recognize the Lutheran experience of the terror of sin and the joy of faith "brought to life by the gospel or absolution" in Hamann's retelling of his story.[24]

From this overwhelming experience of divine grace Hamann went on to read through the entire Bible making notes and comments as he went along,[25] prefacing his own notes with what he had found to be the essentials of biblical hermeneutics.[26] He summarizes this in the statement that God is an author. He has given us a book and that is what authors do. This divine authorship implies a condescension ("Erniedrigung und Herunterlassung") that equals the work of the Father in creation and the work of the Son in incarnation. It reveals the pattern of divine action.[27] In creation, we see God in the context of the temporal and finite; in the incarnation, we see his Son as a human being. In a similar way, what we see in the Bible, is God reduced to the level of an author. There is thus a close parallel between the hiddenness of the Creator, the crucifixion of the Saviour and the Spirit of wisdom in the Bible, and since biblical revelation is what explains the pattern, the latter is the key to the former two.

To this condescension from God's side corresponds humility from the side of the human; this is the attitude ("Gemüthsverfassung") with which the Bible is to be read. Reading the Bible while being unaware of this pattern of condescension and humility, and for that reason unable to recognize the pattern of divine

---

24 Cf. the experience of repentance as retold in the Augsburg Confession art. 12, here quoted from Robert Kolb and Timothy J. Wengert, eds., *The Book of Concord* (Minneapolis, Minn.: Fortress Press, 2000), 45. On Hamann's appreciation of Luther, see further Brose, *Hamann und Hume*, I, 168–90.

25 These notes are printed in N 1,7–249; BW 65–311.

26 "Über die Auslegung der Heiligen Schrift"; N 2,5–6; BW 59–61. These works were not intended for publication, and were not printed until after Hamann's death.

27 After having returned from London, Hamann was acquainted with writings of Luther that let him develop this aspect of his thought even further. See Tom Kleffmann, "Luther und Hamann als Theologen des Kreuzes," in *Johann Georg Hamann: Religion und Gesellschaft*, ed. Manfred Beetz and Andre Rudolph (Berlin: de Gruyter, 2012), 208–27.

action it uncovers, is for Hamann "the peak of atheism and the greatest magic of disbelief".[28]

Considering the Bible as revelation implies that its origin is the eternal, immutable God. Itself being a part of the perishable world, the human mind cannot relate directly to the reality of the eternal One in any other way than as to the unknown.[29] However, God chose the Jews to reveal both the corrupt nature of humans and God's own justice and mercy in dealing with it,[30] and the consummation of this revelation is the story of Christ. Human reason can to some extent accept the unknowability part. It respects Socrates, who admitted that he did not know anything and even "the father of the newer philosophy" (Descartes) had to reject everything he knew. It is the acceptance of revelatory condescension with its accompanying obligation of human humility that is the hard part. As is shown in the case of Descartes, one rather prefers to replace it with a construction of "revamped and newly accepted errors".[31]

The form of biblical revelation is divine condescension; its content, however, is the divine but hidden lordship over both nature and history which unfolds according to the pattern revealed in the story of the Jews and of Christ.[32] The biblical narrative is thus the key to understanding in both these areas of human knowledge. As a historian one will find God's wise government; as a scholar of nature one will find God's wise omnipotence. The reduction to blind chance or eternal laws is as wrong in the one area as it is in the other.[33] This is not intended as a critique of science and scholarship; Hamann appreciated the work both of Newton and the historian. However, they are both touched by God's wise government and should therefore also acknowledge it.

The Bible is written by the Creator and is therefore the key to the understanding of the world. For Hamann, the Bible is therefore not only the source of dogmatics; it is even the source of our understanding of epistemology.

---

28 "Der Gipfel der Atheisterey und die größte Zauberey des Unglaubens" (N 1,5). The translations from Hamann's work are my own.
29 N 1,224; BW 286.
30 N 1,11; BW 69.
31 N 1,222; BW 284.
32 The Christological typology of the London writings is explored in detail in Friedemann Fritsch, *Communicatio Idiomatum: Zur Bedeutung einer christologischen Bestimmung für das Denken Johann Georg Hamanns*, Theologische Bibliothek Töpelmann 89 (Berlin: de Gruyter, 1998), 9–105.
33 N1,9; BW 67.

4 The Limit of Reason

Returning from London, Hamann was met with opposition from his rationalist friends, the most famous of which was Immanuel Kant, who tried to reconvert him to the cause of Enlightenment rationality. Hamann's answer was the essay *Sokratische Denkwürdigkeiten*,[34] where he criticizes the Enlightenment understanding of reason through a meditation on the work of Socrates who was recognized as the wisest of all men despite his own admission that he knew nothing.[35] The Enlightenment rationalists had neglected this aspect of Socratic wisdom, but Hamann considers it highly significant.

Hamann identifies the Socratic humility on behalf of his own knowledge with the attitude of Paul who wrote that "if anyone imagines that he knows something, he does not yet know as he ought to know."[36] For Hamann, Socrates is thus a prophet who led the Greeks to worship the unknown God, thus letting us know that God is the God of the gentiles too (77). Among his contemporaries, however, it is only in Hume that Hamann finds the same admission of the inability to establish reliable, reason-based knowledge. Hamann thus equates Socratic ignorance with Hume's understanding of perception ("Empfindung", 73).

For Hume, there are two kinds of perceptions, namely ideas and impressions. Ideas are sense experience and impressions are memories and reflections on these experiences. The implication is that there is nothing in the human mind that is not reducible to perception (E 2–4). We never know in advance what we will experience. The notion of a necessary, experience-based truth is thus incoherent. The perceptions in the human mind are either conceptual truisms ("bachelors are unmarried"; Kant called this analytical statements) or founded on contingent facts that could have been different. The Enlightenment idea of a consistent worldview established through the rational exploration of experience is thus reduced to a pile of unfounded nonsense. Our behaviour is

---

[34] N 2,57–82; numbers in parenthesis in this section refer to this work. For English translations, see James C. O'Flaherty, ed., *Hamann's Socratic Memorabilia: A Translation and Commentary* (Baltimore: Johns Hopkins University Press, 1967), and Gwen Griffith Dickson, *Johann Georg Hamann's Relational Metacriticism*, Theologische Bibliothek Töpelmann 67, (Berlin, New York: de Gruyter, 1995), 375–400.
[35] For the account of the ignorance of Socrates as retold by himself, see *Apology* 21–3 (Plato, *Complete Works*, ed. D. S. Hutchinson and John M. Cooper (Indianapolis: Hackett, 1997), 21–2): Socrates was the wisest, because he understood that his knowledge was worthless.
[36] 1 Cor 8:2 (ESV); Hamann quotes in Greek (74).

determined by our passions which, for Hume, are a subset of our perceptions and not by an alleged rationality.[37]

Our perception of reality therefore does not in itself entail knowledge. It consists of disconnected facts that according to the criteria of a coherent rationality appear as mere ignorance. Compilations of facts are therefore useless. Adopting this view, Hamann maintains that one will not learn to philosophize from studying the history of philosophy any more than one will learn to govern by embracing a statue of a statesman (62). In describing Socrates, one often takes his mother's occupation as one's point of departure and presents him as a midwife facilitating the birth of understanding. Hamann prefers to present him from his father's occupation as a sculptor who cuts away what impedes reality (i.e., ignorance) from exposing itself (66). There is nothing unusual in this metaphor; the sculptor who lets inherent beauty appear by carving away what obstructs our seeing it is an image with a long pedigree. It is even found in Luther who was probably Hamann's source.[38] What is unique to Hamann, however, is to find David Hume as the incarnation of the spirit of Socratic unknowability.[39] As Socrates was the unlikely but God-sent prophet among his contemporaries, Hume acts as a Saul among the prophets in Hamann's own time.[40]

The folly of rationalism makes one indifferent to reality to the extent that one blindly follows the position of the majority. The public thus becomes an idol and rationalists are nothing but idol worshippers who cater to the expectation of the crowd. Hamann's critical epistemology thus also entails a critical analysis of the power structures of the allegedly enlightened society. Idols may be exposed, however, by letting them devour sacrifices they cannot stomach. By this allusion to the story of the idol in Bel and the Dragon, an apocryphal addition to the Book of Daniel, Hamann presents his own essay as an attempt at exposing the idolatrous superstition of the rationalists (59–60).

---

[37] Kenny, *History of Philosophy*, 564. Hume thus comes quite close to Luther's understanding of faith as affection and his insistence on reason as subservient to one's basic affection. This is a connection of which Hume is unaware and Hamann does not explore. On this aspect of Luther's thought, see Birgit Stolt, *Martin Luthers Rhetorik des Herzens* (Tübingen: Mohr Siebeck, 2000), 53–61; Alfsvåg, *Christology as Critique*, 44.

[38] Alfsvåg, *Christology as Critique*, 65.

[39] This is also contrary to established Hume scholarship. There is, however, a recent attempt at exploring Socratic ignorance as a central element in Hume's thought; see Bernard Freydberg, *David Hume: Platonic Philosopher, Continental Ancestor* (Albany: State University of New York Press, 2012).

[40] N 3,316 (Golgotha und Scheblimini, 1783).

People do not like being exposed in this way. The critics of merely apparent knowledge are therefore invariably met with heavy opposition. In Hamann's view, it is therefore no coincidence that both Socrates and Jesus were executed by the people they criticized. In both cases, the conflict was exacerbated by the proponents of truth being humble and unpretentious; nobody expects truth to appear in the disguise of a tortured man (as in the case of Jesus) who admits his own ignorance (as in the case of Socrates, 67–8). This is obviously an allusion to the principle of divine condescension that is so heavily emphasized in the London writings.

However, the critique of rationalism does not entail scepticism either for Hume or for Hamann. For Hume, it entails the endorsement of belief established through nature and/or custom – Hume is not always entirely clear on this point (E 5,7–14).[41] There is nothing wrong in relating to reality within the framework of an idea of its totality; the problem occurs when we think of this idea as established through rational proof. Hume occasionally expresses a kind of despair concerning this situation.[42] On the whole, however, he seems content with his notion of belief.

Hamann is aware that Hume's notion of belief is quite different from his own; in Hume, "faith loses as much as it wins," he writes. What Hamann finds irrefutable in Hume, is his subversion of reason and advocacy of ignorance; that Hume goes on to reject the entire edifice of Christian faith as he understood it, does not worry him. In Hamann's view, faith is not founded on rational arguments any more than tasting and seeing are (73–4).[43] If Hume sees even religion as perception-based rationality, he is wrong and his refutation uninteresting apart from the fact that it is spot on as far as the misconceptions of the Enlightenment religionists are concerned. Hamann thus reads Hume against Hume[44] while being sensitive to the cracks in Hume's own argument that lets the reality of divine transcendence shine through.

Hamann thus finds Hume an ally in his fight to replace Enlightenment rationality with a consistent, i.e., faith-based exploration of experience. This lets him long for a person that could do for history what Francis Bacon has done for

---

41 Brose, *Hamann und Hume*, I, 219–22.
42 Cf. the part of Hume's *Treatise* which Hamann translated and published in 1771 as "Nachtgedanken eines Zweiflers"; David Hume, *A Treatise on Human Nature* ([S.l.]: The Floating Press, 2009), 414–27 (T 1,4,7); Hamann's translation is found in N 4,364–70.
43 There may be an allusion to Psalm 34:8 here: "Taste and see that the LORD is good!" (ESV).
44 So also Thomas Brose, *Johann Georg Hamann und David Hume: Metaphysikkritik und Glaube im Spannungsfeld der Aufklärung*, vol. II (Frankfurt a M; Berlin; Bern; Bruxelles; New York; Oxford; Wien: Lang, 2006), 409–11.

physics (65), i.e., to establish a sound methodology for experience-based scholarship. This remark may sound as confusing as Hamann's praise of Hume; nowadays Bacon is remembered (and praised or criticized according to one's own preferences)[45] as the one who reduced science to the manipulation of nature for the benefit of humans. Still, Bacon had a theological framework for his scientific work; he saw it as the fulfilment of a divine vocation.[46] It is probably this faith-based openness for being exposed to reality as it appears that Hamann has in mind.[47] His own worldview was shattered and rebuilt through his experience of the unexpected. He had met God in the context of experienced reality. In Hamann's view, we cannot meet God in any other way. The rejection of reason-based speculation is thus only trustworthy when it is combined with a methodologically sound exploration of experienced reality as the area of divine presence. Our experience of God-given reality is only trustworthy when interpreted as an encounter with the divine. The Bacon of history is thus no other than Hamann himself.

Experience-based, logically necessary truths do not exist. This is the principle on which Hume and Hamann agree completely.[48] Reality can thus only be consistently approached through what Hume calls belief and Hamann calls faith. Hidden behind this apparent agreement, however, is a profound difference. Whereas Hume has no notion of creation and for that reason must replace rationality with the jetsam and flotsam of customary beliefs, Hamann has a theology of creation that allows experienced events to appear as significant. They are transparent for the reality of the divine which is what grounds reality in so far as it exists at all. For Hamann, this is not a perspective that is established through induction from experienced events – then he would find himself as the target of Hume's critique. On the contrary, it is a perspective that is given with the existence of the world and which lets existence itself appear as the unavoidable task of intellectual reflection. Faith is not established through induction; it is a reflection on the conditions of our being able to perform inductions.

---

[45] For an attempt at doing both at once, see Tyson, *Returning to Reality*, 50.

[46] Stephen A. McKnight, *The Religious Foundations of Francis Bacon's Thought* (Columbia, Mo: University of Missouri Press, 2006); Steven Matthews, *Theology and Science in the Thought of Francis Bacon* (Abingdon: Ashgate, 2008).

[47] On Hamann's appreciation of Bacon, see Sven-Aage Jørgensen, "Hamann, Bacon, and Tradition," *Orbis Literarum* 16 (1961): 48–73, and Dickson, *Relational Metacriticism*, 79.

[48] Kant's critique of this principle is his *Kritik der reinen Vernunft*; Hamann's critique of Kant's critique is his *Metakritik über den Purismum der Vernunft* (N 3,281–9). For a discussion of this work, see Alfsvåg, *Christology as Critique*, 95–105.

Sokratische Denkwürdigkeiten rejects a one-sidedly reason-based world view, but this work does not explore the alternative in any detail. Hamann is here mainly interested in letting Socrates in the shape of David Hume expose the irrationality of rationalism. For a deeper view, we will have to go to his other works.

5 The Significance of a Christological Worldview

In 1762, Hamann published his essay "Aesthetica in Nuce" as part of a collection of essays called *Kreuzzüge der Philologen*.[49] The origin of the word "aesthetics" is the Greek verb αἰσθάνομαι, "to perceive". What we have in this work is Hamann's understanding of perception, i.e., his own experience-based epistemology. Following in Plato's footsteps,[50] he insists that the condition of perception ("Empfindung") is light, but for Hamann this light is the light that flows from the divine "let there be light!" on the first day of creation (197). To perceive is thus to find oneself on the receiving end of God's creative work. The world is divine communication.[51]

This is an important starting point but the interpretation of this communication is no easy task. Divine communication in creation appears for us as what Hamann calls "turbatverse und disiecti membra poetae" (jumbled verses and the scattered limbs of the poet; 198). We therefore need helpers, of which there are three kinds: Scholars like Bacon, who collect the scattered signs, philosophers, who interpret them, and poets, who imitate and restore them (199).

One of the implications of this approach is that Hamann understands divine communication through the Bible as nothing but a variation of divine communication through creation; the origin, the message and the task of the interpreter are identical. Hamann thus follows the Enlightenment insistence on the significance of natural theology, but he rejects the attempt at understanding it according to the principles of anthropocentric rationality and is very critical of the biblical scholars who let this kind of natural theology guide their reading of

---

[49] N 2,113–245; "Aesthtetica in Nuce" is found on pp. 195–217, and numbers in parenthesis in the following refer to this work. For English translations, see Dickson, *Relational Metacriticism*, 409–31, and Johann Georg Hamann, *Writings on philosophy and language*, trans. Kenneth Haynes (Cambridge: Cambridge University Press, 2007), 60–95.
[50] Cf. the parable of the sun in *Republic* 508a–509b. For a discussion of Hamann's nuanced appreciation of Plato, see Sparling, *Hamann and the Enlightenment Project*, 196–201.
[51] "Die Schöpfung [ist] eine Rede an die Kreatur durch die Kreatur" (creation is speech from the created to the created, 198).

the Bible. For this reason, Hamann is very critical of biblical interpreters who content themselves with the registration of historical and philological facts but are uninterested in interpreting them as transparent for the divine light. The target of Hamann's critique is Johann David Michaelis, who in 1757 had published his book *Beurtheilung der Mittel, welche man anwendet, die ausgestorbene hebräische Sprache zu verstehen* ("Evaluation of the means to be employed for understanding the dead Hebrew language").[52] Michaelis is Wolff's disciple to the extent that his linguistic ideal is the precise, objectifying description. As a philologist, Hamann certainly appreciates Michaelis's work with the Hebrew language, but Michaelis is in Hamann's view blind to its rhetorical power and theological significance.[53] In this way, Michaelis commits what Hamann calls "the mathematical original sin" (202); he reduces significant observations to mathematical points without theological significance. In another essay, Hamann gives a similar critique of the work of Johann August Starck and Hermann Samuel Reimarus.[54]

Hamann elaborates his critique of Michaelis with a quotation from Book IX of Bacon's *De Augmentis Scientiarum* from 1638 where Bacon contends that there are two kinds of excess biblical interpretation. One is to insist on a hidden meaning behind the text unrelated to what it says as is done, for example, in cabbalistic interpretations. The other is to disgrace Scripture by interpreting what is divinely inspired in a merely human way. One should observe context, occasion, and the writer's intention in interpreting a biblical text. However, it is even more important that one does not forget that the biblical texts are divine and thus contain doctrines that transcend the circumstance of their occasion (202).[55] This forgetful-

---

[52] Critique of Michaelis is the main topic of "Kleeblatt Hellenistischer Briefe" (Cloverleaf of Hellenistic Letters, N 2,167–193), another of the essays in the *Kreuzzüge*-collection (English translation in Hamann, *Writings*, 33–59). For an introduction to the work of Michaelis, see John Sandys-Wunsch, "Early Old Testament Critics on the Continent," in *Hebrew Bible/Old Testament: The History of Its Interpretation II: From the Renaissance to the Enlightenment*, ed. Magne Sæbø (Göttingen: Vandenhoeck & Ruprechts, 2008), 971–84.

[53] On Hamann's critique of Michaelis, see Fritsch, *Communicatio Idiomatum*, 89, 154–5, and Jens Wolff, "Ästhetische Nuss oder Reliquie: Hamanns christologischer Symbolismus," in *Johann Georg Hamann: Religion und Gesellschat*, ed. Manfred Beetz and Andre Rudolph (Berlin: de Gruyter, 2012), 334–45.

[54] See Alfsvåg, *Christology as critique*, 85–6. In Hans W. Frei, *The Eclipse of Biblical Narrative: A Study in Eighteenth and Nineteenth Century Hermeneutics* (New Haven: Yale University Press, 1975), a critique similar to Hamann's is seen as generally relevant for this period.

[55] According to Matthews, *Theology and Science in Bacon*, 88–9, one can discern an influence from Luther in Bacon's hermeneutics, something a keen Luther reader like Hamann surely observed and appreciated.

ness is precisely what Hamann finds in Michaelis's (and Reimarus's) writings. Hamann wants the text interpreted as divine communication but he has no patience with those who dispense with sound exegetical philology in their mining for depths of meaning hidden behind the surface of the text.

The scholars who are supposed to interpret the communication of God through nature, however, basically commit the same error. Though the dialects are different, the message of divine majesty and condescension is the same in both areas (204) and nature mediates this message through our senses and passions ("Leidenschaften").[56] When these instruments are mutilated, however, nature is not perceived; it is not experienced as nature. The address of Hamann's critique is here the scientists who in his view flay nature through their abstractions, thus paralyzing the nerve fibres through which nature is supposed to connect with human perception.[57] Nature therefore sighs under the tyranny of humans (206).[58] Hamann's metaphors imply a perception of nature as a living organism existing in a symbiotic relationship with humans. The "mathematical original sin" therefore leaves nature suffering under the loss of everything meant to serve as an instrument for divine-human communication.

The key to the interpretation of both nature and history is the person of Jesus, who is the ultimate manifestation of divinity within the context of the historical and natural. The light of creation is primarily manifest in Christ, its firstborn,[59] and when this light is dimmed, the colours of the world fade away (206). Christ is thus the Alpha and Omega of the world; a non-Christological worldview is as void of meaning as texts that omit the first and last letters of the alphabet (207). Nature and writing are the materials of the Spirit (210), but they have been reduced to nothing. The task is thus to revive them (211), and this can only be done through the proclamation of the name of Jesus (212). Elaborating on this point, Hamann quotes Augustine who maintains that the reading of the prophetic books without Christ having been understood is an insipid and futile

---

56 According to Hume, passions are impressions as they determine human behaviour; see note 37. According to Fredrick C. Beiser, *The Fate of Reason: German Philosophy from Kant to Fichte* (Cambridge, Massachusetts and London: Harvard University Press, 1987), 37, Hamann's view of nature inspired the Romantics.

57 For Hamann, nature is not reducible to its mathematically explorable structures; on this point, see Ulrich Moustakas, *Urkunde und Experiment: Neuzeitliche Naturwissenschaft im Horizont einer hermeneutischen Theologie der Schöpfung bei Johann Georg Hamann*, Theologische Bibliothek Töpelmann 114, (Berlin; New York: de Gruyter, 2003), 213. Even here, Bacon is the authority for Hamann's critique.

58 An allusion to Rom 8:21–22.

59 Cf. Col 1:15.

project, but with this understanding the reading becomes virtually intoxicating.⁶⁰ However, this intoxication is not an experience one simply can decide to have. Quoting Luther's Preface to Romans, Hamann insists that one must be dead to be able to receive this kind of wine (212–3).⁶¹

Hamann's approach is here obviously informed by his appreciation of the Lutheran doctrine of law and gospel which also was the framework for his understanding of his conversion experience. What is peculiar to Hamann is thus not the interpretation of faith as *creatio ex nihilo* as this belongs to the basics of Lutheran theology.⁶² What is peculiar to Hamann is his complete lack of soteriological myopia; he insists that this is the point of orientation for the adequate understanding of the world.⁶³ Christ is God's final word that confirms what God has said "through nature and scripture, through creatures and seers, through reasons and figures, through poets and prophets" (213). This should come as no surprise. After all, the Father of the Son is the Creator of heaven and earth who can be expected to show a certain consistency in his dealings with his creatures.

For this reason, there is no adequate approach to the world but the one given in prayer and worship. God is the world's origin and his presence in the world is discernible through the incarnation of his Son and the work of the Spirit. For those who know how to look, all of the world's phenomena, both in nature and history, with the Bible being the most important manifestation of the latter, are transparent for transcendence.⁶⁴ We are, however, dependent on God opening our eyes that we may perceive and proclaim it.

For Hamann, it is therefore the doctrine of *Communicatio idiomatum* that is the key to the understanding of the world.⁶⁵ In the same way as the two natures of Christ according to the Council of Chalcedon are united "without mixture and without separation", all phenomena in the world in Hamann's view have the

---

60 Hamann does not give the source of the quotation, which is taken from Augustine's Lectures on the Gospel of John, IX, 3.
61 Martin Luther, *Werke: Kritische Gesamtausgabe* (Weimar: H. Bühlau, 1883–1990), Deutsche Bibel, vol. 7, 25.
62 On this aspect of Luther's thought, see Alfsvåg, *What no Mind has conceived*, 212–20.
63 Luther comes close to a similar emphasis when he in his discussion of the relation between faith and reason in *Disputatio de homine* insists that the doctrine of justification is the definition of the human (Luther, *Werke*, 39 I, 176).
64 For Hamann, creation and revelation are coextensive; so Dickson, *Relational Metacriticism*, 146.
65 See Fritsch, *Communicatio Idiomatum*, 89, and Gregory A. Walter, "The Crucified Body Signified by All," in *Johann Georg Hamann: Religion und Gesellschaft*, ed. Manfred Beetz and Andre Rudolph (Berlin: de Gruyter, 2012), 292–306.

same dual nature; they are as natural events manifestations of divinity. The significance of this point of orientation is explored by Hamann in several contexts. He is not willing to accept the evolvement of human language either through direct divine intervention or as a development from purely natural causes. As divine communication, creation is meaningful, i.e., linguistic, in its structure; the language of humans is thus nothing but human appreciation of the world as a divine gift.[66] Neither is he willing to accept the idea of a natural, neutral state from which the Enlightenment philosophers developed the idea of human liberty and human rights. For Hamann, human existence is a part of divine creation and is, for that reason, graced from the outset.[67] For Hamann, the idea of a neutral state prior to the manifestation of existence as graced implies that humans make all the important decisions in God's absence. This amounts to a kind of Pelagianism which in Hamann's view is as deficient in social theory as it is in theology.[68]

6 Perceiving the Light of Creation

Hamann's task as a scholar and a human is the experience-based investigation of reality as the manifestation of the light of divine creation. This entails an epistemology that can be described as empiricism without nominalism. Hamann thus defends a radical openness toward reality as it appears for us. The idea of scientific theories being criticized for their alleged lack of compatibility with theological orthodoxy is completely foreign to Hamann. However, he rejects the emphasis on mere factuality he finds among his contemporaries both in natural science and biblical scholarship. While his appreciation of nature as a living organism should endear him to ecologically informed theologians and philosophers, this leaves us with questions with which we still struggle today. Are the metaphysical commitments of science and biblical scholarship under modernity as dubious as those attacked by Hamann? If this is indeed the case, how do we disentangle their obvious achievements from these commitments?

---

[66] Alfsvåg, *Christology as Critique*, 79–83. From a philosophical point of view, this expresses Hamann's subscription to Plato's insistence that meaning precedes perception; see Gerson, *Ancient epistemology*, 42. Hume's debunking of the Enlightenment idea of an experience-based rationality makes the same point from the other end.
[67] There is thus no opposition between grace and nature in Hamann's thought; so also Dickson, *Relational Metacriticism*, 45.
[68] Alfsvåg, *Christology as Critique*, 87–94.

Post-modern thinkers have found Hamann fascinating as they well should; he is, after all, the one who gave them their catchword "metacritique".[69] But what are we to make of his insistence that we do not appreciate anything adequately until we have seen it as transparent for the light of divine creation?[70] What are the precise methodological implications of this point of departure for a hermeneutics of nature and history?

While waiting for a Bacon (or Hamann) who could do this for us today, we may recuperate the leads Hamann gives us as far as they take us. Understanding reality as the manifestation of the light of creation, Hamann insists that creation is carried by divine love and mercy despite our experiences of sin and tragedy. The biblical narrative of the life, death and resurrection of the Son of God is here our basic and irreplaceable point of orientation, but we will not grasp its significance without having experienced divine love through the tragic realities of our own life. This insistence on the necessity of having met the reality of divine love through one's own misery is closely connected to, and certainly also inspired by, the same emphasis in Luther's thought.[71]

Both for Luther and for Hamann, this entails a rejection of the human attempt at finding one's way to God, and thus to a rationally coherent worldview through a reason-based exploration of experience. Human reason is an indispensable tool for our attempts at interpreting the interrelatedness of created phenomena, but it will neither give us a reliable overview of the world nor present us with a consistent understanding of the Creator. We will never be able to establish a reason-based natural theology in a consistent way. Both our limitation as finite beings and the ambiguity of our experience of the world are here insurmountable hurdles. For none of Luther, Hamann or Hume, is faith (Hume would say belief) the outcome of a rational weighing of the relevant evidence. Faith is created when humans are overwhelmed by reality.

Luther explored this perspective through his critique of what he called the second use of the law. The first use of the law is to build workable human societies and, in that capacity, the law is to be revered as a divine gift.[72] When given a second use, though, as the foundation of one's relationship with God, it fails

---

69 Cf. note 48.
70 For an attempt at a serious discussion of this question informed more by Thomas Aquinas than by Hamann but still in a quite Hamanesque spirit, see Michael Hanby, *No God, No Science? Theology, Cosmology, Biology* (Oxford: Wiley-Blackwell, 2013).
71 Alfsvåg, *What no Mind has Conceived*, 210.
72 Cf. Rom 7:12, also emphasized in Luther's *Disputatio de homine* (note 63)

miserably.⁷³ A sound relationship with God will only be established when humans find themselves at the receiving end of God's creative power. Hamann applies this evaluation of the benefits and shortcomings of the law on the understanding of reason and enlists the service of Hume in his deconstruction of reason as the foundation of a credible and consistent worldview. In Hamann's published works, this connection between Paul, Luther and Hume is merely implied, but in some of his letters he is explicit about the parallel he finds between law and reason in this respect.⁷⁴ There is a first and second use even of human reason and while the first use is indispensable, its second use is disastrous as is made abundantly clear in Hume's critique of the rationalists. Both Paul and Hume belong among the prophets after all.

Both Luther and Hamann struggled with the secularizing implications of a nominalist worldview that would not let them see either nature or (biblically recorded) history as transparent for transcendence, and they were unyielding in their emphasis that this worldview has to be eradicated for an experience-based and biblically informed theology to develop. Hamann was living in a time when historically oriented biblical scholarship was beginning to emerge and he was relentless in his critique of this enterprise, founded as it was on a worldview he considered atheist in its implications. However, his critique of a historically informed biblical scholarship is not founded on a need for making the distance between factual reality and biblical narrative as short as possible. For Hamann, the divine incarnational condescension into the messy world of human experience is as real as it gets. Ideals of perfection are at variance with the principle of divine condescension and, for that reason, counterproductive both in relation to revelation and its transmission. Furthermore, faith in creation entails the appreciation of precisely this messy world as the area of divine presence, the understanding of which is resolved according to the pattern made manifest through the biblical narrative.

Biblical interpretation is therefore in Hamann's view the key to any kind of understanding of the world that has the aspiration of evolving beyond the mere registration of facts without dissolving into incoherence. The challenge Hamann places before us as readers and interpreters of the Bible is thus that we should

---

73 Cf. Rom 3:20. From this perspective, the law describes what cannot be done; so Andrea Vestrucci, *Theology as Freedom: On Martin Luther's "De servo arbitrio"* (Tübingen: Mohr Siebeck, 2019), 128.
74 See Elfriede Büchsel, "Paulinische Denkfiguren in Hamanns Aufklärungskritik: Hermeneutische Beobachtungen zu exemplarishcen Texten und Problemstellungen," *Neue Zeitschrift für systematische Theologie und Religionsphilosophie*, no. 30 (1988): 269–84, and Brose, *Hamann und Hume*, I, 187–90.

present before the reading public interpretations that indeed make sense according to this criterion. If Hamann is to be believed, our reliability and relevance as theologians depend on our being equal to the challenge.

References

Alfsvåg, Knut. *Christology as Critique: On the relation between Christ, Creation and Epistemology*. Eugene: Wipf and Stock, 2018.
Alfsvåg, Knut. "Contra Philosophos: The Lutheran Reformation as Critique of the Rationality of Modernity." In *Justification in a Post-Christian Society*, edited by Göran Gunner and Carl-Henrik Grenholm, 192–206. Eugene: Pickwick Publications, 2014.
Alfsvåg, Knut. "'These Things Took Place as Examples for Us': On the Theological and Ecumenical Significance of the Lutheran Sola Scriptura." *Dialog* 55 (2016): 202–9. https://doi.org/10.1111/ dial.12256.
Alfsvåg, Knut. *What no Mind has Conceived: On the Significance of Christological Apophaticism*. Studies in philosophical theology 45. Leuven, Paris, Walpole: Peeters, 2010.
Bayer, Oswald. *A Contemporary in Dissent: Johann Georg Hamann as Radical Enlightener*. Translated by Roy A. Harrisville and Mark C. Mattes. Grand Rapids: Eerdmans, 2012.
Beiser, Fredrick C. *The Fate of Reason: German Philosophy from Kant to Fichte*. Cambridge, Massachusetts and London: Harvard University Press, 1987.
Betz, John R. *After Enlightenment: The Post-secular Vision of J. G. Hamann*. Malden, Mass; Oxford; Chichester: Wiley-Blackwell, 2009.
Brose, Thomas. *Johann Georg Hamann und David Hume: Metaphysikkritik und Glaube im Spannungsfeld der Aufklärung*. 2 vols., Frankfurt: Lang, 2006.
Bultmann, Christoph. "Early Rationalism and Biblical Criticism on the Continent." In *Hebrew Bible/ Old Testament: The History of Its Interpretation II: From the Renaissance to the Enlightenment*, edited by Magne Sæbø, 875–901. Göttingen: Vandenhoeck & Ruprecht, 2008.
Büchsel, Elfriede. "Paulinische Denkfiguren in Hamanns Aufklärungskritik: Hermeneutische Beobachtungen zu exemplarishcen Texten und Problemstellungen." *Neue Zeitschrift für systematische Theologie und Religionsphilosophie*, no. 30 (1988): 269–84.
Dickson, Gwen Griffith. *Johann Georg Hamann's Relational Metacriticism*. Theologische Bibliothek Töpelmann 67. Berlin, New York: de Gruyter, 1995.
Frei, Hans W. *The Eclipse of Biblical Narrative: A Study in Eighteenth and Nineteenth Century Hermeneutics*. New Haven: Yale University Press, 1975.
Freydberg, Bernard. *David Hume: Platonic Philosopher, Continental Ancestor*. Albany: State University of New York Press, 2012.
Fritsch, Friedemann. *Communicatio Idiomatum: Zur Bedeutung einer christologischen Bestimmung für das Denken Johann Georg Hamanns*. Theologische Bibliothek Töpelmann 89, Berlin: de Gruyter, 1998.
Funkenstein, Amos. *Theology and the Scientific Imagination from the Middle Ages to the Seventeenth Century*. Princeton, N.J.: Princeton University Press, 1986, 1986.
Gerson, Lloyd P. *Ancient Epistemology*. Cambridge: Cambridge University Press, 2009.
Gregory, Brad S. "No Room for God? History, Science, Metaphysics and the Study of Religion." *History and Theory* 47 (2008): 495–519.

Hahn, Scott W., and Benjamin Wiker. *Politicizing the Bible: The Roots of Historical Criticism and the Secularization of Scripture 1300–1700*. New York: Crossroad, 2013.
Hamann, Johann Georg. *Londoner Schriften*, edited by Oswald Bayer and Bernd Weissenborn. München: C. H. Beck, 1993.
Hamann, Johann Georg. *Sämtliche Werke*, edited by Josef Nadler. 6 vols. Wien: Herder, 1949–1957.
Hamann, Johann Georg. *Writings on Philosophy and Language*. Translated by Kenneth Haynes. Cambridge: Cambridge University Press, 2007.
Hanby, Michael. *No God, No Science? Theology, Cosmology, Biology*. Oxford: Wiley-Blackwell, 2013.
Hayes, John H. "Historical Criticism of the Old Testament Canon." In *Hebrew Bible/Old Testament: The History of Its Interpretation II: From the Renaissance to the Enlightenment*, edited by Magne Sæbø, 985–1005. Göttingen: Vandenhoeck & Ruprecht, 2008.
Hume, David. *An Enquiry Concerning Human Understanding*. Oxford World's Classics, edited by Peter Millican. Oxford: Oxford University Press, 2007.
Hume, David. *A Treatise on Human Nature*. [S.l.]: The Floating Press, 2009.
Hägglund, Bengt. *History of theology*. Translated by Gene J. Lund. St. Louis, Mo.: Concordia Publishing House, 2007.
Jørgensen, Sven-Aage. "Hamann, Bacon, and Tradition." *Orbis Literarum* 16 (1961): 48–73.
Kenny, Anthony. *A New History of Western Philosophy*. Oxford: Oxford University Press, 2010.
Kleffmann, Tom. "Luther und Hamann als Theologen des Kreuzes." In *Johann Georg Hamann: Religion und Gesellschaft*, edited by Manfred Beetz and Andre Rudolph, 208–27. Berlin: de Gruyter, 2012.
Kobusch, Theo. "Nominalismus." In *Theologische Realenzyklopädie*, edited by Gerhard Müller, 589–604. Berlin, New York: de Gruyter, 1994.
Kolb, Robert, and Timothy J. Wengert, eds. *The Book of Concord*. Minneapolis, Minn.: Fortress Press, 2000.
Luther, Martin. *Werke: Kritische Gesamtausgabe*. Weimar: H. Bühlau, 1883-1990.
Matthews, Steven. *Theology and Science in the Thought of Francis Bacon*. Abingdon: Ashgate, 2008.
McKnight, Stephen A. *The Religious Foundations of Francis Bacon's Thought*. Columbia, Mo.: University of Missouri Press, 2006.
Moustakas, Ulrich. *Urkunde und Experiment: Neuzeitliche Naturwissenschaft im Horizont einer hermeneutischen Theologie der Schöpfung bei Johann Georg Hamann*. Theologische Bibliothek Töpelmann 114. Berlin, New York: de Gruyter, 2003.
O'Flaherty, James C., ed. *Hamann's Socratic Memorabilia: A Translation and Commentary*. Baltimore: Johns Hopkins University Press, 1967.
Plato. *Complete Works*, edited by D. S. Hutchinson and John M. Cooper. Indianapolis: Hackett, 1997.
Sandys-Wunsch, John. "Early Old Testament Critics on the Continent." In *Hebrew Bible/Old Testament: The History of Its Interpretation II: From the Renaissance to the Enlightenment*, edited by Magne Sæbø, 971-84. Göttingen: Vandenhoeck & Ruprecht, 2008.
Smith, Ronald Gregor. *J. G. Hamann: A Study in Christian Existence*. London: Collins, 1960.
Sparling, Robert Alan. *Johann Georg Hamann and the Enlightenment Project*. Toronto: University of Toronto Press, 2011.
Stolt, Birgit. *Martin Luthers Rhetorik des Herzens*. Tübingen: Mohr Siebeck, 2000.

Tyson, Paul. *Returning to Reality: Christian Platonism for Our Times*. Eugene, Oregon: Cascade Books, 2014.
Vestrucci, Andrea. *Theology as Freedom: On Martin Luther's "De servo arbitrio"*. Tübingen: Mohr Siebeck, 2019.
Walter, Gregory A. "The Crucified Body Signified by All." In *Johann Georg Hamann: Religion und Gesellschaft*, edited by Manfred Beetz and Andre Rudolph, 292–306. Berlin: de Gruyter, 2012.
Wolff, Jens. "Ästhetische Nuss oder Reliquie: Hamanns christologischer Symbolismus." In *Johann Georg Hamann: Religion und Gesellschaft*, edited by Manfred Beetz and Andre Rudolph, 334–45. Berlin: de Gruyter, 2012.

Alison Milbank
Let Everything that Hath Breath Praise the Lord

Eco-Theology and the Bible in the Poetry of Henry Vaughan and Christopher Smart

Abstract: In contrast to the mechanistic philosophy that came out of the scientific revolution, in which animals can be considered as mere automata, this paper argues for an alternative tradition through a biblical poetics. Recourse to the Hebrew poetry of the Psalms was made by the poet Henry Vaughan at the time of the Commonwealth in England, when Anglican worship was proscribed, and he turned to nature to provide a divine liturgy akin to the Book of Common Prayer. Influenced by Robert Lowth's Lectures on the Sacred Poetry of the Hebrews, Christopher Smart adopted his taxonomy of Hebrew poetic tropes in the long poem, Jubilate Agno, in which creatures and humans were paired to reveal divine perfections and offer an antiphonal liturgical offering. Through this psalmic poetry, then, a more active understanding of the participation of all living forms in the divine life became possible in what we would now recognise as an eco-theology.

Keywords: Henry Vaughan, Christopher Smart, Robert Lowth, Natural agency, Psalms

1 Introduction

From Lynn White's influential attack on Genesis 1.28's language of dominion as leading directly to the ecological crisis to the various contestations today between defenders and critics of the scriptural evidence, the Bible has been central to recent ecological debates.[1] Most discussion ignores any historical dimension, apart from frequent reference to Francis Bacon's assertion of human dominion as a God-given technological task, which is viewed as providing the

---

[1] Lynn White Jnr, "The Historical Roots of Our Ecological Crisis," *Science* 155 (1967): 1203–7.

Alison Milbank, University of Nottingham, alison.milbank@nottingham.ac.uk

driver of the scientific revolution.[2] It is known that many members of the Royal Society, such as Hooke and Robert Boyle, practised vivisection cheerfully, claiming that same dominion, so that objections were 'a discouraging impediment to the empire of man over the inferior creatures of God'.[3] Descartes' views were particularly influential in which natural forms are essentially inert: 'since art copies nature, and people can make various automata which move without thought, it seems reasonable that Nature should even produce its own automata, which are more splendid than the artificial ones – namely the animals.'[4]

While this negative approach to animals as mere machines in the seventeenth century is well known, this essay will demonstrate that a converse new respect for creatures arose at the same time, questioning Cartesian dualism, and having recourse to that same Bible and particularly the psalter for a more respectful and theological understanding of the natural order and a different construal of the human role towards it. While this more positive view can be found in some natural philosophers, I shall argue that the poets go even further, including the animal, vegetable and even mineral creation in liturgical *poiesis*. While the positive apprehension of the natural world in Henry Vaughan and Christopher Smart has been noticed by critics, I shall make new links between their writing and the method and theology of the Hebrew verse of the book of Psalms, and in particular, for Smart, the researches of Robert Lowth into Hebrew stylistics.

While Isaac Newton had a view of natural forms as inherently passive, he also, according to Voltaire, had a respectful view of animals and was a careful reader of the clerical naturalist, John Ray (1627–1705), who argued for the intrinsic worth of other creatures.[5] Ray's development of botanical taxonomy preceded, and in some senses went beyond, that of Linnaeus and he was also a proponent of physico-theology, a blend of science and theology, seen in his celebrated work, *The Wisdom of God Manifested in the Creation* of 1691 and the posthumously published *Three Physico-theological Discourses* of 1713. Like the poets to be examined here, Ray has frequent recourse to the Psalms where nature is presented as witness to God's wisdom and ordering power. This biblicism

---

[2] *Works of Francis Bacon*, trans. James Spedding *et al.* (London: Longmans Green, 1875), 14 vols, 4, Book 1, Aphorism 129 (129).
[3] Quoted in Margaret Boden, *Mind as Machine: A History of Cognitive Science* (Oxford: Oxford University Press, 2006), vol. 1, 73.
[4] René Descartes, Letter to Henry More, 5 Feb. 1649, in *Selected Correspondence of Descartes*, ed. by Jonathan Bennett, https://www.earlymoderntexts.com/assets/pdfs/descartes1619_4.pdf.
[5] See his "Eléments de la philosophie de Newton", in: *Oeuvres completes de Voltaire*, vol. 22 (Paris: Garnier, 1879), 422.

as method is clearly shown in his Preface, which is a catena of biblical and psalmic reference.

> The vast Multitude of Creatures, and those not only small, but immensely great, the Sun and Moon, and all the Heavenly Host, are Effects and Proofs of His Almighty Power. The Heavens declare the Glory of God, and the Firmament sheweth His Handy- Work, Psal. xix. 1. The admirable Contrivance of all and each of them, the Adapting all the Parts of Animals to their several Uses, the Provision that is made for their Sustenance, which is often taken Notice of in Scripture, Psal. cxlv. 15, 16. The Eyes of all wait upon Thee: Thou givest them their Meat in due Season. Thou openest Thy Hand, and satisfieft the Desire of every living Thing. Matth. vi. 26. Behold the Fowls of the Air, for they sow not, neither do they reap nor gather into Barns yet your Heavenly Father feedeth them. Psal. cxlvli. 9. He giveth to the Beast his Food, and to the young ravens when they cry. And, Lastly, Their mutual Subserviency to each other, and unanimous conspiring to promote and carry on the Publick Good, are evident Demonstrations of His Sovereign Wisdom. [6]

Furthermore, it is this biblicism that enables Ray to move beyond the Cambridge Platonist understanding of Henry More and Ralph Cudworth in an immanent but irrational spirit within nature, since the indwelling wisdom of God in the Hebrew Bible is active and intentional for Ray, as can be seen in the active verbs of the above passage. Notably, his creatures not only exhibit virtue but "unanimously conspire" to promote the Common Good. Most originally, Psalm 104:24 – "O Lord, how manifold are thy works! In wisdom hast thou made them all: the earth is full of thy riches" – leads Ray to justify the existence of flies, which serve no human purpose (as it was then believed) but are made by God's free creative power *ex nihilo*, "to enjoy themselves".[7]

This is in stark contrast to the kind of natural philosophy which seeks utility only in order to prove God's creative hand at work and which was then prevalent. Although Ray approves of Descartes, who was considered to have given new arguments in favour of divine order in the world, this concept of animal delight and enjoyment is quite new. I would argue that it is the language of Psalms and other poetic parts of the Old Testament, which encourages this new attention to creaturely agency. The same psalm which frames the fly, Psalm 104:26, also contains an idea of a great sea monster enjoying himself, without any concept of utility: "there go the ships, and there is that great Leviathan: whom thou hast made to take his pastime therein." As we shall see, it is Bible interpretation that often drives new envisioning of natural forms and creatures.

---

[6] John Ray, *The Wisdom of God Manifested in the Works of the Creation* (London: Samuel Smith, 1691), 6–7.
[7] Ray, *Wisdom of God*, 128.

It is God's wisdom (based on Proverbs and the Wisdom of Solomon) which enables creatures to act for the public good, which accords them some sort of intuitive moral agency.

2 Henry Vaughan and the Liturgy of Nature

The earliest example of this creaturely agency can be found in the work of a religious poet, Henry Vaughan (1621–95), who was a contemporary of Ray. Vaughan was an Anglican (his twin brother was an Anglican priest and alchemist) who turned in the period of the Civil War and Republican Presbyterianism to nature as the only possible site for a sacramental worship now proscribed in the church building. His poetry takes biblical tropes to form poetic liturgies of praise and his 'church' is now the natural world of creatures and forms. In "The Morning Watch," nature's sounds form "hymning circulations" as "birds, beasts, all things / Adore him in their kinds" and "all is hurled / In sacred *hymns*, and *order*, the great *chime* / and *symphony* of nature."[8] Where church bells and musical liturgies fall silent, the chime of the different natural forms of life and their varied song fills the liturgical lacuna.

Vaughan naturally invokes the language of the scriptures to describe this creaturely liturgy, as in "The Bird":

> All things that be, praise him; and had
> Their lesson taught them, when first made.
> So hills and valleys into singing break,
> And tho' poor stones have neither speech nor tongue,
> While active winds and streams both run and speak,
> Yet stones are deep in admiration.[9]

Like John Ray who uses the psalms to describe the active agency of nature, here Vaughan also imitates scripture's employment of moving forms. In Psalm 114:4 "the mountains skip like rams" and in Isaiah 55:8 the mountains also sing, leading to "hills and valleys into singing break". The warrant for stones' participation lies in the words of Christ himself in Luke 19.40 where stones are a witness: "And he answered and said unto them, I tell you that, if these should hold their peace, the stones would immediately cry out."

---

[8] Henry Vaughan, "The Morning-Watch," *The Complete Poems*, edited byAlan Rudrum (Harmondsworth: Penguin, 1983), 179.
[9] Vaughan, "The Bird," *Complete Poems*, 261.

Here even the seeming inanimate is actually contemplating the divine plenitude, and understanding itself as stone, in the manner of his contemporary, the philosopher Ann Conway, for whom all nature including humankind meditates through its material instantiation.[10] Vaughan frequently makes analogies between humankind and the mineral orders, seeing humans as basically "dust" and stones, and the very mortality of human nature is aided by the divine call to stones to witness: "So that both stones, and dust, and all of me / Jointly agree / To cry to thee".[11] This poem is again quasi-liturgical, entitled, "Church-Service," in imitation of George Herbert's organising form of "The Temple" for his divine poems, with individual lyrics imitating different parts of the structure, including the floor.[12] So human and stones here are "jointly", jointed as if parts of a stone floor of a church, as well as jointed like a body, evoking also Ezekiel 37's vision of the valley of the dry bones, requiring a divine voice to animate them. Elsewhere, this liturgical role for birds leads to an understanding of their nature that is far from Descartes' automaton, as in "Cock-Crowing:"

> Father of lights! What sunny seed
> What glance of day hast thou confined
> Into this bird? To all the breed
> This busy ray thou hast assigned;
> Their magnetism works all night,
> And dreams of Paradise and light.[13]

"Father of lights" is a quotation from James 1:17, referring to the divine origin of all gifts but Vaughan is also employing the hermetic language of his brother Thomas, the priest and practical alchemist:

> For she [the *anima* or soul] is guided in her operations by a spiritual metaphysical grain, a seed or glance of light, simple and without any mixture, descending from the first Father of lights. For though his full-eyed love shines on nothing but Man, yet everything in the world is in some measure directed for his preservation by a spice or touch of the first intellect.[14]

---

10 See Anne Conway, *The Principles of the most Ancient and Modern Philosophy*, translated by Allison Coudert and Taylor Corse (Cambridge: Cambridge University Press, 1996), 9, 9, 70 on stones.
11 Vaughan, "Church Service," *Complete Poems*, 182.
12 George Herbert, "The Church Floor," in *The Temple, The Complete English Poems*, edited by John Tobin (London: Penguin, 1991), 60.
13 Vaughan, "Cock-crowing," *Complete Poems*, 251.
14 Thomas Vaughan, *Anima Magica Abscondita*, cited in Vaughan, *Complete Poems*, 597.

In this hermetic discourse of "seeds" and "magnetism", creatures fulfil their divinely gifted role by instinct, but Thomas Vaughan describes this more actively as "a touch of the first intellect". And his brother suggests that the cock's own dreams are of Paradise, and that a divine ray or seed of intellect visits the bird. If this seems somewhat unorthodox for Anglican thought, note how it is allied to a reference to "full-eyed love", which is a quotation from Anglican cleric George Herbert's highly orthodox poem, "The Glance," where in Paradise, God "shalt look us out of pain" by the glance of "full-eyed love".[15]

Although the hermetic elements look forward to a proto-Romantic view of nature Vaughan's is a specifically biblical vision, which allies with theological accounts of the psalms. Gerald Blidstein asserts quite strongly that contemplation of nature is not the focus of the psalms. Rather the reader "revel[s] in that existence to which nature points".[16] Janet Soskice also affirms that attention to creation in the Bible is generally about the Creator whom it signifies.[17] Furthermore, Terence Fretheim suggests that it is to avoid natural forms being treated as gods that the Psalms have this strong focus on nature praising God, to avoid natural creatures or living forms receiving worship themselves.[18] For Vaughan, nature's doxology is so important because it offers the liturgical and ecclesial community he so lacks and in the process he offers the role of contemplation even to the inanimate. In making praise the mode of connection between plants and creatures, wind and rivers, Vaughan presents in a union of biblical and Neoplatonic form the panoply or *pleroma* of a rich diverse and multiple reality unified by its created status. Creation *ex nihilo* here becomes itself a mode of intimate relation rather than the distant clock-winding of the deistic divine who then withdraws, allowing immutable laws to operate.

3 The Study of Hebrew Poetry and Poetic Practice

Compared to other religious poets of the seventeenth century, from Donne and Herbert to Marvell and Milton, Vaughan stands out in his understanding of the active participation of creatures and in his melding of biblical theology and hermeticism. What makes such a vision of an active agency in nature possible in the

---

15 Herbert, "The Glance," *Complete English Poems*, 163.
16 Gerald J. Blidstein, "Nature in *Psalms*," *Judaism* 13, 1 (Winter, 1964): 29–36 (30).
17 Janet Martin Soskice, "Creation and the Glory of Creatures", *Modern Theology* 29, 2 (2013): 172–85 (174).
18 Terence Fretheim, "Nature's Praise of God in the Psalms," *Ex Auditu* 3 (1987): 18–30 (36).

next century is, in my opinion, a renewed critical interest in Hebrew Poetry. From the Reformation onwards, as various studies have shown, biblical poetic paraphrase became the preferred mode for a protestant and puritan poetic practice, such as that of Sir Philip Sidney and his sister.[19] At the same time the psalms were often recited or sung in British church services in the metrical translations of Sternhold and Hopkins. The eighteenth century followed the example of Isaac Watts, who produced a whole psalterful of translations in the late seventeenth century, with a plethora of psalm translation appearing in print.[20]

The eighteenth century also witnessed an increasing scholarly interest in Hebrew poetry. David Norton's study shows that Robert Lowth was not the first in this field (where several French studies preceded him), but his lectures from 1741–51 as Oxford Professor of Poetry, *Praelectiones Academicae de Sacra Poesi Hebraeorum* (*On the Sacred Poetry of the Hebrews*), first published in Latin in 1753 and in English in 1787, were highly influential throughout Europe.[21] Necessarily, he focused a great deal on the psalms, and paid careful attention to their use of parallelism, defining, in his later study of Isaiah, three main sorts in Hebrew poetry: synonymous, in which a first phrase is repeated in different words; antithetic, in which a contrary is expressed to the first phrase; and synthetic, in which the first phrase is echoed.[22] Interestingly, he saw this structure as liturgical from the beginning, for he viewed the Hebrew word for poetry, *mizmor* as involving a separation or cesura, as was appropriate for music and dancing in worship being "performed by two choirs, taking their parts alternately in each".[23]

The possible sublimity of biblical language had been noted by Longinus, in *On the Sublime*, which came back into popularity with French and English translations in the late seventeenth and early eighteenth century. He wrote: "A similar effect was achieved by the lawgiver of the Jews—no mean genius, for he both understood and gave expression to the power of the divinity as it deserved—when he wrote at the very beginning of his laws, and I quote his words: 'God

---

19 See Hannibal Hamlin, *Psalm Culture and Early Modern English Literature* (Columbus OH: Ohio State University Press, 2007).
20 See Rivkah Zim, *English Metrical Psalms: Poetry as Praise* (Cambridge: Cambridge University Press, 2003) and Roger Lund, "Making an Almost Joyful Noise: Augustan Imitation and the Psalms of David," *Journal for Eighteenth-Century Studies* 39:1 (March 2016): 121–39.
21 David Norton, *A History of the Bible as Literature*, 2 vols. (Cambridge: Cambridge University Press, 1993), 2, 59–72. Robert Lowth, *Lectures on the Sacred Poetry of the Hebrews*, 2 vols (London: L. J. Johnson, 1787).
22 Robert Lowth, Isaiah. A New Translation; with a Preliminary Dissertation (London, J. Nichols, 1778), x–xi.
23 Lowth, *Isaiah*, 1.

said,'—what was it?—'Let there be light, and there was. Let there be earth, and there was.'"[24] It was the brevity and concision of the Genesis verse that rendered it sublime and transporting, qualities Lowth too emphasizes in Hebrew poetry, along with the grandeur of thought and passion of feeling such tropes induce: "literary excellence capable of arousing feelings of sublimity".[25]

It was, above all, natural forms of life which enabled sublime feeling in Longinus and similarly in Lowth's analysis of Hebrew Poetry. Lecture VI is devoted to "Poetic Imagery from the Objects of Nature" and Lowth notes that there are upwards of 250 botanical terms used in the Psalms, with great emphasis on such sublime sources as mountains and seas.[26] This poetic nature is animated by the poet and seen as constitutive of a divine temple, especially in Lowth's insightful interpretation of the celebrated nature psalm, Psalm 104, which we have already seen as central to Ray's vision of wisdom in creation, as expressive of various aspects of the tabernacle. So "stretching out the heavens as a curtain" refers to the veil across the holy of holies, "making the clouds his chariot" to the cloudy pillar before the ark and so on.[27]

4 The Influence of Lowth on Christopher Smart's Cosmic Liturgy

By this architectural and liturgical reading of natural imagery, Lowth begins to elide nature and culture, as each, as he states, is emblematic of the divine artist. He encourages, thereby, the idea that water, air and stars participate in a universal worship. Among his appreciative readers, none was more effusive than the poet Christopher Smart, who described the Latin version of Lowth's *Sacred Poetry* as "for its elegance, novelty, variety, spirit, and (I had almost said) divinity [...] one of the best performances that has been published for a century."[28] Smart was already a poet of divinity, with a series of Seaton prize poems published on diverse divine attributes. The prize was the bequest of a cleric, Thom-

---

24 Longinus, *On the Sublime*, in *Classical Literary Criticism: Aristotle, Horace, Longinus*, trans. T. S. Dorsch (Harmondsworth: Penguin, 1965), 9, 9 (111).
25 Lowth, *Lectures*, 1, 115.
26 Lowth, *Lectures*, 1, 78, 87.
27 Lowth, *Lectures*, 110–2. Psalm 104:2–3. All translations of the Psalms are taken from *The Book of Common Prayer* (London: Cambridge University Press, nd).
28 Christopher Smart, 'S', "De Sacra Poesi Hebraeorum Praelectiones Academicae a Roberto Louth", *Universal Visiter and Monthly Memorialist* 1, no 1 (Jan 1756): 23–27 (23).

as Seaton, a fellow of Clare College, Cambridge, whose own poem, "Hymn XLII", on the role of creatures, was decidedly Cartesian, and indicates the kind of approach that Vaughan's poetry moved away from:

> Why is all Nature dumb but we?
> A base, ungrateful Train,
> Whose Tongue is rarely form'd to praise
> And therefore formed in vain.
>
> O that the Birds and Beasts say I
> And every Insect small,
> Knew the wise Hand that form'd 'em thus
> They'd on their maker call.[29]

Creatures in Cartesian mode lack language and reason and are therefore unable to praise God. Instead, the speaker must offer praise on behalf of the whole natural order. In his early Seatonian poems, Smart is already being more speculative and appreciative of the role of animals and plants. In "On the Omniscience of the Supreme Being", he employs the language of the hierarchical chain of being paradoxically:

> Woeful vicissitude! When Man, fall'n Man,
> Who first from Heav'n from gracious God himself
> Learn'd knowledge of the Brutes, must know by Brutes
> Instructed and reproach'd, the scale of being;
> By slow degrees from lowly steps ascend,
> And trace Omniscience upwards to its spring![30]

Implied here is the fact that, although taught by God to name the creatures, humankind falls in the chain of being as a result of having obeyed the serpent rather than God. Yet now, by observing divine wisdom at work in the created order, humanity must ascend in knowledge from the creatures back to their Maker. Indeed, humans are "reproach'd" by the better behaviour of animals and instructed by them in a way not possible in a Seatonian universe of dumb beasts. Furthermore, in "On the Power of the Supreme Being", a poem orches-

---

29 Quoted in Chris Mounsey, Christopher Smart, *The Clown of God* (Bucknell University Press), 211-12. See also Thomas Seaton, *A Compendious View of the grounds for Religion Both Natural and Revealed in Two Dissertations* (London: L. J. Robert, 1734). Seaton already seeks to ally natural and revealed religion as relying on the same foundation (2).
30 Christopher Smart, "On the omniscience of the Supreme Being," *Selected Poems*, edited by Karina Williamson (London: Penguin, 1990), 25–30 (29).

trating cataclysmic natural upsurgings of divine power, in which forests are uprooted and mountains hurled, natural living forms are addressed directly by the speaker as interlocutors:

> Ye thunders, earthquakes, and ye fire-fraught wombs
> Of fell Volcanos, whirlwinds, hurricanes
> And boiling billows hail! In chorus join
> To celebrate and magnify your Maker.[31]

The model here is from the Benedicite, the canticle from Morning Prayer in the Anglican service, the words from Daniel 3:23 in the Septuagint version of that book, usually entitled, "The Song of the Three Children" in the furnace. It begins, "O all ye works of the Lord, bless ye the Lord: praise him and magnify him for ever" and then moves to call on various natural phenomena and creatures, including humankind, with the same refrain.[32] The authority for this invocation in Smart's poem is therefore biblical, and the poem begins, "Tremble, thou earth! Th'anointed poet said", quoting Psalm 114:7, where King David, anointed king and inspired prophet, gives the warrant to address nature. Later in the poem, nature is compared to a vast machine, but one that consciously feels in every spring and wheel. Smart's theological and poetic vision is straining under the mechanical orthodoxy as did many in the light of the London earth tremors of 1750, three years earlier. The physical sound of thunder and volcanic irruption usually seen as God's voice, can turn creaturely through the authority of the Benedicite. Note how the Bible is thereby the motor which allows the beginnings of a more inclusive attitude to other natural beings, as well as the Book of Common Prayer, which was, of course, equally important for Vaughan.

As for other religious poets of the time, King David would become Smart's ideal of the poet of divinity, and as such, the poet of nature.[33] He would later write his own psalm paraphrases, compose hymns on the liturgical year and address "A Song to David". Yet his poetic fame now rests less on these than on works composed while he was a patient in an asylum for the mentally ill from 1758/9 to 1763, his incarceration precipitated, ironically for someone so concerned with the liturgical in his verse, by his incessant public prayer. These poetic sequences, entitled, *Jubilate Agno,* were only brought to light and pub-

---

31 Smart, "On the Power of the Supreme Being," *Selected Poems,* 30-34 (32).
32 *Book of Common Prayer,* 8–10.
33 See Joanne Murray, "*Jubilate Agno* as Psalm," *Studies in English Literature 1500-1900* 20:3 (Summer 1980): 249–50.

lished in 1939 and they show a development in Smart's study of Hebrew poetic structure.

In imitation of the Hebrew poetry as translated in the Authorised Version of the Bible, the poems are unrhymed. The title for the fragments (as such they are, and their order is disputed) is also taken from the psalms. "Jubilate Deo" is the title of Psalm 100, which begins "O be joyful in the Lord, all ye lands: serve the Lord with gladness, and come before his presence with a song".[34] It is included as a canticle in the Anglican service of Morning Prayer. Here, the praise is addressed to Christ as the Lamb, stressing the Christian nature of the praise offered, with Christ addressed as the Lamb of God in John 1:29 and worshipped in this form in Revelation 5, where in verses 13–14 all created things in heaven, earth, the sea and under the sea cry praises, to which the four living creatures respond, Amen. Again, this offers a biblical warrant and authority for the inclusion of creatures apart from the human as liturgical participants, and with a voice, which Seaton had denied them.

In the structure of the poem, Smart makes use of Lowth's presentation of Hebrew poetry as that of call and response between two groups, but in contrast to the Anglican liturgical arrangement of cantoris and decani groups of choristers, who sit on the cantor's or dean's side of a cathedral, and who sing the psalms antiphonally across the quire, the main two groups for this poetic litany are humans and non-human creatures, ranging in the latter group from porcupines to sea-shells. For the opening lines declare: "let man and beast appear before him and magnify his name together".[35] Fragment A has sections all beginning with "let" and match a person with a creature that illuminates his or her character; the human figures are presented in roughly chronological order through the Old Testament. The employment of the jussive subjunctive, "let", is a hortatory form much in use in the Coverdale psalm translation of the psalms in the Anglican Prayer Book. Its grammatical form is important because it takes the subjunctive form as far in the direction of command as it can go. What the subjunctive element adds is an idea of co-operation and freedom, since it is, after all, subjunctive and not an actual imperative, as it is in the Hebrew. Another meaning, moreover, of the verb to "let" is to allow to happen, which further stresses the fact that to call to praise is to enable the flourishing of the person addressed. And although most examples in the psalm translations refer to people, some are addressed to non-human entities, as in Psalm 98:8-9: "Let the

---

34 *Book of Common Prayer*, Psalm 100, 613 in the Psalter and 77–8 as part of the office of Morning Prayer.
35 Smart, "Jubilate Agno," *Selected Poems*, A3, 43.

sea make a noise and all that therein is: the round world, and they that dwell therein. Let the floods clap their hands, and let the hills be joyful together before the Lord." The most famous biblical "let" in the English Bible is that same Genesis 1:3, "let there be light" that Longinus found so productive of the sublime. In Genesis the voice is divine and creative; the human "let" in Smart's poem is the speaker calling the natural and human worlds to respond: to demonstrate that to be created is to be called into relation with God.

Here is an example of a typical grouping of "let" exhortations in *Jubilate Agno*:

> Let Barzillai bless with the Snail – a friend in need is as the balm of Gilead, or as the slime to the wounded bark.
> Let Joab with the Horse worship the Lord of Hosts.[36]

Barzillai the Gileadite helped King David in his flight from Absalom in 2 Samuel 19:32, offering consolation, Smart suggests, the "balm of Gilead" spoken of in Jeremiah 8:22. It is extracted from trees as a resin and so Smart imagines the snail's slimy trail on the tree as consoling the tree for its lost oil. Man, creature and tree are equally bringers of comfort. Joab, on the other hand is a brave and astute general for King David in 2 Samuel but colludes with him over the killing of Uriah, deserts David for Adonijah and kills his replacement as general. He is part of the liturgical action but the pairing with a horse, in my view, suggests his moral limitations. Psalm 147:10 is apposite here: "He [the Lord] has no pleasure in the strength of an horse: neither delighteth he in any man's legs." As a figure of strength and ability Joab is impressive, but physical ability alone is not enough in horse or man. Moreover, horses are obedient, which Joab proved not to be. However, the ability and courage of Joab in battle allies him with the power of God: "the Lord of Hosts". There is also a Christological reference in that in Revelation 19:11-16 Christ appears on a white horse with a sword as a warrior, with "Lord of Lords and King of Kings" on his vesture (v.16).[37]

In these two cases, as in many others in Fragment A, the creature and plant are descriptors of or comments upon the human being, rather like an emblem or a medieval bestiary in which a creature represents both virtue and vice. In such bestiaries, the warlike temperament of the horse is emphasized, while his virtue is often shown in loyalty to his rider: a virtue that Joab signally lacks.[38] By these

---

36 Smart, *Jubilate Agno*, Fragment A, A59–60, 46.
37 On the horse emblem and its Christological use, see Louis Charbonneau-Lassay, *The Bestiary of Christ*, trans. and abridged D. M. Dooling (New York: Parabola, 1991 [1940]), 100–1.
38 Charbonneau-Lassay, *Bestiary of Christ*, 96.

pairings, Smart articulates a typology in which each human character is judged or celebrated by analogy with his or her creaturely partner. In effect, he is employing the mode of biblical parallelism which Lowth identified, in synonymous mode, but in this way the creatures are equivalents of the human agents. Smart refers to Lowth's taxonomy of parallelism directly in the poem:

> For the relations of words are in pairs first.
> For the relation of words are sometimes in oppositions.
> For the relations of words are according to their distances from the pair.[39]

The Fall means that meaning is sometimes distanced, even agonistic, in opposition, as we shall see below. And just as Vaughan saw the scale of being disturbed by the Fall, so that now humanity must learn from those originally lower in the chain, so must Smart's characters, who are either aided, illuminated or put in their place by the pairing with an example of the natural creation. His version of the Benedicite, therefore, does not move from inanimate to animate to human, but to and forth between human and creatures as equivalents, with Fragment A ending with the blackbird, whose sincerity and whole-hearted praise urges humans "to be of good cheer".

At certain points in the poem, Smart makes reference to Hebrew, most notably the latter *lamed* and there has been some critical discussion about the extent of his Hebrew studies.[40] It has never been suggested before, but it is possible he knew the Hebrew work, *Perek Shiruh*, an ancient Hebrew song or prayer, in which different parts of the creation, animals, plants and even places, speak verses of the scriptures, for example, "The Bat is saying: 'Comfort My people, comfort them, says your Lord.'" (Isaiah 1:40).[41] Whereas some of the words are highly appropriate, so that the raven says: "Who prepares food for the raven, when his young ones cry out to God?" (Job 38:41), the bat's role in comfort has no biblical warrant, since bats are unclean creatures, and are also associated with fearful places in Isaiah 2:20, but there may be a hint in the Hebrew meaning of the word as "one who flies in the dark". God's presence in the dark brings comfort, so that it seems the writer's purpose is to derive a divine pres-

---

[39] Smart, *Jubilate Agno*, B598–600, 100. Italics here and elsewhere are in the original printing of the poem.
[40] See Charles Parish, "Christopher Smart's Knowledge of Hebrew," *Studies in Philology* 58:3 (July 1961): 516–32 and Karina Williamson's notes on Smart's use of Hebrew in the Oxford edition of the poems.
[41] *Perek Shirah*, trans. at http://zootorah.com/assets/media/perek-shirah-booklet.pdf, accessed May 24, 2021.

ence everywhere, just as Smart seeks to do in his *lamed* section, where El or God is found in surprising places.

> For the letter ל [*lamed*] which signifies GOD by himself is on the fibre of some leaf in every Tree.
> For ל is the grain of the human heart and on the network of the skin.
> For ל is in the veins of all stones both precious and common.
> For ל is upon every hair both of man and beast.
> For ל is in the grain of wood.
> For ל is in the ore of all metals.
> For ל is on the scales of all fish.
> For ל is on the petals of all flowers.
> For ל is upon on all shells.
> For ל is in the constituent particles of air.
> For ל is on the mite of the earth.
> For ל is in the water yea in every drop.
> For ל is in the incomprehensible ingredients of fire.
> For ל is in the stars the sun and in the Moon.
> For ל is upon the Sapphire Vault.[42]

Note how the mark of the divine, the trace or *vestigium* to use the language of Bonaventure, is in everything from mites to water-drops, in parallel with the *Perek Shirah*'s universal reach but going further in its immanence.[43] For Smart's poem is highly Christological both in its sense of the Son as Creative Word forming language and world, and also in its incarnational theology, in which the Word takes on human nature and even, symbolically, the animal creation also in being called, the Lamb.

Fragment B, from which the "El" section is taken, is the longest of the four parts of the poem and the most complex. Smart now adds a clause beginning "for" to his initial "let" exhortation. Again, this is a common pattern in psalm translation, as in Psalm 95, which is a part of the Anglican service of Morning Prayer as the opening canticle, the Venite:

> O come, let us sing unto the Lord; let us heartily rejoice in the strength of our salvation.
> Let us come before his presence with thanksgiving: and show ourselves glad in him with psalms.
> For the Lord is a great God: and a great King above all Gods.[44]

---

42 Smart, *Jubilate Agno*, B477–91, 94–5.
43 See Philip L. Reynolds, "Bonaventure's Theory of Resemblance," *Traditio* 58 (2003): 219–55, where he predicates a common being to all created things.
44 *Book of Common Prayer*, 72.

This is a very clear example of parallelism of synchrony and echo, with its two "comes" and varied expressions of praise, and a cumulative synchrony in verse 3. The "for" verse gives a reason for the activity as it introduces a description of God's power in creation, which is followed by another "O come" and "for" sequence, which emphasizes the privileged role for Israel in his care.

Smart's usage is very similar to this, as new pairings of human and non-human are called to praise, and a reason based on scripture is offered in the "for" section:

> Let Abigail rejoice with Lethophagus – God be gracious to the widows indeed.
> For the Fatherless Children and widows are never deserted of the Lord.[45]

In 1 Samuel 25 Abigail's husband, Nabal churlishly refused aid to David, who had helped him in the past. The situation was only saved by Abigail's prompt action in offering help herself, although when Nabal is told of it, he falls dead and Abigail becomes the beloved wife of David. God was, indeed, gracious to this widow and her fate illustrates the prevalent biblical expression of God's care for the fatherless and the widow. Her story then validates the divine compassion. The lethophagus aids in a rather different way, as a worm that feeds off the bodies of the dead, and so enables the dissolution of the body of Abigail's unsatisfactory first husband. Fragment B is full of such examples of the "lower" creation as active participants in providential action, including shellfish such as winkles, and even a mermaid, while the human actors now include a range of classical figures as well as biblical and historical characters, including people known personally to Smart.

As the canvas of activity grows ever more cosmic, so too does the theological understanding of creatures and the non-human. The opening of Fragment A had already echoed Psalm 150:6: "let everything that hath breath: praise the Lord". Yet whereas the psalm is calling every person to praise, "all souls" or *ha-neshamah* in Hebrew, Smart interprets it as *ha-neshimah*, meaning, let every breath, for which there is some warrant in Jewish tradition.[46] So, Smart's speaker calls "every Creature, in whom is the breath of Life" to praise.[47] From B160 onwards, he develops this understanding of an animated universe in contradistinction to the 'vain deceit' of secular science, justifying it as based on scripture:

---

[45] Smart, "Fragment B," *Selected Poems*, B70, 58. Italics in the original as is the case in later quotations.
[46] See Shaul Wagschal, *The Practical Guide to Teshuvah* (New Brunswick NJ: Targum Press, 1991) 53.
[47] Smart, "Jubilate Agno," in *Selected Poems*, A2, 42.

"For I am inquisitive in the Lord, and defend the philosophy of the scripture against vain deceit."[48] For Smart, the Bible offers a more vitalist account of the Spirit active in living things as against the more passive account of matter in Newtonian physics in which the *vis insita* or power of resistance by an inert object is the most positive conception.[49] Smart's is a complex engagement, which is fruitfully and carefully articulated in Harriet Guest's study, but I believe what is at stake for him is the importance of witnessing to the activity of the Creative Word, the Logos, in nature, which is conceived as a plenitude in comparison with Newton's concept of the Void.[50] This can be seen in the following verses:

> Let Barsabas rejoice with Cammarus – Newton is ignorant for if a man consult not the WORD how should he understand the WORK?
> For there is infinite provision to keep up the life in all the parts of the Creation.[51]

As Guest points out, there is ample evidence of Newton's Bible study, but it is his failure to take his view of nature from a theological understanding of creation that is at issue. The Bible just does not present a world of dead matter but participation in a divine cosmic liturgy, which we have seen described in Lowth's interpretation of Psalm 104. For this reason, Smart was unwilling to accept the evidence of a vacuum in air-pump experiments, since God's spirit fills the whole world.[52] Instead he developed a more Hermetic understanding of resistance as the power of evil seeking to frustrate the divine spirit: *"For FRICTION is inevitable because the Universe is FULL of God's works."*[53] Thus, creatures are praising God but also witnessing by their praise to a rejection of evil.

This can be seen at work in the final section of Fragment B, which is the most well-known part of the poem, in the form of an extended description of Smart's only companion in the madhouse, his cat, Jeoffry. First, Jeoffry is involved in praise of God:

---

[48] Smart, "Jubilate Agno," in *Selected Poems*, B130, 64.
[49] Isaac Newton, *Newton's Principia: The Mathematical Principles of Natural Philosophy*, translated by Andrew Motte (New York: D. Adee, 1846), 73.
[50] Harriet Guest, *A Form of Sound Words: The Religious Poetry of Christopher Smart* (Oxford: Oxford University Press, 1989), 205 and 196–240 on the natural philosophy. See also Rosalind Power, "Christopher Smart's *Systema Natura*: Anti-Newtonianism and the Categorical Impulse," *Journal for Eighteenth-Century Studies* 37:3 (2014): 361–73.
[51] Smart, "Jubilate Agno," in *Selected Poems*, B220, 75.
[52] Smart, "Jubilate Deo," in *Selected Poems*, B219, 74.
[53] Smart, "Jubilate Deo," in *Selected Poems*, B185, 70.

> For at the first glance of the glory of God in the East he worships in his way.
> For this is done by wreathing his body seven times round with excellent quickness.
> For then he leaps up to catch the musk, which is the blessing of God on his prayer.[54]

Whereas in the psalms the primary focus had been on creatures witnessing to their divine making by their natural actions, Smart names a range of deliberate feline habits as constitutive of worship. Moreover, the numbering of the cat's circlings, significantly seven, the number of the complete virtues, consisting of four cardinal and three theological, as well as the seven gifts of the Spirit, accords to this worship a symbolic character. It also implies a deliberate ritual, with a blessing completing it as in any Anglican service. Then like a good follower of the golden rule of Matthew 7:12, having shown his love for God, Jeoffry loves his fellow-cat:

> For having consider'd God and himself he will consider his neighbour.
> For if he meets another cat he will kiss her in kindness.[55]

Even the mouse is shown mercy by being given a chance. Then at night his work of resistance begins:

> For he keeps the Lord's watch in the night against the adversary.
> For he counteracts the powers of darkness by his electrical skin and glaring eyes.
> For he counteracts the Devil, who is death, by brisking about the life.[56]

The cat's nocturnal perambulations as well as his very physical instantiation, ward off evil, while his "brisking", his giving himself to active living, denies the Devil, who is characterized in patristic tradition, as death itself. Where some eighteenth-century anti-Newtonianism was potentially atheistical in its vitalism, Smart employs such a natural philosophical stance for orthodoxy, for a fallen world, but one of universal life and agency, inspired by the Spirit. *"For the divine spirit comes about his body to sustain it in complete cat."*[57]

---

[54] Smart, *Jubilate Deo*, in *Selected Poems*, B697–9, 105.
[55] Smart, *Jubilate Deo*, in *Selected Poems*, B713–4, 106.
[56] Smart, *Jubilate Deo*, in *Selected Poems*, B717–20, 106.
[57] Smart, *Jubilate Deo*, in *Selected Poems*, B742, 107.

5 Smart's Presentation of a Biblical Divine Immanence

As with Henry Vaughan, Smart has recourse to Hermetic conceptions of matter and spirit in order to defend Christian orthodoxy and the doctrines of analogy and participation against reductive conceptions of creatures. The Oxford edition of the poem, indeed, cites Vaughan's brother Thomas a source for this spiritualised nature: "for Nature is the Voice of God, not a mere sound or command but a substantial active breath, proceeding from the Creator and penetrating all things."[58] Such a view denies the separation of human and creaturely realms and also of natural and revealed religion, since God is revealing himself actively through the natural order. As Smart puts it: *"For Earth which is an intelligence hath a voice and a propensity to speak in all her parts."*[59] This goes further than John Ray in identifying agency and intellect within nature, but it is still biblical. Psalm 100 begins: "O be joyful in the Lord all ye lands" while Psalm 96 has several references: "sing unto the Lord, all the whole earth" (v.1); "let the whole earth stand in awe of him" (v. 9); "let the heavens rejoice and let the earth be glad; let the sea make a noise" (v. 11). It might be argued that the use of earth or land here is a metonym for the people, but the Hebrew gives the word for earth long before that of the people in Psalm 96. Moreover, the pressure away from idolatry and towards the oneness of God in the Hebrew scriptures tends to render the physical universe as a series of signs rather than referents. To return to the remarks of Blidstein and Fretheim earlier in this paper, such is the theological method of the psalmist, but it has the effect of enabling an expression of God's immanence as well as his transcendence, or rather, in wholly orthodox fashion, the two go together.

The role of the speaker, which had earlier been that of a Davidic psalmist, awakening a congregation to worship, is now one of contemplation, as a Solomon who can see truly because he has the gift of divine wisdom. This contemplation of nature is particularly evident in the apocryphal book, The Wisdom of Solomon, which has always been part of the Anglican lectionary. In Chapter 7 Solomon gives a paeon of praise to Wisdom as she enables him to understand creation, from the orders of the seasons to the ways of birds and beasts. There she is described as "the breath of the power of God" and as "the brightness of

---

[58] Thomas Vaughan, *Works*, 84, cited in *The Poetical Works of Christopher Smart, Volume 1, Jubilate Agno*, edited by Karina Williamson (Oxford: Oxford University Press, 1980), 51.
[59] Smart, "Jubilate Deo," in *Selected Poems*, B234, 76.

the everlasting light, the unspotted mirror of the power of God" (Wisdom 7:25–26). There is no longer, in the later sections of Fragment B, a need for "let" phrases, for the creatures are already praising by their very life and activities, and contemplation is all that is necessary of a dynamic universe of divine plenitude, an "unspotted mirror".

6 Conclusion

In this essay we have come a long way from the automaton view of creatures and the inertness of matter, as well as from the dominatory interpretations of Genesis 1.28 that fuelled the scientific revolution.[60] In the poetry of Christian writers such as Henry Vaughan and Christopher Smart, rather than the Bible being the source of bad attitudes to creatures, it was the very same Scriptures, which they took as their hermeneutic for interpreting nature, that led to a new relationship between human beings and the natural order, which we might fairly see as implicitly ecological. Language and reason, the two characteristics seen as marking the human from the non-human, are identified in their poetry with the whole created order, although exhibited by habit and behaviour in the case of cats and earthworms. Nor is the human voice the only raised in articulate praise, for in this cosmic liturgy, all matter is sacramental and significatory: indeed, Smart's poetry in particular exhibits a kind of hylomorphism by which spirit shapes and pervades all matter. In Vaughan's poetry, nature performs the liturgy which human pride has neglected, while in both poets, natural forms teach, rebuke and lead the human. Above all, their poetry speaks of the natural order as one single web of complex relations. I wonder if the Romantic poet, Coleridge, had Vaughan and Smart in mind when he wrote his celebrated comparison of Greek and biblical poetry:

> It must occur to every Reader that the Greeks in their religious poems address always the Numina Loci, the Genii, the Dryads, the Naiads, &c, &c, – All natural Objects were dead – mere hollow Statues – but there was a Godkin or Goddessling included in each - In the Hebrew Poetry you find nothing of this poor Stuff ... In the Hebrew Poets each Thing has a

---

[60] See, for example, Francis Bacon, *Novum Organum*, edited by Joseph Devey (New York: Collier, 1902), Aphorism 3, 11: "Knowledge and human power are synonymous, since the ignorance of the cause frustrates the effect; for nature is only subdued by submission." See also the whole debate in Peter Harrison, *The Bible, Protestantism and the Rise of Natural Science* (Cambridge: Cambridge University Press, 1998).

Life of it's [sic] own, & yet they are all one Life. In God they move and live, and have their Being not *had*, as the cold System of Newtonian Theology represents but *have*.[61]

Studies of the religious poetry of this period have acknowledged its biblical basis, and even sometimes its critique of Newton in the case of Smart, but they have rarely united these themes or acknowledged the influence of the nascent literary study of the Psalms by Robert Lowth.[62] In beginning to trace this synergy, I hope to have demonstrated that in this later poetry, as well as in biblical poetics, the theology of the natural world is one which allows it agency and participation with human beings in the life and worship of God.

References

Bacon, Francis. *Novum Organum*, edited by Joseph Devey. New York: Collier, 1902.
Bacon, Francis. *Works of Francis Bacon*. 14 vols., edited by James Spedding. London: Longmans Green, 1875.
Blidstein, Gerald J. "Nature in *Psalms*." *Judaism* 13, 1 (Winter, 1964): 29–36.
Boden, Margaret. *Mind as Machine: A History of Cognitive Science*. Oxford: Oxford University Press, 2006.
Charbonneau-Lassay, Louis. *The Bestiary of Christ*, translated and abridged by D. M. Dooling. New York: Parabola, 1991 [1940].
Conway, Anne. *The Principles of the most Ancient and Modern Philosophy*, translated and edited by Allison Coudert and Taylor Corse. Cambridge: Cambridge University Press, 1996.
Descartes, Rene. *Selected Correspondence of Descartes*, edited by Jonathan Bennett, at https://www.earlymoderntexts.com/assets/pdfs/descartes1619_4.pdf, accessed 14 July, 2022.
Fretheim, Terence. "Nature's Praise of God in the Psalms." *Ex Auditu* 3 (1987): 18–30.
Griggs, Earl Leslie. *Collected Letters of Samuel Taylor Coleridge*. Oxford: Clarendon Press, 1956–71.
Guest, Harriet. A Form of Sound Words: The Religious Poetry of Christopher Smart. Oxford: Oxford University Press, 1989.
Harrison, Peter. *The Bible, Protestantism and the Rise of Natural Science*. Cambridge: Cambridge University Press, 1998.
Herbert, George. *The Temple, The Complete English Poems*, edited by John Tobin. London: Penguin, 1991.
Lowth, Robert. *Lectures on the Sacred Poetry of the Hebrews*, 2 vols. London: L. J. Johnson, 1787.

---

[61] *Collected Letters of Samuel Taylor Coleridge*, edited by Earl Leslie Griggs (Oxford: Clarendon Press, 1956–71), 2 #457.

[62] On Smart's critique of Newton see Powell, "Christopher Smart's Systema Naturae: Anti-Newtonianism and the Categorical Impulse in *Jubilate Agno*," and on the biblical imitation of the period, see Lund, "Making an Almost Joyful Noise". Many poets celebrated Newton, as James Thomson, in *Poem Sacred to the Memory of Sir Isaac Newton* (London: Andrew Millar, 1741).

Lowth, Robert. *Isaiah. A New Translation; with a Preliminary Dissertation.* London, J. Nichols, 1778.

Lund, Roger. "Making an Almost Joyful Noise: Augustan Imitation and the Psalms of David." *Journal for Eighteenth-Century Studies* 39:1 (March 2016): 121–39.

Newton, Isaac. *Newton's Principia: The Mathematical Principles of Natural Philosophy*, translated by Andrew Motte. New York: D. Adee, 1846.

Norton, David. *A History of the Bible as Literature*, 2 vols. Cambridge: Cambridge University Press, 1993.

Parish, Charles. "Christopher Smart's Knowledge of Hebrew." *Studies in Philology* 58:3 (July 1961): 516–32.

Perek Shirah at http://zootorah.com/assets/media/perek-shirah-booklet.pdf, accessed 24 May 2021.

Powell, Rosalind. "Christopher Smart's Systema Naturae: Anti-Newtonianism and the Categorical Impulse in *Jubilate Agno*." *Eighteenth-Century Studies* 37: 3 (2014): 361–76.

Ray, John. *The Wisdom of God Manifested in the Works of the Creation.* London: Samuel Smith, 1691.

Reynolds, Philip L. "Bonaventure's Theory of Resemblance." *Traditio* 58 (2003): 219–55.

Smart, Christopher. *The Poetical Works of Christopher Smart. Volume 1: Jubilate Agno*, edited by Karina Williamson. Oxford: Oxford University Press, 1980.

Smart, Christopher. *Selected Poems*, edited by Karina Williamson London: Penguin, 1990.

Soskice, Janet Martin. "Creation and the Glory of Creatures." *Modern Theology* 29, 2 (2013): 172–85.

Thomson, James. *Poem Sacred to the Memory of Isaac Newton.* London: Andrew Millar, 1741.

Vaughan, Henry. *The Complete Poems*, edited by Alan Rudrum. Harmondsworth: Penguin, 1983.

Voltaire, (François-Marie Arouet). *Eléments de la philosophie de Newton*, in *Oeuvres completes de Voltaire*, vol. 22. Paris: Garnier, 1879.

Wagschal, Shaul. *The Practical Guide to Teshuvah.* New Brunswick NJ: Targum Press, 1991.

White, Lynn. "The Historical Roots of Our Ecological Crisis." *Science* 155 (1967): 1203–7.

Zim, Rivkah. *English Metrical Psalms: Poetry as Praise.* Cambridge: Cambridge University Press, 2003.

Brandon K. Watson
The Divine Forwards: Karl Barth's Early Exegesis of the Pauline Epistles

Abstract: Karl Barth's identification of the divine life *in se* and *pro nobis* has been the subject of wide debate in Barth scholarship. The thesis outlined in this chapter is that Barth's mature doctrine of election is not a material departure from an earlier position but a more dogmatically elaborate position of his early biblical exegesis, particularly of Paul's epistles. The basis for Barth's innovative interpretation of the doctrine of election is not simply found in 1936(9) whereby Jesus is claimed to be the subject of election but in his reading of Paul in the 1920s. To support this claim, Barth's early exegetical lectures in both Göttingen and Münster are analyzed. In so doing, the chapter contributes to a growing field of scholarship mapping the development of Barth's doctrine of election and its consequences for theological construction.

Keywords: Karl Barth, Pauline Epistles, Biblical Exegesis, Trinity, Election, Doctrine of God

1 Introduction

Theology *is* exegesis or, as John Webster would have it, "theology is derivative from and governed by exegesis and directed toward exposition".[1] The two cannot be separated from one another; they are both mutually informative. How exegesis and theology work together can be seen clearly from Karl Barth's early engagement with Scripture and the Christian tradition. The importance of the biblical text to Barth's dogmatic formulation has been noted on numerous occasions. Outside of Barth's *Römerbrief*, however, little research has been devoted to Barth's early exegesis itself. His biblical exegesis permeates not only the University lectures he offered but, as the fine print sections of the *Kirchliche Dogmatik* attest, his entire dogmatic enterprise.[2] The dogmatic innovation would

---

[1] John Webster, "Relation beyond all Relations," in Karl Barth, *The Epistle to the Ephesians*, edited by R. David Nelson, transl. by Ross M. Wright (Grand Rapids: Baker Academics, 2017), 73.
[2] Cf. Gerhard Bergner, *Um die Sache willen: Karl Barths Schriftauslegung in der Kirchlichen Dogmatik* (Göttingen: Vandenhoeck & Ruprecht, 2015), esp. 120–61.

Brandon K. Watson, University of Münster, Germany, brandon.watson@uni-muenster.de

https://doi.org/10.1515/9783110768411-012

not be possible without Barth's basic conviction that the God to whom the Bible bears witness is self-determined and fully revealed in God's self-revelation of Jesus Christ as Lord. One of Barth's well-known innovations is his revision of the doctrine of election, construed as the self-election of Jesus Christ. Barth does not derive such language to speak of the mystery of election from thin air, nor does he simply correct the anthropological focus of the reformers; rather, he seeks to understand the mysteries of the God about whom the writers of the Bible spoke. For example, as support for the self-electing God in his mature doctrine of election, just after grounding his doctrine of election in John 1, Barth interprets Galatians 4:4, Ephesians 1:10, 23; 3:9, Philippians 2:10, and Colossians 1:15, 19; 2:9 among other key biblical texts such as 1 Corinthians 15:20, 2 Corinthians 4:4, and Hebrews 1:2–3.[3]

The aim of this chapter is to uncover evidence of Barth's trinitarian and christological understanding of election from within his biblical exegesis. The guiding question is: What evidence, if any, is there of Barth's radical reformulation of election in Barth's early exegetical lectures? Rather than focusing exclusively on Barth's dogmatic development as seen in his dogmatic publications, this chapter focuses on the root of Barth's dogmatic belief system and development: how he understood Paul to formulate a christological relationship between Trinity and election. Suffice it to say, Barth's biblical exposition has not been taken into careful consideration regarding key theological developments.[4] What is to be shown in this chapter is how Barth's theological exegesis of the Pauline epistles developed on the heels of the *Römerbrief* period.[5] The common treatment sidesteps Barth's early biblical exegesis, which is in large part due to availability of published resources.[6]

---

3 Karl Barth, *Die Kirchliche Dogmatik: Die Lehre von Gott*, II/2 (Zürich: EVZ, 1959), 106.
4 To claim as much is not to negate the work done on Barth's hermeneutics. See, for example, Richard Burnett, *Karl Barth's Theological Exegesis: The Hermeneutical Principles of the Römerbrief Period* (Tübingen: Mohr Siebeck, 2001), 125–220; and Michael Trowitzsch, "Pfingstlich genau. Zur Hermeneutik Karl Barths," in *Karl Barth in Deutschland (1921-1935)*, edited by Christian Link and Michael Trowitzsch (Zürich: TVZ, 2005), 363–91.
5 In Bonn, these exegetical lectures tapered off as he began work on the *KD*. Barth offered two more exegetical lectures in Basel in the winter semester [WS] 1937/38 on Colossians and in the summer semester [SS] 1938 on 1 Peter. See Christiane Tietz, *Karl Barth: Ein Leben im Widerspruch* (München: C.H. Beck, 2018), 491 n.16–21; Bruce L. McCormack, *Karl Barth's Critically Realistic Dialectical Theology* (Oxford: Clarendon Press, 1995), 416–17. For background during the Bonn years as well as after returning to Switzerland in July 1935, see Tietz, *Karl Barth*, 107–273; 273–318; and Eberhard Busch, *Karl Barths Lebenslauf* (München: Chr. Kaiser, 1975), 213–75; 276ff.
6 The availability of sources has of course had an effect on the historical reconstruction and tracing of theological development. The continuous publications made available in the

Such a filling in the gaps can assist treatments of Barth's development in the 1920s and 30s. What can be learned from Barth's treatment of Paul's epistles? How are early forms of Barth's doctrine of the Trinity and the Trinity's relationship to election informative for his dogmatic accounts and theological development? These particular questions are the focus of this chapter while keeping in mind the genre of the texts as lectures presented, not commentaries written, nor dogmatics developed. It is the contention of this chapter that while Barth's doctrine of election would later be deepened and sharpened, the christological foundations are laid in the 1920s and are largely Pauline in nature.

2 Barth's (Paul's?) Trinitarian Theology of Election

Before turning to the exegetical analysis, it is helpful to outline key insights gleaned from interpreting Barth's early exegesis of Paul's epistles. The present chapter does not aim at NT exegesis proper but seeks to understand how Barth understood Paul to conceive God, the God-world relation, and how Barth's understanding of election was evidenced as he sought to work out the trinitarian God of the Bible and Christian tradition as *in se* and *pro nobis*. To undertake a reading of the NT letters themselves with particular reference to the nuances of Barth's own "scientific exegesis" is a task for a later date.[7]

The developmental aspect of these lectures and works of Barth's early career is consequential. Barth's christocentrism was the consequence of Barth's reading of Paul. God's will, as seen from Barth's lectures in the 20s and 30s, is

---

Gesamtausgabe do indeed allow us to "draw new connections". Donald Wood, *Karl Barth's Theology of Interpretation* (New York: Rutledge, 2007), 175. Barth's lectures on Paul, however, are given scant treatment by Wood as evidence of Barth's overall exegetical trajectory. Cf. Donald Wood, "Exegesis," in *The Oxford Handbook of Karl Barth*, edited by Paul Dafydd Jones and Paul T. Nimmo (Oxford: Oxford University Press, 2019), 263–76. Barth's biblical exegesis (outside of *Der Römerbrief*) is not considered in some recent treatments of Barth on election. Cf. Wolf Krötke, "Erwählungslehre," in *Barth Handbuch*, edited by Michael Beintker (Tübingen: Mohr Siebeck, 2016), 221–6. At the same time, recent treatments highlight the importance and lack of attention to Barth's biblical exegesis in the discussion without delving into the exegesis itself. See Michael Gibson, "Barth on Divine Election," in *Wiley Blackwell Companion to Karl Barth*, edited by George Hunsinger and Keith L. Johnson (Hoboken: Wiley Blackwell, 2020), 53.
[7] Cf. Bruce L. McCormack, "The Significance of Karl Barth's Theological Exegesis of Philippians," in *Orthodox and Modern* (Grand Rapids: Baker Academic, 2008), 89–105.

single, free, and gracious. Without explicitly stating that Jesus is the object and subject of election as we find later in Barth's fully revised doctrine of election in 1936(9)–1942, which has proved to be the determining factor in tracing Barth's development, the grounds for Barth's innovation are evident in his interpretation of the biblical text.[8] There has been an emphasis on the role Pierre Maury played in Barth's doctrinal development, particularly given Barth's claim in the Foreword to Maury's 1957 *Predestination and other Papers*, where he says: "One can certainly say that is was he who contributed decisively to giving my thoughts on this point their fundamental direction."[9] Barth's doctrine of God is not speculative but concrete. The will of God to be gracious is the will of God grounded in God's becoming; the two cannot be separated just as the doctrine of creation cannot be separated from the doctrine of reconciliation. Barth's christological concentration and specification of God's being as an event cannot, likewise, be abstracted from how he interpreted the biblical texts themselves. Barth's later formulations may be preferred over those of Barth's earlier account given its descriptive specificity, but the roots, the grounding of Barth's developmental moves in the doctrine of God and Christology, are seen throughout his lectures on Paul's epistles. More attention to Barth as biblical exegete illuminates the material dogmatic moves Barth makes. At the very least, tracking the doctrine of election in Barth's development has to take into account his biblical lectures and exegesis *in addition to* his *Römerbrief* and subsequent dogmatic publications.

The significance of these early lectures of Barth cannot be overstated. As will be shown, the movement of God in Christ is the decisive factor throughout Barth's exegesis. The participatory nature of humanity being "in Christ" is pred-

---

[8] Having depended on Ingrid Spiekermann's dating of Barth's dialectical phase as ending in 1936, McCormack has since adjusted his dating to 1939 based on Matthias Gockel's study, which convincingly shows that "Barth's 'mature' doctrine of election did not emerge until he advanced the thesis that Jesus Christ is the subject of election ... (winter semester 1939–1940)". Bruce L. McCormack, "Forward to the German Edition of *Critically Realistic Dialectical Theology*," in *Orthodox and Modern*, 291–304, here 303. See Matthias Gockel, *Barth and Schleiermacher on the Doctrine of Election* (Oxford: Oxford University Press, 2006), esp. 104–97; McCormack, *Critically Realistic*, 455–63; Pierre Maury, *Election, Barth, and the French Connection*, 2nd edition, edited by Simon Hattrell (Eugene: Pickwick, 2019); and Matthew J. Aragon Bruce, "Election," in *The Oxford Handbook of Karl Barth*, edited by Paul Dafydd Jones and Paul T. Nimmo (Oxford: Oxford University Press, 2019), 309–24.

[9] Karl Barth, "Foreword," in Pierre Maury, *Predestination and other Papers*, translated by Edwin Hudson (Chatham: W.J. Mackay & Co, 1960), 15–18, here 16. Barth is referring to how he developed his thinking in the lecture material eventually becoming *KD* II/2 on the heels of lectures he and Pierre Maury held in 1936.

icated on the historical reality of the human Jesus. Abstracted from this historical person, the "in Christ" loses significance. Thus, the "in Christ" carries implications not only for the ontology of human nature and salvation. The Pauline phrase is also consequential for God's being and essence. The "in Christ" of Paul, as Barth sees it, is not directed to a pre-temporal bodiless deity. The being of God "in Christ" is always *in concreto* the human Jesus of Nazareth. God's being contains, and makes room for, human history within it. How the logical and ontological aspects of this particular understanding hold up to scrutiny is important. The way to discuss the historical enfleshment of the second person of the Trinity cannot, if one wishes to follow Barth, fall back on an abstract notion of a God behind God, of a *Deus absconditus* behind the *Deus revelatus*. The eternal being of God is contained in the closed circle of Jesus Christ as pneumatic human flesh. The being of God between the times cannot be scrutinized using human notions of historical analysis. In sum, God's being, both eternally and historically considered, in some way contains within it the enfleshment, the embodiment of the human Jesus. To unpack these claims, we will undertake a close reading of Barth's early exegesis of Paul.

3 Barth Interprets Paul

As Barth transitioned from local parish ministry to academic life, taking up the position of Professor of Dogmatics and New Testament Exegesis at the University of Göttingen, he coupled his treatment of the reformed tradition and dogmatics with exegetical lectures on Paul's epistles.[10] The claim that Barth does not make material connections between his dogmatic lectures and his biblical exegesis while in Göttingen is only partially true.[11] Fundamentally, Barth saw the conversation and cross-referencing to be done within the biblical text themselves, in particular the Pauline texts. His early biblical lectures provide evidence of how Barth was always thinking across the disciplines of dogmatics and exegesis. It was during the first lecture cycles in Göttingen that Barth undertook

---

[10] It wasn't only Paul's epistles, but for the sake of this chapter, these particular lectures are the focus. Critical themes regarding Barth's understanding of God's being and election can be found especially in his lectures in winter semester 1925/26 on John's Gospel, also repeated in Bonn in summer semester 1933. Cf. Karl Barth, *Erklärung des Johannes-Evangeliums*, Gesamtausgabe 2.9 (Zürich: TVZ, 1976).

[11] Christopher Asprey, *Eschatological Presence in Karl Barth's Göttingen Theology* (Oxford: Oxford University Press, 2010), 17.

work on Paul's Epistle to the Ephesians (WS 1921/22), Philippians (SS 1924), and Colossians (WS 1924/25).[12] Barth would repeat the courses on Philippians and Colossians back-to-back as Professor of Systematic Theology and New Testament Exegesis at the University of Münster four years later: Philippians (WS 1926/27) and Colossians (SS 1927). During the same semester, Barth held a Seminar on Paul's letter to the Galatians (SS 1927–WS 1927/28).[13]

Given Barth's repetition of the same lecture courses, the chapter follows the historical trajectory as much as possible. Beginning in 1921/22 with Barth's lectures on Ephesians, the chapter then moves into Barth's work on Philippians in 1924. Picking up just a semester later, in the Winter Semester 1924/5, Barth's interpretation of Colossians will be addressed and finally Barth's work on Paul's Epistle to the Galatians in 1927/28 will be explored.[14] Each of these lecture cycles is explicated with a particular focus on how Barth understands God's trinitarian being and election while being attentive to the historical and contextual elements.

3.1 Ephesians

Alongside a lecture course on the Heidelberg Catechism, Barth offered a one-hour exegetical lecture on Ephesians.[15] The entire course in WS 1921/22 was spent on the first chapter of Ephesians, save the last lecture on February 23, 1922 where he outlined the contents of chapters 2–6 and indicated the close of chap-

---

12 For background to Barth's Göttingen years, see Eberhard Busch, *Die Anfänge des Theologen Karl Barth in seinen Göttinger Jahren* (Göttingen: Vandenhoeck & Ruprecht, 1987).
13 For background and context to Barth's work during these years in Münster, cf. Busch, *Karl Barths Lebenslauf*, 178–211; Wilhelm Neuser, *Karl Barth in Münster 1925–1930* (Zürich: TVZ, 1985); and Tietz, *Karl Barth*, 163–85.
14 Presenting the material in this order, while chronologically ideal, is also difficult given the material used in each section is pulled from the various lecture series he held on the same book. However, most of the material remains largely consistent throughout each time he held the course. Cf. Karl Barth, *Barth-Thurneysen Briefwechsel: Band II 1921–1930*, Gesamtausgabe 5.4 (Zürich: TVZ, 1974), 741–2; hereafter cited as *Bw.Th.II*; Tietz, *Karl Barth*, 175, and for the lectures in Bonn, see Tietz, *Karl Barth*, 475 n.9; Karl Barth, *Barth-Thurneysen Briefwechsel: Band III 1930–1935*, Gesamtausgabe 5.34 (Zürich: TVZ, 2000), 981–2, hereafter cited as *Bw.Th.III*; and McCormack, *Critically Realistic*, 293–4, 378.
15 For a treatment of the lectures on the Heidelberg Catechism as well as how Barth developed a theology of confession, see Hanna Reichel, *Theologie als Bekenntnis: Karl Barths kontextuelle Lektüre des Heidelberger Katechismus* (Göttingen: V&R, 2015), here 29–92. Barth was also slated to offer a lecture course on Hebrews, but he had too much on his plate at the time. Cf. Barth, "(Rundbrief), 2. April 1922," in *Bw.Th.II*, 65.

ter 3 to be the high point of the epistle.[16] These lectures were based on earlier sermons, confirmation instruction, and detailed exegetical work. Barth wrote to Eduard Thurneysen on March 3, 1918 regarding his work with the confirmands: "I dared to do it, to do a cursory reading of the entire book of Ephesians with the confirmands. It didn't need anything more than a very aphoristic explication, which did not really do the entirety of the book any justice from afar."[17] From May 4, 1919 to September 7, 1919, Barth devoted a series of 18 sermons to the book of Ephesians.[18] The subsequent exegetical lectures were clearly influenced by the tremendous amount of work and time Barth had already devoted to the text. The decision to lecture on Ephesians was also motivated by practical reasons such as the move to Göttingen and finishing up his second edition of *Der Römerbrief*.[19] Given that the lectures have been published, one can clearly see Barth's christological development.

Paul's letter to the Ephesians is filled with language surrounding predestination, election, and adoption, most of which is contained in the first chapter. We first encounter Barth's understanding of Paul's "in Christ" from Ephesians 1:1–4, which sets the tone for the entire epistle, even central to Paul's overall thought.[20] Barth is already redirecting attention to whom Paul pointed in election rather than to the human recipients, claiming that Paul's doctrine of predestination is more sharply defined than one finds in either Augustine or the

---

16 Karl Barth, *Erklärung des Epheser- und des Jakobusbriefes 1919–1929*, Gesamtausgabe 2.46 (Zürich: TVZ, 2009), xii–xvi, 152; hereafter cited as *Epheserbrief*.
17 Barth, "Barth-Thurneysen, 5. März 1918," in Karl Barth, *Barth-Thurneysen Briefwechsel: Band I 1913–1921*, Gesamtausgabe 5.3 (Zürich: TVZ, 1973), 267–9; hereafter cited as *Bw.Th.I*. All translations in this chapter are the author's.
18 Karl Barth, *Predigten 1919*, Gesamtausgabe 1.39 (Zürich: TVZ, 2003), 173–334. Cf. Barth, *Epheserbrief*, x. Barth also wrote to Thurneysen that the book of Ephesians gave him enough material for the entire summer, and he spent a lot of energy and time with the text. Cf. Barth, "Barth-Thurneysen, 21. Mai, 1919," in *Bw.Th.I*, 327–8. Jörg-Michael Bohnet points to five separate times between the years of 1918–1920 where Barth was directly dealing with a translation and detailed notes to Ephesians. Cf. Jörg-Michael Bohnet, "Vorwort," in Barth, *Epheserbrief*, ix–xii.
19 Cf. Nina Dorothee Mützlitz, *Gottes Wort als Wirklichkeit: Die Paulus-Rezeption des jungen Karl Barth (1906–1927)* (Neukirchen-Vluyn: Neukirchener, 2013), 179–94.
20 Cf. Barth, "Safenwil, Sonntag, den 4. Mai 1919," in *Predigten 1919*, 178–80. Here, Barth goes into Paul's eschatological background in his use of the "in Christ" motif and is worth citing here at length: "Everything Paul has to say to us is short, sweet, and simple, *maintained* in the always repeated phrase: *in him*. In him, in Christ, Paul wants to say, is the change. We only have to look to Christ, since we can *no longer* confuse God with death, since *we only known him* as the living one, the creator, the mover. *Christ speaks* the living Word and *awakens* the living faith … the change that happens to us … understood in this way, is exhaustive as possible." Barth, "Safenwil, Sonntag, den 4. Mai 1919," in *Predigten 1919*, 178–9.

Reformers.²¹ Barth's intent, carried over from his work on *Der Römerbrief*, remained the same: to "understand *with* Paul".²² To overcome human-centered preoccupations, Barth suggests collapsing election, salvation, and hope into the One, as he understands Paul to be doing. In typical Barth fashion, a geometrical relation is used to show how the anticipated insight is only one sector in the entire circle thus far described, however, this one sector, the real insight of the blessing of God in Christ, is the sector of "a *circle*".²³ The synthesis, the enclosed circle if you will, of God's being and the being of the world is the encounter in Jesus Christ, where the only coherence is found.²⁴ Paul's consolidation into the One is not attributing a condition to God, but rather a reference to the "decisive moment of the *freedom* of God through which God differentiates God's self ... we should not confuse *this* conditionality with any conditionality in the *kosmos*, since this conditionality is the conditionality through the unconditional one doing the conditioning (*Bedingtheit durch den unbedingt Bedingenden*)."²⁵ This language of conditioning directs the reader of Barth away from ascribing anthropological necessities to election and to the divine self-differentiation in God's free electing activity.

Second, Barth interprets Paul's use of *agape* in Eph. 1:5 as the medium by which God determines God's self for humanity. He asserts: "The sovereign freedom and ruling power of God, whose outworking to us is always only grasped as electing, reveals itself in Jesus Christ as love, love of the *Deus absconditus* as our Father."²⁶ We are redirected to the source, the origin of the human-being, but ultimately the source of all being, God's love. God's love presents an entirely new disclosure of human existence. The election of elected-*being* is in Christ, the absolute Word of love as God's determination about humanity which comes "to *word* in the cross of Christ but comes as *God* to word in Christ's resurrec-

---

21 Barth, *Epheserbrief*, 91–5; 99.
22 Eberhard Busch, "Barth in Germany (1921–1935)," in *The Oxford Handbook of Karl Barth*, edited by Paul Dafydd Jones and Paul T. Nimmo (Oxford: Oxford University Press, 2019), 34–51, here 35.
23 Barth, *Epheserbrief*, 94.
24 Cf. Barth's 1919 sermon on Eph. 1:15–23, where he claims: "The world does not have its own life without God, separated from God ... The world is through God and in God, from God and to God. God is the life of its life, the power of its powers, the basis of its bases." Barth, "Safenwil, Sonntag, den 11. Mai 1919," in *Predigten 1919*, 182.
25 Barth, *Epheserbrief*, 99.
26 Barth, *Epheserbrief*, 102.

tion."[27] The evidence of the mystery that is God's eternal being is pre-determined, elected to come to speech, to *word*, in the historical existence of Jesus Christ. If discussion of God's pre-determined being is abstracted from the love that grounds God's very self-determined being, exegesis of Paul ceases as does dogmatic construction.

As Barth often warns, speaking of God having completely revealed God's reality in the person of Jesus Christ is not saying too much nor saying too little.[28] For, to say something, there has to be a subject who says it. And, for God to speak, God must be a subject. The presence of God in time, God's involvement in history, is not something to take lightly. Barth takes Paul at his word when he speaks about death and life. When he says these two words, he is referring to them in their entirety in God. Barth works out the logic of life-death and time-eternity in a progressive fashion from within the framework of resurrection, asserting: "Who says *time*, says body (*Leib*), and who says *eternity* in time, says the resurrection of the body (*Leib*). Embodiment (*Leiblichkeit*) is materiality (*Dinglichkeit*). Without materiality there is no individual. Without an individual, without a subject, there is no relation to God."[29] The real embodied flesh of Jesus Christ is eternity in time, God's eternal election of historical embodiment. The resurrection, according to Paul, is the location of eternity in time. The mystery of God's being *asarkos* is God's being self-elected in time *ensarkos*: God's being is a protologically conceived embodied being.

Barth closes his lecture on Ephesians 1:7–14 with a plea to the students not only to empathize, but to think after (*nachdenken*) the object of perception, whereby "we are relocated into the simultaneity with Paul, up until the point" where the object itself has to explain and address itself, the object understood as the incommensurable Jesus Christ.[30] God's self-moved being presented as a

---

27 Barth, *Epheserbrief*, 106. It is the resurrection of Christ that provides the grounds for the noetic standpoint to think or observe this One, according to Westerholm, in that "Christ's history presents the material points of reference that orient those who occupy this standpoint." Martin Westerholm, *The Ordering of the Christian Mind* (Oxford: Oxford University Press, 2015), 127.
28 Barth, *Epheserbrief*, 118. In fact, the notion of saying anything is a play into the theological dialogue Barth uses during these early lectures as an encounter between God and human beings. Cf. Asprey, *Eschatological Presence*, 24–6.
29 Barth, *Epheserbrief*, 144.
30 Barth, *Epheserbrief*, 133. The living word of God and the living faith in this word brings a fundamental change to the existence of the human person: "*this is the gospel*". Barth, "Safenwil, Sonntag, den 4. Mai 1919," in *Predigten 1919*, 178.

subjective object of perception is never still; it remains dynamic, which is and becomes, as Barth says, the "great divine *forwards!*"[31]

3.2 Philippians

Barth first lectured on Philippians in Göttingen in SS 1924 alongside his first course on the prolegomena to dogmatics.[32] Barth repeated his lectures on Philippians from Göttingen two and a half years later while at the University of Münster. The lectures on Philippians from WS 1926/27 are what exist in print and show Barth's intentions to make the "work readable for non-theologians".[33]

On the whole, Barth's lectures on Philippians follow a standard procedure. He engages in textual analysis throughout, weaving together exegesis of Paul's letter with his other writings, especially Romans, while at the same time engaging the Reformers as well as modern biblical interpreters. Before diving into the realities of God's justifying work in Phil. 3, Barth seems to find a rhythm in Phil. 2. In the Christ hymn, Barth directs attention to the self-elected agency of Jesus to humiliate himself in the form of human flesh. This humility of Jesus is concretely consequential for the people in Philippi living together in the faith. Humility is not treated by Paul in the abstract; when a person is self-absorbed, it is done *a priori*, not *a posteriori*.[34] If humility is treated abstractly then the abstraction turns into pride. The concrete ethical treatment Barth is after here is predicated on the reason and ground of all mutual respect and recognition: the self-humbling of Jesus. Jesus humbled himself, which is the infinite qualitative distinction of the *self*-humbling of Jesus Christ, who took on sin-ruled flesh.[35] Jesus was the active subject, not a recipient of the passive voice action; it was not a

---

[31] Barth, *Epheserbrief*, 147. Cf. Barth, "Safenwil, Sonntag, den 11. Mai 1919," in *Predigten 1919*, 184. In his dogmatic lectures in 1924/25, he relates the divine forwards to the purposes of God's rejection as always working from damnation to election, never the other way around: "God wants to go *forwards* with us, *not* backwards!" Karl Barth, *Unterricht in der christlichen Religion II: Die Lehre von Gott/Die Lehre vom Menschen 1924/1925*, Gesamtausgabe 2.20 (Zürich: TVZ, 1990), 193, hereafter cited as *UcR II*.
[32] Published as Karl Barth, *Unterricht in der christlichen Religion: Prolegomena 1924*, Gesamtausgabe 2.17 (Zürich: TVZ, 1985); hereafter cited as *UcR I*.
[33] Karl Barth, *Erklärung des Philipperbriefes* (München: Chr. Kaiser, 1928), Vorwort; hereafter cited as *Philipperbrief*.
[34] Barth, *Philipperbrief*, 50.
[35] Barth, *Philipperbrief*, 57.

fate that came over him but a step into un-recognizability, of being (and becoming) *incognito*.³⁶

Barth plays further with the concept of recognition in this passage. Jesus discards the knowability of his being by taking on flesh where the Father recognizes him and, at the same time, Jesus recognizes himself. Jesus' procession into the unrecognizable is based and grounded in the sovereign free will of God. Where the explication, the recognition of his procession, occurs is at Golgotha, or as Barth says, it comes to appearance or erupts to indicate the meaning of the self-humiliation of the eternal Son to take on flesh. There is no other Christ than the one who became human. Moreover, there is no second-subject of the divine will who raised Jesus from the dead and gave him the name above all names.³⁷ The recognition of oneself as completely lost, yet simultaneously justified and standing before God, is also predicted on the *one* encounter between God and human flesh. The human being is always a being in becoming.³⁸

Transitioning from Phil. 2 into Phil. 3, one feels the urgency with which Barth lectured as he explored the movement of God from eternity into time in the enclosure of human flesh and the ramifications thereof.³⁹ At the outset, Barth titles Phil. 3:1b–4:1 as "Justice from God". Paul's use of the first-person singular in Phil. 3:4–14 stands in contrast to Paul's use in Romans and Galatians, the significance of which is the immediate sublation of the subject through the irreversible relation of Christ to Paul and not of Paul to Christ.⁴⁰ Paul's knowledge of Jesus Christ as his Lord is the decisive factor indicating the self-grounding subject of the knowledge. The content of justification based in faith and not on the law is the point where Paul differentiates between physical-mystical and ethical-juridical approaches to redemption.⁴¹ Barth spends time developing the difference between self-justification and external-justification,

---

36 Barth, *Philipperbrief*, 57–9. Barth also uses the language of Jesus as *Inkognito* earlier in Göttingen. See Barth, *UcR II*, 174–7.
37 Barth, *Philipperbrief*, 59–61.
38 Barth, *Philipperbrief*, 102–3.
39 Barth held a lecture series over Phil. 3 in Danzig in 1926 along with Bultmann and others. Barth's lectures remain unknown. Cf. Barth, "Barth–Bultmann, 3. Dezember, 1925," in *Karl Barth–Rudolf Bultmann Briefwechsel 1911-1966*, Gesamtausgabe 5.1 (Zürich: TVZ, 1994), 60–1, hereafter cited as *Bw.B-B*. See also Barth, "Barth–Thurneysen, 8. Januar, 1926 (aus Danzig)," in *Bw.Th.II*, 393–4.
40 Barth, *Philipperbrief*, 91. Barth later claims that the contrast in Phil. 3:19–20 is similar to that of Colossians, yet the eschatological determination of such a contrast is more palpable here than in Galatians and Romans. Barth, *Philipperbrief*, 112–3.
41 Barth, *Philipperbrief*, 95–6.

ultimately interpreting Paul as offering a forensic account of justification in Phil. 4:9.[42] It is the subjectivity of God, the self-justification of God in Christ, where the origin of faith is located, where the positive notion of faith relativizes all religion, where faith is only understood as an act of failure.[43]

Barth closes his lectures with extended treatment of Paul's repeated "in Christ" in Phil. 4:7. Rather than indicating a biblical ethic here with Paul's closing exhortations, Barth dives into the true existence of the Christian, which is decisive in the event of being guarded, of a wall built around oneself.[44] When the commandment is good and the commandment is held, it converts the knowledge (*Wissen*) of the good commanded into knowledge of God (*Erkenntnis Gottes*).[45] The letter of Paul ends where it began: bearing witness to the event which encloses the entirety of humanity.[46] What is to be said regarding God's relation to the world in election and God's self-constituted being from Barth's exposition of Philippians? Two brief comments are worth noting. First, Barth likens, once again, the being of God in the coming of Jesus Christ to an enclosed circle. The human being of Jesus is enclosed, encompassed by the eternal being of God's triunity: there is no other Christ than the enfleshed Jesus. Second, Jesus' work of justification on the cross and in the resurrection, while a free and completely subjective act of God, originates in the eternal, single divine decree as mutual recognition.

---

[42] For a treatment of Barth's *Römerbrief* in this regard, see Bruce L. McCormack, "Longing for a New World: On Socialism, Eschatology and Apocalyptic in Barth's Early Dialectical Theology," in *Theologie im Umbruch der Moderne: Karl Barths frühe Dialektische Theologie*, edited by George Pfleiderer and Harald Matern (Zürich: TVZ, 2014), 135–49. The development McCormack draws out in Barth's *Römerbrief* is also contained in his interpretation of Paul's Epistles.

[43] Barth, *Philipperbrief*, 97–9. While the objectification of God's justification occurs here, Barth still recognizes a form of progressive sanctification. Along the way of the Christian life, there is an increasing grasping after while always remaining an "already not yet"; however, the grasping is not continuous personal progress: we are grasped by Christ Jesus, the singular subject who enables, not negates, human subjectivity. Cf. Barth, *Philipperbrief*, 103–5. Regarding the eschatological existence of the person Paul describes in Philippians, see McCormack, "The Significance of Karl Barth's Theological Exegesis of Philippians," in *Orthodox and Modern*, 102–5.

[44] Barth, *Philipperbrief*, 121–3: "God then steps in like a wall around the human with God's peace, secures the human heart, human thoughts, and Godself as the center of one's existence." Barth, *Philipperbrief*, 121.

[45] Barth, *Philipperbrief*, 123.

[46] Barth, *Philipperbrief*, 126.

3.3 Colossians

In WS 1924/25, while in Göttingen, Barth lectured on Paul's Epistle to the Colossians.[47] These lectures were repeated in SS 1927 in Münster, again in WS 1934/35 in Bonn, and for the last time in WS 1937/38 in Basel.[48] Corresponding to each of these lecture cycles Barth lectured on constructive dogmatics.[49] Since we are dealing with multiple years and lecture fragments, the interpretation takes a different method compared to the other sections. The larger strokes of Barth's dealings with Colossians are taking into account rather than treating isolated years or lecture series.

Reading Barth's lectures on Colossians is like watching a surgeon perform a precise incision. Every line is filled with cross-reference from Paul's other letters, acute Greek intertextual exegesis where the biblical text is self-interpretive, and references to a range of biblical scholars, philosophers, and theologians. Barth approaches the text with presuppositions, of course, yet these presuppositions are placed under critical scrutiny. In Barth's exegesis, he is also seeking something beyond Paul, something beyond the literal word of the apostle. Weaving together the tapestry, Barth addresses the historical-critical issues questions without attaching too much significance to them.[50] The canonical question carries more weight for Barth than does authorship. The fact that Colossians is canonical is an act of faith by the church first and foremost and bears the weight of the letter being a witness to divine revelation. The interpreter reads *with* and thinks *after* Paul.[51] The prevalent feature in Barth's work on Colossians is the freedom and grace of God. The Pauline "in Christ" plays, once

---

47 I am grateful to Kait Dugan, the Director of the Center for Barth Studies at Princeton Seminary, in Princeton, New Jersey. She helped me locate Barth's lecture manuscripts on Colossians and the surrounding lecture cycles for context as well as the typescript of portions of these lectures. Barth's lectures will be cited with *Kolosserbrief* followed by the corresponding year.
48 Thurneyson wrote to Barth that his 1924/25 Colossians lectures were sitting in front of him, presumably to give Barth feedback before he repeated the lectures in the coming months. See "Thurneysen-Barth, 13. April, 1927," *Bw.Th. II*, 495.
49 The first offering of these lectures in 1924/5 was at the same time as Barth's published UcR II. The second offering of these lectures coincided with his unpublished lectures Dogmatik I as well as his seminar on Galatians discussed in the next section. The Colossians lecture cycle in Bonn in 1934/35 corresponded with his lecture entitled Prolegomena 6. The final offering in Basel in WS 1937/38 corresponded to a seminar on natural theology and the continuation of his Kirchliche Dogmatik.
50 Barth, *Kolosserbrief 1924–25*, 2–5; Barth, *Kolosserbrief 1927*, 1–6; and Barth, *Kolosserbrief 1937–38*, 3–5.
51 Barth, *Kolosserbrief 1927*, 7; Barth, *Kolosserbrief 1937–38*, 2–5.

again, an important role in how Barth understands the concrete revelation of God in the human Jesus where the certainty of election lies.⁵² The truth of the gospel of Jesus Christ is identical with the word of God, the word of truth, and the foundation of the church. To hear the proclamation spoken is an act and occurrence of the same subject. The word is identical with the crucified and resurrected one. In Christ, faith, hope, and love are constitutively brought to the human being.⁵³

Barth references Paul's letter to the Corinthians and the significance of the aorist and future tenses of the resurrection of the dead which always stand behind Paul's speech regarding his apostleship.⁵⁴ The correlation of moments in time is, as Barth notes, an occurrence between the times in that the entirety of humanity, regardless of religious affiliation, has been transferred into the embodied existence of Jesus: the past event and the future expectation are one.⁵⁵ Throughout Barth's lectures, he builds his case based on Paul's writings regarding the eternal, yet concrete event of Jesus. As he shows in his simultaneous dogmatic lectures, "the election and not the damnation of all persons is the *aim* of the ways of God".⁵⁶ How is it that everything God has done can be contained in the objective event of a human being? According to Col. 1:15–17, it is because Jesus is with God, as God, and Godself the Lord of all creation.

God is self-differentiated from created reality. Despite God's invisibility "before the foundation of the world", God is not alone. Barth offers, on the basis of his interpretation of Col. 1:15, a communal and relational understanding of God as triune. He does not, however, use language of personhood. In God's own being, God has an otherness, a movement toward an other, and a self-repetition of who God essentially is in Godself.⁵⁷ The identity between God and the world, between God and humanity, is singularly located in the Son of God as the rescuer of the world. We are not dealing here with two separate "Sons of God", one temporally older than the other, but with the same Son, in whom the essence of God is grounded. As the Son of God, Jesus, the firstborn of all creation according to Paul, is the grounded impossible possibility where God differentiates Godself from the world. Barth ensures not to make creation necessary to God but grounds God's

---

52 Barth, *Kolosserbrief 1927*, 7; Barth, *Kolosserbrief 1937–38*, 10. Cf. also Barth, *UcR II*, 207.
53 Barth, *Kolosserbrief 1937–38*, 14.
54 Barth, *Kolosserbrief 1927*, 9; Barth, *Kolosserbrief 1937–38*, 16. Cf. also Karl Barth, *Die Auferstehung der Toten* (München: Chr. Kaiser, 1926), 60–63.
55 Barth, *Kolosserbrief 1924–25*, 12–3; Barth, *Kolosserbrief 1937–38*, 27–8, 41.
56 Barth, *UcR II*, 211.
57 Barth, *Kolosserbrief 1937–38*, 29–30.

being and act in love and freedom.⁵⁸ The hinge of Col. 1:18 works to correlate the ecclesiological (vv. 18–20) description of the function of the Son of God and the God-world relation (vv. 13–17). The significance of the pneumatic flesh of God has a complete substitutionary function and exists within the plan of God from eternity (not conceived as abstract timelessness) into time.

To say Barth offers *only* an objective account short-circuits Barth's dialectics. Barth clearly sees Paul as a (dialectical) witness to the reality of God's self-revelation of God in Jesus Christ. The mystery of God to which Paul rightly speaks is identical with the reality revealed in Jesus. Barth does not see God as eternally deliberating whether or not to create (or to enter into the same creation *ex nihilo*) as if there were an empty "idea" of God or a world without God: "In Christ, God is (God's entire essence correspondingly!) present as Godself and the world justified, in that God has taken up residence (*Wohnung genommen*) in Jesus."⁵⁹ The embodiment of flesh is eternity contained in time—a movement of God between the times. The correlations Barth builds dogmatically between God's being and eternity are based in his reading of Paul, which remain dialectical all the way through.

3.4 Galatians

To undertake a study on Barth's work on Galatians, one would need to take into account his entire life's work.⁶⁰ For our purposes here, we will focus on the material available for Barth's seminar on Galatians at the University of Münster. Barth's seminar on Galatians in 1927/28 lacks a full manuscript. The work done here on this seminar pulls from the student protocol of these seminar offerings as well as other works during these two semesters.⁶¹ The seminar was offered with a particular focus on Galatians "in the hands" of Luther and Calvin. Barth held a lecture course in Dogmatics on Mon., Tue., Thurs., and Fri. from 7a–8a, lectured in an exegesis of Colossians course (indicated above) on Wednesday

---

58 Barth, *Kolosserbrief 1924–25*, 15–18; Barth, *Kolosserbrief 1937–38*, 31.
59 Barth, *Kolosserbrief 1937–38*, 71.
60 For Barth's most extensive treatment of Galatians, see Karl Barth, *Die Kirchliche Dogmatik: Die Lehre von der Versöhnung*, IV/1 (Zollikon, Zürich: EVZ, 1953), 712–8.
61 I am grateful for the work and cooperation of Dr. Peter Zocher, the archivist of the Barth-Archiv in Basel, Switzerland. Working through a pandemic presents its own particular set of problems, especially regarding travel and enclosed spaces. When cited, the Protocol will be followed by the date of the seminar meeting. The originals of the Protocol are contained in the Karl-Barth-Archiv in Basel.

from 7a–8a, and held the dogmatic seminar on Galatians on Friday from 6p–8p.[62] Before we move into how Barth interpreted Galatians during this time, a few procedural remarks are in order.

The main questions to be dealt with in the seminar were: How is something like theological exegesis possible? How can biblical exegesis bring the remarks of the text in its own time to be heard?[63] Outside of a few exceptions, the procedure of the seminar followed the same basic pattern: verse by verse historical critical background to the section, verse by verse exegetical commentary alternating between Luther and Calvin, 19th century treatment, followed by concluding remarks. Barth covered Galatians 1 through 2:10 in the first 11 sessions in SS 1927, which began on April 29, 1927 and ran through July 28, 1927. Picking up where he left off, Barth managed to work from Gal. 2:11ff through Gal. 3:6 beginning on November 4, 1927 and finishing the WS 1927/28 on February 24, 1928. It is difficult to trace material dogmatic connections and developments based solely on the protocol. Nonetheless, a few remarks can be made regarding the seminar sessions themselves. First, Barth showed fluency with the Greek text, Luther's Latin, and Calvin's Latin/French. There is a seamless representation of the biblical text interlaced with secondary literature. Second, Barth worked mainly with the 1919 and 1935 texts of Luther's Galatians Commentary and supported his work on Calvin's shorter commentary through Calvin's sermons and the *Institutes* from time to time.[64]

Barth did not, however, limit his work during this time on Galatians, nor his work on Luther and Calvin to this one seminar. Reformational themes permeated his work during this time particularly as he engaged with Friedrich Gogarten and Rudolf Bultmann over the "old, never fully resolved Lutheran-Reformed

---

[62] Cf. Westfälische Wilhelms-Universität Münster, *Vorlesungsverzeichnis*, Sommerhalbjahr, (1927): 29, urn:nbn:de:hbz:6:1-337836. Presumably, Barth offered the lecture on Dogmatics from 7–8 in the morning on Fridays and the Galatians seminar on Friday evenings from 6–8 given they could not occur during the same time. For an analysis of the dogmatic lectures during this semester, see Amy Marga, *Barth's Dialogue with Catholicism in Göttingen and Münster* (Tübingen: Mohr Siebeck, 2010), 91–122; and Bruce L. McCormack, "Trinity," in *The Oxford Handbook of Karl Barth*, edited by Paul Dafydd Jones and Paul T. Nimmo (Oxford: Oxford University Press, 2019), 227–45. Barth analyses Calvin and Luther (and Zwingli) earlier in 1922. He claims that Luther's theology leaves the cross open or at least "loosely" open, whereas Calvin understands a completely closed reality of the cross. Karl Barth, *Die Theologie Calvins 1922*, Gesamtausgabe 2.23 (Zürich: TVZ, 1993), 93–171, here 103–4.
[63] Galatians Protocol, 29.04.1927.
[64] Barth had also translated Calvin's sermons over the birth of Jesus which were published. Cf. Karl Barth, "Predigt über die Geburt Jesu Christi, gehalten am Weihnachtstag vor der Feier des heiligen Abendmahles," *ZdZ*, Jg. 5 (1927): 465–78.

controversies".⁶⁵ Coincidentally, Barth and Bultmann both offered a two-hour seminar on Galatians in the same semester.⁶⁶ Moreover, as Barth reworked and revised his earlier dogmatics into a Prolegomena, published as *Die christliche Dogmatik im Entwurf 1927*, the lectures offered one semester prior to his seminar on Galatians, he continued to be plagued with the intensive question regarding God's triune being.⁶⁷

During this time, Barth also held a lecture entitled "Rechtfertigung und Heiligung".⁶⁸ It was delivered for the first time after months of consideration on January 3–5, 1927.⁶⁹ Barth held the same lecture in six different locations, the last of which was held in Putbus/Rügen on June 9–10, 1927. The lectures in

---

65 Barth, "Barth–Bultmann, 28.04.1927," in *Bw.B–B*, 71. Such questions were not unique to Barth during this time but became more focused as he engaged heavily with the two traditions in comparison. Cf. Georg Plasger, "Luther und Calvin," in *Barth Handbuch*, edited by Michael Beintker (Tübingen: Mohr Siebeck, 2016), 37–42.

66 The title of Bultmann's seminar is also telling of the continued focus on the Reformed-Lutheran divide. Whereas Barth's was titled "Lektüre des Galaterbriefs an Hand der Kommentare Luthers und Calvins," Bultmann's seminar was titled "Luthers Kommentar zum Galaterbrief." See Bultmann, "Bultmann–Barth, 01.05.1927," in *Bw.B–B*, 74.

67 As Barth prepared these lectures and worked intensively on the question of God's "hypostatic character" *ad intra* and *ad extra*, he was also doing extensive reading in Luther's 1516 *Römerbrief* in comparison with K. Holl's, *Die Rechtfertigungslehre in Luthers Vorlesung über den Römerbrief*. Cf. Barth, "Barth–Thurneysen, 29. November, 1926" and "Barth–Thurneysen, 26. Dezember, 1926," in *Bw.Th.II*, 448–51. We also get a glimpse in WS 1926/27, the semester prior to his Galatians seminar, of how Barth was heavily invested in reading Luther and Calvin on Galatians, particularly as it pertains to the human response of faith and obedience to God's justifying work as God's work in the human person. Cf. Karl Barth, *Die christliche Dogmatik im Entwurf: Die Lehre vom Worte Gottes. Prolegomena zur christlichen Dogmatik 1927*, Gesamtausgabe 2.14 (Zürich: TVZ, 1982), 417–34.

68 The essay first appeared as Karl Barth, "Rechtfertigung und Heiligung," *ZdZ*, Jg. 5 (1927): 281–309, and was later reprinted in the Gesamtausgabe as Karl Barth, "Rechtfertigung und Heilung 1927," in *Vorträge und kleinere Arbeiten 1925–1930*, edited by Hermann Schmidt Gesamtausgabe 3.24 (Zürich: TVZ, 1994), 57–98. Barth would later treat the reformed doctrine of justification at Münster in WS 1929/30 and then in Bonn in WS 1933/34. The relationship between justification and sanctification in Barth's theology, particularly his refusal of placing justification at the forefront for dogmatic thinking, deserves further treatment which cannot be undertaken here. Cf. Hinrich Stoevesandt, "Die Grundspannung von Rechtfertigung und Heiligung bei Karl Barth," in *Solidair en Solide. In gesprek met H.W. de Knijff*, edited by E. Dekker (Kampen: VbK Media, 1997), 110–117; and Hinrich Stoevesandt, "Die Göttinger Dogmatikvorlesung Grundriß Karl Barths," in *Karl Barth in Deutschland (1921–1935)*, edited by Christian Link and Michael Trowitzsch (Zürich: TVZ, 2005), 77–98, see particularly 89–93.

69 Barth wrote to Thurneysen in an ambivalent tone as to how much unread material awaits him as he prepares for the series of three lectures to be delivered over the Christmas holiday. Cf. Barth, "Barth–Thurneysen, 8. November, 1926," in *Bw.Th.II*, 440–4.

Holland were coupled with his lecture first given in Aaurau on March 9, 1927, entitled "Das Halten der Gebote".⁷⁰ All five of the previous lectures were held prior to the start of the summer Semester 1927 outside of this last lecture held during a two-week gap in the Friday course on Galatians. In this essay, Barth offers nine thesis statements regarding the relationship between justification and sanctification.⁷¹ An entire exegesis of this essay will not be undertaken here, but a few points are worth drawing out which correspond to Barth's exegesis of Galatians during this time as well as how Barth relates God's being and election. First, Barth places a heavy emphasis on Paul's oft cited, "in Christ".⁷² Justification and sanctification are the carrying out of grace in God's election and calling "with God and through Jesus Christ in the truth of the Holy Spirit".⁷³ The sinner is the one saved because the person is, in Christ, elected, called, and loved; there is one divine will: God's eternal self-willing to become flesh.⁷⁴ The entirety

---

70 The essay was first printed in *ZdZ*, Jg. 5 (1927): 208–27, then later in 1957 in Karl Barth, *Theologische Fragen und Antworten* (Zollikon: TVZ, 1957), 32–53, and finally in the Gesamtausgabe in 1994 as Karl Barth, "Das Halten der Gebote," in *Vorträge und kleinere Arbeiten 1925–1930*, edited by Hermann Schmidt, Gesamtausgabe 3.24 (Zürich: TVZ, 1994), 99–139. There is clear material overlap between the two texts. However, in this essay, Barth is mainly concerned with Calvin, yet it also evidences Barth's work on Galatians and God's election.

71 A year later in WS 1928/29 at the University of Münster and then repeated in Bonn in WS 1930/31, we see the engagement furthered and building heavily on Luther and Calvin, while carrying out his critique of Osiander, Beck, and Holl. See Karl Barth, "Das Gebot Gottes des Versöhners," in *Ethik II*, Gesamtausgabe 2.10 (Zürich: TVZ, 1978), 9–68. In its mature expression in 1955, Barth builds on his previous years of studying Calvin and Luther: "Sanctification is not justification! ... Justification is not sanctification! ... therefore, there is no justification without sanctification! ... but most certainly: there is also no sanctification without justification!" Karl Barth, *Die Kirchliche Dogmatik: Die Lehre von der Versöhnung*, IV/2, (Zürich: EVZ, 1964), 570–3.

72 Barth underlined significant words and phrases in the handwritten manuscript of this essay. It is presumably an indication of Barth returning to this lecture manuscript as he wrote § 66 in *KD* IV/2. Of particular significance is that he underlined "in Christ" in section 8 of this manuscript and he wrote "*endlich!*" (finally!) in the marginalia. The editor indicates it is perhaps also indicative of why Barth titled a 1957 lecture (2 years after *KD* IV/2) "Das Halten der Gebote" rather than "Rechtfertigung und Heiligung". However, despite the publication of the lecture in Aarau reprinted later in 1957, the lecture itself was only given three times in Aarau and Holland (Leiden and Utrecht) in 1927. Cf. the introductory notes by Hermann Schmidt, "6. Putbus/Rügen 9.–10. Juni 1927," in *Vorträge und kleinere Arbeiten 1925–1930*, edited by Hermann Schmidt, Gesamtausgabe 3.24 (Zürich: TVZ, 1994), 60–2. In fact, the "in Christ" is a central material connection from 1927 all the way until Barth's fully developed Christology in *KD* IV. Cf. also Karl Barth, "Gottes Gnadenwahl," *Theologische Existenz heute* 47 (1936): 11–7.

73 Barth, "Rechtfertigung und Heiligung," 62.

74 Barth, "Rechtfertigung und Heiligung," 81.

of the being of humanity and the nature of the human is located in the love that constitutes God's being, that is, the eternal and created order are subsumed into the divine love, in which all of humanity is located and saved in Jesus Christ.[75] Second, Barth differentiates between eternity and time throughout the essay, even demarcating justification as the eternal side and sanctification the temporal side of the work of God's "love for sin".[76] These two sides of the same act of grace (as with election and calling) find their relation ultimately in Christ himself. The love of God is not contingent on human decision making, nor is a human decision a condition of God's love. The decisive condition is the preceding, eternal love of election.[77] Over and against the either/or of human decision making, God is self-determined in eternal love in the character of an event. It is God's grace and love which clearly preoccupy Barth's thinking during this time as he exegetes the scriptures and the Christian tradition while formulating God's trinitarian being *ad intra* and *ad extra*—the two, he finds, are contained within the other.

4 Conclusion

After engagement with Barth's early exegetical lectures during his two professorships in Göttingen and Münster, the chapter teased out theological implications from Barth's exegesis of Paul. The implications affirm the self-giving, self-humiliating of God in Jesus Christ. Using Barth as a resource for biblical studies has proven to be a fruitful engagement and has shown how his biblical insights not only influenced his dogmatic work, but also how his focus on the Word of God spurs constructive consideration of God's self-revelation. Important for further development is finding sufficient language to speak of the self-differentiated being of God in eternity as containing human flesh while main-

---

75 Barth, "Rechtfertigung und Heiligung," 95–6.
76 Barth, "Rechtfertigung und Heiligung," 86.
77 Barth, "Rechtfertigung und Heiligung," 86–96. Cf. also Barth, "Das Halten der Gebote," 122–3. Barth claims the love of God is God not wanting to be without the world. God's being is sufficient in itself, but out of the love God is and has, God wills not to be without humanity. Cf. Barth's deaconess chapel sermon on Jeremiah 31:3 in Münster on February 13, 1927, "Gottes Liebe," in *Predigten 1921–1935*, Gesamtausgabe 1.31 (Zürich: TVZ, 1998), 169, here 163. Cf. also Barth's Gifford lectures over the 1560s Scottish Confession in 1937/38, where he claims the exact same: "This is the love of God, that God, who has no need of it, does not want to be without the world nor without humanity." Karl Barth, *Gotteserkenntnis und Gottesdienst nach reformatorischer Lehre* (Zollikon: EBZ, 1938), 70.

taining a God-world distinction. Barth found the language to do so in Paul, in Paul's description of God's graceful and free existence in the pneumatically filled human flesh of Jesus Christ. Perhaps, following Barth, affirming as much is not saying too much nor saying too little.

References

Asprey, Christopher. *Eschatological Presence in Karl Barth's Göttingen Theology*. Oxford: Oxford University Press, 2010.
Barth, Karl. *Die Auferstehung der Toten*. München: Chr. Kaiser, 1926.
Barth, Karl. "Predigt über die Geburt Jesu Christi, gehalten am Weihnachtstag vor der Feier des heiligen Abendmahles." *ZdZ*, Jg. 5 (1927): 465–78.
Barth, Karl. "Rechtfertigung und Heiligung." *ZdZ*, Jg. 5 (1927): 281–309.
Barth, Karl. *Erklärung des Philipperbriefes*. München: Chr. Kaiser, 1928.
Barth, Karl. "Gottes Gnadenwahl." *Theologische Existenz heute*, no. 47 (1936): 11–7.
Barth, Karl. *Gotteserkenntnis und Gottesdienst nach reformatorischer Lehre*. Zollikon: EBZ, 1938.
Barth, Karl. *Die Kirchliche Dogmatik: Die Lehre von der Versöhnung*. IV/1. Zollikon-Zürich: EVZ, 1953.
Barth, Karl. *Theologische Fragen und Antworten*. Zollikon: TVZ, 1957.
Barth, Karl. *Die Kirchliche Dogmatik: Die Lehre von Gott*. II/2. Zürich: EVZ, 1959.
Barth, Karl. "Vorwort." In Pierre Maury. *Predestination and other Papers*. Translated by Edwin Hudson, 15–18. Chatham: W.J. Mackay & Co, 1960.
Barth, Karl. *Die Kirchliche Dogmatik: Die Lehre von der Versöhnung*. IV/2. Zürich: EVZ, 1964.
Barth, Karl. *Karl Barth–Eduard Thurneysen Briefwechsel: Band I (1913–1921)*, edited by Eduard Thurneysen. Gesamtausgabe 5.3. Zürich: TVZ, 1973.
Barth, Karl. *Karl Barth–Eduard Thurneysen Briefwechsel: Band II (1921–1930)*, edited by Eduard Thurneysen. Gesamtausgabe 5.4. Zürich: TVZ, 1974.
Barth, Karl. *Erklärung des Johannes-Evangeliums*, edited by Walter Fürst. Gesamtausgabe 2.9. Zürich: TVZ, 1976.
Barth, Karl. *Ethik II*, edited by Dietrich Braun. Gesamtausgabe 2.10. Zürich: TVZ, 1978.
Barth, Karl. *Die christliche Dogmatik im Entwurf: Die Lehre vom Worte Gottes. Prolegomena zur christlichen Dogmatik 1927*, edited by Gerhard Sauter. Gesamtausgabe 2.14. Zürich: TVZ, 1982.
Barth, Karl. *Unterricht in der christlichen Religion: Prolegomena 1924*, edited by Hannelotte Reiffen. Gesamtausgabe 2.17. Zürich: TVZ, 1985.
Barth, Karl. *Unterricht in der christlichen Religion II: Die Lehre von Gott/Die Lehre vom Menschen 1924/1925*, edited by Hinrich Stoevesandt. Gesamtausgabe 2.20. Zürich: TVZ, 1990.
Barth, Karl. *Die Theologie Calvins 1922*, edited by Hans Scholl. Gesamtausgabe 2.23. Zürich: TVZ, 1993.
Barth, Karl. *Karl Barth–Rudolf Bultmann Briefwechsel: 1911–1966*, edited by Bernd Jaspert. Gesamtausgabe 5.1. Zürich: TVZ, 1994.
Barth, Karl. *Vorträge und kleinere Arbeiten 1925–1930*, edited by Hermann Schmidt. Gesamtausgabe 3.24. Zürich: TVZ, 1994.

Barth, Karl. *Predigten 1921–1935*, edited by Holger Finze-Michaelsen. Gesamtausgabe 1.31. Zürich: TVZ, 1998.
Barth, Karl. *Barth–Thurneysen Briefwechsel: Band III (1930–1935)*, edited by Eduard Thurneysen. Gesamtausgabe 5.34. Zürich: TVZ, 2000.
Barth, Karl. *Predigten 1919*, edited by Hermann Schmidt. Gesamtausgabe 1.39. Zürich: TVZ, 2003.
Barth, Karl. *Erklärung des Epheser- und des Jakobusbriefes 1919–1929*, edited by Jörg-Michael Bohnet. Gesamtausgabe 2.46. Zürich: TVZ, 2009.
Bergner, Gerhard. *Um der Sache willen*. Göttingen: Vandenhoeck & Ruprecht, 2015.
Bruce, Matthew J. Aragon. "Election." In *The Oxford Handbook of Karl Barth*, edited by Paul Dafydd Jones and Paul T. Nimmo, 309–24. Oxford: Oxford University Press, 2019.
Burnett, Richard. *Karl Barth's Theological Exegesis: The Hermeneutical Principles of the Römerbrief Period*. Tübingen: Mohr Siebeck, 2001.
Busch, Eberhard. *Karl Barths Lebenslauf*. München: Chr. Kaiser, 1975.
Busch, Eberhard. *Die Anfänge des Theologen Karl Barth in seinen Göttinger Jahren*. Göttingen: Vandenhoeck & Ruprecht, 1987.
Busch, Eberhard. "Barth in Germany (1921–1935)." In *The Oxford Handbook of Karl Barth*, edited by Paul Dafydd Jones and Paul T. Nimmo, 34–51. Oxford: Oxford University Press, 2019.
Gibson, Michael. "Barth on Divine Election." In *Wiley Blackwell Companion to Karl Barth*, edited by George Hunsinger and Keith L. Johnson, 47–58. Hoboken: Wiley Blackwell, 2020.
Gockel, Matthias. *Barth and Schleiermacher on the Doctrine of Election*. Oxford: Oxford University Press, 2006.
Krötke, Wolf. "Erwählungslehre." In *Barth Handbuch*, edited by Michael Beintker, 221–6. Tübingen: Mohr Siebeck, 2016.
Marga, Amy. *Barth's Dialogue with Catholicism in Göttingen and Münster*. Tübingen: Mohr Siebeck, 2010.
Maury, Pierre. *Election, Barth, and the French Connection*, edited by Simon Hattrell. Eugene: Pickwick, 2019.
McCormack, Bruce L. *Karl Barth's Critically Realistic Dialectical Theology. Its Genesis and Development 1909–1936*. Oxford: Clarendon Press, 1995.
McCormack, Bruce L. *Orthodox and Modern: Studies in the Theology of Karl Barth*. Grand Rapids: Baker Academic, 2008.
McCormack, Bruce L. "Longing for a New World: On Socialism, Eschatology and Apocalyptic in Barth's Early Dialectical Theology." In *Theologie im Umbruch der Moderne: Karl Barths frühe Dialektische Theologie*, edited by George Pfleiderer and Harald Matern, 135–49. Zürich: TVZ, 2014.
McCormack, Bruce L. "Trinity." In *The Oxford Handbook of Karl Barth*, edited by Paul Dafydd Jones and Paul T. Nimmo, 227–45. Oxford: Oxford University Press, 2019.
Mützlitz, Nina Dorothee. *Gottes Wort als Wirklichkeit: Die Paulus-Rezeption des jungen Karl Barth (1906–1927)*. Neukirchen-Vluyn: Neukirchener, 2013.
Neuser, Wilhelm. *Karl Barth in Münster 1925–1930*. Zürich: TVZ, 1985.
Plasger, Georg. "Luther und Calvin." In *Barth Handbuch*, edited by Michael Beintker, 37–42. Tübingen: Mohr Siebeck, 2016.
Reichel, Hanna. *Theologie als Bekenntnis: Karl Barths kontextuelle Lektüre des Heidelberger Katechismus*. Göttingen: Vandenhoeck & Ruprecht, 2015.

Stoevesandt, Hinrich. "Die Grundspannung von Rechtfertigung und Heiligung bei Karl Barth." In *Solidair en Solide. In gesprek met H.W. de Knijff*, edited by E. Dekker, 110–17. Kampen: VbK Media, 1997.

Stoevesandt, Hinrich. "Die Göttinger Dogmatikvorlesung Grundriß Karl Barths." In *Karl Barth in Deutschland (1921–1935). Aufbruch — Klärung — Widerstand*, edited by Michael Beinkter, Christian Link, and Michael Trowitzsch, 77–98. Zürich: TVZ, 2005.

Tietz, Christiane. *Karl Barth: Ein Leben im Widerspruch*. München: C.H. Beck, 2018.

Trowitzsch, Michael. "Pfingstlich genau. Zur Hermeneutik Karl Barths." In *Karl Barth in Deutschland (1921–1935). Aufbruch — Klärung — Widerstand*, edited by Michael Beinkter, Christian Link, and Michael Trowitzsch, 363–91. Zürich: TVZ, 2005.

Webster, John. "Relation beyond all Relations." In Karl Barth, *The Epistle to the Ephesians*, edited by R. David Nelson and translated by Ross W. Wright, 31–49. Grand Rapids: Baker Academic, 2017.

Westerholm, Martin. *The Ordering of the Christian Mind*. Oxford: Oxford University Press, 2015.

Wood, Donald. *Karl Barth's Theology of Interpretation*. New York: Rutledge, 2007.

Wood, Donald. "Exegesis." In *The Oxford Handbook of Karl Barth*, edited by Paul Dafydd Jones and Paul T. Nimmo, 263–76. Oxford: Oxford University Press, 2019.

Georg Fischer
Karl Rahner's Use of the Bible

Abstract: The article gives a first report and information about the research project "Karl Rahner and the Bible," granted by the Austrian Science Fund. It focuses on the backgrounds and characteristics of his approach to Scripture, exposes its roots in the Spiritual Exercises and his philosophical formation. There an ambivalence in his attitude towards the Bible can be seen; on one hand marked with high esteem, on the other with preference for the tradition of the Church. This affects also Rahner's stance towards the Old Testament and Judaism.

Keywords: Karl Rahner; Bible in Systematic Theology; Christological focus; Jewish-Christian Relations

1 Introduction

This article intends to provide a *first report and initial information* about a larger research project,[1] granted by the "Fonds zur Förderung der wissenschaftlichen Forschung" ("The Austrian Science Fund," FWF) in Austria, on "Karl Rahner and the Bible." Benedikt Collinet and I are investigating Karl Rahner's use of Scripture throughout his entire œuvre.[2] This task is important not only because of Karl Rahner's position as an eminent theologian, but even more so because of his influence on the Second Vatican Council, as official theological consultant of Franz Cardinal König, and, unofficially, also of Julius Cardinal Döpfner. As we can already observe, taking Karl Rahner as a prominent example, the findings offer a specific view of the relationship between Scripture and Theology in the last century.

---

[1] This article was originally delivered as paper at the S&T online conference in June 2020 (planned for Bologna) and reflects mainly the status at that time. Meanwhile many new results are available in: Benedikt J. Collinet and Georg Fischer (Hg.), *Karl Rahner und die Bibel. Interdisziplinäre Perspektiven*, QD 326, Freiburg: Herder, 2022.

[2] The time for this research is fortunate as the publication of nearly all of Rahner's writings has been completed in the critical edition of *Sämtliche Werke* (= abbreviated henceforth *SW*). It comprises 40 volumes, published by Herder in Freiburg, Germany, starting with volume 19 (!) in 1995, and ending in 2018 with the final volume 32/2, containing the indexes.

Georg Fischer, Theological Faculty, University of Innsbruck, Austria, georg.fischer@uibk.ac.at

https://doi.org/10.1515/9783110768411-013

After the death of Karl Rahner, the topic of our research project has received only *little direct attention* up to now.³ There have been only three articles, with a gap of more than 30 years. *Karl Heinz Neufeld* has addressed the issue in an early contribution.⁴ He gives an overview structured around four headings. First, he investigates biblical traces regarding the life and thought of Rahner. Then he focuses on the Bible's explicit role in his work. Afterwards, Neufeld tackles concrete themes with increased biblical references. Finally, he treats the delicate question of "Die eine Bibel und der Unterschied von Neuem und Altem Testament." This last issue, the difference between the New and the Old Testament, and especially the role of the latter, remains in Neufeld's view an important topic for further investigation.

A few years later, *Rainer Kampling* dealt anew with Rahner's relationship with the Bible.⁵ He understands it based upon the background of the development within the Catholic Church in the first half of the Twentieth Century and contradicts the accusation that Rahner's theology was "unbiblisch." In Rahner's works, however, he can verify that they are laden with biblical language, motifs, and images and that Holy Scripture is a "gewußte und geglaubte Voraussetzung" within them.⁶ Kampling finally describes Rahner as "Förderer und Forderer der Exegese."⁷

Recently, *Albert Raffelt* has published the article "Karl Rahner und die Bibel."⁸ He focuses on how exegetes appreciated Rahner's help concerning their

---

3 However, in a celebration in Freiburg on February 11th–12th of 1984 for Rahner's approaching 80th birthday (March 4th), shortly before his death on March 30th, Rudolf Pesch already gave a paper related to our theme, on "Gegen eine doppelte Wahrheit. Karl Rahner und die Bibelwissenschaft." It was published in: *Vor dem Geheimnis Gottes den Menschen verstehen*, ed. Karl Lehmann (Freiburg, München, Zürich: Schnell & Steiner, 1984): 10–36.
4 Karl Heinz Neufeld, "Die Schrift in der Theologie Karl Rahners," *JBT* 2 (1987), 229–246.
5 Rainer Kampling, "Exegese und Karl Rahner," in *Theologie aus Erfahrung der Gnade. Annäherungen an Karl Rahner*, eds. Mariano Delgado and Matthias Lutz-Bachmann (Berlin: Morus 1994), 267–283. This article and the entire book originated from a series of lectures to remember Rahner's 90th birthday and 10th year of his death.
6 Kampling, "Exegese" (note 5), 270, in English: "a known and believed precondition". Kampling continues to affirm that the Bible was integrated into Rahner's life and that this is reflected in his writings.
7 Kampling, "Exegese" (note 5), 272–279: ... somebody who promotes and challenges exegesis.
8 Albert Raffelt, "Karl Rahner und die Bibel," in *Anstöße der Theologie Karl Rahners für gegenwärtige Theologie und Kirche*, eds. Karsten Kreutzer and Albert Raffelt (Freiburg: Katholische Akademie der Erzdiözese 2019), 187–198. This collective volume comprises the contributions of a conference held under the same title in Freiburg on September 28–29 in 2018. Raffelt added his article to the book; it was not part of the conference. Maybe, as an editor, he felt that something would be missing, if this issue was not addressed.

struggles about the acceptance of their research in the middle of the past century.[9] Raffelt goes on to show Rahner's familiarity with the Bible, beginning with his studies and formation. He points out that the Biblical Index of the *SW* testifies to Rahner's use of *all* biblical writings; even Nahum, missing up until the last stages of editing, showed up in the last published volume.[10] Raffelt continues with Rahner's interest in the results of newer exegesis, picking up also the form-critical approach and even asking biblical scholars for specific contributions, as a help in clarifying systematic topics. At the end, Raffelt admits that the role of the Old Testament is significantly less to the New Testament in Rahner's writings, but he counters the reproach of "Bibelferne" directed against Rahner.[11]

To sum up: Less than 30 pages in more than 30 years since Rahner's death on such an important issue as the relationship of one of the most eminent theologians of the last century to God's word invites an investigation of this theme more deeply. Throughout his life,[12] Rahner has published thousands of pages using the Bible or referring to it, thus this study is both necessary and rewarding. It may also contribute to the larger theme "Scripture and Theology," taking Rahner as an example of the use of God's revelation by a productive, important theologian. In the following, I wish to *give an overview* of some major insights and developing traces in the research on this topic so far.

---

9 Raffelt, "Rahner" (note 8), 187–189.
10 Raffelt, "Rahner" (note 8), 190–191. See also *idem*, "Rahners Lektüreliste," *HK* 73/3 (2019), 50–51.
11 Raffelt, "Rahner" (note 8), 196.
12 One of Rahner's early articles is on "Theos im Neuen Testament" (from 1942; see *SW* 4, 346–403), where he picks up the respective contribution from *TWNT* edited by Kittel, a sign that he is open to research done by 'protestants'. Already before, in 1936, Rahner had written his theological dissertation on a biblical topic: *E latere Christi* (cf. *SW* 3, 3–84). In Rahner's late writings, from his last years, biblical themes and passages are present, too, e.g. in *SW* 29, 120–123, an article on "Schriftlesung" (Reading Scripture), or in *SW* 30 a contribution on "Buch Gottes und Buch der Menschen," dealing with the interrelationship of God and humans in the formation of the Bible.

2 A Few Indications on the Biographical Background

This is not the place to discuss Rahner's life; it can easily be found in other sources.[13] He was born on March 5th, 1904, in a Catholic family, and had a pious grandmother who was influential on his religious education. He entered the *Society of Jesus* in 1922 in Tisis, close to Feldkirch in Austria, following his elder brother Hugo who had already joined the same order on January 11th of 1919. The formation in the order included, after the novitiate,[14] philosophical and theological studies. Having received a theological doctorate and written a Habilitation[15] in Innsbruck, Rahner started to teach systematic theology in 1937 at Innsbruck as well.

According to Karl-Heinz Neufeld SJ, one of his closest collaborators,[16] and to Elfriede Oeggl, Rahner's last secretary,[17] Rahner possessed *no Bible* of his own with which he would have constantly worked. When he needed to quote a biblical passage, he used one, which was available in the given situation, mostly a German translation / version.[18] He knew Latin very well, also because he prayed the breviary daily in that language. He taught New Testament Greek in the Jesuits' formation program in Tisis, a language he himself had learned only after

---

[13] For example in *SW* 1, XII–XXX; *SW* 32, 29–32, and, in an extended manner, Karl Heinz Neufeld, *Die Brüder Rahner* (Freiburg: Herder, ²2004).

[14] A major focus of Jesuit novitiates lies on spiritual formation. Part of it is a long retreat of 30 days with biblical meditations, the original form of "spiritual exercises", going back to St. Ignatius of Loyola. Rahner would, later in his life, refer often to this experience and also himself give similar, shorter retreats to others (cf. for confirmation *SW* 13 and 25).

[15] *Sünde als Gnadenverlust in der frühkirchlichen Literatur*, *SW* 11, 3–42; it appeared originally as an article in the *ZKTh* 60 (1936), 471–510.

[16] Karl Heinz Neufeld SJ (see note 4) is also one of the main editors of Rahner's "*Sämtliche Werke*" and redacted personally several volumes.

[17] Elfriede Oeggl served Rahner as his assistant, secretary and driver in the years 1981 to 1984, up to his death.

[18] At Christmas in 1981, he gave to Elfriede Oeggl, as a present, a copy of the German Bible in the version of the "*Einheitsübersetzung*." Rahner did have a Greek New Testament, which he could read easily and often used. German translations available to Rahner were those of Eugen Henne and Konstantin Rösch, also called "Paderborner Bibel," from 1934, and, for the New Testament, of Otto Karrer, a friend of his brother Hugo.

High School. It seems that he was not acquainted with Hebrew[19] or Aramaic. Nevertheless he, however rarely, alludes to original readings.

Other sources of Rahner's *familiarity with the Bible* are the daily Eucharist and prayer, viz. meditation, which he regularly observed, already very early in the morning (4–5a.m.). When the Nazis banished the Jesuits from Innsbruck in 1939, Rahner went to Vienna where he collaborated in the Pastoral Institute of the Archdiocese. The last year of the Second World War, with the Russian army approaching Vienna, he spent as a chaplain in a parish in Bavaria, where he had to give homilies on biblical texts constantly. In later years, too, he preached very often and received many requests for this.[20] He used mainly the text of the gospels, as the volumes with selected homilies show.[21]

Rahner came back to *Innsbruck* as a professor in 1948 and stayed there until 1964, when he accepted a call to Munich, and later to Münster. In 1981, he returned to Innsbruck again for his last years. He died on March 30th 1984, in the Sanatorium of the Kreuzschwestern in Hochrum, a village close by, and is buried in the crypt of the Jesuit church of the Holy Trinity in Innsbruck. Conducting this research on "Karl Rahner and the Bible" in Innsbruck continues his legacy in the city where he became extraordinarily productive and spent more years of his life than at any other place.

3 Roots of Rahner's Orientation

As usual in Jesuit formation, the young members have to study philosophy as well as theology. In Rahner's time, the centre was at Valkenburg in the Netherlands. There, Albert Rembold SJ[22] and Augustin Bea SJ, later Rector of the Pontifical Biblical Institute in Rome and Cardinal, were among his teachers. The list of

---

19 According to the former theological curriculum, an at least rudimentary knowledge of Hebrew was required for a doctorate in theology. However, no testimony of such a course or an exam by Rahner in Hebrew is extant.
20 Several times newly ordained priests asked him to preach at their first masses ("Primiz"). In one of these occasions, Rahner gave the homily in the first mass of Balthasar Schmerl on July 5th 1953 even in Außervillgraten, a very small, remote village in Eastern Tyrol.
21 See, among other examples, *SW* 1, 361–410, *SW* 14, 221–345, and parts of *SW* 23 (esp. 431–469). Benedikt Collinet, "Anmerkungen zur Bibelauslegung in Karl Rahners frühen Predigten," *GuL* 94 (2021), 64–69, deals with aspects of the background of Rahner's early homilies.
22 Fr. Rembold edited in 1932 various fascicles of the series "*Aus den Schatzkammern des Alten Testaments*," on Micah, Song of Songs, Ben Sira, God as almighty creator and God as fountain of wisdom.

Rahner's readings comprises 388 titles, among them little more than 20 touching the field of the Bible.[23] This is rather typical for the time and for the *insistence on systematic theology*, rather than on exegetical studies,[24] which is characteristic of Jesuit formation.

The start of Rahner's academic career was a failure. The order had planned that he should become a professor of philosophy and sent him to Freiburg for a doctorate. However, his "Doktorvater" Honecker did not accept Rahner's dissertation on the metaphysics of Saint Thomas Aquinas,[25] partly maybe due to its openness towards new ideas – those of Martin Heidegger, Edmund Husserl, and others. The *closeness to philosophy* and the interest in anthropology remain as characteristics of Rahner's thinking throughout his life. A quote may underline this orientation: Rahner perceives as danger "das Werden der Kirche zum konfessionellen Verein."[26]

After this disappointment, Rahner's provincial sent him to Innsbruck to complete a thesis in theology, where he also wrote a "Habilitation," both within less than a year (1936–37; see above note 15). "E latere Christi," his doctorate, shows a typological interpretation of John 19:34. In it, he quotes biblical passages frequently, also many from the OT.[27] Rahner's procedure is close to the *exegesis of the Fathers of the Church*; like his brother Hugo, Karl, too, was familiar with their writings and published substantially about them.[28] Soon afterwards, he became a professor of dogmatic theology and remained in this position up to his retirement in 1971.

---

[23] A similar relationship of approximately 1:20 appears in the frequency of Old and New Testament quotes. In the early article "Von der Wachsamkeit des Christen" (*SW* 1, 355–356), e.g., where Rahner refers 38 times to the Bible, only 2 quotes are from the OT.

[24] A small sign for the priority of systematic theology: In *SW* 13, 633, exegesis ranks only in the fourth place among the theological disciplines, whereas dogma occupies the first place, with moral theology and canon law following next.

[25] Rahner published it later, 1939, as *Geist in Welt*. Johann Baptist Metz, a disciple of Rahner, redacted and augmented the 2nd edition in 1957 (for both versions see *SW* 2, 3–300). In a letter to his provincial, Rahner gave as a reason for Honecker's rejection that the latter regarded his thesis as "too modern" (*SW* 2, XXVII, note 57).

[26] *SW* 4, 575 (trans.: that the church becomes a confessional club).

[27] He mentions Zech 12:10, too, and sees John 19:34–35 as its fulfillment (*SW* 3, 30–31). Rahner does not quote the text of Zech 12, nor discuss the text-critical problem, namely the original reading "gaze at *me* whom they pierced," with God speaking.

[28] His first major theological work is on the "Five spiritual senses of Origen" (*SW* 1, 16–65; originally in French). In the tractate *De gratia Christi* (*SW* 5/1, 239–491 and *SW* 5/2, 605–1361), which he read for the first time in 1937, he regularly refers to the Fathers of the Church, etc.

In order to evaluate justly Rahner's merits, *further aspects* have to be kept in mind. Up until the 1960s, the Biblical Commission in Rome hampered an open discussion or exchange with modern biblical sciences.[29] Moreover, at his time exegesis and the methods of biblical interpretation were not that developed or helpful as nowadays; historical-critical approaches prevailed[30] and caused dissatisfaction and insecurity among theologians. In addition, it was common to use the Bible for "Schriftbeweise" (scriptural testimonies) to prove the truth of one's position. Rahner had done so himself in his early years[31] yet explicitly desisted from such an approach later several times.[32] He had realized the danger of fundamentalist ways of reading God's word and fought against them.

---

29 Rahner himself became a target of traditionalist circles. His lecture at the Salzburger Hochschulwochen on June 1st in 1962 "Löscht den Geist nicht aus!" (= Do not extinguish the Spirit!) led to a Papal prohibition of publication; however, it was not executed and later revoked. Benedikt Collinet, "Die Autorität der Schrift im Wechselspiel mit dem katholischen Lehramt. Anmerkungen zum komplexen Verhältnis von Bibelwissenschaft und lehramtlicher Autorität am Beispiel der Päpstlichen Bibelkommission," in *Religious Authority. Autorität und Religion*, edited by Liborius Lumma, Wilhelm Rees et al. (Innsbruck: University Press, 2022), 33–58, deals with the influence of the official doctrinal authority on the Biblical Commissions and the interplay between them.
30 This may explain Rahner's remark in his article on "Exegese und biblische Theologie," presenting as an aim, Catholic theology "von der protestantischen Exegese unabhängig machen" (trans.: to make it independent from protestant exegesis; *SW* 4, 512). – The difference between exegesis and biblical theology, although not always expressed clearly, is an important issue. Rahner preferred the latter (see his statements from *SW* 22 and 26 below in part 5, especially notes 60 and 63).
31 See the tractates on grace and on penance (in *SW* 5/1+2, and 6/1+2).
32 Two examples: Instead of starting with Scripture for talking on the Holy Spirit, he intends "jetzt einen ein wenig anderen Meditationsweg einzuschlagen versuchen" (= to try to open a slightly different, meditative way: *SW* 29, 38). For the issue of "Law and Justice" Rahner starts with rhetorical questions, whether to begin with Saint Paul, or with the Old Testament, only to set off in another direction (*SW* 30, 536). – Rahner's presentations of the "Gotteslehre" (teaching about God) in *SW* 22/1, B, offer further confirmations for this approach. In the first four contributions he either does not mention biblical texts, or alludes to them only very scarcely. In *SW* 15, the article "Hören auf Gottes Wort" is similarly void of biblical passages, as well as the one on "new earth," a motif introduced by Isa 65:17.

4 A Preference for Jesus and the "Gospel"

In Rahner's writings, the balance between the three 'persons' of the Trinity is uneven.[33] Certainly, he deals with all of them, but his central interest lies in the *person of Jesus Christ*. This is partly due to Jesuit spirituality[34] but probably to a similar extent also due to the common sentiment in circles of faithful at his time. *SW* 5/1+2, the tractate "*De gratia Christi*," concentrates on the grace which Jesus has brought. The codex "*De paenitentia*" (*SW* 6/1+2) would have offered many opportunities to introduce God's mercy and willingness to forgive already in the Old Testament; however, Rahner does this only rarely.[35] The rich messages of reconciliation or divine mercy in the OT would have added momentum to the theological reasoning – but there are, if any, only scarce allusions to them. A quote from the "*Grundkurs*" may make evident Rahner's Christological focalization: "(die Uroffenbarung) … immer schon umfangen und überholt … durch den absoluten Willen Gottes zu seiner Selbstmitteilung auf Jesus Christus hin und von ihm her."[36] His emphasis on the "heart of Jesus" offers another argument to underline this from early on in his writings.[37]

Yet, there is an interesting observation on a *diachronic level*. In his first ever recorded prayer, Rahner addresses God, as the first person within the Holy Trinity, directly,[38] and he also does so a few years later in his book "*Worte ins Schweigen*."[39] The tractate on "creation" naturally required Rahner to talk about God as the creator; however, even here the grace (of Christ) appears to be an

---

[33] This finds confirmation in the volume with the indexes: The list of texts on God and the Holy Trinity is little more than one page long, whereas the one on Jesus Christ and Christology fills three entire pages (*SW* 32/2, 606–610).

[34] The Spiritual Exercises of Saint Ignatius of Loyola (cf. note 14) contain many meditations on Jesus' life. Out of their four phases, called "weeks," the last three focus on Jesus Christ nearly exclusively. Rahner was familiar with them since the novitiate, and normally a Jesuit would do them, in a shorter form, every year. For his rootedness in Ignatian spirituality, see *SW* 13.

[35] See, for example, the references to the OT in dealing with repentance (*SW* 6/2, 155).

[36] *SW* 26, 158, paraphrased in English: God's absolute will for the communication of his self, directed towards Jesus Christ and coming from him, has always already embraced and surpassed the original revelation. The testimony of Elfriede Öggl (see above 2, and note 17), in a conversation (January 23th, 2020), confirms that Rahner in his very last days could feel Jesus very close to him, in deep piety.

[37] One of Rahner's first articles is asking whether this concept already appears in Origen (*SW* 1, 164). See also five contributions to this topic in part 4 of *SW* 13.

[38] *SW* 1, 3: "der Heilige, Ewige" (= the Holy, Eternal one).

[39] Republished in *SW* 7, 3–38.

organizing principle.⁴⁰ Yet, towards the end of his life, we can find a kind of "return" to the initial orientation. "To adore and love God" is Rahner's deep concern.⁴¹ And in an interview which was published only after his death, he states: "Die (Antwort) heißt Gott".⁴²

In between, in many of his writings, Rahner concentrates mostly on Jesus, and God appears less, if so, predominately as the "father" of Jesus. There is *no equal balance* in the attention given to both of them.⁴³ That "Christianity properly knows only very few statements / testimonies about the absolute mystery called God"⁴⁴ is difficult to sustain when one considers how much the Bible, as a whole, talks about him and depictures him as the central figure.

As a logical continuation of his focus on Jesus, Rahner has a preference for the "Gospel." He gives *priority to the New Testament* over the Old, and especially to the "Evangelium." The concentration on the Gospel/gospels⁴⁵ is clearly visible in the number of passages, as well as their relevance in his arguing. The "hearer of the word" becomes the "hearer of the Gospel."⁴⁶ The focus on the New Testament is present throughout his entire work and Rahner is firm in it and often refers to it.⁴⁷ He even uses the word "evangelize" and most of his homilies and meditations are on passages of the gospels.⁴⁸

The Scripture index in *SW* 32/2 contains references to all biblical books.⁴⁹ Several times Rahner quotes or refers to books of the *Old Testament*, and his

---

40 Thus Karl Heinz Neufeld, in *SW* 8, XV: "von der Gnadenlehre aus entfaltet."
41 "Die große Sorge: dass Gott angebetet und geliebt wird," *SW* 31, 234.
42 *SW* 31, 356 (also 341, as title): "The answer is God." Cf. also *SW* 26, 500 and 512, where Rahner calls God "Geheimnis" (mystery) and "umfassender Grund" (encompassing foundation).
43 This is equally valid for the third 'person' of the Trinity, the Holy Spirit.
44 *SW* 15, 706: "Das Christentum macht nun hinsichtlich dieses – Gott genannten – absoluten Geheimnisses eigentlich nur ganz wenige Aussagen ... ."
45 John's gospel is Rahner's favorite. He also quotes Pauline letters often. The emphasis on the New Testament becomes obvious in the Scripture index in *SW* 32/2, too: 17 pages refer to passages of the Old Testament (818–834), 54 pages, that is more than thrice as much, mention New Testament texts (834–887). As the OT is more than three times longer than the NT, Rahner gives the latter more than 10 times more attention than the former with respect to their lengths.
46 The monograph *Hörer des Wortes* (see *SW* 4, 1–281) could hint at a topic that humans are listeners of God's word, yet it is based on his doctoral studies in philosophy in Freiburg and thus has another orientation. "Hörer des Evangeliums" occurs in *SW* 19, 226, in Rahner's dealing with the approach to the message of salvation.
47 *SW* 4, 346–403, presents his early article on "Theos im Neuen Testament," *SW* 12, 193–208, contains an article on "Theology in the New Testament", etc.
48 See, e.g., *SW* 23, 269, and in part C therein exclusively 431–472.
49 Albert Raffelt, "Karl Rahner" (note 8), 190–191. He interprets it as a sign that Rahner knew and used the entire Bible.

understanding is often appropriate. Here are some examples: The passage in Num 20, where Moses and Aaron do not fulfil exactly God's command to bring out water from the rock at Meribah command and have to bear the consequences, serves for Rahner as an example that God may inflict timely limited evils as punishment.[50] For a homily on the Holy Night, he uses Psa 74:13, explaining it with "auch die Nacht gehört Gott".[51] Among the 45 selected sermons in *SW* 14 there is only one concerning an OT text, namely Psa 23, but Rahner renders the Hebrew expression שׁבט in this context exactly with "Keule" (club).[52] In discussing "the true prophet," he refers to Deut 18, the key passage in the OT.[53]

However, the balance between Old and New Testament is *uneven*. There is a significant weakness in Rahner's use of the Old Testament.[54] In treating God and his heart,[55] he writes about Jesus' heart – yet, passages like Gen 6:6, the first text in the Bible speaking of God's heart, or Hos 11:8, where it is stirred up, do not occur. In "Buch Gottes und Buch der Menschen" Rahner tackles the issue of the relationship between divine and human contributions to the formation of Scripture; only very late in bis argument does he address the OT, which would have offered the first and most challenging examples to discuss it.[56] Similarly, the article "Das christliche Verständnis der Erlösung" contains only few allusions to biblical texts and no references to the OT.[57]

Looking back on this part, Rahner's concentration on Jesus Christ and the Gospel is, on one hand, *a strength*, very well developed and shining with many facets. On the other hand, however, the role of God, his first revelation in the Books of the OT and the rich messages in it are *underestimated*. This leads, fac-

---

50 *SW* 6, 646: "zeitliche Übel als Strafe."
51 *SW* 7, 388, in translation: The night, too, belongs to God.
52 *SW* 14, 314–316; this interpretation astonishes, as it is unusual and received support years later by a specialist: Othmar Keel, *Die Welt der altorientalischen Bildsymbolik und das Alte Testament. Am Beispiel der Psalmen* (Zürich: Benziger, 1972; Göttingen: Vandenhoeck & Ruprecht, [3]1984), 208. Maybe Rahner consulted an OT exegete for this homily on Psa 23, as he is also very sensitive for other details of this outstanding text.
53 *SW* 25, 59.
54 George Vass, *A Pattern of Doctrines 1: God and Christ. Understanding Karl Rahner, volume 3* (London: Sheed & Ward, 1996), 128; similarly Christoph Theobald SJ (Paris), in an oral communication on December 4th, 2019.
55 "Der liebe Gott und sein Herz," *SW* 25, 378–379.
56 *SW* 30, 178–187, esp. 184: "Nachträglich muß nun noch etwas über das Alte Testament gesagt werden" (= additionally something has to be said about the OT). To assign only a kind of complementary role to the first divine revelation does not do justice to its value.
57 *SW* 30, 346–358.

tually, to an imbalance in the appreciation of the entire Bible and to limitations in theological thought.

5 A Discrepancy between Theory and Reality

Several facts indicate that Rahner *highly esteemed Scripture*. He sees it, in the tradition of the church, as "the soul of theology."[58] He regards the "Dienst am Wort" as the primary function of the Church.[59] He started, together with Heinrich Schlier, the series "*Quaestiones disputatae,*"[60] with the aim of fostering the exchange and understanding between biblical and systematic theologies. Very often, and more so in his early writings, he refers to Scripture, and all biblical books show up somewhere in his œuvre. In his life, he had daily contact with the Bible through the readings in the Masses and praying the breviary. Rahner had picked up new developments regarding the Bible, knowing e.g. about "Formgeschichte." He was also sensitive to the difference between "Sache" and "Veranschaulichung"[61] and to various concepts of biblical theology.[62] His many homilies testify to a constant interest in and exchange with biblical, mainly New Testament passages. At the beginning of his Grundkurs he makes some revealing remarks. Rahner hopes that he "in genügender Weise von den Fragestellungen und Ergebnissen der heutigen Exegese und Bibeltheologie Kenntnis genommen hat."[63]

---

58 *SW* 16, 488, n28. Rahner quotes the Encyclica *Providentissimus Deus* (1893); on this cf. *Herders Theologischer Kommentar zum Zweiten Vatikanischen Konzil*, edited by Peter Hünermann and Ernst J. Hilberath, vol. 3 (Freiburg: Herder, 2005), 800.
59 "Service of the Word," *SW* 19, 151.
60 *QD* 1 in 1958, originally in *ZKTh* 78 (1956), 137–168, now in *SW* 12, 3–58, as "Grundlegung der Dogmatik. Über die Schriftinspiration." In "Zur Methode der Theologie" Rahner states "der systematische Theologe … kann nicht darauf verzichten, Bibeltheologe zu sein" (*SW* 22/1a, 305: a systematic theologian cannot dispense from being a biblical theologian).
61 Highlighted by Pesch, "Gegen eine doppelte Wahrheit" (note 3), "matter and its illustration"; Rahner discerned thus "Aussageweise" (expression) and "Aussageinhalt" (content), necessary for an adequate comprehension of the meaning of biblical texts; see his "Theologische Prinzipien der Hermeneutik eschatologischer Aussagen," in *SW* 12, 489–510, esp. 509.
62 An important insight regards the distinction between a theology of the entire Bible and of the individual theologies of single biblical scrolls: "Über die Schriftinspiration," *SW* 12, 57. A realization of this program, for the OT, is mine *Theologien des Alten Testaments*, NSK-AT 31 (Stuttgart: Katholisches Bibelwerk, 2012).
63 *SW* 26, 8, in paraphrase: "to have sufficiently engaged with the questions and results of present-day exegesis and biblical theology;" shortly before he writes: "… um keinen Preis den

On the other hand, Rahner nearly always gives *primacy to dogmatic theology*.[64] In his reasoning, e.g. in the tractate "*De paenitentia*," he regularly begins with the "teaching of the Church," and afterwards adduces scriptural passages for confirmation.[65] A principle in the background of Rahner's stance towards the Bible comes to the fore in this quote: "Darüber hinaus bekennen wir, daß absolute Sicherheit dem Schriftargument nur im Licht der Tradition zukommt."[66] The conflict with Norbert Lohfink, his Jesuit confrere, in 1968, is a further example of Rahner placing the Bible in second rank.[67]

Rahner expressed his high esteem for the Bible several times, yet did not always keep pace with it. This difference is revealing. It shows that Rahner, theoretically, affirms the *priority of divine revelation* above human thinking and personally lives according to it in many ways. His works, however, often do not correspond to this preference. One may see two main reasons for this inadequacy, a biographical and a contextual one: Rahner's philosophical background and his desire to show the reasonability of faith led him to lay more weight on systematic thinking and theology. Further, in his time, the (Catholic) Church was still reluctant and unsteady in giving the Bible the deserved importance. Only in the wake of the Second Vatican Council did this start to change for the better.[68]

Eindruck erwecken, er sei ein Exeget" (= he wants at no cost to give the impression to be an exegete).

64 In "Gesellschaft Jesu und Studium," *SW* 13, 633, Rahner gives this sequence of theological subjects: "Dogma, Moral, Kirchenrecht, Exegese" (cf. note 24).

65 *SW* 6/1 and 6/2, presenting lectures regularly repeated between 1945 and 1960. In one instance, however, in part III in *SW* 6/2, 612, the Bible receives the first place for the *probatio* (argumentation).

66 *SW* 6/2, 156, in English: "Further we confess that the argument from Scripture receives absolute certainty only in light of the tradition." This statement emphasizes still more the dimension of the Church in the traditional 'Catholic' position of "Schrift und Tradition."

67 "Die Exegese im Theologiestudium: eine Antwort an Norbert Lohfink," in *SW* 16, 456–462.

68 A first step towards a higher appreciation of the Bible and biblical sciences was the encyclical "Divino afflante Spiritu" of Pope Pius XII in 1943; for its background see especially Michael Florian Pfister, *Ein Mann der Bibel – Augustin Bea SJ (1881–1968) als Exeget und Rektor des Päpstlichen Bibelinstituts in den 1930er und 1940er Jahren* (Regensburg: Schnell & Steiner 2020), 465–562.

6 The Delicate Relationship with the "Synagogue"

The aspect treated last *concerns the rapport with the Jews* and their religion, too. Rahner concentrates on the Church as the intended community of God's faithful, whereas from the Book of Exodus the "people of YHWH" are a main focus of the Bible in its entirety.[69] Although Rahner often picks up actual debates,[70] the Shoah seems to be absent. Later however, in 1961, he writes the introduction to the book: "Dein verkannter Bruder. Ein Jude sieht uns Christen. Eine Einführung zu André Neher." It is particularly impressive concerning a new attitude towards Jews.[71] Therein he demands to listen to "the lament and accusation" of those who have suffered injustice.[72] Close to the end of his life, the discussion with Pinchas Lapide, too, makes Rahner change towards a still more comprehensive stance regarding Jewish religion and traditions.[73] This is a sign of an important development and of his openness to a process, which had begun in the Second Vatican Council, strongly incited by Augustin Cardinal Bea,[74] one of his early teachers (see above 3, Roots).

Our research project has produced some initial results: A general esteem for Scripture does not find an equivalent expression in its concrete realization. Possible reasons for this imbalance are the marked philosophical orientation of Rahner and the preference for Jesus and the New Testament vis-à-vis the entire divine revelation. The latter was usual at his time among the majority of Christians, especially in Catholic circles, and affected also the attitude towards Judaism. It is a sign that the appreciation of the Old Testament at the time of the Second Vatican Council was limited and God (father) as the source of all revela-

---

[69] See the critique of Filippo Manini, "Una postilla a Rahner sull'ispirazione," *RivBib* 66 (2018), 481–491.
[70] To give some examples: Rahner wrote about the Beatles, the conflict in Biafra, the landing on the Moon (*SW* 24/1, part G), on Liberation Theology (*SW* 28, 69–73), answered the questions of young people (*SW* 28, 378–452), etc. ... Rahner was very interested, even curious when coming into touch with new things – this was the experience of others and my personal one in living with him in Munich in the 1970s.
[71] *SW* 27, 31–35.
[72] *SW* 27, 31.
[73] *SW* 27, 397–453; their talks took place in the Jesuitenkolleg in Innsbruck, in July and October 1982.
[74] Cardinal Augustin Bea SJ was first president of the Pontifical Council for Promoting Christian Unity in 1960, and therefore also one of those responsible for the editing of Nostra Aetate, Unitatis Redintegratio and Dignitatis Humanae.

tion did not find the deserved attention. Only later, in the 1980s, did Brevard S. Childs with his "canonical approach" and Erich Zenger,[75] among others, succeed in overcoming this deficit.

References

Collinet, Benedikt. "Anmerkungen zur Bibelauslegung in Karl Rahners frühen Predigten." *GuL* 94 (2021): 64–69.
Collinet, Benedikt. "Die Autorität der Schrift im Wechselspiel mit dem katholischen Lehramt. Anmerkungen zum komplexen Verhältnis von Bibelwissenschaft und lehramtlicher Autorität am Beispiel der Päpstlichen Bibelkommission." In *Religious Authority / Autorität und Religion*, edited by Lumma, Liborius, Wilhelm Rees *et al.*, 33–58, Innsbruck: University Press, 2022.
Collinet, Benedikt J., and Georg Fischer, eds. *Karl Rahner und die Bibel. Interdisziplinäre Perspektiven*. Quaestiones Disputatae 326. Freiburg: Herder, 2022.
Fischer, Georg, *Theologien des Alten Testaments*, Neuer Stuttgarter Kommentar: Altes Testament 31, Stuttgart: Katholisches Bibelwerk, 2012.
Henne, Eugen, and Konstantin Rösch. *Die Heilige Schrift des Alten und Neuen Testamentes*. Paderborn: Schöningh, 1934.
Hünermann, Peter and Ernst J. Hilberath, eds. *Herders Theologischer Kommentar zum Zweiten Vatikanischen Konzil*, vol. 3. Freiburg: Herder, 2005.
Ignatius von Loyola. *Geistliche Übungen*, translated by Peter Knauer. Würzburg: Echter, ⁵2021.
Kampling, Rainer: "Exegese und Karl Rahner." In *Theologie aus Erfahrung der Gnade. Annäherungen an Karl Rahner*, edited by Mariano Delgado and Matthias Lutz-Bachmann, 267–283. Berlin: Morus 1994.
Karrer, Otto. *Neues Testament*. München: Ars Sacra/Josef Müller, 1949.
Keel, Othmar. *Die Welt der altorientalischen Bildsymbolik und das Alte Testament. Am Beispiel der Psalmen*. Zürich: Benziger, 1972; Göttingen: Vandenhoeck & Ruprecht, ³1984.
Manini, Filippo. "Una postilla a Rahner sull'ispirazione." *Rivista Biblica* 66 (2018): 481–491.
Neufeld, Karl Heinz. "Die Schrift in der Theologie Karl Rahners." *Jahrbuch für biblische Theologie* 2 (1987): 229–246.
Neufeld, Karl Heinz. *Die Brüder Rahner*. Freiburg: Herder, ²2004.
Pesch, Rudolf. "Gegen eine doppelte Wahrheit. Karl Rahner und die Bibelwissenschaft." In *Vor dem Geheimnis Gottes den Menschen verstehen*, edited by Karl Lehmann, 10–36. Freiburg, München, Zürich: Schnell & Steiner, 1984.
Pfister, Michael Florian. *Ein Mann der Bibel – Augustin Bea SJ (1881–1968) als Exeget und Rektor des Päpstlichen Bibelinstituts in den 1930er und 1940er Jahren*. Regensburg: Schnell & Steiner, 2020.

---

[75] Erich Zenger, *Das Erste Testament. Die jüdische Bibel und die Christen* (Düsseldorf: Patmos 1991, several editions since then).

Raffelt, Albert. "Karl Rahner und die Bibel." In *Anstöße der Theologie Karl Rahners für gegenwärtige Theologie und Kirche*, edited by Karsten Kreutzer and Albert Raffelt, 187–198. Freiburg: Katholische Akademie der Erzdiözese, 2019.

Rahner, Karl. *Sämtliche Werke 1–32/2* (= *SW*). Freiburg: Herder, 1995–2018.

Rembold, Albert. *Aus den Schatzkammern des Alten Testaments*. Valkenburg, Limburg: Ignatiusverlag, 1932.

Vass, George. *A Pattern of Doctrines 1: God and Christ. Understanding Karl Rahner*, vol. 3. London: Sheed & Ward, 1996.

Zenger, Erich. *Das Erste Testament. Die jüdische Bibel und die Christen*. Düsseldorf: Patmos, 1991.

Part 3: **Informing Theological Discourse: Systematic Perspectives**

Boubakar Sanou and John C. Peckham
Canonical Theology, Social Location and the Search for Global Theological Method

Abstract: This chapter sets forth a proposal outlining one way constructive theology might be approached in light of the rapid globalization of Christianity. Could there be such a thing as a global theological method? If so, what might it look like? How might global theological method be conceived (in broad strokes) so as to avoid (or at least mitigate) the danger of privileging and imposing particular philosophical, doctrinal, or other frameworks that are the fallible product of a given context or social location? To address these questions, the chapter first discusses the importance of social location and its impact on theological interpretation, construction, and reception. Then, the discussion turns to the question of the uniquely normative authority of Scripture relative to theological method by way of a brief discussion of some core commitments of canonical theological method, which revolve around the common commitment of most Christians to Scripture as the final standard of orthodoxy. Finally, the chapter discusses potential implications for approaching and doing constructive theology that upholds the uniquely normative authority of Scripture, could be affirmed and practiced by most Christians across the globe, and might assist in fostering a context for mutual theological dialogue without the imposition of one fallible context as the ground of such theological method.

Keywords: Theological method, Canonical theology, Global theology, Social location, Hermeneutics

1 Introduction

Theology is never done in a vacuum. Both the construction and reception of theology take place in particular contexts. Indeed, as Michael Goheen puts it, all readings of Scripture "are located readings that cannot escape their own cultural and historical limitations."[1] In this regard, James Cone adds, "one's social

---
[1] Michael W. Goheen, "A History and Introduction to a Missional Reading of the Bible," in

Boubakar Sanou, Andrews University, Berrien Springs MI, USA, sanou@andrews.edu,
John C. Peckham, Andrews University, Berrien Springs MI, USA, jpeckham@andrews.edu

https://doi.org/10.1515/9783110768411-014

and historical context decides not only the questions we address to God but also the mode or form of the answers given to the questions."[2]

In this and many other respects, while Christian theologies done in different contexts may address many common questions, such theologies will inevitably also address different issues and questions – particularly those that are perceived as most relevant to specific contexts. This has massive implications relative to the way constructive theology might be approached in light of the rapid globalization of Christianity, particularly now that, as Fernando Segovia puts it, "the myth of a systematic and universal theology, as well as the myth of an objective and universal interpretation, have been exposed."[3] In this regard, while the center of gravity has shifted such most Christians now live in the Global South, John Mbiti laments that there does "not seem to be corresponding shift toward mutuality and reciprocity in the theological task facing the universal church."[4] Marilyn Naidoo adds: "The dominant Eurocentric universality claim must continue to be challenged and dismantled in order to make room for other theological traditions to become included as partners in an authentic and mutual dialogue."[5] From this perspective, rather than competing over the seal of theological orthodoxy, theologians from various parts of the world should be called to acknowledge their need for one another.

Much theological discourse is driven by theological questions and categories that may be foreign to much of the Majority World (aka the Global South), sometimes overlooking questions and issues of importance to Majority World

---

Reading the Bible Missionally, ed. Michael W. Goheen (Grand Rapids: Eerdmans, 2016): 9. See also Michael Barram, "The Bible, Mission, and Social Location: Toward a Missional Hermeneutic," *Interpretation: A Journal of Bible and Theology* 61/1 (2007): 58; and George R. Hunsberger, "Proposals for a Missional Hermeneutic," in *Reading the Bible Missionally*, ed. Michael W. Goheen (Grand Rapids: Eerdmans, 2016): 309-321.

2 James H. Cone, *God of the Oppressed* (New York: Seabury Press, 1975), 14-15.

3 Fernando Segovia, "Two Places and No Place on Which to Stand: Mixture and Otherness in Hispanic American Theology," in *Mestizo Christianity: Theology from the Latino Perspective*, ed. Arturo J. Bañuelas (Maryknoll: Orbis, 1995), 29.

4 John Mbiti, "Theological Impotence and the Universality of the Church," as quoted in Timothy C. Tennent, *Theology in the Context of World Christianity: How the Global Church Is Influencing the Way We Think about and Discuss Theology* (Grand Rapids: Zondervan, 2009), 16.

5 Marilyn Naidoo, "Overcoming Alienization in Africanising Education," *HTS Teologiese Studies/Theological Studies* 72/1 (2018): 2. Cf. Perry W. H. Shaw, "'New Treasures with the Old': Addressing Culture and Gender Imperialism in Higher Level Theological Education," *Evangelical Review of Theology* 38/3 (2014): 265-79.

Christians.⁶ On the other hand, as Timothy Tennent puts it relative to the work of Majority World theologians, "new questions are being posed to the text within the larger context of poverty, powerlessness, pluralism, and the inevitable challenges that occur when vernacular languages begin to wrestle with theological issues."⁷

This situation raises numerous issues relative to theological method, including relative to how various questions and issues of theology should be pursued in various global contexts. Some approaches to theological method set forth in the West appear to require that Christians in various global contexts first adopt and imbibe particular conceptual frameworks, theological dogmas, and ways of reading the text that have been established in the theological discourse of the Christian tradition.

To take one recent example that we take to be representative of a chorus of contemporary voices on theological method, Craig A. Carter has recently proposed that Christian theology should be approached by way of what he calls the "Christian Platonism of the Great Tradition," which he states "was developed in order to express the metaphysical implications of the doctrine of God that emerged from pro-Nicene scriptural exegesis in the fourth century, and as a result the exegesis, the dogma, and the metaphysics are all intertwined together."⁸

Without attempting here an evaluation of the specifics of Carter's proposal, the positive claim he makes regarding the place of "Christian Platonism" itself raises numerous significant questions, particularly when one considers theological method in global perspective. One such major question is why a Christian in South Korea or Ghana or Guatemala should give priority to Platonic philosophy as a normative conceptual framework for theological interpretation, construction, and reception. As Frederick Wanjala notes: "The categories of thought employed in a philosophy necessarily determine the concepts inherent in the

---

6 In this regard, Steve Bevans adds: "A theology that honors the experience of context will be one that is not tied to Western ways, themes and methods of theology." Steve Bevans, *Essays in Contextual Theology* (Leiden: Brill, 2018), 108. Cf. the discussion in O. S. Olagunju, "An Evaluation of Bevans' Models of Contextual Theology and Its Contributions to Doing Theology in the 21st Century Church," *Ogbomoso Journal of Theology* 17/2 (2012): 37-57.

7 Timothy C. Tennent, *Theology in the Context of World Christianity*, 17. In this regard, see Emiola Nihinlola's call for a contextual theology that will "respond theologically and practically to the social, economic, political and religious needs of the people." Emiola Nihinlola, "A Contextual Theology of Christian Mission in Contemporary Africa," *Practical Theology* 1 (2008): 14.

8 Craig A. Carter, *Interpreting Scripture with the Great Tradition: Recovering the Genius of Premodern Exegesis* (Grand Rapids: Baker Academic, 2018), xiii.

evolving theology," which raises questions regarding the adoption and usage of "alien philosophies."[9]

While many Christian theologians, particularly in the West, advocate a kind of Christian Platonism and/or an Aristotelian-Thomist metaphysical framework, many other Christian theologians have claimed that such approaches are alien frameworks that are incompatible with the teachings of Scripture.[10] It is beyond the scope and goal of this essay to address the debate over whether such frameworks are compatible or incompatible with biblical teachings. However, the very fact that this is a significant point of controversy among Christians, coupled with the fact that many Christian theologies privilege such philosophical frameworks as requisite to Christian orthodoxy, raises significant methodological questions. Such methodological questions are not unique to Platonic or Aristotelian-Thomist philosophical frameworks, but extend to any framework or lens that is afforded methodological authority.

Quite apart from specific evaluations regarding the soundness of any particular philosophical or dogmatic framework, the privileging of any such framework raises significant worries relative to theological method generally and even more so with respect to the search for a common core of theological method that might serve as a shared context for constructive theological dialogue, engendering the kind of "shift toward mutuality and reciprocity in the theological task facing the universal church" for which Mbiti has rightly called.

Specifically, the privileging of any philosophical or theological framework relative to global theology faces at least the following two concerns:
(1) the potential undermining of the uniquely normative authority of Scripture that the vast majority of Christians across the globe affirm, and
(2) the danger of privileging and imposing particular philosophical, doctrinal, or other frameworks that are the fallible product of a given context or social location.

These two concerns will be taken up in the following two sections, beginning with a discussion of the importance of social location and its impact on theological interpretation, construction, and reception, then turning to the question of

---

9 Frederick Wanjala, "Contextual Theology: An Essential Pillar for the Success of the Church's Mission," *African Ecclesial Review* 58/3-4 (2016): 256. To be clear Wanjala is not here specifying any particular alien philosophy as the problem, but calling for the usage of more indigenous philosophies particularly in the task of evangelization.
10 Cf. the view of Justo L. González regarding what he considers the problematic theological conceptions of divine impassibility and strict immutability. González, *Mañana: Christian Theology from a Hispanic Perspective* (Nashville: Abingdon, 1990).

the uniquely normative authority of Scripture relative to theological method by way of a brief discussion of some core commitments of canonical theological method, which revolve around the common commitment of most Christians to Scripture as the final standard of orthodoxy. Finally, this paper will turn to a discussion of some potential implications for approaching and doing constructive theology that upholds the uniquely normative authority of Scripture, could be affirmed and practiced by most Christians across the globe, and might assist in fostering a context for mutual theological dialogue without the imposition of one fallible context as the ground of such theological method.

2 Social Location and Theological Method

2.1 Social Location: A Brief Overview

Social location refers to the sum total of human experiences that contribute to and shape a person's overall perspective on life. These human experiences not only include a person's physical location in age, gender, race, and community, but also the moral, intellectual, emotional, and spiritual atmosphere they live in, their social class, marital status, political convictions, language, nationality, history of the communities they belong to, etc. There is therefore no human life that is lived outside of a concrete social location. The various factors of a social location contribute to make each individual in society distinct from others. As members of a generation live through the same historical period and share similar experiences, a generation could even be considered as "a social location of thought."[11] This social locatedness creates in each person a specific "lens through which a vision of life and social order is expressed, experienced, and explored."[12] Thus, this specific lens, or worldview, equips each person with a unique overall outlook on life from which what they perceive as reality is seen, interpreted, evaluated, and interacted with. With time, this perception which

---

[11] Vernon K. Robbins, "The Social Location of the Implied Author of Luke-Acts," in *The Social World of Luke-Acts: Models for Interpreters*, edited by Jerome H. Neyrey (Peabody, MA: Hendrickson Publishers, 1991), 307.

[12] Kevin J. Vanhoozer, "What Is Everyday Theology? How and Why Christians Should Read Culture," in *Everyday Theology: How to Read Cultural Texts and Interpret Trends*, ed. Kevin J. Vanhoozer, Charles A. Anderson, and Michael J. Sleasman (Grand Rapids: Baker Academic, 2007), 26.

may have only been cognitive at the beginning, becomes engrained in a person to the point of influencing also the affective and evaluative dimensions of their daily life. In a sense, a person's social locatedness affects their overall reasoning about reality, which in turn programs them to believe and live in a certain way.

2.2 The Impact of Social Location on Theological Interpretation

In 2004 Mark Allan Powell published the results of his research on the impact of social location on the reading and interpretation of Scripture.[13] In the first phase of this research, he surveyed two groups of seminary students, one in the United States and the other in St. Petersburg, Russia. The experiment consisted in asking them to read the story of the Prodigal Son in Luke 15:11-32, close their Bibles, and then recount it from memory as accurately as possible to each other in their respective groups. He discovered two major differences in the oral recounting of this parable. On one hand, while only six percent of the American students remembered the famine mentioned in verse 14, 84% of the students in St. Petersburg made reference to it. On the other hand, 100% of the American students emphasized the prodigal son's squandering of his inheritance whereas only 34% of the Russian students remembered this detail.

For the American students the mention of the famine in the parable seems to be an extra detail that adds nothing fundamental to the story. Because they had no recent recollection of famine, they all emphasized the squandering of wealth as irresponsible behavior. However, for the Russian students, who lived and interacted with some of the survivors of the 900-day German army siege to the city of St. Petersburg in 1941 which triggered a famine that killed up to 670,000 people, the mention of the famine was a significant detail that added a lot to the story.

In the second phase of his research, Powell surveyed the famine detail in scholarly exegesis of this parable. After reviewing fifty-five Western biblical scholars' writing on this parable, he found that 67% of them (37 out of 55 scholars) made no mention of the famine at all, or just mentioned it but without any comment. The remaining 33% of the authors (18 out of 55) mention the famine but

---

13 Mark Allan Powell, "The Forgotten Famine: Personal Responsibility in Luke's Parable of the 'Prodigal Son'" in *Literary Encounters with the Reign of God,* ed. Sharon H. Ringe and H. C. Paul Kim (New York: T&T Clark, 2004), 265-287.

only as a negligible detail, which when omitted has no impact whatsoever on the significance of the story other than to intensify the already dreadful situation.[14]

This experiment is a good illustration of the unavoidable reality of a person's social location's impact on their reading and interpretation of Scripture. A person's social location influences how they see the world, conceptualize reality, or interpret Scripture. Thus, whenever we approach Scripture, our social location programming "tells us what to notice and what is not worth noticing."[15] That may explain why the New Testament contains four accounts of the only one Gospel as the same gospel story was packaged by each of the four authors in a different way for the consumption of their selected audiences. Their audiences provided them with the contexts within which the content of the Gospel was reformulated.

2.3 Toward a Transformative Theological Interpretation

Because of the formative nature of every person's social locatedness on their ontological and epistemological perspective on the world and their own lived experiences, it is inevitable that their social locatedness will also inform their reading and theological interpretation of Scripture,[16] and ultimately their faith in and relationship with Jesus. In other words, whether they like it or not, each Christian's social location shapes their understanding of what they read in the Bible and how they conceptualize it theologically.[17] Therefore, because biblical interpretation never takes place in a social and cultural vacuum, understanding the social location of the recipients of the gospel must not be overlooked in biblical hermeneutics.[18] Since effective communication is not only about what is said but also about what is heard, to avoid miscommunicating the principles of Scripture, theologians should be concerned both about what they say and what

---

14 Powell, "The Forgotten Famine," 265-274.
15 E. Randolph Richards and Brandon J. O'Brien, *Misreading Scripture with Western Eyes: Removing Cultural Blinders to Better Understand the Bible* (Downers Grove: InterVarsity, 2012), 71. See also Elisabeth Schüssler Fiorenza, "The Ethics of Biblical Interpretation: Decentering Biblical Scholarship," *Journal of Biblical Literature* 107/1 (1988): 5.
16 Bruce L. Bauer, "Social Location and Its Impact on Hermeneutics," *Journal of Adventist Mission Studies* 12/1 (2016): 75; Kevin J. Vanhoozer, *Hearers and Doers: A Pastor's Guide to Making Disciples Through Scripture and Doctrine* (Bellingham, WA: Lexham Press, 2019), xii-xiii.
17 Craig G. Bartholomew, *Introducing Biblical Hermeneutics: A Comprehensive Framework for Hearing God in Scripture* (Grand Rapids: Baker Academic, 2015), 216.
18 Barram, "The Bible, Mission, and Social Location," 58.

their intended audiences hear given the realities of their social locatedness. It should always be remembered that "if theology is the ministry of the Word to the world, it follows that theologians must know something about the world to which they are ministering."[19]

For any approach to theological interpretation to be effective in contributing to the transformation of people's worldviews, in any context, it must be hermeneutically sound. But it must also be "culturally relevant and receiver-oriented thus minimizing rejection by and alienation of the people to whom it is presented."[20] In other words, for the gospel to meaningfully engage recipients with the purpose of transforming their worldviews, its communicators must encode the biblical and theological message in such a way that its content remains faithful to the standard of biblical warrant (see the further discussion of this standard later in this chapter), but also makes sense to its receptors in terms of its relevance in order to challenge them given their social location. The rationale for this is that people cannot be confronted with things that are beyond their frame of reference and be expected to respond positively to them. As such, for biblical interpreters to make a lasting impact on their readers, especially outside of academia, they need to pay attention to the social location assumptions of those readers.[21] Just as people can run into the danger of misreading Scripture if they neglect basic principles of biblical interpretation, theologians can also run into the danger of misapplying Scripture if they neglect basic principles of cultural hermeneutics.

How can Scripture be faithfully presented in a pluralistic age for the worldviews of its hearers to be transformed? Our approach to this question is that besides prayerfully engaging in a rigorous exegesis and theological interpretation of biblical texts, biblical scholars must also diligently strive to achieve some degree of proficiency in cultural literacy as this would help them understand the various factors affecting their intended audiences' reading and theological interpretation of the Bible, the reasons behind those factors, and how to respond in ways that are biblically faithful and contextually relevant so that those readers can make intelligent, life-changing decisions in favor of the gospel.

Since one purpose of theological interpretation is to seek to understand Scripture for a specific context, it must always be rooted in Scripture as its

---

[19] Vanhoozer, "What Is Everyday Theology?" 8.
[20] Boubakar Sanou, *Motivating and Training the Laity to Increase their Involvement in Ministry in the Ouaga-Center Adventist Church in Burkina Faso* (DMin diss., Andrews University, 2010), 42.
[21] Glenn Rogers, *The Bible Culturally Speaking: The Role of Culture in the Production, Presentation and Interpretation of God's Word* (Bedford: Mission and Ministry Resources, 2004), 27, 36, 41.

source of truth and always connected to a context as the setting where the biblical truth is applied and expressed.[22] Theologians must also endeavor to recover theological interpretation from a mere credal or critical academic reading of the Bible and put more emphasis on helping their readers grow as faithful disciples of Jesus Christ. Kevin Vanhoozer argues that because culture is "a powerful means of spiritual formation," the process of making disciples must involve "both deprogramming (exposing, critiquing, and correcting the pictures and stories we live by) and reprogramming (replacing the "old self" and the social imaginaries that funded our former way of life with the social imaginary generated by Scripture and the gospel.)"[23] This means that theological interpreters need not be content with only rightly articulating truth as it is found in the Bible. Since the ultimate truth is in the person of Jesus and not in mere concepts (John 14:6), scholars should care about suggesting practical, culturally relevant ways of growing in Christ, normed by Scripture. By successfully bridging the gap between lectern and pew, their hearers and readers will know how the Bible relates to their daily life and hopefully be equipped to "negotiate their way carefully, following the one way of Jesus Christ through a variety of cultural byways."[24] In other words, by being able to understand how what is happening in contemporary culture affects their readers, scholars will be better equipped to help those readers "leave [their] mark on culture rather than passively submit to cultural conditioning."[25]

Faithful theological interpretation should be far more than simply presenting biblical truth no matter how crucial that truth is. While cognitive knowledge is important to a life of faith, cognitive knowledge alone is not enough to transform a person's worldview. Jesus himself spent an important part of his ministry in teaching truth (e.g., the Sermon on the Mount in Matt 5-7; the parables: Luke 15, 18:1-14, 19:11-26; Matt 13:1; Luke 4:31-32; John 15:1-17). His intention was for his hearers to grow in their understanding of the person and will of God in order for them to have an informed and better relationship with him. Yet, Christ taught the truth as knowledge grounded in a relationship and experience with God (John 8:32, 15:1-10). He always challenged his hearers, especially his disci-

---

[22] David K. Clark, "Biblical and Theological Foundations of Marriage and Family," in *Handbook of Family Religious Education*, ed. Blake J. Neff and Donald Ratcliff (Birmingham, AL: Religious Education Press, 1995), 21.
[23] Vanhoozer, *Hearers and Doers*, xiii, 15.
[24] Vanhoozer, "What is Everyday Theology?" 7.
[25] Vanhoozer, *Hearers and Doers*, xii.

ples, to apply their intellectual knowledge to their day-to-day experiences (Matt 7:24-27).

Hearing and accepting cognitively the truth as it is in the Bible is not the end of the Christian experience. Alongside continually seeking to better understand the truth that Scripture teaches, believers need to be constantly challenged to pay close attention to their experiential growth in Christ (2 Pet 3:18). Since a loyal allegiance to Jesus is a hallmark of being his disciples (Luke 16:13), one of the dangers in biblical interpretation is to make truth something that is merely discussed rather than something that practically relates to believers' daily experiences and moves them into allegiance to Christ. Since "biblical truth is meant not just to be studied but more to be applied in life-changing ways,"[26] providing contextually relevant but biblically faithful applications of theological truth to life's situations should be an important goal of faithful, transformative theological interpretation. Consequently, scholars should endeavor to help their readers understand not only what particular scriptural passages teach, but should theologically interpret Scripture in a way that relates to how theological truth may impact their relationship with Christ.

The end goal of faithful theological scholarship should be to give strong roots to the teachings of Scripture within the various contexts of our ever-changing world. The understanding of biblical truth must be cognitive, affective, and evaluative for it to have a life-changing impact on its hearers' deep-seated worldview assumptions.[27] It needs "to make practical application of each passage to the individual life [...] in order to bring the hearers or readers to salvation and an ever closer, personal relationship with God."[28] Jiří Moskala succinctly sums up the primary goal of biblical interpretation:

> the *raison d'être* of biblical interpretation is not primarily to understand biblical history, though this is crucial, or to know doctrine, even though doctrine is indispensable for an intelligent following of Christ. The primary reason to interpret the Bible is to be engaged in a personal relationship with the loving and holy Lord and to grow in Him, in the experiential knowledge of His character and saving actions.[29]

---

[26] Grant R. Osborne, "Hermeneutics," in *Evangelical Dictionary of World Mission*, ed. A. Scott Moreau (Grand Rapids: Baker Books, 2000), 432.
[27] Osborne, "Hermeneutics," 432.
[28] Richard M. Davidson, "Interpreting Scripture: An Hermeneutical 'Decalogue,'" *Journal of the Adventist Theological Society* 4/2 (1993): 109.
[29] Jiří Moskala, "Toward Consistent Adventist Hermeneutics: From Creation through De-Creation to Re-Creation," in *Women and Ordination: Biblical and Historical Studies*, ed. John W. Reeve (Nampa, ID: Pacific Press, 2015), 7.

With this understanding of social location and its relevance to theological interpretation in place, we are now in a position to turn to the issue of the uniquely normative authority of Scripture relative to theological method.

3 The Normative Authority of Scripture and Canonical Theology

The vast majority of Christians over the ages have affirmed the uniquely normative authority of Scripture – that Scripture is the prime standard or norm of faith and practice. This is especially true of Majority World theologians, whose affirmation of "the authority of Scripture stands as a powerful bulwark against the winds of skepticism that have swept across much of the Western academy and church."[30] However, as briefly noted earlier, the way that some approaches to Christian theology privilege particular philosophical frameworks – and the theological dogmas and textual interpretations that flow from them – seems to undermine the uniquely normative authority of Scripture that the vast majority of Christians across the globe affirm.

Specifically, if a given *kind of* extra-biblical conceptual framework (e.g., Christian Platonism) is privileged as a lens through which Scripture should be read and a rule according to which theology should be constructed, then that given conceptual framework possesses functional priority over Scripture – serving as an interpretative norm. Scripture cannot reform or correct any such lens or rule insofar as the very reading of Scripture is normed by such a lens or rule. This runs afoul of the widespread Christian view that Scripture is the norm that is not normed and replaces the uniquely normative authority of Scripture, which most Christians take to be infallible, with an external norm that is fallible and derived from a particular context that is foreign to many Christians across the globe. Of course, Scripture itself is the product of particular contexts, but – in the view of most Christians – Scripture is unique in that it is the product of special divine revelation and inspiration and, thus, should not only be regarded as uniquely normative, but should also *function theologically* as uniquely normative – as the final standard or norm by which theological claims are measured, judged, and (when necessary) reformed.

---

30 Tennent, *Theology in the Context of World Christianity*, 14.

3.1 Canonical Authority

Elsewhere, one of us has made a case for a canonical approach to theological method that flows from recognizing the authority of Scripture as the unique and final norm of theological interpretation and construction.[31] The core commitments of a canonical approach could be practiced among and across the vast range of Christian communities because nearly all Christian communities across the globe recognize the common core of the biblical canon.[32] While some Christians recognize more books, nearly all Christians affirm the uniquely normative (i.e., "canonical") authority of the 39 books of the Hebrew Bible or Old Testament and the 27 books of the New Testament. This common core of the biblical canon is by far the most widely attested rule of Christian thought, enjoying nearly universal reverence among Christians.

The core commitments of this canonical approach are in large part just the working out of a way to approach theology such that Scripture *functions* as uniquely normative, or *canonical*, at every step.[33] Canonical theology treats Scripture as *canonical* in virtue of the belief that Scripture is divinely revealed and inspired and is the divinely commissioned and thus unified collection of writings that God has commissioned to function as the uniquely normative rule of faith and practice.[34] Accordingly, canonical theology employs the entirety of

---

[31] See John C. Peckham, *Canonical Theology: The Biblical Canon, Sola Scriptura, and Theological Method* (Grand Rapids: Eerdmans, 2016). See also John C. Peckham, "The Rationale for Canonical Theology: An Approach to Systematic Theology After Modernism," *Andrews University Seminary Studies* 55/1 (2017): 83-105.

[32] In this regard, Jay Wesley Richards avers that "commitment to biblical normativity" is itself "the norm among Catholic and Orthodox" and Protestant theologians. *The Untamed God: A Philosophical Exploration of Divine Perfection, Simplicity, and Immutability* (Downers Grove, IL: InterVarsity, 2003), 32.

[33] The canonical theological method employs the following steps: (1) identify the issues/questions by extensive literature review (subject to change based on canonical investigation), (2) attempt to table known presuppositions that impinge upon the theological issues/questions and conduct an inductive reading of the canon and extract for further study any texts/passages that even touch on the questions, (3) pore over the data derived from the inductive reading, analyzing and organizing it according to discernible canonical patterns, (4) based on the analysis of the data, construct a minimal model that addresses the theological issues/questions, and, finally, (5) systematize the model by situating the tentative theological conclusions within the context of the wider theological landscape, with openness to further investigation and correction. For a more detailed discussion of these steps and the theory behind them, see Peckham, *Canonical Theology*.

[34] This involves recognizing Scripture as "canonical" in three primary ways: (1) the basic sense of the term "canon" as the rule or standard of theology – the norm over which there is no

the biblical canon as the formal *and* functional rule of theology by which all theological interpretations and claims should be continually measured and normed.[35]

3.2 Scripture Rules over Readers' Understandings

From the view that Scripture is divinely commissioned to be the uniquely normative (i.e., canonical) rule of faith and practice, it follows that Scripture should actually *rule* relative to theological interpretations and judgments. If Scripture is to *function* as such, one's view or that of one's community cannot be allowed to rule over Scripture. This requires that one recognizes that one's views (and those of one's community) may be in need of correction and reform by Scripture (understanding that one's reading of Scripture is itself impacted by one's social location such that this process involves an ongoing, hermeneutical spiral).[36]

In this regard, canonical theology deliberately recognizes that all theologians always and unavoidably bring their fallible conceptual frameworks to the theological task and that such frameworks are greatly impacted by one's social location. At the same time, canonical theology affirms that the teachings of Scripture set forth an overarching conception of the nature of reality and how to understand it, which undergirds the narratives and claims of Scripture. This we

---

norm (except God), hermeneutical or otherwise, (2) recognizing the canon as the rule in virtue of recognizing it as the divinely commissioned corpus of Scripture, and (3) reading the canon as a unified (but not uniform) corpus, consisting of spiritual things that are to be spiritually discerned. See Peckham, "The Rationale for Canonical Theology."

35 As David Yeago puts it, recognizing "the biblical canon as inspired Scripture" means to approach "the texts as the discourse of the Holy Spirit, the discourse therefore of one single speaker, despite the plurality of their human authors" such that "the church receives the canon, in all its diversity, as nonetheless a *single* body of discourse." "The Bible: The Spirit, the Church, and the Scriptures," in *Knowing the Triune God*, ed. David Yeago and James Buckley (Grand Rapids: Eerdmans, 2001), 70. Further, Kevin Vanhoozer states, there is a "properly theological unity implicit in the idea that God is the ultimate communicative agent speaking in Scripture," the "divine author" of the canon. *The Drama of Doctrine: A Canonical-Linguistic Approach to Christian Theology* (Louisville: Westminster John Knox Press, 2005), 177, 181. Accordingly, "we must read the Bible canonically, as one book. Each part has meaning in light of the whole (and in light of its center, Jesus Christ)." *Drama*, 178.

36 In this regard, as Thomas H. McCall puts it: "We should be faithful to proclaim all that Scripture teaches, but we should be cautious about going *beyond* it." McCall, "Is the Wrath of God Really Satisfying?" *Christianity Today*, 29.03.2018, https://www.christianitytoday.com/ct/2018/march-web-only/is-wrath-of-god-satisfying-good-friday-cross.html.

might refer to as a *core* conceptual framework.[37] Accordingly, the method of canonical theology aims at progressively shaping and reforming the theologian's fallible conceptual framework by sustained attention to the core conceptual framework that can be discerned in the biblical canon itself, seeking illumination by the Holy Spirit and recognizing that this aim is an imperfect and continual process since one's reading of Scripture is itself always impacted by one's fallible conceptual framework.[38]

Despite the illumination of the Spirit, the subjectivity and social location of any reader of Scripture cannot be excluded from their interpretation of what they read. Said differently, a Spirit-enlightened interpretation of Scripture in no way negates the impact of the interpreters' social location on their scholarship since their social locatedness is inseparably linked to their frame of reference. Therefore, readers' understanding of Scripture should not be permitted to supersede Scripture itself as normative. Diligent study and reliance on the Holy Spirit for discernment has the potential to lead an interpreter to more light on a passage of Scripture.[39] The same Holy Spirit who inspired Scripture in the first place will also illuminate Scripture so that contemporary readers can understand and apply its principles to their daily lives (1 Cor 2:11-14; cf. John 16:13).[40]

---

[37] Such an approach does not expect to arrive at a fully articulated philosophical metaphysical framework or epistemology as if such is taught by Scripture, but involves minimal overarching claims that flow from what Scripture discernibly and demonstrably affirms.

[38] Although the phrase "conceptual framework" is used in various ways, we use it here to refer to the framework within which one conceptualizes anything about which they think.

[39] See Roy B. Zuck, "The Role of the Holy Spirit in Hermeneutics," *Bibliotheca Sacra* 141/562 (1984): 120-130; Gary L. Nebeker, "The Holy Spirit, Hermeneutics, and Transformation: From Present to Future Glory," *Evangelical Review of Theology* 27/1 (2003): 47-54.

[40] To comfort his grief-stricken disciples after announcing to them his imminent departure to heaven, Jesus promised them the omnipresence of the Holy Spirit. The Holy Spirit, as the Helper (παράκλητος, *parakletos*), will abide with the disciples not only to bring to their remembrance what Jesus previously taught them (John 14:16, 26, 15:26), but also to guide them into all truth (John 16:13). Because the Holy Spirit is "the Spirit of truth" (John 14:17) who inspired the writing of Scripture (2 Pet 1:20-21; 2 Tim 3:16) and guides believers "into all truth" (John 16:13), his involvement in the transformative hermeneutical process is not optional. Although careful study should be highly valued in biblical interpretation, it should also be strongly emphasized that because faithful biblical hermeneutics is a spiritual enterprise, the intended meaning of a scriptural passage and its contemporary significance and application cannot be ascertained only by rational processes apart from the enlightenment of the Holy Spirit. Carefully following the principles of both biblical and cultural hermeneutics should go hand in hand with total dependence on the guidance of the Holy Spirit in seeking to comprehend Scripture. There is a connectedness between the role of the Holy Spirit in revealing Scripture and his role in faithfully interpreting and applying it. As the author of Scripture, the Holy Spirit is definitely its best

Yet, once again, reliance on the Holy Spirit's guidance in the process of theological interpretation does not mean that biblical scholars or theologians can claim infallibility for their interpretation of Scripture simply by claiming that they were led by the Holy Spirit. Infallibility is a characteristic quality of Scripture (cf. 2 Tim 3:16; 2 Pet 1:20-21), but not of its interpreters. The work of the revelation and inspiration of Scripture is a complete superintended work of the Holy Spirit. The Spirit's illumination as it relates to the interpretation of Scripture is an ongoing process. For one thing, finite human interpreters can only have partial glimpses of what can be known about God (1 Cor 13:9-12). Moreover, since we cannot entirely escape the limitations of our own deep-seated worldview assumptions, we can never arrive at absolute objectivity in our reading and interpretation of Scripture.[41] Thus, despite the illumination of the Spirit, the subjectivity and social location of any reader of Scripture always affects (to some degree) the reader's interpretation of what they read.

Rather than (intentionally) privileging a particular conceptual framework or theological understanding that is inevitably impacted by one's subjectivity and social location (or that of particular communities), however, the method of canonical theology attempts to continually subject all conceptual frameworks and theological interpretations to being measured and normed by the claims discernible in the canon of Scripture itself.[42] This involves subjecting all relevant beliefs and claims to the twin standards of canonical correspondence and canonical coherence, which themselves flow from commitment to the uniquely normative authority of Scripture.[43]

---

expositor. Diligent study and reliance on the Holy Spirit for discernment has the potential to lead an interpreter to more light on a passage of Scripture. In this process of unfolding the truth of Scripture (cf. John 16:13), the Holy Spirit takes what God wanted to convey through biblical authors and actualizes it so that contemporary readers can apply its principles to their daily lives. In this way, the Spirit's conviction of sin, righteousness, and judgment (John 16:8) continues to be a present-day reality. For further reading, see Zuck, "The Role of the Holy Spirit in Hermeneutics"; Nebeker, "The Holy Spirit, Hermeneutics, and Transformation."

41 Vanhoozer, "What Is Everyday Theology?" 36.
42 Of course, given that we all read and interpret from a particular social location, we inevitably privilege some conceptual framework, but such unintentional privileging can be mitigated methodologically.
43 For further discussion of these standards, see Peckham, *Canonical Theology*, 206-212. As *Canonical Theology* was written primarily for an audience of Western academic theologians, our claim is not that the book is immediately employable in all global contexts, but that the core commitments set forth therein might be immediately practicable.

3.3 Canonical Correspondence and Coherence

The standard of canonical correspondence refers to whether and to what extent a particular claim corresponds to what the biblical canon affirms.[44] A claim fails the standard of canonical correspondence if it is not discernible, demonstrable, and defensible on the basis of what is affirmed in the text of Scripture.[45] Another way of speaking of this standard is in terms of biblical warrant. A biblically warranted claim is one that is adequately grounded in what Scripture affirms. The complementary standard of canonical coherence requires that theological claims be coherent with one another, following from the view that, as divinely revealed and inspired, Scripture does not *affirm* contradictory teachings. As such, if one's theological interpretations and claims adequately correspond to Scripture, such interpretations and claims will not include contradictions.

Yet, given the ruling authority of Scripture, one should not synthetically smooth out apparent tensions in Scripture, but should patiently look for an understanding of all relevant texts and passages that is consistent while resisting the temptation to twist, distort, or negate what any text of Scripture actually claims. Relative to both standards, theological interpretations and claims should continually be subjected back to the test of whether they correspond to the teachings of Scripture. While competent theologians may disagree about whether a given claim is biblically warranted or consistent with Scripture, such claims can be checked and dialogued over in community (local and global) according to the rule of Scripture as canon.[46]

---

[44] We recognize the irony of a paper arguing for biblically normed theological interpretation that does not itself give much in the way of biblical engagement. One of us has elsewhere laid out a biblical case for this, but the scope of this brief essay does not allow for both a summary and consideration of this method and a constructive biblical case for this approach. For this, see Peckham, *Canonical Theology*.

[45] In this regard, as Christopher Seitz put it, canonical reading "shares a concern for the objective reality of the text and for its intentional direction and ruled character." "Canonical Approach," in *Dictionary for Theological Interpretation of the Bible*, ed. Kevin J. Vanhoozer (Grand Rapids: Baker Academic, 2005), 100.

[46] "Different theologies emerge because different cultures ask different questions and the contextual responses tend to be highly influenced by practical problems in the local cultures and their worldviews. Different theologies may be complementary, but their theologies must be connected with Christian universal beliefs and examination of the Scriptures. Thus, the presence of so many contextual responses in the globalization process should be illuminated in the light of the universal Christian beliefs. All theology in the local context must attempt to be contextualized without the loss of Christian identity or of truth. 'Globalizing theology' presents how to incarnate faithfully Christian truth in the contemporary globalizing world." Young Sub

3.4 Micro-exegesis and Macro-exegesis

As Fernando Canale has emphasized in his work, any task of theological interpretation and construction that aims at attending to the teachings of Scripture involves the following three levels of theological thinking, each of which are impacted by one's social location:
(1) the level of the theological reading of individual texts and passages of Scripture
(2) the level of particular theological doctrines, and
(3) the level of overarching (philosophical) conceptions of the nature of reality – regarding the divine nature, the nature of creation, and the relationship between Creator and creation.[47]

These three levels greatly impact one another. One's overarching conceptions regarding the nature of reality will greatly impact one's doctrinal affirmations and one's reading of Scripture. Conversely, it follows from commitment to the ruling (i.e., "canonical") authority of Scripture that one's doctrinal affirmations and overarching conceptual framework should be informed and reformed by the individual texts and passages of Scripture.

In order to navigate these three levels (the textual, doctrinal, and philosophical), canonical theology employs two levels of exegesis.[48] First, canonical theology employs the procedures of grammatical-historical exegesis at the level of individual passages, while recognizing such procedures do not exhaust the task of theological interpretation.[49] This first level of exegesis might be called micro-exegesis. Second, canonical theology seeks to consider the entirety of Scripture relative to a given issue or question, seeking what Scripture affirms at the levels of doctrinal claims (the doctrinal level) and overarching conceptions

---

Song, "Cultural Context of Globalization and 'Globalizing Theology' as a Christian Response to the Globalization Process," *Korean Journal of Christian Studies* 81 (2012): 259.

47 Fernando Canale refers to these three levels as macro-hermeneutical principles, meso-hermeneutical principles, and micro-hermeneutical principles, respectively. See Fernando Luis Canale, *Back to Revelation-Inspiration: Searching for the Cognitive Foundation of Christian Theology in a Postmodern World* (Lanham, MD: University Press of America, 2001), 148–49.

48 This approach, articulated in more technical detail in Peckham, *Canonical Theology*, draws on and expands Fernando Canale's crucial distinction between [micro]hermeneutical and [macro]phenomenological exegesis. Canale, *Back to Revelation-Inspiration*, 148-49.

49 It follows from the view that Scripture is divinely commissioned to function as the rule of faith that one should pay close attention to the syntax and grammar of the text and anything that can be known with confidence about the history of the text. On the biblical basis for such an approach, see Davidson, "Interpreting Scripture," 95-114.

of the nature of reality (the philosophical level), without assuming that Scripture answers any given issue or question the theologian might raise.[50] This second level may be called macro-exegesis, which is exegetical in the sense that it aims at drawing conclusions from the biblical canon rather than reading conclusions into the biblical canon.

Ideally, these two levels of exegesis operate in tandem – in a kind of ongoing spiral of theological interpretation that moves from the trees (individual passages of Scripture) to the forest (Scripture as a whole) and back again.[51] The exegetical reading of individual texts and passages is the basis for any consideration of what Scripture as a whole may affirm relative to a given claim and, in turn, consideration of what Scripture teaches as a whole sheds light on the reading of any individual texts and passages. Alongside this, canonical theology deliberately recognizes that one's exegetical reading of any individual text or passage is unavoidably affected by the conceptual framework and doctrinal beliefs that one comes to the text with (and one's social location as a whole), but seeks to continually subject one's known beliefs to criticism and correction by Scripture (which itself involves a process of interpretation in a hermeneutical spiral) such that (ideally) one's consideration of what Scripture (as a whole) affirms will progressively reform one's conceptual framework and doctrinal beliefs.

Such a continual process is necessary because, as Marc Cortez puts it, "a completely objective 'God's-eye' view of the world will never be available to us."[52] Accordingly, canonical theology does not attempt to construct a totalizing and immovable cathedral-like systematic theology, but via the ongoing process of micro-exegesis and macro-exegesis, aims at constructing dynamic and ambulatory models – always moving and reforming according to further consideration of Scripture, analogous to Israel's traveling wilderness tabernacle.[53]

---

[50] Further, the questions the theologian asks should themselves be reformed via consideration of Scripture.
[51] Cf. Grant Osborne's view, wherein "continuous interaction between text and system forms a spiral upward to theological truth." *The Hermeneutical Spiral* (Downers Grove: IVP Academic, 2006), 392.
[52] Marc Cortez, "Context and Concept: Contextual Theology and the Nature of Theological Discourse," *Westminster Journal of Theology* 67 (2005): 89.
[53] See Peckham, *Canonical Theology*, 220-221.

3.5 The Priority of What Is in the Text

From the commitment to the ruling authority of Scripture, it follows that instead of presupposing the truth of this or that conceptual framework or doctrinal claim, all such frameworks and claims should be *continually* tested according to the standard of biblical warrant (or canonical correspondence). In this regard, approaches to the theological interpretation of Scripture often distinguish between what is in the text – the actual writings of Scripture – from what is referred to as what is "behind the text" and what is "in front of the text."[54] What is behind the text refers to what can be known about the context and way in which the text originated, including questions of authorship, date, and the situation of life that the writing first addressed. What is in front of the text refers to the way post-biblical Christians have interpreted the text of Scripture – the way the text has been received and understood by Christians throughout the ages.[55]

Consideration of both what is behind the text and what is in front of the text can yield crucial insights and are very valuable and worthwhile areas of study. However, if the biblical canon itself is to function as uniquely normative for theological construction, both what is behind the text and what is in front of the text must be ruled by what is in the text.[56] As such, without neglecting consideration of what is behind the text and what is in front of the text, canonical theology gives priority to what is in the text.

This is crucial for the context of global theology in at least two primary respects. First, if what is in the text is to function as *canonical*, then consideration of what is behind the text could greatly illuminate the potential meaning in the text, but such consideration cannot be allowed to override what the text says. That is, consideration of what is behind the text can be used to shed light on what the text conveys, but never in a way that runs counter to what the text actually says – that is, the grammar and syntax of the text. This rules out the kind of modernistic biblical criticism that treats the biblical text as a merely human production and which tends to focus on attempting to reconstruct the origins of the text on the basis of merely humanistic, and largely speculative, considerations that often run counter to what is in the text itself. Further, from

---

54 Cf. Kevin J. Vanhoozer, "What Is Theological Interpretation of the Bible?" in *Dictionary for Theological Interpretation of the Bible*, ed. Kevin J. Vanhoozer (Grand Rapids: Baker Academic, 2005), 19.
55 What about textual criticism? Canonical theology operates by consideration of the best results of textual criticism.
56 Put differently, what is in the text matters most, but what is behind and in front of the text also matters, but both matter in a way that has to be ruled by the text itself.

the recognition that Scripture is a divinely revealed and inspired corpus, it follows that the meaning in the text cannot be limited to what humans at the time may have thought apart from divine inspiration. This recognition widens the task of theological interpretation to consideration of the divinely intended meaning that is discernible in the text in its immediate and canonical context.

Second, if Scripture itself is to function as canonical, what is in front of the text – the interpretations of Scripture and theologies of Christians down through the ages – must be normed by what is in the biblical text itself. As such, while canonical theology recognizes the great value of studying and learning from Christian theologians throughout the ages, canonical theology reserves final, normative authority for the biblical canon itself such that past and present Christian interpretations and theologies should always be subjected to the standard of biblical warrant.

As Marc Cortez puts it, the "theological formulations of other historical contexts (e.g., creeds, confessions, etc.) [...] should be listened to very carefully" and treated with "respect and dignity," but "we must deny that such formulations have an authoritative function beyond that of a historically reliable theology. Our contextual dialogue must therefore include these historical contexts but must not feel itself constrained by the assertions, assumptions, and articulations provided by those contexts."[57] This excludes the normative privileging of a given philosophical framework or theological system as a lens that governs the reading of Scripture. While canonical theology greatly values the proper role of community, it does not afford *normative* authority to communal interpretations or theologies. This is because the adoption of community-normed theological interpretation would undermine the functional ruling ("canonical") authority of Scripture.

Not only that, the implementation of community-normed interpretation requires that one first identify which tradition and/or community is adequate to function as such a norm and whose interpretations are best.[58] In this regard, Hyung Jin Kim Sun rightly points out that traditional theological "sources are not self-explanatory; someone has to do the work of interpreting them, a process that always is informed by the social location and intellectual outlook of

---

57 Cortez, "Creation and Context: A Theological Framework for Contextual Theology," 362.
58 On some problems faced by community-normed approaches, particularly relative to answering the questions, which tradition and whose interpretation, see Peckham, *Canonical Theology*, 104-108. See, further, the discussion of the relationship between tradition and theological method given a perspective that privileges Scripture as uniquely normative in Kwabena Donkor, *Tradition, Method, and Contemporary Protestant Theology: An Analysis of Thomas C. Oden's Vincentian Method* (Lanham, MD: University Press of America, 2003).

the person doing the interpreting."⁵⁹ Accordingly, the implementation of community-normed theological interpretation not only amounts to giving normative authority to a fallible community and/or tradition that may foster false teachings, but also engenders the imposition of one context and social location on other Christians of all other times and places.

3.6 Doing Theology within Community and across Communities

Canonical theology does not, on the other hand, give license to isolationist readings – that is, readings that individuals undertake (or attempt to undertake) in isolation from the influence of other people or resources. In fact, as briefly alluded to earlier, canonical theology emphasizes that no theological interpretation can actually be done in a way that is free from any extra-biblical influence and every theological interpretation is impacted by the conceptual framework that one brings to the text. As such, one who attempts to do theology in isolation is far more susceptible to idiosyncratic interpretations that flow from one's own fallible conceptual framework, which is itself greatly impacted by one's social location.

Recognition of the ruling authority of Scripture should engender humility and self-criticism.⁶⁰ If the canon is to rule, then one's fallible interpretation of it cannot rule, but one should deliberately submit one's interpretation of the text to be measured against what is discernible and demonstrable in the text itself. As such, one should be at least as critical of one's own interpretations as one is of the interpretations of others, recognizing that "all theologies are contextual," which "is not to say that all theology is relative" but "to acknowledge that every theological perspective [including one's own and that of one's community] has emerged in a particular time and space, in engagement with specific cultures, issues, and events."⁶¹

---

59 Hyung Jin Kim Sun, "Intercultural Global Theology," *Vision: A Journal for Church and Theology* 19/2 (2018): 87. In context, he is addressing specifically the sources of his own Mennonite tradition, but the point he makes applies to all theological sources and traditions.
60 Recognizing that far more than methodological procedures are at work in doing theology, canonical theology is committed to a humble interpretive posture and orientation toward the text and theology, the practice of ethical and charitable reading, and recognition of the limits of human language and interpretation. See the discussion in Peckham, *Canonical Theology*, 218-225.
61 Hyung Jin Kim Sun, "Intercultural Global Theology," 82.

Further, it is crucial to note that while Scripture may be read and interpreted in various ways, so too might *any* text – including any text of any given tradition. What some people see as the "problem" of hermeneutical diversity, then, is not a problem unique to a canonical approach, but (as has been argued elsewhere) an unavaoidable byproduct of the hermeneutical circle.[62] Whereas some propose that hermeneutical diversity might be assuaged by adopting a community-determined normative standard of interpretation (such as a creed or set of creeds), such a proposal faces numerous difficulties. Given the fact that the Christian tradition is far from monolithic, one such difficulty is the considerable problem of reaching consensus regarding which tradition or part thereof should be adopted as interpretatively normative; indeed, many Christians object to the adoption of any interpretatively normative standard outside of the canon of Scripture in the first place. Even if this massive difficulty could be overcome, any standard that might be adopted would itself be subject to various interpretations – itself just as susceptible to hermeneutical diversity.[63] Moreover, any such standard that could plausibly enjoy such broad consensus – save the biblical canon itself – would likely not address the vast majority of the issues regarding which the plethora of Christian denominations differ.[64] Given such difficulties, I do not see see how the adoption of any such standard could *actually function* to assuage the problem of hermeneutical diversity.[65] No standard is more widely accepted than the common canonical core of Scripture itself and I see no reason to believe any other standard would fare better relative to the "problem" of hermeneutical diversity, particularly if subjected to the amount of scrutiny as Scripture has been over the ages.

Given this situation, instead of encouraging isolationist readings on the one hand or community-normed readings on the other, canonical theology contends that theological interpretation should take place within community *and* across

---

[62] See the extensive discussion of this issue in Peckham, *Canonical Theology*, chapters 4-7.
[63] "In fact, hermeneutical diversity may be a greater problem within communitarian approaches, which add diverse interpretation of Christian tradition to that of Scripture," including what appear to be "mutually exclusive interpretations of Scripture and mutually exclusive explanations regarding doctrines, including self-identified disputes between theologians in the tradition." Peckham, *Canonical Theology*, 186.
[64] Could any plausibly ecumenical consensual rule adequately adjudicate between the different interpretations of Roman Catholics, Lutherans, Baptists, and Methodists (and others), for example? What of the differences among Roman Catholics themselves, Lutherans themselves, Baptists themselves, and Methodists themselves?
[65] Take for example the recent debate over universalism, which many of its proponents claim holds considerable support in the patristic tradition.

various communities, alongside the deliberate "attitude that our perspective is limited and we can learn from others."[66] Doing theology within community with such an attitude may help guard against individualistic and idiosyncratic interpretations and illumine one's own blind spots and some of the ways in which one's conceptual framework – and social location more broadly – may be unduly influencing one's reading and thus undermining the ruling authority of Scripture.

A text that one has always read one way due to one's social location may be read very differently by someone from a very different social location. Rather than expecting others to read Scripture as if they are from one's own social location (or vice versa), if one reads and interprets in community and across communities one will be obliged to recognize that an interpretation of Scripture or theological construction that seems obvious to oneself (or is taken as obvious in one's tradition) may not be obvious after all. Ideally, this will bring one to consider what presuppositions one may be bringing to the text and to the task of theology, to recognize other possible ways of reading and thinking, and to continually subject all interpretations (especially one's own) to the question of whether and to what extent such interpretations correspond to what is in the biblical text itself. In this regard, Jesus himself asked, "What is written in the Law? How does it read to you?" (Luke 10:26, NASB).

This is one reason why it is so valuable to invite others – particularly those from vastly differing contexts – to the table, not only for the sake of inclusion, but also because of the great value the perspectives of others will bring to the theological dialogue. In this regard, the core commitments of canonical theology can be coupled with the recognition of the importance of "self-theologizing," understood (in the words of Young Sub Song) as "the right and responsibility of indigenous Christians to interpret the Bible and to find applicable theology in their own cultural contexts."[67]

Much more should be said about what canonical theology is and just how to do it as a theological method. Hopefully, enough has been said here to consider some ways in which the approach of canonical theology might be helpful relative to the discussion of theological method for a global context, to a discussion of which we now turn.

---

66 Hyung Jin Kim Sun, "Intercultural Global Theology," 83.
67 Young Sub Song, "Cultural Context of Globalization," 254. Here, Young Sub Song is referring to and interacting with Paul Hiebert's conception of self-theologizing.

4 The Core Commitments of Canonical Theology as a Way Forward?

Might the core commitments of canonical theology, akin to what has been briefly articulated above, offer the outline of a helpful approach for theology in various contexts across the globe? In this regard, we want to be very clear that we do not mean to propose that canonical theology as we conceive of it or practice it should itself be a standard that others should follow. We take the core commitments of canonical theology that we have attempted to articulate here to be an outworking of the common commitment held by most Christians to the uniquely normative authority of Scripture, from which it follows that Scripture should actually function as such in the doing of theology.

If this is so, the core commitments of canonical theology are eminently applicable/translatable to, and modifiable by, various global theologians – most of whom already share the common commitment to the uniquely normative authority of the canon of Scripture. In this regard, theologians from various global contexts need not be expected to adopt and implement the core commitments of canonical theology as we have articulated them here (which is undoubtedly impacted by our own conceptual frameworks and social locations), but may recognize ways of implementing something like these commitments that may better fit their contexts (adapted to and shaped by the questions, issues, and categories most relevant to local contexts) while still upholding the uniquely normative (i.e., canonical) authority of Scripture. Likewise, theologians in various global contexts should not be expected to adopt this or that conceptual framework or set of doctrinal claims (other than the minimal claim of biblical authority itself), but every such framework or set would itself be subject to the standard of *continual* testing according to what is in the text of Scripture – both relative to individual passages and the biblical canon as a whole.[68]

As far as we can see, the core commitments of canonical theology are also eminently *practicable* in various contexts around the globe. What is *in the text* is both most immediately accessible to the most global Christians and considered

---

[68] This approach to theology would not sideline the particular kinds of questions and interests in particular metaphysical issues or approaches, but would not privilege particular extra-canonical questions and metaphysics, instead welcoming any theological questions and inquiries that might be brought to the text from any context and which are all equally subject to the authority of text.

by the vast majority of Christians past and present to be uniquely normative.[69] As such, it makes sense to focus on the text as the most crucial locus of theological interpretation, without neglecting or sidelining what is accessible and can be ascertained regarding what is behind the text and in front of the text, respectively. As Uche Anizor puts it, "Christian theologians have almost universally assumed" that "a theological claim can be true only insofar as it is drawn from or at least coheres with Scripture."[70] He goes on: "Even where theologians diverge on the relation of Scripture to tradition, reason, or experience, they agree on the centrality and authority of Scripture for Christian theology."[71]

In this way, rather than imposing a conceptual framework or theological system from one global context (e.g., the West) upon other global context, the core commitments of canonical theology make room for encouraging theologians across the globe to do theology from within their own context, subjected to testing according to the commonly held standard of the biblical canon itself and thus not engendering anything like theological relativism.[72] Such "testing" itself would not be outsourced to any one particular Christian community or community-determined norm, but could take place via an ongoing mutual and reciprocal theological dialogue among and across various Christian communities, centered around the commonly held standard of the canon and the core commitments that flow from shared recognition of the biblical canon as uniquely normative.[73]

---

[69] In this regard, Hank Voss notes that we must not neglect "the testimony of pastors serving among the world's more than one billion urban poor. Many of these leaders will never be able to afford more than three or four books beyond their Bible. The exegetical fruits of these teachers of the church, who almost always rely upon the canon for their 'commentary' on a pericope, is not to be quickly despised." Hank Voss, "From 'Grammatical-historical Exegesis' to 'Theological Exegesis': Five Essential Practices," *Evangelical Review of Theology* 37/2 (2013): 146. For example, Voss notes, "I think of conversations on 'suffering' with leaders of persecuted house churches in China, or on 'citizenship' (Acts 22:38; Eph. 2:19; Phil. 3:20) with pastors whose congregations consist of undocumented workers in the United States." Voss, 146, n36.

[70] Uche Anizor, *How to Read Theology: Engaging Doctrine Critically and Charitably* (Grand Rapids: Baker Academic, 2018), 60. Further, Anizor writes: "The strength and plausibility of every formulation are tied to how much they directly engaged with the Bible." Anizor, *How to Read Theology*, 85.

[71] Anizor, *How to Read Theology*, 60.

[72] While interpreters may differ, they might nevertheless "come together and check one another against the standard of the Scripture." D. A. Carson, "The Role of Exegesis in Systematic Theology," in *Doing Theology in Today's World: Essays in Honor of Kenneth S. Kantzer*, ed. by J. D. Woodbridge and T. E. McComiskey (Grand Rapids: Zondervan, 1991), 53-54.

[73] Cf. Kwabena Donkor's discussion of the problem of community-normed interpretations, illustrated by the problems faced relative to some "traditional African communities" that hold

In this regard, theologians from across the globe may not only participate in "testing" and refining theological proposals by asking whether and to what extent any given claim meets the twin standards of biblical warrant (i.e., canonical correspondence) and internal coherence, participating theologians would also be positioned to learn from one another and be alerted to biblically warranted claims that they had overlooked or which might not have seemed significant to them previously due to their different social location. As Tennent puts it, ideally an "open and honest exchange will help us to recognize some of our own, less obvious, heresies and blind spots."[74] In this regard, Hank Voss adds, we might seek to "avoid the western academic captivity of the Bible by dialoguing with global exegetes whose location outside of the West allows new insights to emerge."[75]

One example of a blind spot that affects much of Western theology is a reticence to consider the reality and impact of evil spirits, despite the fact that it is a significant motif in Scripture.[76] In Majority World contexts, conversely, the reality and impact of evil spirits is seldom questioned. In this regard, Kabiro wa Gatumu explains that "some scholars regard the Western church as having failed" to "give sufficient or serious attention to the topic of supernatural powers" due to "anti-supernaturalistic prejudice."[77] In this and other ways, theolo-

---

to "aspects that would be deemed superstitious by biblical, Christian standards" such as "ancestral theology." He notes that: "Requiring these communities to purge themselves of these 'errors,' even in a dialogical setting, would seem to require the setting up of" some "global" standard "that would arise outside of the traditional community's interpretive framework." Kwabena Donkor, "Postconservatism: A Third World Perspective," in *Reclaiming the Center: Confronting Evangelical Accommodation in Postmodern Times*, ed. Millard J. Erickson, Paul Kjoss Helseth, and Justin Taylor (Wheaton: Crossway, 2004), 218-219. With Donkor, we believe the finally normative standard in this and other respects should be the canon of Scripture itself.

74 Tennent, *Theology in the Context of World Christianity*, 18.
75 Voss, "From 'Grammatical-historical Exegesis' to 'Theological Exegesis,'" 151.
76 As Brian Han Gregg notes, "the conflict between God and Satan is clearly a central feature of Jesus' teaching and ministry." *What Does the Bible Say About Suffering*? (Downers Grove: IVP Academic, 2016), 66.
77 Kabiro wa Gatumu, *The Pauline Concept of Supernatural Powers: A Reading from the African Worldview*. Paternoster Biblical Monographs (Milton Keynes: Paternoster, 2008), 52, 51. Cf. Robert Ewusie Moses, *Practices of Power: Revisiting the Principalities and Powers in the Pauline Letters* (Minneapolis: Fortress, 2014), 221-24. Consider further the story told by John Mbiti of a man who returns home after ten years of theological education unable to respond to his community's view that his sister had become possessed by a spirit. As Mbiti tells the story, the newly minted scholar "*looks around. Slowly he goes to get Bultmann, looks at the index, finds what he wants, reads again about spirit possession in the New Testament. Of course he gets the answer: Bultmann has demythologised it. He insists that his sister is not possessed. The people*

gians from outside of the Western context tend to be much more attuned to, and experienced in dealing with, religious pluralism.[78]

Another example, crucial in the West today and regarding which large swaths of Westernized Christianity is failing, is the biblical theme of social justice. As Timothy Tennent puts it: "Majority World Christians are more likely to be sensitive to the Christian responsibility to address issues related to poverty and social justice."[79] However, these issues are often "conveniently ignored [...] in our large, [Western], seeker-driven, and entertainment-oriented middle-class churches."[80] Even a cursory reading of the Hebrew prophets reveals that there is no shortage of biblical passages that emphasize the importance of social justice. Yet much Westernized theology does not sufficiently emphasize the concerns of Scripture in this regard – the concerns of "justice and mercy and faithfulness" that Jesus calls the "weightier provisions of the law" (Matt 23:23, NASB). Sadly, such concerns are foreign to and ignored by some affluent, Western Christians that are "rich" and "have need of nothing" (Rev 3:17) and thus operate with a kind of Laodicean theology that fosters turning a blind eye to injustice.

5 Conclusion

Of course, the core commitments of canonical theology should not be thought of as a panacea for theological shortcomings or as guaranteeing success relative to global theological method.[81] As explained above, the primary core commitment

---

shout, 'Help your sister, she is possessed!' He shouts back, 'But Bultmann has demythologised demon possession.'" John Mbiti, "Theological Impotence and the Universality of the Church," quoted in Perry W. H. Shaw, "'Treasures With the Old': Addressing Culture and Gender Imperialism in Higher Level Theological Education," 265.

78 Tennent, *Theology in the Context of World Christianity*, 14-15, adds: "Majority World Christians are experienced at articulating the uniqueness of the gospel in the midst of religious pluralism." He goes on, "because of their own backgrounds as well as their close proximity to other living faiths, Majority World Christians understand more profoundly the relationship of Christianity to non-Christian religions. They often approach the continuities with less defensiveness while, at the same time, are surprisingly frank and candid about the glaring discontinuities that inevitably arise when other religions fail to recognize the true dignity of Jesus Christ."
79 Tennent, *Theology in the Context of World Christianity*, 14.
80 Tennent, *Theology in the Context of World Christianity*, 14.
81 This may advance the search for an approach to global theological method that is (ideally) not beholden to a conceptual framework or set of dogmatic conclusions that come from a particular (post-biblical) context, but one that is continually subject to testing by the canon of Scripture itself.

of canonical theology is to the uniquely normative authority of Scripture, from which it follows that Scripture should actually function as such in the doing of theology. From this, it further follows that neither one's own conceptual framework, doctrinal commitments, or textual interpretations, nor those of a particular community, should be allowed to rule. Shared attention to these and other core commitments of canonical theology might foster a common dialogue among global theologians that affirm the uniquely normative authority of Scripture, perhaps contributing to a context for mutual theological dialogue that increasingly avoids the imposition of one fallible context upon another as a ground of theological method.

References

Anizor, Uche. *How to Read Theology: Engaging Doctrine Critically and Charitably*. Grand Rapids: Baker Academic, 2018.
Barram, Michael. "The Bible, Mission, and Social Location: Toward a Missional Hermeneutic." *Interpretation: A Journal of Bible and Theology* 61/1 (2007): 42–58.
Bartholomew, Craig G. *Introducing Biblical Hermeneutics: A Comprehensive Framework for Hearing God in Scripture*. Grand Rapids: Baker Academic, 2015.
Bauer, Bruce L. "Social Location and Its Impact on Hermeneutics." *Journal of Adventist Mission Studies* 12/1 (2016): 74–83.
Bevans, Steve. *Essays in Contextual Theology*. Leiden: Brill, 2018.
Canale, Fernando Luis. *Back to Revelation-Inspiration: Searching for the Cognitive Foundation of Christian Theology in a Postmodern World*. Lanham, MD: University Press of America, 2001.
Carson, D. A. "The Role of Exegesis in Systematic Theology." In *Doing Theology in Today's World: Essays in Honor of Kenneth S. Kantzer*, edited by J. D. Woodbridge and T. E. McComiskey, 39–76. Grand Rapids: Zondervan, 1991.
Carter, Craig A. *Interpreting Scripture with the Great Tradition: Recovering the Genius of Premodern Exegesis*. Grand Rapids: Baker Academic, 2018.
Clark, David K. "Biblical and Theological Foundations of Marriage and Family." In *Handbook of Family Religious Education*, edited by Blake J. Neff and Donald Ratcliff, 5–35. Birmingham, AL: Religious Education Press, 1995.
Cone, James H. *God of the Oppressed*. New York: Seabury Press, 1975.
Cortez, Marc. "Context and Concept: Contextual Theology and the Nature of Theological Discourse." *Westminster Journal of Theology* 67 (2005): 85–102.
Davidson, Richard M. "Interpreting Scripture: An Hermeneutical 'Decalogue,'" *Journal of the Adventist Theological Society* 4/2 (1993): 95–114.
Donkor, Kwabena. "Postconservatism: A Third World Perspective." In *Reclaiming the Center: Confronting Evangelical Accommodation in Postmodern Times*, edited by Millard J. Erickson, Paul Kjoss Helseth, and Justin Taylor, 199–221. Wheaton, IL: Crossway, 2004.
Donkor, Kwabena. *Tradition, Method, and Contemporary Protestant Theology: An Analysis of Thomas C. Oden's Vincentian Method*. Lanham, MD: University Press of America, 2003.

Fiorenza, Elisabeth Schüssler. "The Ethics of Biblical Interpretation: Decentering Biblical Scholarship." *Journal of Biblical Literature* 107/1 (1988): 3–17.

Gatumu, Kabiro wa. *The Pauline Concept of Supernatural Powers: A Reading from the African Worldview*. Paternoster Biblical Monographs. Milton Keynes: Paternoster, 2008.

Goheen, Michael W. "A History and Introduction to a Missional Reading of the Bible." In *Reading the Bible Missionally*, edited by Michael W. Goheen, 3–27. Grand Rapids: Eerdmans, 2016.

González, Justo. *Mañana: Christian Theology from a Hispanic Perspective*. Nashville: Abingdon, 1990.

Gregg, Brian Han. *What Does the Bible Say About Suffering?* Downers Grove, IL: IVP Academic, 2016.

Hunsberger, George R. "Proposals for a Missional Hermeneutic." In *Reading the Bible Missionally*, edited by Michael W. Goheen, 309–21. Grand Rapids: Eerdmans, 2016.

Mbiti, John. "Theological Impotence and the Universality of the Church." *Lutheran World* 21/3 (1974): 251–60.

McCall, Thomas H. "Is the Wrath of God Really Satisfying?" *Christianity Today*, 29.03,2018, https://www.christianitytoday.com/ct/2018/march-web-only/is-wrath-of-god-satisfying-good-friday-cross.html.

Moses, Robert Ewusie. *Practices of Power: Revisiting the Principalities and Powers in the Pauline Letters*. Minneapolis: Fortress, 2014.

Moskala, Jiří. "Toward Consistent Adventist Hermeneutics: From Creation through De-Creation to Re-Creation." In *Women and Ordination: Biblical and Historical Studies*, edited by John W. Reeve, 1–38. Nampa, ID: Pacific Press, 2015.

Naidoo, Marilyn. "Overcoming Alienization in Africanising Education." *HTS Teologiese Studies/Theological Studies* 72/1 (2018): 1–8.

Nebeker, Gary L. "The Holy Spirit, Hermeneutics, and Transformation: From Present to Future Glory." *Evangelical Review of Theology* 27/1 (2003): 47–54.

Nihinlola, Emiola. "A Contextual Theology of Christian Mission in Contemporary Africa." *Practical Theology* 1 (2008): 7–17.

Olagunju, O.S. "An Evaluation of Bevans' Models of Contextual Theology and Its Contributions to Doing Theology in the 21st Century Church." *Ogbomoso Journal of Theology* 17/2 (2012): 37–57.

Osborne, Grant R. "Hermeneutics." In *Evangelical Dictionary of World Mission*, edited by A. Scott Moreau, 430-32. Grand Rapids: Baker Books, 2000.

Osborne, Grant R. *The Hermeneutical Spiral*. Downers Grove: IVP Academic, 2006.

Peckham, John C. *Canonical Theology: The Biblical Canon, Sola Scriptura, and Theological Method*. Grand Rapids: Eerdmans, 2016.

Peckham, John C. "The Rationale for Canonical Theology: An Approach to Systematic Theology After Modernism." *Andrews University Seminary Studies* 55/1 (2017): 83–105.

Powell, Mark Allan. "The Forgotten Famine: Personal Responsibility in Luke's Parable of the 'Prodigal Son.'" In *Literary Encounters with the Reign of God*, edited by Sharon H. Ringe and H. C. Paul Kim, 265–87. New York: T&T Clark, 2004.

Richards, E. Randolph and Brandon J. O'Brien. *Misreading Scripture with Western Eyes: Removing Cultural Blinders to Better Understand the Bible*. Downers Grove, IL: InterVarsity, 2012.

Richards, Jay Wesley. *The Untamed God: A Philosophical Exploration of Divine Perfection, Simplicity, and Immutability*. Downers Grove, IL: InterVarsity, 2003.

Robbins, Vernon K. "The Social Location of the Implied Author of Luke-Acts." In *The Social World of Luke-Acts: Models for Interpreters,* edited by Jerome H. Neyrey, 305–22. Peabody, MA: Hendrickson Publishers, 1991.

Rogers, Glenn. *The Bible Culturally Speaking: The Role of Culture in the Production, Presentation and Interpretation of God's Word.* Bedford, TX: Mission and Ministry Resources, 2004.

Sanou, Boubakar. *Motivating and Training the Laity to Increase their Involvement in Ministry in the Ouaga-Center Adventist Church in Burkina Faso.* DMin diss., Andrews University, 2010.

Segovia, Fernando. "Two Places and No Place on Which to Stand: Mixture and Otherness in Hispanic American Theology." In *Mestizo Christianity: Theology from the Latino Perspective,* edited by Arturo J. Bañuelas, 26–40. Maryknoll: Orbis, 1995.

Seitz, Christopher. "Canonical Approach." In *Dictionary for Theological Interpretation of the Bible,* edited by Kevin J. Vanhoozer, 100–2. Grand Rapids: Baker Academic, 2005.

Shaw, Perry W. H. "'New Treasures with the Old': Addressing Culture and Gender Imperialism in Higher Level Theological Education." *Evangelical Review of Theology* 38/3 (2014): 265–79.

Song, Young Sub, "Cultural Context of Globalization and 'Globalizing Theology' as a Christian Response to the Globalization Process." *Korean Journal of Christian Studies* 81 (2012): 243–63.

Sun, Hyung Jin Kim, "Intercultural Global Theology." *Vision: A Journal for Church and Theology* 19/2 (2018): 81–89.

Tennent, Timothy C. *Theology in the Context of World Christianity: How the Global Church Is Influencing the Way We Think about and Discuss Theology.* Grand Rapids: Zondervan, 2009.

Vanhoozer, Kevin J. *Hearers and Doers: A Pastor's Guide to Making Disciples Through Scripture and Doctrine.* Bellingham, WA: Lexham Press, 2019.

Vanhoozer, Kevin J. *The Drama of Doctrine: A Canonical-Linguistic Approach to Christian Theology.* Louisville: Westminster John Knox Press, 2005.

Vanhoozer, Kevin J. "What Is Everyday Theology? How and Why Christians Should Read Culture." In *Everyday Theology: How to Read Cultural Texts and Interpret Trends,* edited by Kevin J. Vanhoozer, Charles A. Anderson, and Michael J. Sleasman, 15–61. Grand Rapids: Baker Academic, 2007.

Vanhoozer, Kevin J. "What Is Theological Interpretation of the Bible?" In *Dictionary for Theological Interpretation of the Bible,* edited by Kevin J. Vanhoozer, 19–25. Grand Rapids: Baker Academic, 2005.

Voss, Hank. "From 'Grammatical-historical Exegesis' to 'Theological Exegesis': Five Essential Practices." *Evangelical Review of Theology* 37/2 (2013): 140–52.

Wanjala, Frederick. "Contextual Theology: An Essential Pillar for the Success of the Church's Mission." *African Ecclesial Review* 58/3-4 (2016): 244–57.

Yeago, David. "The Bible: The Spirit, the Church, and the Scriptures." In *Knowing the Triune God,* edited by David Yeago and James Buckley, 49–93. Grand Rapids: Eerdmans, 2001.

Zuck, Roy B. "The Role of the Holy Spirit in Hermeneutics." *Bibliotheca Sacra* 141/562 (1984): 120–30.

Hans Burger
Quadriga without Platonism

In Search for the Usefulness of the Fourfold Sense of Scripture in Dialogue with Hans Boersma

Abstract: Proponents of the 'theological interpretation' of Scripture plead for a re-evaluation of the quadriga, the traditional idea of the fourfold sense of Scripture. This article analyses Hans Boersma's view of the quadriga. It gives an analysis of the theological beliefs required by this exegetical practice of such a sacramental reading of Scripture. For Boersma, the quadriga presupposes that Christ and the new Christ-reality are present in the Old Testament. The article discusses furthermore whether it is necessary to accept a sacramental and Platonic ontology, claiming the existence of the Platonic forms or ideas in the eternal Logos. The Platonic worldview has a 'gravitational pull' that is 'upward' and is not helpful to understand the salvific historical dynamics of Scripture. Building on Oliver O'Donovan's criticism of Platonism, the article proposes to understand the quadriga differently in the light of a model of interpersonal communication that does more justice to the creativity and abundance of God's loving interaction with humanity in history. In a next step, the article analyses more in detail the multiplicity of meaning in a spiritual reading of Psalm 22 using the concepts of sense, reference and significance. Finally, the article discusses whether such a practice of spiritual reading could be called sacramental. The concept of sacrament is interpreted as a soteriological and Christological concept with as its centre Jesus Christ as the 'primordial sacrament'. In a sacrament Christ is present and Christ is communicated. Thus this practice of spiritual reading is sacramental indeed although it does not presuppose a sacramental ontology.

Keywords: Hans Boersma, Fourfold sense of Scripture, Platonism, Theological hermeneutics, Sacramental reading, Christian reading of the Old Testament

---

Hans Burger, Theological University Kampen, Utrecht, The Netherlands,
jmburger@tukampen.nl

1 Introduction

In the contemporary quest in theology and the church for the understanding of Scripture, the so-called 'theological interpretation' of Scripture is an important voice. Many of its proponents plead for a revaluation of the *quadriga*, the traditional idea of the fourfold sense of Scripture. One of the is Hans Boersma, who has extensively studied patristic exegesis. Boersma builds on the Nouvelle Théologie (Henri de Lubac and Jean Daniélou) as part of a larger project of the reconstruction of a sacramental or participatory ontology.[1] For Boersma's view of the fourfold sense of Scripture, two important building blocks have to be distinguished: the conviction that Christ is present in the Old Testament and his Christian-Platonist participatory ontology. In this article, I will argue for an interpretation of the fourfold sense of Scripture that builds on the presence of Christ in the Old Testament but without a Christian-Platonist ontology.

I will start with an overview of Boersma's position (section 2). Next, I will evaluate Boersma's Platonist ontology and argue that this ontology is somewhat problematic (section 3). I will then give my own alternative interpretation of the four senses of Scripture continuing with Boersma's other building block, the presence of Christ in the Old Testament (section 4). Finally, I will also explain why I continue to refer to this presence as 'sacramental' (section 5).

2 Hans Boersma

Boersma's central thesis is that behind the exegesis of the church fathers stands one central belief: Christ and the new Christ-reality are present in the Old Testament. The use of typological, allegorical, and sacramental interpretation is not due to philosophical ideas but arises from a specific Christian perspective. Boersma writes, "The reason why the church fathers practiced typology, allegory and so on is that they were convinced that the reality of the Christ event was already present (sacramentally) within the history described within the Old

---

[1] Hans Boersma, *Nouvelle Théologie and Sacramental Ontology: A Return to Mystery* (Oxford: Oxford University Press, 2009); Hans Boersma, *Heavenly Participation: The Weaving of a Sacramental Tapestry* (Grand Rapids: Eerdmans, 2011); Hans Boersma, *Sacramental Preaching: Sermons on the Hidden Presence of Christ* (Grand Rapids: Baker Academic, 2016); Hans Boersma, *Scripture as Real Presence: Sacramental Exegesis in the Early Church* (Grand Rapids: Baker Academic, 2017).

Testament narrative."² Thus, this exegetical practice requires several theological beliefs.
1. Christ is present in the Old Testament: What the church fathers do in their exegesis is search for Christ who is hidden in the Old Testament like a treasure hidden in the field.³

This implies two further beliefs:
   1.1 In his providence, God reigns over the history of salvation in a Christ-shaped way rather than in an arbitrary way. The way in which the history of salvation unfolds is in line with the incarnation of the eternal Word of God so that we can discern his shape already in earlier events.⁴
   1.2 In a sacramental way, texts and events of the history of salvation before Christ participate in the reality of Christ. The relationship between Christ and earlier events is not merely nominal but sacramental. Just as it is believed that Christ is really present in the sacrament of the Eucharist, Christ as the *res* is really present in the Old Testament texts and events as *signum*.⁵

The sacramental-christological reading involves more than just the allegorical-dogmatic reading which finds Christ himself in Scripture. The tropological-moral and the anagogical-eschatological meanings presuppose that the church, believers and their future can be found in the text as well. Consequently, this practice of reading implies more beliefs:
2. Those who are in Christ share in his reality. Christ cannot be separated from his body or from those who are incorporated in him. Christ is always the *totus Christus*.

Accordingly, this implies two further beliefs:
   2.1 Where Christ is present, his church is present as well.

---

2 Boersma, *Scripture as Real Presence* (note 1), 12. See further xv, 15, 17, 82, 103, 130. In this point, Boersma builds on Lubac and Daniélou who both in different ways emphasized also that the spiritual reading of the Old Testament presupposed the presence of Christ in the Old Testament. See Boersma, *Nouvelle Théologie and Sacramental Ontology* (note 1), 149–90; Boersma, *Heavenly Participation* (note 1), 138, 151.
3 This image was used by Irenaeus; see Boersma, *Scripture as Real Presence* (note 1), xv, 17, 130.
4 Cf. Boersma, *Scripture as Real Presence* (note 1), 24–5.
5 Cf. Boersma, *Nouvelle Théologie and Sacramental Ontology* (note 1), 155–57, 174, 180–83; Boersma, *Heavenly Participation* (note 1), 149–150; Boersma, *Scripture as Real Presence* (note 1), xiii, xv, 17, 79, 96, 102–3, 178, 184.

2.2 Because Christ or the Christ-reality is present sacramentally in the Old Testament, the church can be found in the Old Testament, too.⁶

These other beliefs also concern the future:
3. Part of the reality of Christ is the eschatological goal of history, the heavenly reality of the beatific vision.

Consequently, two other convictions are implied:
3.1 We have to read Scripture in the light of this ultimate supernatural purpose.
3.2 We have to read Scripture as part of a spiritual movement in service of the virtuous transformation of our lives and oriented towards this eschatological future.⁷

What this makes clear is that the practice of sacramental reading with the four senses (literal, allegorical, tropological and anagogical) is an implication of beliefs about the reality of Jesus Christ as the eternal and incarnate Word of God. As the pre-existing Word, he was already present sacramentally in the history of salvation before his incarnation, and the providence of God could give events their Christ-like form. Moreover, since the believers share in Christ, who is now seated in heaven, they can read Scripture as part of a spiritual and transformational process of participation in Christ, searching for doctrinal truth, for transforming direction in their way of life, and for eschatological orientation.

For Boersma, this is closely connected with a sacramental or participatory ontology. He writes: "The Platonist-Christian synthesis made it possible to regard creation, history, and Old Testament as sacramental carriers of a greater reality. Creation, history and Old Testament had significance throughout most of the Christian tradition precisely because they pointed to and participated in a greater reality: what the Platonists called 'Forms' or 'Ideas' and what the Christians insisted was the Word of God himself."⁸ So, according to Boersma, the practice of sacramental-christological reading implies another belief.

---

6 Cf. Boersma, *Heavenly Participation* (note 1), 148, 151; Boersma, *Scripture as Real Presence* (note 1), xv–xvi, 19, 24, 89, 113–18, 148, 152.
7 Cf. Boersma, *Nouvelle Théologie and Sacramental Ontology* (note 1), 153–55; Boersma, *Heavenly Participation* (note 1), 138; Boersma, *Scripture as Real Presence* (note 1), xii, 19–22, 112, 122, 131–58, 249–72.
8 Boersma, *Heavenly Participation* (note 1), 38. On participation in the history of the Platonist-Christian tradition, see the overview in Wolter Huttinga, *Participation and Communicability:*

4. Our reality has to be understood in terms of a sacramental and Platonic ontology, claiming the existence of the Platonic forms or ideas in the eternal Logos.

To be more specific:
   4.1 As the incarnation of the eternal Logos, Christ is the heavenly reality.
   4.2 Because the eternal Logos is sacramentally present in the history of salvation, he gives this history meaning, coherence, and unity.
   4.3 The heavenly and eternal Logos has to be identified with the Platonic forms or ideas.
   4.4 The entire created reality participates sacramentally in the eternal Logos, who gives creation its meaning, coherence, and unity.[9]

According to Boersma, a two-fold coherence is necessary, although he does not make this distinction himself: the coherence in time of the history of salvation and the coherence of the created reality. For the sake of the latter coherence a Christian Platonism is necessary. In Boersma's reconstruction of the history of theology and philosophy nominalism caused both the horizontal fragmentation of history into disconnected events as well as the vertical separation of created objects from their transcendent and eternal origins.[10] The impact of this vertical separation concerns not just the interpretation of Scripture but is far deeper, leading to voluntarism and relativism in the field of ethics.

3 Is Platonism Necessary?

The question is, however, if both forms of meaningful coherence are necessary or if it is possible to continue the practice of spiritual interpretation without Platonism.

In search for an answer to this question, I will start with Psalm 22. Reading Psalm 22 with the story of the cross and resurrection of Jesus Christ in mind, the

---

Herman Bavinck and John Milbank on the Relation between God and the World (Amsterdam: Buijten en Schipperheijn Motief, 2014), 39–75.
9 Cf. Boersma, *Heavenly Participation* (note 1), 23–51; Boersma, *Scripture as Real Presence* (note 1), 3–6, 9–12.
10 Cf. Boersma, *Nouvelle Théologie and Sacramental Ontology* (note 1), 16; Boersma, *Heavenly Participation* (note 1), 21–39, 67, 76–81, 88–94; Boersma, *Scripture as Real Presence* (note 1), 7–8, 96.

Psalm proves to be mysterious. The analogies between this Psalm and the story of Jesus Christ are many. It is hard, if not impossible, to imagine that this Psalm was written without God's providential care or inspiration of his Holy Spirit. It is, therefore, not surprising that the early church said that allusions to Jesus Christ were already present in this Psalm.

Let us presuppose a Christian position, believing that the God of Israel is the triune God of the Christian faith and that this God is actively involved in our world that is also his creation. Let us also assume for this article that God the Father is acting providentially in history, that God the Son is the eternal and pre-existent Word of God, and that God the Spirit has inspired the prophets that have written Scripture. Moreover, this God gives eternal salvation in the history of Jesus Christ. If these assumptions are true, I have no problems with the above implied beliefs 1, 2 and 3:

1. Christ is present in the Old Testament.
2. Those who are in Christ, share in his reality.
3. Part of the reality of Christ is the eschatological goal of history, the heavenly reality of the beatific vision.

When these three beliefs and their implications are true, the practice of spiritual reading can be continued.

This practice of spiritual reading is a Christological reading. It presupposes that God is able to do things in a Christlike manner in the history of salvation before Christ, and that his Spirit is able to inspire human authors to write Scriptural texts that reveal Christ before his incarnation. Furthermore, Christ is seen as the representative of Israel and of humanity but also as the embodiment of what God has to say (the incarnation of the Word of God). Moreover, in the community of the church as the body of Christ, believers participate in Christ. This means that they receive a Christlike character more and more in a lifelong process of transformation until Christ returns at the last day.

But does this practice imply a Christian form of Platonism? This is the case in belief 4 in my reconstruction:

4. Our reality has to be understood in terms of a sacramental and Platonic ontology claiming the existence of the Platonic forms or ideas in the eternal Logos.

Within the movement of 'Nouvelle Théologie', Jean Daniélou has claimed that we need to distinguish between typology and allegory within patristic exegesis. On the one hand, there is good Christological typology that does justice to the text. On the other hand, there is the problematic allegorical reading that gives everything a symbolic meaning and has the Platonism of Philo as its source.[11] Henri de Lubac, however, had no problems with the allegorical reading.[12] Craig Bartholomew supports Daniélou, distinguishing between typology, which follows the history of salvation and has an eschatological pull, and allegory, which has a strong tendency towards a Platonist vertical pull.[13] Both Boersma and Ypenga, however, conclude that the distinction of typology and allegory is not helpful in understanding patristic and medieval exegesis.[14] Still, apart from the terms of typology and allegory, it is important to distinguish the salvation-historical eschatological movement and the Platonic upward movement. The first is connected with the historical unity and coherence of the history of salvation, while the second is connected with the ontological unity and coherence of the created reality. Do we need both of them, or can we suffice with a coherent and united view of the history of salvation? What conclusions, exactly, follow from the presence of Christ in the Old Testament?

Boersma understands this presence as sacramental presence. Let us presuppose that Christ is really present in the sacrament (which I believe is the case). This implies further beliefs.

5. God can use elements from his creation for meaningful and saving communication and communion with human beings. God can use a Psalm, an Old Testament story, or bread and wine to communicate his salvation with us. Accordingly, it is logical to hold the following conviction, as well.
6. God has created this world and events in the history of salvation so that he can use them for meaningful and saving communication and communion.

Thus, God uses specific elements from the created and historical reality in specific situations to be present with us in a specific way and to communicate his saving presence with us in a specific communicative act. It is a possibility that God chooses to be sacramentally present in particular events or texts.

---

11 Cf. Jean Danielou, *From Shadows to Reality: Studies in Biblical Typology of the Fathers* (London: Burns & Oates, 1960), 64–5, 111–12, 149, 226, 287–88.
12 On this discussion, see Boersma, *Nouvelle Théologie and Sacramental Ontology* (note 1), 180–190; Anko Ypenga, *Sacramentum: Hugo van St.-Victor ([d.] 1141) en zijn invloed op de allegorische interpretatie van de liturgie en de sacramentele theologie vanaf 1140 tot aan Durandus van Mende ([d.] 1296)* (Doctor of Philosophy Thesis, University of Groningen, 2002), 45–53.
13 Cf. Craig Bartholomew, *Introducing Biblical Hermeneutics: A Comprehensive Framework for Hearing God in Scripture* (Grand Rapids: Baker Academic, 2015): 130–31, 141–42.
14 Cf. Boersma, *Nouvelle Théologie and Sacramental Ontology* (note 1), 188–190; Ypenga, *Sacramentum* (note 12), 47–8, 52–3.

According to Boersma, this justifies a generalization: God is sacramentally present in the created reality as a whole, for the entire created reality participates in the eternal Logos. Here an important shift is made.

We start with a model of *interpersonal communication*. God communicates meaningfully with humanity and uses elements of his creation to communicate personally with us. In Scripture, in the Eucharist and the church, and even in creation, God's Word can be heard and read so that we can consciously live in God's presence. In this historical model, God can be seen as a dynamic God coming from the *eschaton* in Christ the redeemer.

According to Boersma, God's use of words and events in a historical event (becoming) implies a participatory, ontological relationship between created words and events, on the one hand, and a divine reality (being) on the other.[15] From a model of personal interaction a shift is made to a model of a *participatory ontology*. According to this model, our creation is a meaningful one because the natural world sacramentally participates in the supernatural world, that is, the temporal participates in the eternal. Now impersonal categories are used. The danger looms that the emphasis is no longer on history but on vertical relationships between time and eternity. This is related to another impending shift of emphasis – the historical Christ becomes the eternal Logos who, as the mediator of creation, can be identified with the Platonic ideas or forms.

However, I have some problems with this Platonism. First, it presupposes a cycle of *exitus* and *reditus*. This reality is perceived as a cyclic movement from eternal unity to temporal plurality and back to eternal unity. Human history is re-plotted, accordingly, as what Oliver O'Donovan has called an "ecstatic and self-gathering movement of being" and is perceived in the light of a vertical dynamics between the natural and the supernatural. O'Donovan further remarks that the return to God is a "confirmation of the *first* movement of our being".[16] This means that the origin of the movement is emphasized. In the movement, "There is self-transcendence, but it is intellectual; it is not the historical transcendence of end over beginning".[17] Furthermore, the historical character of the dynamics of God's interaction with his creation and with humanity are ignored and the possibility of eschatological newness or a surprisingly unexpected act of God's love is excluded. Moreover, the liturgical act of

---

15 In the conclusion of *Scripture as Real Presence*, Boersma uses this word pair of becoming and being. See Boersma, *Scripture as Real Presence* (note 1), 237–79.
16 Oliver O'Donovan, *Entering into Rest* (Grand Rapids: Eerdmans, 2017), 10.
17 O'Donovan, *Entering into Rest* (note 16), 11.

worship, including the Eucharistic movement of praise and thankfulness, is seen as part of this ontological cycle.

But love and liturgy are more than what is ontologically necessary. A model of interpersonal communion can more completely do justice to the freedom, creativity and abundance of this 'more'. Love does not do only what is necessary but also what is unexpected, new and generous. Love brings something into existence that did not exist before. This is true of the eschatological act of God as well as the Eucharistic act of the human liturgy. The sacrifice of praise and thankfulness in which the creation is sanctified is not just ontologically necessary. It is more – a free act of interpersonal communication.

Second, Platonism offers a solution to a metaphysical problem and answers the question which world is the real world. The real world is not our world of time and change but the world of eternity and immutability. The result of this solution is the upward pull from time to eternity that has already been mentioned. The Platonic ideas provide an ontological fundamental to our world, giving extra certainty to our existence. However, this leads to a deterministic view of our world. The immutable divine ideas determine our reality. Moreover, it does not help us understand how human uses of signs and language develop.

Our use of signs and language is our way of participating in our world, and its development is guided by changing practical and contextual interests. Our knowledge has a constructive aspect, whereas reality has a certain plasticity. More importantly, God has created a world of temporal, spatial, embodied creatures, and that world is good. We need no higher reality. Furthermore, God's creation is contingent. Although this created reality originates in God's thoughts (God's thoughts are relevant) and although God has created an ordered reality with creatures made according to their kind, his thoughts are free and more is possible than we have seen in this creation until now. God's thoughts are greater than our thoughts.

Where Platonism understands the relationship between God and his creation within a model of ontological participation, an alternative ontology is possible: an ontology of God's communicative and powerful speech acts and of God's loving presence. In Scripture, we find such personal and communicative categories (Heb 1:3) as well as the importance of the presence of God's Spirit (Ps 104:30). It is enough that the Creator creates by his Word and is present in his creation, faithfully sustaining his creation. I do not see why, before sin came into the world, an extra guarantee was necessary to give stability to the relationship between God and his creation: neither a platonic ontology of participation nor a voluntarist covenant ontology.[18] God speaks and enters into a personal relationship of loving nearness. Consequently, that the creation bears witness to the creator should be understood in a communicative model. God wants to communicate his majesty and his loving presence. In his work of art, the artist demonstrates his creativity; in the same way, the creation is an expression of God's glory.

Thus, such a communicative model does not imply a voluntarist separation of God's will from his character and his thoughts. For Boersma, Platonism is necessary to solve the problematic consequences of modern nominalism and voluntarism in Christian ethics. That is, our preferences determine what is good or evil. Indeed, God's creation is not empty or meaningless in a moral sense. However, the work of Oliver O'Donovan shows that the problems caused by voluntarism can be solved in another way by using the concept of a created moral order instead of the Platonic theory of forms or ideas. With this idea of a moral order, O'Donovan maintains, on the one hand, the real existence of teleological and generic relations, and, on the other hand, the freedom of the Creator and the contingency of creation.[19]

Third, the doctrine of the eternal ideas requires that the eternal Logos is more real than created reality. It might be the case that God is the source of reality, but, still, the significance of events in human history is great. According to the narrative of Scripture, human acts – human sin, the obedient acts of the incarnate Son in his human life on earth, the renewal of humanity in the Spirit – have crucial impact on the future of creation. How is it possible that events in human history have this impact, and why was the incarnation of the Logos important if Platonism is true? Platonism finds the real reality above history, according to the narrative of Scripture, what is decisive for created reality happens in history.

That believers participate in the heavenly Christ does not change this. Moreover, that believers participate in the mind of Jesus Christ should not be understood as a participation in the eternal Logos. It is true that all treasures of wisdom and knowledge are hidden in Christ, but that is not the eternal *logos asarkos* but Jesus Christ, died and risen, who is the incarnate Logos, the embod-

---

18 With the concept of the covenant of works, Reformed theology has opted for a voluntarist covenant ontology. On the covenant of works, see Hans Burger, "Theology without a covenant of works. A Thought Experiment," in *Covenant: A Vital Element of Reformed Theology. Biblical, Historical and Systematic-Theological Perspectives*, ed. Hans Burger, Gert Kwakkel, Michael Mulder (Leiden: Brill 2022), 325–48.
19 Cf. Oliver O'Donovan, *Resurrection and Moral Order: An Outline for Evangelical Ethics*. Second Edition (Leicester: Apollos, 1994), 31–45.

iment of what God has to say and in whom God's fullness dwells. With O'Donovan, I would understand Christians' participation in the mind of Christ in a non-Platonic way.[20] Following O'Donovan, my alternative proposal would be something like what follows. God has made an ordered creation with creatures created with an inherent meaning, according to their own nature. Knowing is our human way to participate in the order of creation. In the act of knowing, human beings participate constructively in the existence of reality with our linguistic acts. Thus, the reality that God has created, has a certain plasticity. Entities are partly linguistic constructions. Accordingly, the quality of our linguistic acts and of our human mindset (our *nous*, in Greek Biblical terms) is crucial for the way in which we as humanity, with our acts of knowing, participate in the kosmos created by God. Here sin has destructive noetic consequences. We rebuild God's reality in accordance with our interests, following our idols. At the same time, transforming participation in the mindset or *nous* of Christ is salutary, both for human beings and for the non-human created reality. To conclude, it is necessary that we as human beings participate in the human mind of the incarnate Word, through whom God saves and creates.

These three problems all show that Platonism has a de-historicizing tendency. Platonism emphasizes the eternal reality of the immutable ideas and moves away from the world of time and change. It stimulates a focus on the eternal Logos instead of the incarnate Son, Jesus Christ. It leads to a re-plotting of the Biblical story that is not helpful for understanding the dynamics of the history of salvation and God's loving interaction with fallen humanity.[21] To offer a solution to metaphysical problems, Platonism proposes a participatory ontology, where I would prefer a model of interpersonal communication that does more complete justice to the creativity and abundance of God's loving interaction with humanity in history.

---

20 See Hans Burger, "Receiving the mind of Christ: Epistemological and hermeneutical implications of participation in Christ according to Oliver O'Donovan," *Journal of Reformed Theology* 10/1 (2016): 52–71.
21 When Boersma is dealing with some problems of (Neo)platonism for the Christian faith, he does not seem to see this problem; see Hans Boersma, "All One in Christ: Why Christian Platonism Is Key to the Great Tradition," February 2020. https://www.hansboersma.org/articles-1/all-one-in-christ-why-christian-platonism-is-key-to-the-great-tradition.

4 The Presence of Christ in Scripture and Multiplicity of Meaning

For modern people, deeply influenced by nominalism, the spiritual reading of Scripture seems an impossible practice because we do not share the view of a cosmos filled with signs that refer to a divine reality.[22] Nevertheless, I want to continue with the central conviction of the patristic exegesis, which is the other building block of Boersma's view of sacramental reading: the presence of Christ in the Old Testament. In the final step of this article, I will sketch an alternative proposal of a theological view that can support this spiritual reading.

Again, I will start with Psalm 22. This Psalm is a poetic prayer that later became part of the book of Psalms and Old Testament Scripture. The Psalm is ascribed to David but it is difficult to reconstruct the original context of the Psalm. We may presuppose that the Psalm was used many times when it was sung or recited. Within the meaning of the Psalm as part of the book of Psalms, it is possible to specify in more detail. I will distinguish between sense (the meaning of an expression that is language-internal; related to the world of the text), reference (the relation between an expression and an extra-linguistic entity; related to the world behind the text), and significance (secondary meanings, emotional and personal associations of an expression; related to the world in front of the text).

- *Sense*: Together, the Hebrew words of the Psalm create the world of the text.
- *Reference*: The Psalm refers to a situation of loneliness before God, enemies, illness and threats, any experience of liberation, or any future generation. Every time this Psalm was reread and reused it may have been used with other references.
- *Significance*: The text has meant something to persons who read or prayed this Psalm, as it evoked emotions, memories, and thoughts.

It is evident that the reference and the significance of the Psalm can change from situation to situation. However, the sense is relatively stable, even though changes in reference and significance also influence the sense of the text.

According to the gospels of Matthew, Mark and Luke, Jesus quoted the second verse of the Psalm during his crucifixion. Jesus had read the Hebrew Scriptures and applied these texts to his own messianic role. Several times, he used texts

---

[22] Cf. Ypenga, *Sacramentum* (note 12), 33.

from Scripture to model his own acts accordingly.[23] It must be presupposed that he had read Scripture to find his own destination. It is well possible that when he announced his own death and resurrection, he had read Psalm 22 and found hope in it for his own resurrection after his crucifixion. In any case, Jesus knew this Psalm and used it at the cross. It must have been a meaningful Psalm to him.

- *Sense*: It might be that for Jesus the words of the Psalm already denoted death and resurrection.
- *Reference*: Likely, for Jesus the words of the Psalm more and more referred to his own future suffering, death, and resurrection, until the moment came that the loneliness, mocking, enmity, nakedness, thirst, and God-forsakenness became his own experience.
- *Significance*: The Psalm must have been personally meaningful to Jesus, evoking expectations, images of his own death and resurrection, and strong emotions.

In the perspective of Easter and Pentecost, Jesus' followers have read Psalm 22 as a prophetic Psalm that is fulfilled in Jesus Christ. The events of Jesus' death and resurrection clearly have influenced their understanding of the meaning of the Psalm.

- *Sense*: The sense of the Psalm is influenced slightly. For example, the abandonment by God became a reality in a special way during Jesus' crucifixion.
- *Reference*: The Psalm can be used to refer first to the events of Jesus' crucifixion, death, and resurrection, but it can still be used to refer to other experiences of suffering, as was the case before Jesus. But, in the second half of the Psalm, other possible references come into view, like worldwide mission, a worldwide people praising God, the universal kingship of Jesus, and an eschatological meal.
- *Significance*: For different people in different situations of more or less suffering, the Psalm will have a variety of meanings. It might help to connect one's suffering to Christ's suffering, to hope for God's answer to suffering, or to praise God for his salvation.

Within the historical processes of the use and reuse of the text, the figure of Jesus is crucial. It is important to see what he does and who he is when he acts. The Gospels recount how Jesus used passages from Scripture, applied them to

---

[23] Examples are Zech 9:9–10 (Mk 11:1–8), Psalm 110 (Mark 12:35–37), the exodus-narrative (Mark 14:22–25) and Dan 7:13–14 (Mark 14:62). Cf. N. T. Wright, *Jesus and the Victory of God* (Minneapolis: Fortress Press, 1996), 490–93, 507–9, 527–28, 554–63, 586.

himself, or modelled his life accordingly to claim a connection between himself and words from Scripture. At the same time, what happens during Jesus' life goes beyond what he can model actively as a human person. This becomes clear in the fulfilment of the prophetic Psalm 22: Jesus quotes verse 2 on the cross, but it went beyond his reach that the soldiers act in accordance with verse 18, dividing his clothes and casting lots. According to Luke, after his resurrection Jesus said to his disciples that the Law of Moses, the Prophets, and the Psalms wrote about him (Lk 24:27, 44). The apostolic Gospels and letters substantiate this in a variety of ways. The New Testament shows him as the Messiah of Israel who represents his people and, as such, embodies, fulfils, and realizes their Scriptures. Jesus the Messiah is the fulfilment of the law, the prophets, and the psalms. Moreover, as the incarnation of the eternal word of God, he is the decisive embodiment of what God has to say. God spoke his word to Israel but Israel had a mission to be a blessing to the world. As representative of Israel, Jesus is also the last Adam who represents a new humanity.[24] His reality includes the reality of the renewed Israel, renewed humanity, and the renewed creation.

If this is true, this has several implications for the relationship between Jesus Christ and the meaning of Scripture. First, Jesus the Messiah is the climax of the story of Israel, the fulfilment of the Scriptures of Israel, and the definitive embodiment of what God has to say. Within the salvation-historical process, Jesus the Messiah gives the Scriptures of Israel their final meaning. Without Jesus as the Messiah, Israel's Scriptures have an openness and ambiguity that disappears in Jesus. As fulfilment and embodiment of the Word of God, he gives the Scriptures their final and definitive meaning. But, Jesus himself is a living person and not a text; he remains extra-textual, Scripture receives its meaning in its relationship with this extra-textual person, the living Christ.

Second, if Jesus Christ is the definitive embodiment and fulfilment of what God has to say, he is also the incarnation of the pre-existent eternal Word of God. Thus, he can be found in the works of the *Tanakh* and is already present in those words.[25] The one who is the final fulfilment of Scripture can already be

---

[24] See Hans Burger, *Being in Christ: A Biblical and Systematic Investigation in a Reformed Perspective* (Eugene: Wipf & Stock, 2008), 457–64.

[25] When Peter Enns writes about the interpretation of the Old Testament in the New Testament, he emphasizes that the authors of the New Testament follow the interpretative methods of the Second Temple and gives this eschatological hermeneutic the lable 'christotelic'. What he fails to see in his historical approach is that Christ as the eternal Word of God can be present sacramentally already in the Old Testament before his incarnation. See Peter Enns, *Inspiration and Incarnation: Evangelicals and the Problem of the Old Testament* (Grand Rapids: Baker Academic, 2015), 103–52. – In the theological tradition of Kampen (both Boersma and I come

found in ambiguous but still Christomorphic passages, like Psalm 22. Accordingly, in the interpretation of passages like Psalm 22 it can be argued that a Christological interpretation is not arbitrary. This implies the belief that God who fulfils the Scriptures of Israel in Christ was already in the eternal Word involved in the formation of the *Tanakh*.

To conclude, Jesus Christ, the Word of God himself, is no text. It is important to emphasize that Christ as the centre of Scripture remains extratextual, external to the book. He resolves the ambiguities and openness of the *Tanakh* and gives the Scriptures a clarity that goes beyond the text alone. At the same time, knowing Jesus as the Messiah, he can be found in the Scriptures of Israel, for he is sacramentally present for us in Scripture.[26]

Thus, we can read Scripture in two directions. We can read Scripture in a literal or historical reading where we follow the direction of time, trying to reconstruct the meaning of a text in its original context. In this reading, we follow the dynamics of the history of salvation with its tensions, disappointments, hopes, surprises and all its unexpected newness.[27] Hence, the *sensus literalis* of

---

from that tradition), a Christological reading of the Old Testament was suggested that emphasized the historical relationship to Jesus Christ and the similarity between the (character of) the God of the Old Testament and the God whom we get to know in Jesus Christ. Still, this leads to a historical distance between the church and the Old Testament reality that has to be bridged. More recently, this has been done by narrative means. Boersma's emphasis on the sacramental presence of (the reality of) Christ in the Old Testament repairs the problems of this Kampen approach at a more fundamental level. See Boersma, *Scripture as Real Presence* (note 1), xiv. On the Kampen approach of the Old Testament, see Koert van Bekkum and Gert Kwakkel, "De theologische boodschap van oudtestamentische teksten: Oorsprong en actualiteit van de Kamper aandacht voor de heilshistorie," in *Gereformeerde theologie stroomopwaarts. Terugkijken op 75 jaar vrijmaking*, ed. Erik de Boer, Geranne Tamminga, and Dolf te Velde (Amsterdam: Buijten & Schipperheijn, 2021): 79–94.

26 Dalferth has rightly emphasized the extra textual character of Christ as the centre of Scripture. However, this leads in his theology to a tension between Christ and Scripture. This tension is solved when we see that Christ is sacramentally present in Scripture. See Ingolf U. Dalferth, "Die Mitte ist außen: Anmerkungen zur Wirklichkeitsbezug evangelischer Schriftauslegung," in *Jesus Christus als die Mitte der Schrift: Studien zur Hermeneutik des Evangeliums*, ed. Christof Landmesser, Hans-Joachim Eckstein, and Hermann Lichtenberger (Berlin, New York: Walter de Gruyter, 1997): 173–98, in particular 186–98; Ingolf U. Dalferth, *Wirkendes Wort: Bibel, Schrift und Evangelium im Leben der Kirche und im Denken der Theologie* (Leipzig: Evangelische Verlagsanstalt, 2018), 292–320.

27 For interesting examples of such a reading, see Eep Talstra, "God: Biografie van een overlever," *Kerk en Theologie* 67 (2016): 97–112; and Eep Talstra, "The Spirit as Critical Biblical Scholar," in *The Spirit Is Moving: New Pathways in Pneumatology: Studies Presented to Professor*

a passage is a combination of the sense that this passage had in the original situation, the first reference (the reality the human author of the text wanted to refer to when he produced the text), and the significance that the text had for the original audience.

In a spiritual reading we look back knowing the story of Jesus the Christ. This spiritual or sacramental reading of Scripture is fundamentally a Christological reading. It is a reading in the light of Easter and the Spirit at Pentecost, a reading in the light of the fulfilment of Israel's Scripture in Jesus the Messiah. Still, the reality of Christ is a complex reality for several reasons. First, Christ is God and man who exists eternally as the Word of God. Second, primarily Jesus is the Messiah and embodiment of Israel; secondarily he is the representative of the new humanity and the head of the new creation.[28] Third, the differentiation of head and body results both in a diversity of persons and, second, in an eschatological tension. What is already the case with the head, living with a spiritual body in the heavenly glory of God, is not in the same way the case with the members of his body. And, fourth, this eschatological tension is connected as well with the timely differences between Christ's first coming and his representative act, the time of the church (the 'in between' with its tension of the 'yet and not yet'), and Christ's second coming with the completion of history.

Accordingly, a Christological reading is a reading with various interests, as the *quadriga* demonstrates. The allegorical-dogmatic reading is interested in the reality of Christ, the new covenant, the new Israel, and the church as the fulfilment of Scripture. The moral-tropological reading searches for the ongoing realization of the mysterious unity with Christ in the life of the congregation and the believers. Finally, the anagogic-eschatological reading longs to perceive the complete and public fulfilment of participation in Christ in the eschatological kingdom of God. De Lubac has emphasized that the four senses of Scripture constitute an organic whole.[29] The four senses refer to the coming of God in Christ and the realization of the Christ-reality. Consequently, the four senses can be understood as various reading strategies that follow each other as part of a mystagogical path: the discovery of Christ and the mystery of life in union with him (faith), the ongoing transformation by participation in him (love), and the desire for the eschato-

---

Cornelis van der Kooi on the Occasion of His Retirement, ed. Gijsbert van den Brink, Maarten Wisse, and Eveline van Staalduine-Sulman (Leiden: Brill, 2019): 23–35.
28 For a contemporary rendition of the spiritual reading, it is a challenge to develop a non-supercessationist version that does not forget Israel.
29 Henri de Lubac, *Exégèse médiévale, les quatre sens de l'Écriture*. Vol. 1 (Paris: Aubier, 1959), 643–56; Ypenga, *Sacramentum* (note 12), 35.

logical life with him (hope).³⁰ Because this complexity leads to a multiplicity of meaning it is important to further analyse this multiplicity.

1. Christ and his reality can be present in various ways in a text. Firstly, this variety is related to different references. The text can be used to refer to Christ, to his cross and resurrection, to the restoration of Israel, to the church, to a life of participation in Christ, and to the kingdom of God. Further, it is important to note that the reuse of texts started already before Christ in Scripture itself (e.g. the use of the exodus to refer to a future liberation)³¹ and in Jewish exegesis (e.g. the reading of the Song of Songs to refer to the relationship between God and Israel).³²

Secondly, the variety of genres is important as well. In historical texts persons (David) or events (exodus) can be a type. Legal prescriptions can be fulfilled in a moral or public life in Christ. Cultic laws can be a sign of the fulfilment in Christ as high priest. Promises or prophecies can refer more or less explicitly to restoration or to Christ. Psalms, Proverbs or the Song of Songs evoke their own way of spiritual or mystagogical reading.³³

In some passages, the text itself explicitly speaks about a future figure like Christ.³⁴ In other passages, Christological reuse/relecture of the passage is like the use of words in a metaphor, creating new meaning by using the passage in a Christological context.

2. At the level of the sense of the text, the change of meaning is smallest. Still, during the process of the development of Scripture in the work of editors, in the reuse of texts in later books of Scripture, or in the translation of the Septuagint, the sense of passages has undergone changes. The use of a text with

---

30 Cf. Annemieke de Jong-van Campen, *Mystagogie in werking. Hoe menswording en gemeenschapsvorming gebeuren in christelijke inwijding* (Zoetermeer: Boekencentrum, 2009), 106–12, 307–310; Jacob van Bruggen, *Het kompas van het christendom*, 170–72.
31 Boersma, *Scripture as Real Presence* (note 1), 83–92; Danielou, *From Shadows to Reality* (note 11), 153–60.
32 Boersma, *Scripture as Real Presence* (note 1), 190.
33 Cf. Lubac, *Exégèse médiévale* (note 29), I:173–74. Hans Boersma shows in his book how the variety of genres in Scripture colours the sacramental reading of Scripture, see Boersma, *Scripture as Real Presence* (note 1).
34 On the development of Messianic expectations and Messianic re-interpretations of passages in the Old Testament, see Walter H. Rose, "Messiaanse verwachtingen in het Oude Testament: Oorsprong en ontwikkelingen in de tijd na de ballingschap," in *Messianisme en eindtijdverwachting bij joden en christenen*, ed. Gerard C. den Hertog and Simon Schoon (Zoetermeer: Boekencentrum, 2006), 17–36.

new references influences its sense as well.³⁵ This means that the sense of the text as a feature of the text itself is not completely stable.

If it is true that Jesus Christ is the centre of Scripture, this development of sense receives its end point in the work of the authors of the New Testament. As the definitive Word of God, Christ adds new meaning to the *Tanakh* that cannot be found yet in the Old Testament. Thus, the Christological meaning of the Old Testament is not static, although Christ is present in the old words but the meaning can only be understood completely as the result of a salvation-historical process in which old words receive new meaning. At the same time, this development finds its end in Christ. In him, God has said what he wants to say. Accordingly, the closure of the canon implies that within the intertextual web of the canon the sense of a passage receives its final stability.

3. More change of meaning is possible at the level of reference. Passages can be used to refer to the reality of Christ with all its aspects: his person, the events of his life, his present role as high priest and king, the new Israel and the church, his presence in the life of believers participating in him, and the future to be revealed at his return. Still, the number of new possible references is not endless. They all must concern the reality of Christ.

4. By far, the most new meanings emerge at the level of significance. In new contexts and new situations passages from Scripture speak to many people who receive instruction, wisdom, consolation, encouragement, empowerment, inspiration, etc. from Scripture.³⁶ It would be misleading to search for the variety of meaning especially within the text. The variety of meaning that can be found in the practice of spiritual reading is not text immanent. Only the sense of a text is a feature of the text itself. Reference and significance are a result of the reuse / relecture of text in a variety of situations by many different persons.³⁷ They only slightly influence the sense of the text.

---

[35] Compare 1 Cor 15:55 with Hos 13:14; but also 'virgin' in Matt 1:23 with 'virgin' in Is 7:14; 'son' in Matt 2:15 with 'son' in Hos 11:1. On the influence of the LXX and how this translation made a Christological use more easy see, e.g., N. T. Wright, *The Resurrection of the Son of God* (Minneapolis: Fortress Press, 2003), 147–50.

[36] The diversity of meaning is emphasized especially in pentecostal and charismatic hermeneutics and theology. See, e.g., Craig S. Keener, *Spirit Hermeneutics: Reading Scripture in Light of Pentecost* (Grand Rapids: Eerdmans, 2016). But see also Frank D. Macchia, *Jesus the Spirit Baptizer: Christology in Light of Pentecost* (Grand Rapids: Eerdmans, 2018), 56–64.

[37] Theo Hettema argues in a similar way that a rehabilitation of the model of the fourfold sense of Scripture is possible if the plurality of meaning is not seen as text-immanent but as referential; cf. Theo L. Hettema, "De viervoudige schriftzin: passage of slotzin? Lezing blok-

Finally, this multiplicity of meaning is not arbitrary, giving every reader the opportunity to create her own meaning. In the first place, the practice of spiritual reading has a clear theological legitimization in the sacramental presence of Christ in the text. Secondly, this practice has a clear theological purpose – to live in communion with Christ.

5 Sacramental Reading without Platonism

The practice of spiritual reading in search for a Christological meaning can be continued today. To do this an alternative to the Platonism of the patristic and medieval theologians is necessary. Since the reading practice is a combination of several reading strategies motivated by theological convictions about Jesus Christ and the new reality that can be found in him, it is important to be explicit about these theological beliefs.

It is fundamental that God is able to communicate with us, that he can act within history, and that he can use elements of his creation (words, events) to communicate with us. Without this divine interaction with us at a personal level the practice of sacramental reading is meaningless. Moreover, the practice of spiritual reading presupposes that Jesus is the risen Messiah, the decisive embodiment of what God wants to communicate with us, and the incarnation of the eternal pre-existent divine Word. Still, it has to be decided whether this reading practice is 'sacramental.' This is not the case if the Reformed tradition is followed. According to the Reformed tradition, a sacrament is a material sign and seal of the Word of God that follows the Word and is instituted by Jesus Christ himself.[38] However, an alternative approach is possible. Originally, the word '*sacramentum*' is the translation of *musterion* in 1 Tim 3:16. It refers to Christ, who is the mystery of salvation. Following Walter Kaspar and Eberhard Jüngel, Jesus Christ can be conceived of as 'Ursakrament', the primordial sacrament.[39] Consequently, sacrament is a Christological and soteriological concept. Moreover,

---

week Noster godsdienstfilosofie Hoeven 16 juni 2004," http://home.kpn.nl/tlhettema/pdf/Viervoudig.pdf.

[38] For a Reformed understanding of sacraments, see e.g. J. Todd Billings, "Sacraments," in *Christian Dogmatics: Reformed Theology for the Church Catholic*, ed. R. Michael Allen and Scott R. Swain (Grand Rapids: Baker Academic, 2016): 339–62.

[39] Eberhard Jüngel, *Wertlose Wahrheit: Zur Identität und Relevanz des christlichen Glaubens*. Theologische Erörterungen 3 (München: Kaiser, 1990), 273, 315, 333; Walter Kasper, Theologie und Kirche (Mainz: Matthias-Grünewald, 1987), 245.

it is a communicative concept. The sacrament communicates the mystery of salvation and gives the knowledge, wisdom and life that is in Jesus Christ.[40] Thus, a sacrament can be understood as a sign that refers to the mystery of salvation in Jesus Christ, the primordial sacrament, and that mediates and communicates the presence of Christ and his salvation, thus enabling us to live in union with Christ and to participate in him. In this communication of the mystery of salvation in Christ, Christ is represented and present in Scripture, the church, the proclamation of the gospel, and baptism and the Eucharist. Accordingly, these means of communication can be called sacraments that all refer to Christ as the 'Ursakrament'. This does not mean that all divine communication is sacramental or even that human speakers are sacramentally present in their texts. What is present and what is communicated in the sacraments, is more specific: in them, Christ is sacramentally present, and Christ is communicated sacramentally with those who receive him in faith. Such a concept of sacrament does not contradict the *solus Christus*, the *extra nos* of Jesus Christ, or the *prima scriptura* of the Reformation. Because Christ is sacramentally present in Scripture, a spiritual and Christological reading of Scripture can be called a sacramental reading as well.

God's sacramental presence in particular persons, moments, events, texts, and his communication and presence with us in Christ means that he comes, shows his merciful love, makes himself present to us, and even chooses to live in human beings by his Spirit. This coming is part of God's saving acts and always implies a reaction to human sin.

Theologically speaking, it is part of soteriology and eschatology. This has to be distinguished from ontology or protology. Sacrament is a soteriological concept, not metaphysical or ontological. Consequently, God's sacramental presence in his Word, in baptism and the Eucharist, or in his people does not imply a sacramental ontology. Neither does participation in Christ imply a participatory ontology. Instead of a Platonic ontology that understands everything in the light of an "ecstatic and self-gathering movement of being"[41] and that understands humanity in the light of the first movement of our being, I would propose an eschatological ontology. In such an ontology God, his Word, and his Spirit are coming from his future that is full of creativity, newness, and surprise.

At the same time, this loving God is the eternal God. Coming from the eschaton, he is already present from the beginning. For this reason, his eternal Word already is present in Scripture before his incarnation.

---

40 Eberhard Jüngel, *Ganz werden: Theologische Erörterungen 5* (Tübingen: Mohr Siebeck, 2003), 274–87.
41 O'Donovan, *Entering into Rest* (note 16), 10.

If this is all true, it is possible to continue the practice of sacramental reading in search of a Christological meaning. At the same time, it is possible to avoid the problems of a Platonic worldview – a worldview with a 'gravitational pull' that is 'upward'[42] and not helpful to understand the salvific historical dynamics of Scripture.[43]

References

Bartholomew, Craig G. *Introducing Biblical Hermeneutics: A Comprehensive Framework for Hearing God in Scripture*. Grand Rapids: Baker Academic, 2015.

Billings, J. Todd. "Sacraments." In *Christian Dogmatics: Reformed Theology for the Church Catholic*, edited by R. Michael Allen and Scott R. Swain, 339–62. Grand Rapids: Baker Academic, 2016.

Boersma, Hans. "All One in Christ: Why Christian Platonism Is Key to the Great Tradition," February 2020. https://www.hansboersma.org/articles-1/all-one-in-christ-why-christian-platonism-is-key-to-the-great-tradition.

Boersma, Hans. *Heavenly Participation: The Weaving of a Sacramental Tapestry*. Grand Rapids: Eerdmans, 2011.

Boersma, Hans. *Nouvelle Théologie and Sacramental Ontology: A Return to Mystery*. Oxford: Oxford University Press, 2009.

Boersma, Hans. *Sacramental Preaching: Sermons on the Hidden Presence of Christ*. Grand Rapids: Baker Academic, 2016.

Boersma, Hans. *Scripture as Real Presence: Sacramental Exegesis In the Early Church*. Grand Rapids: Baker Academic, 2017.

Burger, Hans. *Being in Christ: A Biblical and Systematic Investigation in a Reformed Perspective*. Eugene: Wipf & Stock, 2008.

Burger, Hans. "Receiving the mind of Christ: epistemological and hermeneutical implications of participation in Christ according to Oliver O'Donovan." *Journal of Reformed Theology* 10/1 (2016): 52–71.

Burger, Hans. "Theology without a Covenant of Works. A Thought Experiment." In *Covenant: A Vital Element of Reformed Theology. Biblical, Historical and Systematic-Theological Perspectives*, edited by Hans Burger, Gert Kwakkel, and Michael Mulder, 325–348. Leiden: Brill, 2022.

Dalferth, Ingolf U. "Die Mitte ist außen: Anmerkungen zur Wirklichkeitsbezug evangelischer Schriftauslegung." In *Jesus Christus als die Mitte der Schrift: Studien zur Hermeneutik des Evangeliums*, edited by Christof Landmesser, Hans-Joachim Eckstein, and Hermann Lichtenberger, 173–198. Berlin, New York: Walter de Gruyter, 1997.

---

42 Bartholomew, *Introducing Biblical Hermeneutics* (note 13), 141.
43 The author thanks Hans Boersma, Kevin Vanhoozer, and Wolter Huttinga for their comments on an earlier version of this article.

Dalferth, Ingolf U. *Wirkendes Wort: Bibel, Schrift und Evangelium im Leben der Kirche und im Denken der Theologie*. Leipzig: Evangelische Verlagsanstalt, 2018.
Danielou, Jean. *From Shadows to Reality: Studies in Biblical Typology of the Fathers*. London: Burns & Oates, 1960.
De Jong-Van Campen, Annemieke. *Mystagogie in werking. Hoe menswording en gemeenschapsvorming gebeuren in christelijke inwijding*. Zoetermeer: Boekencentrum, 2009.
Enns, Peter. *Inspiration and Incarnation: Evangelicals and the Problem of the Old Testament*. Grand Rapids: Baker Academic, 2015.
Hettema, Theo L. "De viervoudige schriftzin: passage of slotzin? Lezing blokweek Noster godsdienstfilosofie Hoeven 16 juni 2004," http://home.kpn.nl/tlhettema/pdf/Viervoudig.pdf, retrieved 11.06.2020.
Huttinga, Wolter. *Participation and Communicability: Herman Bavinck and John Milbank on the Relation between God and the World*. Amsterdam: Buijten en Schipperheijn Motief, 2014.
Jüngel, Eberhard. *Wertlose Wahrheit: Zur Identität und Relevanz des christlichen Glaubens. Theologische Erörterungen 3*. München: Kaiser, 1990.
Jüngel, Eberhard. *Ganz werden. Theologische Erörterungen 5*. Tübingen: Mohr Siebeck, 2003.
Kasper, Walter. *Theologie und Kirche*. Mainz: Matthias-Grünewald, 1987.
Keener, Craig S. *Spirit Hermeneutics: Reading Scripture in Light of Pentecost*. Grand Rapids: Eerdmans, 2016.
Lubac, Henri de. *Exégèse médiévale: Les quatre sens de l'Écriture*. Vol. I. Paris: Aubier, 1959.
Macchia, Frank D. *Jesus the Spirit Baptizer: Christology in Light of Pentecost*. Grand Rapids: Eerdmans, 2018.
O'Donovan, Oliver. *Entering into Rest*. Grand Rapids: Eerdmans, 2017.
O'Donovan, Oliver. *Resurrection and Moral Order: An Outline for Evangelical Ethics*. Second Edition. Leicester: Apollos, 1994.
Rose, Wolter H. "Messiaanse verwachtingen in het Oude Testament: Oorsprong en ontwikkelingen in de tijd na de ballingschap." In *Messianisme en eindtijdverwachting bij joden en christenen*, edited by Gerard C. den Hertog and Simon Schoon, 17–36. Zoetermeer: Boekencentrum, 2006.
Talstra, Eep. "God. Biografie van een overlever." *Kerk en Theologie* 67 (2016): 97–112.
Talstra, Eep. "The Spirit as Critical Biblical Scholar." In *The Spirit Is Moving : New Pathways in Pneumatology: Studies Presented to Professor Cornelis van Der Kooi on the Occasion of His Retirement*, edited by Gijsbert van den Brink, Maarten Wisse, and Eveline van Staalduine-Sulman, 23–35. Leiden: Brill, 2019.
Van Bekkum, Koert, and Gert Kwakkel. "De theologische boodschap van oudtestamentische teksten. Oorsprong en actualiteit van de Kamper aandacht voor de heilshistorie." In *Gereformeerde theologie stroomopwaarts. Terugkijken op 75 jaar vrijmaking*, edited by Erik de Boer, Geranne Tamminga, and Dolf te Velde, 79–94. Amsterdam: Buijten & Schipperheijn, 2021.
Van Bruggen, Jacob. *Het kompas van het christendom: ontstaan en betekenis van een omstreden bijbel*. Kampen: Kok, 2002.
Wright, N. T. *Jesus and the Victory of God*. Minneapolis: Fortress Press, 1996.
Wright, N. T. *The Resurrection of the Son of God*. Minneapolis: Fortress Press, 2003.
Ypenga, Anko. *Sacramentum: Hugo van St.-Victor ([d.] 1141) en zijn invloed op de allegorische interpretatie van de liturgie en de sacramentele theologie vanaf 1140 tot aan Durandus van Mende ([d.] 1296)*. Doctor of Philosophy Thesis, University of Groningen, 2002, https://pure.rug.nl/ws/portalfiles/portal/7066873/thesis.pdf.

Arnold Huijgen
Reinventing the Quadriga

Connecting Biblical Exegesis and Systematic Theology through the Anagogical-Eschatological Sense of Scripture

Abstract: The present article seeks to promote the rapprochement between systematic theology and Biblical studies by retrieving the classical *Quadriga* or fourfold sense of Scripture in a new key. The anagogical or eschatological sense is key in bringing Biblical studies and systematic theology closer together. Traditional understandings of the anagogical sense focus on the future glory of believers, the beatific vision of God, but this article argues for reinterpreting the anagogical sense in terms of 20th century understandings of eschatology. The eschatological nature of God's presence under the Old Testament, the New Testament eschatological expectations, the eschatological nature of truth as promise, and the idea of Christ as centre of Scripture are aspects of the eschatological sense of Scripture that are not only theologically viable but also stimulating for the interplay between systematic theology and Biblical studies. This approach overcomes the problems of Platonic approaches and can accommodate historical-critical methods, thereby narrowing the gap between Biblical studies and systematic theology.

Keywords: Hermeneutics, Old Testament, Trinity, Eschatology, Bible.

1 Introduction

The relation between biblical exegesis as a scholarly enterprise and systematic theology as reflection on Christian doctrine is a complex one. Ever since Gabler liberated exegesis from dogmatic shackles, exegetes have defended their independence against dogmatic imperialism.[1] This independence has been instrumental for impressive scholarly results and ongoing specialisation, and the field

---

[1] Ioannes Philippus Gabler, *De iusto discrimine theologiae biblicae et dogmaticae, regundisque recte utriusque finibus: oratio qua recitata...* (Altorf: Monath, 1787). Cf. Johann Salomo Semler, *Versuch einer freiern theologischen Lehrart* (Halle: Hemmerde, 1777), 294–8.

Arnold Huijgen, Protestant Theological University, Amsterdam, The Netherlands, a.huijgen@pthu.nl

of Biblical studies has become a mélange of historical, linguistic, philological, sociological, archaeological and many other studies.[2] The natural research partner for the Biblical scholar is often not the theologian but the historian or the philologist. Meanwhile, systematic theologians were confronted with an ever-increasing complexity of Biblical scholarship that made it more and more difficult to base theological convictions on Scriptural passages. Awareness of the historical distance, the hermeneutical complexities and the plurality of Biblical voices has further complicated the understanding of the Bible in theological contexts.[3] The times on which theologians lined up a number of Bible quotations from various Biblical sources as proof-texts for their positions are long gone.[4] Rather, the primary discussion partners for systematic theologians are philosophers. So, methodological differences, academic and societal developments as well as ongoing specialisation have deepened the rift between Biblical studies and theology.

A contrary movement is also visible, often under the heading of "Theological Interpretation of Scripture."[5] Many Biblical scholars and systematic theologians are dissatisfied with the distance between the fields for three reasons.

---

[2] See Judith M. Lieu and J.W. Rogerson, *The Oxford Handbook of Biblical Studies* (Oxford: Oxford University Press, 2008).

[3] See the various contributions to *Sola Scriptura: Biblical and Theological Perspectives on Scripture, Authority, and Hermeneutics*, ed. Hans Burger, Arnold Huijgen, and Eric Peels (Leiden: Brill, 2017).

[4] The so-called *loca probantia* (or: prooftext) method is found examplary in the high point of Reformed scholastic theology, the 1625 Leiden *Synopsis purioris theologiae*, recently edited: *Synopsis Purioris Theologiae = Synopsis of a Purer Theology: Latin Text and English Translation: Volume 1: Disputations 1–23*, ed. Dolf te Velde e.a., SMRT 187 (Leiden: Brill, 2013); *Synopsis Purioris Theologiae = Synopsis of a Purer Theology: Latin Text and English Translation: Volume 2: Disputations 24–42*, ed. Henk van den Belt e.a. SMRT 204 (Leiden: Brill, 2016); *Synopsis Purioris Theologiae = Synopsis of a Purer Theology: Latin Text and English Translation: Volume 3: Disputations 43–52*, ed. Harm Goris e.a. SMRT 222 (Leiden: Brill, 2020).

[5] See *Dictionary for Theological Interpretation of Scripture*, ed. Kevin J. Vanhoozer e.a. (London: SPCK, 2005); Mark Alan Bowald, "The Character of Theological Interpretation of Scripture," *International Journal of Systematic Theology* 12 (2010): 162–83; Daniel J. Treier, "What is Theological Interpretation? An Ecclesiological Reduction," *International Journal of Systematic Theology* 12 (2010):144–161; Stephen E. Fowl, *Theological Interpretation of Scripture* (Carlisle: Paternoster Press, 2010); Stanley E. Porter, "What Exactly Is Theological Interpretation of Scripture, and Is It Hermeneutically Robust Enough for the Task to Which It Has Been Appointed?," in *Horizons in Hermeneutics: A Festschrift in Honor of Anthony C. Thiselton*, ed. Stanley E. Porter and Matthew R. Malcolm (Grand Rapids: William B. Eerdmans Publishing Company, 2013), 234–67.

First, the Bible as such presents itself as a literary unity.[6] While historical-critical dissection of texts makes sense it can also destroy the significance of the text itself. Second, the fact that Biblical texts receive the amount of attention they do cannot be separated from the importance the Bible has for its primary reading community, the Church.[7] The primary context of Bible reading is the liturgy, and personal Bible reading is only derived from that centuries-old practice. The Church as reading community, both synchronically and diachronically, must be taken into account to understand the importance of Biblical texts.[8] Third, the Bible presents itself as a text about God. It is a theological text which requires theological means to make sense of it.[9] Of course, the theological approach should not be the only lens through which the Bible is read, but it surely cannot be dispensed with, to exactly understand the literal meaning of the text. So, the canonical form of the text, the theological content, and the actual reading community (the Church) are arguments in favour of a rapprochement between Biblical studies and systematic theology. The question remains how this is to be done.

Promising attempts to reconnect Biblical studies and theology often pivot on patristic theology. Pre-modern, pre-critical readings of the Bible respect the canonical form, read the Bible within the Church, with full attention for its theological content. Three examples of these kinds of studies may suffice. First, Matthew Bates has advocated Trinitarian readings of the Old Testament by way of "prosopological exegesis": under the Old Testament dispensation, a divine Person (often the eternal Son) could speak in the figure of other persons.[10] While

---

[6] This is often connected to a so-called "Canonical Approach." See Brevard S. Childs, *Introduction to the Old Testament as Scripture* (Minneapolis: Fortress Press, 1979); Brevard S. Childs e.a. *The Bible as Christian Scripture: The Work of Brevard S. Childs* (Atlanta: Society of Biblical Literature, 2013).

[7] E.g., Stanley Hauerwas, *Unleashing the Scripture: Freeing the Bible from the Captivity to America* (Nashville: Abingdon Press, 1993); cf. Darren Sarisky, *Scriptural Interpretation: A Theological Exploration* (Malden: Wiley, 2012).

[8] Theological interpretation of Scripture coheres with a reorientation on premodern, particularly Patristic, exegesis. Cf. Fowl, *Theological Interpretation*, 54.

[9] John Webster, *Holy Scripture: A Dogmatic Sketch* (Cambridge: Cambridge University Press, 2003), 6: "both the texts and the processes surrounding their reception are subservient to the self-presentation of the triune God, of which the text is a servant and by which readers are accosted, as by a word of supreme dignity, legitimacy and effectiveness."

[10] Matthew W. Bates, *The Birth of the Trinity: Jesus, God, and Spirit in New Testament and Early Christian Interpretations of the Old Testament* (Oxford: Oxford University Press, 2015), 28, 33. Bates derives this terminology from Carl Andresen, "Zur Entstehung und Geschichte des trini-

the author of the epistle to the Hebrews employs this exegetical technique within the Biblical corpus, Church Fathers used this procedure extensively to interpret both the Old and New Testaments.[11] Bates emphasises the importance of divine authorial intent over human authorial intent.[12] Second, Hans Boersma has explored sacramental exegesis in the early church, in which Scripture is regarded as the means of God's real presence in a sacramental way.[13] Boersma derives diverse ways of reading Scripture from the reading practice of Church Fathers: besides literal readings, interpretation can (and, according to Boersma, should) be hospitable, allegorical and doctrinal, incarnational, harmonious, prophetic, and beatific.[14] Thus, Boersma connects the postmodern emphasis on the reader and the practice of reading with the traditions of the early church, bypassing the modern focus on historical issues. Third, Darren Sarisky has presented a constructive proposal of theological semiotics and an ontology of the reader based on a careful study of Augustine's model of signs.[15] The result is the idea of the Bible as icon, which is not meant to be looked *at*, which historical-critical methods do, but to be looked *through*, to the divine reality, which is the spiritual practice of reading the Scriptures.[16] All three examples lean on a Platonic understanding of reality: behind the phenomenal world exists the ideal world, concretely: the world of God. Boersma explicitly declares his adherence to "Christian Platonist convictions."[17]

Retrieval of patristic forms of exegesis comes with an apparent disadvantage: the connection with present-day Biblical studies is only made in the field of the history of interpretation, not with respect to actual Biblical interpretation. In other words, retrieval of patristic exegesis does not bridge the gap with Biblical studies but rather widens it. Bates explicitly disavows historical-critical methods, as not apt for the task of reading Holy Scripture.[18] Moreover,

---

tarischen Personsbegriffes," *Zeitschrift für die neutestamentliche Wissenschaft und die Kunde der älteren Kirche* 52 (1961): 1–39.

11 Hebrews 10:5, quoting Psalm 39:7–9 LXX (=Psalm 40:6–8); Bates, *The Birth of the Trinity*, 86.
12 Bates, The Birth of the Trinity, 191–2.
13 Hans Boersma, *Scripture as Real Presence: Sacramental Exegesis in the Early Church* (Grand Rapids: Baker Academic, 2017).
14 Boersma, *Scripture as Real Presence*, 56, 131, 219, 249.
15 Darren Sarisky, *Reading the Bible Theologically* (Cambridge: Cambridge University Press, 2019).
16 Sarisky, Reading the Bible Theologically, 239.
17 Boersma, *Scripture as Real Presence*, 1. See Hans Burger's article in the present volume for a critique of this Platonic approach, and for an alternative.
18 Bates, *The Birth of the Trinity*, 175–202.

the fact that Christian doctrine defines the reading of the text would lead Biblical studies back to their pre-Gablerian servanthood to dogmatic theology. Of course, Biblical scholars would not be willing to do that. Besides, the question is whether the Patristic approach of texts, with its implied or explicit Platonism, leads to viable theological results. So, not only from the perspective of Biblical studies, but also from that of systematic theology, there are problematic aspects in theologies of patristic retrieval.

For the present author, the advantages and solid results of critical Biblical scholarship are evident. The emphasis on the literal, grammatical, and historical meaning of the text in the times of Renaissance and Reformation led to no less than a rediscovery of the Bible.[19] The Enlightenment also led to achievements that should not be abandoned: critical research has led to a more profound knowledge of Biblical texts and their backgrounds. Admittedly, rationalist tendencies in the Enlightenment laid the Bible on a Procrustean bed, since it cannot answer scientific questions with mathematical precision. But the results of modern Biblical scholarship are impressively sound. It is worthwhile to seek for an integration of modern Biblical studies and systematic theology rather than a bypass of modern exegesis to pre-modern theologies.

The present article seeks to promote the rapprochement between systematic theology and Biblical studies by retrieving the classical *Quadriga* or fourfold sense of Scripture in a new key. In the Middle Ages, this fourfold sense was summed up in the rhyme: *littera gesta docet, quid credas allegoria, moralis quid agas, quo tendas anagogia* – "The literal sense teaches you what happened, the allegorical what you should believe, the moral what you should do, the anagogical what you should hope for (=what you should reach for)."[20] Of these four, the allegorical or doctrinal meaning was considered most important, although all four senses should be kept together. To the mind of the present author, the anagogical or eschatological sense is key in bringing Biblical studies and systematic theology closer together.

---

[19] This rediscovery went along with a renewed interest in Patristic theology, see: Jan den Boeft, "Erasmus and the Church Fathers," in *The Reception of the Church Fathers in the West: From the Carolingians to the Maurists*, ed. Irena Backus (Leiden: Brill, 2001), 537–72 and other contributions in that volume.

[20] Augustinus de Dacia, *Rotulus Pugillaris* 1. Cf. Henri de Lubac, *Exegèse médiévale: Les quatre sens de l'Écriture* 1.1 (Paris: Aubier), 23.

2 Renewal of Anagogical-eschatological Interpretation

2.1 Eschatology Connects Biblical Studies and Systematic Theology

The retrieval of patristic exegesis generally proceeds in ways similar to the allegorical, or doctrinal, sense of Scripture to draw out meanings of the texts. The presupposition is that God exists and that his existence defines the situation of interpretation. As Darren Sarisky writes: "Th[e] determination of the aim of interpretation begins with a doctrine of God in place from the outset: a doctrine of the Trinity is operative; faith in God is not written off as mere prejudice that infects and distorts the practice of reading."[21] The subject matter of the text is Christ, and readers of the Bible should read for the sake of engaging with Jesus Christ. While critical exegesis aims at objectivity and thus excludes faith as a bias that may hinder understanding, theological interpretation of Scripture regards faith as valid. In Boersma's terms, Scripture is God's "real presence."[22] To read as if he were absent would miss the very essence of the text. This position can be characterized as an emphasis on the allegorical sense of Scripture, because doctrine drives the interpretation.

What is the character of God's real presence in Scripture? This question lays bare the implicit or explicit Platonism in the ideas of Boersma and others. The reality of God is a reality behind or beyond the present reality. It is pictured in spatial and metaphysical rather than temporal terms. Modernity has impressed Westerners with the awareness of the historical nature of their existence but in Platonic thought spatiality is more important than temporality. This difference is crucial for the relation between systematic theology and Biblical studies because Biblical studies cannot dispense with historicity as the central category. To the mind of the present author, systematic theology can benefit from an emphasis on historicity but only if this is defined in Christian terms. Theologically speaking, time does not simply exist, it is not merely *chronos*. It is primarily *kairos*, the time in which God acts decisively.

Traditional understandings of the anagogical sense focus on the future glory of believers, the beatific vision of God. I propose to reinterpret the anagogical

---

21 Sarisky, *Reading the Bible Theologically*, 288.
22 Boersma, *Scripture as Real Presence*.

sense in terms of 20th century understandings of eschatology.²³ Eschatology is not merely about what exactly happens at the end of times but it is the expectation of God as the coming one into this world. Hope, faith and expectation are the human correlates of this coming of God.

On three levels an emphasis on eschatology, God's coming into the world and human expectancy, can stimulate the interplay between Biblical studies and systematic theology.²⁴ First, the eschatological coming of God fits the Old Testament better than a Triune real presence in the Platonic sense. Throughout the Bible God is the coming one, the one to be expected. Whenever he comes, he makes things new. After the fall he comes to Adam with a promise of future renewal.²⁵ He comes to Abram and makes his life into eschatological existence: Abram's life is guided by God's promise, the Word that shapes his life into expectation of what he cannot see.²⁶ The central categories are the ones of promise and deliverance. The central notions of the exodus and the Babylonian exile are narrations of hope amid oppression.

In Christian understanding the history of God and Israel, the dialectic of promise and God's coming, culminates in the coming of God in the human flesh, the incarnation. The coming of Jesus Christ is the *kairos* par excellence. The position of the Christian Church is typically between the incarnation and the eschaton, between the first and second coming of Christ. For Christ has not only come, he has gone to heaven also, giving way to the Spirit. The final verses of the Bible express the Christian hope well: "The Spirit and the bride say, 'Come!'"²⁷ This is the second level where eschatology connects Biblical studies and systematic theology: according to the New Testament, the Church lives in eschatological expectation. "In keeping with his promise we are looking forward to a new heaven and a new earth, where righteousness dwells."²⁸ When

---

23 Ernst Troeltsch, *Glaubenslehre: Nach Heidelberger Vorlesungen aus den Jahren 1911 und 1912* (München/Leipzig: Duncker & Humblot, 1925), 36 famously wrote: "A modern theologian says: the eschatological office is mostly closed nowadays." Since then, it has been working extra hours (Hans Urs von Balthasar), particularly because of dialectical theology, mainly in Rudolf Bultmann and Karl Barth.
24 The present proposal draws important stimuli from the theology of Wolfhart Pannenberg, for instance: *Offenbarung als Geschichte*, ed. Wolfhart Pannenberg (Göttingen: Vandenhoeck & Ruprecht, 1961).
25 Genesis 3:15.
26 Genesis 12:1–3; Hebrews 11:8–10.
27 Apocalypse 22:17 (New International Version).
28 2 Peter 3:13.

the Church is thus defined by hope, this hope in turn will stamp the way the Church reads the Scriptures.

The third level is the most fundamental: the eschatological character of truth. According to the Christian creed, Jesus Christ will come to judge the living and the dead. He will then speak truth: the final judgment and verdict about every truth claim ever expressed in history and about every individual. The ultimate truth will then come to light. This means that every truth claim in the present age is provisional, dependent on the ultimate truth which is yet to be revealed. Meanwhile, the truth that will be revealed can be known already, albeit in part. Jesus Christ will be the eschatological judge but in the incarnation God had already revealed his purposes. So there is an eschatological tension in every truth claim, spanning from God's revelation in the incarnation to the ultimate judgment by Christ.

The eschatological character of truth fits the Biblical theology of the New Testament well. Note that in the New Testament the Holy Spirit is the downpayment of the coming glory, and as such represents the presence of the future.[29] The New Testament emphasises the *kairos* of Christ's coming to the extent that it does not explicitly distinguish between Christ's first and second comings.[30] He is the coming one, the truth in person.

2.2 Advantages of the Eschatological Emphasis

When the eschatological sense of Scripture is taken as the first of the spiritual senses, instead of the allegorical or moral senses, the historical dynamic of the drama between God and his people under the Old Testament and the eschatological tension between the present and the not-yet in the New Testament can tie Biblical studies and systematic theology together. Aspects of salvation history under the Old Testament and New Testament pneumatology fit in more naturally than is the case in the various retrievals of patristic theology. This can be exemplified in three advantages of the eschatological emphasis.

First, God's eschatological presence fits the reading situation of the Bible. Whereas modern, critical readings of the Bible tend to be disengaged readings, as if God were not present, adherents of theological interpretation of Scripture have emphasized that reading the Bible takes place in the real presence of God. This real presence needs to be qualified however. In Platonist understandings,

---

[29] 2 Corinthians 1:22; Ephesians 1:14.
[30] Cf. Apocalypse 1:7–8.

God is present behind the text, in some instances speaking 'in the person' of a Psalmist or other author of a Biblical text. This presence is a mere presupposition, and is static in nature. Rather, the eschatological sense of Scripture qualifies God's presence as an act of coming. He is not merely present in or behind the text in the same way a human person can be present in a room. God's presence is not self-evident. If it was to the Church Fathers, it has lost its self-evidence in modernity. Rather, when the Church reads the Scriptures, she does so hoping that God will be present, believing his promise. This means that the text does not refer to a reality behind the text, and behind the present reality, but that it refers forward to the coming of God. This means that the presence of God is a matter of faith in God's promise. The notion of promise is crucial in this respect. It is a word that has a future behind it; it invites believing anticipation of what is surely to come. This is the exact situation where Bible reading takes place, in the liturgy where the future touches the present. But there is no need to refer to a metaphysical realm behind the text.

Second, the idea of truth as eschatological reality is apt for the study of the Bible and for Christian doctrine. It is important to note that an eschatological understanding of truth provides a middle way between two dangers: for Biblical studies, the idea that "truth" is what can be established by historical means, and for theology, the idea that "truth" lies behind the text, in a metaphysical dimension. Rather, truth is eschatological: it manifests itself in history, but not in terms of clock-time *chronos* but in terms of the decisive *kairos*. The eschaton is the defining moment for all truth claims in all of history. Truth is proven to be reliable in a world full of lies, and revelation is the history God makes with his people. Truth is faithfulness, *èmèt*.[31] This eschatological understanding of truth matches the New Testament notion that Jesus Christ has been proven to be the Son of God in his resurrection from the dead.[32] The fact of his resurrection is presently not demonstrable in the way scientific findings are demonstrable: by repeating the experiment in laboratory settings. Still, if Jesus Christ has risen from the dead, this changes everything: the understanding of human life and death, and even of all reality. The New Testament invites people to believe the Gospel of Jesus Christ and thus to live eschatologically, expecting his coming to judge the living and the dead. By consequence, this is the way the Scriptures need to be read: expecting the coming of Jesus Christ in this world through his Spirit. This eschatological understanding of the hermeneutical situation matches some of the patristic elements brought forward by Hans Boersma, particular-

---

31 Cf. Exodus 34:6.
32 Romans 1:4.

ly the hospitable reading. But its understanding of time and reality is distinctly non-Platonic but rather eschatological. This is what happens when the analogical, eschatological sense of Scripture becomes the primary lens instead of the allegorical sense.

Third, the anagogical sense of Scripture is apt to express that Christ is the centre of Scripture, and how he is so. Of course, the Christ event is central to the New Testament, particularly the cross and resurrection. But the relation between Christ and the Old Testament has been a matter of much debate. Matthew Bates has demonstrated that Church Fathers found Christ present under the Old Testament, under the person of agents in the text.[33] This comes with the evident disadvantage of ahistorical readings, and with the oblivion of Israel as primary addressee of the text. The eschatological sense of Scripture helps in two regards: first, because Old Testament texts can be read backwards from the New Testament reality.[34] This is what the canonical gospels and Paul's letters do: they declare that Jesus' life, particularly his death and resurrection, took place "according to the Scriptures."[35] They reinterpret Old Testament texts in light of later events, as texts with a forward tendency. This procedure is neither "prosopological" nor metaphysical, but it pivots on time and eschatology. Second, the nature of Christ's centrality of the Bible becomes clear.[36] Christ is not part of the text of the Bible: his nature is not textual, but personal. Scripture is centred on Christ, points and relates to Christ, but Christ and Scripture are distinct. Christ is the centre of the Scriptures, not in semantic or thematic terms, but in a distinctly theological sense. He is neither the summary, nor the implicit or explicit theme of the Scriptures. It is a statement of the Church that he is the centre of Scripture. "So, the centre of scripture is not found in the horizon of semantic meanings of biblical texts, but in the horizon of pragmatic use in the Christian church."[37] Exactly because Christ is person and not text, he functions as the

---

[33] Bates, *The Birth of the Trinity*, 115–35.
[34] Richard B. Hays, *Reading Backwards: Figural Christology and the Fourfold Gospel Witness* (Waco: Baylor University Press, 2014); cf. Richard B. Hays, "Christ Prays the Psalms: Israel's Psalter as Matrix of Early Christology," in *The Conversion of the Imagination: Paul as Interpreter of Israel's Scripture* (Grand Rapids: William B. Eerdmans, 2005), 101–18.
[35] 1 Corinthians 15:3; cf. Mathew 26:54; Luke 24:27.
[36] See Ingolf U. Dalferth, "Die Mitte ist außen: Anmerkungen zum Wirklichkeitsbezug evangelischer Schriftauslegung," in *Jesus Christus als die Mitte der Schrift: Studien zur Hermeneutik des Evangeliums*, ed. Christof Landmesser et al., BZNW 86 (Berlin: de Gruyter, 1997), 173–98.
[37] Arnold Huijgen, "Alone Together: *Sola Scriptura* and the Other Solas of the Reformation," in *Sola Scriptura*, 96.

external centre of Scripture, which gives the text its relation to reality.[38] This reality does not lie behind the text but in front of the readers of the text: it is not the reality of the Platonic idea, but of the eschatological coming of God. The truth of Scripture is grounded in the historical reality of the man Jesus from Nazareth. Therefore, the Old Testament is to be read forward. Jesus Christ fulfils and validates the Old Testament. Because of His resurrection the past has received a new future. But also under the New Testament the Church reads forward, in view of Christ's judgment, the final word on all of humanity.

The centrality of the eschatological sense of Scripture presupposes a certain kind of reader, or rather: a specific attitude of the reader of Scripture. The famous rhyme from the Middle Ages rightly says: "quo tendas anagogia," "the anagogical sense teaches you what you need to reach for." Reading Scripture always takes place between the place where the readers are and the coming Kingdom of God. God's promise connects the two, spanning an arc of tension. Therefore, Bible reading primarily belongs in the liturgy where Christ's resurrection is celebrated, and believers practice their hope for the Kingdom of God. The invocation of God and prayerful receptivity characterise the attitude of the intended reader of Scripture. Thus, reading Scripture is transformative: the powers of the coming Kingdom renew the reader through the Holy Spirit.

The priority of the eschatological sense of Scripture puts the other senses in perspective. The literal sense does not merely relate what happened. This is where the rhyme from the Middle Ages is less apt. This literal sense is part of a history. The moral or tropological sense, that teaches what readers must do, is affected by the eschatological sense, because the right acts are the one that fit the coming Kingdom. The allegorical sense, which was considered the most important in the Middle Ages, teaches what to believe. The priority of the eschatological sense redefines the truths of faith as promises. Remarkably, the *Heidelberg Catechism*, one of the Reformed confessions, contains a hint of this. The answer to the question "What then must a Christian believe?" is: "All that is promised us in the gospel, a summary of which is taught us in the articles of our universal and undisputed Christian faith."[39] The articles of the Apostles' Creed are thus regarded as promises. The Dutch Reformed theologian Oepke Noordmans comments in this regard: "The word 'promise' contains everything. Prom-

---

[38] Dalferth, "Die Mitte ist außen," 173: "Wirklichkeitsbezug."
[39] *Heidelberg Catechism*, Question and Answer 22.

ise means that we are not saying everything; there is a future still to come; and a Person is concealed in that promise."[40]

3 The Old Testament: Trinitarian Interpretation

The viability of the renewal of the Quadriga proposed in the present article can be demonstrated with respect to the interpretation of the most difficult part of the Bible, the Old Testament. Traditionally, this has been the focal point of allegorical interpretations which made spiritual sense of texts that contained no spiritual message at first sight. Unfortunately, Israel as addressee of the Old Testament was often forgotten, and the results of allegorical interpretation can strike the modern reader as less than plausible, although they conformed to exegetical standards of the time. For the present argument, it is important that Old Testament studies are not burdened with dogmatic presuppositions that would harm the freedom of exegesis, while the Old Testament also must be relevant for systematic theological studies. A good example of the difficulties that can arise lies in the doctrine of the Trinity: most systematic theologians will claim that God has not begun to be Triune at some point in time but that he is eternally Triune. Then under the Old Testament God also was Triune and the question is whether traces of the Trinity can be found in the Old Testament.[41] The eschatological sense of Scripture helps in this question.

Traditionally, there are mainly two ways to find the Trinity in the Old Testament, or to prove the doctrine of the Trinity from the Old Testament. First, the doctrine of the Trinity has been undergirded by Old Testament proof texts that would allude to plurality in God, such as the threefold invocation of the Holy God in Isaiah's vision of the seraphs, or the three lines of the Aaronic blessing.[42] Texts that refer to Israel or the king as "son of God" belong to the same category. The three men that came to Abraham are the most famous example and a favourite proof text for the Trinity in Church Fathers.[43] Of course, these pluralities can well be explained differently than in a Trinitarian perspective. The Reformer

---

40 Oepke Noordmans, *Herschepping* (Amsterdam: Holland, 1934), in *Verzamelde Werken Deel II: Dogmatische peilingen, Rondom Schrift en Belijdenis* (Kampen: J.H. Kok, 1979), 222. An English translation of Noordmans' main work, "Recreation", is in progress.
41 See also: Arnold Huijgen, "Traces of the Trinity in the Old Testament: From Individual Texts to the Nature of Revelation," *International Journal of Systematic Theology* 19 (2017): 251–70.
42 Isiah 6:1–3; Numbers 6:24–26.
43 Genesis 18:1–22.

John Calvin therefore did away with all these Old Testament proof texts, except the plural reference in Genesis: "Let us make mankind."[44] Second, personifications such as God's Wisdom, Word, or Spirit, were regarded as indication of the second or third Person of the Trinity. Also, agents such as the "Angel of the Lord" were regarded as Old Testament prefigurations of the incarnate Son.[45] But exegetically, this "Angel" is no more than a messenger, even when he refers to God in the first person singular: this was common practice among messengers.[46] Besides, while Wisdom, Word, and Spirit are vehicles of divine agency, that does not render these themselves divine.[47] They perform a communicative function. All in all, the traditional avenues to find the Trinity in the Old Testament prove unconvincing in light of modern exegesis.

The nature of revelation under the Old Testament provides a more solid account of the Trinity under Old Testament conditions. In the Old Testament, God is both transcendent and he condescends. On the one hand, he stands above everything that happens on the earth, but on the other hand, he really comes down to engage in the history he makes with humans.[48] The Old Testament has no problem whatsoever with anthropomorphic descriptions of God, and does not feel the need to characterise these as mere accommodations, to safeguard a clean idea of the God of traditional metaphysics, who cannot be corporeal because corporeality implies limitation.[49] Meanwhile, the Old Testament consistently distinguishes God from creation. This is the sense of the second commandment which prohibits images of God for he cannot be unqualifiedly identified with his creation, or any part of creation.[50] God is not identified by an object in space but by the history he makes over time. This is the fundamental distinction between Israel's religion and the other religions of the Ancient Near East. God is "the living God"[51] who is not defined by the confinement of an im-

---

[44] Genesis 1:26.
[45] Larry W. Hurtado, *One God, One Lord: Early Christian Devotion and Ancient Jewish Monotheism* (Philadelphia: Fortress Press, 1988), 17–18.
[46] Genesis 44:10; cf. A.S. van der Woude, "De Mal'ak Jahweh: Een godsbode," *Nederlands Theologisch Tijdschrift* 18 (1963): 1–30.
[47] See the contributions in *Presence, Power and Promise: The Role of the Spirit of God in the Old Testament*, ed. David G. Firth and Paul D. Wegner (Nottingham: Inter-Varsity Press, 2011).
[48] E.g., Genesis 11:5; 8:21; cf. Psalm 93:9.
[49] Cf. Benjamin D. Sommer, *The Bodies of God and the World of Ancient Israel* (Cambridge: Cambridge University Press, 2009).
[50] Christian Link, "Das Bilderverbot als Kriterium theologischen Redens von Gott," *Zeitschrift für Theologie und Kirche* 74 (1977): 58–85.
[51] Psalm 42:2; Jeremiah 10:10.

age, but who defines himself by identifying with the history of his people. Therefore, God does not reveal his "being" in the Old Testament, but his "name." Name is not a category, it is specific and personal, presupposes a context of communication, and its meaning is shaped by the history of the person bearing the name.[52] God's name in particular is a promise: "I am who I am" is a promise of a consistent loyalty and faithful friendship.

At this point, the eschatological sense of Scripture proves to be fitting and helpful for there is an eschatological tendency in God's dealings with his people. In his history with Israel, God employs ever new strategies, moves ever closer, until he becomes human under the New Testament. The history of God and Abraham, Isaac, Jacob, and Israel is a history of promises, kept by God but forgotten by the people. Besides the dynamic between God's transcendence and his condescendence, there is the tension between the actual state of affairs and the situation as promised by God. This structure of God above (transcendence), below (condescendence), and moving forwards towards the future is the closest parallel to a "proof" of the Trinity in the Old Testament, of Father, Son, and Holy Spirit. Traces of the Trinity under the Old Testament are not found on the level of phenomena or objects but in God's history with Israel. The doctrine of the Trinity, Israel, and eschatology are connected in Biblical theology to the extent that they are substantially one.

Note that Trinitarian interpretation of the Old Testament is allegorical in a specific sense: doctrine helps to interpret Biblical texts. But because the eschatological sense is primary, the allegorical sense does not consist in identification of phenomena with specific parts of doctrine but it refers to the history of the living God with his people, directed towards the incarnation. This allegorical sense does not need to find a spiritual meaning in, or rather behind, the actual text. Its reference to history safeguards that this allegory stays within the bounds of the letter.[53]

Within Trinitarian interpretation the role of the Spirit is crucial. He drives the eschatology by moving salvation history forward. In different phases God uses different instruments. At one time kingship is forbidden. Then it is allowed

---

[52] Christian Link, "Die Spur des Namens: Zur Funktion und Bedeutung des biblischen Gottesnamens," in *Die Spur des Namens: Wege zur Erkenntnis Gottes und zur Erfahrung der Schöpfung: Theologische Studien* (Neukirchen-Vluyn: Neukirchener Verlag, 1977), 37–66.

[53] Arnold Huijgen, "Allegory Within the Bounds of the Letter: Toward a Pneumatological Reorientation of Protestant Interpretations of the Old Testament," in *The Spirit is Moving: New Pathways in Pneumatology: Studies Presented to Professor Cornelis van der Kooi on the Occasion of his Retirement*, ed. Gijsbert van den Brink, Eveline van Staalduine-Sulman, and Maarten Wisse (Leiden: Brill, 2019), 77–90.

and soon David appears, the man after God's heart. The Spirit employs persons and institutions as forms to picture God's intentions for Israel, but no form can ultimately suffice, because God is God and humans are sinners. Then the Spirit disrupts the form to open up the future with a new form. This shaping and disrupting is typical for the work of the Spirit under the Old Testament. Every reconfiguration, every new shape, holds only until the tension between God above and God in his intricate history with Israel reaches a climax. The Spirit drives history towards the eschaton.

4 Conclusion

The present author has argued for the priority of the eschatological sense of Scripture as a redefinition of the anagogical sense of the traditional fourfold sense of Scripture. The eschatological nature of God's presence, truth as promise, and the idea of Christ as centre of Scripture are aspects of the eschatological sense of Scripture that are not only theologically viable but also stimulating for the interplay between systematic theology and Biblical studies. The disadvantages of recent proposals for theological interpretation of Scripture can be overcome once a Biblical, eschatological understanding of history replaces Platonist metaphysics. Truth cannot be had without history: not history in general or in an objectified sense but the actual history of the living God of Israel with his people. The truth is historical and eschatological. Against this background, allegorical interpretations may be viable, in the sense that doctrine (particularly the doctrine of the Trinity) helps to find aspects of meaning in Biblical texts.

Importantly, the renewal of the Quadriga advocated in the present article combines well with historical-critical methods of Biblical interpretation. History and truth should not be at odds. Besides, the emphasis on the Spirit as eschatological downpayment is Pauline and the interpretation proposed here does not shy away from the intricacies and paradoxes of the Old Testament: these are all part of the history God makes with his people. Still, whether the Trinitarian-eschatological interpretation of Scripture is viable, must be decided in discussion with Biblical scholars, and it must be tested in exegetical practices.

References

Andresen, Carl. "Zur Entstehung und Geschichte des trinitarischen Personsbegriffes." *Zeitschrift für die neutestamentliche Wissenschaft und die Kunde der älteren Kirche* 52 (1961): 1–39.

Bates, Matthew W. *The Birth of the Trinity: Jesus, God, and Spirit in New Testament and Early Christian Interpretations of the Old Testament*. Oxford: Oxford University Press, 2015.

Belt, Henk van den and others, editors. *Synopsis Purioris Theologiae. Synopsis of a Purer Theology: Latin Text and English Translation: Volume 2: Disputations 24–42*. Studies in Medieval and Reformation Traditions 204. Leiden: Brill, 2016.

Boeft, Jan den. "Erasmus and the Church Fathers." In *The Reception of the Church Fathers in the West: From the Carolingians to the Maurists*, edited by Irena Backus. Leiden: Brill, 2001, 537–72.

Boersma, Hans. *Scripture as Real Presence: Sacramental Exegesis in the Early Church*. Grand Rapids: Baker Academic, 2017.

Bowald, Mark Alan. "The Character of Theological Interpretation of Scripture." *International Journal of Systematic Theology* 12 (2010): 162–83.

Burger, Hans, Arnold Huijgen, and Eric Peels (editors), *Sola Scriptura: Biblical and Theological Perspectives on Scripture, Authority, and Hermeneutics*. Studies in Reformed Theology 32. Leiden: Brill, 2017.

Childs, Brevard S. *Introduction to the Old Testament as Scripture*. Minneapolis: Fortress Press, 1979.

Childs, Brevard S. and others. *The Bible as Christian Scripture: The Work of Brevard S. Childs*. Atlanta: Society of Biblical Literature, 2013.

Dalferth, Ingolf U. "Die Mitte ist außen: Anmerkungen zum Wirklichkeitsbezug evangelischer Schriftauslegung." *Jesus Christus als die Mitte der Schrift: Studien zur Hermeneutik des Evangeliums*, edited by Christof Landmesser and others. BZNW 86. Berlin: de Gruyter, 1997, 173–98.

Firth, David G. and Paul D. Wegner, editors. *Presence, Power and Promise: The Role of the Spirit of God in the Old Testament*. Nottingham: InterVarsity Press, 2011.

Fowl, Stephen E. *Theological Interpretation of Scripture*. Carlisle: Paternoster Press, 2010.

Gabler, Ioannes Philippus Gabler. *De iusto discrimine theologiae biblicae et dogmaticae, regundisque recte utriusque finibus: oratio qua recitata...* Altorf: Monath, 1787.

Goris, Harm and others, editors. *Synopsis Purioris Theologiae. Synopsis of a Purer Theology: Latin Text and English Translation: Volume 3: Disputations 43–52*. Studies in Medieval and Reformation Traditions 222. Leiden: Brill, 2020.

Hauerwas, Stanley. *Unleashing the Scripture: Freeing the Bible from the Captivity to America*. Nashville: Abingdon Press, 1993.

Hays, Richard B. "Christ Prays the Psalms: Israel's Psalter as Matrix of Early Christology." In *The Conversion of the Imagination: Paul as Interpreter of Israel's Scripture*. Grand Rapids: William B. Eerdmans, 2005, 101–18.

Hays, Richard B. *Reading Backwards: Figural Christology and the Fourfold Gospel Witness*. Waco: Baylor University Press, 2014.

Huijgen, Arnold. "Alone Together: Sola Scriptura and the Other Solas of the Reformation." In *Sola Scriptura: Biblical and Theological Perspectives on Scripture, Authority, and Hermeneutics*, edited by Hans Burger, Arnold Huijgen and Eric Peels. Studies in Reformed Theology 32. Leiden: Brill, 2017, 79–104.

Huijgen, Arnold. "Traces of the Trinity in the Old Testament: From Individual Texts to the Nature of Revelation." *International Journal of Systematic Theology* 19 (2017): 251–70.

Huijgen, Arnold. "Allegory Within the Bounds of the Letter: Toward a Pneumatological Reorientation of Protestant Interpretations of the Old Testament." In *The Spirit is Moving: New Pathways in Pneumatology: Studies Presented to Professor Cornelis van der Kooi on the Occasion of his Retirement*, edited by Gijsbert van den Brink, Eveline van Staalduine-Sulman, and Maarten Wisse. Leiden: Brill, 2019, 77–90.

Hurtado, Harry L. *One God, One Lord: Early Christian Devotion and Ancient Jewish Monotheism*. Philadelphia: Fortress Press, 1988.

Lieu, Judith M. and J.W. Rogerson, *The Oxford Handbook of Biblical Studies*. Oxford: Oxford University Press, 2008.

Link, Christian. "Das Bilderverbot als Kriterium theologischen Redens von Gott." *Zeitschrift für Theologie und Kirche* 74 (1977): 58–85.

Link, Christian. "Die Spur des Namens: Zur Funktion und Bedeutung des biblischen Gottesnamens." In *Die Spur des Namens: Wege zur Erkenntnis Gottes und zur Erfahrung der Schöpfung: Theologische Studien* Neukirchen-Vluyn: Neukirchener Verlag, 1977, 37–66.

Lubac, Henri de. *Exégèse médiévale: Les quatre sens de l'Écriture*. Paris: Aubier.

Noordmans, Oepke. "Herschepping." Amsterdam: Holland, 1934. In *Verzamelde Werken Deel II: Dogmatische peilingen, Rondom Schrift en Belijdenis*. Kampen: J.H. Kok, 1979.

Porter, Stanley E. "What Exactly Is Theological Interpretation of Scripture, and Is It Hermeneutically Robust Enough for the Task to Which It Has Been Appointed?" In *Horizons in Hermeneutics: A Festschrift in Honor of Anthony C. Thiselton*, edited by Stanley E. Porter and Matthew R. Malcolm. Grand Rapids: William B. Eerdmans, 2013, 234–67.

Sarisky Darren. *Scriptural Interpretation: A Theological Exploration*. Malden: Wiley, 2012.

Sarisky, Darren. *Reading the Bible Theologically*. Cambridge: Cambridge University Press, 2019.

Semler, Johann Salomo. *Versuch einer freiern theologischen Lehrart*. Halle: Hemmerde, 1777.

Sommer, Benjamin D. *The Bodies of God and the World of Ancient Israel*. Cambridge: Cambridge University Press, 2009.

Treier, Daniel J. "What is Theological Interpretation? An Ecclesiological Reduction." *International Journal of Systematic Theology* 12 (2010):144–161.

Troeltsch, Ernst. *Glaubenslehre: Nach Heidelberger Vorlesungen aus den Jahren 1911 und 1912*. München, Leipzig: Duncker & Humblot, 1925.

Vanhoozer, Kevin J. and others, editors. *Dictionary for Theological Interpretation of Scripture*. London: SPCK, 2005.

Velde, Dolf te, and others, editors. *Synopsis Purioris Theologiae. Synopsis of a Purer Theology: Latin Text and English Translation: Volume 1: Disputations 1–23*. Studies in Medieval and Reformation Traditions 187. Leiden: Brill, 2013.

Webster, John. *Holy Scripture: A Dogmatic Sketch*. Cambridge: Cambridge University Press, 2003.

Woude, A.S. Van der. "De Mal'ak Jahweh: Een godsbode." *Nederlands Theologisch Tijdschrift* 18 (1963): 1–30.

Mark W. Elliott
The Theological Art of Scriptural Interpretation: Lessons from von Balthasar

Abstract: This paper first describes the context into which the thoughts of Hans Urs von Balthasar appeared, principally those works of Schlier and Rahner with their distinctive approach to "biblical theology". It will then look at Balthasar's contribution to the Catholic multi-authored volume *Mysterium Salutis* of 1967, before moving to consider some thematic elements in his *Herrlichkeit* (translated as *Glory of the Lord*). These include the notion of the pressure of Divine Glory coming to be focused in Jesus and then through him into the New Testament and then onwards into Christian reflection. Moreover, it is important to understand "covenant" as more than something written but rather as that which drove action within earthly history, which subsequently and consequentially took literary expression in the canon. Also, the continuity of the New Testament with the Historical Jesus and the importance of a form which need not be static (Israel, Jesus Christ, canon) are important emphases. There is accordingly a brief account of Balthasar's 1976 reflections on the relationship between biblical exegesis and dogmatics. The paper will conclude with a consideration of the related questions of "canon" and "theological encyclopaedia". It will argue that the bible needs to be heard more than "made use of" in theology, that it at least *includes* teaching that is properly called "doctrinal", rather than seeing it as mere question-raising in the manner of fundamental theology, with too much respect being paid to anthropological and existential issues.

Keywords: Biblical Theology, Exegesis, Dogmatics, Divine Glory, Covenant

1 Catholic Biblical Theology in the Late 1950s

The entry "Biblische Theologie" in the third edition of the *Lexikon für Theologie und Kirche* (II: 1958) might well be illuminating for the present task because it is illustrative of *a* if not *the* mainstream position on that topic just prior to the time Balthasar was writing. (His volume *Theologie: Alter Bund* appeared in 1967.) In the article the larger part, written by Heinrich Schlier, makes it clear that any

---

Mark Elliot, University of the Highlands and Islands, Scotland, UK, mark.elliott@uhi.ac.uk

unity between the Testaments is to be found in the one plan of salvation, thus allowing for typology and *sensus plenior* to operate. Both testaments point forward to an eschatological fulfilment. The incompleteness of the OT is to be seen in its overemphasis of ritual, its being too much tied up with nationalism, together with the covenant sign of circumcision, in its ethical deficiency, in the cloudy ideas around "the Beyond", in an all-too-political notion of Messianic hopes and even in an imperfect conception of God. In the New Testament things will be clarified: the "antiquated torso" of the rabbinic-formalist Judaism is certainly not the appropriate continuation of the OT.

Now this prevailing pre-"New Perspective" notion of an "upgrading" that arrives with the New Testament feels wrongheaded sixty years on. Surely the NT jumps off the platform the OT provides for it and not all of the OT is matched by corresponding NT "improvements". However, as though aware of the objection of "supersessionism", Schlier adds that we do not have to go so far as Wilhelm Vischer, who thinks Christ can be seen *in* the OT itself as mediator of salvation (even if from a dogmatics point of view it is objectively the case that justification and grace come from Christ). First and at least before moving on to the NT, he insists, the OT must be given its own value, as it was for the believers "within the OT" who read it.

However, a question needs to be posed to Schlier: who were these very people who "read the OT"? The characters of the Old Testament themselves, such as Jeremiah reading Moses? The writers? The compilers? "The community of faith"? In any case, Schlier is prepared to assert about the OT that "es ist Morgenröte, nicht Tageshelle, 'Schatten des Zukünftigen' (Hebr. 10,1)" (1958: 441). For that reason dogmatic and ethical proof-texting from the Old Testament cannot provide any theological norm in a definite and positive way. After all the OT is a mere pedagogue (here an interesting appeal to Galatians 3:23 is made, substituting "Old Testament" where Paul wrote ὁ νόμος). Indeed a *History of Religions* approach makes one sensitive to development, with the Religion of the Patriarchs first, although Schlier disapproves of this as sacrificing continuity between testaments and forgetting theology. Yet, he observes, even the theological responses of Protestant OT Theology writers are not united in approach and sometimes are too dependent on Systematic Theology in their search for a unity of the OT. We need, Schlier insists, something more organic and some have tried to do this. These works are more focused on the Old Testament as relating life and history not doctrine (1958:442), and Schlier appreciates Gerhard von Rad's "history of traditions" approach particularly on this: also, it makes for a structural unity of the OT with the NT. The Biblical theology of the Old Testament is very much tied up with a historical treatment of the stream of *Geist*. Only with

WW1 did the evolutionary approach cease, as in E. König's 1922 *Theologie des Alten Testaments*. And then in his contribution "II. Biblische Theologie des *Neuen* Testaments", Schlier provided a longer list of catholic scholarly works.[1] The main concern discussed here is the extent to which a biblical theology of the New Testament can or should be descriptive or prescriptive. Rather than more conceptual arguments or evaluations Schlier gives a helpful list of fairly unknown yet significant catholic attempts at biblical theology of the OT.[2]

All this was by Schlier, Rahner's co-founder of the *Quaestiones Disputatae* series, whose first number was *Über die Schriftinspiration*. It is only for the final section of "Biblische Theologie", on the theme of the relationship of Biblical Theology to Systematic Theology that Karl Rahner then stepped in to take over the baton as anchor-runner or *Dirigent*, with a tone that was assertive, even combative, echoing themes and phrases from the fuller introduction to the volume *Quaestiones Disputatae* 1.[3] To wit: it just won't do for *Biblische Theologie* to stand in the way of *Systematische Theologie* getting to work directly with Scripture. For Systematic Theology has its own questions to put to Scripture and means hearing the word within the church (and maybe putting its own "dogmatic" questions to the bible[4])—Biblical Theology will be only a part of that,

---

[1] To give the highlights from Schlier's list of biblical theologies: C. Hayman wrote a *Biblische Theologie* (1708/1768) against scholastic theology, as did A.F. Büsching, 1758. Then there was that of K.F. Bahrdt, 1785 (who stressed awareness of the *genus historicum* of the work) and more recently that by F. C. Ceuppens, *Theologia biblica suivant l'ordre de la Somme de saint Thomas*), Rome, 1938.

[2] Schlier then offers some attempts at a theology of the Old Testament (only) that he seems to favour: P. Scholz, *Handbuch der Theologie des Alten Bundes*, 1862; N. Peters, *Theologia Biblica*, 1948-50; and, contemporaneous with Schlier himself, the attempts by P. Heinisch (*Theology of the Old Testament*, 1955) and P. van Imschoot (*Théologie de l'Ancien Testament*, 1954).

[3] Karl Rahner, *Über die Schriftinspiration*, Quaestiones disputatae Band 1, Freiburg im Breisgau: Herder Verlag, 1958. (An English translation appeared in 1961.)

[4] See Karl H. Neufeld, "Die Schrift in Der Theologie Karl Rahners," *Jahrbuch für Biblische Theologie* 2 (1987): 229–46, 232, who points to the Spiritual Exercises and 'the mysteries of the life of Jesus', and to a view of the bible as 'constitution' for the early church. Neufeld admits that Rahner's Old Testament education was 'spärlich', although it might have been advantageous that an OT Theology such as that of P. Heinisch was structured around Dogmatic categories and he saw the conflict or incompatibility of the presuppositions of exegetes and of systematicians. Yet he wished exegetical theologians to be full partners and not be subordinated to Fundamental Theology. Neufeld concludes that for Rahner Scripture had to do with faith and salvation, whereby 'die Schrift als solche unvermeidlich relativiert.' As Wilhelm Thüsing explained it: 'Es handelt sich um das Problem, weshalb zum AT mit seinem nicht nur theologischen, sondern auch anthropologischen Reichtum das NT (als Kerygma von Jesus als 'Mittler' und 'absolutem Heilbringer') hinzukommen darf and letzlich muß.'—it is the same *faith* the OT

though a special part. Then Rahner moves into the realm of ecclesial theology in his employment of the term *Dogmatik*, which is not identical with the content of Scripture, since it comes from the Magisterium. Biblische Theologie is *part* of *Dogmatik* only when *Dogmatik* tries to understand the words of Christ in Scripture. Scripture is not one source (*Quelle*) among others but it is certainly *the* source for *the knowledge of* Dogmatics ("Quelle der Erkenntnis der Dogmatik"). Whatever else Scripture is, it is the norm for the kerygmatic proclamation of Christ today. There is the possibility of a pre-dogmatic fundamental theological type of Biblical Theology. Tradition is never as pure from human additions (*Zutaten*) as Scripture is, and hence Scripture is a pure source, even though the Magisterium must still interpret with the Spirit's assistance (*Beistand*). *Dogmatik* has to listen to Scripture and to Biblical Theology, albeit that these are not the same thing. *Dogmatik* is not to judge as it tended to do in the past; but rather Biblical Theology has a critical function for *Dogmatik*. Biblische Theologie is to be the *hegemonikon* of *Dogmatik*, as Leo XIII insisted, but it is also tasked with rejuvenating theology as it returns to it (scripture: so, Pius XII).

For Rahner then, biblical theology had to constitute a moment in Systematic Theology itself and is not to be seen as owned by historical theology. This stops any necessary mediation by historical theology – *contra* Schleiermacher.[5] Rahner himself would not risk taking a step back from Fundamental Theological Questions (the nature of Revelation, the contribution of Religion to theology, the place of Reason, etc.) into actually taking on the biblical theological task. Even if he thought the boundaries were porous, the great Jesuit knew his own limitations as a scholar-theologian. But even biblical theology should not stand in the way of a Systematic Theology as it used Scripture to illuminate even as it

---

shares with the NT and indeed it shapes the NT's Christology by setting up a framework of call and response. The OT's covenant has been fulfilled, so it does not really operate now (*contra* Norbert Lohfink), although via the NT one can see important themes and include them. Scripture testifies as a norm to the originary religious and sets the tone for tradition (237). Like every person the exegete is addressed to be active in response. The overall "revelation' of God himself is prior to any particular textual *Urkunde* (Neufeld, "Schrift," 239). There is some appeal to scripture in Rahner's famous 'Theos im NT article': particularly just after the War did one see the fruits of working with biblical theology on sin and salvation in particular, even if that fruit lacks detail. The equally programmatic 1954 essay in the *Chalkedon* volume (edited by Alois Grillmeier) declared that the church's formulae left room for a wider biblical Christology to be explored, It is the biblical Jesus and none other who calls Christians today (cf. the Münster Christology lectures).

5 See Karl Rahner, "Heilige Schrift und Theologie," *Schriften VI*, 111-20, 118; also "Zur Theologie der Heiligen Schrift," *Sacramentum Mundi* IV, 439.

asks questions of it, in a living way that the bible writers did themselves of scripture (Schlier).

Not so with Hans Urs von Balthasar, at least not in the 1960s. The biblical material lay pristine, inviting.

2 Balthasar in *Mysterium Salutis*: Alter Bund as *Praeparatio evangelii*

Balthasar was famous for his trilogy, consisting of (1) *Herrlichkeit* (ET, *Glory of the Lord*), where he considered how glory is expressed in beauty, with the latter reconfigured by the former, not least in light of the covenantal history, (2) *Theodramatik* (ET, *Theodrama*) a casting of the economy of salvation in the context of Trinitarian relations) understood in terms of dramatic theory with an emphasis on the dynamic and inter-personal and (3) *Theologik* (ET: *Theo-logic*) which moves to a theological philosophy or a philosophical theology. There is exegesis within the volumes of his chief project, especially in his foundational *Herrlichkeit*, as we shall see.

To begin with, however, one should note that most impressive and most curious of post-Vatican II projects, the monumental work, *Mysterium Salutis*, to which a diverse array of Catholic academics contributed. Volume 1 (1965) was dedicated to Balthasar himself, and the entry on "Heilsgeschichte" was written (at length) by Herbert Haag. Volume 2: *Die Heilsgeschichte vor Christus* deals with The Trinity, and then the Trinity in light of salvation history; then comes Rahner on the Trinity as transcendental ground of *Heilsgeschichte*; then there are entries on creation, theological anthropology and the history of humanity before Christ in terms of need and preparation for salvation, world religions; and finally Joseph Scharbert's "Heilsgeschichte und Heilsordnung des Alten Testaments" (Vol 1: 1076-1142), which is very much a 1960s-style biblical theology informed by critical insights and with acceptance of the different emphases of J,E,D, and P. Revelation as the meaning of the facts of salvation history are mediated by traditions with built-in awareness of typological connections. This essay by Scharbert is a much more clearly theological version than that which Haag offered in the previous volume.

It fell to Balthasar himself to write the very first essay in this second volume himself, an essay called "Der Zugang zur Wirklichkeit Gottes". On p. 38 he insists that, according to the bible, Nature is not pure and has no claim on grace, for there is no state of pure nature. God comes towards Nature in grace and is

Himself the hidden but present salvation for all. Pre-Christian religions can serve as vehicles for such revelation, and indeed Revelation uses them but also corrects them. Even Ezekiel 14:14 recognized certain pagans as wise and righteous. (Balthasar 1967: 43); and Hebrews 11:1, 3, 6 include some righteous "pagans". However there needs to be through the cross a displacement of the religions for them only to become wise ("Mitverörtung der Religionen, um erst wahrhaft weise zu werden"). Acts 17, he observes, is here quite different from Romans 1-2. For Acts, natural religion is a mixed blessing, whereas Paul in Romans 1-2 is more negative towards it. Surely on balance the bible affirms that God makes a divine 'way of being' available to thinking people, and thereby reveals himself even though as ungraspable, yet in *tanta similitudine* (DS 806). Bubbling under the surface of this essay is the question of the Old Covenant as preparation for the New Covenant (not the books of the Old Testament as such). It is at least that *praeparatio*, but it is more, as we see in the employment of the Ezekiel quotation as an authority that has no less standing as holy Scripture than any New Testament text.

3 Biblical Theology of Glory/Herrlichkeit, Leading towards a Dogmatics

As one who declared himself to be first a scholar of literature, when it came to almost 400 pages dedicated to *Herrlichkeit* III, 2.1 *Alter Bund* it is perhaps not surprising that he sensed a healthy humanism in biblical studies and, guided by the likes of Martin Noth and Gerhard von Rad, immersed himself in the research of the time. He remarked that the bible itself contains its own humanism, manifested not least in the OT's demythologising of ANE myths and with its openness to Greek philosophical thinking (*Herrlichkeit* III, 2, 24). Philosophy's provisionality (*Vorlaufigkeit*) is similar to that of the OT. Connected to this and something that was also *de jour* at the time was the realisation of the ecumenical (hence or since cross-cultural) potential of biblical theology: "Die biblische Theologie öffnet sich abschließend zu einer kirchlichen (ökumensichen) Theologie" (*Herrlichkeit* III, 2, 25).

One should perhaps note Balthasar's disclaimer on the last page of the volume that this was not meant to be an attempt at an OT Theology let alone a biblical theology, not least since too many biblical themes were missing. A biblical theology of *X*, where "*X*" stands for a doctrine or theme, does not really qualify as biblical theology. Also, rather than a systematic dogmatics an *ecu-*

menical dogmatics can arise with *Gloria Dei* at the centre. What we have is a dogmatics based on the theme of *Herrlichkeit Gottes* rather than a biblical theology as such. This means that Balthasar intended to do what Rahner too wanted done: to offer something biblical towards or as part of dogmatics, not a mediating pan-biblical theology as such.

3.1 The *Kabod* Weight or Force of the Living God

To summarise the contents *Teil I, Alter Bund*: Glory is the formal grounding character of Scripture. Before any dialogue can begin, Balthasar contends, there has to be a "being touched" (*Betroffensein*) by the "glorious" aspect of God. As Matthias Scheeben had already insisted, theology is not about mysterious heavenly truths but is about the living God in his glory, meaning the absolute Subject creating a covenantal relationship that fosters a sobriety of life in obedient response. Now of course *kabod* has to do with Revelation and so is itself a fundamental theological category. *Kabod* can mean the centre of gravity (Gen 49:6) in the case of a human person, but with God that does not appear to be the case. *Kabod* is *not* God's core but rather that which comes from him, and which draws human attention. It is inseparable from its effects, being a spiritual component from God himself, who as in his core absolute subject is free to appear. *Kabod* is indeed an abstract in the sense of mystery in itself, yet by definition it moves to take a step to appear in form (Hegel) (*Herrlichkeit* III, 2, 36). Moses experienced a dialectic of knowing/unknowing that corresponded to divine manifestation/non-manifestation.

3.2 The Element of *Doxa* (Repute/Name) in LXX on the Way to Neuer Bund

The LXX translation *doxa* expands the semantic range of *kabod* to include "reputation", which will be important for the NT gospel. As creatures in the image of God we creatures contain a longing to rise up to meet the agapeic descent of glory in the realm of the senses. Embodiment is included in that image, which is that of being worldly in God's presence (*Bild als Weltlichsein vor Gott*). There is a 'terrible' side to God's radiance (*Glanz*) which would confound any Romantic aesthetical theology. Balthasar's Neo-Platonism[6] (often self-acknowledged, hence hardly an *unconscious* baleful influence) is reflected in statements as on S. 133: "Die 'kosmische Liturgie' war im Grunde nichts als die Rückgabe aller Herrlichkeit durch das geschaffene Du an das absolute Ich." God appears as the beautiful, but the presence of the Good joins in to hold it and the True together. In fact, the ethical Good is the core of God's ethical-reliability; later Jewish writers and the NT would use *doxa* with its ethical connotations more widely than the OT does. God's good action to the world bathes the world in goodness—communicating it to the world as a speech-*act*, not just saying forensically that it is good. Grace reaches inwards into each person; but Grace is also clothing for it is what the nations *see* (*Herrlichkeit* III, 2, 136).

Moses' "seeing God's back" means seeing God go or pass by *in his deeds*. God brings Israel into his own space; it is not about God giving humans a new quality. Balthasar likes to employ the terminology of transplantation (the process of *Entrückung* and *Geborgenheit* as the result). Now there might well be an image of God in people; yet at the same time there is a huge gap that qualifies this family resemblance and necessitates a covenant within an estranged family. God's covenantal *chesed* can be translated by the Greek *charis*: "the person who stands in the sphere of the covenant is justified" (*Herrlichkeit* III, 2, 155). This gives one a confidence to behave in a righteous way, from the indefectibility of the divine source of life. Abraham had a readiness to obey; it came out of love towards the gracious initiating God. *Mishpat* is an ordering justice that has its source in God, just like a light that is radiated (Hosea 6:5). Directed towards the poor it is the fruit of compassion. *Geborgenheit* with God is a source of life (*Herrlichkeit* III, 2, 170).

3.3 Glory Internalised in the Prophetic Heart, then Radiated outwards

One might expect the throne-room vision of Isaiah to be significant and so it proves to be, but it is not treated at great length. The vision is what makes the prophet send-able; the vision of Glory is half-way between Sinai and the escha-

---

[6] One should note that Neoplatonism is not the same as Platonism. Put (very) simply, Neoplatonism operates with an epistemological but not an ontological dualism, since what is primary is Mind, and it emphasises the movement from the mental-invisible and truly real towards the visible and physical, to associate with it and draw it upwards. It is ultimately monist. See Christian Wildberg, "Neoplatonism," in Edward N. Zalta (ed.), *The Stanford Encyclopedia of Philosophy* (Winter 2021 Edition), https://plato.stanford.edu/archives/win2021/entries/neoplatonism/.

tological glory, and the prophet shuttles between. The vision was not an end in itself in this double sense (*Herrlichkeit* III, 2, 229). Jeremiah will accompany the people (Is 29:21: the Lord's "strange work") into the wilderness. God is revealed through lives placed at his disposal. In silence there can be a receiving of the purifying work of God. In Jeremiah God appears in the struggle with the prophet (*Herrlichkeit* III, 2, 238). Jeremiah did not receive a vision of glory but instead a reassurance of his calling and a fire in his heart; the glory burned there without Jeremiah knowing it was such but knowing it as love that others could have in the New Covenant. Of all the prophets, it is probably actually Ezekiel who is most appreciated for his vision of the strange God and the Temple, which exceeds anything in the stock traditions of Israel, who is a dumb-struck prophet as the place of mediation between the people's humiliation and the lowering of God's glory in judgment. Thus the fire in the temple becomes glorious again after a burning presence, on the way to the vision of John the Divine in the NT (*Herrlichkeit* III, 2, 254f). In arriving at these insights use is made of the Old Testament research of Fohrer, Eichrodt and Zimmerli (181). W.T. Dickens observes: "His treatment of the book of Isaiah provides a striking example. He discussed 1–3 Isaiah as discrete units, nowhere giving serious consideration to the theological significance of their editorial conjoining. This diachronic approach remains a significant, though much less common, feature of his volume in 'The Glory of the Lord on the New Covenant'."[7] It is probably fair to say that Balthasar was not really interested in the sequence of books as much as in the symphonic nature of their content and so he went for spotting similar themes within 1–3 Isaiah without necessarily saying who owed what to whom.

3.4 Religious Experience of Transcendence on Earth: Bund, not "Testament"

Yet the resulting Theology of Glory in this post-exilic OT sense (which has prophetic, apocalyptic and wisdom expressions) is a theology that has moved on from darkness and terrors of judgement, but without integrating them: "es ist eine Theologie, die die Nächte und Schrecken des Gerichtes irgendwo hinter sich gebracht und nicht in der Tiefe integriert hat." The corollary is that the NT will bring an integrative judgement that is also restoration.

---

[7] W.T. Dickens, "Balthasar's biblical hermeneutics," in *Cambridge Companion to von Balthasar*, edited by Edward T. Oakes (Cambridge: Cambridge University Press, 2004): 175–86, 182.

Perhaps one of the most interesting sections lies towards the end of *Herrlichkeit* III.2.1. After reviewing the exilic prophets, Balthasar observes that the post-exilic works like Ezra, Nehemiah and Chronicles were fairly sterile and backward looking. In them there is no more prophecy and a lot of uncertainty, not even an experience of God's absence like Ezekiel; just silence and a meditative pause (*Herrlichkeit* III.2.1, 338). Perhaps surprisingly he sees theology of the cult and the word as somewhat marking time, keeping the show on the road during the *Leere Zeit*. Between the two poles of clinging to the past (with the "theologically empty" temple built in detail to resemble the former one) and of hoping for a violent reconditioning of the cosmos "apocalyptically" (just a few could see this glory shut up in heaven/mysteries, with a heavy moralising, exclusivism and asceticism), there lies what might be the high point of the OT in Balthasar's eyes: the humble poor looking towards the heavenly Jerusalem (in later Isaiah, Sirach and Wisdom of Solomon) where glory and the beauty of creation get mixed together, just as history seems to have failed. God as friend of life (Wis 11:26) accompanies all with providence (Wis 14.3); the immortal illumination of Torah is identified with *kabod*. Life beyond Sheol is promised (Wis 3:4) and there is the first appearance of immortality (*Unsterblichkeit*). *Pace* Hegel, God is not limited by creation (see *Herrlichkei* III/2.1,911), for God is the non-Other (*non-Aliud*). Wisdom is the outbreath of Glory and it moves things. The NT will expand on this one-many; wisdom is ready to be found (Wis 6:13-16). Eros reaches out to God's agape, and Eros loves Wisdom because it is beautiful but more profoundly so because God loves her. Eschatology presents an either-or to moral living, yet it is one that is philosophically informed. Balthasar's exposition here (*Herrlichkeit* III.2.1, 317-36) is sustained by the Wisdom of Solomon) perhaps more than any piece of Scripture, including Ezekiel.

There is importantly to be "no return to Sinai", except as a past symbol of present attachment or rootedness, yet which needs always to look forward to a transformation in history from outside history (*Herrlichkeit* III.2.1, 317-36373): "Dieser Befund kennzeichnet das ganzen Alten Bund als 'figura', als eine 'ästhetische Wirklichkeit' gegenüber einer 'ethischen', endgültig inkarnierten." ("This discovery [that the Messiah takes over from the 'Son of Man' image] characterizes the whole Old Covenant as 'figure', as an aesthetic reality, over against an ethical, sufficiently incarnated one.") One problem is that in the OT death still lies between God and people. Holy Saturday is required to deal with that; and the force of the *dei* of Lk 24:26, that Christ *had to* suffer before entering glory, is a necessity at the level of the human, if not the divine. By the reference to *Bundesverhältnis* the people in the OT are more than themselves since they are recipients and vessels of grace (and not literary, universal types). The same goes for the church.

3.5 OT Images Re-presented in NT

Just what of the Old is the New fulfilling? Of course we need the OT for "the whole biblical theology to be conveyed in its full form" ("die ganze biblische Theologie vermittelt in einer Gesamtgestalt"); but the experiences of glory to which the texts witness are what is important, not the OT text in itself. The lack of interest shown by Balthasar in the question of the shape of the canon or formal questions about literary composition (and hence the whole *Quelle-Gattung-Tradition-Redaktion* enterprise) reinforces the impression that the topic is not *Altes Testament* but rather *Alter Bund*, part of Ancient Israel's *realia*; likewise with the *Neuer Bund* for the church. In his essay, "Balthasar's Biblical Hermeneutics", W.T. Dickens was critical of Balthasar's criticism (in *Glory of the Lord* I, 37) of diachronic approaches (a criticism that would be defended by Edward Oakes) and Balthasar's insistence on the need for any interpreter (including the biblical scholar) to be somehow "inspired". With Nietzsche, Balthasar believed History should really be about love and art, as that which plumbs the inner depth of our being, indeed, art is more concrete and particular than recorded events, having better access to the reality of Christ.[8] One only ends up controlling the text by over-contextualizing it, as those who see exegetes primarily as historians tend to do. Instead, the canon allows diverse inspired texts to interact in shaping the reader's understanding and *that* is the point.

The bipartite covenant flows into the one-sided Covenant which had always preceded it;[9] and Balthasar found himself disagreeing with Bultmann[10] for whom there was no original unilateral covenant. The idea is that Israel's failure is not one that ends in the finitude of being but in the very God who presented the choice of choosing life or death. Christ breaks through that "death barrier" that Israel repeatedly chose in an unseen way. Even if exact verbal parallels

---

[8] Edward T. Oakes, "Balthasar's Critique of the Historical-Critical Method," in *Glory, Grace, and Culture: The Work of Hans Urs von Balthasar*, edited by E. Block, New York: Paulist, 2005, 150–74, 153.
[9] Cf. *Herrlichkeit* III.2.1, 376–7: "Aber Israels scheitern ist von anderer Art: es scheitert nicht vor allem an der Endlichkeit des Daseins, sondern an Gott, der es in die Entscheidung zwischen Leben und Tod, Segen und Fluch gestellt hat (Dt 30,19)."
[10] Rudolf Bultmann, "Ursprung und Sinn der Typologie als hermeneutischer Methode," *Theologische Literaturzeitung* 75 (1950): 205–12.

with the OT are sketchy, still there is imagic re-presentation. The End that is declared is not timelessness but through eternity entering time it is the entry of real time (*echter Zeit*) into eternity. It is not about opposition of the two testaments, but about the NT making the OT appear as not so much a failure (Bultmann's *Geschichte des Scheitern*) but as the epistemological introduction to the understanding of the New nevertheless in need of reconfiguring: the point of the metaphor of *Trümmer*, "rubble" (*Herrlichkeit* III.2.2, 29; cf. Barth, *Dogmatik in Umriss*, Intro.) that is much used here is not pejorative but literally a constructive one: that the strewn-around content of the Alter Bund is picked up and re-used for a new building; yet the OT foundation is used (*Herrlichkeit* III.2.2, 35). The Incarnate One will draw all peripheral to him. It is not that Christ's primary interest is in fulfilling the OT,[11] as though that ground level history is what demands that of him. Jesus has a Trinitarian liberty, which in turn lends us "decisionality". This plays into life in the quotidian, not the transcendental dimension. The gap between Father and Son is wider than that between God and sinners, and so mediation operates as inclusion. There is a theodramatic action that lays a bridge, but there is no preparation on the side of creation, for all happens between Father and Son.[12]

3.6 The NT is the Written Impression of Christ Mediated through Easter Faith

There is no space except to briefly outline the heart of the companion volume *Der Neue Bund*. Jesus reveals God's hiddenness: the pre-Easter Jesus is like that. Any "visible, objective glory" is only subjectively visible even as God Incarnate redefines "beauty" and operates a dislocation of rapture (*Entrückung*) of the viewer. Balthasar might be accused of making too much of a pre-Easter/post-Easter contrast; any link to the OT in order to fulfil passes through the Father's sovereign will. It requires the Trinity raising him up to glory for there to be any glory; the historical Jesus is therefore somewhat overlooked. It is a theology based on the Trinitarian revelatory experience in post-Easter communities. Therefore, Balthasar claims that the historical Jesus "did not at all anticipate his glorification by the Father" (*Herrlichkeit* III.2.2, 330). He can only be approached

---

[11] *Glory of the Lord VII*, Edinburgh: T.&T. Clark, 1990, 372.
[12] Vincent Holzer, *Le Dieu Trinité dans l'histoire. Le différend théologique Balthasar–Rahner*. Cogitatio Fidei 190, Paris: Cerf, 1995, 222.

through faith as exalted in his self-consciousness. *A fortiori* the OT has little direct validity of its own:

> A necessity existed, like the necessary link between promise and fulfilment, but there was also a sovereign freedom that was obedient to the Father alone, and not to the historical structures of the prophecies. From an earthly point of view the boundlessness of the imagining love in Cross and Hell is absolutely withheld from sight—and in being absolutely withheld from sight, it makes the incomprehensibility of the divine love of the Father "visible". (*Glory* VII, 283)

There is an overall progressive view of the development in the NT writings, one that grows in stages towards Johannine theology, the *Flucht- und Zielpunkt* of NT Theology (*Herrlichkeit* III.2.2, 10). The church's developing convictions and thoughtfulness leads to the fullness of the (ultimately inexpressible) reality.

4 Later Considerations

In his famous 1976 essay, "Exegese und Dogmatik", Balthasar pondered as to what is left of gospel passages relationship to Jesus' words and deeds, after the historical critics have had their way.[13] Are we (the church and her theologians) building our dogmatic house on sand? Jesus was in his lifetime certainly the incorporation of God's kingdom on its way to realization, crucified under Pontius Pilate. Yet there is a transposition of the Word in Jesus into the Word by the Holy Spirit in the faith of the early church, even as the latter can grasp that Word only partially. There is an objective unity in the personal address of the Word and the one faith of the church. Exegetes are also to pay attention to the implicit theology in the biblical texts, as these lead them in Erasmian fashion with a focus on the plain grammatical sense. Any synthesis of diverging NT texts is trans-historical (*übergeschichtlich*) because Christ's rising and returning to the Father contains history within it. *Dogmatik* has to consider whether it can take on this role of synthesis, while realising it is always inchoate (the Truth is a person), and its job is to make sure the churches receive the fullness of truth. Accordingly it should not read texts in a discrete way ("geschlossene") but as open to and linked to each other, yet not *intégraliste*. He ends the essay with the example of the consciousness of Jesus: did he mislead his followers with talk of

---

[13] Hans Urs von Balthasar, "Exegese und Dogmatik," *Internationale katholische Zeitschrift Communio* 5 (1976): 385–92.

an imminent End? It is surely no interim ethic but an ethic of obedience to the World-end of the cross and on to Easter as new life. It is a happy mistake that Paul and others mistook this and therefore preached with urgency in light of an imminent end. What Jesus was about dogmatically was his human obedience: "Sein Horizont war 'ökonomisch' eingeengt auf seine im Gehorsam zu vollbringende Sendung."[14] There is not an urgency for the sake of running out of time but a steady going at the Father's pace, as a *human* mission in time to bring the old world to an end. Dogmatics can be saved from many apparent problems by deep exegesis. Here once more in Balthasar is the Johannine Eschatology of the Cross to the fore with Jesus as the man exercising trust, whoever else he was in Trinitarian terms.

5 The Importance of Canon and "Fixedness"

Matthew Levering has recently observed that for Balthasar it *has to be* the historical Jesus if he is to engage our senses and our suffering as well as mind.[15] So the historical form of the creature matters. And to quote Balthasar himself, the accent would seem to lie with the *Logos ensarkos*, but that includes his presence to the church: "Only John has dared to cast a bridge over the distance that is held open in the Gospels by the flight of the disciples, and in Paul by faith." (ET: *Glory* VII, 196.) The form is that of the Lord, not of some human *prosopon*. The grace that radiates forth is from the Logos when "raised up"—on the cross as the Johannine ascension. Eternity lives a temporal life, and there is no place for a transcendental Christology; *qua* human he is "blind" during his earthly life, a silencing of the Word, "the empty space through which the δόξα can send its rays" (ET: *Glory* VII, 147)—which happens in exaltation and hence in the form given to it in the expressed faith of the New Testament Scriptures. And yet that space is a shaped and dimensioned one. It has a form since God has form and yet the form that can be perceived appears in creaturely dimensions.

Something of this "top-down and descending" aspect to the choice of Glory as a dominant theme in Balthasar's oeuvre is pinpointed by Rowan Williams in an early essay at the time of the Anglophone first reception of Balthasar. In contrast to Rahner's transcendental, bottom-up Christology the downward out-

---

14 Ibid., 392.
15 Matthew Levering, *The Achievement of Hans Urs von Balthasar*, Washington; CUA Press, 2019, 14.

ward *ekstasis* of participation[16] is that preferred by Balthasar. As we recognize our place too (Heidegger and Gadamer are waved towards), there is a call to dramatic participation and not mere spectating. In his later *Theodramatik* I, 22, he even speaks of Scripture as libretto; the drama is indeterminate in that it has to be lived out. What Balthasar actually wrote was: "Und jenes Libretto des Heilsdramas Gottes, das wir Heilige Schrift nennen, ist wertlos in sich, falls es nicht im Heiligen Geist die immerwährende Vermittlung zwischen dem Drama dort und dem Drama hier ist." There is more here about the communication between past and present church. Williams is however correct to conclude that this means "biblical calling" is somewhere between predetermined and totally free – avoiding "pure (structuralist) functionalism, without simply taking refuge in a static essentialist dogma or a privatized existentialism".[17] In accord with this (as per *Glory of the Lord* VII, 268): "The God of the Bible is neither a *tremendum* nor a *fascinosum*, but first of all an *adorandum*."

Cyril O'Regan has written that what Balthasar sees scripture supplying is "the view of the divine as a free self-communicating 'I' [...], the perception of the self as constituted in the free response of faith and praise, and the vision of creation as graced, at once radically mysterious in terms of origin and suffused by divine presence. Christ is understood to be the unsurpassable rendering of the free personal God, to provide the archetype for faith in its basic description and way of life and to illuminate and complete the order of creation without compromising its integrity."[18] This is a useful summary of Balthasar's work, which finds an echo in Rowan Williams' recent monograph, *Christ the Heart of Creation*.[19] Is it a fundamental theology as Dulles and Hans Hübner[20] want to see biblical theology? It is too exegetical for that, it is too intertextual, it is too much based on spiritual experience. There is a metaphysic of sin in the sense that it goes deep into all of *created* reality: even the essence of the church as *casta meretrix*.

In fact, to suppose that biblical theology could be or take its place as a source of Revelation in order to provide a chastening fundamental theology, to keep systematic theology "honest", seems like a category mistake to some.

---

[16] Rowan Williams, "Balthasar and Rahner," in *The Analogy of Beauty*, edited by John Riches (Edinburgh: T&T Clark, 1986), 11–34, 26.
[17] Rowan Williams, "Balthasar and Rahner," 27.
[18] Cyril O'Regan, *Anatomy of Misremembering: Von Balthasar's Response to Philosophical Modernity. Volume 1: Hegel*, New York: Crossroads, 2013, 74.
[19] Rowan Williams, *Christ the Heart of Creation* (London: Bloomsbury, 2018).
[20] Avery Dulles, *Models of Revelation*, Maryknoll, N.Y.: Orbis Books, 1992; Hans Hübner, *Evangelische Fundamentaltheologie: Theologie der Bibel*, Göttingen: Vandenhoeck & Ruprecht, 2006.

Hence, according to Benoît Bourgine, a *Theologie de coordination* fits with Rahner's approach of a "faith seeking understanding" as to how the Word is to be heard,[21] such that a biblical theologian deals in both explication and application. Biblical theology lies between exegesis and Systematic Theology and gets affected by both; hence biblical theology should thus influence systematic theology but at the same time not to be too far removed from the concerns of now, with its existentialist commitment: "Le rôle régulateur de l'Écriture, vibrante de la victoire sur le péché et la mort, est à même de la ramener vers les rivages du vécu."[22] However my view is that this seems to let Systematics off rather lightly, even by-passing it to get to practical theology engaging with culture and leaving a void where doctrine used to be.[23] It is theology that needs to be coordinated with the bible-interpreted tradition and not just bible-interpreting, and for Systematics to relate to contemporary culture and philosophy but only as the dialogue is two-way and the intentions are shaped by evangelical concerns. Seeing the form of revelation in Scripture is a contemplation that by sharpening our eyes of faith in the world keeps our intentions that bit purer.

References

Balthasar, Hans Urs von. "Exegese und Dogmatik." *Internationale katholische Zeitschrift Communio* 5 (1976): 385–92.
Balthasar, Hans Urs von. *Herrlichkeit III/2. 1 Alter Bund. 2. Neuer Bund*. Einsiedeln, 1967–69.
Balthasar, Hans Urs von. *Glory of the Lord VI: The Old Covenant*, Edinburgh: T. & T. Clark, 1990.
Balthasar, Hans Urs von. *Glory of the Lord VII: The New Covenant*, Edinburgh: T. & T. Clark, 1990.

---

[21] B. Bourgine, "Pour une théologie biblique/Towards a Biblical Theology," *Revue d'Histoire et de Philosophie religieuses* 99 (2019):227–36, 227: "La théologie biblique, définie comme le rapport établi entre le texte biblique et la vie chrétienne aujourd'hui."

[22] Ibid., 224. Bourgine reports Konrad Schmid's criticism of C. Dohmen and R. Kratz in his "Sind die Historisch-Kritischen kritischer geworden? Überlegungen zu Stellung und Potential der Bibelwissenschaften," *Jahrbuch für Biblische Theologie* 25 (2011) 63–78. To balance this, he noted the work by Karsten Lehmkühler, *Kultus und Theologie. Dogmatik und Exegese in der religionsgeschichtlichen Schule*, Forschungen zur systematischen und ökumenischen Theologie 76, Göttingen, Vandenhoeck & Ruprecht, 1996: every liberal has their own dogma. Systematic theology is to build on the foundations of biblical theology (Barth, KD I/1,15; cf. Rahner, *Theological Investigations I*, 154).

[23] Bourgine has developed this in his recent book, *Bible oblige. Essai de théologie biblique*. (Paris: Cerf, 2019). His conclusion proposes a biblical revelatory firmament for culture and life which nourishes and guarantees them.

Bourgine, Benoît. "Pour une théologie biblique/Towards a Biblical Theology." *Revue d'Histoire et de Philosophie religieuses* 99 (2019): 227–236.
Bourgine, Benoît. *Bible oblige. Essai de théologie biblique.* Paris: Cerf, 2019.
Bultmann, Rudolf. "Ursprung und Sinn der Typologie als hermeneutischer Methode." *Theologische Literaturzeitung* 75 (1950): 205–12.
Dickens, W. T. "Balthasar's biblical hermeneutics," in *Cambridge Companion to von Balthasar*, edited by Edward T. Oakes, Cambridge: Cambridge University Press, 2004, 175–86.
Dulles, Avery. *Models of Revelation*, Maryknoll, N.Y.: Orbis Books, 1992.
Holzer, Vincent. *Le Dieu Trinité dans l'histoire. Le différend théologique Balthasar–Rahner.* Paris: Cerf, 1995.
Hübner, Hans. *Evangelische Fundamentaltheologie: Theologie der Bibel*, Göttingen: Vandenhoeck & Ruprecht, 2006.
Lehmkühler, Karsten. *Kultus und Theologie. Dogmatik und Exegese in der religionsgeschichtlichen Schule*, Forschungen zur systematischen und ökumenischen Theologie 76. Göttingen: Vandenhoeck & Ruprecht, 1996.
Levering, Matthew. *The Achievement of Hans Urs von Balthasar.* Washington, DC: CUA Press, 2019.
Mengus, Raymond. "L'"Épilogue' de Hans Urs von Balthasar (1905-1988)." *Revue des Sciences Religieuses* 62 (1988): 252–64.
Neufeld, Karl H. "Die Schrift in der Theologie Karl Rahners." *Jahrbuch für Biblische Theologie* 2 (1987): 229–46.
Oakes, Edward T. "Balthasar's Critique of the Historical-Critical Method." In *Glory, Grace, and Culture: The Work of Hans Urs von Balthasar*, edited by Ed Block Jr., New York, Paulist Press, 2005, 150–74.
O'Regan, Cyril. *Anatomy of Misremembering: Von Balthasar's Response to Philosophical Modernity. Volume 1: Hegel*, New York: Crossroads, 2013
Rahner, Karl. 'Heilige Schrift und Theologie', *Schriften VI.* Einsiedeln/Zürich/Köln, Benziger Verlag, 1965, 111–20.
Rahner, Karl. "Zur Theologie der Heiligen Schrift." In *Sacramentum Mundi* IV, Freiburg: Herder, 428–49.
Rahner, Karl. *Über die Schriftinspiration, Quaestiones disputatae Band 1*, Freiburg im Breisgau: Herder Verlag, 1958.
Schmid, Konrad. "Sind die Historisch-Kritischen kritischer geworden? Überlegungen zu Stellung und Potential der Bibelwissenschaften." *Jahrbuch für Biblische Theologie* 25 (2011): 63–78.
Van Erp, Stephan. *The Art of Theology: Hans Urs von Balthasar's Theological Aesthetics and the Foundations of Faith.* Studies in Philosophical Theology 25. Leuven: Peeters, 2004.
Wildberg, Christian. "Neoplatonism." In *The Stanford Encyclopedia of Philosophy* (Winter 2021 Edition), edited by Edward N. Zalta,
https://plato.stanford.edu/archives/win2021/entries/neoplatonism/.
Williams, Rowan. "Balthasar and Rahner." In *The Analogy of Beauty*, edited by John Riches, Edinburgh: T&T Clark, 1986, 11–34.
Williams, Rowan. *Christ the Heart of Creation.* London: Bloomsbury, 2018.

Ida Heikkilä
The Holy Scriptures as a Recognition- and Witnessing-Authority

The German Lutheran—Catholic Dialogue "Communio Sanctorum: The Church as the Communion of Saints"

Abstract: This chapter deals with the role and authority of the Holy Scriptures in the life of the church. The topic is approached through an analysis of the German Catholic–Lutheran dialogue document "Communio Sanctorum. Die Kirche als Gemeinschaft der Heiligen" (2000, transl. "Communio Sanctorum: The Church as the Communion of Saints"). In this dialogue, the Scriptures are understood as one of five authorities of witness and recognition (*Bezeugungsinstanzen*), authorities through which the church can recognize the truth and witness to it. The chapter shows how this approach leads to a theological model where the Scriptures coordinate the other authorities but can, nevertheless, never be interpreted outside of the interplay with the other authorities. It also shows how the unwillingness to lift one of the witnessing authorities above the others makes way for a strong pneumatology, where the right balance between the authorities is maintained by the Holy Spirit. The chapter further argues that Communio Sanctorum submits all five witnessing authorities, the Scriptures included, to the one, apostolic Tradition. It recognizes remarkable commonalities between the statements of Communio Sanctorum and Catholic teaching on the one hand and, on the other, agrees with those Protestant critics who claim that the document's emphasis on the Scriptures' embeddedness in the rest of the ecclesial tradition is quite problematic from the Lutheran point of view.

Keywords: Witnessing authorities, Scripture, Tradition, Ecclesial normativity, Recognition and mediation of revelation, Catholic–Lutheran dialogue

1 Introduction

In the disputes between the Roman Catholic Church and the churches of the Reformation, different understandings of the relationship between Scripture

---

Ida Heikkilä, University of Helsinki, mrs.ida.heikkila@gmail.com

https://doi.org/10.1515/9783110768411-018

and tradition have, from the beginning, been one of the central reasons for tension and division. Moving forward to contemporary times, the opposition has eased to some extent, but the relationship continues to puzzle the academy, the churches and the ecumenical movement.

In Germany, an ecumenical attempt to see this relationship from a new perspective was made in the year 2000. The bilateral working group of the Roman Catholic German Bishops' Conference (*Deutsche Bischofskonferenz*) and the church leadership of the United Evangelical Lutheran Church of Germany (*Vereinigte Evangelisch-Lutherische Kirche Deutschlands*) introduces in its dialogue document *Communio Sanctorum. Die Kirche als Gemeinschaft der Heiligen*[1] (2000; transl. *Communio Sanctorum: The Church as the Communion of Saints*[2] (2004)) a new theological concept into the ecumenical discussion: the *witnessing authorities*[3] (*Bezeugungsinstanzen*).[4] There are five of these witnessing authorities: the Holy Scriptures, tradition, the *sensus fidelium* or, alternatively, the priesthood of all believers, the teaching office and theology.[5] The aim of this paper is to interpret the theology of the witnessing authorities and to reflect on its implications for the understanding of the role of the Holy Scriptures in the life of the church.

The reception of *Communio Sanctorum* (hereinafter CS) has not proceeded without obstacles. Some of the results of the dialogue, especially the treatment of the Petrine ministry (papacy), have met with strong resistance within the

---

1 Bilaterale Arbeitsgruppe der Deutschen Bischofskonferenz und der Kirchenleitung der Vereinigten Evangelisch-Lutherischen Kirche Deutschlands, *Communio Sanctorum. Die Kirche als Gemeinschaft der Heiligen* (Paderborn: Bonifatius, 2000).

2 Mark W. Jeske, Michael Root and Daniel R. Smith, eds., *Communio Sanctorum. The Church as the Communion of Saints*, Unitas Books Series (Collegeville: Liturgical Press, 2004).

3 "Witnessing authorities" is the term used in the English translation of the document. The German term can also be translated with the more neutral "witnessing entities," but as "witnessing authorities" describes the function and role of the "*Bezeugungsinstanzen*" quite well and is already established in the theological discourse, it is preferred here. In this paper, the translations of the German text are the author's own, i.e., not taken from the translation mentioned.

4 The term "Bezeugungsinstanz" is occasionally used already in the German dialogue *Verbindliches Zeugnis* ("binding testimony") of the Ecumenical Working Group of Protestant and Catholic Theologians (*Ökumenischer Arbeitskreis evangelischer und katholischer Theologen*) in the 1990s. In this dialogue, however, the concept is not yet fully developed, and no attention is drawn to the use of it. See, e.g., Ökumenischer Arbeitskreis evangelischer und katholischer Theologen, *Verbindliches Zeugnis I: Kanon – Schrift – Tradition*, Dialog der Kirchen (Göttingen: Vandenhoeck & Ruprecht, 1992), 394.

5 In German, the witnessing authorities are as follows: Heilige Schrift, Tradition, Glaubenssinn der Gläubigen bzw. Priestertum aller Gläubigen, kirchliches Lehramt, Theologie (CS 11).

German Protestant churches and the academy. The attitudes towards the system of witnessing authorities have been more varied.[6] The reactions on the Roman Catholic side have, in general, been positive.[7] Despite the many stimuli it contains, CS has been almost forgotten in later ecumenical theology.[8] Nevertheless, the theological originality of the document was not nullified with its unsuccessful ecumenical reception and deserves our attention still today.

Communio sanctorum focuses primarily on questions related to the nature of the church and church fellowship. This it does from the vantage point of the church as the communion of saints. The listing of the witnessing authorities is produced as a by-product of these ecclesiastical considerations. In the understanding of the dialogue group, the witnessing authorities serve both the recognition and mediation of revelation. They have a "joint effect in finding and proclaiming the truth of the Gospel" (p. 11) or "the revealed truth" (CS 7). It is the communion of saints, the "faith and witness community" (CS 50), that receives the truth and witnesses to it through the witnessing authorities.

This chapter offers a detailed analysis of the system of the authorities of witness and recognition in CS, focusing especially on their normativity in relation to each other. At the end of the chapter, the analysis is brought into conversation with the reception of the document in the dialogue churches. The concluding section then reflects on the implications of the described system for the understanding of the role of the Holy Scriptures within the church as a witness community.

2 Witness as the Transmission of Revelation

In CS, the witnessing authorities are considered under the heading "The Attestation [*Bezeugung*] of the revelation in the church" (p. 32). This position informs us of the first basic elements of CS's understanding of the witnessing authori-

---

[6] For the Protestant reactions, see Oliver Schuegraf and Udo Hahn, eds., *Communio Sanctorum: Evangelische Stellungnahmen zur Studie der Zweiten Bilateralen Arbeitsgruppe der Deutschen Bischofskonferenz und der Kirchenleitung der VELKD* (Hannover: Vereinigte Evangelisch-Lutherische Kirche Deutschlands, 2009).

[7] For the Roman Catholic responses, see Deutsche Bischofskonferenz, *Stellungnahme der Deutschen Bischofskonferenz zur Studie "Communio Sanctorum"*, Die deutschen Bischöfe 52 (Bonn: Sekretariat der Deutschen Bischofskonferenz, 2003).

[8] Robert Svatoň, "Differentiated Consensus in Anthropology as the Basis of 'Ecumenical Ethics'? Catholic-Lutheran Example," *Acta Missiologica* 12.2. (2018): 50–60, on p. 58.

ties: firstly, their function is to witness to revelation and, secondly, the place where they operate is the church.

In the understanding of the bilateral dialogue group, the church is at the same time receiver and agent "of the universal transmitting of revelation" (CS 44). The dialogue group states that the church in its members and in its entirety is a "witness to the salvific power of God in the world, an advocate for the 'new creation' in the passing old world." In other words, the church is a "sign and carrier of divine salvation for the world" (CS 12). The dialogue group indicates (CS 44) that in this sense, the church is a mediator that stands over against the individual believer. In the previous citations, "witness," "sign" and "carrier" come very close in meaning. The formulations suggest that bearing witness to revelation means transmitting and mediating it or at least that these actions are very closely intertwined.

The description of the church as "receiver" of the truth draws our attention to the fact that the church needs to find out and accept the truth before it can mediate it. The five witnessing authorities serve both these ends as they have a "joint effect in finding and proclaiming the truth" as already mentioned. Accordingly, CS calls the witnessing authorities occasionally "authorities of recognition and witness" (*Erkenntnis- und Bezeugungsinstanzen*; CS 45, 59). The balance of these two aspects, recognition and witness, will be evaluated in the conclusion of this chapter.

According to CS, "[r]evelation is transmitted through the witnessing word. This word is experienced [*erfahren*] as the word of God" (CS 42). This formulation suggests that the witnessing word is constitutive of all the witnessing authorities. The expression "witnessing word" does not apparently refer only to the oral or written witness borne by the church since CS also speaks of the witness borne through a Christian life (CS 17, 125, 229). According to the dialogue group, the acceptance of the witnessed word as God's word cannot be realized without the prevenient and assisting grace of God and the inner work of the Spirit (CS 41).

The dialogue group emphasizes that witnessing to the truth does not mean handing over any strictly defined doctrine or teaching; it is primarily and basically life with the word of God:

> Transmitting the truth of the revelation is not a mere passing on of immutable clauses, rites and practices, but it is much more conveying that experience, knowledge and those decisions that the church has made in history on the basis of the word of God in its thought and life. In this way, tradition [*Überlieferung*] can contribute to the fullness of the word of God being revealed more and more. (CS 55.)

In CS's theology of witness, the apostles have a special and unique role. According to CS, the basic content of faith (in the meaning of *fides quae*) is God and his salvific act in Jesus Christ. This content "has a basic form: the witness of the first witnesses within the fellowship of the church" (CS 41). It is unclear whether this first witness is oral or written but it is clearly equated with the witness of the apostles: "As eyewitnesses to the Risen One, the apostles provide a unique and elementary meaning" (CS 142), CS argues. "Through the giving of the Holy Spirit they [the Twelve] are enabled to go into the whole world as his witnesses and to proclaim the Gospel to all peoples" (CS 136), the document adds. The document does not discuss the role of those eyewitnesses who were not apostles.

According to CS (CS 142), the proclamation of the apostles is always normative for the church. As the apostles are not among the witnessing authorities listed by the dialogue group, their witness must have been preserved under one or several of the witnessing authorities listed by CS, the most obvious alternatives being the Holy Scriptures, tradition and the teaching office. This question is elucidated especially in the analysis of the fourth witnessing authority, the teaching office.

3 The Interplay of the Witnessing Authorities

In the life of the church, the witnessing authorities are simultaneously independent and dependent. The Scriptures, tradition, the *sensus fidelium*, the teaching office and theology "have an independent and, in that sense, unchangeable and irreplaceable task. In the faith community of the church they are dependent upon and refer to each other, follow on from each other and act upon each other, yet each in their own specific way" (CS 72). *Communio sanctorum* admits that conflicts and tensions between the witnessing authorities cannot always be avoided within the churches themselves or in ecumenical encounters. In fact, "[t]he described interaction of the witnessing authorities is possible only through the influence of the Holy Spirit, and it cannot be understood without His impact" (CS 73), the group remarks. The document concedes that the church's "recognition of and witness to the truth remain incomplete" (CS 44). The previous citations show that the Holy Spirit has a central role in the interaction of the witnessing authorities. Precisely this pneumatological point of view has by some been regarded as the reason for the "great innovative courage" shown in CS's new theological solution.⁹

The strong reliance on pneumatology can, however, also be seen as one of the central weaknesses of the system of the witnessing authorities; it seemingly enables the dialogue group to develop its theology of the individual witnessing authorities without having to fully solve the tensions that are born between the claims of the authorities. Through the pneumatological shift, the often very practical problems that are born in the interaction between the authorities of witness and recognition become quite abstract and can no longer be discussed critically.

Even if the system with the witnessing authorities does not belong to the most central theological themes addressed explicitly in CS, the model has factual influence on the way the central themes are being dealt with. This can be seen, for example, in the historical description of papacy, where the factual realization of the Petrine ministry is not brought back to one single witnessing authority or theological principle but is seen as a "multidimensional agglomerate of theological-normative, pastoral-imperative and political-contingent factors," which relate to each other in new ways at different times.¹⁰

4 The Holy Scriptures as the Primary Witnessing Authority

Communio Sanctorum calls the Holy Scriptures "the original witness to the truth of the living God that was revealed to us fully and clearly in Jesus Christ" (CS 46). The document also states that "[t]he Holy Scriptures are the first and basic

---

9 See Beinert, "Weltweite Gemeinschaft der Christenheit. Zum Dokument 'Communio Sanctorum – Die Kirche als Gemeinschaft der Heiligen'." *Stimmen der Zeit* 219 (2001): 89–98, on p. 91.

10 Beinert, "Weltweite Gemeinschaft der Christenheit", 96. Beinert (93–94) welcomes the heuristic approach of CS and argues that it is not enough to merely place the confessional doctrinal statements and thematic complexes side by side and to review their ability to reach consensus, as has been done before. A specific confession must be reviewed rather from the perspective of to what extent it is compatible with Christianity including different forms of the faith. In this, an elaborate theoretical instrument of recognition is needed. Beinert sees Melanchthon's doctrine of the loci (*Loci-Lehre*) as an instrument that can be drawn on and, to him, this is precisely what CS does, only with modern modifications. In the view of Beinert, the decisive differences in the history of Christianity have been born when the uniqueness of the individual witnessing authorities has been transformed into an application of a single authority.

[*grundlegend*] witnessing form [*Bezeugungsgestalt*] of the word of God" (CS 72). Further, the dialogue group claims that the Scriptures are the witnessing authority that lies the closest to revelation (CS 48), probably referring to their historical closeness to the life of Jesus Christ. These statements seem to ignore the apostolic eyewitness and claim that the scriptural texts are the first witness to God's revelation. The tension is resolved by the dialogue group's conviction that in the Scriptures "the witness of the apostles and prophets, to whom God has entrusted his word, is summarized validly" (CS 46). Thus, all that is said of the Scriptures as a witnessing authority is eventually based on the apostolic witness to the word of God.

The previous formulations make the distinction between the revelation of God in Jesus Christ and the Scriptures as a witness to it clear. The Scriptures are chronologically and logically secondary in relation to revelation. However, the dialogue group is convinced that the books of the Scriptures teach the truth "reliably, faithfully and without error" since they "have been recorded under the breath of the Holy Spirit" (CS 47). In the life of the church, the Scriptures are the "ultimate norm of faith," the "*norma normans non normata*," since "God himself witnesses to his truth through them" (CS 48). Hence, it is God himself, not any ecclesiastical authority, who guarantees that the original witness is preserved in the Scriptures. The self-witness of God and the "breath of the Holy Spirit" ensure that the scriptural witness is not only a historical preservation of the apostolic witness but a living witness. "By virtue of the truth of God that is attested in them, the Holy Scriptures assert themselves from the beginning and again and again in the church (CS 49). The truth that is attested in the Scriptures determines them to the extent that the dialogue group is able to say that revelation is given in the Scriptures (CS 198).

It must be noted that the composition of the text leaves open the possibility of the original apostolic witness being transmitted reliably through some other media than the Scriptures. In fact, stating that the Scriptures contain a summary of the original witness suggests that the original witness is broader, deeper or more detailed than the one found in the Scriptures. The dialogue group disclaims such conclusions only partly when it declares that the Holy Scriptures contain the revelation sufficiently (*hinreichend*) and are, therefore, not in need of supplementation (material sufficiency; CS 53).

The conviction that the Scriptures are the ultimate norm of faith for the church means that they are also "the basic and decisive criterion for all the other witnessing authorities" (CS 271). The other witnessing authorities should orient themselves bindingly to the Bible "when they interpret it, meditate deeply on it, apply it to the prevailing situation and make it fruitful for the Christian life" (CS

72). However, even though the witness of the Scriptures is materially sufficient, as was noted above, it cannot be grasped without the other authorities. In order for the church to receive and recognize the truth and witness to it "the different authorities of recognition and witness must act together" (CS 45). Thus, "[t]he Scriptures can never be consulted in isolation, but in the context of the faith and witness community of the church. These, in turn, must be measured against the Holy Scriptures themselves" (CS 50), the dialogue group explains.

5 Tradition as a Witnessing Authority

In the dialogue group's listing of the witnessing authorities, tradition or the transmission of faith comes second. There are two factors that make an analysis of this second authority complex: Firstly, the fact that all nouns are capitalized in German makes it difficult to determine whether the correct English translation in each case is "Tradition" or "tradition".[11] Secondly, CS uses two different words, which in English are translated only into one ("tradition"), namely *Tradition* and *Überlieferung*. The second authority is referred to as *"Tradition"* three times (p. 11, CS 7, 72), *"die Überlieferung des Glaubens"* (the transmission of faith) with an additional *"Tradition"* in brackets once (CS 45), *"Überlieferung"* with *"Tradition"* in brackets also once (p. 35) and *"Überlieferung"* with an explanation "that is, the 'transmission of the normative apostolic message'" in brackets once as well (CS 271). As a result of this variation, it is difficult to determine whether it is the apostolic Tradition, the process of transmitting this Tradition or human tradition that has the role of a witnessing authority.

It was concluded above that, in the dialogue group's understanding, witness to the truth and to revelation is basically life with the word of God. In this

---

[11] The English translation by Jeske, Root and Smith translates the German *Tradition* in some contexts with "Tradition" and in others with "tradition". This is congruent with the understanding of CS, where the Holy apostolic Tradition of the church is distinguished from tradition as the unfolding of this message (CS 52). However, the translators use a small initial letter on many occasions where CS refers to the apostolic Tradition of the church (e.g., CS 19, 52, 56, 72) and are not consistent in their use of the capitalized "Tradition" either: for example, the expression "Tradition of the church" is used in CS 53 and the formulation "tradition of the church" in CS 196 and 209, respectively. For this reason, I improve on Jeske et al. in consistently using the capitalized "Tradition" when the original text refers to the normative apostolic Tradition of the church, while I use "tradition" when it refers to human traditions or the process of transmitting the faith (*Überlieferung*). The evaluation of when this is the case is, of course, an integral part of the analysis.

process, tradition as the transmission of faith has its own specific role: it "preserves the living interaction of the faith community with the Word of God in the past for the present and the future" (CS 72). The bilateral dialogue group agrees on that all baptized Christians are part of the transmitting of the faith (CS 57). However, in the process of transmission, CS differentiates between the mediation of the "normative [*verbindlich*] apostolic message" and the different ways this message unfolds in the church and in the lives of individual Christians. The former is "apostolic Tradition," the latter "human traditions," which are not generally binding (CS 52). The witnesses of individual Christians are presumably expressions of the "different ways this message unfolds in the church and in the lives of individual Christians". As a conclusion, the tradition process realizes in two distinct ways: primarily as preservation and transmission of the apostolic witness and, on a secondary level, as transmission of the witnesses of individual Christians. The apostolic witness is born out of a direct and personal encounter with Jesus Christ, the Word of God, whereas the witnesses of the rest of the witnessing community have been born out of an encounter with the Word as mediated through the witnessing authorities.

CS calls tradition (here *"Tradition"*) a "medium of the word of God" (CS 56), apparently referring to its transmitting of the apostolic witness, i.e., the first witnesses' interaction with the Word of God, Jesus Christ. According to the dialogue group, the question of whether tradition transmits the Word of God correctly and wholly is determined by the witness of the Holy Scriptures. The dialogue group concedes that tradition (*"Tradition"*) "is always in need of critical interpretation, so much as it itself is a critical authority to the church: As medium of the Word of God it is a critique of the current church; as a historical medium it is to be addressed critically on the basis of the Scriptures" (CS 56). CS also states that tradition is interpretation of the Word of God and therefore stands under the norm of the Scriptures (CS 72). These formulations point to the conclusion that the second witnessing authority is identified with the transmitting of the faith (Lat. *tradere*); it is not the normative apostolic witness, Tradition, but the process of transmitting this witness that should be interpreted critically and measured against the norm of the Scriptures.

6 The Witness of God's People (*Sensus Fidelium*) as a Witnessing Authority

The study of the second witnessing authority led us to asking how the transmitting of the apostolic witness relates to the transmitting of the witnesses of other Christians. The third witnessing authority grows directly out of the second, focusing on the witness of the whole people of God. What makes the understanding of this third witnessing authority difficult is that is goes by three different names. In the introduction of CS, the third authority is called "the sense of the faith of the faithful" (CS 7). This is a term stemming from the Roman Catholic tradition. By the sense of the faith of the faithful or *sensus fidelium*, the Catholic dialogue party means "the perception *[Wahrnehmung]* of and witnessing *[Bezeugung]* to faith through the entire church" (CS 58). In the preface to the document, in turn, the third witnessing authority is called "sense of the faith of the faithful, i.e., the priesthood of all believers" (p. 11), combining the Catholic term with a Protestant one.[12] On still another occasion, the authority is named "the witness of the entire people of God (sense of the faith of the faithful)" (CS 45). The actual dealing with the third witnessing authority takes place under the heading "The witness of the entire people of God" (p. 37). This last formulation obviously tries to involve all the terms mentioned.

CS's treatment of *sensus fidelium* and the priesthood of all believers as synonyms is problematic. The Faculty of Protestant Theology at the University of Tübingen points out that, from a Reformation perspective, all members of the people of God are called not only to witness to the Gospel but also to judge all teaching according to its congruence with the Gospel. In this sense, believers participate in the ecclesial teaching office. The Roman Catholic *sensus fidelium*, in turn, is not part of the teaching office and can, because of that, never reject its official statements.[13]

---

[12] The assessment of the term as Protestant (*evangelisch*) is the dialogue group's own (CS 130). Luther himself did not use the term in his writings. Timothy Wengert, "The Priesthood of All Believers and Other Pious Myths," *Institute of Liturgical Studies Occasional Papers* 117 (2006): 92–115, on p. 92. Since the Second Vatican Council, the Roman Catholic Church speaks of the common priesthood of the faithful. CS 129.

[13] Evangelisch-Theologische Fakultät der Eberhard-Karls-Universität Tübingen, [Statement on CS], in *Communio Sanctorum. Evangelische Stellungnahmen zur Studie der Zweiten Bilateralen Arbeitsgruppe der Deutschen Bischofskonferenz und der Kirchenleitung der VELKD*, edited by Oliver Schuegraf and Udo Hahn (Hannover: Amt der VELKD, 2009): 211–266, on pp. 234–235.

The common understanding of the dialogue parties is that the main function of the *sensus fidelium* is the transmitting of the Gospel for future generations. The sense of the faith "recognizes and confesses the faith, the norm of which is the Scriptures, the form of which tradition has shaped [*geprägt hat*], which the magisterium witnesses to openly and which theology clarifies critically" (CS 72). CS underlines that the *sensus fidelium* is more than the mere assent to the other authorities of witness and recognition: "As a charism of the inner conformity [*Übereinstimmung*] with the content of faith it is itself such an authority, through which the church in its entirety recognizes the content of faith and confesses it in its conduct of life (CS 59). The dialogue group believes that, by the aid of the Holy Spirit, the totality of the believers will remain in the truth (CS 57).

The dialogue group's explicit dealing with the third witnessing authority is limited to five paragraphs only (CS 57–60, 72) but the witness borne by the whole people of God is a theme that runs through the whole document. *Communio Sanctorum* is clear that the receiving and recognizing of and witnessing to the truth is a commission given to the whole church (CS 45). The dialogue group declares that the Risen One "...takes all who believe in him in his service of witnessing to him in history throughout the centuries" (CS 41) and calls people to the obedience of faith.[14] The church goes to the whole world in the power of the Holy Spirit "with the witness that faith in Jesus Christ is the way to salvation opened up by God" (CS 16).

Interestingly, in the previous citations, the witness of the church is understood solely as mediation of the Gospel, whereas the third witnessing authority, "The witness of God's people," includes also the aspects of recognition of the truth and conformity with it. As a matter of fact, calling the third witnessing authority "the witness of God's people" is misleading in that CS's description of the witness community of the church meets only the other criterion of a witnessing authority: the transmitting function. Calling the third witnessing authority simply *sensus fidelium* would make the system of the witnessing authorities more logical but certainly also more difficult for the Lutheran dialogue party to embrace.

---

14 The calling of all the members of the church is seen also in the following citations: "Witnessing now already to the new life in the communion of saints belongs essentially to the calling of all the members of the church [...]" (CS 221); "All are called and sent to witness prophetically to the Gospel of Jesus Christ, to worship and serve people together" (CS 126).

7 The Ecclesial Teaching Office as a Witnessing Authority

On the bilateral dialogue group's listing of witnessing authorities, the ecclesial teaching office comes fourth. Similarly with the previous witnessing authorities, the naming of this authority is not completely consistent in the document: on the one hand, the authority is called "the ecclesial teaching office" (p. 11, CS 72) or "the teaching office" (CS 7), and, on another occasion, "ecclesial office" with "teaching office" in brackets (CS 45, p. 38). Regardless of the variation in the naming of the authority, the dialogue group's dealing with the fourth witnessing authority makes clear that it is the responsibility for the teaching within the church that is under scrutiny. Still, using only the term "ecclesial teaching office" would be recommendable, as "ecclesial office" usually involves also other aspects of ministry than teaching, e.g., the administration of the sacraments, and is therefore misleading in this context. The bilateral group is open about the fact that the ecclesial teaching office is realized in different ways in the churches in dialogue (CS 72) but does not explicate the differences.

According to the dialogue group, the teaching office in its different forms "has the task of preserving the content of the word of God through interpretation and preaching, defending it against errors and, in that way, serving unity". CS is clear on that the teaching office "stands under the word of God and is only allowed to interpret the Scriptures and, in that way, to transmit the apostolic Tradition" (CS 72).[15] The document reminds that "[t]he ministry's responsibility for teaching is bound to the witness of faith of the whole church" (CS 61). Even the Pope cannot determine faith (CS 173).[16] These formulations make clear that the normative apostolic witness does not, as such, continue in the witness of the teaching office, a possibility previously left open in this analysis, but that the latter stands under the norm of the former. However, in the understanding of the Lutheran dialogue party, the described view stands in tension with the Catholic conviction that only the *magisterium* is allowed to interpret God's word in a normative manner. The concern on the Protestant side is that the ecclesial teaching office is detached from the other witnessing authorities and, in fact, lifted above them (CS 182).

---

[15] CS 61 states similarly that the teaching office stands under the norm of the Gospel.
[16] The statement is given indirectly, when pointing out in a critical tone that the First Vatican Council and Roman Catholic theology directly preceding it understood papacy in this meaning.

Finally, another factor that complicates the understanding of the fourth witnessing authority is that CS also mentions a "ministry of governance" (*Leitungsamt*) that "...participates in the authority of the apostles and sees to the proper transmission of the apostolic Tradition. In this constant reference back to the apostles it is itself "*apostolic*" (CS 19).[17] The dialogue group points out that the service of the ministry of governance is measured against the fundamental proclamation of the apostles (CS 142) – notably not against the Holy Scriptures. The fact that the ministry of governance is not listed among the witnessing authorities leaves open the possibility to interpret the text to indicate that the apostolic ministry of governance operates outside of and above the interaction of the witnessing authorities, thus being the primary medium for the transmission of the apostolic witness.

At this point, it has become clear that CS's tendency to offer several, slightly different names or titles for the individual authorities of witness and recognition is problematic. The differences might not look significant when treated individually but when put together they result in remarkable variation in theological understanding; as a matter of fact, they enable two parallel paths of "thinking through" the individual authorities, paths that have quite different outcomes.

8 Theology as a Witnessing Authority

Finally, we shall deal with the fifth of the witnessing authorities, theology. Of the five witnessing authorities, it is perhaps the least obvious, as it could easily be assimilated with the fourth authority, the teaching office of the church. In the dialogue group's understanding, the independent role of theology as a witnessing authority lies in its task of making the foundation of faith, which is in itself inaccessible, as discernible or knowable (*erkennbar*) as possible, as well as in formulating the content of faith for the contemporary life. This it does by means of methodically exact argumentation (CS 69). Theology draws on the Scriptures and tradition, the witness of the teaching office and of the whole people of God (CS 72). Its task, however, is clearly more than the organizing, transmitting and interpreting of the witnesses borne by the other authorities: "...its task is also to actualize the content of faith, to establish [*durchdringen*] it scientifically and to make it ecumenically fruitful..." (CS 71), that is, so to say, to take the already existing witnesses one step further. These citations suggest that theology is

---

[17] For a similar emphasis, see CS 142.

responsible for the presenting of the content of faith in its final form, that is, for making the witness of the other witnessing authorities understandable and accessible. In this way it fulfils the task of finding and proclaiming the revealed truth; the task that defines all the witnessing authorities (CS 7).

Theology also has a critical function in the church. Its task is to measure the factuality (*Sachgerechtigkeit*) of the other witnessing authorities against the norm of the Scriptures and to point out and correct deficiencies and deformations in the transmitting of the revealed truth (CS 69, 70). CS even proposes that theology has a responsibility for the correctness of doctrine (CS 69). The critical function of theology has, however, its limits. It is always committed to the maintaining of the unity of faith in the church (CS 71). It can be argued that this last remark undermines the critical function of theology altogether as it disallows it to operate outside of the harmony of the other witnessing authorities. By and large, the theology characterized in the document is clearly an ecclesial theology in service of the Christian community, not an independent academic discipline operating outside of it. This is logical, as the witnessing authorities actualize per definition in the church.

9 Reactions to *Communio Sanctorum*

After the publication of *Communio Sanctorum*, the document was widely discussed in the churches in dialogue and in the German academy. In 2003, a 42-page statement on the dialogue results was published by the Roman Catholic German Bishops' Conference (DBK). By and large, DBK's assessment of the dialogue document was very positive. The Bishops' Conference judged that ecumenical progress had been made in a whole range of problematic fields. It also acknowledged that the Roman Catholic representatives of the dialogue had succeeded in presenting the Catholic faith without it losing any substance.[18]

The Bishops' Conference's positive evaluation is based on a recognition of remarkable commonalities between the statements of CS and Catholic teaching. According to DBK, both the naming and weighting of the witnessing authorities stand in compliance with Catholic doctrine. DBK agreed with CS's description of the relationship between Scripture and tradition, the distinction between apostolic Tradition and human tradition (or, *traditio* and *traditiones*, as DBK ex-

---

18 *Stellungnahme der Deutschen Bischofskonferenz* (see note 7): 40.

presses it) and the theology of *sensus fidelium* which are all expressed in terms in accordance with the Second Vatican Council.[19]

In its response to CS, DBK paid a great deal of attention to the question of the apostolic ministry. The Bishops' Conference assessed that the meaning of the teaching office of the church among the other witnessing authorities needs further clarification. It pointed out that, according to the Catholic understanding, the promise of Jesus enables called teachers, standing in the succession of the apostles, to witness to the truth of the Gospel. Such an understanding of the teaching office of the church, perceived (*wahrgenommen*) by the bishops, does not relativize the meaning of the other witnessing authorities, DBK argues.[20] Neither does it undermine the meaning of the apostles whose ministry as "eye-witnesses to the Risen" is unique.[21] On the one hand, The Bishops' Conference remarked that the scriptural canon cannot be pitted against the teaching of the church since, firstly, a text and a personal ministry are not commensurate and, secondly, the fixing of the canon is a result of the ecclesial teaching, which, in turn, is based on the teaching of the apostles. On the other hand, DBK underlined that the teaching of the church must always "bind the church to the word of God as it fundamentally [*grundlegend*] witnesses to itself in the Scriptures".[22]

The Bishops' Conference was especially pleased with CS's acknowledgement that the church is the recipient, carrier and mediator of revelation. When the church hears God's word and teaches it, it is a "subject of witness," DBK states. According to the Bishops' Conference, an agreement on the witnessing authorities is finally dependant precisely on the understanding of the role of the church in the salvific work of Jesus.[23] Finally, the bishops reaffirmed that the apostolic Tradition stands under the scriptural promise of being able to recognize the truth and witness to it.[24]

On the Protestant side, the statements of different committees of VELKD, individual member churches of VELKD and Protestant faculties and institutes were compiled into one volume.[25] The statements witness to a "broad resonance" with the suggestions of CS, a resonance which is, all the same, out-

---

19 *Stellungnahme der Deutschen Bischofskonferenz*, 12–3.
20 *Stellungnahme der Deutschen Bischofskonferenz*, 41.
21 *Stellungnahme der Deutschen Bischofskonferenz*, 30.
22 *Stellungnahme der Deutschen Bischofskonferenz*, 18.
23 *Stellungnahme der Deutschen Bischofskonferenz*, 20–2.
24 *Stellungnahme der Deutschen Bischofskonferenz*, 13.
25 Cf. *Evangelische Stellungnahmen* (see note 6).

weighed by critical observations.[26] The commentators are quite unanimous in their critical stance towards the dialogue group's treatment of the Petrine ministry as well as the veneration of saints and Mary. As for the witnessing authorities, the reactions vary remarkably.[27]

According to the Commission of Professors at the Faculty of Protestant Theology of the Ludwig Maximilian University of Munich, *Communio Sanctorum* asserts the normativity of the Scriptures in a way that corresponds to the core of Lutheran teaching. The faculty identified the assurance of the self-witness (*Selbstbezeugung*) of the risen Crucified as the constitutive precondition for the understanding of the interaction of the witnessing authorities.[28] In contrast to Munich, the Faculty of Protestant Theology at the University of Tübingen did not find the Lutheran interpretation of *norma normans non normata* in CS. The faculty argued that the dialogue group placed the Holy Scriptures and ecclesial tradition on the same level of authority; the witness of the whole people of God and the ecclesial teaching office are then given the right to judge between these two authorities.[29] The statement of the Centre of Ecumenical Research at the University of Munich, in turn, was largely positive towards CS's understanding of the relationship between Scripture and tradition but pointed out that there are still clear differences in the understanding of the scriptural *claritas* and self-interpretation.[30] The Theological Chamber of the Evangelical Church in Germany criticized CS's understanding of the teaching office, pointing out that the

---

[26] Friederike Nüssel, "Einleitung zu den Stellungnahmen der Bilateralen Arbeitsgruppe der Deutschen Bischofskonferenz und der Kirchenleitung der Vereinigten Evangelisch-Lutherischen Kirche Deutschlands 'Communio Sanctorum. Die Kirche als Gemeinschaft der Heiligen'", in *Evangelische Stellungnahmen zur Studie der Zweiten Bilateralen Arbeitsgruppe der Deutschen Bischofskonferenz und der Kirchenleitung der VELKD*, edited by Oliver Schuegraf and Udo Hahn (Hannover: Amt der VELKD, 2009): 19–50, on p. 20.

[27] Nüssel, "Einleitung zu den Stellungnahmen", 48.

[28] Kommission des Professoriums der Evangelisch-Theologischen Fakultät der Ludwig-Maximilians-Universität München, [Statement on CS], in *Evangelische Stellungnahmen zur Studie der Zweiten Bilateralen Arbeitsgruppe der Deutschen Bischofskonferenz und der Kirchenleitung der VELKD*, edited by Oliver Schuegraf and Udo Hahn (Hannover: Amt der VELKD, 2009) 179–91, on pp. 183–4.

[29] Tübingen, [Statement on CS], 231–233.

[30] Zentrum für ökumenische Forschung der Ludwig-Maximillians-Universität München, [Statement on CS], in *Evangelische Stellungnahmen zur Studie der Zweiten Bilateralen Arbeitsgruppe der Deutschen Bischofskonferenz und der Kirchenleitung der VELKD*, edited by Oliver Schuegraf and Udo Hahn (Hannover: Amt der VELKD, 2009): 267–293, on p. 276.

apostolate does not continue in a continuous ecclesial ministry but in the scriptural canon.[31]

The faculty of Tübingen pointed out that, in CS, there is no word of God outside of the interplay of Scripture, tradition and the teaching office and, thus, the self-interpretation of the word of God is only self-interpretation of this interplay. This means that there can never be a contradiction between the Scriptures and the teaching office since the Scriptures can unveil their true meaning only within this interaction, that is, when interpreted authentically by the teaching office. The faculty sees here a sharp contrast to Reformation thought where the self-assertion of the word of God basically means the self-assertion of the Scriptures, the only critical norm for the process of transmission in the church.[32]

10 Conclusions

Based on our previous study, DBK's and Tübingen's assessment that CS has been greatly influenced by Roman Catholic tradition, whereas the influence of the Lutheran tradition is weaker, can be largely confirmed. This is seen in that, in accordance with the Catholic faith, the document gives great value to the ecclesial teaching office, emphasizes the boundedness of the Scriptures to the other witnessing authorities and undergirds in many ways the importance of Tradition.

This study has shown that the dialogue group avoids contrasting the different witnessing authorities, emphasizing their harmony and interplay instead. The arrangement of the witnessing authorities does, however, reflect the degree of authority ascribed to them. The naming of the Scriptures as the first authority expresses the dialogue group's conviction that all the other witnessing authorities are bound to this original witness to the apostolic Tradition. The placing of *sensus fidelium* third, before the teaching office, indicates their willingness to value the witness of the whole people of God. Placing theology last, after the teaching office, undergirds the role of the church as the primary place for doing theology. One of the central findings of this analysis is that the second witnessing authority, tradition, does not refer to the holy, apostolic Tradition of the

---

[31] Kammer für Theologie der Evangelischen Kirche in Deutschland, [Statement on CS], in *Evangelische Stellungnahmen zur Studie der Zweiten Bilateralen Arbeitsgruppe der Deutschen Bischofskonferenz und der Kirchenleitung der VELKD*, edited by Oliver Schuegraf and Udo Hahn (Hannover: Amt der VELKD, 2009): 143–160, on p. 152.
[32] Tübingen, [Statement on CS], 230.

church but rather to the transmitting of that Tradition. The apostolic Tradition is above all the five witnessing authorities; it is the stream of life that the witnessing authorities are embedded in. In fact, the main reference point of the witnessing authorities is not Scripture but Tradition: the Scriptures summarize the apostolic Tradition, tradition transmits it, the *sensus fidelium* recognizes it, the magisterium interprets it bindingly and theology makes it fruitful for the contemporary life.

In the understanding of the dialogue group, all the authorities of witness and recognition have two functions: they find the truth and they mediate it. The access to the truth is enabled by the Holy Spirit. CS does not really explain how the witnessing authorities can find or recognize the truth independently. In general, the focus of the dialogue lies on the mediating or witnessing function of the authorities rather than on the recognizing function. Moreover, the reactions of the churches and university faculties concentrate on the question of who has the final teaching authority in the church and not so much on where the church is to find God's revelation. It can be argued that the question of mediating the truth should be secondary in relation to that of finding it for if the process of mediation is right but the content that is mediated is wrong, it has nothing to offer the recipient.

In CS, the church is clearly something separate from the witnessing authorities; the church *has* the witnessing authorities. The authorities of witness and recognition work in two steps. Through these, the church first finds out the truth and then mediates it to the world. The world cannot find out the truth by itself, without access to the witnessing authorities realized in the church. Eventually, the primary witnessing authority is the church itself. This means that the church and the world are placed on different levels as recipients of revelation.

The dialogue group's interpretation of the principle *norma normans non normata* is problematic from the Lutheran point of view. In CS, Scripture does represent the most authoritative tradition but it is, nevertheless, one of the witnessing authorities, all standing under the norm of the apostolic Tradition. The normativity of the apostolic witness, in turn, is justified with quite thin arguments, mainly with the apostles being eyewitnesses to the Risen One. To the dialogue group, the witness of the Scriptures is, albeit materially sufficient, not strong enough without the other witnessing authorities. The raising of the Scriptures to a higher level than the other witnessing authorities is based on them being historically closest to the apostolic witness. Based on this historical closeness, the Scriptures are to coordinate and arrange the later witnesses of the other authorities.

Communio Sanctorum's system with the witnessing authorities is an original and open-minded attempt to answer the question of who has the final say in the church and how the different authorities relate to each other. However, the theology of the witnessing authorities is quite unsystematized considering the substantial themes it explicitly and implicitly deals with. The document specifies the different witnessing authorities and describes their mutual relationships briefly but does not explain profoundly enough what the witnessing system means for the understanding of divine revelation or the Scriptures. The dialogue shows once again that the ecumenical difficulty does not primarily consist of forming an agreement on individual theological loci but in creating a tension-free system of all the individual pieces.

References

Beinert, Wolfgang. "Weltweite Gemeinschaft der Christenheit. Zum Dokument 'Communio Sanctorum – Die Kirche als Gemeinschaft der Heiligen'." *Stimmen der Zeit* 219 (2001): 89–98.

Bilaterale Arbeitsgruppe der Deutschen Bischofskonferenz und der Kirchenleitung der Vereinigten Evangelisch-Lutherischen Kirche Deutschlands. *Communio Sanctorum. Die Kirche als Gemeinschaft der Heiligen*. Paderborn: Bonifatius, 2000.

Communio Sanctorum. The Church as the Communion of Saints. Unitas Books Series, edited by Mark W. Jeske, Michael Root and Daniel R. Smith. Collegeville: Liturgical Press, 2004.

Deutsche Bischofskonferenz. *Stellungnahme der Deutschen Bischofskonferenz zur Studie "Communio Sanctorum"*. Die deutschen Bischöfe 71. Bonn: Sekretariat der Deutschen Bischofskonferenz, 2003.

Evangelisch-Theologische Fakultät der Eberhard Karls Universität Tübingen. [Statement on CS] In *Communio Sanctorum. Evangelische Stellungnahmen zur Studie der Zweiten Bilateralen Arbeitsgruppe der Deutschen Bischofskonferenz und der Kirchenleitung der VELKD*, edited by Oliver Schuegraf and Udo Hahn. Hannover: Amt der VELKD, 2009. 211–66.

Kammer für Theologie der Evangelischen Kirche in Deutschland. [Statement on CS]. In *Communio Sanctorum. Evangelische Stellungnahmen zur Studie der Zweiten Bilateralen Arbeitsgruppe der Deutschen Bischofskonferenz und der Kirchenleitung der VELKD*, edited by Oliver Schuegraf and Udo Hahn. Hannover: Amt der VELKD, 2009. 143–60.

Kirchenleitung der VELKD. "Votum der Kirchenleitung der VELKD zum Diskussionsprozess über 'Communio Sanctorum'." In *Communio Sanctorum: Evangelische Stellungnahmen zur Studie der Zweiten Bilateralen Arbeitsgruppe der Deutschen Bischofskonferenz und der Kirchenleitung der VELKD*, edited by Oliver Schuegraf and Udo Hahn. Hannover: Amt der VELKD, 2009. 13–17.

Kommission des Professoriums der Evangelisch-Theologischen Fakultät der Ludwig-Maximilians-Universität München. [Statement on CS]. In *Communio Sanctorum. Evangelische Stellungnahmen zur Studie der Zweiten Bilateralen Arbeitsgruppe der Deutschen Bischofskonferenz und der Kirchenleitung der VELKD*, edited by Oliver Schuegraf and Udo Hahn. Hannover: Amt der VELKD, 2009. 179–91.

Nüssel, Friederike. "Einleitung zu den Stellungnahmen der Bilateralen Arbeitsgruppe der Deutschen Bischofskonferenz und der Kirchenleitung der Vereinigten Evangelisch-Lutherischen Kirche Deutschlands 'Communio Sanctorum. Die Kirche als Gemeinschaft der Heiligen'." In *Communio Sanctorum. Evangelische Stellungnahmen zur Studie der Zweiten Bilateralen Arbeitsgruppe der Deutschen Bischofskonferenz und der Kirchenleitung der VELKD*. Edited by Oliver Schuegraf and Udo Hahn. Hannover: Amt der VELKD, 2009. 19–50.

Svatoň, Robert. "Differentiated Consensus in Anthropology as the Basis of 'Ecumenical Ethics'?: Catholic-Lutheran Example." *Acta Missiologica* 12.2. (2018): 50–60.

Wengert, Timothy. "The Priesthood of All Believers and Other Pious Myths." *Institute of Liturgical Studies Occasional Papers* 117 (2006): 92–115.

Zentrum für ökumenische Forschung der Ludwig-Maximillians-Universität München. [Statement on CS]. In *Communio Sanctorum. Evangelische Stellungnahmen zur Studie der Zweiten Bilateralen Arbeitsgruppe der Deutschen Bischofskonferenz und der Kirchenleitung der VELKD*, edited by Oliver Schuegraf and Udo Hahn. Hannover: Amt der VELKD, 2009. 267–93.

Elisabeth Maikranz
The Relationship of Scripture and Tradition in the Light of God's Revelation

Abstract: The question of the normativity and thus the critical function of Scripture is an unfinished debate in theology. It is precisely the plurality of biblical writings and inner-biblical traditions that makes an answer difficult. Moreover, different traditions are justified in recourse to the biblical testimony. The chapter adresses the complexity of the processes of tradition within the Bible and starting there it seeks to form an understanding of the critical function of Scripture. To this end, it takes up the debate within the ecumenical movement where a differentiated and comprehensive understanding of tradition has been developed. Compatible with this is the tradition-historical approach of the Lutheran theologian Wolfhart Pannenberg. For him, the New Testament record has a normative function, as it is the 'historical source' for the revelation of God in the story of Jesus of Nazareth. It documents the hermeneutical processes through which the first Christians interpreted the life and destiny of Jesus. Taking Pannenberg as a starting point, the chapter reinterprets the critical function of Scripture: The critical function of Scripture cannot be described as a static measure but is rather a dynamic process in which inner-biblical processes of interpretation are translated into the present in order to convey the special significance of the biblical events of revelation.

Keywords: Wolfhart Pannenberg, Critical function of Scripture, Transmission history, Hermeneutics, Ecumenical dialogue

1 Introduction

The biblical Scriptures are considered to be the "only rule and guiding principle for judging teachings and teachers"[1] according to the Formula of Concord,

---

[1] My translation from Irene Dingel, ed. *Die Bekenntnisschriften der evangelisch-lutherischen Kirche*. Vollständige Neuedition (Göttingen: Vandenhoeck & Ruprecht, 2014), 1216: "einige Regel und Richtschnur, nach welcher zugleich alle Leren und Lerer gerichtet und geurteilet werden sollen".

Elisabeth Maikranz, Heidelberg University, elisabeth.maikranz@oek.uni-heidelberg.de

thereby establishing their normative function in Protestant Theology.[2] However, the implementation of this status is difficult as Scripture is not given without contradiction, tensions, and inconsistencies and the biblical texts are expanded texts containing different stages of interpretative redactions (*Fortschreibung*).[3] Moreover, taking the biblical text as a starting point, the different Christian confessions developed their own theological traditions by transmitting the salvific message of the Gospel in different contexts. In the history of reception of the Gospel, the diversity of traditions grew apart from the Canon.[4] The question of the relation of Scripture and tradition stands in this tension. On the one hand, the normative function of the biblical texts is asserted despite there being different 'teachings and teachers' in Scripture itself which found expression and transmitted their interpretation of the salvific revelation of God in Jesus Christ. On the other hand, Scripture and tradition are part of an overall Christian transmission process proclaiming the salvation of humanity through Jesus Christ. In the following, both dimensions are reflected in order to fruitfully integrate both perspectives to provide further conclusions for theological thinking.

This chapter argues for an understanding of the critical function of Scripture that takes into account different dimensions of tradition as the Bible consists of traditions. In doing so, it refers, on the one hand, to the ecumenical discussion that perceived the diversity of tradition processes already in the 1960s (section 2). On the other hand, the tradition-historical thinking of the Lutheran theologian Wolfhart Pannenberg can show how the tradition processes within Scripture can be taken into account for a consideration of the critical function of Scripture (section 3). In a third step, the implications of the connection between Scripture and tradition for theological thinking will be unfolded (section 4).

---

[2] For an overview of the state of the art concerning the *sola scriptura* see Frederike van Oorschot, Friedrich-Emanuel Focken, and Elisabeth Maikranz, "Einführung," in *Schriftbindung evangelischer Theologie*, edited by Frederike van Oorschot and Friedrich-Emanuel Focken, Forum Theologische Literaturzeitung 37 (Leipzig: Evangelische Verlagsanstalt, 2020): 15–40, especially 16–21.
[3] Jörg Lauster offers an analysis of the development of the doctrine of Scripture reflecting on the definition of Scripture as principle in its methodological challenges; cf. Jörg Lauster, *Prinzip und Methode: Die Transformation des protestantischen Schriftprinzips durch die historische Kritik von Schleiermacher bis zur Gegenwart*, Hermeneutische Untersuchungen zur Theologie 46 (Tübingen: Mohr Siebeck 2004).
[4] Cf. Ernst Käsemann, "Begründet der neutestamentliche Kanon die Einheit der Kirche?" in *Exegetische Versuche und Besinnungen 1*, edited by Ernst Käsemann (Göttingen: Vandenhoeck & Ruprecht, ²1960), 214–23.

2 The Relationship of Scripture and Tradition as Challenge

Inquiring into the relationship of Scripture and tradition has to start with a reflection on the framework in which this inquiry takes place. In most cases, the description of this relation is oriented by the denominational tradition of the reflecting theologian. From the Orthodox perspective, Scripture and tradition form a fundamental unit; for Roman Catholics the relation between Scripture and tradition is expanded by their relation to the magisterium; and a Protestant position emphasizes the priority of Scripture over tradition and the magisterium.[5] Already in this short juxtaposition, it becomes obvious that the perspective on the relationship of Scripture and tradition is linked to a 'meta-tradition' and that a characterization of the relationship has to start with a reflection on each of the two concepts. For Scripture, this task is easily fulfilled. Although the biblical Canon contains different orderings and volumes of biblical books in the different Christian confessions, the extent of Scripture generally has more commonalities than differences. Despite the fact that every denomination has its own Canon which originates from the translation of the biblical texts,[6] 'Scripture' is generally identified with the Christian Canon. Speaking about tradition instead provokes more questions as tradition can be understood in various ways and has to be clarified. Especially in the context of the ecumenical movement in the first half of the 20th century, it became obvious that tradition is more than simply doctrines.[7] Tradition is the entire process in which Christianity is lived in a 'typical' denominational way and, therefore, tradition is also the whole process of transmitting the Gospel and faith in Jesus Christ. Thus, the term 'tradi-

---

5 Cf. Ulrich H. J. Körtner, *Arbeit am Kanon: Studien zur Bibelhermeneutik* (Leipzig: Evangelische Verlagsanstalt 2015), 17.
6 Cf. Körtner, *Arbeit*, 24–31. Therefore, Ulrich Körtner calls the canon a "Hybrid."
7 Cf. Albert C. Outler, "The Renewal of the Christian Tradition: The Report of the North American Section," in *The Report of the Theological Commission on Tradition and Traditions*, edited by the World Council of Churches and Commission on Faith and Order, Faith and Order Paper No. 40 (Geneva 1963), 12, where Outler states: "The tradition of a particular denomination is an extremely complex entity, forming a denominational 'mind' which manifests itself in characteristic ways of 'seeing' and 'hearing' and speaking. Their political and social histories interact with their specifically doctrinal emphases to shape and mold traditional patterns and these are surprisingly tenacious, even in the midst of conscious protestations on behalf of *sola Scriptura*." (Italics in the original.)

tion' needs some further explanation.⁸ There can be at least three dimensions involved in describing the concept of tradition. *First*, 'tradition' can indicate church doctrines and teachings and involve a judgement whether the content of a tradition or practice is positive (e.g., early church and apostolic tradition) or negative (e.g., Luther's rejection of the Roman Catholic tradition as *traditio humanis*). Especially when the term 'tradition' is used in the plural, the content dimension is evident. This dimension understands 'tradition' as a "phenomenological term which covers the various concrete *forms* actually taken by the traditionary *process*."⁹ This leads to the *second* dimension: The term 'tradition' can refer to the process of transmission and describe a traditionary process (e.g. 'tradition of the Gospel'). Here, "tradition is the transitive process by means of which the Christian past is renewed in the living present and made available to the open future."¹⁰ The term used in the singular often addresses this process dimension. *Third*, these two dimensions are combined when, in scriptural interpretation, exegetes work out the transmission history (*Traditionsgeschichte*) of a text and observe the content and motifs of tradition as well as the traditionary process. In this case, 'tradition' manifests itself in Scripture which has to be further developed.

Taking into account the different dimensions of 'tradition,' the relationship between Scripture and tradition occurs on two levels. From an inner perspective, Scripture itself consists of different traditions, which can be observed by implicit and explicit intertextual reference. Intertextual references themselves occur on different levels:¹¹ There is intertextual reference to texts and myths from the Ancient Near East and Hellenistic area that are adopted and transformed in Old Testament texts. Besides, there is intra-biblical intertextuality, when for example, newer texts interpret older ones or when Old Testament

---

8 Cf. Outler, "Renewal," 15f. For the following see also Elisabeth Maikranz and Carolin Ziethe, "Kapitel D: Schrift und Tradition," in *Schriftbindung evangelischer Theologie*, edited by Frederike van Oorschot and Friedrich-Emanuel Focken (Leipzig: Evangelische Verlagsanstalt, 2020): 155–89, in particular 155–62.
9 Outler, "Renewal," 17.
10 Outler, "Renewal," 17.
11 Intertextuality means for a text that "it is an intertext, i.e. simultaneously post-text and pre-text." Heinrich F. Plett, "Intertextualities," in *Intertextuality*, edited by Heinrich F. Plett, Research in Text Theory 15 (Berlin, New York: de Gruyter, 1991), 17. This understanding of intertextuality describes also the biblical texts and the different reference-relations. "Whenever a new text comes into being it relates to previous texts and in its turn becomes the precursor of subsequent texts." Plett, "Intertextualities," 17.

motifs are used to explain the sense of Jesus of Nazareth as the Son of God.[12] Inner-biblical references can especially be explicit by quoting another verse directly and implicit by an indirect allusion.[13] The intertextuality in the Bible shows the formation of the texts as a process that deals with and discusses traditions and motifs from its environment. This intra-perspective leads to an outward level, as it shows how Scripture is embedded in and, at the same time, generates tradition by adopting, transferring and even omitting traditions.[14] On a textual level, this process stops with the formation of the canon but, considering the perception of the biblical texts, it continues up until the present. 'Post-Canonical' traditional processes are inspired by the biblical texts and narrations and disseminate via different media (exegesis in sermons, cultural expressions such as art, music, literature etc.). This intertwining of Scripture, traditions, and traditionary processes shows that – as Scripture itself is part of and constituted by traditions – the relationship between Scripture and tradition is dynamic in a sense that both are elements of a process of updating and transferring meaning through time.

These dynamics were also considered at the fourth World Conference on Faith and Order at Montreal in 1963.[15] After a period of using the method of "compara-

---

[12] For examples of primary ways the New Testament uses the Old Testament, see Greg K. Beale *Handbook on the New Testament Use of the Old Testament: Exegesis and Interpretation* (Grand Rapids: Baker Academic, 2012), 55–93.

[13] See Beale, *Handbook*, 31: "An 'allusion' may simply be defined as a brief expression consciously intended by an author to be dependent on an OT passage. In contrast to a quotation of the OT, which is a direct reference, allusions are indirect references (the OT wording is not reproduced directly as in a quotation)."

[14] Different ways of reception have been identified, for example, by Carolin Ziethe, *Auf seinen Namen werden die Völker hoffen: Die matthäische Rezeption der Schriften Israels zur Begründung des universalen Heils*, Beihefte zur Zeitschrift für die neutestamentliche Wissenschaft 233 (Berlin, Boston: de Gruyter, 2018), 28–30. She speaks of legitimizing/authoritative, re-accentuating, transformative, and negative reception. See also Plett, "Intertextualities," 19, who speaks of "affirmative," "negative," "inverted," and "relativistic" intertextuality.

[15] The Faith and Order Movement and, along with it, the Life and Work Movement and the International Missionary Council, emerged from the World Missionary Conference in Edinburgh 1910, where three general objectives for the Ecumenical Movement were defined: Cooperation in mission, unity in the proclamation of Jesus Christ and the common service to the world. Especially the second objective was considered to be elaborated in the Faith and Order Movement. In 1948, Faith and Order and Life and Work became affiliated to become the World Council of Churches and continued their work inside this umbrella organization.

tive ecclesiology"[16] in order better to understand each other, the separating mentality of the different denominations behind the disuniting doctrines became an issue. Thus, the Movement of Faith and Order started to work on the question of the relationship of the different denominational traditions to the traditionary process and the one tradition of Jesus Christ. In this context, the relationship of Scripture and tradition was considered using Scripture as a common basis which was crucial for finding ways of unity.[17] The report of the Montreal Conference has rarely been explicitly adopted in Protestant theology[18]. However, it enlarges upon the dynamic between Scripture and tradition. In the report of Section II on *Scripture, Tradition and Traditions*,[19] the relation of tradition and Scripture is explained by their relation to the Tradition (written with a capital T), which means "the Gospel itself, transmitted from generation to generation in and by the Church, Christ himself present in the life of the Church."[20] This Tradition of God's revelation was inaugurated by the testimony of prophets and apostles: "The once-for-all disclosure of God in Jesus Christ inspired apostles and disciples to give witness to the revelation given in the person and work of Christ."[21] This witness was initially oral but was also written down and "under the guidance of the Holy Spirit led to the formation of Scriptures and to the canonization of the Old and New Testaments as the Bible of the Church."[22] Thus, Scripture is the Tradition in its written form and the fact that "Tradition precedes the Scriptures points to the significance of tradition, but also to the Bible as the treasure of the Word of God."[23] Starting with the initialization of a witness and traditionary process by the revelation of God, a whole transmission process becomes clear, entrusting the Scriptures to be a witness of the Gospel. Thus, Scripture is essential for elaborating the meaning of revelation while at the same time it cannot be separated from its traditional background and transmission and the traditionary process. As all different denomina-

---

16 That is "the effort to separated Christians to explain themselves to each other in the hope that they would thereby remove stultifying misconceptions and also discover hitherto unregistered areas of agreement." Outler, "Renewal," 7.
17 Cf. Lauster, *Prinzip*, 347: As all confessions emphasize the importance of the Scripture, it can serve as "basaler Minimalkonsens der ökumenischen Verständigung" ("basic minimal consensus of ecumenical communication", my translation).
18 Cf. Lauster, *Prinzip*, 360f.
19 *The Fourth World Conference on Faith and Order: Montreal 1963*, edited by Patrick C. Rodger and Lukas Vischer, Faith and Order Paper No. 42 (London: SCM Press, 1964), 50–61.
20 Rodger and Vischer, *Montreal*, 50.
21 Rodger and Vischer, *Montreal*, 51.
22 Rodger and Vischer, *Montreal*, 51.
23 Rodger and Vischer, *Montreal*, 51.

tional traditionary processes can be ascribed to the initiation by the revelation and passing on of the Gospel from one generation to another, the Tradition occurs only in *different forms of traditions*: "The traditions in Christian history are distinct from, and yet connected with, the Tradition. They are the expressions and manifestations in diverse historical forms of the one truth and reality which is Christ."[24] Yet, here lies the problem of tradition: the historical forms "*can* be a faithful transmission of the Gospel, but also a distortion of it."[25] This hermeneutical crucial point concerns traditionary processes as well as the interpretation processes of Scripture.

The ecumenical discussion of the topic of Scripture and tradition does not end with Montreal but entails further studies. In Bristol in 1967, the role of Scripture and tradition in the hermeneutical process was discussed, drawing on the different methods of interpretation, especially historical criticism.[26] Here, the variety and plurality in scriptural interpretation became obvious which relate to the self-revelation of God in its plural historical action.[27] Unity in this diversity was considered to be in a common reference point rather than in a uniform interpretation.[28] At Bristol, the question for a definition of a cross-denominational authority of the Bible rested unanswered but was taken up in Leuven in 1971.[29] Here, a threefold authority of Scripture was described:[30] *First*, the Bible as a literary document has history- and culture-making power. *Second*, as a historical document, it is the epistemological starting point for understanding God's revelation. *Third*, as the Bible contains God's word to humanity, its authority derives from the authority of God himself. Thus, the authority of Scripture is relational as it always refers to God. As God's action of self-revelation which accumulates in the event of Christ is only accessible through human interpretation of the event transmitted in the biblical texts, the 'center of Scripture' (*Mitte der Schrift*) has to be described as a dynamic Christological "center

---

24 Rodger and Vischer, *Montreal*, 52.
25 Rodger and Vischer, *Montreal*, 52, my emphasis.
26 Cf. *Bristol 1967: Studienergebnisse der Kommission für Glauben und Kirchenverfassung*, edited by Reinhard Groscurth and Lukas Vischer, Beihefte zur Ökumenischen Rundschau 7/8 (Stuttgart: Evangelischer Missionsverlag, 1967), 46–58.
27 Cf. Groscurth and Vischer, *Bristol*, 49.
28 Cf. Lauster, *Prinzip*, 356f.
29 Cf. *Löwen 1971: Studienberichte und Dokumente der Sitzung der Kommission für Glauben und Kirchenverfassung*, edited by Konrad Raiser, Beihefte zur Ökumenischen Rundschau 18/19 (Stuttgart: Evangelischer Missionsverlag, 1971), 8–21.
30 Cf. Raiser, *Löwen*, 12.

of relation" (*Beziehungsmitte*).[31] While the ecumenical discussion introduced an authoritative understanding of Scripture that is integrated in the process of Tradition and linked to different forms of traditions, the still unresolved question is about the critical function of Scripture in relation to tradition.[32] For the ecumenical debate as well as for Protestant theology, the overall remaining question is *how* the critical function of Scripture can be conducted.[33] As in the ecumenical discussion in the 1960s and 1970s, a differentiated comprehension of the relationship of Scripture and tradition was introduced, so it can serve as a starting point for further reflection on this topic that extends especially the perception of tradition. The reflection on the Christian transmission history by the Lutheran theologian Wolfhart Pannenberg can be considered as a continuation of these thoughts. Pannenberg's methodological approach offers new stimuli regarding how the Scripture can be critical to traditions.

3 Wolfhart Pannenberg's Perception of the Relation of Scripture and Tradition

Wolfhart Pannenberg is an interesting interlocutor for further elaborating the complexity of the relationship of Scripture and tradition as he reflects comprehensively on the Christian transmission history (*Überlieferungsgeschichte*) and the meaning of Scripture for this traditionary process. He relates Scripture to an encompassing traditionary process and describes the written records as a "condensation of a transmission history" (*Niederschlag einer Überlieferungsgeschichte*).[34] Locating Scripture in the transmission history, he refers to the discussion concerning the relationship between Scripture and tradition in the 1950s and 1960s which becomes apparent given one of his references is the Danish Lu-

---

[31] Cf. Raiser, *Löwen*, 16.
[32] Cf. for a detailed reconstruction of the ecumenical discussion on Scripture and tradition see Matthias Haudel, *Die Bibel und die Einheit der Kirchen: Eine Untersuchung der Studien von 'Glauben und Kirchenverfassung'*, Kirche und Konfession 34 (Göttingen: Vandenhoeck & Ruprecht, 2012).
[33] Cf. Lauster, *Prinzip*, 211–13.
[34] Wolfhart Pannenberg, "Was ist eine dogmatische Aussage? (1962)," in *Grundfragen systematischer Theologie: Gesammelte Aufsätze*, edited by Wolfhart Pannenberg (Göttingen: Vandenhoeck & Ruprecht, ³1979), 162.

theran theologian and member of Faith and Order, Kristen Ejner Skydsgaard.[35] Skydsgaard rejects a Protestant understanding of tradition that regards tradition in opposition to an original and undistorted Scripture.[36] Referring to Old and New Testament Studies, Skydsgaard acknowledges the important role of tradition: before Scripture, there was tradition.[37]

Alongside the perception of Scripture as a result of a traditionary process, Pannenberg emphasizes the normative function of Scripture. It results from the origin of the Scriptures of the New Testament and the consolidation of the canon which structures the whole Christian transmission history.[38] Since the formation of the canon of the New Testament, all traditions, creeds as well as church doctrines, are imparted and take place with respect to the canon.[39] Referring to Skydsgaard, Pannenberg describes the function of Scripture within tradition as "guardianship"[40] and assumes Scripture as the "primordial witness of the Tradition per se" (*Urzeuge der Tradition schlechthin*).[41]

This normative and thus structural function of Scripture for the Christian transmission history becomes implicitly evident in Pannenberg's understanding of history and revelation. The Christian transmission is inextricably linked with the resurrection: "Only by referring to the resurrection of Jesus in the context of the intellectual situation of Early Christianity, does the story of faith in Christ from its beginning till the emergence of the confession of the deity of Jesus Christ become comprehensible."[42] It is the resurrection of Jesus that reveals God

---

35 Pannenberg refers to Kristen E. Skydsgaard, "Schrift und Tradition: Bemerkungen zum Traditionsproblem in der neueren Theologie," *Kerygma und Dogma* 1 (1955): 161–79.
36 Cf. Skydsgaard, "Schrift," 169.
37 Cf. Skydsgaard, "Schrift," 170: "Bevor es Schrift gab, gab es Tradition." Cf. Pannenberg, "Aussage," 162, Fn. 15.
38 Cf. Pannenberg, "Aussage," 162.
39 Cf. Pannenberg, "Aussage," 162.
40 Pannenberg, "Aussage," 162, Fn. 16. See Skydsgaard, "Schrift," 177, who understands the guardianship ("Wächteramt") of Scripture as "die Kirche und ihre Tradition, ihre mancherlei Traditionen immer wieder 'zur Sache zu rufen', immer wieder reinigend und lehrend Christus selbst als dem Herrn der Tradition Platz zu schaffen" ("calling the church and its tradition, its many traditions to the point, again and again purifying and teaching and making room for Christ himself as Lord of the tradition", my translation).
41 Skydsgaard, "Schrift," 178. Cf. also Pannenberg, "Aussage," 162, Fn. 16.
42 My translation from Wolfhart Pannenberg, "Die Krise des Schriftprinzips (1962)," in *Grundfragen systematischer Theologie: Gesammelte Aufsätze*, edited by Wolfhart Pannenberg (Göttingen: Vandenhoeck & Ruprecht, ³1979), 16: "Nur von der Auferstehung Jesu her wird, im Rahmen der geistigen Situation des Urchristentums, die Anfangsgeschichte des Christusglaubens bis hin zur Entstehung des Bekenntnisses zur Gottheit Jesu verständlich."

in the life and fate of Jesus of Nazareth and thus the crucial point of God's revelation is the historicity of the resurrection.[43] Only if the resurrection can be considered as a historical event, the reality of God can truly have entered history and have an impact on history. History, according to Pannenberg, does not consist of *bruta facta*, because human history is always interlaced with understanding which relies on hopes and memories.[44] As such, perception and comprehension of reality spans between past and future and the transformation of understanding itself is a historical event. Thus, a historical event always exists with meaning that emerges from the context in which it occurs. Therefore, historical events cannot be separated from their meaning and Pannenberg assumes that history itself is always a history of traditions: "The events of history speak their own language, the language of facts; however, this language is understandable only in the context of the traditions and the expectations in which the given events occur."[45]

For Pannenberg, history and tradition are inextricably linked and traditions are necessary for understanding historical events. This structure relies on the biblical texts where God's promises are fulfilled by his deeds in history.[46] The preceding promises are an interpretive framework for understanding God's indirect acts of self-revelation in history. Promises and their fulfilments are an ongoing process that continues until the end of the history, for only then can

---

[43] Cf. Wolfhart Pannenberg, *Systematic Theology: Volume 2* (Grand Rapids: Eerdmans, 1994), 346–63. On page 360f, Pannenberg relates facticity and historicity: "The claim to historicity that is inseparable from the assertion of the facticity of an event simply involves the fact that it happened at a specific time." While assertion of the historicity of an event does not necessarily mean its indisputably facticity, regarding the resurrection Pannenberg states on page 361: "In the case of the resurrection of Jesus, all Christians must realize that the facticity of the event will be contested right up to the eschatological consummation of the world because its uniqueness transcends an understanding of reality that is oriented only to this passing world and because the new reality that has come in the resurrection of Jesus has not yet universally and definitively manifested itself."

[44] Cf. Wolfhart Pannenberg, "Dogmatic Theses on the Concept of Revelation," in *Revelation as History*, edited by Wolfhart Pannenberg (London: Sheed and Ward, 1979), 152: "History is not composed of raw or so-called brute facts. As the history of man, the history of revelation is always bound up with understanding, in hope and remembrance. The development of understanding is itself an event in history. In their fundamental givenness, these elements are not to be separated from history; history is also the history of the transmission of history."

[45] Pannenberg, "Theses," 152f.

[46] Cf. Wolfhart Pannenberg, "Heilsgeschehen und Geschichte (1959)," in *Grundfragen systematischer Theologie: Gesammelte Aufsätze*, edited by Wolfhart Pannenberg (Göttingen: Vandenhoeck & Ruprecht, ³1979), 25f.

God be fully understood.⁴⁷ However, Pannenberg sees a difference between the promises and fulfilments, so that a change in the promises happens through the fulfilment events.⁴⁸ He integrates this change of meaning into his understanding of history when he understands the change of meaning itself as a historical event and thus history as history of transmission.⁴⁹ This is the structural background for Pannenberg's concept of the revelation of God. In terms of the resurrection as the self-revealing deed of God in history, Pannenberg assumes the prophetic-apocalyptic tradition as the expectation that builds the interpretative framework for discovering the presence of God in Jesus Christ. By relating the event of the resurrection to its traditional context it can show its meaning which lies within itself. The prophetic-apocalyptic traditions contain three aspects:⁵⁰ (1) the final revelation of God at the end of time, (2) the idea that the end of history can be seen in extraordinary visions, and (3) the expectation of the resurrection of the dead at the end of history. The first expectation lays the ground for the other two and constitutes the universality of the revelation by understanding the whole history as affected by a revelation of God at the end of history. Pannenberg finds this final revelation in the message of Jesus himself: Jesus' preaching of the near Kingdom of God locates itself in the end time.⁵¹ Here, his claim for authority became obvious as he "proclaimed the impending end, not just as a judgement calling for repentance but in a manner that presented himself as the eschatological salvation."⁵² The eschatological salvation already begins with the appearance of Jesus but, as with an apocalyptic vision, Jesus' claim to power required confirmation.⁵³ Here lies a second commonality with the apocalyptic tradition. According to Pannenberg, this need for legitimation is fulfilled by the resurrection of the dead. Thus, "[i]t is only within this tradition of prophetic and apocalyptic expectation that it is possible to understand the resurrection of Jesus and his pre-Easter life as a reflection of the eschatological self-vindication of Yahweh."⁵⁴ It is the primitive Christian community that, in

---

47 Cf. thesis 2 "Revelation is not comprehended completely in the beginning, but at the end of the revealing history" and its explanation, Pannenberg, "Theses," 131–35.
48 Cf. Pannenberg, "Heilsgeschehen," 35.
49 Cf. Pannenberg, "Theses," 152.
50 Cf. Pannenberg, "Theses," 126f.132f.141–143; Wolfhart Pannenberg, *Grundzüge der Christologie* (Gütersloh: Gütersloher Verlagshaus Mohn, ⁷1990), 61–105.
51 Cf. Pannenberg, *Grundzüge*, 55–57; Pannenberg, *Systematic Theology*, 326–34.
52 Pannenberg, "Theses," 145f. See also Pannenberg, *Systematic Theology*, 326–34.
53 Cf. Pannenberg, *Grundzüge*, 57.
54 Pannenberg, "Theses," 127.

light of the encounters with the resurrected,[55] metaphorically interprets the special event of the 'resurrection' in reference to the expectation of the awakening of the dead at the end of time.[56] The expectation of the general resurrection makes the event comprehensible and the resurrection of Jesus appears as part of the final revelation of God at the end of time: "It is through the resurrection that the God of Israel has substantiated his deity in an ultimate way and is now manifest as the God of all men."[57] The apocalyptic character of the Christ-event establishes the prolepsis of God's revelation at the end of history. Although, the final verification is yet to come at the end of time, this prolepsis offers already a new perspective on reality: In light of Jesus Christ, the reality and being of God becomes comprehensible, despite the fact that we do not stand at the end of history.[58] With the proleptic end of history, history as a whole, as universal history, comes into sight and thus the interpretative framework for each following event is set out.[59] If we look at Pannenberg's reconstruction of the mutual interpretation of earlier traditions and the historical event, it becomes clear that the revelation of God is constitutively dependent on this correlation. According to Pannenberg, it is precisely because the eschatological expectations are fulfilled by a historical event that final revelation takes place. For the post-Easter context, this revelation becomes the interpretive framework for the interpretation of human reality from now on.

For Pannenberg, the hermeneutical interpretation processes are essential for conceiving the revelation of God in history. Thus, the early Christian transmission history can be understood as further unfolding the implicit meaning of the cross and resurrection of Jesus. Nonetheless, according to Pannenberg, further interpretation always has to be related to the event and its interpretation

---

55 Cf. Pannenberg, *Grundzüge*, 85–97; Pannenberg, *Systematic Theology*, 352–59.
56 Cf. Pannenberg, *Systematic Theology*, 346f.
57 Pannenberg, "Theses," 142.
58 Cf. Pannenberg, "Theses," 142: "And, only in the sense that the perfection of history has already been inaugurated in Jesus Christ is God finally and fully revealed in the fate of Jesus. With the resurrection of Jesus, the end of history has already occurred, although is does not strike us in this way."
59 Pannenberg's universal-historical hermeneutics are presented in Pannenberg, "Heilsgeschehen," and in Wolfhart Pannenberg, "Hermeneutik und Universalgeschichte (1963)," in *Grundfragen systematischer Theologie: Gesammelte Aufsätze*, edited by Wolfhart Pannenberg (Göttingen: Vandenhoeck & Ruprecht, ³1979), 91–122. They rely on the hermeneutical tension between piece and whole: the piece is only comprehensible in light of the whole and the whole only in light of its pieces. See also Wolfhart Pannenberg, "Die Bedeutung der Kategorien 'Teil' und 'Ganzes' für die Wissenschaftstheorie der Theologie," *Theologie und Philosophie* 53 (1978): 481–97.

dynamics. For Christology, Pannenberg describes the task of a "theory of the Christological tradition" (*Theorie der christologischen Tradition*)[60] which has to reconstruct the intrinsic development of the Christological creed. Central to this reconstruction is the biblical record because, for the historical person Jesus of Nazareth as well as for his meaning, the New Testament writings are in a double sense a 'historical source': "As a historical source, they do not only tell us 'what was once believed', but at the same time they also reveal something about Jesus himself, in whom the Christian believes".[61] For Pannenberg, it is crucial that the New Testament report is perceived with its historical as well as kerygmatic level and that both remain related to each other. "The historical reconstruction of the figure and proclamation of Jesus is always obliged to explain how the early Christian proclamation of Christ could arise from the fate of Jesus."[62] All post-Easter talk about Jesus of Nazareth must be based on what can be said about the life and work of the earthly Jesus as historically probable, if it is not to appear as a product of faith.[63] Thus, according to Pannenberg, the unity of the early Christian transmission history and the New Testament is derived from the Christ-event itself.[64]

This determination of the New Testament scriptures is supported by Pannenberg's re-interpretation of the biblical texts as the word of God. "The biblical

---

60 Pannenberg, *Grundzüge*, 11; Pannenberg, *Systematic Theology*, 282.
61 Pannenberg, *Grundzüge*, 18 (my translation); in the original German: "Als historische Quelle sagen sie nämlich nicht nur, 'was früher einmal geglaubt wurde', sondern sie lassen zugleich auch etwas erkennen über Jesus selbst, an den der Christ glaubt."
62 Pannenberg, *Grundzüge*, 17 (my translation): "Die historische Rekonstruktion der Gestalt und der Verkündigung Jesu ist immer verpflichtet zu erklären, wie vom Geschick Jesu her die urchristliche Christusverkündigung entstehen konnte."
63 Cf. Pannenberg, *Grundzüge*, 20.
64 Cf. Pannenberg, "Aussage," 171: "Bezogen auf seinen ursprünglichen Geschehenszusammenhang – dazu gehören die Erwartungen des Judentums der Zeit Jesu mitsamt ihrem alttestamentlichen Hintergrund, vor allem aber das Auftreten und die Botschaft Jesu selbst – trägt das Geschehen der Auferweckung Jesu und von daher auch seine Kreuzigung seine Bedeutung in sich selbst, und so wird von ihm her die urchristliche Überlieferungsgeschichte als Entfaltung der diesem Geschehen innewohnenden Bedeutung verständlich, aber auch überprüfbar. So empfängt die urchristliche Überlieferungsgeschichte und damit das NT selbst vom Christusgeschehen her seine Einheit." ("In relation to the original context of the event – which includes the expectations of Judaism at the time of Jesus with their Old Testament background, but above all the appearance and message of Jesus himself – the event of Jesus' resurrection and therefore also his crucifixion carries its meaning in itself, and thus the early Christian history of tradition becomes understandable, but also verifiable, as the unfolding of the meaning inherent in this event. In this way, the early Christian history of tradition, and thus the NT itself, receives its unity from the event of Christ." My translation.)

traditions are to be related to the same God who brings the events of history into being"[65] and thus are received as authorized by God and described as 'word of God.' In the biblical traditions, the word of God "relates itself to revelation as foretelling, forthtelling, and report,"[66] as Pannenberg maintains. As prophetic word and promise, the word of God foretells the revelation; as forthtelling in law and commandment it is a result of divine self-vindication.[67] In the New Testament, 'word of God' is considered as kerygma, e.g. apostolic proclamation.[68] As this 'type' of God's word is initiated by the appearances of Jesus (Gal 1:12; 15f.) it is God who releases the kerygma. Therefore, Pannenberg understands the apostolic proclamation as "the report of the revelation of God in the fate of Jesus"[69] that has to be 'reported', e.g. transmitted "in every language, culture, and situation as the decisive act of God's salvation."[70] According to Pannenberg, the word of the kerygma itself is "an element in the accomplishment of the revelation event."[71] The eschatological event of revelation "activates a universal proclamation through which it is also made explicit"[72] and which is essential for the universal revelation. For Pannenberg, there is no need for a special inspiration as the events show their self-evidence "as they stand within the framework of their own history."[73]

Considering this correlation of biblical tradition and revelation, Scripture itself has only a derived critical authority for Pannenberg: It is the witnessed event which the New Testament scriptures narrate and report that becomes the criterion for the expressions and attribution of meaning unfolded subsequent to the event itself. The New Testament affirms the connection of event and meaning because it bears witness to it. As witness of the revelation of God in Jesus Christ, Scripture is the source for the primitive Christian Jesus tradition and thus is for Pannenberg *instrumentum doctrinae* to proof statements of faiths and dogmatic hypotheses about Jesus Christ.[74] However, this normative function is

---

[65] Pannenberg, "Theses," 153.
[66] Pannenberg, "Theses," 152.
[67] Cf. Pannenberg, "Theses," 153f.
[68] Cf. Pannenberg, "Theses," 154f.
[69] Pannenberg, "Theses," 154. Report does not mean an objective and solely chronological description of the event, but is essentially proclamation.
[70] Pannenberg, "Theses," 154.
[71] Pannenberg, "Theses," 154f.
[72] Pannenberg, "Theses," 155.
[73] Pannenberg, "Theses," 155.
[74] Cf. Pannenberg, "Aussage," 177f. For the hypothetical character of dogmatic propositions see Pannenberg, "Aussage," 176 and 180.

closely related to the witnessed event itself as Pannenberg considers the New Testament scriptures as a historical source. Behind the witness lies the witnessed event that has to be comprehended in its context of traditions and expectations.

4 The Impact of the Observations on Theological Reflection

For Pannenberg, the meaning of the event of revelation can only be worked out by considering its context in the transmission history as the event is understood within this context of meaning. By linking meaning and historical event, Scripture and the Gospel itself become the starting point and material by which to understand the historical event. Exploring how the event of the revelation affected the (faith) traditions of its transmission context, Pannenberg observes how the revelation of God formed, corrected and altered traditions while at the same time creating new traditions through which the meaning of the event became explicit. For Pannenberg, this process of change of meaning is the basis of his theological approach, in which he constantly reviews theological teachings and traditions to determine whether they correspond to the 'original' relation between historical event and formation of meaning. For the above-mentioned question of the critical function of Scripture, this means that the critical function of Scripture lies within its documentation of meaning and event of the revelation in Jesus Christ. This is not a static description as the biblical witness is manifold. According to Pannenberg, Scripture itself is a historical and kerygmatic source through which this intertwining can be studied. In this respect, the critical function of Scripture can be understood as a permanent pointer back to the connection between meaning and historical event. The critical function is thus not described as a static norm but as one that is usually given by the biblical authors themselves. As the biblical authors interpreted the historical person of Jesus of Nazareth and placed him in a context of tradition, interpretive structures can be discovered in the biblical testimony that can be placed in relation to contemporary interpretive processes. Thus, the critical function is understood as a dynamic process. It reminds the interpreter to look for structural analogies, for it is precisely the change in meaning that shows how God's revelation spoke into or interrupted the understanding of the time. Thus, the question arises how the change in meaning of the traditions can be made explicit today, so that the particularity of God's revelation can be conveyed. However, taking seriously the plurality of the interpretations and their conditionality on the historical context, a more detailed statement on the critical function can hardly be made. This determination of the critical function opens room for discussion in which the leading principles for interpretation have to be named in order to illuminate the way of interpreting and describing the formation of meaning.

As a result, it means that theology has to consider the transformation of meaning in the Christian history of traditions. Therefore, according to Pannenberg, theology has to combine biblical interpretation with historical research into its hermeneutics. For both approaches, Scripture is the starting point as it is the historical source for the Christ event and, at the same time, it documents the significance and interpretation process of the event.[75] In order to grasp this process of meaning transformation through the development of traditions at least two dimensions of tradition play an important role. *First*, the contextual dimension of the different traditions and, *second*, the question of the execution of the traditionary process which forms, corrects and alters traditions while at the same time creating new traditions through which meaning becomes explicit.

The biblical writings themselves are always embedded in and consist of tradition, but the processes of transmission do not end with the formation of the canon. Rather, the meaning of revelation is continually reinterpreted in relation to the biblical texts, and 'leading' traditions develop that function as a 'hermeneutical key' for the interpretation of Scripture (e.g., the Lutheran doctrine of justification). In order to bring together both the inner-biblical and the post-biblical dimensions of tradition, theological reflection must relate both developments to each other and examine the relationship between the two processes of transmission. This task is always limited by the temporal gap between past and present. This gap cannot be eliminated, but it can be 'filled' by looking at the history of transmission. In order to obtain a comprehensive picture, the various 'actors' in this process must be taken into account: The medium that transmits meaning, i.e., the biblical texts; the further development of language; the reader with his or her horizon of experience and formed thinking; leading methodological approaches and theories that affect the acquisition of meaning. Scripture and tradition are part of the interplay of the different actors. Their

---

75 Thereby the biblical text is more than "a document of a mundane occurrence and human religiosity" ("Dokumente profaner Begebenheiten und menschlicher Religiosität") and the "very content" ("eigentlicher Inhalt") which is the witnessed action of God can be 'surveyed', cf. Wolfhart Pannenberg, "Kerygma und Geschichte," in *Studien zur Theologie der alttestamentlichen Überlieferungen*, eds. Rolf Rendtorff and Gerhard von Rad (Neukirchen: Neukirchener Verlag, 1961), 133. Pannenberg states that this meaning of the biblical scriptures was already emphasized by kerygmatic theology in opposition to the historical methods and practice.

different roles and functions need to be reflected because they lead to different hermeneutic approaches, such as historical criticism, literary criticism or reader-response criticism. It is not one approach alone that discloses an understanding of the salvific reality of God revealed in Jesus Christ. Transformations of meaning and significance can lie at different levels and can be conditioned by different perspectives, and each approach detects transformation according to its methodological background. Theological reflection must account for its attachment to traditions in order to take traditions seriously as traditions and make room for new interpretations.

In connection with Pannenberg, three main points can be made regarding the relation between Scripture, tradition, and theology. *First*, theology needs to take into account the complexity of tradition in Scripture in an effort to elucidate transmission processes to understand the formation of meaning. By tracking the different interpretations and attribution of significance processes, theology can achieve a deeper understanding of the Christian faith and its different shades and renew a contemporary comprehension. *Second*, transmitting the content of the revelation of God is always linked to Scripture and seeks expressions to translate its meaning into new contexts. Given that Scripture is the permanent reference for the significance of the Christ event, every new expression has to be proven in reference to the biblical Scriptures as they attest to the earliest interpretation processes. Nonetheless, the gap between present and past interpretation will rest and challenge every new interpretation. By trying to elaborate how the historical event was interpreted initially, later transmission processes can be related to the interpreting processes that occurred earlier. As transmission processes are translation processes that explicate, alter, or even reduce the handed down tradition into a current cultural and intellectual situation, the process itself has to be reflected upon and decisions of interpretation have to be critically questioned. *Third*, expressing the reality of God in reference to Scripture and tradition cannot disclose a definite and final expression of this reality. Expressions always rely on language, semantics and cultural background. As language changes, the meaning contexts of outmoded expressions must also be opened up anew. Accordingly, the salvific dimension of God's revelation in Jesus Christ requires processes of translation and transmission in order to reveal the reality of God to people of all times. In the course of such transmission, theological reflection opens up space for interpretations that preserve tradition and enable a renewal of the forms of proclamation of the Gospel.

References

Beale, Greg K. *Handbook on the New Testament Use of the Old Testament: Exegesis and Interpretation*. Grand Rapids: Baker Academic, 2012.
Dingel, Irene, ed. *Die Bekenntnisschriften der evangelisch-lutherischen Kirche*. Vollständige Neuedition. Göttingen: Vandenhoeck & Ruprecht, 2014.
Groscurth, Reinhard and Lukas Vischer, eds. *Bristol 1967: Studienergebnisse der Kommission für Glauben und Kirchenverfassung*. Beihefte zur Ökumenischen Rundschau 7/8. Stuttgart: Evangelischer Missionsverlag, 1967.
Haudel, Matthias. *Die Bibel und die Einheit der Kirchen: Eine Untersuchung der Studien von 'Glauben und Kirchenverfassung'*. Kirche und Konfession 34. Göttingen: Vandenhoeck & Ruprecht, ³2012.
Käsemann, Ernst. "Begründet der neutestamentliche Kanon die Einheit der Kirche?" In *Exegetische Versuche und Besinnungen 1*, edited by Ernst Käsemann, 214–23. Göttingen: Vandenhoeck & Ruprecht, ²1960.
Körtner, Ulrich H. J. *Arbeit am Kanon: Studien zur Bibelhermeneutik*. Leipzig: Evangelische Verlagsanstalt, 2015.
Lauster, Jörg. *Prinzip und Methode: Die Transformation des protestantischen Schriftprinzips durch die historische Kritik von Schleiermacher bis zur Gegenwart*. Hermeneutische Untersuchungen zur Theologie 46. Tübingen: Mohr Siebeck, 2004.
Maikranz, Elisabeth, and Carolin Ziethe. "Kapitel D: Schrift und Tradition." In *Schriftbindung evangelischer Theologie: Theorieelemente aus interdisziplinären Gesprächen*, edited by Frederike van Oorschot and Friedrich-Emanuel Focken, 155–89. Forum Theologische Literaturzeitung 37. Leipzig: Evangelische Verlagsanstalt, 2020.
Outler, Albert C. "The Renewal of the Christian Tradition: The Report of the North American Section." In *The Report of the Theological Commission on Tradition and Traditions*, edited by the World Council of Churches and Commission on Faith and Order, 5–29. Faith and Order Paper No. 40. Genf, 1963.
Pannenberg, Wolfhart. "Kerygma und Geschichte." In *Studien zur Theologie der alttestamentlichen Überlieferungen: FS Gerhard von Rad zum 60. Geburtstag*, edited by Rolf Rendtorff and Gerhard v. Rad, 129–40. Neukirchen: Neukirchener Verlag, 1961.
Pannenberg, Wolfhart. "Die Bedeutung der Kategorien 'Teil' und 'Ganzes' für die Wissenschaftstheorie der Theologie." *Theologie und Philosophie* 53 (1978): 481–97.
Pannenberg, Wolfhart. "Die Krise des Schriftprinzips (1962)." In *Grundfragen systematischer Theologie: Gesammelte Aufsätze*, edited by Wolfhart Pannenberg, 11–21. Göttingen: Vandenhoeck & Ruprecht, ³1979.
Pannenberg, Wolfhart. "Dogmatic Theses on the Concept of Revelation." In *Revelation as History*, edited by Wolfhart Pannenberg, 123–58. London: Sheed and Ward, 1979.
Pannenberg, Wolfhart. "Heilsgeschehen und Geschichte (1959)." In *Grundfragen systematischer Theologie: Gesammelte Aufsätze*, edited by Wolfhart Pannenberg, 22–78. Göttingen: Vandenhoeck & Ruprecht, ³1979.
Pannenberg, Wolfhart. "Hermeneutik und Universalgeschichte (1963)." In *Grundfragen systematischer Theologie: Gesammelte Aufsätze*, edited by Wolfhart Pannenberg, 91–122. Göttingen: Vandenhoeck & Ruprecht, ³1979.

Pannenberg, Wolfhart. "Was ist eine dogmatische Aussage? (1962)." In *Grundfragen systematischer Theologie: Gesammelte Aufsätze*, edited by Wolfhart Pannenberg, 159–80. Göttingen: Vandenhoeck & Ruprecht, ³1979.

Pannenberg, Wolfhart. *Grundzüge der Christologie*. Gütersloh: Gütersloher Verlagshaus Mohn, ⁷1990.

Pannenberg, Wolfhart. *Systematic Theology: Volume 2*. Grand Rapids: Eerdmans, 1994.

Plett, Heinrich F. "Intertextualities." In *Intertextuality*, edited by Heinrich F. Plett, 3–29. Research in Text Theory 15. Berlin, New York: de Gruyter, 1991.

Raiser, Konrad, ed. *Löwen 1971: Studienberichte und Dokumente der Sitzung der Kommission für Glauben und Kirchenverfassung*. Beihefte zur Ökumenischen Rundschau 18/19. Stuttgart: Evangelischer Missionsverlag, 1971.

Rodger, Patrick C. and Lukas Vischer, eds. *The Fourth World Conference on Faith and Order: Montreal 1963*. Faith and Order Paper No. 42. London: SCM Press, 1964.

Skydsgaard, Kristen E. "Schrift und Tradition: Bemerkungen zum Traditionsproblem in der neueren Theologie." *Kerygma und Dogma* 1 (1955): 161–79.

Van Oorschot, Frederike, Friedrich-Emanuel Focken, and Elisabeth Maikranz. "Einführung." In *Schriftbindung evangelischer Theologie: Theorieelemente aus interdisziplinären Gesprächen*, edited by Frederike van Oorschot and Friedrich-Emanuel Focken, 15–40. Forum Theologische Literaturzeitung 37. Leipzig: Evangelische Verlagsanstalt, 2020.

Ziethe, Carolin. *Auf seinen Namen werden die Völker hoffen: Die matthäische Rezeption der Schriften Israels zur Begründung des universalen Heils*. Beihefte zur Zeitschrift für die neutestamentliche Wissenschaft 233. Berlin, Boston: de Gruyter, 2018.

Michael Borowski
Deriving Theology from Scripture

An Account based on the Work of Kevin J. Vanhoozer

Abstract: How can theology be derived from Scripture? This chapter assumes that such a theology "derived from Scripture" is desirable, but difficult to achieve. Building on Kevin J. Vanhoozer's work, the chapter outlines an account of developing doctrine as a way of deriving theology from Scripture. It locates the task of developing doctrine in Vanhoozer's overall 'agenda' and reflects on Vanhoozer's conception of the nature of doctrine, in order to then argue for three components of doctrinal development: the turn to Scripture, the formulation of doctrine, and the renewal of doctrine. The paper presupposes that outlining one's own approach for doing theology not only necessitates reflection on that particular account, but also allows for dialogue between this and other accounts practitioners of theology may maintain.

Keywords: Kevin J. Vanhoozer, Scripture and theology, Drama of doctrine, Development of doctrine, Nature and function of doctrine, Dogmatics

1 Introduction

While we may agree that Christianity relates to the Bible, it is less clear how theology can be derived from Scripture. In other words: If the Bible is central to Christianity, what does it mean to 'be biblical' in one's theology? The challenge implied by this question is how to relate Scripture to theology. For in many academic contexts, biblical studies and theology are overall separated. There are reasons for such a separation, and overcoming it might represent a challenge of its own. Yet there is a further initial challenge, one that has been less prominent in this volume so far. For what unites both questions – the one concerning theology as well as the one concerning faith – is their applicational focus: In asking how theology can be derived from Scripture we imply not only a certain relationship between the two – we also imply that there is some 'doing'; a doing that may somehow lead from Scripture to theology.

Michael Borowski, VU Amsterdam, The Netherlands, michael.borowski@gmx.de

https://doi.org/10.1515/9783110768411-020

The aim of this chapter is to offer an exemplary account on how to derive theology from Scripture. Outlining such an account does not represent a reflection on the details of one's theological method, but rather the big picture of how one may construe, or obtain, theology from Scripture. The purpose of this is to make transparent how theological proposals can be established – not to suggest that this is the only way for doing so, but to offer an example that makes transparent the aims and standards to which this account aspires, thereby inviting reflection of one's own account, as well as dialogue between differing accounts.[1] With this in mind, this chapter summarizes the work of a particular theologian by applying a particular focus; and in implicitly affirming this account, the chapter also represents an exercise in accountability.

To accomplish the aim of offering an account on how to derive theology from Scripture, I turn to the US-American theologian Kevin J. Vanhoozer, who has not only worked on the issue of deriving theology from Scripture extensively, but has done so consistently by expressing a concern for the praxis of theology. I argue that by drawing on Vanhoozer, three components for the task of doing theology can be summarized, and that they can function as an orienting example and a basis for discussion on how to derive theology from Scripture. In section 2, I offer an account of the bigger picture according to Vanhoozer (i.e., the broader theodramatic context for the particular agenda of this chapter), and then zoom in on Vanhoozer's characterization of doctrine (section 3) and his particular agenda for developing doctrine (section 4). In this fourth section, I will propose three components of Vanhoozer's theological programme of developing doctrine: the turn to Scripture, the formulation of doctrine, and the renewal of doctrine. All sections can be understood as an attempt to systematize Vanhoozer's extensive work on developing theology from Scripture, and hence the outcome of this attempt resembles a proposal for deriving doctrine from Scripture, based on the work of Vanhoozer.[2]

---

1 Cf. Mike Higton, and Jim Fodor, *The Routledge Companion to the Practice of Christian Theology* (Abingdon: Routledge, 2015), 723.
2 For practical purposes, I will refrain from explicitly referring to Vanhoozer in every given sentence. Yet my claim is that Vanhoozer's work can be sketched in the way this chapter proposes, and I argue in particular for certain components in his work.

2 The Bigger Picture: Doctrine between Drama and Discipleship

According to Vanhoozer, the quest for the development of doctrine should be located within the bigger picture, which in turn can be characterized as a drama: the church responding to the good news of the gospel.[3] Why drama? Because this is the set-up we find ourselves in, and in which we – and others – must act. Starting from Plato's concept of time as a moving image of eternity, one can think of God in time as a "moving image" of the way God himself is in eternity; that the economic Trinity (i.e., what the Father, Son and Spirit do in history) is a dramatic representation of what God's eternal life is, and of his eternal disposition toward the world.[4] What God is and does is captured in the Bible, which is why the essence of the Bible – which is the gospel – is theodramatic (i.e., reporting on the matter of what God (*theos*) has said and done (*drao*) in history –, for at "the heart of Christianity is not merely an idea of God but rather God's self-communicating words and acts"[5]). History is therefore always theodramatic, representing a "series of divine entrances and exits, especially, as these pertain to what God has done in Jesus Christ."[6]

What God is and does is captured in the Bible – a book like any other on the one hand, but, from a faith perspective, a text authored ultimately by God with Christ as its ultimate content and with the Holy Spirit as its ultimate interpreter.[7] For Christians and the church, the Bible is Scripture – but hence also is script, for it demands to be played out:[8] Humans (and, in particular, Christians) are called to participate within the drama; not to be hearers only, but doers of the word.[9] However: *How* to perform Scripture is not that easy – we find ourselves

---

[3] Kevin J. Vanhoozer, "A Drama-of-Redemption Model," in *Four Views on Moving Beyond the Bible to Theology*, edited by Gary T. Meadors and Stanley N. Gundry (Grand Rapids: Zondervan, 2009), 155.
[4] Kevin J. Vanhoozer and Daniel J. Treier, *Theology and the Mirror of Scripture: A Mere Evangelical Account* (Grand Rapids: InterVarsity Press, 2015), 65.
[5] Kevin J. Vanhoozer, *Faith Speaking Understanding: Performing the Drama of Doctrine* (Louisville: Westminster John Knox Press, 2014), 20.
[6] Kevin J. Vanhoozer, *The Drama of Doctrine: A Canonical-Linguistic Approach to Christian Theology* (Louisville: Westminster John Knox Press, 2005), 31.
[7] Vanhoozer and Treier, 73.
[8] Vanhoozer, *The Drama of Doctrine*, 115.
[9] Cf. Kevin J. Vanhoozer, *Hearers and Doers: A Pastor's Guide to Making Disciples through Scripture and Doctrine* (Bellingham: Lexham Press, 2019).

in ever new situations, and disciples must learn to discern how to *do* the word in a way that fits the gospel, that is, not only *thinking* more biblically, but eventually *being* more biblical.[10]

The overall theodramatic agenda, then, explicates the implications from the God of the gospel, and addresses the church, so that it will grow into the full stature of Christ.[11] Doctrine is the means that fosters such growth. The theologian's (i.e., the dramaturge's) task can be construed as supporting the church's pastors in unfolding the script (i.e., Scripture) towards a fitting performance of the church.

3 The Theologian's Primary Mission: Contributing to the Development of Doctrine

Before this background, I will now outline how – again, in this account based on Vanhoozer – theology can be derived from Scripture; a way of doing theology by developing doctrine. I start with some notes on the general character of doctrine in this section, and then move on to three crucial components for developing doctrine in the following one.

What are we referring to when speaking of 'doctrine'? *Doctrina, didaskalia* means 'teaching, instruction' – yet, what is being taught, why, and by whom is it taught, and who is being taught? Most uncontroversial may be here the participants in play; for it is a given Christian church that is being taught by its given authorities. More controversial, however, will be the 'what' and 'why'. 'What' is being taught, then, could traditionally be summarized as doctrines (here including historical, narrative, kerygmatic and apologetical elements) as informative truth, claims about objective realities ('traditional view'). Other approaches could be found in Schleiermacher (i.e., doctrine as articulations of human experiences) or Lindbeck (i.e., doctrine as intersubjective grammatical rules for church language and church life).[12]

In this account, however, doctrine "is the reward that faith finds at the end of its search for the meaning of the apostolic testimony to what God was doing

---

[10] Kevin J. Vanhoozer, *Is There a Meaning in This Text?: The Bible, the Reader, and the Morality of Literary Knowledge* (New York: HarperCollins, 2009), final chapter.
[11] Vanhoozer and Treier, *Theology and the Mirror of Scripture*, chapter 1 and 2.
[12] Vanhoozer, "A Drama-of-Redemption Model," 87.

in the event of Jesus Christ."[13] It may at times not equal truth in every sense – and may also be seen differently than Scripture in this regard – but it refers to what the church, on the basis of the Bible, believes, teaches and confesses. Doctrine therefore is explicated in creeds and statements of faith, but also in the churches' most characteristic practices.[14] 'Praxis' should be emphasized here – for doctrine in the broad sense can be understood as "direction for the fitting participation of individuals and communities in the drama of redemption."[15] As such, it functions as a special kind of instruction that teaches the head, orients the heart and guides the hand."[16] As not everything in Christian faith functions this way, the nature and the task (i.e., the 'what' and the 'why') are closely connected in this approach.

At the same time, the relation of doctrine and theology may come into focus. There is no consensus either on the matter, nor on the means of theology.[17] Theology can be understood, however, as "exegetical reasoning"; as "biblically informed thinking."[18] The combination of these two phrasings already indicate that theology included both a primary (but not singular) source (i.e., the Bible), and a particular activity (i.e., making judgments via merely cognitive acts, which again involve language and make use of philosophy, etc.).[19] So Christian theology is a discipline that seeks to "refine the dross of mere opinion about God into the gold of knowledge, gold mined largely from scriptural shafts."[20] Theology, then, can be celebrating, coping, criticizing and communicating – yet the point in this account is that theology is perpetuating: it is embodying Christ in one's own life.[21] Theology hence can be defined not only as faith *seeking* understanding, but likewise as faith *speaking* understanding,[22] which is to say that it is not only an analytic task concerned with the Bible, but also a constructive task, addressed towards persons and situations. As to its content, it can be ad-

---

13 Vanhoozer, *The Drama of Doctrine*, 4.
14 Kevin J. Vanhoozer, "Scripture and Theology: On 'Proving' Doctrine Biblically," in *The Routledge Companion to the Practice of Christian Theology*, edited by Mike Higton and Jim Fodor, *Routledge Religion Companions* (Abingdon: Routledge, 2015), 756.
15 Vanhoozer, *The Drama of Doctrine*, 102.
16 Vanhoozer and Treier, *Theology and the Mirror of Scripture*, 107.
17 Kevin J. Vanhoozer, "Systematic Theology," in *The Routledge Companion to Modern Christian Thought*, edited by Chad Meister and James Beilby (London: Routledge, 2013), 716.
18 Kevin J. Vanhoozer, *Remythologizing Theology: Divine Action, Passion, and Authorship*, vol. 18 (Cambridge: Cambridge University Press, 2010), 189.
19 Vanhoozer, *Remythologizing Theology*, 190.
20 Vanhoozer and Treier, *Theology and the Mirror of Scripture*, 141.
21 Vanhoozer, *The Drama of Doctrine*, 15.
22 Vanhoozer, *Faith Speaking Understanding*, 17.

dressed as an attempt to give a loving, reasonable, and faithful description of the gospel and its implications.[23] Theology that is dramaturgical in this way aims for theodramatic performances that "display fittingness with the canon and with the contemporary situation."[24] Doctrine, after all, can be a result of theology and is pursued particularly in the discipline of dogmatics (and biblical theology) – the cognitive science of the church seeking to form the church into a holy nation,[25] and aids the church's attempt to understand the Scriptures.

Examples of doctrinal development could be the church's mature teaching regarding the deity of the Holy Spirit, regarding Christ's descent into hell, and regarding the salvation of unbaptized infants. In the first case, Basil of Caesarea's arguments – in particular those pertaining to Scripture's ranking of the Spirit in relation to God the Father and God the Son – can be understood as an example of doctrinal development, leading to the confession: the Spirit "with the Father and the Son together is worshipped and glorified" in the Council of Constantinople in 381.[26] The second case of doctrinal development also made its way into the (Apostles') Creed – a phrase that some Christians will recite with conviction, while others may choose to remain silent.[27] Regarding the third case, there would be a variety of opinions even in the Reformed tradition alone – for instance, because a given church may not presume upon God's election.

These examples already indicate various functional levels of importance within a given church: Level-1 doctrines identify the God who works salvation; they therefore represent doctrine on which the "integrity of the gospel itself likewise depends."[28] Level-2 doctrines deal with some aspect of the "history of redemption – not with the divine persons per se, but with that what they have done (and that what humans have or have not done in response)."[29] Level-3 doctrine, finally, refer to doctrines which do not "threaten the integrity of the triune God …, or the gospel …, and over which there is disagreement even with-

---

[23] Vanhoozer, "Systematic Theology," 721.
[24] Vanhoozer, *The Drama of Doctrine*, 262.
[25] Kevin J. Vanhoozer, "Analytics, Poetics, and the Mission of Dogmatic Discourse," in *The Task of Dogmatics: Explorations in Theological Method*, edited by Oliver D. Crisp and Fred Sanders (Grand Rapids: Zondervan, 2017), 47.
[26] Kevin J. Vanhoozer, "Improvising Theology According to the Scriptures: An Evangelical Account of the Development of Doctrine," in *Building on the Foundations of Evangelical Theology: Essays in Honor of John S. Feinberg*, edited by Gregg Allison and Stephen Wellum (Wheaton: Crossway, 2015), 19.
[27] Vanhoozer, "Improvising Theology According to the Scriptures," 22.
[28] Vanhoozer, "Improvising Theology According to the Scriptures," 19.
[29] Vanhoozer, "Improvising Theology According to the Scriptures," 22.

in one's theological tradition."[30] Disagreement over various levels of doctrine hence lead to different outcomes: Disagreement over level-1-doctrines may define issues of heresy, disagreements over level-2-doctrines may lead to the issue of denominations, disagreements over level-3-doctrines may represent diverse opinions within both the church as a whole and a particular denomination.

Structurally, then, doctrine is necessarily developed and taught on all levels and in all types of churches.[31] The immensely more difficult question in play, however, is *how* one may develop doctrine, or: how to do so *well*. To this question I now turn.

4 Three Components of Developing Doctrine

How may one develop doctrine? Vanhoozer has worked on this issue consistently and extensively. Yet his work remains complex. For this reason, the following orientation suggests an outline of how theology can be derived from Scripture according to his work: I suggest three components that seem to be essential in Vanhoozer's thinking: the turn to Scripture, the formulation and the renewal of doctrine. I will speak of three 'components' (and not of 'steps'), as all three of them are part of the same task, taking place at the same time and enduringly so, under the guidance of the Spirit, and on the various levels and in the various forms of the church and its institutions.

4.1 The Turn to Scripture

Turning to Scripture may require a certain metaphysical commitment on our part, i.e., one that allows for Christ to be understood as the mirror image (εἰκών/*eikon*) that reflects the Glory of God.[32] Scripture can be approached as a verbal εἰκών of what is in Christ: "as Christ is an icon of God (as visible mirror image of the invisible), so Scripture is a verbal icon (a textual mirror) of Christ."[33] As Christ, Scripture not only bears witness of what the triune God *does*

---

30 Vanhoozer, "Improvising Theology According to the Scriptures," 24.
31 Kevin J. Vanhoozer, "May We Go Beyond What Is Written after All? The Pattern of Theological Authority and the Problem of Doctrinal Development," in *The Enduring Authority of the Christian Scriptures*, edited by Donald A Carson (London: Inter-Varsity Press, 2016).
32 Vanhoozer and Treier, *Theology and the Mirror of Scripture*, 104.
33 Vanhoozer and Treier, *Theology and the Mirror of Scripture*, 105.

in space and time, but also represents what the triune God *is* in eternity: "As Christ is an icon of God (i.e., a visible mirror image of the invisible), so Scripture is a verbal icon (i.e., a textual mirror) of Christ."[34] Such a metaphor of a mirror would not only refer to Paul (1 Corinthians 13:12) and James (James 1:23), but do justice to the fact that mirrors reflect both images and light – the icon, then, does not call attention to itself, but reflects what lies beneath or beyond the surface. It is a witness to transcendence.[35] In the biblical writings, the divine personal presence shines through the text. This characterization of Scripture in itself bears witness of metaphysical commitment; commitment that runs somewhat contrary to modern demythologizing of metaphysics, namely by remythologizing. Remythologizing does not require abandonment of modern science, but a re-evaluation of both God and Scripture after a re-evaluation of certain developments in historical theology.[36]

As a consequence, remythologization may require a re-evaluation of the academic disciplines of exegesis and theology: biblical exegesis can never be free from theological convictions nor from ideology;[37] allegedly neutral attempts of exegesis may result in theology not derived from the whole of Scripture.[38] An explicitly theological interpretation of Scripture guards against such illusions. On the other hand, our turn towards Scripture must guard against (naïve) biblicism. Such biblicism[39] understands the *sola scriptura* as *solo scriptura* (a grammatically debatable, but considerably widespread phrase in Evangelical discourse meaning something like 'nothing but the Bible'). Yet with *sola scriptura* the Reformers did not mean that Scripture is the *only source* for theology. For such an understanding would not represent any solution, as even those agreeing on *sola scriptura* would not come to a unified understanding, but rather to disagreement on methods, and eventually to the division of churches. Rather, we may state that this praxis did not perceive *sola scriptura* as the only source, but as the ultimate authority. Furthermore, the Reformers understood *sola scrip-*

---

34 Vanhoozer and Treier, *Theology and the Mirror of Scripture*, 105.
35 Cf. Vanhoozer and Treier, *Theology and the Mirror of Scripture*, 95–100.
36 Cf. Vanhoozer, *Remythologizing Theology*.
37 Kevin J. Vanhoozer, *Dictionary for Theological Interpretation of the Bible* (Ada: Baker Academic, 2005).
38 Vanhoozer, "May We Go Beyond What Is Written after All?," 262.
39 Biblicism today is characterized by Vanhoozer by one of the following features: (1) dismissal of extra-biblical knowledge, (2) tendency to understand Bible as a textbook that is a somewhat easy authority over other disciplines, (3) lack of respect for creeds and confessions, and (4) appeal to "proof-texts", which are taken out of historical and literary context. Vanhoozer, "May We Go Beyond What Is Written after All?," 763.

tura as a Praxis rather than just an abstract principle, which takes place in the larger economy of testimony: It begins with the triune God in communicative action, acknowledges first priority to the canonical principle (i.e., Scripture interprets Scripture), but also acknowledges the catholic principle (i.e., the appointed role of church tradition). Reading Scripture with the whole church in a manner of critical biblicism constitutes catholic biblicism.[40]

Yet turning to Scripture as a mirror of what is in Christ within the economy of testimony does not free us from the hermeneutical burden: As one recognizes the complexities of this economy, one of which the theology-ladeness of reading Scripture is only one example, we may find ourselves in need of a hermeneutics of humility and conviction: humility which tempers our knowledge, and conviction which tempers our skepticism.[41] While hermeneutics is not our primary concern in this chapter, we pick up the critical realism displayed in this approach to hermeneutics, and turn to the more constructive component within the development of doctrine: the formulation of doctrine.

4.2 The Formulation of Doctrine

Ultimately, developing doctrine is a matter for the church. However, in doing theology, theologians may formulate initial theological hypotheses – theology that aims to fulfil the purpose of doctrine, and which is explicitly or implicitly formulated as such. For doing so, our concern here is less the exegetical praxis of particular passages, but the construction of biblical accounts based on the whole of the Bible. In other words, our concern is the burden of systematic theology: How do theologians move from Scripture as a multi-genre literary source to highly organized conceptual articulations of Scripture's teachings?[42] This challenge occurs for numerous reasons – for instance, whenever Christians encounter new situations.[43] In the past, attempts at developing doctrine have been made in various ways; most importantly in creeds and dogmatic decisions of the churches. Yet, on the theoretical side, many attempts to conceptualize systematic theology have been made, many rejected, and eventually, the whole enterprise has been put into question.[44] Given our turn to Scripture, we may

---

[40] Kevin J. Vanhoozer, *Biblical Authority after Babel: Retrieving the Solas in the Spirit of Mere Protestant Christianity* (Ada: Baker Books, 2016), 143–6.
[41] Vanhoozer, *Is There a Meaning in This Text?*, 455–68.
[42] Vanhoozer, "Systematic Theology," 714.
[43] Cf. Vanhoozer, *Hearers and Doers*, 40.
[44] Cf. Vanhoozer, "Systematic Theology," 716–8.

evaluate any given systematic theology by assessing how well it helps to understand what the Bible says[45] – but how does one assess which theology is helpful in this way?

This is probably the most crucial, and also the most difficult aspect of our whole enterprise.[46] In our account, we start with the reiteration that formulating doctrine has to take into account the "whole economy",[47] which consists, most importantly, of God, Scripture, and the church. The interplay within the economy can be seen within the recurring features of doing theology over time by attempts to reform the "faith that was once and for all entrusted to God's holy people" (Jude 3). For instance, *sola gratia* and *solus Christus* emphasize the canonical and catholic content of Christian theology, whereas *sola fide* and *sola scriptura* emphasize the canonical and catholic approach towards Christian theology.[48]

In the context of this economy, the primary focus must be on Scripture,[49] which likewise represents the content of Christian theology with its material principle, (i.e., both a strong trinitarianism and crucicentrism) and its approach of Christian theology with its formal principle (i.e., magisterial authority of Scripture and ministerial authority of tradition).[50] Within Scripture, there is a variety of forms of discourses.[51] For formulating doctrine, we might have to follow the way the (biblical) words go – which means appealing to propositions as propositions, images as images, stories as stories, etc.[52] With Webster, the discipline of dogmatics pursues its function as cognitive science of the church by offering "the schematic and analytic presentation of the matter of the gospel."[53]

Yet in our economy, formulating doctrine is not a mere cognitive task. Most importantly, presenting the matter of the gospel is heavily dependent on one's

---

[45] Vanhoozer, "Systematic Theology," 723.

[46] Putman suggests that this essential question might not have been answered Cf. Rhyne R. Putman, *In Defense of Doctrine: Evangelicalism, Theology, and Scripture* (Minneapolis: Augsburg Fortress Publishers, 2015), 174. This might be due to the publication date.

[47] Vanhoozer speaks of the economy in various ways. The "whole economy" here is a reference to the various agents, acts and aids to achieve God's redemptive aims.

[48] Cf. Vanhoozer, *Biblical Authority after Babel*, 232–3.

[49] Vanhoozer, "Scripture and Theology: On 'Proving' Doctrine Biblically," 141.

[50] Vanhoozer and Treier, 123.

[51] That is, in particular, principles, images, data and testimony.

[52] Vanhoozer, "Scripture and Theology: On 'Proving' Doctrine Biblically," 148.

[53] Vanhoozer, "Scripture and Theology: On 'Proving' Doctrine Biblically," 153.

view of God,⁵⁴ and it aims for the shaping of the identity of the church and its individual believers.⁵⁵ Formulating doctrine well may not therefore be about the right methods (alone), but (also) about becoming the right person.⁵⁶ Within virtue ethics, habits are of importance.⁵⁷ For formulating doctrine, we may name three: *Imitation* of biblical judgments is required, since doctrine must cohere with Christ's mind (Phil 2:5), and in this sense the "reach of the apostolic discourse" can – and often must – be continued within the pattern of that very mind.⁵⁸ *Imagination*, then, is required, as the "mind of Christ" cannot function as a concrete criterion, but rather as the framework of understanding. Following also C.S. Lewis, imagination can be understood as the "organ of meaning." Hence it is via imagination that the church reads Scripture, seeing beyond the words, and what is in Christ.⁵⁹ Finally: Responding to what is seen both in Scripture and in a given context requires response, and hence *improvisation* – not by producing innovation, but rather to progressively discover "the full meaning potential of the divine authorial discourse intrinsic to and implicit in the Bible."⁶⁰

4.3 The Renewal of Doctrine

Doctrine does not only need to be developed; it also can – or even must – be renewed. Arguments for such a renewal include the following: For one, if doctrine serves to "teach the head, orient the heart and guide the hand,"⁶¹ it functions as a "grammatical rule of the body-language" of the church.⁶² It follows that change in doctrine might be necessary given new situations requiring adjusted teaching, orientation and guidance. Secondly, while Scripture represents a disposition of faith once and for all in written form, doctrine represents a construal created from those writings. Hence, like a theory might be adjusted given

---

54 Vanhoozer refers here to what he terms "Kelsey's rule", i.e., that one's view on Scripture is "tied up" with one's view of God (and vice versa); cf. Vanhoozer, "Scripture and Theology: On 'Proving' Doctrine Biblically," 146.
55 Vanhoozer, "Scripture and Theology: On 'Proving' Doctrine Biblically," 148.
56 See also Vanhoozer and Treier's emphasis on developing a mind like Christ and the connection to wisdom, e.g. Vanhoozer and Treier, *Theology and the Mirror of Scripture*, 131–57.
57 Vanhoozer, "May We Go Beyond What Is Written after All?," 777.
58 Vanhoozer, "May We Go Beyond What Is Written after All?," 780.
59 Vanhoozer, "May We Go Beyond What Is Written after All?," 781. Cf. Vanhoozer and Treier, 105.
60 Vanhoozer, "May We Go Beyond What Is Written after All?," 784.
61 Vanhoozer and Treier, *Theology and the Mirror of Scripture*, 107.
62 Vanhoozer, "Analytics, Poetics, and the Mission of Dogmatic Discourse," 48.

the same available data, doctrine might be adjusted. This perspective echoes the approach of critical (hermeneutical) realism;[63] it allows for a distinction between *sacra doctrina* (i.e., the teaching of the Bible itself) and *doctrine* (i.e., what the church believes, teaches, and confesses).[64] Thirdly, what has been said so far has given way to an account that both requires and allows for both continuity *and* discontinuity.[65] Such an account to develop doctrine calls for organic development of doctrine: Scripture relates to doctrine like an acorn to an oak – the DNA remains the same, while the function and appearance change.[66] Two applications are apparent: For one, in developing doctrine, the nature of Scripture must stay the same, while the appearance and function of doctrine might change. For another, the renewal of doctrine should not result in the retraction of former doctrine.[67]

Yet how can we determine if, or in how far a particular doctrinal development represents genuine growth and hence a faithful improvisation rather than a misunderstanding or false innovation? Naturally, reflecting on the previous two components – the application of both turning to Scripture and the formulation of doctrine – is essential. However, there may be three particular criteria for *testing* doctrine. First, we may test whether a particular doctrine exemplifies *canon sense*:[68] With John Henry Newman, the Christian tradition is not seen as an immutable deposit nor as a series of relativistic revolutions, but something living and growing: "What we have in Scripture is a seed – a seminal idea, to be precise – which eventually blossoms into a mature plant."[69] Yet while in other accounts Scripture and tradition may hence represent the same level of authority, this is not the case in our account. Scripture always represents the highest authority, while tradition represents our construal of it. Construals may change – Scripture does not. So time and again, doctrine must prove its canon sense. In other words: While there is sameness (i.e., the continuity of the gospel), we aim

---

63 Cf. Vanhoozer, *Is There a Meaning in This Text?*, 420.
64 Vanhoozer, "May We Go Beyond What Is Written after All?," 756.
65 Such development rejects approaches in which doctrine seeks to state always exactly the same (which has proven not to be possible even for the proponents) as well as approaches in which doctrine can be revised in their essence (which makes Christianity subject to any given ideology or personal agenda). Cf. Vanhoozer, "Improvising Theology According to the Scriptures," 26–8.
66 Vanhoozer, "Improvising Theology According to the Scriptures," 29.
67 The distinction between change and retraction is crucial, for whenever actual retraction is on the table, the quest for heresy might likely be, too.
68 Cf. Vanhoozer, "May We Go Beyond What Is Written after All?," 788.
69 Vanhoozer, "Improvising Theology According to the Scriptures," 28.

for a genre of doctrine that acknowledges genuine growth and otherness as well.[70] Secondly, we may test whether a particular doctrine exemplifies *catholic sensibility*.[71] The church is not only both local and translocal, it is also transtemporal: the saints include people from all tribes and epochs – and all their insights matter. One can make the argument that "early creedal formulation in particular command respect, because for centuries, despite diverse contexts, [many] have found these creeds to be faithful mirrors of Scripture."[72] Finally, we may test whether a particular doctrine exemplifies *contextual sensitivity*:[73] Does doctrine fit into a particular context? Does it enlighten our understanding and the influence of God's kingdom? Revaluating doctrine on its various levels via these criteria should help to guide a critical analysis of the grammar one suggests for the "body-language of the body of Christ."

5 Conclusion

The aim of this chapter was to offer an exemplary account of how one may seek to derive theology from Scripture. Based on the work of Vanhoozer, I have offered some reflection on the nature of doctrine, and then identified three components for developing doctrine well – the turn to Scripture, the formulation of doctrine, and the renewal of doctrine. Given the brevity of this chapter, many details are in need of further elaboration – most importantly, I believe, the aspect of formulating doctrine needs to be analysed more deeply, and here the quest for what Webster addressed as "the schematic and analytic presentation of the matter of the gospel".[74]

---

70 Vanhoozer, "Improvising Theology According to the Scriptures:, 39.
71 Cf. Vanhoozer, "May We Go Beyond What Is Written after All?," 788–9.
72 Vanhoozer and Treier, *Theology and the Mirror of Scripture*, 125.
73 Cf. Vanhoozer, "May We Go Beyond What Is Written after All?," 789–90.
74 My thanks to Kevin J. Vanhoozer and an anonymous reviewer for their comments on earlier versions of this paper. Likewise I want to thank Tomas Bokedal, John C. Peckham and the Research Group 'Reformed and Evangelical Theology' of the Herman Bavinck Center at the VU Amsterdam.

References

Higton, Mike, and Jim Fodor. *The Routledge Companion to the Practice of Christian Theology.* Abingdon: Routledge, 2015.

Putman, Rhyne R. *In Defense of Doctrine: Evangelicalism, Theology, and Scripture.* Minneapolis: Augsburg Fortress Publishers, 2015.

Vanhoozer, Kevin J. "Analytics, Poetics, and the Mission of Dogmatic Discourse." In *The Task of Dogmatics: Explorations in Theological Method*, edited by Oliver D. Crisp and Fred Sanders. Grand Rapids: Zondervan, 2017.

Vanhoozer, Kevin J. *Biblical Authority after Babel: Retrieving the Solas in the Spirit of Mere Protestant Christianity.* Ada: Baker Books, 2016.

Vanhoozer, Kevin J. *Dictionary for Theological Interpretation of the Bible.* Ada: Baker Academic, 2005.

Vanhoozer, Kevin J. *The Drama of Doctrine: A Canonical-Linguistic Approach to Christian Theology.* Louisville: Westminster John Knox Press, 2005.

Vanhoozer, Kevin J. "A Drama-of-Redemption Model." In *Four Views on Moving Beyond the Bible to Theology*, edited by Gary T. Meadors and by Stanley N. Gundry. Grand Rapids: Zondervan, 2009.

Vanhoozer, Kevin J. *Faith Speaking Understanding: Performing the Drama of Doctrine.* Louisville: Westminster John Knox Press, 2014.

Vanhoozer, Kevin J. *Hearers and Doers: A Pastor's Guide to Making Disciples through Scripture and Doctrine.* Bellingham: Lexham Press, 2019.

Vanhoozer, Kevin J. "Improvising Theology According to the Scriptures: An Evangelical Account of the Development of Doctrine." In *Building on the Foundations of Evangelical Theology: Essays in Honor of John S. Feinberg.* Edited by Gregg Allison and Stephen Wellum. Wheaton: Crossway, 2015.

Vanhoozer, Kevin J. *Is There a Meaning in This Text? The Bible, the Reader, and the Morality of Literary Knowledge.* New York: HarperCollins, 2009.

Vanhoozer, Kevin J. "May We Go Beyond What Is Written after All? The Pattern of Theological Authority and the Problem of Doctrinal Development." In *The Enduring Authority of the Christian Scriptures.* Edited by Donald A Carson. London: Inter-Varsity Press, 2016.

Vanhoozer, Kevin J. *Remythologizing Theology: Divine Action, Passion, and Authorship.* Vol. 18. Cambridge: Cambridge University Press, 2010.

Vanhoozer, Kevin J. "Scripture and Theology: On 'Proving' Doctrine Biblically." In *The Routledge Companion to the Practice of Christian Theology.* Edited by Mike Higton and Jim Fodor. Routledge Religion Companions. Abingdon: Routledge, 2015.

Vanhoozer, Kevin J. "Systematic Theology." In *The Routledge Companion to Modern Christian Thought.* Edited by Chad Meister and James Beilby. London: Routledge, 2013.

Vanhoozer, Kevin J., and Daniel J. Treier. *Theology and the Mirror of Scripture: A Mere Evangelical Account.* Grand Rapids: InterVarsity Press, 2015.

List of Contributors

Knut Alfsvåg is professor of systematic theology at VID Specialized University, Stavanger, Norway. Research interests include theology of the Reformation, apophatic theology, and the relation between theology and science.

Beatrice Victoria Ang is a faculty member of the Biblical Seminary of the Philippines and of the Asia Graduate School of Theology ThM/PhD program in Theological Studies and Church History. Her research interests—in Systematic Theology and Patristics—focus chiefly on John Chrysostom and Christianity in late antiquity.

Tomas Bokedal is Associate Professor in New Testament and Early Christianity at NLA University College, Norway, and Lecturer in New Testament at King's College, University of Aberdeen, UK. Bokedal's primary fields of research concern Christian origins and the relation between Scripture and Theology. He is the author of *The Formation and Significance of the Christian Biblical Canon: A Study in Text, Ritual and Interpretation* (2014) and *Christ the Center: How the Rule of Faith, the Nomina Sacra, and Numerical Patterns Shape the Canon* (2023).

Francis Borchardt is Associate Professor of Hebrew Bible in the department of Theology, Religion, and Philosophy at NLA University College. He researches on subjects related to book history within early Judaism and early Christianity.

Michael Borowski writes on the interface of theology, science and culture, and their relation to the church and the public square. A current project is his dissertation at the VU Amsterdam, *Being Human in an Age of Science*. He also coordinates the plattform "Scripture & theology".

Hans (J.M.) Burger is professor of systematic theology at the Theological University Kampen / Utrecht (the Netherlands). His research in systematic theology focusses on theological hermeneutics, the doctrine of Scripture, soteriology (participation in Christ), and the doctrine of the covenants.

Torleif Elgvin is emeritus professor in Biblical and Jewish Studies, NLA University College, Oslo. His main research interests are Qumran and early Jewish tradition, Hebrew Bible, the Song of Songs, and late editing of biblical books. He has published Qumran texts in Discoveries in the Judaean Desert and is involved in the advanced research project "The Lying Pen of Scribes. Manuscript Forgeries, Digital Imaging, and Critical Provenance Research" (University of Agder, The Research Council of Norway).

Mark W. Elliott is Professor of Biblical and Historical Theology at the University of the Highlands and Islands and Professorial Fellow, Wycliffe College, University of Toronto. He specialises in the relationship of Biblical theology and Christian doctrine, including the history of exegesis and theology.

Georg Fischer SJ is Professor emeritus for Old Testament Biblical Sciences and Ancient Oriental Languages at the Theological Faculty of the Leopold-Franzens-University in Innsbruck. Together with Benedikt Collinet he was responsible for the research project "Karl Rahner and the Bible". His main fields are Jeremiah, Genesis, Biblical Theology and Hermeneutics.

Ida Heikkilä has recently received the degree of Doctor of Theology from the University of Helsinki. Her main research interests lie in Lutheran-Catholic ecumenical dialogues, German theology and the relationship between Scripture and Tradition.

Arnold Huijgen is Professor of Dogmatics at the Protestant Theological University in Amsterdam (The Netherlands). His research centers on hermeneutics, the Trinity, Mary, and eschatology.

Ludger Jansen is Cusanus Professor for Philosophy at the Philosophical-Theological College in Bressanone (Italy) and adjunct Professor of Philosophy at the University of Rostock (Germany). His main research interests are in Metaphysics, Philosophy of Science, and Philosophy of Religion, including the philosophical reflection of exegesis and revelation.

Elisabeth Maikranz is a research associate and lecturer at the Ecumenical Institute of Heidelberg University. Her main research interests include fundamental theology, ecumenical theology, hermeneutics, value discourses and theology, and theological responses to contemporary issues.

Alison Milbank is Professor of Theology and Literature in the Department of Theology and Religious Studies at the University of Nottingham. Her main research interests are in the relation of religion and culture, especially the Gothic, fantasy, Dante and Ruskin.

Jeanine Mukaminega is Professor of Old Testament at the Faculty of Protestant Theology in Brussels. In her research she focusses on the societal impact of biblical exegesis and on how biblical hermeneutics is challenged by multiculturality and postmodernism.

John C. Peckham is Professor of Theology and Christian Philosophy at the Seventh-day Adventist Theological Seminary, Andrews University.

Willibald Sandler is Associate Professor of Dogmatics at the Faculty of Catholic Theology of the University of Innsbruck. His main fields of research are Dramatic theology, theology of grace and of events of grace, the theological discernment of new spiritual movements, Christian spirituality and spiritual theology.

Boubakar Sanou is Associate Professor of Mission and Intercultural Leadership at the Seventh-day Adventist Theological Seminary, Andrews University.

Brandon K. Watson is Academic Assistant at the Chair of Systematic Theology at the University of Münster. He is the author of *Karl Barth on Faith: A Systematic Exploration*, forthcoming with de Gruyter, and the translator of Markus Mühling's *Post-Systematic Theology II: God's Trinitar-*

ian Love Adventure, forthcoming with Brill. His main research interests are in 20th century Philosophy and Theology, Hermeneutics, and Philosophy of Religion.

Luuk van de Weghe (PhD, University of Aberdeen) is the author of *The Historical Tell: Patterns of Eyewitness Testimony in the Gospel of Luke and Acts* (2023). His research has been published in preeminent peer-reviewed journals in biblical studies, including *New Testament Studies*, *Tyndale Bulletin*, and *Bulletin for Biblical Research*.

www.ingramcontent.com/pod-product-compliance
Lightning Source LLC
Chambersburg PA
CBHW031748220426
43662CB00007B/321